Africa and World War II

This volume considers the military, economic, and political ___ ___ Africa during World War II. The essays feature new research and inno___ ___ oaches to the historiography of Africa and bring to the fore issues of race, ge___ er, and labor during the war, topics that have not yet received much critical attention. It explores the experiences of male and female combatants, peasant producers, women traders, missionaries, and sex workers. The first section offers three introductory essays that give a continent-wide overview of how Africa sustained the Allied effort through labor and resources. The six sections that follow offer individual case studies from different parts of the continent. Contributors offer a macro and micro view of the multiple levels on which Africa's contributions shaped the war as well as the ways in which the war affected individuals and communities and transformed Africa's political, economic, and social landscape.

Judith A. Byfield is Associate Professor of History at Cornell University, teaching African and Caribbean history. She is coeditor of *Gendering the African Diaspora: Women, Culture and Historical Change in the Caribbean and Nigerian Hinterland* (2010) and author of *The Bluest Hands: A Social and Economic History of Women Indigo Dyers in Western Nigeria, 1890–1940* (2002). She is a former president of the African Studies Association (2011) and is on the editorial board of the Blacks in the Diaspora series published by Indiana University Press.

Carolyn A. Brown is Associate Professor of History at Rutgers University. She is the author of *We Are All Slaves: African Miners, Culture, and Resistance at the Enugu Government Colliery, Nigeria, 1914–1950* (2001). She is coeditor, with Paul Lovejoy, of *Repercussions of the Atlantic Slave Trade: The Interior of the Bight of Biafra and the African Diaspora* (2010). She is on the editorial board of Cambridge University Press's African Studies series and is a senior editor of the labor journal *International Labor and Working Class History*.

Timothy Parsons holds a joint appointment as Professor of African History in the history department and in the African and African American studies program at Washington University in St. Louis, where he also directs the international and area studies program. His primary publications include *The Rule of Empires: Those Who Built Them, Those Who Endured Them, and Why They Always Fall* (2010); *Race, Resistance and the Boy Scout Movement in British Colonial Africa* (2004); and *The 1964 Army Mutinies and the Making of Modern East Africa* (2003).

Ahmad Alawad Sikainga is Professor of History at the Ohio State University. He is the author of *City of Steel and Fire: A Social History of Atbara, Sudan's Railway Town, 1* ___ *___ Slaves into Workers: Emancipation and Labor in Colonia___* ___ *___hazal under British Rule, 1898–1956* (199___ ___ *___in and Role, 1925–1955* (1983). He is coe___ *___ ___n Africa* (2006) and *Civil War in Sudan* (19___

Africa and World War II

Edited by

JUDITH A. BYFIELD

Cornell University

CAROLYN A. BROWN

Rutgers University–New Brunswick

TIMOTHY PARSONS

Washington University in St. Louis

AHMAD ALAWAD SIKAINGA

Ohio State University

CAMBRIDGE
UNIVERSITY PRESS

CAMBRIDGE
UNIVERSITY PRESS

32 Avenue of the Americas, New York, NY 10013-2473, USA

Cambridge University Press is part of the University of Cambridge.

It furthers the University's mission by disseminating knowledge in the pursuit of education, learning, and research at the highest international levels of excellence.

www.cambridge.org
Information on this title: www.cambridge.org/9781107630222

First published 2015

Printed in Great Britain by Clays Ltd, St Ives plc

A catalog record for this publication is available from the British Library.

Library of Congress Cataloging in Publication Data
Africa and World War II / Judith Byfield, Cornell University, Carolyn A. Brown, Rutgers University–New Brunswick, Timothy Parsons, Washington University in St. Louis, Ahmad Sikainga, Ohio State University.
pages cm
ISBN 978-1-107-05320-5 (hardback) – ISBN 978-1-107-63022-2 (Paperback)
1. World War, 1939–1945 – Africa. 2. Africa – History – 1884–1960. I. Byfield, Judith A. (Judith Ann-Marie), editor, author. II. Brown, Carolyn A. (Carolyn Anderson), 1944– editor, author. III. Parsons, Timothy, 1962– editor, author. IV. Sikainga, Ahmad Alawad, editor, author.
D766.8.A473 2015
940.53'6–dc23 2014027894

ISBN 978-1-107-05320-5 Hardback
ISBN 978-1-107-63022-2 Paperback

Additional resources for this publication at http://www.cambridge.org/academic/subjects/history/african-history/africa-and-world-war-ii

We would like to dedicate this volume to several mentors, colleagues, and friends who passed in 2014: Jacob Ade Ajayi, George Bond, Patrick Chabal, Ali Mazuri, and Ivor Wilks. Together they helped pioneer the field of African Studies and we hope to continue in their footsteps.

Contents

List of Contributors

Giulia Barrera, Directorate General of Archives, Rome, Italy

An archivist and an Africanist historian, Barrera has published finding aids and articles on archival matters as well as articles on interracial sexual relations, mixed race children, women's history, and the construction of racial hierarchies in colonial Eritrea.

Catherine Bogosian Ash, Independent Scholar, Detroit, MI, USA

Bogosian Ash has taught courses on the history of women, colonialism, and popular culture and protest in Africa at Wayne State University. She has published articles on forced labor in French West Africa and the evolution of a labor army in postcolonial Mali.

Carolyn A. Brown, Rutgers University, New Brunswick, NJ, USA

An historian of labor slavery and urban social history, Brown's publications include *We Are All Slaves: African Miners, Culture, and Resistance at the Enugu Government Colliery, Nigeria, 1914–1950* (Heinemann, 2003), which won the Book of the Year Prize from the International Labor History Association, and the coedited volume with Paul Lovejoy, *Repercussions of the Atlantic Slave Trade: The Interior of the Bight of Biafra and the African Diaspora* (Africa World Press, 2011).

Judith A. Byfield, Cornell University, Ithaca, NY, USA

An associate professor of African history, Byfield's publications include *The Bluest Hands: A Social and Economic History of Women Indigo Dyers in Western Nigeria, 1890–1940* (Heinemann, 2002) and *Cross Currents: Building Bridges Across American and Nigerian Studies* (Bookbuilders [Nigeria], 2009).

Suryakanthie Chetty, University of South Africa, Pretoria, South Africa

Chetty teaches courses on colonial South African and African history as well as courses on "Empires of the Modern World." She has published articles on settler masculinity and South African propaganda practices during the Second World War.

William G. Clarence-Smith, School of Oriental and African Studies, University of London, London, UK

A professor of the economic history of Asia and Africa and chief editor of the *Journal of Global History*, Clarence-Smith's publications include *Slaves, Peasants and Capitalists in Southern Angola, 1840–1926* (Cambridge University Press, 1979) and *Islam and the Abolition of Slavery* (Oxford University Press, 2006).

Barbara M. Cooper, Rutgers University, New Brunswick, NJ, USA

A professor of history, Cooper's publications include *Marriage in Maradi: Gender and Culture in a Hausa Society in Niger, 1900–1989* (Heinemann, 1997) and *Evangelical Christians in the Muslim Sahel* (Indiana University Press, 2006), for which she won the Melville J. Herskovits Prize of the African Studies Association.

Ruth Ginio, Ben Gurion University, Negev, Israel

Ginio, a professor of history, is the author of *French Colonialism Unmasked: The Vichy Years in French West Africa* (University of Nebraska Press, 2006) and coeditor of *Shadows of War: A Social History of Silence in the Twentieth Century* (Cambridge University Press, 2010).

Louis Grundlingh, University of Johannesburg, Johannesburg, South Africa

A professor in the department of historical studies, Grundlingh teaches courses on urban history and the history of leisure and has published numerous articles on the racial and politicized experiences of black South African soldiers who participated in the Second World War.

Hailu Habtu, Institute of Ethiopian Studies, Addis Ababa University, Addis Ababa, Ethiopia

As a senior research Fellow, Habtu has published widely on Ethiopian Christianity, language, and culture. He also teaches graduate courses on Ethiopian oral and written literature.

Allen M. Howard, Rutgers University, New Brunswick, NJ, USA

Professor emeritus of history, Howard is the coauthor of *Community Leadership and the Transformation of Freetown, 1801–1976* (Mouton, 1978) and coeditor of *The Spatial Factor in African History: The Relationship of the Social, Material, and Perceptual* (Brill, 2005).

Daniel Hutchinson, Belmont Abbey College, Belmont, NC, USA

Hutchinson, an assistant professor of history, teaches courses on the history of the United States, African American history, military history, race, and ethnicity, as well as on U.S. foreign relations. He has published articles on the experiences of prisoners of war during World War I in Alabama.

Eric T. Jennings, University of Toronto, Toronto, Canada

A professor of history, Jennings's publications include *Vichy in the Tropics* (Stanford University Press, 2001), *Curing the Colonizers* (Duke University Press, 2006), and *Imperial Heights: Dalat* and *the Making and Undoing of French Indochina* (University of California Press, 2011). He has also received the Alf Heggoy and Jean-François Coste book prizes.

Driss Maghraoui, Al Akhawayn University, Ifrane, Morocco

Maghraoui, a professor of history and international relations, has published numerous articles and chapters and is the editor of *Revisiting the Colonial Past in Morocco* (Routledge, 2003).

Malyn Newitt, King's College London, London, UK

Professor emeritus of history, Newitt's publications include, *A History of Mozambique* (Indiana University Press, 1995) and *Portuguese Overseas Expansion, 1400–1668* (Routledge, 2004).

Timothy Parsons, Washington University, St. Louis, MO, USA

Parsons, a professor of African and African American studies, is the author of *The Second British Empire: In the Crucible of the Twentieth Century* (Rowan & Littlefield, 2014) and *Race, Resistance, and the Boy Scout Movement in British Colonial Africa* (Ohio University Press, 2004).

Carina Ray, Fordham University, Bronx, NY, USA

An associate professor of African and the Black Atlantic history, Ray is the author of *Crossing the Color Line: Race, Sex, and the Contested Politics of Colonialism in Ghana* (Ohio University Press, 2015) and coeditor of *Darfur and the Crisis of Governance in Sudan* (Cornell University Press, 2009).

Raffael Scheck, Colby College, Waterville, ME, USA

Scheck, a professor of history, is the author of *Hitler's African Victims: The German Army Massacre of Black French Soldiers in 1940* (Cambridge University Press, 2006), *Mothers of the Nation: Right-Wing Women in Weimar Germany* (Berg Press, 2004), and *French Colonial Soldiers in German Captivity during World War II* (Cambridge University Press, 2014).

Elizabeth Schmidt, Loyola University Maryland, Baltimore, MD, USA

Schmidt, a professor of African History, is the author of several books, including *Cold War and Decolonization in Guinea, 1946–1958* (Ohio University Press, 2007), for which she received the African Politics Conference Group's 2008 Best Book Award, and *Mobilizing the Masses: Gender, Ethnicity, and Class in the Nationalist Movement in Guinea, 1939–1958* (Heinemann, 2005).

Ahmad Alawad Sikainga, Ohio State University, Columbus, OH, USA

A professor of history and African studies, Sikainga's publications include *Slaves into Workers: Emancipation and Labor in Colonial Sudan* (University of Texas Press, 1996) and *City of Steel and Fire: A Social History of Atbara, Sudan's Railway Town, 1906–1984* (Heinemann, 2002).

Carol Summers, University of Richmond, Richmond, VA, USA

Summers, a professor of history and international studies, is author of *Colonial Lessons: Africans' Education in Southern Rhodesia, 1918–1935* (Heinemann, 2002) and *From Civilization to Segregation: Social Ideals and Social Control in Southern Rhodesia, 1890–1934* (Ohio University Press, 1994).

Thaddeus Sunseri, Colorado State University, Fort Collins, CO, USA

Sunseri, a professor of African history, is the author of *Wielding the Ax: Scientific Forestry and Social Conflict in Tanzania, c. 1820–2000* (Ohio University Press, 2009), a finalist for the African Studies Association's 2010 Melville J. Herskovits Award, and *Vilimani: Labor Migration and Rural Change in Early Colonial Tanzania, 1884–1915* (Heinemann, 2001).

Acknowledgments

This volume is the outcome of many discussions; a workshop at Rutgers University, New Brunswick, NJ, in 2008, *Re-Evaluating Africa and World War II*; a conference at Cornell in 2009, *Re-Evaluating Africa and World War II*; as well as the patience and good humor of many colleagues. A project of this magnitude is only successful because along the way many people and organizations decide that they want to help. To the tens of people who helped in multiple ways, big and small, we thank you from the bottom of our hearts.

We enjoyed support from three institutions over the course of this process – Rutgers University, Cornell University, and Columbia University. We must acknowledge the generosity in spirit and resources from the following departments, programs, and institutes. Rutgers University: ARESTY Research Center for Undergraduates; Center for Race and Ethnicity; Black Atlantic Seminar; Center for African Studies; the Rutgers University Libraries; Department of History; Dean, School of Arts and Sciences; Research Council, Office of Research and Economic Development; Vice President of Undergraduate Education; Vice President of Academic Affairs. Columbia University: Institute of African Studies. Cornell University: Africana Studies and Research Center; The Carl Becker House; De Bary Mellon Interdisciplinary Writing Group; John Henrik Clarke Library; Cornell Cinema; Cornell Society for the Humanities; Departments of Anthropology, Government, History, and Development Sociology; European Studies; Kroch Library, Division of Rare and Manuscript Collections; Mario Einaudi Center for International Studies; Feminist, Gender and Sexuality Studies; Institute for Comparative Modernities; and the Institute for Social Sciences.

We also owe an enormous debt to several individuals who went above and beyond the call of duty to ensure the success of the workshop and conference. They include: Jamila Crowther, Renée DeLancey, Shelley Feldman, Sandra Greene, Robert L. Harris, Salah Hassan, Raj Krishnan, Stacey Langwick, Nancy Lawler, Dan Magaziner, Fouad Makki, Gregg Mann, Kwame Siriboe,

Rebecca Snyder, and Nicolas van de Valle. Filmmakers Steve White and John F. Schwally shared their outstanding work *761st Tank Regiment* and *FDR's Secret Air Force*, respectively, with our audiences. We are grateful to the presenters at both the workshop and the conference and to the many people who shared in the conversations and discussions.

Putting together a volume of this magnitude requires many eyes and many hands. LaRay Denzer merits extra thanks for adding her editorial acumen to the mix. She brought a critical second eye to the articles in this collection, while Laura Ann Twagira rendered order to the materials for the Web site and Naomi Bland and Moyagaye Bedward helped us stay on top of a tsunami of details. Our readers offered the right mix of encouragement and advice. Ashley Jackson at Kings College London and David Killingray provided insight and encouragement at critical moments. Although he subsequently left Cambridge University Press, we have to say a special "Thank you!" to Eric Crahan, who strongly encouraged us to pursue this project from the very beginning, and to his successor, William Hammell, who continued the support. Finally, we thank our families, who invariably shared all phases of this volume and probably do not want to hear another interesting story about World War II.

Preface

Judith A. Byfield

The genesis of this volume was a simple Sunday morning conversation with Carolyn Brown. I had attended a preview of the first episode of Ken Burns's documentary, *The War*, at Dartmouth College, and I shared my observations with her. We both planned to include chapters on World War II in our respective monographs, and as we discussed our mutual concern with the largely superficial treatment of Africa in European and American accounts of World War II, and our conversion to the idea that World War II deserved much greater attention in African studies, the idea for a conference took root.

We convinced Gregg Mann and Ahmad Sikainga to join us as co-organizers in the project, and we brought together twenty-six participants from around the globe for a workshop at Rutgers University, New Brunswick, NJ, March 27–30, 2008. Following that workshop we organized a conference at Cornell University, September 18–20, 2009, as well as three panels at the 2010 meeting of the American Historical Association. This has been a long process, and along the way the composition of organizers changed as well; Gregg Mann left and Timothy Parsons joined us. In the multiple steps that brought us to this point, the numerous meetings and rewrites, our conviction in this project has been reinforced, for each of us learned something new at the end of the day.

Why Revisit World War II?

In the documentary *The War*, Ken Burns did an admirable job in illustrating the complexity and grand scale of World War II as well as the personal experiences of individuals who witnessed its horrors and victories. While fully deserving of the praise it garnered, the series also illustrates the concerns that drive this collaborative project – the inadequate attention to Africa's role in World War II. This early version of episode one importantly included discussion of Italy's invasion of Ethiopia in 1935 but then replicated the standard discussion of the North Africa campaigns, largely focusing on the actions of Generals Montgomery and Rommel. The same is true in texts on the war. The continent and especially sub-Saharan Africa are absent from the major works such as *The Second World War: A Complete History* by Martin Gilbert and *A World At Arms: A Global History of World War II* by Gerhard Weinberg.[1] Unfortunately, this dominant narrative betrays a superficial understanding of the critical role that Africa and its peoples played in this war. This project seeks to intervene in this narrative by making available new scholarship that will facilitate a richer understanding of Africa's role and impact on this global conflict. In addition, this volume will bring the historiography of World War II and African historiography into greater dialogue as it illuminates the distinctive ways in which the drive to secure Africa's resources for the war shaped African lives and livelihoods.

A small but critical number of historians have focused on Africa's role in World War II;[2] however, most Africanist historians gloss over the period by giving a cursory discussion of the numbers of African troops in South Asia and Western Europe or treating it as just a prelude to nationalist movements in the postwar era. The contributors to this project argue that Africa's contribution to the war was signal to the Allied victory and that the war years require more systematic analysis for a number of reasons. The demands of the war brought unprecedented interventions into the daily lives of Africans by colonial powers and transformed social and economic relations within households and communities. Additionally, the new importance of the colonies for the war effort was not lost on the men and women who were put in the position of sacrificing their lives and economies to give others in Europe the freedoms that they did not enjoy. For men and women across the continent, the war was not just a distant event; rather, it transformed their lives, made them agents in a global struggle for democracy, and left an indelible imprint on their history. The contributors to the volume also utilize insights from a variety of fields of inquiry such as spatial analysis, gender

---

[1] Martin Gilbert, *The Second World War: A Complete History* (New York: Holt Paperbacks, 2004); Gerhard Weinberg, *A World At Arms: A Global History of World War II* (New York: Cambridge University Press, 2005).

[2] For example, see Myron Echenberg, *Colonial Conscripts: The Tirailleurs Senegalais in French West Africa, 1857–1960* (Portsmouth, NH: Heinemann, 1991); Ashley Jackson, *Botswana 1939–45: An African Country at War* (Oxford: Clarendon Press, 1999); David Killingray and Richard Rathbone (editors), *Africa and the Second World War* (New York: St. Martin's Press, 1986); Nancy Ellen Lawler, *Soldiers, Airmen, Spies and Whisperers: The Gold Coast in World War II* (Athens: Ohio University Press, 2002); Gregory Mann, *Native Sons: West African Veterans and France in the Twentieth Century* (Durham: Duke University Press, 2006); G. O. Olusanya, *The Second World War and Politics in Nigeria, 1939–1953* (London: Evans Bros. for University of Lagos Press, 1979); Timothy Parsons, *The African Rank-and-File: Social Implications of Colonial Military Service in the Kings Rifles, 1902–1964* (Portsmouth, NH: Heinemann, 1999).

studies, cultural studies, and environmental history. Consequently, this volume will help chart new ways of thinking about and capturing Africa's role in World War II.

Africa and World War II

The contributions to this volume highlight three critical issues – periodization, colonial policies, and the impact of the war on African individuals and communities. Periodization is critical in understanding the consequences the war imposed on African communities as well as Africa's impact on critical moments during the war. Contributors identify signal events that had the most sustained impact on African communities, such as the fall of France and Japan's conquest of South East Asia. They illustrate Africa's vital role in sustaining the Allied cause, especially after the fall of South East Asia. This attention to periodization allows for more comparative analyses both within and across regions and refines our analyses of changes in colonial policy. For example, Britain did not make the recruitment of African soldiers a priority until Japan's victories in the Far East, and then quickly moved to put 80,000 British West African troops in Burma.[3] France, on the other hand, relied heavily on West African soldiers in Europe and other parts of the empire, recruiting more than 100,000 men. These men on the frontlines were the most visible expression of Africa's role in the war; however, combat was just one dimension of Africa's contribution, for as the war expanded demands on African communities increased significantly. Nancy Lawler notes that Britain and France in particular "looked to their overseas territories to continue to fulfill their well-established role in the imperial systems . . . the colonies were expected not only to support themselves, but to provide resources, both natural and human, for the good of the respective metropoles."[4]

In many ways African resources sustained the Allied effort especially after 1942 but came at a high cost. What were the consequences for African communities as they supported their war-ravaged metropoles, the war effort, and themselves? Several contributors to this volume explore this question in depth by examining the social, cultural, political, and economic changes on the continent. One of the most critical areas of concern for colonial officials was labor. Not only did colonial powers use African soldiers to augment their forces in Europe and Asia, they needed African labor to maintain those economic sectors in Africa deemed essential to the war effort, such as coal mining and rubber production. In addition, entire communities had to be mobilized to provide rice and other foodstuffs for the troops, starch for

---

[3] For more on African troops in Burma, see John A. L. Hamilton, *War Bush: 81 (West African) Division in Burma* (Wilby, Norwich, UK: Michael Russell, 2001).

[4] Lawler, *Soldiers, Airmen, Spies and Whisperers*, 1.

uniforms, and palm products necessary for the manufacturing of soaps and margarine in Europe.

The mobilization of communities to provide labor, food, and other resources for the war exacerbated some of the contradictions of colonialism, thus making World War II an equally significant watershed in African history. Colonial regimes faced rising tensions as some communities experienced food shortages in the wake of the redeployment of agricultural labor or the redirection of food to troops. Price controls on food, as well as restrictions on shipping and the movement of imported goods such as kerosene, helped fuel hyperinflation, especially in urban centers. In a period when control was paramount, colonial officials had to devise new strategies and policies to secure the resources necessary for the war while keeping the lid on social and economic unrest.

Despite the hardships, many African men and women took to heart the stated aims of the Allied forces and volunteered to support the war in numerous ways in order to demonstrate their commitment to the shared ideals of the cause. They raised money for local and international charities, prayed for Allied victories, and financed airplanes. Nigerians, for example, contributed £210,999 to the war effort through the Nigeria War Relief Fund.[5] Regardless of where or how individuals and communities contributed, the war changed their lives. Many women shouldered new responsibilities and exercised new freedoms as men and a few women went off to fight. The pace of urbanization increased, leading to greater pressure on housing and other urban resources as well as an expanded social base for critiques of colonial rule. In addition, in Liberia, Senegal, and Nigeria the war brought many people into contact with black Americans and helped foster new ways of thinking and new cultural expressions.

In many areas the war exacerbated existing social tensions. Urbanization, for example, made it increasingly difficult for households and communities to maintain control over young people, especially young women. In the cities, which were exciting cauldrons of new cultures, political activism, and temptations, women and girls could evade the attempts of fathers and husbands to restrict their movement. Similarly, young men could evade the control that older men had over their ability to marry. New sexual mores, the anonymity of urban life, and the opportunities for wage earning challenged generational privileges, deprived communities of the labor of their youths, and deepened a range of health issues.

The war also intensified political consciousness and awareness of the contradictions of imperialism. The contradictions became more glaring as

---

[5] Gloria Chuku, "'Crack Kernels, Crack Hitler': Export Production Drive and Igbo Women during the Second World War," in Judith A. Byfield, LaRay Denzer, and Anthea Morrison (eds.), *Gendering the African Diaspora: Women, Culture and Historical Change in the Caribbean and Nigerian Hinterland* (Bloomington: Indiana University Press, 2010).

the war unfolded for not only did colonial subjects champion the self-determination and democracy of the people who ruled them, but Africa, specifically Brazzaville, became the capital of De Gaulle's Free France. These contradictions resonated especially strongly with African soldiers for whom the mystique of white superiority fell victim to the brutality they saw Europeans inflict upon each other. Moreover, they cringed under the racial discrimination within their own army command as well as that of prisoner of war camps. Racism also played out on the continent in different ways, and several contributors examine racism in policies and practice. These contributions on racism will be significant to the historiography of World War II for as John Dowers argues, "apart from the genocide of the Jews, racism remains one of the great neglected subjects of World War Two."[6]

People on the home front who saw their sacrifices during the war as a down payment for their own self-determination also came to realize the contradictions between the ideals of the war and the effort to relegitimize colonialism. The continuation of wartime economic policies deepened the conditions for social discontent among workers, farmers, traders, and elites. World War II, in many instances, helped galvanize the militant nationalism of the postwar period as African men and women increasingly demanded their place in deciding their futures, their rights as workers, and an end to the indignities of racism. The war also contributed to the pace of decolonization, for the years of conflict left Britain and France economically weak. At its conclusion both colonial powers were initially committed to reforming imperialism through development and greater African political participation. However, their weakened economies and the cost of reforms ultimately contributed to their willingness to relinquish political control of their African colonies.[7]

Africa supplied troops, funds, and materials, as well as a location from which to plan for a Free France; thus it played a critical role in the Allied victory. The themes discussed here – mobilizing troops and resources, the experience of combat, changing gender roles, racial discrimination, democracy – all resonate with other world regions as well. Thus this volume will give scholars of North America, Europe, and Asia the tools to integrate Africa into their discussion of the war. They will have the resources to incorporate African voices and experiences from different parts of the continent, and to make comparative analyses within Africa and between Africa and other regions.

The insights and resources in this volume will enable us to teach World War II in its global complexity. For example, a global vantage point

[6] John Dower, *War without Mercy: Race and Power in the Pacific War* (New York: Pantheon Books, 1986), 4.
[7] Frederick Cooper, *Decolonization and African Society: The Labor Question in French and British Africa* (New York: Cambridge University Press, 1996).

complicates the seemingly simple issue of dating the start of the war. At the conclusion of the war in Europe, Italy and the United Nations signed a treaty in which all parties agreed that World War II in Ethiopia began with Italy's invasion of the country on October 3, 1935.[8] This detail forces us to problematize the dominant narrative of the war that begins and ends in Europe. In addition, this volume enables us to refine our understanding of the similarities and resonances of racial policies and practices among Allied and Axis forces. Britain, France, the United States, Germany, and Italy shared racial ideologies that demonized and infantilized people of African descent, and practiced racial discrimination at home and abroad. Therefore, both Allied and Axis states had to balance their need of black bodies for the war effort against their desire to maintain racial hierarchies and social separation. Finally, a global perspective reminds us that the discussions of what would come in the wake of the war had many contributing voices before competing power blocs reduced those voices to a bipolar Cold War. Ultimately, this volume will help to restore the "world" to the study of the Second World War.

A Note on Structure

This volume is organized into six sections. The first section offers three introductory essays that attempt to give a continent-wide overview of the centrality of Africa's human and material resources to the war effort. The remaining sections offer individual case studies from different parts of the continent. Section Two, *Colonial Subjects and Imperial Armies*, examines the experience of African men recruited for the military from French West Africa, South Africa, Morocco, and Kenya. Section Three, *Mobilizing Communities and Resources for the War Effort*, examines the largely coercive strategies imperial governments used to obtain resources such as rubber, lumber, minerals, or agricultural products from their African colonies and African resistance to them. Section Four, *Race, Gender, and Social Change in a Time of War*, draws on material from Eritrea, Gold Coast, Nigeria, South Africa, and France to illustrate how the war built on certain ideas about race and gender and changed gender relations as it created new opportunities, especially for young men and women. Section Five, *Experiencing War in Africa and Europe*, examines the wartime experiences of female combatants in Ethiopia, African American and African soldiers, French women, and missionaries. Finally, in Section Six, *World War II and Anticolonialism*, case studies from Guinea, Uganda, and Sudan consider the varied ways in which

---

[8] Richard Pankhurst, "Italian Fascist War Crimes in Ethiopia: A History of Their Discussion from the League of Nations to the United Nations (1936–1949)," *Northeast African Studies*, new series, 6 (1999), 109–11.

the war shaped the anticolonial and nationalist movements that intensified after the war. Together they offer a macro and micro view of the multiple levels on which African contributions shaped the war as well as the ways in which the war affected individuals and communities and transformed Africa's political, economic, and social landscape.

ONE

INTRODUCTION

The Military Experiences of Ordinary Africans in World War II

Timothy Parsons

Ordinary African men and women are largely missing from grand narratives of the Second World War. Most histories of the global conflict pay scant attention to Africa and Africans because they focus primarily on the European and Asian theaters, but this lacuna is also due in part to the imperial powers' explicit efforts to downplay and obscure the extent to which they relied on their African subjects to fight and win the war. Faced with severe manpower shortages as the Axis overran much of Europe and Asia between 1939 and 1942, British and French military planners desperately looked to their African colonies to supply combat troops, military laborers, and specialist units. As the tide of the war turned in their favor after 1943, the British and Free French used African formations to augment their overextended forces. Their goal was to "win the peace" by restoring their national honor and reclaiming lost imperial territories before they could fall into the American or Soviet spheres of influence. Mindful that the brutality of the Axis version of imperialism and the egalitarian promises of the Atlantic Charter had made formal empires less reputable after the war, the African imperial powers had good reason to understate the extent to which they had drawn subject populations into a war that did not directly concern them. African soldiers, and the women who interacted with them, are therefore usually consigned to the footnotes of the official histories of the Second World War.

In reality, ordinary Africans were deeply involved in every major theater of the war. Indeed, colonial African troops played central roles in two of the major conflicts that historians conventionally date as preceding the formal outbreak of the conflict in 1939. The Italian forces that invaded Ethiopia in 1935 included approximately 40,000 Somalis, Eritreans, and Libyans.[1] One year later, Francisco Franco began his attempted coup d'état against

---

[1] Harold Nelson, *Somalia: A Country Study*, 3rd ed. (Washington, D.C.: US Government Printing Office, 1982), 24.

the Spanish Republican government by sending Moroccan soldiers from the
Armée d'Afrique to Spain. Some 62,000 Moroccans had fought on the Fascist side by the end of the civil war, and British and French military observers
estimated that they suffered a staggering 40 percent casualty rate.[2] Italy and
Spain were both minor African powers, but their relatively inexpensive and
expendable colonial forces gave Benito Mussolini and Franco the means to
pursue the imperial ambitions that helped touch off the Second World War
in Europe.

By comparison, French African soldiers played a much more central
role in making France a great power. More significantly, French strategists in both world wars relied on the Armée d'Afrique, the army of French
North Africa, and Troupes Coloniales, commonly known as the *Tirailleurs
Sénégalais*, drawn from the West and Equatorial Africa federations, Madagascar, and Indochina as a counterweight to the much larger German Army.
In the spring of 1940, they deployed twelve North African and eight other
colonial divisions (roughly 100,000 Africans in all) against the Germans
in western France. In practice, French generals broke down many of these
larger formations into companies and integrated them with metropolitan
French units. Consequently, the Tirailleurs suffered heavy losses when the
Nazi blitzkrieg broke through the French lines and forced the leaders of
the Third Republic to request an armistice. Records of this chaotic period
are incomplete, but it appears that Germans killed approximately 17,500
African soldiers and took 15,000 more as prisoners of war (POWs) in the
months of May and June 1940.[3] Marshall Philippe Petain's Vichy regime
repatriated some Tirailleurs to Africa, but it sent the more intact African
regiments to garrison French colonies in North Africa and Syria. Moreover, many Tirailleurs continued to languish in hastily constructed camps
in southern France. Petain's government did little to look after the African
POWs who often experienced brutal and humiliating treatment at the hands
of their Nazi capturers.[4]

In West Africa, French imperial officials moved solidly into the Vichy
camp after the Royal Navy bombed the French fleet at the Algerian port
of Mers el-Kebir to keep it out of German hands and the Free French
attacked Dakar. Seeking to expand their West African garrison and lay
the groundwork for the invasion of Britain's West African colonies, Vichy
commanders impressed tens of thousands more Africans into the Tirailleurs

---

[2] Gervase Clarence-Smith, "The impact of the Spanish Civil War and the Second World War
on Portuguese and Spanish Africa," *Journal of African History*, 26 (1985), 324.

[3] Anthony Clayton, *France, Soldiers and Africa* (London: Brassey's Defence Publishers, 1988),
6–7, 124; Myron Echenberg, *Colonial Conscripts: The Tirailleurs Senegalais in French West
Africa, 1857–1960* (Portsmouth, NH: Heinemann, 1991), 88; Gregory Mann, *Native Sons:
West African Veterans and France in the Twentieth Century* (Durham, NC: Duke University
Press, 2006), 111.

[4] See Scheck, Chapter 22, this volume.

Sénégalais.[5] Similarly, North African officials continued to conscript men for units of the Armée d'Afrique.[6] Ironically, Charles de Gaulle's generals did much the same thing in French Equatorial Africa. Most western-focused histories of the Second World War overlook the reality that Brazzaville was the de facto capital of Free France until the Allied invasion of North Africa in 1942 and that the bulk of de Gaulle's forces in the early years of the war consisted of conscripted Equatorial African Tirailleurs. Very few African soldiers in the Vichy and Free French forces had a direct stake in the ideological divisions that split the French empire and put them on opposing sides in the global war.

The same could be said for the Nigerians, Gold Coasters, Sierra Leoneans, and Gambians who joined the Royal West Africa Frontier Force (RWAFF), which was Britain's West African colonial army. Alarmed by threat of a Vichy attack, British military planners rapidly expanded the RWAFF from a collection of lightly armed independent companies intended for colonial self-defense into a modern military formation. Although the French invasion never materialized, the British War Office used the expanded RWAFF to shore up the empire in Africa and Asia.

This was also the case in Northeast Africa where the West Africans were part of a larger African and Indian force fighting to drive the Italians from the Horn of Africa. Caught off guard by the Italian invasion of Ethiopia in 1935, British strategists launched a crash mobilization campaign to upgrade their colonial forces in East Africa and the Sudan.[7] Nevertheless, they were still unprepared for Italy's entry into the war in 1940, powerless to prevent Mussolini from threatening Red Sea communication routes by overrunning British Somaliland.

To meet this threat, the War Office took direct control of the King's African Rifles (KAR) and followed the West African template in transforming it into frontline infantry units. Where the interwar KAR consisted of six small, territorially based battalions drawn from Kenya, Uganda, Tanganyika (now Tanzania), and Nyasaland (now Malawi), it too expanded markedly under metropolitan control. The Northern Rhodesia Regiment and the Somaliland Camel Corps – similar to KAR battalions – were also part of the imperial forces confronting the Italians. As in West Africa, the War Office raised an extensive array of armored car, artillery, medical, educational, transportation, engineering, and other specialist units that allowed

---

[5] Estimates for the numbers of men conscripted in French West Africa between 1940 and 1942 range from 25,000 to 125,000. Nancy Ellen Lawler, *Soldiers of Misfortune: Ivoirien Tirailleurs of World War II* (Athens: Ohio University Press, 1992), 133–14; Echenberg, *Colonial Conscripts*, 88.

[6] See Maghraoui, Chapter 5, this volume.

[7] K. D. D. Henderson, "The Sudan and the Abyssinian campaign," *Journal of the Royal African Society*, 42 (1943), 14; Ahmad al-Awad Muhammad, *The Sudan Defence Force: Origin and Role, 1925–1955* (Khartoum: Institute of African and Asian Studies, c. 1980), 80.

these colonial African battalions to operate as brigades and divisions. Kenya served as the staging area for the liberation of Northeast Africa in 1939. To provide support for the frontline combat troops, the Kenyan government raised two uniformed labor units, which it called pioneer battalions. Recognizing the need to ensure that civilian laborers did not come under enemy fire, imperial planners worked with Kenyan officials to establish the much larger East Africa Military Labour Service (EAMLS) one year later.

Units of the South Africa's Union Defence Force (UDF) formed the core of the forces that invaded Italian East Africa from Kenya. Brushing aside the opposition Nationalist Party's call to remain neutral, Prime Minister Jan Christiaan Smuts took the dominion into the conflict on the side of the Allies in 1939. Nevertheless, Smuts's generals took pains to ensure that wartime mobilization did not disrupt institutionalized racial segregation in South Africa. Consequently, they refused to recruit non-Europeans into the UDF and shunted Africans into the unarmed Native Military Labour Corps (NMLC). The NMLC's officers, who were drawn from the South African Native Affairs Department, were often as concerned with upholding the Union's segregationalist ideals as they were with defeating the Axis. The authorities in Namibia raised a similar unarmed and segregated African labor unit that joined the men of the NMLC on guard duty (often armed only with spears) and menial labor assignments throughout southern Africa. Nonetheless, South African racial sensibilities did not prevent the UDF combat units from serving alongside RWAFF and KAR battalions in two integrated African divisions during the invasion of Italian East Africa.

Indeed, allowing for the presence of two divisions of the Indian Army, the East African campaign, which began in February 1941, was a pan-African conflict that included units of the Sudanese Defence Force, a Free French detachment of Chadian Tirailleurs, elements of the regular Ethiopian army and pro-British Ethiopian "Patriots," and even a small Belgian Congolese combat detachment and medical unit. Belgian officials insisted that elements of their colonial army, the Force Publique, take a nominal part in the operation to strike back against the Axis after the Germans overran their homeland. They also deployed a brigade to Nigeria in 1941 to guard against a potential Vichy attack. Additionally, Lord Hailey, the head of the British Military and Economic Mission in Stanleyville (now Kinshasa), arranged for the No. 10 Belgian Casualty Clearing Station to be attached directly to the British East African forces as a way of keeping the Congo firmly in the Allied camp.[8]

These imperial units faced an Italian force more than 250,000 strong that was roughly 71 percent African. While the opposing forces were equally

---

[8] Bruce Fetter, "Changing war aims: Central Africa's role, 1940–41, as seen from Leopoldville," *African Affairs*, 87 (1988), 388–9; Kenya governor to general officer commanding East Africa, GH 4/690/1, November 27, 1945, Kenya National Archives (hereafter KNA), Nairobi.

matched in terms of weaponry and materiel, one of the keys to the relatively easy Allied victory was the fact that Britain's African colonial formations were far superior to their Italian counterparts in terms of leadership, training, and morale. Most of the Somalis, Ethiopians, and Eritreans wearing Italian uniforms were unwilling and restive conscripts who had no sympathy for Mussolini's grand imperial designs in Africa. Consequently, many Italian units rebelled or melted away during the fighting, and by July 1941, the Ethiopian capital of Addis Ababa was in Allied hands. British military and civil officials took the superior performance of their African troops as an affirmation of their superiority as an imperial power, but there was no reason for the Africans in either colonial army to fight each other apart from their different uniforms and officers. Moreover, the British and Italian officers made it clear that race trumped wartime animosities by socializing with each other on equal terms after the Italian surrender.[9] Similarly, many African soldiers angrily noted that Italian POWs lived better than they did.

With Northeast Africa secure in 1942, British military planners looked for ways to use African resources and manpower in the much more strategically important Mediterranean theater. Pressed by Axis victories in Libya and western Egypt that threatened the Suez Canal, they faced a serious manpower shortage after the loss of considerable numbers of imperial troops in the fall of Greece and Crete and the redeployment of Australian units to defend British interests in Asia after the Japanese attack on Pearl Harbor. The South African formations that had fought in Ethiopia replaced some of the Australians on the frontlines, but imperial strategists looked primarily to British Africa for uniformed military laborers to provide logistical support for the Allied Forces operating in North Africa and the Middle East. Unlike their counterparts in the uniquely distinct colonial infantry regiments, the Africans who served in this capacity joined a much larger metropolitan military unit. Formed at the start of the war to support the British forces fighting in France, the Royal Pioneer Corps expanded to draw on the manpower of the empire. By 1942, there were pioneers from Africa, Cyprus, Palestine, India, Mauritius, and the Seychelles serving in the Middle East, but civil officials in Africa insisted that their "natives" could not be treated as regular British troops. Consequently, the Directorate of Pioneers and Labour for the Middle East Forces created the African Auxiliary Pioneer Corps (AAPC) to accommodate colonial sensibilities.

While there were West African pioneer companies, the bulk of the AAPC came from Kenya, Uganda, and the High Commission Territories (HCTs)

---

9 G. Gifford, "The Sudan at war: The Composite Infantry Battalion of the Eastern Arab Corps, Sudan Defence Force, the Abyssinian Campaign," *Journal of the Royal African Society*, 42 (1943), 164; Neil Orpen, *South African Forces in World War Two* (Cape Town: Purnell, 1971), 342; "History of the war in the Northern Frontier District, 1 June–31 August 1940," PC NFD 4/1/11, KNA, Nairobi. See also Barrerra, Chapter 14, this volume.

of Bechuanaland (now Botswana), Basutoland (now Lesotho), and Swaziland. In the East African case, Kenyan and Ugandan officials recruited most of their companies from men already serving in the EAMLS. In southern Africa, British district officers and African elites in the HCTs welcomed the opportunity for their men to enlist in an imperial formation that provided a welcome alternative to the degrading and unpopular South African Native Military Labour Service. Ever mindful that the South Africa government hoped to incorporate them into the Union, the Sotho, Swazis, and Tswana hoped to maintain their autonomy by placing the British empire in their debt. Thus, the "native authorities" in these protectorates strongly supported the imperial recruiting efforts.

The AAPC's primary mission was to provide logistical support for the British Eighth Army's campaign against the Germans and Italians in North Africa. African pioneer companies repaired tanks, assembled trucks, served as dockworkers and built railway lines, roads, and water pipelines. While the AAPC companies had some combat training, their officers never actually expected them to fight because their official role was to work behind the front lines. This was an unrealistic assumption in the Egyptian and Libyan deserts, where the fortunes of war shifted constantly in the first half of 1942. In 1942, the Axis forces captured several hundred East African pioneers after they overran the fortified Libyan port of Tobruk. Later that month, forty more East Africans burned to death when the Germans bombed the oil depot at the Abu Hagag railway station.[10] Given the intensity of the fighting, it was hardly surprising that several East African companies broke under the stress of the British retreat back into Egypt. More than 200 pioneers ended up in first Italian and then German POW camps where they often suffered the same brutal treatment experienced by the Tirailleurs who fell into German hands after the fall of France.[11]

While most of the Eighth Army was in disarray during this difficult period, colonial political concerns placed additional strain on East Africans. Most of their officers were former members of the colonial administration who lacked military experience and insisted that the AAPC follow "native custom" to ensure that the pioneers did not become "detribalized" during their military service. Morale understandably sank as the East Africans realized that this meant that their rations and service conditions were decidedly inferior to other imperial units. Similar tensions simmered in the South African forces where the civil authorities insisted on digging up the graves of white

[10] Kenyan secretariat minute, July 28, 1942, MD 4/5/66/24; Report by Lt. J. E. V. Ross, welfare officer, July 27, 1942, MD 4/5/66/26a, KNA. Nairobi.

[11] Kenyan chief native commissioner, minute, 1943, MD 4/5/66/38, KNA, Nairobi; Private Pherison Batton, Camp 85/VI to native commissioner (Chiradzulu, Nyasaland), January, 1943, S45 3/2/2, National Archives of Malawi (hereafter NAM), Zomba; Bildad Kaggia, *Roots of Freedom*, 1921–1963 (Nairobi: East Africa Publishing House, 1975), 56.

soldiers who were buried alongside members of the NMLC.[12] The West African and High Commission Territory AAPC companies missed most of the fighting in the months before the British victory at El Alamein in August 1942, and therefore had a better reputation than their East African counterparts. Nonetheless, the pioneer experience during this difficult time demonstrated that colonial racial sensibilities undermined the military effectiveness of Britain's African troops.

French African soldiers in the Middle East served under equally difficult conditions. There was a Tirailleur battalion with the Free French forces attached to the Eighth Army in Egypt, and Tirailleurs fought on both sides when the Allies seized Vichy-controlled Syria in June 1941. Knowing nothing of the larger political divisions that led one French force to go to war against another, Ivoirians in the Vichy garrison were shocked to find that their attackers were French Equatorial Africans. As Namble Silue told Nancy Lawler: "De Gaulle's men attacked us. The Camerounians attacked us. We were amazed because they weren't Germans. They were black. Why were they attacking us?"[13] When Silue and his comrades surrendered, de Gaulle's generals simply dressed most of them in new uniforms and incorporated them into the Free French forces on the assumption that conscripted Africans were not entitled to choose sides in the war.

This is how large numbers of French African subjects again found themselves fighting on European soil as the Allies rolled up the Nazi empire in the later years of the war. Although they are largely missing from the grand French narrative of self-liberation from the Germans, colonial troops from North, West, and Equatorial Africa made up a significant portion of the Free French forces fighting in Italy and then France.[14] Seeking to obscure the role that Africans played in freeing France from Nazi rule, de Gaulle ordered the *blanchissement* (whitening) of the Second Free French armored division before the liberation of Paris in August 1944 by replacing Africans with members of the French resistance. As winter approached he further obscured the role that non-European troops had played in the liberation by redeploying some 20,000 African soldiers to southern France.[15] The Free French government had every intention of reclaiming the French empire after the war and therefore did not want to acknowledge that it owed any debt to its imperial subjects.

---

[12] Ashley Jackson, "African soldiers and imperial authorities: Tensions and unrest during the service of High Commission Territories soldiers in the British army, 1941–46," *Journal of Southern African Studies*, 25 (1999), 648–9; Kenneth Grundy, *Soldiers Without Politics: Blacks in the South African Armed Forces* (Berkeley: University of California Press, 1983), 81.

[13] Lawler, *Soldiers of Misfortune*, 143.

[14] See Maghraoui, Chapter 5, this volume.

[15] Anthony Beevor and Artemis Cooper, *Paris after the Liberation, 1944–1949*, 2nd ed. (New York: Penguin Books, 2004), 31; Lawler, *Soldiers of Misfortune*, 179.

Most British imperial officials opposed using colonial troops in Europe for just this reason. This was particularly true in East Africa where the colonial governments barred the War Office from using their AAPC companies in the 1943 Italian campaign. Citing concerns over cold weather and promises to keep African troops in Africa, they rejected the Middle East Command's proposals to free up European manpower by assigning African pioneers to support roles in Italy. In opposing this "dilution" of regular British Army formations with East African pioneers, a senior Kenyan official serving with the Middle East forces made it clear that postwar political concerns trumped military necessity: "Someone has to do the manual work. If we allow ourselves to think for a moment that manual work is in any sense derogatory, what is to happen to these thousands of Pioneers after the war?... Their living must for many years be on the land, either their own or a European farm."[16]

The HCTs, which did not have to answer to politically connected settlers, were more willing to allow their pioneers to serve alongside British troops. The Swaziland government bowed to the wishes of Paramount Chief Sobhuza II in insisting that Swazi troops had to stay together, but Sotho and Tswana soldiers became antiaircraft gunners, smoke generator operators, firemen, sentries, and frontline support troops in metropolitan units throughout the Middle East and Italy. Sotho troops serving with a heavy artillery battalion of the Essex Regiment even wore its regimental badge. The dilution experiment was largely successful, but the South African parliament was so alarmed that racial mixing might threaten the racial order in the Union that it passed a law making it illegal for African noncommissioned officers to give orders to European privates.[17]

British colonial governments in East and West Africa met the War Office's demands for African manpower and avoided these thorny sorts of racial problems by only allowing their troops to serve in Asia where, in theory, they would be exposed to fewer contaminating influences. In October 1939, the inspector general of the KAR and RWAFF made plans for the deployment of African troops to defend British interests in the Middle and Far East, and after the Italian surrender in Ethiopia the commander-in-chief of imperial forces in India formally requested African reinforcements.[18] The KAR

---

[16] Lt. Colonel E. L. Brooke Anderson to chief secretary, East African Governors' Conference, October 16, 1942, MD 4/5/137/125a, KNA, Nairobi.

[17] R. A. R. Bent, *Ten Thousand Men of Africa: The Story of the Bechuanaland Pioneers and Gunners, 1941–1946* (London: HMS Stationery Office for Bechuanaland Government, 1952), 89; Brian Gray, *Basuto Soldiers in Hitler's War* (Maseru: Mojira Printing Works for Basuto Government, 1953), 63; Ashley Jackson, "Supplying the war: The High Commission Territories' military-logistical contribution in the Second World War," *Journal of Military History*, 66 (2002), 652.

[18] Hubert Moyse-Bartlett, *The King's African Rifles* (Aldershot: Gale & Polden, 1956), 480; commander-in-chief (India), to War Office, December 1, 1941, CO 968/11/5, The National Archives (TNA), Kew.

formed the core of the Eleventh (East Africa) Division and two independent brigades, which also included the Congolese Tenth Casualty Clearing Station and battalions of the Northern Rhodesia Regiment and the Rhodesian African Rifles. Colonial officials in Rhodesia raised the later regiment in 1942 over the vociferous objections of the Rhodesian settlers, who shared the South African objections to arming and training Africans. In the West African colonies, where there were no settlers, it was much easier to expand the RWAFF and its support units to create the Eighty-first and Eighty-second (West Africa) Divisions for service in Asia.[19]

Initially, an East African brigade replaced Indian garrison troops in Ceylon (now Sri Lanka) in late 1941. Several months later, another KAR brigade took part in the invasion of Madagascar to ensure that the Vichy administration did not open the Diego Suarez naval base to Japanese submarines. As in Ethiopia and Syria, ordinary Africans once again fought each other simply because they were serving in opposing colonial armies. In this case, the Madagascar garrison consisted of 500 Tirailleurs, a local artillery unit, Reunioais engineers and medical units from Indochina, Syria, and Morocco. After an initial landing by British and South African troops, the East Africans seized the rest of the island for the Allies after some fairly stiff resistance from the Tirailleurs.[20]

Such fratricidal combat was merely a prelude to the much more intense fighting that colonial African troops faced in Southeast Asia. Seeking to defend India, reopen supply routes to the nationalist forces in southern China, and reclaim Burma and Malaya for the postwar empire, British imperial forces waged a three-year-long campaign against the Japanese in the jungles of Burma. Although military historians have rediscovered this "forgotten war," the roughly 90,000 Africans (9 percent of the imperial troops in Southeast Asia) who fought in it still remain out of the spotlight.[21] When they went into action in early 1944, the tide had largely turned against the Japanese, but African troops played a central role in filling out the overstretched Fourteenth Army. The West African divisions operated for months on air-dropped supplies in Burma's coastal Arakan region, while the Eleventh (East Africa) Division seized a vital bridgehead over the Chindwin River in central Kabaw valley during the summer 1944 offensive.

[19] W. V. Brelsford, *The Story of the Northern Rhodesia Regiment* (Lusaka: Government Printer, 1954), 87; A Haywood and F. A. S. Clarke, *The History of the Royal West African Frontier Force* (Aldershot: Wellington Press, 1964), 374; Christopher Owen, *The Rhodesian African Rifles* (London: Leo Cooper, 1970), 1–4, 16.

[20] "An account of the operations of 22 (EA) Bde, 10 September–6 November 1942," VIII/5, Dimoline Papers, Liddell Hart Centre, King's College London; A. G. F. Monro, "Madagascar Interlude," *Army Quarterly*, 53 (1947), 212; Clayton, *France, Soldiers and Africa*, 136.

[21] David Smurthwaite, *The Forgotten War: The British Army in the Far East, 1941–1945* (London: National Army Museum, 1992), 17, 67.

Both operations entailed brutally intimate jungle fighting, which often exposed and inflamed the blatant inequities of colonial military service. Dissatisfaction with poor rations, low pay, and inferior equipment even spread to the British officers who led African troops. The Eleventh Division's unofficial nickname became "half-price" in a grumbling reference to its inferior treatment in comparison to the Indian Army divisions that it served with in the Burma campaign. The Northern Rhodesia Regiment's official motto was *Diversi genere fides pares* (different in race, equal in loyalty), but this was not the case for African troops in the Southeast Asia Command. The same colonial political considerations that undermined morale in the East African AAPC companies in North Africa were at play in Burma where African troops faced the added burden of receiving difficult assignments based on their senior commanders' romanticized tribalistic stereotypes that Africans were "natural" jungle fighters. While many African soldiers and their officers, particularly metropolitan junior officers, won decorations and promotions for fighting bravely and tenaciously, some battalions experienced incidents of "mass refusals" and blatant insubordination as they nearly collapsed under the stress of combat.[22]

A mixed record of heroism and indiscipline was hardly limited to African units and occurred to varying degrees in every army that took part in the Second World War. Nevertheless, it is entirely understandable to ask why a colonial soldier should accept the hardships or personal risks of wartime service to an authoritarian empire. Some Nyasalanders serving in the King's African Rifles were personally insulted when European officers suggested that they were apolitical mercenaries: "It really makes us rather ashamed to hear that we only want to earn money as we do in ordinary work."[23] Regardless of the colonial army in question, it is safe to say that some African soldiers were genuine volunteers while others were obvious conscripts, but there were also less clear-cut cases where chiefs, civil officials, and employers coerced men into joining colonial militaries. These categories are important, for the circumstances under which a man became a particular kind of colonial soldier were usually the primary factor in determining how he viewed the nature of his service and behaved in combat.

At the official level, there appeared to be clear distinctions between the recruiting philosophy and practices of the various African powers in World War II. The French system was relatively straightforward, for the French unapologetically made conscription the primary basis of recruitment in both the peace and wartime Tirailleurs Sénégalais. Similarly, the Italians used conscription to impress 60,000 Eritreans (roughly 40 percent of the able-bodied

---

[22] Lt Col M. W. Biggs to General Mansergh, commander, 11th (EA) Division, January 3, 1945, M. W. Biggs private papers.

[23] Native Authority Mbelwa, "Complaints laid down by askaris, December 14, 1944, S41 1/23/4/53a, NAM, Zomba.

adult male population) into their East African colonial army.[24] Invoking the Jacobian ideal that all citizens and subjects had a duty to serve the republic, French colonial officials depicted conscripted military service as a civilizing influence on primitive peoples. To this end, they conducted an annual lottery that sent tens of thousands of young men into either the Tirailleurs or the *deuxième portion* (second portion), which was essentially a semimilitarized labor unit.[25] By the 1930s, the stigma and unpleasant consequences of being consigned to the *deuxième portion* led many men to volunteer for military service, but French officials actually preferred to meet their manpower targets through conscription because enlistment bonuses for volunteers were too expensive. Other potential conscripts avoided serving the republic altogether by fleeing the annual dragnet: Roughly 20 percent of the men on the annual recruiting census lists failed to turn up between 1923 and 1946.[26] Some draft dodgers were not averse to joining a colonial army; rather, they simply wanted better terms of service. Consequently, the British RWAFF, which usually offered superior wages and benefits, drew heavily on men from French West Africa (FWA).

The efficiency and invasiveness of the French recruiting system allowed both Vichy and Free French officials to conscript tens of thousands of Africans even after France had fallen to the Germans.[27] The Vichy regime in West Africa, in particular, impressed approximately 20,000 laborers into the *deuxième portion* between 1941 and 1943.[28] Few soldiers had the education or access to information to make sense of these metropolitan political divisions, which explains how they found themselves serving on both sides of the conflict. Some men also crossed freely back and forth between the French and British colonial forces on their own initiative. The Tirailleurs of the Bataillon Sénégalais de Marche No. 10, which mutinied in Madagascar when faced with deployment to French Indochina, sent the following note to a very surprised British officer:

> Some of us have served in the Royal West African Frontier Force, before we deserted to get better pay with the French Army. We have never had any pay, nor have we had the opportunity of fighting the enemy as we were promised . . . Now we say to you, English Colonel, that all the men of the B. M. 10 are willing to serve in the English Army.[29]

This appeal was not particularly remarkable or unique; British recruiters were generally unconcerned with a man's origins so long as he met their physical standards for enlistment.

[24] See Barrerra, Chapter 14, this volume.
[25] See Ash, Chapter 6, and Schmidt, Chapter 23, this volume.
[26] Echenberg, *Colonial Conscripts*, 60–1, 70, 74–6.
[27] See Schmidt, Chapter 23, this volume.
[28] See Ash, Chapter 6, this volume.
[29] Monro, "Madagascar interlude," 216.

British colonial officials took pride in distinguishing themselves from their French counterparts in asserting that all their combat troops were volunteers, an important and necessary distinction, for the claim that they ruled African colonies as the benevolent trustees of primitive peoples made overt conscription politically impossible. Dragging supposedly simple "tribesmen" into a brutal global war would have undermined the fundamental legitimizing ideology of British rule in Africa. Consequently, imperial military doctrine held that all frontline colonial combat soldiers served the empire voluntarily. Therefore, recruiting advertisements emphasizing this appeal for the Rhodesian African Rifles were the norm in most British colonies: "Those who wish to serve their King should apply to the nearest Native Commissioner's office . . . Rates of pay are [generous]. Conditions of service also include free cloths, rations and quarters."[30] Similarly, Afrikaner opposition to the war in South Africa meant that members of the UDF voluntarily took a special oath to serve abroad with the imperial forces.[31]

On paper, these provisions created the appearance that the members of Britain's colonial combat formations were indeed volunteers, but in practice, many Africans who served in the KAR, the RWAFF, and other colonial infantry units were de facto conscripts. In most colonies district officers told the native authorities to bring in a set number of recruits each month and were not particularly concerned with how the chiefs met their quotas. This was the case in South Africa, where civil officials imagined that "tribal chiefs" had the customary authority to muster tribesmen for combat.[32] Not surprisingly, chiefs throughout colonial Africa used conscription to get rid of rivals and intimidate their constituents. In West Africa, private employers ordered their workers to join the military, particularly after several mines shut down for the duration of the war. In West and East Africa, press gangs under the command of African noncommissioned officers operated. An overly large schoolboy in central Kenya, Jackson Mulinge, who would go on to command the independent Kenya Army, fell victim to one such gang. Recruiters also used more subtle tactics to coerce men into the military. In western Kenya, a district officer forced a defiant young man to dress like a woman until he volunteered in an effort to recover his masculinity.[33]

In attempting to make a sharp distinction between combat and labor units, British colonial authorities argued that it was morally acceptable to conscript Africans for theoretically safer unarmed service behind the front

---

[30] Owen, *The Rhodesian African Rifles*, 6; see also Byfield, Chapter 2, this volume.
[31] See Chetty, Chapter 16, this volume.
[32] See Grundlingh, Chapter 4, this volume.
[33] K. L. Hunter, "Memoirs of an administrative officer," Mss.Afr.S. 1942, Rhodes House Library, Bodleian Library of Commonwealth and African Studies, Oxford University; interview with Jackson Mulinge, Nairobi, 1993; Wendell Holbrook, "Oral history and the nascent historiography for West Africa and World War II: A focus on Ghana," *International Journal of Oral History*, 3 (1982), 158–60; Kaggia, *Roots of Freedom*, 21.

lines. Conscription also gave them a way to better manage African man-power, ensuring that military recruiting did not draw off labor from strate-gically important industries and politically connected settlers. The HCTs accepted that the AAPC paid lower wages than the South African mines, and Basutoland's resident commissioner insisted that "compulsion, naked and unashamed" was the only fair way to manage the protectorate's work-force and share the burden of service. In Namibia, recruiters privileged the interests of European employers by operating primarily in the northern native reserves, while in East Africa the Kenyan settlers managed to shut down most military labor recruiting after 1943.[34]

From an African perspective, the politics and practice of British con-scription and recruiting policies were complex. Conscripts sometimes found themselves working for civilian employers, while conscripted pioneers – theoretically noncombatants – often found themselves on the frontlines in North Africa, Italy, and Burma. In many cases the men who resisted con-scription into the unarmed labor units willingly volunteered for the KAR and RWAFF to secure better pay and affirm their masculinity. In South Africa, even the NMLC attracted willing recruits because it paid far more than civil employers.[35] Moreover, there were many cases where educated men, who had a much better understanding of the Axis powers' more virulent brand of racism, willingly answered Britain's call for volunteers. Ganda nobles and royal family members demonstrated their commitment to the empire by enlisting in a special territorial battalion that became the frontline Seventh KAR.[36] John Henry Smythe, who voluntarily joined the Royal Air Force in Sierra Leone, spoke for many Africans when he explained that Hitler's racist ideology, which he encountered in *Mein Kampf*, "would put any black man's back right up and it put mine up."[37]

Anger with Hitler and distrust of the Axis did not mean that African soldiers willingly accepted unequal treatment or inequitable service. They were not particularly more restive than other Allied troops; however, pop-ular narratives of World War II as a "good war" tend to obscure the real-ity that all military institutions experience some level of disobedience and insubordination. African units were beset by a variety of colonialism-related

[34] Robert Gordon, "The impact of the Second World War on Namibia," *Journal of South-ern African Studies*, 19 (1993), 153–4; Hamilton Sipho Simelane, "Veterans, politics and poverty: The case of Swazi veterans in the Second World War," *South African Historical Journal*, 38 (1998), 161; Timothy Parsons, *The African Rank-and-File: Social Implications of Colonial Service in the King's African Rifles, 1902–1964* (Portsmouth: Heinemann, 1999), 74; Jackson, "Supplying the war," 731.

[35] See Grundlingh, Chapter 4, this volume.

[36] See Summers, Chapter 25, this volume.

[37] Quoted in David Killingray, *Fighting for Britain: African Soldiers in the Second World War* (Woodbridge, Suffolk: James Currey, 2010), 53.

disciplinary problems over the course of the war that stemmed directly from the subordinate status of their rank-and-file soldiers.

At the individual level, men fortunate enough to be stationed in their home colonies simply fled the military when they were dissatisfied with the circumstances of their enlistment or terms of service. As a Nyasaland Signaller explained to a friend: "I am now tired of signal work and I want to run away so if you hear nothing at all you will know that I have hit the trail for a place from where I will not return."[38] In East Africa, there were 14,000 men absent without leave in March 1945, while South African authorities listed 2,693 men as missing from the NMLC by the end of the war.[39] The ease of desertion probably kept tensions manageably low: Recordkeeping was so spotty in colonial Africa that deserters rarely faced any form of sanction or punishment despite a concerted effort by the military authorities to round them up as the pool of recruits shrank at the end of the war. Nyasalanders helped thwart government attempts to capture deserters by spreading rumors that the military police seeking missing soldiers were actually kidnapping people to make quinine from their blood and brains.[40]

Discontent could become dangerous when escape was not an option. After the liberation of Ethiopia, an entire brigade of East African troops (roughly 6,000 men) refused to board ships for the invasion of Madagascar in February 1942 on the grounds that their officers had promised they could go home after defeating the Italians. As tensions simmered a battalion commander received an ominous letter promising that "if we go to war again we ourselves will shoot you." Similarly, another soldier in the brigade openly questioned why he and his fellows had to fight for Britain: "You Europeans say you help us. But do you? It is us black men who help you. We have not got an Empire to defend. You have."[41] In North Africa, AAPC members echoed these sentiments in protesting that they received inferior wages and rations in comparison to British and Indian troops: "If one offers himself to become his Majesty's soldier and agrees to his Government that he is prepared to meet his death if necessary, is it right that this man should be treated like a slave?"[42]

---

[38] Signaler R. Alex Nyallapah to W. M. Nyallapah, September 29, 1943, S45/3/2/2, NAM, Zomba.

[39] African Manpower Conference, March 6, 1945, DEF/15/29/118a, KNA, Nairobi; Louis Grundlingh, "'Non-Europeans should be kept away from the temptations of towns': Controlling black South African Soldiers during the Second World War," *International Journal of African Historical Studies*, 25 (1992), 555.

[40] *Political Intelligence Bulletin*, No. 4, 1943, located in S34/1/4/1, NAM, Zomba.

[41] Anonymous letter to commanding office, February 1942, 2/4 KAR, VP, KNA, Nairobi; Commanding officer 2/3 KAR to HQ 25 Brigade, February 17, 1942, WO 169/6965, TNA, Kew.

[42] Petition of the 442 Motor Transport Company, February 14, 1943, MD 4/5/137/144e, KNA, Nairobi.

These festering grievances explain the violence and mass insubordination that plagued the Eleventh (EA) Division in Burma. Grenade and rifle attacks by angry African soldiers killed at least three British officers and NCOs and wounded fifteen more in more poorly run battalions. Writing frankly in a top secret report, the commander of the Fourteenth Army admitted he was "anxious" about the division and warned that if the soldiers' demands for leave were not addressed, the African division would become "a liability and a constant anxiety to whatever formation it belongs."[43]

Colonial political considerations also produced problems in French-speaking African units, particularly when soldiers believed they were being cheated or abused. In 1940, a contingent of Guinean Tirailleurs, who were fortunate enough to return home after the fall of France, attacked French civil officials in Conakry when their back pay was not forthcoming.[44] When a contaminated smallpox vaccine killed a number of recruits in the Belgian Congo, rumors flew through the Force Publique that the rations of canned meat with a smiling African on the label contained their dead comrades. In late 1944, these stories convinced the members of the Luluabourg garrison to join an aborted civil conspiracy to overthrow Belgian rule. Six months later, mutinous Tirailleurs, who hoped to transfer to the British colonial forces in Madagascar, stoned their commander when he tried to explain why they were not eligible for hardship pay.[45]

Disciplinary incidents over terms of service were relatively common in all colonial forces, but much more serious problems emerged among the Tirailleurs stranded in France after the Allied liberation in 1944. Like the restive British African soldiers in Burma, they wanted to go home, but the Allies could not find sufficient shipping. Consequently, thousands of survivors of German POW camps and the 20,000 Tirailleurs that de Gaulle withdrew from combat as he whitened the Free French forces seethed over poor food, inadequate housing, unpaid wages, and racial insults by sub-standard temporary officers.[46] At least fifteen strikes and mutinies erupted in ramshackle army camps throughout southern France in the second half of 1944. Unquestionably, the most serious incident took place at a transit camp in the Dakar suburb of Thiaroye where some 500 Tirailleurs struck when the French colonial authorities tried to convert their saved wages from metropolitan to colonial francs. On December 1, 1944, the mutineers, certain they were being cheated because of confusing exchange rates, refused to board trains for Bamako and tried to take up arms. The French killed thirty-five of them in putting down the insurrection.[47]

---

[43] Lt. General Slim, commander 14th Army to HQ Allied Land Forces South East Asia, February 1, 1945, WO 203/1794, TNA, Kew.

[44] See Schmidt, Chapter 23, this volume.

[45] Bruce Fetter, "The Luluabourg revolt at Elisabethville," *African Historical Studies*, 2 (1969), 272–4; Monro, "Madagascar interlude," 216.

[46] See Scheck, Chapter 22, this volume.

[47] Echenberg, *Colonial Conscripts*, 100–1; Mann, *Native Sons*, 116–17.

As was the case in many World War II-era armies, tensions over women was another key cause of these disciplinary incidents, but here too colonial political considerations made the situation worse by attempting to dictate which women African soldiers could and could not interact with. In trying to control the intimate relations of rank-and-file troops, civil and military officials tried to ensure that wartime military service did not undermine gendered racial distinctions that were central to European rule in Africa. Consequently, the French authorities tried to keep the Tirailleurs away from French women, and British military censors were alarmed to discover that Africans serving in North Africa and Asia believed that they were having sex with "white" women. British and French officers also worried that unsuitable women would infect their African soldiers with venereal diseases, subversive political ideas, and unacceptable notions of social and racial equality.

Yet most colonial military authorities believed that African men had to have sex and worried that even more serious disciplinary problems would result if they insisted that their troops remain chaste for the duration of the war. This was a gross overgeneralization, but like most soldiers, many Africans who fought in the Second World War believed that their service affirmed their masculinity. Writing of the accomplishments of his fellow soldiers during the war, Robert Kakembo declared: "The African [soldier] has proved to Europeans that he is a man. He can and does reveal his ability for amazing feats of exertion."[48] Many African soldiers believed that their accomplishments in combat entitled them to have relationships with women, and this was one of the main reasons that the military labor units were so unpopular. Many soldiers believed that women would mock them as cowards if they didn't fight or carry weapons. Afrikaner men, who had little sympathy for the British empire, joined the UDF for similar reasons.[49]

Colonial officers therefore looked for acceptable ways to meet these expectations without compromising military health or discipline. Given that 32,400 soldiers (both African and European) in East Africa received treatment for venereal disease in 1943, this was also a tactical and strategic concern.[50] One solution was to bring women within the bounds of military discipline by setting up supervised brothels. A senior British medical officer argued that: "Absolute continence in the young African far removed from his home and natural surroundings is not easy to inculate . . . It is surely better to offer him a mistress who has been under medical supervision than to

[48] Robert Kakembo, *An African Soldier Speaks* (Kampala: George C. Turner, 1944), 2. The original manuscript was censored by the East Africa Command, but it was eventually published by George C. Turner (Kampala) and the Livingstone Press (London) in 1947.
[49] See Chetty, Chapter 16, this volume.
[50] EAC Standing Committee for Combating VD, March 3, 1944, BY 13/91/19a, KNA, Nairobi.

trust to the doubtful efficiency of preventive ablution to save him from the inevitable [consequences] of clandestine appointments with ... harlots."[51] This was not a controversial position for the French military, which ran officially sanctioned Bordels Mobiles de Campagne (mobile brothels) for its imperial troops. But British notions of morality forced colonial units to be far more discreet in setting up similar institutions for their men. Over the vociferous objections of military chaplains, many of whom were missionaries in peacetime, pragmatic junior officers established covert brothels under the supervision of cooperative military doctors. While these measures actually did relatively little to reduce VD infection rates, they served a secondary function of further isolating African soldiers from the civil population.[52]

These policies reflected a strong misogynistic thread running through colonial military policies towards women. Both British and French officers considered them threats to discipline and military effectiveness, which placed the women living near military installations or in operational areas at some risk. Harkening back to the Victorian-era Cantonment Acts, many colonies adopted legislation empowering the police to detain and inspect women "loitering" near camps or railway stations.[53] While some of these people were indeed prostitutes, others were wives, lovers, family members, or simply friends. For women who were mere bystanders, it could be quite dangerous to get too close to these installations, for spotty discipline and weak leadership often made sexual assault a serious problem in colonial armies.

Yet it would be a mistake to view the relations of African soldiers with women solely through the lens of commerce and predation. Ethiopian women served directly with the irregular Patriot formations during the liberation of Ethiopia.[54] Some Tirailleurs stranded in France formed strong emotional ties to local women in spite of the best efforts of the French authorities to enforce gendered racial segregation.[55] Many men serving with French and British forces in Europe and Southeast Asia were committed family men who grew dangerously restive at the end of the war because they desperately wanted to go home.

[51] Deputy director of medical services, quarterly report, 12 (A) Division, October–December 1942, WO 222/1808, TNA, Kew.

[52] Clayton, *Soldiers and France in Africa*, 15; interviews with R. S. N. Mans and G. W. H. Goode, London, 1994; G. K. Young, Mss.Afr.s.1715/309, Rhodes House Library, Bodleian Library of Commonwealth and African Studies, Oxford University; Consultant Venereologist Lees, Middle East Forces, Report for 4th quarter, 1943, February 21, 1944, WO/222/1302, TNA, Kew.

[53] For example, see the Defence (Amendment Compulsory Treatment of Venereal Diseases) Regulations, 1944, S40/1/8/4/35a, NAM, Zomba. See also Ray, Chapter 18, this volume.

[54] See Habtu and Byfield, Chapter 20, this volume.

[55] See Ginio, Chapter 17, this volume.

Unfortunately, the inferior status of African troops put them at the end of line for repatriation after the Axis surrender. Lacking a responsive government to intervene on their behalf with the military authorities, they often had to stand in as imperial garrison troops for the more privileged metropolitan citizen soldiers who got to go home first. As a frustrated medic in Southeast Asia complained in early 1946: "We have been told the war is finished, but that . . . we will have to wait five or six months . . . The Europeans are selfish, most of them are demobilised, and if you ask them when the African troops are going back they just say there are no ships."[56] Tswana and Sotho in the AAPC similarly found themselves guarding British military installations in the Middle East long after the war was over, and several companies were caught in the crossfire of the Zionist guerilla war against the British in Palestine. Thus, the demobilization process lasted well into 1948 in most African colonies.

Two years later, an official British government report boasted of repatriating 350,000 eastern, central, and southern African ex-servicemen, but it is impossible to know precisely how many Africans served in the Second World War, much less how many came home from it. This was particularly true for the Tirailleurs Sénégalais because three different regimes oversaw their conscription, but it is safe to estimate that more than 200,000 Africans, and possibly as many as 350,000, fought for one of the French factions over the course of the conflict. Roughly 155,000 men served in the RWAFF and its various support arms, while the British recruited an additional 4,900 West Africans for the Royal Air Force and 4,200 more for the Royal Navy. The fact that many of these soldiers actually came from French West Africa further complicated the demobilization process. Recruiting records for the AAPC are scanty, but it is likely that at least 250,000 East and Central Africans served in British colonial military units over the course of the war. In southern Africa, approximately 36,000 pioneers from the HCTs served in AAPC companies, while the South African NMLC numbered 76,000 men. Allowing for an estimated 40,000 men in the wartime Force Publique, 40,000 in the Sudan Defence Force, and approximately 140,000 Northeasterners fighting for the Italians, this means that just short of a million Africans were veterans of the Second World War.[57]

While this figure represents an educated guess, it is even harder to determine how many African soldiers died or suffered permanent injury as a

[56] "Report of morale of British, Indian and colonial troops of Allied Land Forces, Southeast Asia, January 1946," WO/203/2268, TNA, Kew.
[57] "Report of the Demobilisation and Resettlement Committee, 12 July 1945," DEF 10/39/77a, KNA, Nairobi; William Platt, "East African forces in the war and their future," *Journal of the Royal United Services Institute*, 93 (1948), 409; John Keegan, *World Armies* (London: Macmillan, 1979), 57; Muhammad, *The Sudan Defence Force*, 99; Echenberg, *Colonial Conscripts*, 88; Grundlingh, "'Non-Europeans should be kept away from the temptations of towns,'" 539; Jackson, "African soldiers and imperial authorities," 645.

result of their wartime service. Myron Echenberg estimates that French West African units suffered a 12 percent casualty rate. There is no comparable statistic available for the British colonial African forces, but the decidedly incomplete records available indicate that in the West and East African formations in Burma, 858 men were lost and 4,266 wounded. Civil authorities in East Africa listed 7,301 soldiers as deceased over the course of the war, but this figure does not fit with casualty reports from individual colonies and specific units. The torpedoing of troopships carrying Sotho pioneers to Malta and East African artillerymen to Southeast Asia alone resulted in nearly 1,500 deaths.[58] Disability figures for African veterans are even more problematic. The Kenyan government listed roughly fifty ex-servicemen as permanently disabled in 1945, but a civil official for a single Kenyan province reported more than 1,000 permanently incapacitated World War II veterans five years later.[59]

Poor recordkeeping was understandable, given the rudimentary nature of wartime colonial bureaucracies, but obscuring the service and sacrifices of African soldiers paid an admittedly unplanned political dividend in undercutting veterans' demands for recognition and compensation for their contribution to the Allied victory. Many of these men were aware of the egalitarian (and implicitly anti-imperial) promises embedded in the Atlantic and United Nations Charters and expected them to apply to colonial Africa. Few thought in terms of national independence; rather, they generally expected political rights, economic opportunity, and social equality. Like most veterans, they wanted to believe that they had fought and sacrificed for some greater good.

The Tirailleurs who fought on French battlefields in 1940 and 1944 believed that they deserved special consideration because they had done a better job of defending the republic than metropolitan troops and insisted that "equal sacrifices" meant "equal rights." While the postwar French government disagreed, it was impossible to discount their contributions. Theoretically, French African veterans received a limited franchise in 1939, but in 1946 they represented only 5 percent of the electorate that selected African representatives for the Fourth Republic's Constituent Assembly.[60] The British empire never allowed subject peoples to participate in metropolitan politics, and so African veterans focused on gaining political representation

---

[58] "East African report to the colonial secretary, July 1947," DEF 10/43/93, KNA, Nairobi; Louis Allen, *Burma: The Longest War* (London: J. M. Dent and Sons, 1986), 642; Brian James Crabb, *Passage to Destiny: The Sinking of the S.S. Khedive Ismail in the Sea War Against Japan* (Stamford: Paul Watkins, 1997), 78; Gray, *Basuto Soldiers in Hitler's War*, 29; Echenberg, *Colonial Conscripts*, 88.

[59] "Kenyan disabled veterans," 1945, DEF, 10/26/57; Civil reabsorption officer to welfare officer (African), November 13, 1951, DC/KSM, 1/22/67/233, KNA, Nairobi. See also Parsons, Chapter 7, this volume.

[60] Echenberg, *Colonial Conscripts*, 149.

at the local level. A Ugandan soldier, who wanted the right to elect members of the Gandan Lukiko (advisory council), declared: "The point is it is cheating sending our men to the front to fight for democracy only to come back to find the government autocratic and bureaucratic."[61]

Most veterans, particularly those who were less educated, simply sought better lives. Those who managed to claim their accumulated pay and demobilization benefits (which was not always easy) often had commercial ambitions. Many soldiers stranded overseas in 1945 and 1946 spent their time setting up bus and trucking companies, agricultural cooperatives, and trading ventures. Robert Kakembo's Kawonawo Trading Company planned to pool the resources of 250 veteran investors to fund repair shops, newspapers, agricultural marketing cooperatives, and entertainment centers throughout the Uganda Protectorate.[62] The majority of these ventures either failed to materialize or floundered because their founders had difficulty raising capital and securing government licenses.

Less ambitious former soldiers would have been content with modest service and disability pensions, but a common grievance of most African veterans, regardless of nationality or unit, was that the imperial powers never delivered these fundamental benefits. British military officers flatly denied that they had ever promised service pensions, and civil officials initially resisted making disability payments on the grounds that "tribes" had a collective responsibility to look after their injured men. Moreover, disabled veterans who did secure disability pensions soon found that postwar inflation reduced their value substantially. Overall, the greater political influence of French colonial soldiers meant than they fared substantially better than their English-speaking counterparts. Seeking the military vote, the new cohort of African politicians helped veterans win reserved civilian jobs, loans, subsidized housing, and more generous pensions. Conversely, British officials went out of their way to stress that ex-servicemen were not entitled to special benefits and cited higher metropolitan casualty rates and the German bombing of Britain to rebut claims that the empire owed a special debt to African soldiers.[63]

There is considerable debate over how much these simmering grievances and unmet expectations politicized African veterans of the Second World War. To be sure, many of the angry men would have been more active in pressing their claims for rights and benefits, but most lacked the means and opportunity to do so. Guinean ex-Tirailleurs challenged chiefly authority

[61] Report of chief censor, Nairobi, March 3, 1945, February 22, 1945, CS 1/17/23/291a, KNA, Nairobi.

[62] Robert Kakembo to the editor of *Gambuze*, c. 1945, CO 822/118/4, TNA, Kew.

[63] "Ugandan propaganda for Africans in the pre-demobilization period," August 3, 1945, DEF/10/64/39a, KNA, Nairobi; Great Britain, *Report of the Commission of Enquiry into Disturbances in the Gold Coast* (London: H.M. Stationery Office, 1948), 21.

and backed the more radical political parties that sprang up in FWA, but in Mali only younger short-service veterans engaged in militant politics.[64] Moreover, it is telling that apart from Léopold Senghor, who served in the regular French military, none of the men who won seats in the postwar French constituent assembly were veterans.

In British Africa ex-servicemen had even less political influence. This was due in part to the success of the colonial governments' "reabsorption" programs. The Kenyan government hired former army officers as "civil absorption officers" to keep an eye on discharged soldiers, and in most colonies the only legal veterans' organization was a closely monitored African affiliate of the British Legion. Seeking to protect the integrity of "tribal society," British administrators sought to turn former soldiers back into "tribesmen" with minimum social disruption. This meant that while cooperative and reliable ex-NCOs often had first call on civil service jobs, most World War II veterans received no extra benefits or considerations and there was little that they could do about it. Deep resentment over these policies did lead to an infamous ex-servicemen's riot in the Gold Coast in 1948, but this was the only significant case of organized veterans' unrest in British Africa. Historians and popular Kenyan nationalists have significantly overestimated the role of former soldiers in the Mau Mau Emergency. While leaders such as Dedan Kimathi, Stanley Mathenge, and Waruhiu Itote ("General China") were veterans, most served in support units and had very little combat training.[65] This may well explain why the Kenya Land Freedom Army was a relatively ineffective fighting force.

---

[64] Echenberg, *Colonial Conscripts*, 149; Mann, *Native Sons*, 110; see also Schmidt, Chapter 23, this volume.

[65] The Kenyan authorities considered the Kikuyu too politicized to join the KAR. Kimathi deserted from the EAMLS after six months of service, while Itote was a mess steward in Burma. Similarly, most of the members of the militant 40 Group that formed the core of the revolt had been clerks, storemen, artisans, and military laborers. Henry Kahinga Wachanga, *The Swords of Kirinyaga: The Fight for Land and Freedom* (Nairobi: Kenya Literature Bureau, 1991), xvi, 26, 42; interview John Nunneley, London, 1994.

2

Producing for the War

Judith A. Byfield

The production of agricultural, forestry, and mineral resources in Africa proved central to the prosecution of World War II. Without Africa's resources, especially after 1942, Britain and the United States would not have been able to produce the technology or provide the transportation their armies required. Equally important, African resources helped maintain Britain's national economy both during and after the war.[1] This chapter considers the central role that African resources played in the prosecution of the war and in the survival of European powers. Further, it supports Ashley Jackson's contention that the rapid mobilization of African resources enhanced the continent's value in the eyes of imperial powers.[2]

Africa's central role unfolded on the ground in distinctive ways not fully appreciated by an earlier generation of scholars. In an address given at Chatham House on October 24, 1944, social anthropologist Meyers Fortes attempted to assess the impact of World War II on British West Africa. After considering the political and social implications of the war, he declared that the "impact of the war on West Africa has been most powerful in the economic sphere."[3] He noted that even within the economic sphere, the impact was uneven. The greatest impact was in the sector producing raw materials for the world market while the subsistence sector experienced the least. Meyers built his analysis on the notion that production for subsistence

---

[1] Michael Cowen and Nicholas Westcott, "British imperial economic policy during the war," in David Killingray and Richard Rathbone (eds.), *Africa and the Second World War* (New York: St. Martin's Press, 1986), 20–22.

[2] Ashley Jackson, *The British Empire and the Second World War* (New York: Hambledon Continuum), 177.

[3] Meyers Fortes, "The impact of the war on British West Africa," *International Affairs*, 21 (1945), 211.

This paper was completed while I was on leave at the Institute for Advanced Studies (IAS), School of Historical Studies, Princeton. I enjoyed the generous support of the IAS Fund for Historical Studies and a Professional Development Grant from Cornell University.

occurred in an arena that was separate and apart from production for the world market; however, subsistence production and the production of raw materials for the world market were integrally linked. In fact, we can argue that the link between subsistence production and the production of raw materials for the world economy intensified during the war years because the war effort also required increasing production of food crops. The war brought about unanticipated and sometimes contradictory outcomes in Africa. Ultimately this chapter helps us to better understand the dynamics between the macro and micro planes of analysis as Africa and the imperial powers that controlled it engaged in total war.

Periodizing Demand

The first sentence of the 1941 treaty between Britain and Ethiopia declared, "The liberation of Abyssinia is the first victorious fruit of the War,"[4] even though Italy's invasion of Ethiopia in 1935 failed to generate a response from Britain or the League of Nations. As a result, Ethiopia's demand for resources falls outside the classic periodization of World War II and historical studies fail to take note of the resources African communities sent to Ethiopia. Men and women from across Africa and the African diaspora raised funds for the Ethiopian Red Cross, guns, and munitions as they struggled against the much larger and better-armed Italian army.[5] Elements of this mobilization would continue after war in Europe began in 1939.

When World War II began in Europe, it was not clear how African colonies would be affected or called upon, nor to what extent. For example, British officials anticipated that their African colonies would be affected only tangentially. They expected that the basic materials for war production – iron ore, timber, machinery, cloth, and food – would be drawn from the dominions and Far East. In November 1939, Britain bought the total wool production from Australia and New Zealand, the total colonial sugar production for the duration of the war and one year after, as well as the entire output of copper from Northern Rhodesia on an annual basis.[6] However, as the war unfolded, the imperial powers increasingly looked to Africa to supply a range of raw materials. Demand for these raw materials varied with the shifting fortunes of the Allied, Axis, and neutral powers. Britain and France, members of the Allied forces, controlled by far the majority

---

[4] "Treaty with Abyssinia," *Journal of the Royal African Society*, 41 (1942), 1.

[5] For a fuller discussion of the consequences of disconnecting Italy's invasion of Ethiopia from World War II, see Judith A. Byfield, "Beyond impact: Toward a new historiography of Africa and World War II," in Thomas Zeiler with Daniel DuBois (eds.), *A Companion to World War II* (Malden, MA: Wiley-Blackwell, 2013), vol. II, 653.

[6] Cowen and Westcott, "British imperial economic policy during the war," 41. See also Malcolm McKinnon, "Equality of sacrifice': Anglo-New Zealand relations and the war economy, 1939–45" *Journal of Imperial and Commonwealth History*, 84 (1984), 54–75.

of African colonies. Italy was the only Axis power with African colonies: Libya, Eritrea, and recently captured Abyssinia/Ethiopia.[7] This gave Germany access to the human and raw materials of Italy's colonies as well as proximity to British and French colonies and the Suez Canal.[8] Spain and Portugal declared neutrality; nonetheless, their economies and those of their colonies had to respond to the shifting landscape.

Demand was directly tied to the victories and defeats of Allied and Axis powers; consequently, certain dates loom especially large in the history of Africa's role in World War II. Open conflict in Europe began September 1939, but as early as July 1939 the British government started making contingency plans in the event of war. The imperial government restricted imports and exports in order to achieve four main goals: "conserve supplies for use in Britain or Allied countries; prevent British exports from reaching the enemy; bring pressure to bear on neutral governments and firms; and guide exports to particular countries in the interests of exchange."[9] However, the invasions of Belgium and France and their subsequent surrenders to Germany in May and June 1940, respectively, forced Britain to rethink a host of plans and strategies in Africa. Once France fell, new contingencies had to be created because many French and British colonies, especially in West Africa, shared lengthy borders.

As countries fell to invasion by the Axis forces the economic and political landscapes changed significantly. France's surrender to Germany in 1940 led to the creation of two French governments. While Marshal Philippe Pétain's Vichy government advocated the country's surrender, Charles de Gaulle's Free French government with its capital in Congo Brazzaville sought to end Germany's occupation of France.[10] The colonial governors in France's African colonies were divided between the competing French governments. Between 1940 and December 1942, the governors of French West Africa (FWA/AOF), Mauritius, and North Africa supported the Vichy regime while the governors of French Equatorial Africa (FEA/AEF) supported de

---

[7] David Killingray, *Fighting for Britain: African Soldiers in the Second World War* (Woodbridge, Suffolk: James Currey/Boydell & Brewer, 2010), 7.

[8] Michael Crowder, "The Second World War: Prelude to decolonisation" in Michael Crowder (ed.), *The Cambridge History of Africa* (Cambridge/New York: Cambridge University Press, 1984), vol. VIII, 16.

[9] Ayodeji Olukoju, "'Buy British, sell foreign': External trade control policies in Nigeria during World War II and its aftermath, 1939–1950," *International Journal of African Historical Studies*, 35 (2002), 365.

[10] With the signing of the Boisson-Eisenhower agreement on December 7, 1942, French West Africa agreed to cooperate with the Americans, but not with General de Gaulle. See Ruth Ginio, *French Colonialism Unmasked: The Vichy Years in French West Africa* (Lincoln: University of Nebraska Press, 2006), xv. French West Africa included Senegal, Ivory Coast, Niger, Dahomey (now Benin), French Sudan (now Mali), French Guinea, Mauritania, and the mandate territory of Togo. French Equatorial Africa included Cameroon, Chad, Gabon, and Congo Brazzaville.

Gaulle and the Free French. Allied positions were further compromised when Italy joined the Axis powers in May 1940, and by August invaded British Somaliland, as well as sections of Sudan and Kenya.[11]

The Allied governments had to draft additional contingency plans when Japan entered the war. Japan's campaign in Southeast Asia between December 1941 and March 1942 produced several dramatic developments which significantly altered Africa's role in the war. At the end of this campaign, Britain and the United States lost control of their colonies in Asia as well as access to critical markets. The Allied forces lost access to Malaya, the Philippines, Singapore, and North Borneo, all major producers of rubber, fats, and oils for the world market.[12] The Japanese campaign also led to greater U.S. involvement, for the United States dramatically increased its industrial capacity to provide the necessary shipping, fuels, and machinery to keep up with the expanding global conflict. Many items required for U.S. production were already, or could be, produced in Africa. Therefore, demand for African products skyrocketed in order to meet U.S. needs and to fill the void left by Japanese control of the Asian markets.[13] So much so that East Africa, which had been considered marginal in the early years of the war, became economically significant after December 1941.[14]

The attack on Pearl Harbor on December 7, 1941, brought the United States into the war as a combatant; however, Franklin Roosevelt had begun to put in place mechanisms to assist U.S. allies as early as 1938. He crafted an executive order allowing the army to give "older weapons to private contractors, who could then sell them abroad." By spring 1940, following the fall of France, he increased arms production and drew on the 1938 executive order to send weapons and ammunition to the British. In September, he signed an agreement to lend Britain older American ships in exchange for their willingness to lease bases to the United States. As the war raged on, Roosevelt was finally able to convince the Congress to pass the Lend-Lease Act on March 11, 1941. The act empowered the president to provide war material to any country whose defense was also vital to U.S. defense. Countries receiving this support would not have to pay for equipment with cash, but had to use it during the war or return it at the war's conclusion.[15]

---

[11] Crowder, "The Second World War," 16.
[12] Allister E. Hinds, "Government policy and the Nigerian palm oil export industry, 1939–49," *Journal of African History*, 38 (1997), 462.
[13] Gervase Clarence-Smith, "The impact of the Spanish Civil War and the Second World War on Portuguese and Spanish Africa," *Journal of African History*, 26 (1985), 312.
[14] David Anderson and David Throup, "Africans and agricultural production in colonial Kenya: The myth of the war as a watershed," *Journal of African History*, 26 (1985), 335–36.
[15] Mary Dudziak, *War-Time: An Idea, Its History, Its Consequences* (New York/Oxford: Oxford University Press, 2012), 42–43.

The passage of this act could not have come at a more critical time for Britain. The British government experienced a shortage of foreign exchange during the first year of fighting, plus it owed the United States $6 billion for armaments purchased before the passage of Lend-Lease. Under the program Britain did not have to pay for imports with exports, British ships could be repaired in American ports, and food security was ensured for the British population. Nonetheless, many British felt that the conditions attached to the program were quite harsh, for the Americans demanded an audit of all British assets and the expenditure of all Britain's foreign exchange and gold reserves. While the expanding U.S. role in the war proved critical to Britain's survival, the British government also feared this development, which significantly altered the doctrine of Reciprocal Aid that guided cooperation among the Allies.[16]

As Cowen and Westcott explain, the doctrine rested on two principles that increasingly came into conflict as the war progressed. First, each Allied nation was expected to minimize consumption, direct its productive resources to the war, and maximize the use of its resources for the war effort. Thus, all the Allied countries "would equally bear sacrifice for total war." The second principle stipulated that Allied nations would not end the war financially indebted to each other even if there existed a difference in the value of goods imported and exported between these nations. For example, the U.S. exported £4 billion in goods to Britain, but provided Britain grants totaling £5 billion to cover dollar imports. Under the doctrine of Reciprocal Aid, the grant provided by the United States was conditional to the degree it could be demonstrated that "the 'debtor' country was bearing sacrifice for the war effort by maximizing production and minimizing civilian consumption." Despite rations on food and other methods that attested to Britain's sacrifice, officials still feared that Britain would end the war at a distinct disadvantage to the United States. To mitigate this anticipated disadvantage and further fulfill the equality of sacrifice principle, British officials extended the sacrifice principle to the colonies using a range of mechanisms to reduce consumption to a level comparable to that in Britain. These mechanisms included increased taxation, limited consumer goods, price inflation, increased production of materials needed for the war effort, and the transformation of sterling debt owed to the colonies into grants to the metropole.[17]

Officials justified transposing debts into grants by arguing that the colonies and India in particular had not and could not bear equal sacrifice

---

[16] Lizzie Collingham, *The Taste of War: World War Two and the Battle for Food* (New York: Penguin Books, 2012), 104, 108; Charles Kindleberger, *A Financial History of Western Europe*, 2nd ed. (New York/Oxford: Oxford University Press, 1993), 108, 415; Anthony Beevor, *The Second World War* (New York: Little, Brown and Company, 2012), 181.

[17] Cowen and Westcott, "British imperial economic policy during the war," 23–24.

to that which Britain sustained. Transforming sterling debts into grants provided Britain with the financial resources to limit its dollar debts, thus protecting the British national economy during and after the war. This strategy helped; nonetheless, the entire sterling-area dollar deficits increased from $450 million before the war to $1.1 billion in 1948. Oberst argues that much of this debt resulted from "rise in price of American exports, while the price of gold remained constant and the world continued to need American goods."[18]

British indebtedness to the colonies generated a range of concerns. Some officials thought it was fair to draw resources from the colonies given Britain's sacrifice. A colonial official in Uganda commented, "Everybody is overtaxed of course, but if the UK taxpayer is to go on accepting heavy sacrifices . . . it would be only reasonable that the African should accept taxation." Britain's indebtedness to the colonies was not only the result of its economic policies. In Uganda, for example, Native Government officials in the Eastern Province gave Britain thousands of pounds in interest-free loans from their surplus balances. Ugandan loans and fundraising efforts to support the war caused nervousness for some officials, for they "worried about the implications of Ugandans' war contribution for the country's future politics."[19] Nonetheless, Britain's very survival depended on its access to these resources from its African colonies and India.

The fall of France and Belgium, Japan's expansion, and greater U.S. involvement also altered the economic landscape in the Spanish and Portuguese colonies. The British and American forces established a naval blockade in order to impede the Iberian countries from becoming conduits for commodities to Germany and German controlled territories. They tried to control the movement of commodities between the neutral countries and their African colonies by allowing Portugal and Spain to only import goods from their overseas colonies for internal needs and limiting the amount of "nonessential" items that the Iberian countries could import.[20] In recognition of the difficulties these policies posed for Spain and Portugal, the Allies provided some economic aid. Britain encouraged the Portuguese government to sell colonial products to Spain while allowing products from Portuguese colonies to be exported to Britain and its colonies.[21] Britain also provided credits to Spain while the United States agreed to buy sisal produced by German nationals in Portuguese colonies, specifically Angola and Mozambique.[22] Although the African colonies controlled by neutral powers

---

[18] Timothy Oberst, "Transport workers, strikes and the 'imperial response': Africa and the post World War II conjuncture," *African Studies Review*, 31 (1988), 123.

[19] See Summers, Chapter 25, this volume.

[20] Clarence-Smith, "The impact of the Spanish Civil War and the Second World War," 311.

[21] See Newitt, Chapter 12, this volume.

[22] Clarence-Smith, "The impact of the Spanish Civil War and the Second World War," 312. In mid-1940, the Allies introduced navicerts for all exports from the Spanish and Portuguese

did not supply manpower for the war or become theaters of fighting, they were not immune to the war's consequences.

Products for the War Effort

From the earliest days of preparation for war, cloth was considered one of the basic materials for war production. Although the British forced Egypt to cut back on cotton production in order to increase production of grain and vegetables, Egyptian producers still met British demands for fabric and thread. Using records from the Egyptian Ministry of Supplies, Helal argues that between August 1941 and the end of January 1944, British authorities acquired 395,522 spools of thread from the Egyptian Ministry of Rations.[23] Cotton also came from Nigeria and Uganda, but by far the largest contributor of cotton and cloth was India. Kamtekar argues that India's chief industrial contribution during the war was cotton textiles, for it supplied nearly 400 million tailored items and four million cotton-made supply-dropping parachutes. Reports estimated that India supplied 1.2 billion yards of cloth per year to the defense forces.[24]

Rubber, as Clarence-Smith shows, was a crucial strategic resource for the mechanized armed forces of the World War II. It was essential to the production of tires for a host of different vehicles as well as parts for battleships and planes. At the start of the war Africa accounted for 1 percent of the global output of natural rubber, but by 1944–1945 Africa produced nearly 30 percent of global output.[25] The largest producers were Liberia and Nigeria, but rubber also came from Guinea-Conakry, Central African Republic, Ivory Coast, Cameroon, and the Belgian Congo. The war gave a tremendous boost to estate production of rubber in Liberia, parts of Nigeria, and the Belgian Congo. The importance of African rubber was such that Allied forces feared the Germans would try to capture Firestone's rubber plantations in Liberia.[26] Therefore in the fall of 1942, America sent Task

---

colonies, but they refused to provide navicerts for goods produced in those colonies by enemy aliens, most of whom were German planters who had settled in Spanish and Portuguese colonies after World War I.

[23] Emad A. Helal, "Egypt's overlooked contribution to World War II," in Heike Liebau, Katrin Bromber, Katharina Lange, Dyala Hamzah and Ravi Ahuja (eds.), *The World in World Wars: Experiences, Perceptions and Perspectives from Africa and Asia* (Boston: Brill Press, 2010), 232–33.

[24] Individar Kamtekar, "A different war dance: State and class in India 1939–1945," *Past and Present*, No. 176 (2002), 195. India also supplied 25 million pairs of shoes and 37,000 silk parachutes.

[25] Clarence-Smith, Chapter 9, this volume. See also Nancy Lawler, "Reform and repression under the Free French: economic and political transformation in the Cote d'Ivoire, 1942–45," *Africa*, 60 (1990), 88–110.

[26] George "Doc" Abraham, *The Belles of Shangri-La and Other Stories of Sex, Snakes, and Survival from World War II* (New York: Vantage Press, 2000), 7; Daniel Hutchinson,

Force 5889 – seventy-six white men and two thousand black infantry men – to Liberia to protect Firestone's one million acres of rubber trees.[27]

The machinery supplying products for the war required vegetable oils and fats, as did human populations. As with rubber, demand for palm oil increased significantly after 1942. In an important analysis of government policy on palm oil, Allister Hinds found that from the beginning of the war to the collapse of the Allied forces in the Far East in 1942, colonial policy concentrated on restricting export production of palm oil to conserve limited shipping space for vital necessities. After 1942, officials in Nigeria began a concerted effort to increase the production of palm oil, for its export would be "a material factor in determining the fat ration in the UK."[28] To increase production, the colonial government introduced new technology in some areas, such as eastern Nigeria. They introduced oil presses to replace wooden mortars and kernel cracking machines to get to palm kernels from which women producers derived palm kernel oil.[29] Japanese control of Southeast Asia also restricted access to copra, the dried meat or kernel from which coconut oil is extracted. Mozambique became Africa's largest producer of copra, for it had huge groves of coconut palms that were planted during the earlier boom of the 1920s.[30]

Groundnuts (peanuts) were another major source of vegetable oil and all across the continent groundnut production increased, but the geography of its production changed. French West Africa had been a major source of groundnuts before World War II; however, during the Vichy period production declined significantly, for their market shrank considerably. In Senegal the volume for groundnuts fell from 419,000 tons in 1940 to only 114,000 tons in 1942,[31] while in Mozambique export of groundnuts grew to 20,000 tons by 1945.[32] In some regions wartime conditions reoriented trade routes. In Niger, 90 percent of the commercial groundnut crop came from four districts – Maradi, Tessaoua, Matameye, and Magaria – that shared a 1,600-kilometer boundary with northern Nigeria. The region contributed significantly to Niger's economy for it produced from 35 to 50 percent of Niger's total groundnut crop exported to Europe. When France fell to

"Defending the land of their ancestors: African American military experience in Africa during World War II," paper presented at the conference *Re-evaluating Africa and World War II*, Cornell University, September 17–19, 2009.

[27] Abraham, *The Belles of Shangri-La*, 1.

[28] Hinds, "Government policy and the Nigerian palm oil export industry," 462.

[29] Gloria Chuku, "'Crack kernels, crack Hitler': Export production drive and Igbo women during the Second World War," in Judith A. Byfield, LaRay Denzer, and Anthea Morrison (eds.), *Gendering the African Diaspora: Women, Culture, and Historical Change in the Caribbean and Nigerian Hinterland* (Bloomington: Indiana University Press, 2010), 224.

[30] Clarence-Smith, "The impact of the Spanish Civil War and the Second World War," 312.

[31] Michael Crowder, *West Africa under Colonial Rule* (Evanston, IL: Northwestern University Press, 1968), 496.

[32] Clarence Smith, "The impact of the Spanish Civil War and the Second World War," 312.

Germany, the British closed the border between Vichy-controlled FWA and Nigeria. The closure of the border reduced motorized transport between Niger and Nigeria to a trickle, but it did not eliminate trade. Between 1939 and 1946 a large amount of the groundnut crop was sold across the border in Nigeria. In the 1940–1941 buying season, farmers sold 90 percent of Niger's groundnut crop in Nigerian markets and many immigrated to Nigeria as well. Several factors influenced farmers' decisions: harsh wartime demands of the French colonial regime, better prices, cheaper imported merchandise, and larger weekly markets in Nigeria.[33]

The war effort also required forest products and multiple minerals. Forest production, as Cline-Cole argues, reached unprecedented levels during the war. Timber, in particular, was necessary for a range of activities including road, rail, and bridge construction and mineral production, as well as fuel for trains, ships, and cooking. Forests were considered "an indispensable component of the Allied war effort"; therefore, British officials intervened massively in forestry in its African colonies. State intervention included development funds and loans to regional forestry establishments that were used to mobilize technology and labor. The state's policy objective revolved around regional self-sufficiency in timber and fuel requirements, particularly for the armed forces and other services.[34]

As early as 1941, officials became increasingly concerned about the availability of forest products and this was most apparent in Sierra Leone. Freetown, the colony's capital, was a naval base and outpost of the South Atlantic military command. Its population grew rapidly, swollen by "locally stationed and transiting troops, as well as civilians engaged in war-related work, mostly by artisans or labourers." Twenty thousand local conscripts also transited in Freetown over the course of the war. Establishments that catered to servicemen, such as laundries, restaurants, and bakeries, all demanded increasing amounts of fuel wood and charcoal.[35] The military needed large quantities of timber to upgrade or construct military bases, and coal was essential to the tens of cargo ships that steamed into Freetown's port each day.[36] To meet the cascading demand for forest products after the fall of France and the Far East colonies, colonial offices created a hierarchy of consumers: the military, the government, commercial concerns (specifically mines and sawmills), and the general public.[37] The general public experienced an acute shortage of firewood and charcoal for much of the war. This was not unique to West Africa. In East Africa, the demand for forest

[33] John Davison Collins, "The clandestine movement of groundnuts across the Niger-Nigeria boundary," *Canadian Journal of African Studies*, 10 (1976), 260, 262, 264. Collins estimates that between 20 and 40% of Magaria's commercial crop were sold in Nigerian markets.

[34] Reginald Cline-Cole, "Wartime forest energy policy and practice in British West Africa: Social and economic impact on the labouring classes 1939–45," *Africa*, 63 (1993), 56, 58.

[35] Cline-Cole, "Wartime forest energy policy," 62.

[36] Howard, Chapter 10, this volume.

[37] Cline-Cole, "Wartime forest energy policy," 58.

products compelled colonial officials to reopen forest areas that had been claimed by the colonial state. When Italy entered the war in 1940, Britain launched military operations in Libya, Ethiopia, Sudan, and Somalia and began war preparations in Egypt and the Middle East. As a result, demand for African timber increased exponentially. As Sunseri notes, "East African colonies were directed to supply 2,500 tons of timber monthly for Middle East and African operations, and a further 1,500 tons monthly for local military infrastructure."[38] Between 1941 and 1942, Tanganyika alone supplied over 300,000 railway ties each year.

A significant amount of the timber from Africa's forests went to support mining industries. All across the continent mineral production increased for Allied rearmament and munitions production required items such as copper, tin, gold, diamonds, cobalt, and uranium. Dumett argues that "during the peak years of the war, Africa supplied 50% of the world's gold . . . 17% of the copper, close to 90% of the cobalt, all of the uranium and . . . 98% of the world's industrial diamond."[39] Even though the war forced the closure of diamond cutting in northern Europe, diamond sales increased steadily from 1938 and through the war. A 1941 review of the diamond industry reported that the increase was "due to the unprecedented demand for industrials."[40] The United States, the principal buyer, purchased industrial diamonds for its stockpile. The Russian, British, and Canadian governments followed suit. Mineral production could be found in the Gold Coast, Nigeria, South Africa, and Northern and Southern Rhodesia, but the Belgian Congo "supplied the most in terms of quantity and range of products."[41] The governor-general of Belgian Congo, Pierre Ryckmans, maintained the Anglo-Franco-Belgian alliance against Nazism even though Germany occupied Belgium in May 1940.[42] As a result, the colony's valuable resources supported the Allied effort and a substantial amount went to the United States. Higginson noted that the mining giant Union Minière's export of copper and tin to the United States alone increased 1,000 percent.[43]

---

[38] Sunseri, Chapter 13, this volume.

[39] Raymond Dumett, "Africa's strategic minerals during the Second World War," *Journal of African History*, 26 (1985), 382–83. See also Ralph Birchard, "Copper in the Katanga region of the Belgian Congo," *Economic Geography*, 16 (1940), 429–36.

[40] "Diamond industry in wartime, 1941," *Journal of the Royal African Society*, 42 (1943), 130. Reprinted from *The South African Mining and Engineering Journal*. The article was extracted from an annual review of the diamond industry, "The Jeweller's Circular-Keystone," usually prepared by Sidney H. Ball of the engineering firm Rogers, Mayer & Ball (New York).

[41] Dumett, "Africa's strategic minerals," 389.

[42] W. B. Norton, "Belgian-French relations during World War II as seen by Governor General Ryckmans," in *Le Congo Belge Durant La Second Guerre Mondiale: Recueil d'études* (Brussels: Académie royale des sciences d'outre-mer, 1983), 288.

[43] John Higginson, *A Working Class in the Making: Belgian Colonial Labor Policy, Private Enterprise and the African Mineworker, 1907–1951* (Madison: University of Wisconsin Press, 1989), 162.

Ryckmans's determined support of the Allied forces despite Germany's occupation of Belgium safeguarded Allied access to uranium. Technological developments during and after the war suggest that uranium was by far the most important mineral obtained from the Belgian Congo. Belgian prospectors looking for copper discovered uranium ore in 1913. Like copper, uranium was put under the control of Union Minière, the partly government-owned conglomerate. Although they determined that the uranium from the Katanga region of the Belgian Congo was especially rich, the first sizeable quantities of uranium arrived in Belgium only in December 1921.[44] The market for the radium produced from Congolese uranium ore primarily consisted of universities, hospital-based cancer institutes, and medical associations and by 1925 Belgian radium "represented 80% of world consumption."[45]

The development of the atomic bomb, however, put the Congo at the center of policy discussions in both Washington, D.C., and London. American and British policy and defense decision makers concluded that it was in their best interest to uncover and gain control over as much of the world's uranium deposits as possible. U.S. officials approached Union Carbide, which was working through a subsidiary, the Union Mines Development Corporation, to conduct a worldwide search for uranium. Engineers who conducted surveys on behalf of Union Mines rated uranium in the Belgian Congo excellent, while that in the United States, Canada, and Sweden was good. The ore in Czechoslovakia, Portugal, and South Africa rated fair and ore in Madagascar, Australia, Brazil, and England was poor. Since the Belgian Congo was outside of U.S. or British control, these governments created a corporation, the Combined Development Trust, that signed an agreement with the Belgian government in September 1944 granting the United States and the United Kingdom an option on all of the Congo's uranium resources for up to ten years. Negotiators were encouraged to "take whatever steps were necessary to ensure 'joint control' of uranium in the Congo." Therefore, the Trust agreed to a number of concessions, including the purchase of 3.44 million pounds of uranium oxide, payment of $1.45 per pound for high grade oxide, the provision of new equipment to Union Minière in order to reopen and operate the Shinkolobwe mine, and recognition of Belgium's right to participate in any future commercial utilization of Congolese ores in energy production. Although the United States and Britain continued to purchase uranium ore within their respective borders and from

[44] A. Adams. "The origin and early development of the Belgian radium industry," *Environment International*, 19 (1993), 422, 497. The Belgian government held 40% of the capital of Union Minière Haute Katanga and helped in the success of the new radium industry.

[45] Ibid., 499. That same year the last American radium producer was forced to shut down production. Government support, especially with the marketing of radium within and beyond Europe, gave Belgian radium its strong position in the world market.

other countries, the quality of Congo's ore compelled the United States and Britain to assume a controlling role in the production and control of Congolese uranium.[46]

The "war effort" also provided a shield under which imperial countries could transfer products from the colonies to the metropole for non-war-related activities. Portuguese dictator Antonio Salazar used the economic insecurity of the war to advance his goal of imperial autarky or self-sufficiency.[47] Historically Portugal had purchased much of the cotton for its textile industry on the international market. The combination of the Spanish Civil War, which created a market for Portuguese textiles in Spain, the beginning of World War II, and Portugal's enforced neutrality allowed Salazar to vigorously advance cotton production in Mozambique. The state gave out land to concessionary companies, and together the state and the companies forced men and women to grow cotton, often under threat of violence. The number of peasants involved in cotton production increased from 80,000 in 1937 to 445,000 by 1943,[48] while the amount of imports increased from 2,500 tons in 1938 to 18,500 tons by 1942.[49]

Production of the range of resources needed to support the competing European powers as well as the neutral powers drew on vast numbers of African men and women individually or as part of collective work forces. In too many instances officials relied on direct or indirect forms of coercion. Production of rubber, vegetable oils, minerals, and other materials for the war effort was still only one level of Africa's contribution. It could be argued that food production was even more important, for the crops fed the workers in the mines and forests, the military workers, the troops, and the civilian populations. Furthermore, food production, which increased in many places during the war, ensured that peasants and traders could continue to pay taxes, which also directly supported imperial governments.

The Struggle for Food

In many ways, food was one of the most important items provided by African producers. Demand for food increased substantially as both military and civilian populations filed into urban centers such as Freetown and Lagos as the wartime economy expanded. Officials in Freetown estimated that

---

[46] Vincent C. Jones, *Manhattan: The Army and the Atomic Bomb* (Washington, D.C.: Center of Military History, 1985), 293, 295, 296, 300–301 [accessed via Openlibrary.org].

[47] Clarence-Smith, "Impact of the Spanish Civil War and Second World War," 313.

[48] Allen Isaacman and Arlindo Chilundo, "Peasants at work: Forced cotton cultivation in northern Mozambique 1938–1961," in Allen Isaacman and Richard Roberts (eds.), *Cotton, Colonialism, and Social History in Sub-Saharan Africa* (Portsmouth, NH: Heinemann, 1995), 157.

[49] Clarence-Smith, "Impact of the Spanish Civil War and the Second World War," 313.

between 1931 and mid-1941, Freetown's population doubled.[50] Pressure
was put on colonies to be self-sufficient in food. British officials in West
Africa were told that the entire food requirement of the armed forces had
to be met in full locally; however, the type of pressure applied created
consequences that varied from one area to another.[51] In Abeokuta province
in western Nigeria, the resident noted in the 1942 annual report, "the main
war effort in the province is…food production for the military."[52] As
Byfield shows, rice was the designated crop for the military and officials
tasked farmers to produce 3,000 tons of rice although the province produced
only three hundred tons annually before the war.[53]

In FWA/AOF disruption in shipping interrupted rice imports from Southeast Asia. Rice imports fell from 63,000 metric tons in 1940 to 1,000 in 1942.
In order to avert food shortages the Vichy regime diverted attention away
from crops such as cotton in favor of rice.[54] In Ivory Coast, certain communities were ordered to increase rice production through quotas, which
effectively imposed a system of forced production.[55] When production did
not meet the quotas, officials also requisitioned rice. In the Casamance region
of southern Senegal a revolt erupted when "the military demanded that they
hand over seven years' worth of rice reserves, and the army tried to take it
by force."[56]

In Kenya, the Agricultural Production and Settlement Board was granted
executive power in 1941 "to plan and direct an increase of agricultural
production to meet war needs."[57] Settlers received a guaranteed price, a
guaranteed return per acre, and a breaking and clearing grant for maize.
In addition, the price paid to settlers for their maize was almost twice that
paid to African producers. Between January 1941 and June 1942, African
producers received an average of 4/90 shillings per bag from government

---

[50] Howard, Chapter 10, this volume.

[51] Egba division report 1943, ABP 1543, vol. IV, 12. ABE PROF 1, National Archives of
Nigeria (hereafter NAN), Ibadan.

[52] Abeokuta Province Annual Report 1942, ABP 1543, vol. IV, ABE PROF 1, NAN, Ibadan.

[53] Byfield, Chapter 8, this volume.

[54] Monica M. van Beusekom, "Disjunctures in theory and practice: Making sense of change in
agricultural development at the Office du Niger, 1920–60," *Journal of African History*, 41
(2000), 88.

[55] Nancy Lawler, "Reform and repression under the Free French: Economic and political
transformation in the Cote d'Ivoire, 1942–1945," *Africa*, 60 (1990), 96.

[56] Ginio, *French Colonialism Unmasked*, 64; Wilmetta J. Toliver-Diallo, "'The woman who
was more than a man': Making Aline Sitoe Diatta into a national heroine in Senegal," *Canadian Journal of African Studies*, 39 (2005), 338–60. Local colonial authorities erroneously
assumed that Aline Sitoe, the woman who organized rain ceremonies to end the drought
in 1942, led this revolt. She was arrested and sent to Timbuktu, where she disappeared. I
thank Mark Deets for bringing Aline Sitoe Diatta to my attention.

[57] Ian Spencer, "Settler dominance, agricultural production and the Second World War in
Kenya," *Journal of African History*, 21 (1980), 502.

buyers, whereas European farmers received 8/50 s. per bag.[58] As a result, while European farmers sold their maize to the government, many Africans sold their maize on the black market, where they received much higher prices.

The war provided an opportunity for settlers to advance their economic position for the price guarantees were set above prices on the open market, they received low-interest loans, agricultural machinery through the Lend-Lease program, and subsidies for fertilizer. Most importantly, African laborers were conscripted to work on European farms.[59] In Southern Rhodesia, similar policies prevailed, for European farmers received government subsidies, grants, loans, bonuses, and guaranteed prices to entice them to increase their production of maize, wheat, cassava, and other food crops. The Compulsory Native Labour Act, which came into effect on August 1, 1942, opened a "new development in the use of state coercion to secure labor for European farmers" as it legalized the conscription of African men to work in food production.[60]

Egypt also handed over large quantities of food to the Allied forces. Helal reported that the Egyptian Ministry of Supplies delivered 45,000 tons of wheat and maize in 1943 and 20,000 tons of wheat, 6,000 tons of corn, 4,000 tons of barley, and 800 tons of wheat bran in 1944. The ministry also gave British authorities license to receive the surplus rice production in 1942 and 1943, approximately 107,679 tons. Egyptian supplies provided the food rations Montgomery's forces needed in their campaign from El Alamein to Tunis in 1943.[61]

In addition to grains, civilian and military populations needed meat. In her memoir, *Love, Life and Elephants*, Dame Daphne Sheldrick recalled her father's noncombat assignment in World War II. With a staff consisting of two Italian POWs and forty Wakamba men, her father, Bryan Aggett, established a camp at Selengai in the South Game Reserve. There they hunted, butchered, and dried meat from wildebeest and zebra. Their factory-like operation sent more than one hundred sacks of dried meat, or biltong, daily to Nairobi from Emali, the nearest railway station to their camp. She explained that they used all parts of the animals.

The hides... were bound to America, where they were made into machine belting; the bones were ground down into bone meal for animal feed and

[58] Anderson and Throup, "African and agriculture in colonial Kenya," 335, 339.
[59] Spencer, "Settler dominance, agricultural production," 503–04. An Essential Undertakings Board was to define the areas of the economy which would benefit from conscripted labor; however, the board defined virtually the entire agricultural industry as "essential undertaking."
[60] David Johnson, "Settler farmers and coerced African labour in southern Rhodesia, 1936–46," *Journal of African History*, 33 (1992), 119, 121.
[61] Helal, "Egypt's overlooked contribution to World War II," 232.

fertilizer; the hair from the manes and tails were turned into bristles for brushes and brooms . . . the leftover fresh meat – the offal in particular, which was not suitable for biltong . . . my father gave to the Wakamba workers.[62]

Some of the food produced on the continent also went directly to feed European populations. Basic foodstuffs, especially maize and beans from Angola, helped the Portuguese avoid food shortages. The Portuguese state began a rice concession scheme in 1941, which rapidly expanded after Japanese control of Southeast Asia cut off rice imports.[63] In Spain the civil war and state interference in agriculture after the civil war contributed to severe food shortages, and a "flourishing black market for the rich and strict rationing for the poor."[64] Therefore, the Spanish authorities tried to extract as much food as they could from Spain's African territories, especially fish, bananas, tomatoes, potatoes, onions, and other vegetables.

The demand for African commodities for the war effort created severe hardship for many African communities. Since labor was redirected from food production in order to collect rubber, copal, or other commodities deemed essential, famine and food shortages accompanied many production drives. Similarly, labor conscripted to work on European farms also led to food insecurity.[65] In some instances African men from food-growing regions were conscripted to work on European maize farms, an absurdity that was not lost on some officials, who questioned the "rationale of conscripting labour from food-growing areas to produce food on European farms as a method of increasing the colony's food production."[66] The plight of Mozambique illustrates that laborers coerced to grow cotton at the same time that they would ordinarily have weeded their maize and sorghum and prepared their bean fields faced years of hunger, malnutrition, and famine.[67] The insecurity around food during the war years reveals most clearly the interdependency between subsistence production and cash crop production in Africa as well as the ways in which the war affected that interdependence. Yet the impact of food insecurity and famines, as Lizzie Collingham argues, has not been adequately examined even though the number of people who died from hunger and starvation was higher than the number that died in combat. She reports that at least 20 million people died from starvation,

[62] Dame Daphne Sheldrick, *Love, Life and Elephants: An African Love Story* (New York: Farrar, Straus and Giroux, 2012), 42. Biltong is made by cutting the meat into strips and soaking it in a brine of salt, pepper, and vinegar before hanging it to dry overnight. I thank Beth Reiter for bringing this book to my attention.

[63] Newitt, "Portuguese African Colonies during the Second World War," 9.

[64] Clarence-Smith, "Impact of the Spanish Civil War and Second World War," 315.

[65] Spencer, "Settler dominance, agricultural production," 504.

[66] Johnson, "Settler farmers and coerced labour," 123.

[67] Isaacman, *Cotton, Colonialism, and Social History*, 157.

malnutrition, and its associated diseases, while military death claimed 19.5 million people.[68]

Legacies of World War II

In African colonies "the war had both intensified colonial grievances and contributed to economic and social conditions which could only generate unrest."[69] The end of the war in 1945, however, did not radically transform these conditions, for the cost of living and inflation continued to rise and commodity shortages continued, as did price controls. Surveys among British-controlled colonies in 1947 gave a graphic sense of the economic landscape. The 1947 official price index "reached 187 in Dar es Salaam, 198 in Kenya, 211 in the Gold Coast and 229 in Sudan."[70] The high cost of living contributed to the wave of strikes that overtook the continent in the postwar period. In South Africa African mine workers went on strike in 1946, Nigeria experienced a general strike in 1945, Sudanese railway workers went on strike in 1946, and in 1947 railway workers in FWA/AOF stopped work and workers in Kenya held a general strike.[71] Each of these strikes had the support of large cross-sections of the population because so many had been affected negatively by the lack of imports and low commodity prices. As a result these strikes helped galvanize the nationalist movements that began to bear fruit in the 1950s.

The war also intensified competition between European and African traders. In southern Nigeria, for example, African entrepreneurs lost ground to the European trading firms that dominated among the small group of traders given licenses to either export goods or purchase foodstuffs or agricultural products on behalf of the government. Harneit-Sievers argues that there was a significant contraction of the intermediary trading system, with some entrepreneurs losing their business altogether and others joining the already enlarged ranks of petty traders. One of the most lucrative avenues during the war was contracting for military food needs. African firms like the one controlled by Shodipo in Abeokuta thrived providing food, especially rice for the military. In addition, his success relied on the coercive power of the Native Authority system being at his disposal. Food processing also proved lucrative for some African entrepreneurs. Lisabi Mills, an African-owned processing enterprise in Lagos, thrived and

---

[68] Collingham, *Taste of War*, 1.

[69] Oberst, "Transport workers, strikes and the 'imperial response,'" 124.

[70] Ibid.

[71] Ibid., 125–27. For more on these strikes, see: Peter Alexander, *Workers, War and the Origins of Apartheid: Labour & Politics in South Africa 1939–48* (Athens: Ohio University Press, 2000); Frederick Cooper, *Decolonization and African Society: The Labor Question in French and British Africa* (Cambridge: Cambridge University Press, 1996).

was celebrated as an example of import substitution in the nationalist press.[72]

One of the most enduring legacies of the war was the creation of marketing boards, which British Colonial Office official C. Y. Carstairs regarded as a "silent revolution."[73] The United Africa Company (UAC) first proposed the idea of bulk purchasing cocoa and vegetable seeds and oil to protect the import trade if export markets collapsed as well as to protect its own dominant position in both the import and export markets. Given the crisis in 1937–1938, when Gold Coast cocoa farmers essentially went on strike and refused to sell their cocoa at the price the European companies determined, the Colonial Office was highly receptive to the idea of bulk purchase.[74] What began as the Cocoa Control Board in 1939 became the West African Produce Control Board in 1941 and it was responsible for marketing cocoa, palm oil, palm kernels, groundnuts (peanuts), benniseed, and ginger.[75] These marketing boards were not unique to West Africa. In East Africa a sisal control board was established to buy sisal from growers to supply the needs of the Ministry of Supply. Planters dominated the sisal control board and the ministry initially purchased 62 percent of the crop. After the fall of France, however, merchants convinced the state to purchase the entire crop. Consequently, for the remainder of the war the ministry and growers determined the price and marketing of sisal.[76]

During the war, bulk purchasing "provided Britain with an assured and steady supply of food and raw materials at the lowest prices."[77] State control of West African produce also provided a profit, especially from the produce sold to the United States, which also brought in dollars. Economist Kenneth Wright estimated that between 1946 and 1952 the sale of West African produce contributed almost £2 billion to Britain's dollar reserves, thus leading him to conclude the "colonies had been exporting capital to the United Kingdom in the form of dollar exchange."[78] In short, the colonies gave Britain access to funds to prosecute the war, and after the war they provided funds to help reduce Britain's deficit and aid reconstruction.

---

[72] Axel Harnett-Sievers, "African business, 'economic nationalism' and British colonial policy: southern Nigeria, 1935–1954," *African Economic History*, 23 (1995), 101–02. Also see Byfield, Chapter 8, this volume.

[73] Quoted in David Meredith, "State controlled marketing and economic 'development': The case of West African produce during the Second World War," *Economic History Review*, 2nd ser., 39 (1986), 77.

[74] Meredith, "State controlled marketing," 81. For more on the cocoa farmer's strikes or cocoa hold-ups, see Rod Alence, "The 1937–1938 Gold Coast cocoa crisis: The political economy of commercial stalemate," *African Economic History*, 19 (1990–1991), 77–104.

[75] Meredith, "State controlled marketing," 84.

[76] Cowen and Westcott, "British imperial economic policy during the war," 43.

[77] Meredith, "State controlled marketing," 82.

[78] Quoted in Meredith, "State controlled marketing," 89–90; Kenneth M. Wright, "Dollar pooling in the sterling area, 1939–52," *American Economic Review*, 44 (1954), 569–74.

In multiple ways, economic tensions during World War II contributed significantly to the sociopolitical processes that created the coalitions at the forefront of the nationalist movements in the postwar period. In FWA/AOF, where both the Vichy and the Free French governments relied heavily on forced labor, nationalists, who took up the call for an end to forced labor, acted with the support of the vast majority. In February 1946, the group of deputies, including Felix Houphouet-Boigny (future president of Ivory Coast) and Leopold Senghor (future president of Senegal), who wrote to colonial minister that "Millions of men have sent us here giving us a precise mandate, to struggle with all our might to abolish the slavery which is still practiced in Black Africa by men, civil servants and civilians" did not exaggerate.[79] They articulated the disdain for those thousands of men who endured the intensification of forced labor during the war; thousands of whom had the right to vote by the 1950s.

In Nigeria, where produce prices were kept artificially low, while Britain accumulated the surplus from their sale and trading firms like UAC protected their dominant position, issues such as commodity prices, marketing boards, and the fate of Nigerian entrepreneurs became a part of what Harneit-Sievers calls "economic nationalism." He shows that wartime policies created a climate in which political agitation "combined nationalist political issues with problems of business and commerce." Like wage laborers, peasant farmers, and petty traders, the business class became a "'natural' part of the social base of political nationalism."[80]

In a similar vein, the chapters by Schmidt (23), Sikainga (24), and Summers (25) in this volume illustrate how wartime policies and conditions helped create the social base of political nationalism in Guinea, Uganda, and Sudan. They demonstrate some of the similarities as well as the differences in each country's experience. Ugandans, for example, did not face conscription into the army, food rationing, or actual fighting, though 77,000 Uganda served in the army. Some did genuinely volunteer for combat, while a few were "volunteered by local authorities." Uganda's greatest contribution to the war effort was the production of cotton, which allowed cotton growers to make substantial financial contributions to the British government in the form of £1 million sterling through direct lending and £3 million from the Cotton and Coffee Fund.

Guinea, on the other hand, experienced military conscription, forced labor and crop requisition, and heavy taxation, as well as food shortages and inflation. Since chiefs carried out these policies on the local level, the war created great antipathy toward the colonial state and toward chiefs. Schmidt also shows that resistance to the chiefs and the colonial state did not begin in the postwar period, but rather it began during the war years.

---

[79] Quoted in Cooper, *Decolonization and African Society*, 187.
[80] Harneit-Sievers, "African business, 'economic nationalism,'" 86.

The RDA, the main nationalist organization, built its broad-based support by articulating the grievances of veterans, peasants, workers, and urban women; however, as the state addressed the concerns of veterans, they faded into the background, creating a circumstance in which peasants, workers, and urban women dominated the nationalist struggle, in the process giving Guinean nationalism its distinctive radicalism.[81]

Sudan, like Ethiopia and Eritrea, was another major theatre of battle. Equally important, Sudan served as the major supply center and line of communication for the Allied forces in the Middle East and North Africa. Many Sudanese claimed the war as their own and supported the Allied cause completely. Like Ugandans, they expected to be rewarded for their sacrifice; however, British unwillingness to recognize their sacrifice and pave the road toward self-determination gave greater energy to nationalist forces. Railway workers played a prominent role, due in part to their centrality during the war, and, together with peasants and students, they formed much of the social basis of political nationalism. Of the case studies in this volume, Sudanese political nationalism is further distinguished by the fact that Sudan had the second largest communist party on the continent. It was surpassed only by the communist party of South Africa.

Conclusion

Africa produced copious quantities of agricultural, forest, and mineral products that were critical to the success of the Allies. While many imagined themselves as critical allies in this struggle against Nazism and German imperialism, colonial economic policy was predicated on imperial frameworks that viewed Africans solely as colonial subjects. Through the extensive use of coercion, European powers acquired the goods and resources they needed to prosecute the war, feed their populations, and protect their national economies. Africa became integral to the postwar plans for most imperial nations; however, the very strategies that enhanced the value of the African colonies proved to be double-edged swords that generated resistance and social unrest as well. When combined with France and Britain's effort to reform imperialism in the postwar period, the strategies that helped win the war also paved the path to the end of empire.

---

[81] Schmidt, Chapter 23, this volume.

3

African Labor in the Making of World War II

Carolyn A. Brown

"A young girl of 10 or 12 was given twenty-four blows of the *palmatoria*[1] while Sr Amaro stood behind her with a **hippopotamus** hide whip to force her to hold out her hand." A halt was called to this scene "when they saw me." However, he adds for the benefit of his employers, "corporal punishment for the black man is necessary because it is the only thing he fears."[2]

Please note that in [the] future the designation "men" must be substituted for "boys" in all communications referring to the Colliery labour either collectively or individually. No person employed by this department must be addressed as "boy."[3]
          Colliery Manager (Enugu) to Staff, 23 December 1941

For African workers, World War II brought contradictory experiences of "progressive" reform within authoritarian labor systems and the preservation of archaic oppressive systems of labor mobilization and control. The opening quotes illustrate the contrasting strategies that colonial powers used in their search for the best labor regimes to control African labor. There was a clear difference between brutal, coercive systems of labor discipline used, in this instance, by Portuguese planters on Principe and British rejection of incendiary forms of racial address in the British colonies. It was better to make concessions to the gendered sensitivities of African working-class men than to put down a strike whose demand was "respect."[4] But even British

---

[1] A palmatoria is a wide paddle with several holes that is used to beat the palm of the hand or the buttocks. It is interesting that in his explanation of the beating the official would rationalize the brutal punishment of a 12-year-old girl as necessary for a "black man."

[2] Quoted in Newitt, Chapter 12, this volume.

[3] Letter from Colliery Department to all officials and staff – European and African, December 23, 1941, New No. P.1, Nigerian Coal Corporation Files, National Archives of Nigeria, Enugu.

[4] Lisa Lindsay, *Working With Gender: Wage Labor and Social Change in Southwestern Nigeria* (Portsmouth, NH: Heinemann, 2003).

reformers were not adverse to using brutal forms of forced labor and ignor-
ing the rural starvation that it caused, as was the case in the tin-producing
areas of northern Nigeria after the loss of the Far East colonies to the
Japanese.[5] British reform, although often abandoned, came from an embarrassing rash of violent strikes (that spilled over into anticolonial protests)
in the British Caribbean and on the Northern Rhodesian copper belt in the
late 1930s when workers attacked white bosses.[6] These experiences nudged
them along the road to recognizing that Britain did, in fact, have a colonial working-class that *might* quite possibly be controlled by "enlightened"
"modern" systems of worker control and industrial relations used on the
English working-class. Calling an African worker a "boy" and slapping him
around in the workplace may have been an important part of the racialized
labor process of "colonial despotism,"[7] but it was not the way to ensure
the loyalty of colonial workers targeted by Vichy propaganda or exposed to
the unfortunate anticolonial discourse of Britain's ally, the United States.
In the colonies British managers did not immediately understand these
changes and felt betrayed when the state seriously entertained the complaints of African workers against corporeal punishment and demeaning
disciplinary practices.[8] But most colonial powers still assumed that Africans
were too "backward," "primitive," and embedded in "archaic" social structures to be treated as industrial workers in Europe were. Officials felt that
given the weak demand for cash in periods of economic contraction, when
imports were scarce, there were few incentives for men to enter the workforce producing exports for the war. The French had their own preferred
strategy to keep exports up while imports were not coming. They ratch-
eted up the use of forced labor,[9] to such an extent that some rural areas
of French West Africa (FWA) were practically denuded of most of their

---

[5] See Bill Freund, *Capital and Labour in the Nigerian Tin Mines* (Harlow, Essex: Longman,
   1981).

[6] The Fabian socialists took a major interest in these strikes and immediately after the uprising
   sponsored the publication of their own Caribbean specialist, the St. Lucian; W. Arthur Lewis,
   Labour in the West Indies (London: Fabian Society, 1939). Subsequent publications include
   a radical treatment of the largest rebellion in Jamaica; Ken Post's *Arise Ye Starvlings": The
   Jamaican Labour Rebellion of 1938 and Its Aftermath* (The Hague: Nijhoff, 1978). The
   impact of these protests was monumental in the British empire and pushed Whitehall to force
   the colonies to create organizations of worker representation – usually unions – which were
   a requirement for the implementation of "enlightened" systems of collective bargaining and
   industrial relations. For more about the discussion in the Colonial Office see Chapter Four,
   Frederick Cooper, *Decolonization and African Society: The Labor Question in French and
   British Africa* (Cambridge: Cambridge University Press, 1996).

[7] Michael Burawoy, *The Politics of Production: Factory Regimes Under Capitalism and Socialism* (London: Verso Press, 1985), 226–27.

[8] C. A. Brown, *"We Were All Slaves": African Miners, Culture and Resistance at the Enugu
   Government Colliery* (Portsmouth, NH: Heinemann 2003), 250.

[9] Cooper, *Decolonization and African Society*, 110.

working-age men. Thus for most African workers the war experience was both empowering and excruciatingly oppressive.

The essays in this volume include African workers as part of the international *world* of labor created by imperialism and two world wars. In many respects the history of labor during World War II exemplifies the themes that inform the new field of Global Labor History, which examines the integration of global supply chains, transnational coordination of labor policy, and cross-national collaborations between groups of workers.[10] The boundaries between metropolitan and colonial economies or British "working men" and African "native" laborers were more imagined than real.[11] Imperial administrators perceived African workers as "so different" that policy makers could scarcely see what should have been obvious: these were workers and if they wanted to routinize their labor, they needed to treat them as such. As the metropolitan state moved toward wartime coordinated planning and execution of labor policies, it became even more difficult to retain that distinction. The war necessitated the most intensive level of state intervention into the economies of both metropole and colony to ensure that workers produced those goods and services needed for the war. As European states developed new methods of securing, controlling, and reproducing their own national workforces, they also experimented with these methods in their colonies. This experimentation and the communication between colonial and metropolitan workers led colonial workers to demand treatment and wages equal to those of their European counterparts. This dynamic brought colonial policy makers face to face with a fundamental contradiction: they were asking African peoples to give their lives and energies to restore democracy, political rights, and sovereignty to populations in occupied Europe that they themselves lacked. As the war progressed, African workers fully grasped this contradiction and recognized their powerful position in the wartime economy. By the end of the war, nationalist politicians could harvest this discontent and press for increased political participation and eventual independence.

For the French, so divided during most of the war, the labor problem was even more complex. France had always operated under different labor policies than Britain and was more "locked" into its myths of African "backwardness" which, to them, were expressed in the resistance of African men to joining the "modern" labor force. For this reason throughout the colonial period, France made extensive use of a number of coercive labor systems to press-gang African men into the military and workforce. In this volume, Parsons (Chapter 7), Ash (Chapter 6), and Ginio (Chapter 17) define *prestation*,

[10] Amsterdam's Institute of Global History and its research director, Marcel van der Linden, has been in the forefront of this field. *Workers of the World: Essays Toward a Global History* (Leiden: Brill Academic Publishers, 2010).
[11] Brown, "*We Were All Slaves*," 184.

the *indigénat*, and *deuxième portion* as forms of forced labor that plagued subjects of the French empire. Each French government – Vichy, Free France, and Liberated France – used these forms of forced labor. Even when the Free French government met in Brazzaville in 1944 to embark on modest reforms, it kept much of the *deuxième portion* in place. Moreover, they were not convinced that Africans were sufficiently "civilized" to be governed by the Code du Travail that operated in France.[12]

While the chapters in this volume assume the conventional analysis of the war's seminal role in transforming nationalist movements into mass movements, they deepen our discussion of the complex processes and material conditions that underlay this political transformation. Although they vary in focus and topic, these studies assume that the labor of African men women and children was an important determinant in the outcome of the war. Many reflect the new theoretical and empirical contributions of social history and gender studies and also assume that the term "labor" is far broader than the term "working-class." Our contributors recognize as "labor" work performed in forced cultivation schemes and production of those crops requisitioned for export to Europe.[13] Additionally, much of African military recruitment was for laborers who were embedded in the various production systems that underpinned Britain's fighting ability. Scheck examines how the Tirailleurs Sénégalais POWs who survived the massacres following the defeat of France in 1940 were incarcerated in work camps, the *front stalags*, of occupied France.[14] Our chapters also document the work experiences of millions of rural producers forced into hyper-exploitative agricultural projects, such as French Soudan's (Mali) Office du Niger and the Sudan's Gezira Scheme.[15]

Despite the international nature of the war's labor force, most conventional labor historians of World War II focus on the expansion of production in factories, mines, and transport in Europe and North America, barely incorporating what global labor historians call "the imperial labor force," a concept that incorporates those working men, women, and children both in

---

[12] For an excellent analysis of the "twists and turns" in the maneuvers of Free French officials to avoid considering Africans as their equals, see Cooper, *Decolonization and African Society*, Chapter 4.

[13] See Parsons, Chapter 7, and Ash, Chapter 6, this volume.

[14] See Scheck, Chapter 22, this volume.

[15] The literature on both schemes is voluminous. Particularly significant are Victoria Bernal, "Colonial moral economy and the discipline of development: The Gezira Scheme and "modern" Sudan," *Cultural Anthropology*, 12 (1977), 447–79; Jean Filipovich, "Destined to fail: Forced settlement at the Office du Niger, 1926–45," *Journal of African History*, 42 (2001), 239–60; Monica M. van Beusekom, "Disjunctures in theory and practice: Making sense of change in agricultural development at the Office du Niger, 1920–60," *Journal of African History*, 41 (2000), 79–99. See also Ash, Chapter 6, this volume.

the metropole and in the colonies. Perhaps for colonialists the most illuminating revelation of the war was the recognition that African labor was not just an abstract, pliable social category but "real" human beings who had responsibilities and social connections with families and communities, urban and rural, and who *could* imagine a world *without* the colonial governments who exploited and humiliated them. On the other hand, the colonial powers' view of the future was not so sanguine. As Frederick Cooper noted, "The governments which ruled French West Africa and British Africa during the early war years had one characteristic in common: both were planning for futures that did not exist."[16]

African Labor during the Interwar Years

On the eve of World War II the African working class was a small but strategically placed sector of the working population, concentrated in the export-oriented sectors of the agricultural and industrial economy. The most industrialized sectors were in mining, particularly in the copper belt of Northern Rhodesia (now Zambia) and Katanga in the Belgium Congo (now Democratic Republic of Congo) and in the diamond- and gold-producing areas of South Africa. Mine workers in these areas produced 50 percent of the world's gold, 24 percent of its vanadium, 90 percent of its cobalt, and 100 percent of its uranium (including that used for the Manhattan Project and the development of the atomic bomb).[17] These extractive industries required the deployment of labor to build transportation and communication networks that included railroads, deep harbors, connecting road systems, and bridges. Transport workers, a small but strategically placed sector, were among the first to unionize and organize massive strikes in which they galvanized other workers.

Colonial governments, expatriate firms, and settler farmers used the Depression as an opportunity to cut wages that were already below the cost of living. During the recovery in the mid-thirties, rather than restore pre-Depression rates, they chose to use extraordinary forms of coercion – forced labor – to push young men to work under highly unfavorable conditions. When war erupted, governments argued that there were few products to buy at any rate and increased taxation to "pull money out of circulation." With commodity prices plunging in the Depression, rural communities could scarcely support themselves, let alone sustain the reproduction of the working-class. The African working class was, above all, small, reaching only several hundred thousand workers even in large countries such as

---

[16] Cooper, *Decolonization and African Society*, 110.
[17] Raymond Dumett, "Africa's strategic minerals during the Second World War," *Journal of African History*, 26 (1985), 381–408.

Nigeria. But it was located in the most important points of the colony: in transport and on the docks.

Colonial labor systems had a uniqueness largely because of the assumptions officials made about the "difference" in the workplace behavior and goals of African workers. Migrant labor, the preferred system used throughout the continent, assumed that workers' reproduction occurred in the village (i.e., inhabited by old men, women, and underage children). Wages were held deliberately low and not calculated to support the family. Most colonies tried to prevent the development of a stable workforce or the emergence of "detribalized" Africans roaming the cities, existing outside the control of authoritarian village chiefs. As colonial governments struggled with the problem of drawing African young men into the colonial workplace (factories, mines, railroads, docks etc.), plantations, and settler-owned farms, they never considered that higher wages would bring more men to their workplace.

The Depression left its scar on African economies and on the men and women engaged in the new colonial economy. The collapse of trade reduced government revenues that were largely dependent on import and export duties and led to the closure of infrastructural projects, resulting in the dismissal of workers. Farmers found that the prices of their exports had dropped so low it was hardly worth their production.[18] Despite the problems employers were having in securing and controlling African workers, by the outbreak of the war, it had become abundantly clear that the cash economy had penetrated even the most remote areas of the continent. Thus, when commodity prices fell, young men came pouring out of the villages into the cities where they joined previously urbanized workers and the "dangerous classes" – the unemployed and those in the informal economy. Colonial authorities in Africa were confronted with a seemingly intractable dilemma: how to get young African men to come work on their railroads, roads, docks, and plantations without developing a consciousness of themselves as workers and placing demands on the state to support their social reproduction in the cities where they worked rather than in their natal villages. In other words, they strove to create a labor force without a working-class consciousness.

Thus colonial policies ripped communities apart to secure conscripted labor, crushed local food security to force Africans to produce cash crops, and pushed African men into a migrant labor system that treated them as

---

[18] In most cases farmers produced more to compensate for the lower cost per union. However, in the Gold Coast, the behavior of cocoa farmers warned the British that, during the war, they could not assume their support. They held up all supplies of cocoa, demanding higher prices. Gareth Austin, "Capitalists and chiefs in the cocoa hold-ups in South Asante, 1927–1938," *International Journal of African Historical Studies*, 21 (1988), 63–95.

"units of labor." But the colonial workplace was more than an economic experience; it was also social. It was one of the sites where African men were socialized to the power of colonial racism as a system of labor control.[19] At work, assumptions about African backwardness were articulated in a racist discourse in which all the "men" were white and all the "boys" were Africans, as illustrated in the introductory quotations. Disciplinary systems frequently used corporeal punishment, while subhuman work conditions and daily humiliation were considered appropriate for "primitive" workers. In many cases, however, the sheer nature of industrial labor strengthened indigenous models of masculinity and weakened the psychological power of these humiliating practices.[20] In many instances humiliating racist practices became a familiar trigger in inciting collective action during the war, and the colonial authorities and European employers fairly quickly realized the need for reform.[21]

By the mid-1930s, there were signs of a growing working-class consciousness in the British empire. Workers adapted indigenous associations to industrial purposes and created workplace organizations that organized waves of coordinated strikes throughout the empire demanding restoration of Depression wages.[22] Workers were desperate because wages were far below the cost of reproduction of the workforce and the rural economy, buffeted by ever lower prices of agricultural products, offered no respite. Further, many men had become truly urbanized and reliant on wages, despite the colonial myth that they could easily return to their self-sufficient "natal villages." The protests shocked colonial administrators because of their strategic timing, levels of organization, effectiveness in identifying targets, and demographic scope. In many instances these protests spilled out into the streets, successfully mobilizing the discontented, suffering urban poor – that amorphous group of casual workers, unemployed and lumpen, who were ever ready

---

[19] Before the war, African workers were often physically abused, with few protections under colonial legal systems. This began to change in the late 1930s, when workers began to unionize and strike for better working conditions. Michael Burawoy, *The Politics of Production: Factory Regimes under Capitalism and Socialism* (London: Verso Books, 1985).

[20] C. A. Brown, "A 'Man' in the village is a 'boy' in the workplace: Colonial racism, worker militancy and Igbo notions of masculinity in the Nigerian coal industry, 1930–1945," in Lisa Lindsay and Stephan Meischer (eds.), *Men and Masculinities in Modern Africa* (Portsmouth, NH: Heinemann, 2003), 156–74.

[21] Lindsay, *Working with Gender*; John Iliffe, *Honor in African History* (Cambridge: Cambridge University Press 2004), Chapter 17.

[22] In both the Northern Rhodesian Copperbelt and the Enugu (Nigeria), coal mine strikes were organized by indigenous associations adapted to industrial needs: the *Mbeni* dance societies in Northern Rhodesia and the *nzuko ifunaya*, workers' groups modeled on urban "tribal" associations which organized a number of strikes in the mid-1930s. Charles Perrings, *Black Mineworkers in Central Africa* (Portsmouth, NH: Heinemann 1979); Brown, *"We Were All Slaves."*

for any political action. These were the social strata most feared by officials for their elusiveness from control, rejection of capitalist labor regimes, and attraction to crime and radical politics.

The most violent protests were in Britain's West Indian colonies, which became the subject of the *Report of the West India Royal Commission* (commonly known as the Moyne Report), that was so critical that the Colonial Office delayed its publication until the end of the war.[23] Its findings pushed colonial authorities to take more seriously the severity of economic and social conditions in the colonies. In a similar protest in Northern Rhodesia, copper miners also went out on strike and secured some increase in wages.[24] They attacked European supervisors, suggesting that the mystique of white skin was losing credibility. But officials were trapped in their own myths: Were Africans really capable of behaving like "industrial men" or were they so peculiarly different as to render any metropolitan reforms useless? Colonial officials (French, British, Belgian, and Portuguese) held these conflicting ideas to varying degrees. These misconceptions plagued colonial labor policy throughout the war and ill prepared them for the rash of strikes in its wake.

Ports, Rails, and Airfields: African Workers in the Opening Years of the War, 1939–1941

When Hitler's armies marched into Poland, African workers were conducting collective action to restore their meager wages reduced during the Depression. Many protests were led by workers in transport and in construction of strategically valuable war installations, such as ports, airfields, and railways. Workers in the Union of South Africa and some colonies, such as Sierra Leone, the Gold Coast, and Nigeria, had a long tradition of unionization but in others workers continued to use indigenous institutions adapted into associations of labor protest. This was the case in July 1939, when dockworkers in Mombasa, Kenya, the major East African port, used *Beni* dance societies to organize their participation in a rolling strike that began with the public works department and spread to other groups, including the dockworkers.[25] That same year, Gold Coast railway workers struck for the right to have unions and for a wage increase. Although they won a 20 percent increase, by late 1941 the 50 percent inflation rate obliterated this

---

[23] *Report of the West Indies Royal Commission* (London: HMSO, 1945).

[24] Charles Perrings, *Black Mineworkers in Central Africa* (Portsmouth, NH: Heinemann 1979), 207–31; C. A. Perrings, "Consciousness, conflict and proletarianization: An assessment of the 1935 mineworkers' strike on the Northern Rhodesian Copperbelt," *Journal of Southern African Studies*, 4 (1977), 31–51.

[25] Frederick Cooper, *On The African Waterfront: Urban Disorder and the Transformation of Work in Colonial Mombasa* (New Haven, CT: Yale University Press, 1987), 38–39; Terence Ranger, *Dance and Society in Eastern Africa, 1890–1970: The Beni Ngoma* (Berkeley: University of California Press, 1975).

increase, so they downed tools again.[26] In South Africa's Transvaal, 7,000 members of the predominately female Garment Workers Union embarked on a series of actions including sit-down strikes, mass demonstrations, and a three-day lockout.[27] In early 1939, as Britain feverishly fortified the port of Freetown, I. T. A. Wallace-Johnson, a radical journalist and trade unionist, led members of the West African Youth League to mobilize workers in the defense works, the West African Frontier Force (WAFF), and the police. This could not be tolerated in so crucial a city as Freetown, soon to be the largest port in West Africa, in 1939.[28] In response, the government quickly introduced legislation to prevent anticolonial campaigns and labor agitation.[29] Wallace-Johnson was detained for much of the war.

Nonetheless, the colonial powers recognized that their ability to survive the war would depend upon the incorporation of all labor throughout their particular empire. On the eve of war, Britain had begun to implement reforms suggested by the Moyne Report, including recognition of labor unions and the establishment of labor departments. Moreover, Britain, and, to a lesser extent, France, moved towards a consensus that abrogated forms of forced labor and workplace violence. Unfortunately, many of these reforms were suspended or seriously undermined by restrictive war legislation. Some policy makers felt that one way of preventing protest was to segment the workforce, stabilizing the most skilled workers with better wages, housing, and other amenities. This process reflected an international discourse that differentiated between "enlightened" and "uncivilized" ways of mobilizing and controlling colonial workers. But local authorities were always a problem. Even before the war most colonial governments developed astute ways of subverting inquiries about labor conditions and distorted their reporting to downplay both the forms of slavery that they allowed to continue and the various forms of forced labor still in use.

In England, where ideas of labor reform appeared more advanced than those in France, and were certainly more advanced than those in Portugal and Belgium, the "best" ways of controlling African workers had not yet been determined and labor "experts" in the Colonial Office fumbled along, experimenting with the shell of British industrial relations institutions and processes (i.e., trade unions, collective bargaining, and disputes procedures)

---

[26] Cooper, *Decolonization and African Society*, 126–27.

[27] Peter Alexander, *Workers, War and the Origins of Apartheid: Labour and Politics in South Africa 1939–48* (Athens: Ohio Press, 2000), 64–66. For more on the actions of South African women, see Iris Berger, *Threads of Solidarity: Women in South African Industry, 1900–1980* (Bloomington: Indiana University Press, 1992).

[28] See Howard, Chapter 10, this volume.

[29] LaRay Denzer, "Wallace-Johnson and the Sierra Leone labor crisis of 1939," *African Studies Review*, 25 (1982), 159–83; Leo Spitzer and LaRay Denzer, "I. T. A. Wallace-Johnson and the West African Youth League," *International Journal of Historical Studies*, 6 (1973), 413–52, 565–601.

weakened by colonial authoritarianism. Thus unions were legalized, but required to register; laws specified convoluted procedures of wage bargaining, but locked in prohibitions on the right to strike. The right of workers to select their own representatives was compromised when trade union leaders were targeted and often detained, for as soon as war was declared, the British passed the Emergency Powers (Defense) Act that prohibited strikes throughout the empire.[30] Michael Imoudu, leader of the Railway Workers Union in Nigeria, like Wallace-Johnson in Sierra Leone, was detained for most of the war.[31]

In preparation for the war, Britain's Colonial Office established wage-fixing boards and other agencies to coordinate labor and economic policies in the colonies. A resident minister was appointed for West Africa, establishing a point for decision making outside the Colonial Office.[32] A series of West African Labour Conferences brought together governors from the region to discuss policies, set production targets, and determine the best strategies for containing working-class unrest. Social scientists sought to establish the scientific requirements for the reproduction of the workforce and wage-fixing boards were set up in both rural and urban areas. These efforts failed. In every case escalating inflation nullified price controls and wage increases, and only succeeded in mobilizing market women, farmers, and urban populations against the state. Nigerian officials, for example, tried unsuccessfully to regulate the inflationary spiral of food by establishing its own markets, called Pullen Markets, which were universally unpopular because they paid producers lower than market rates and then sold these crops at fixed prices to market women.[33] This could not prevent producers from smuggling foodstuffs to sell on the black market at higher prices nor wholesalers from hoarding.

As soon as hostilities began, the Colonial Office deployed its first "official" labor advisor, Col. Granville St. J. Orde-Browne, a former colonial official of East Africa, to investigate the labor situation in the colonies and make policy recommendations. After an extensive African tour in 1939–1940, he submitted a report that made far-reaching recommendations to the Colonial Labour Advisory Committee, a newly formed agency in the Colonial Office charged to coordinate labor policy, including, for the first time,

---

[30] Gilbert A. Sekgoma, "The Second World War and the Sierra Leone economy: Labour employment and utilisation, 1939–45," in D. Killingray and Richard Rathbone (eds.), *Africa and the Second World War* (London: Macmillan, 1986), 234.

[31] Spitzer and Denzer, "Wallace-Johnson and the West African Youth League"; Michael Omolewa, *Michael Imoudu: A Study in Adventures in the Nigerian Labour Movement* (Ilorin, Nigeria: M. Imoudu Institute for Labour Studies, 1992).

[32] Harold Evans, "Studies in war-time organisation. (2) The Resident Ministry in West Africa," *African Affairs*, 43 (1944), 152–58.

[33] Wale Oyemakinde, "The Pullen Marketing Scheme: A trial in food price control in Nigeria, 1941–47," *Journal of the Historical Society of Nigeria*, 6 (1973), 413–24.

a representative of the British Trades Union Congress (TUC).[34] Although Orde-Browne feared that the economic crisis would develop into a political challenge to the state, he did not believe that African workers were "ready" for trade unions.[35] As Cooper argues, Orde-Browne had problems imagining African workers outside of the restrictive militaristic order that he observed, with satisfaction, in the copper mines of Northern Rhodesia and the Congo.[36] There workers received rations (to ensure that their caloric intake allowed rigorous work) and lived in barracks. West African workers, on the other hand, fed themselves from their wages, and lived in housing that sprung up around their workplace. This was far too much African autonomy for Orde-Browne. When strikes erupted throughout Africa, strikes that resonated with the more familiar ones in England, his assumptions of African "backwardness" meant that he was just as surprised as the "nonexperts."

The summer of 1940 was an anxious period for Britain. In June, France collapsed, its army grossly unprepared for the efficient and precise German intervention. Churchill, distrusting Vichy assurances to the contrary, feared that the French would give Germany access to its large fleet in the Mediterranean, and on July 3 destroyed the French Navy at Mers-el Kébir, killing over 1,200 French sailors and sinking several large warships. While this act convinced the Americans of England's conviction to fight, it also risked pushing the Vichy government closer to Germany and fostered anti-British sentiment throughout France and its territories. Several days later Germany launched the Battle of Britain, sending hundreds of planes in an unsuccessful bid to "soften" Britain for an invasion. In September, Britain again incurred the ire of French West Africa when it joined de Gaulle in an aborted invasion of Dakar to overthrow the Vichy government.[37] By the end of October, Britain had survived the attack, although with 42,000 casualties,[38] hundreds of pilots killed and airplanes destroyed. France's capitulation made Britain anxious that the Vichy government in FWA could influence its West African colonies and possibly invade these territories using its numerous African troops, which far outnumbered Britain's West African troops.[39]

---

[34] This marked a new phase of colonial trade union management in which British TUC advisors were deployed throughout the empire to monitor new unions, establish labor bureaus, and tutor leaders on "responsible trade unionism." See Peter Weiler, "Forming responsible trade unions: The Colonial Office, colonial labor and the Trades Union Congress," *Radical History Review*, 28–30 (1984), 367–92.

[35] Granville St. John Orde-Browne, *Labour Conditions in West Africa*, Cmd. 6277 (London: His Majesty's Stationary Office, 1941), 60.

[36] Cooper, *Decolonization and African Society*, 125–26.

[37] Paul M. Atkins, "Dakar and the strategy of West Africa," *Foreign Affairs*, 20 (1942), 359–66.

[38] R. A. C. Parker, *The Second World War: A Short History*, Oxford University Press, 1997.

[39] See Parsons, Chapter 1, this volume.

Under this threat Britain could not assume the loyalty of its African subjects and used both the "carrot" (propaganda) and the "stick" (prohibitions
on strikes, arrest of union leaders, and draconian laws).[40] Wartime propaganda matured as an instrument of government policy, an important
weapon in the productionist programs of both French and British colonies;
however, propaganda also deepened the contradictions inherent in wartime
policy in ways that accelerated the pace of decolonization. The Gold Coast
administration developed a pilot propaganda project that deployed radio
diffusion sets and trained African broadcasters, training that was later used
to great effect in the successful postwar campaign for independence.[41]

From late 1940 until the United States entered the war in December, 1941,
more than 10,000 African workers prepared the surreptitious Trans-African
Air Ferry Route that enabled the United States to supply the British with
airplanes used in the North African campaigns against German and Italian armed forces.[42] Laborers in the public works departments built roads,
constructed or expanded over thirty airfields, and reinforced ports. African
workers in Freetown transformed the port into the major south Atlantic port
in West Africa, rerouted hinterland water to resupply ships, provided wood,
off-loaded Nigerian coal, and provisioned some 200 convoys a week.[43] In
the strategically important ports of Cape Town and Durban in South Africa,
Africans repaired ships, airplanes, tanks and manufactured munitions and
replacement parts for the war machine.[44] African farmers, whose rice was
conscripted in FWA and whose corn was purchased at below market rates
in Southern Rhodesia, fed troops in North Africa and beyond.[45] Transport
workers, particularly those on the railway and the docks, worked long hours
for little pay bringing important exports to the coast for the home front.
Villagers in French Equatorial Africa suffered under nineteenth-century
conditions, reminiscent of King Leopold's atrocities, to meet quotas of wild

[40] Rosaleen Smyth, "Britain's African colonies and British propaganda during the Second
World War," *Journal of Imperial and Commonwealth History*, 14 (1985), 65–82; Fay
Gadsden, "Wartime propaganda in Kenya: The Kenya Information Office, 1939–1945,"
International Journal of African Historical Studies, 19 (1986), 401–20.

[41] Wendell P. Holbrook, "British propaganda and the mobilization of the Gold Coast war
effort, 1939–1945," *Journal of African History*, 26 (1985), 347–61.

[42] Deborah Ray, "The Takoradi route: Roosevelt's prewar venture beyond the western hemisphere," *Journal of American History*, 62 (1975), 340–58; D. Ray, "The Airport Development Program of World War II," MA thesis, New York University (1964); Anonymous,
"The Sudan's service in a global war: The story of a section of the Trans-African Air Ferry
Route," *Journal of the Royal African Society*, 43 (1944), 16–20; Tom Culbert and Andy
Dawson, *Pan Africa: Across the Sahara in 1941 with Pan Am* (McLean, VA: Paladwr Press,
2010).

[43] See Howard, Chapter 10, this volume.

[44] Dumett, "Africa's strategic minerals."

[45] David Johnson, "Settler farmers and coerced African labour in Southern Rhodesia, 1936–
46," *Journal of African History*, 33 (1992), 111–28.

rubber which, in some cases, was not even grown in their canton.[46] Moreover, the massive buildup of "military labor" corps worked to expand colonial infrastructures.[47]

Sudanese workers were drawn into the war at an early period during the Italian invasion of Ethiopia, because the Sudan held a strategic position vis-à-vis both Egypt and Italian-occupied Ethiopia. It was one of the transit points for the Takoradi Route to Egypt during the North African campaigns[48] as well as part of a second supply route, the African Line of Communications (AFLOC), which crossed the Belgium Congo from Matadi on the Atlantic coast by rail, road, and river; to Juba in southern Sudan; and then down the Nile.[49] Militant railway workers at the terminus of Atbara (Known as "Red Atbara" for its communist-led unions.) had long become conscious of their important role in the war. Their proximity to what would become a front encouraged them to raise grievances about their treatment by European supervisors, disparities in the pay between local and expatriate artisans, and insufficient wages given the rate of inflation.[50]

While the degree of wartime sacrifice became clearer to colonial workers and they increased their protests, military conscription siphoned off the most experienced colonial officials. The few remaining officials were inexperienced and overwhelmed by the task of controlling burgeoning cities that grew astronomically during the war. The crush of rural populations into the city violated residential segregation and urban regulations when shantytowns were built wherever there was space. In South Africa these settlements became arenas for political action and mobilization of the unemployed. The new working class demanded that municipalities provide housing.[51] Similarly, in the workplace white bosses complained that they confronted daily challenges to their authority, which, in many instances, they were powerless to reassert.[52] Clearly, African workers developed a political consciousness

---

[46] See Jennings, Chapter 11, this volume.

[47] D. Killingray, "Labour mobilisation in British colonial Africa for the war effort, 1939–46," in Killingray and Rathbone, *Africa and the Second World War*, 68–96. See also Parsons, Chapter 1, this volume.

[48] Ray, "The Takoradi route," 58.

[49] K. D. D. Henderson, *The Making of the Modern Sudan: The Life and Letters of Sir Douglas Newbold K. B. E of the Sudan Political Service Governor of Kordofan, 1932–1938, Civil Secretary, 1939–1945* (London: Faber and Faber Ltd., 1953); Anonymous, "The Sudan's service in a global war: The story of a section of the Trans-African Air Ferry Route," *Journal of the Royal African Society*, 43 (1944), 16–20; G. S. Brunskill, "Studies in war-time organization. (5) AFLOC," *African Affairs*, 44 (1945), 125–30. See Howard, Chapter 10, this volume.

[50] Ahmad A. Sikainga, *"City of Steel and Fire": A Social History of Atbara, Sudan's Railway Town, 1906–1985* (Portsmouth, NH: Heinemann, 2004).

[51] Phillip Bonner, "The politics of black squatter movements in the Rand, 1944–1952," *Radical History Review*, 46–47 (1990), 89–116.

[52] Fred Cooper, "Introduction," *Decolonization and African Society*, 1–24.

that encouraged them to challenge work practices that managers assumed had become hegemonic.

Meanwhile, colonial economic policies tended to undermine the initiatives that sought to facilitate the cooperation of African workers. These set the context in which workers explored various types of protest. Policies that reduced the volume of imports and siphoned off products (e.g., starch, from cassava, salt, palm oil) from the domestic market increased inflation.[53] For African men and women, the struggles over work and social reproduction during the war created a type of "political accumulation" that strengthened their understanding of their own position within the imperial political economy and assisted them in identifying the most suitable ways of agitating for their interests. This in turn encouraged a trajectory of increasingly sophisticated forms of experimentation in collective action that reflected the maturation of political consciousness. Strikes, boycotts, "goslows," desertion, and sabotage were all used to address the increasingly onerous weight of war policies.[54]

The Turning Point: Workers, the State, and the War, 1942–1945

The year 1942 was a time of heightened worker activism in response to severe economic stress. In virtually every major industry from dock work to mining, strikes and worker protests erupted with a ferocity and determination that caught state officials by surprise. Predictably, they responded by tightening the laws that constrained workers' freedom of movement, deskilled artisan trades, banned the right to strike, and reduced the power of trade unions. The economic impact of war production and restriction caused hardship in both rural and urban areas, prompting workers and nationalist leaders to launch a new wave of protest. There is no consensus on the rate of inflation in individual colonies and urban centers, as estimates range from 75 to 400 percent, but we do know that it was so serious as to push workers action. That year, most colonial cities staggered under impossible rates of inflation caused by import shortages that, in some cases, reached over 300 percent. In other cases, as in Northern and Southern Rhodesia, the redirection of crops to the North African and Middle Eastern campaigns led to food deficiencies and famine throughout the countryside.[55] In West Africa there were additional problems when the traditional foreign markets for agro-exports disappeared. The loss of income pushed farmers into penury. Recognizing

[53] Toyin Falola, "'Salt is gold': The management of salt scarcity in Nigeria during World War II," *Canadian Journal of African Studies*, 26 (1992), 412–36; T. Falola, "Cassava starch for export in Nigeria during the Second World War," *African Economic History*, 18 (1989), 73–98.

[54] See Brown, Chapter 15, this volume.

[55] Johnson, "Settler farmers and coerced African labour."

this crisis, the Colonial Office created the West African Produce Control Board, formerly the West African Cocoa Control Board, to make bulk purchases of all products and to sell them at a profit on the world market; yet these profits were never shared with the producers, who continued to flee to the city in search of better opportunities.[56]

The year 1942 also had special significance to the prosecution of the war itself. On December 7, 1941, the United States entered the war after the Japanese attack on Pearl Harbor. Within three months, Japan conquered and occupied Britain's colony of Singapore, depriving Britain of many tropical resources and threatening strategic waterways to the prized colony of India. Consequently, West Africa became the empire's only reliable source for tropical products and some strategic minerals. From this point on, the region's workers and farmers became the linchpins of British tropical supplies and the Colonial Office elaborated its war restrictions to allow forced labor, to requisition crops, to detain militant trade union leaders, and to limit the right to strike. Propaganda tried to conceal the draconian nature of these initiatives and emphasized "partnership" rather than the "duty to empire" as officials sought to convey the idea that "we're all in this together."[57] West Africans were "encouraged" to work with discipline and loyalty, to produce tin, palm products, cotton, and even salt and cassava for the war effort.[58] The Japanese seizure of Malaya's tin mines, the major source of tin for the United States and England, led to the expansion of the tin mines in Northern Nigeria. The entire output was purchased by a bulk purchasing scheme organized by the Ministry of Supply, which further reduced the wages of workers. The British conscripted 100,887 men for four months, 18,000 at a time, with disastrous consequences. Bill Freund estimates that death rates varied from 4.4 per thousand to an astronomical 25.6 per thousand due to overcrowding, inadequate rations, and infectious diseases.[59]

In 1942, planners in London failed to understand what local authorities knew: that the reproduction of the colonial working class was at risk.[60] Inflation, which pressured already meager wages, was exacerbated by the redirection of consumer goods to supply the war effort, the shortage of shipping space, and fiscal policies that increased taxes as a way of suppressing

[56] Lizzie Collingham, *The Taste of War: World War II and the Battle for Food* (New York: Penguin Press, 2012), 142–44.

[57] Rosaleen Smyth, "The British colonial film unit and sub-Saharan Africa, 1939–1945," *Historical Journal of Film, Radio and Television*, 8 (1988), 285–98; Smyth, "Britain's African colonies and British propaganda."

[58] Michael Crowder, "The Second World War: Prelude to decolonisation in Africa," in Michael Crowder (ed.), *The Cambridge History of Africa* (London and New York: Cambridge University Press, 1984), 8–51.

[59] Bill Freund, *Capital and Labour in the Nigerian Tin Mines* (Atlantic Highlands, NJ: Humanities Press, 1981), 144.

[60] See Byfield, Chapter 2, this volume.

demand. In one tragic instance – Cape Verde – this redirection of shipping priorities led to a famine that killed over 20,000[61] people and pushed others to evacuate their island for the slave-like conditions in plantations of Sao Tome and Principe.[62] To ensure production of commodities essential for the war, the Colonial Office instructed colonial governors to abrogate the right to strike by passing Defense Regulations and Essential Works legislation, using British laws that were being applied against coal miners and other striking groups in the United Kingdom. The designation "essential works" was defined so broadly that virtually the entire colonial working class was included under the law. In 1942 the Compulsory Service (Essential Works) Regulations authorized coerced labor, which in Sierra Leone allowed women to be drafted for noncombatant service as nurses, cooks, food producers, and clerical workers.[63]

Throughout the continent the consensus among imperial policy makers and colonial administrators was that urban overcrowding was creating dangerous slums inhabited by workers and the undisciplined urban poor, thus creating an environment ripe for exploitation by nationalist leaders and radical trade unionists. These cities attracted disgruntled young men and women, chafing under the economic hardship imposed by wartime colonial fiscal and economic policies, and fleeing the authoritarian controls of elders and chiefs who played a key role in coercive projects. These were the "detribalized" youth who officials had feared for decades. As disgruntled youth they joined nationalist politicians, restive workers, militant trade unionists, and the "riff raff" of the city, to give urban politics an unpredictability and political sophistication that created threatening cross-class social movements rooted in the commonalities of overcrowding, deplorable living conditions, and low wages. The exigencies of war suggested that the most necessary and skilled workers be stabilized and Britain made a meager effort using Colonial Development and Welfare funds to construct housing for these workers and assigned the first group of colonial welfare officers to closely monitor these crucial workers. On the Mombasa docks, officials tried to stabilize the workforce by implementing a registration system to prevent casual workers from clustering around the docks in the daily search of work.[64] But the urban population continued to grow and violate urban planning designs.

---

[61] António Carreira, *The People of the Cape Verde Islands* (London: Hurst, 1982), 166. As quoted in Newitt, Chapter 12, this volume.

[62] A Cape Verdean informant recounted how their community in Providence, Rhode Island was unable to ship supplies to their kinfolk because of shipping shortages. Others mentioned relatives who had gone to Principe never to be seen again. For an account of these slave-like conditions, see Catherine Higgs, *Chocolate Islands: Cocoa, Slavery and Colonial Africa* (Athens: Ohio University Press, 2012).

[63] Sekgoma, "The Second World War and the Sierra Leone economy," 239.

[64] Cooper, *On the African Waterfront*, 30–31, 76–78.

A policy of complete labor stabilization, however, was expensive, requiring investments in housing, higher wages, and social amenities. This conflicted with the more dominant philosophy of colonial urban design to depict the Manichean worlds of "colonized" and "colonizer" in stark contrast. The "native town" was dirty, overcrowded, and chaotic. The settlers' part of town was ordered, clean, and spacious. It was this clarity of contrast that made it far easier for urban inhabitants to become politicized than those in the rural areas.[65] Moreover, these inequalities and the suffering of the population contradicted the core values – expressed in propaganda – of the Allied cause, values further enshrined in the provocative Atlantic Charter.

Officials in 1942 were anxious about war production and recognized their powerlessness to control well-disciplined workers. They found strikes hard to resolve. Moreover, many refused to acknowledge that African working men were as concerned as British men about their ability to support their families with dignity on the wages that they were being paid. Protests also focused on discriminatory work policies that often restricted Africans to the lowest level of jobs. Officials responded piecemeal, establishing commissions to study the crisis, arresting strike leaders (though they most often targeted nationalist leaders), and, in some extreme cases, using open violence against strikers.[66] Despite government repression, however, the protests continued, putting officials in an impossible position: How could they meet the very real demands of African workers while guaranteeing the metropole cheap, stable supplies of war material?

The typical pattern of British response to worker unrest in the colonies was displayed in Lagos between 1941 and 1943 when Nigerian workers targeted the cost of living. When government used the Nigerian Defense Regulations to restrict the right to strike, it provoked resistance by the most organized sectors of the nation's working class, the railway workers. The usual process was for unions to present grievances, wait for the government's response, and, when delayed or rejected, to threaten a strike. This was the pattern in the summer of 1943, when working men in Lagos had grown impatient with the gap between wages and the escalating cost of living. They were overworked, burdened by inflation, and restricted by Nigerian Defense Regulations from exercising their right to strike. Meanwhile, the government, having just granted a COLA award, failed to control the spiraling food prices and turned to antiinflationary policies that were being used successfully in England, but were ill suited to Nigeria, where they only further impoverished the population. Fearing that higher wages would lead to spiraling prices, the Colonial Office lowered the minimum annual salary for

---

[65] Frantz Fanon, *The Wretched of the Earth* (New York: Grove Press, 1963); Amilcar Cabral and Africa Information Service Staff, *Return to the Source: Selected Speeches* (New York: African Information Service, 1974).

[66] Cooper, *Decolonization and African Society*, 134. See also Brown, Chapter 15, this volume.

income tax as a way to withdraw money out of circulation. But the national trade union federation became restive and, in June 1943, petitioned the government to make a comprehensive review of salaries, wages, and other conditions of service.[67] They succeeded in getting a wage increase, yet it still did not compensate for the continuing escalation of prices; however, the big protest did not occur until after the war when thousands joined the Nigerian General Strike, which lasted for several months in 1945.[68]

As these protests continued, policy makers realized the limitations on their control over the sociopolitical role workers played within the expanding and politically volatile urban classes. The contradictions were many and acute, the most fundamental being the economy's reliance on the cooperation of African labor and the state's refusal to give labor any meaningful political role in their own country. This guaranteed unrest just when colonial resources were most crucial to the very survival of empire and ensured that economic grievances would be expressed in political ways.

Workers' protests often articulated a discourse of their rights and entitlements as loyal subjects of the empire. Their grievances expressed their sense of what was suitable compensation and treatment in the workplace. Many reformulated gender norms to defend themselves against racist, disrespectful, and brutal forms of labor discipline. In constituting these new gender models they drew on rural forms of masculinity based on fatherhood and elite status and articulated them in a discourse reflecting foreign gender idioms. Thus, they evoked the male breadwinner norm, which may not, in fact, express their actual domestic arrangements, since their wives worked, usually as traders or farmers who did not fully depend on men for support.[69] Workers also expressed a racial consciousness that had sharpened in reaction to the racialized forms of workplace discipline and evoked the discourse of the nationalists who recognized this issue as a powerful mobilizing tool. Disparities between the treatment of British and African household heads became clear when various forms of allowances – family and household – were granted to one and not the other. For example, in the Enugu coal mines, workers demanded an underground allowance that was granted only to British mine supervisors.[70] Additionally, nationalists and trade union leaders watched with interest as Prime Minister Winston Churchill and President Franklin D. Roosevelt engaged in an increasingly raucous public debate on the application of the Atlantic Charter to the

---

[67] Wogu Ananaba, *Trade Union Movement in Nigeria* (New York: Africana Publishing Corporation, 1969), 32.

[68] Wale Oyemakinde, "The Nigerian general strike of 1945," *Journal of the Historical Society of Nigeria*, 7 (1975), 693–710.

[69] Brown, "A 'man' in the village"; Brown, "*We Were All Slaves*"; Lindsay, *Working With Gender*.

[70] Brown, "*We Were All Slaves*", 260–61.

African colonies, underscoring nationalist pressure for self-determination as outlined in Article 3.[71]

Workers incorporated their complaints of workplace discrimination into the public discourse of the nationalists. Political discussions occurred in the workplace and in urban associations of all kinds, where literate clerks, the social strata most involved in the movement, conveyed their ideas to illiterate members. The popular classes in the overcrowded slums and bars joined in. John Iliffe captures the humiliating impact of racism and racial insult in the workplace and the various strategies workers employed to assert their dignity through heroic work cultures.[72] Lurid reports of workplace brutality found an avid audience among the readers of the nationalist papers such as Nnamdi Azikiwe's *West African Pilot* and Wallace-Johnson's *African Standard.*[73]

While urban workers and the unemployed threatened economic stability, other workers engaged in disruptive activities in state and private agricultural projects in the countryside. In the French colonies, some projects forcibly relocated peasants to produce commodities for processing industries in Europe. Others operated on a smaller scale, varying from plantations of sisal and pyrethrum in Tanganyika to settler farms in Kenya and Southern Rhodesia.[74] In both cases settlers secured state support to coerce and exploit cheap African labor, to secure tax-subsidized credit offerings, and to place restrictions on competitive African-grown crops and livestock.[75] Another rural industry was mining, which ranged from the sophisticated gold complex in southern Africa to the copper mines of Northern Rhodesia and the Belgian Congo to the small iron and gold mines in Sierra Leone and the Gold Coast. Regardless of their location, mines tended to disrupt rural productive systems because they were based on migrant labor and too often used coercion to recruit labor, leaving women, children, and the elderly to

[71] See, for example, James Coleman, *Nigeria: Background to Nationalism* (Berkeley: University of California Press, 1958), 231–36. See references.

[72] *Honor in African History,* 286–92.

[73] Spitzer and Denzer, "Wallace-Johnson and the West African Youth League."

[74] For Tanganyika, see Sunseri, Chapter 13, this volume. The literature on Kenya is extensive, two studies particularly relevant to this volume are: John Lonsdale, "The Depression and the Second World War in the transformation of Kenya," in David Killingray and Anthony Atmore (eds.), *Africa and the Second World War* (London: Macmillan Press, 1986), 97–142; Lonsdale "The moral economy of Mau Mau: Wealth, poverty and civic virtue in Kikuyu political thought," in B. Berman and J. Lonsdale (eds.), *Unhappy Valley: Conflict in Kenya and Africa,* Vol. II: *Violence and Ethnicity* (Woodbridge, Suffolk, UK: James Currey, 1992), 466–68.

[75] Tabith Kanogo, *Squatters and the Roots of the Mau Mau Movement,* James Currey, 1987; John Lonsdale, "The Depression and the Second World War in the Transformation of Kenya" in Killingray, 97–142; and on Southern Rhodesia, see David Johnson, "Settler Farmers and Coerced African Labor," and Kenneth P. Vickery, "The Second World War Revival of Forced Labor in the Rhodesias."

produce food for themselves and the city. Protest and resistance took many forms, ranging from desertion to organized crop withdrawals.[76]

Tightening the Chains of Rural Labor: The State and Agricultural Development Schemes

The war brought an intensification of coercive "developmentalist" agricultural schemes that featured brutal policies of colonial social engineering. These schemes were based on a "very thin" scientific foundation and a "rather thick" layer of erroneous assumptions about the backwardness of African rural producers. Two particularly large agricultural development projects exemplify these oppressive forms of labor mobilization and control and destructive intervention into the social organization of the rural areas: the massive Office du Niger irrigation scheme in the French Soudan (now Mali) and the Anglo-Egyptian Sudan's Gezira Scheme. Both relied on forcible relocations of farmers who were put under regimented labor systems as if African farmers were merely machines.[77] Significantly, these schemes relied on family labor, assuming the elasticity of the unit of production, which could be expanded through marriage and biological reproduction.

As Chapter 6 shows, the Office du Niger drew upon the coercive labor policies of the French colonies, the *indigénat*, the *deuxième portion*, and other forms of forced labor.[78] Under each French colonial administration (Popular Front, Vichy, Free France, and the provisional government), the Office used brutal methods of mass relocations and brutal systems of social control. Van Beusekom argues that it never became the agricultural project that French bureaucrats imagined.[79] Rather, African farmers refused to comply with the dictates of these "rationally" ordered production systems that officials assumed they could impose.[80] Nonetheless, during the war years, the mistreatment of displaced communities intensified to levels that, were it not for the war, would otherwise not have been tolerated in the twentieth century.[81] Hundreds died in the process of relocating, which involved forced marches of sometimes 600 kilometers with inadequate food. Villagers evoked the imagery of slavery when speaking of the settlers, whom they called *tubabu jonw* (slaves of the white person). For farmers caught

---

[76] See Jennings, Chapter 11, this volume.
[77] The literature on both projects is extensive, but for the Office of Niger, two important studies are Filipovich, "Destined to fail"; Bernal, "Colonial moral economy and the discipline of development."
[78] See Ash, Chapter 6, this volume.
[79] Van Beusekom, "Disjunctures in theory and practice."
[80] The coercive nature of the work regimes included guards on the roads to prevent farmers from selling harvest to outsiders and enforcing production rules by cutting rations, confiscating fishing nets or physical punishments. Van Beusekom, 84.
[81] Filipovich, "Destined to fail," 255.

in the Office's dragnet, desertion was the most frequently employed and effective strategy. By 1946, 30 percent of the 31,300 settlers had deserted. Others refused to pay taxes or smuggled their crops outside the scheme, where they could get higher prices.

The massive Gezira Scheme in the Sudan shared many of the elements of the Office du Niger. Though it is often cited as an example of a successful mass irrigation scheme, history tells a different story. Bernal argues that it emanated from the same technocratic arrogance as the Office du Niger and presumed a "right" to move people, destroy villages and production systems (many in existence for hundreds of years), and reconstruct the social organization of peasant communities.[82] Village farmers resisted in the same ways as their counterparts in the French Soudan.

Smaller initiatives sought to capture rural villages in a dragnet of forced labor. In Tanganyika rural farmers were conscripted into the plantation workforces to produce sisal, an important wartime product. Sunseri documents how forest dwellers were forced to produce timber for railroad tires and barrack construction.[83] He notes the interplay between the strategies of this East African forestry development project that evicted farmer and pastoral communities from forests and redirected them to work for the coastal sisal and pyrethrum plantations. In the Portuguese territories the Salazar government reached back into the nineteenth century and reintroduced systems of coerced rubber collection using concessionary companies.[84]

Labor exploitation in agricultural formations took many forms, as did the resistance. When we calculate the amount of agro-exports redirected from Africa to the war effort, we can understand the considerable value that African farmers had to the war. It is important to assess their contributions, not just after the loss of Malaysia forced Britain to seek tropical crops and minerals from Africa but to examine the full range of exports produced by African men and women. Concerning the French empire, the shift from Vichy to Free French rule had little impact on the severity of draconian labor recruitment schemes. When Felix Eboué brought French Equatorial Africa into De Gaulle's Free French government in 1940, he assumed he would have some input in labor policies, including regulation of the degrees of exploitation leveled on rural producers and mineworkers. Unfortunately, he did not. Lawler demonstrates that the Free French government was even more compelled to expand the productivity of its few colonies because they constituted its only source of revenue for the war until FWA joined the Free French government in 1943.[85] Since Equatorial Africa was the only

---

[82] Bernal, "Colonial Moral Economy," 453.

[83] See Sunseri, Chapter 13, this volume.

[84] See Jennings, Chapter 11, this volume.

[85] Nancy Lawler, "Reform and repression under the Free French: Economic and political transformation in the Cote d'Ivoire, 1942–45," *Africa*, 60 (1990), 88–110.

area actually controlled by De Gaulle, he had to prove to the Allies that his was a credible government capable of financially supporting itself. He elected to squeeze local farmers to produce exports that would earn foreign exchange to finance his troops, the majority of whom were themselves from Africa.[86] Once again, the cruelty of government rubber quotas and other forest-gathering projects resembled in significant ways the draconian systems that operated in King Leopold's Congo a century earlier.

Despite his debt to Eboué for bringing the territory within his government, de Gaulle rejected many of his suggested reforms and intensified the coercive demands on peasants and workers to such an extent that even Eboué was horrified. When the Vichy governors defected to his side, De Gaulle kept many of their administrators in their posts, from which they spread their militarized production regimes to all French territories.[87]

Colonial officials could only attain a temporary hiatus from African protest in the cities and rural areas. It proved difficult to contain resistance within a definition of "economic issues" and insulate it from the political critique articulated by nationalists. Worker protests spilled beyond the boundaries of labor grievances and broached the political questions imperialists most feared – the issue of self-determination, the very essence of why the war was being fought. Were these ideals limited to Europeans? No one could convince African people that this was the case.

South Africa and Industrial Development during the War

Unlike other states in Africa, South Africa participated in the war economy at multiple levels: as a key supplier of agricultural products, minerals, machine parts, and consumer goods. Its strategic position at the nexus of the ocean routes to Asia privileged it as a refreshment and repair port. Moreover, many strategic minerals so important for the war were found there. This gave the government added leverage to prevent war policies and the deployment of its non-Europeans in military labor from undermining its carefully crafted racial policies.[88] In fact, the war enabled the government to accelerate a process of economic diversification begun in the early 1930s, using gold to finance economic transformation. The sociopolitical effect of these changes was profound, impacting the course of South African politics for several decades. As early as the 1920s the state had created ISCOR, a parastatal that used its ample deposits of iron and coal to develop a national steel industry. ISCOR, as a state body, was subsidized largely by the taxes of African workers.[89]

---

[86] Myron Echenberg, *Colonial Conscripts: The Tirailleurs Sénégalais in French West Africa, 1857–1969* (Portsmouth, NH: Heinemann, 1990).

[87] See Jennings, Chapter 11, this volume.

[88] See Parsons, Chapter 7, Grundlingh, Chapter 4, and Chetty, Chapter 16, this volume.

[89] Dumett, "Africa's strategic minerals."

By World War II, steel facilitated a nascent manufacturing sector, further financed by the rising wartime price of gold that enabled the purchase of capital goods and economic diversification.

The expansion of import substitution manufacturing transformed South African society, incorporating thousands of white, largely Afrikaner women in a multiracial workforce (i.e., including Indians, Africans, Coloureds) with non-European men and women. Wartime labor shortages required a relaxation of some segregation policies that supported the migrant labor system and, offering low wages and harsh conditions, also created the conditions for multiracial workers action.[90] Manufacturing required a different type of working class – made up of semiskilled urban residents, and capable of reproducing itself. Now manufacturers used the thousands of Africans who violated the laws that restricted African access to the cities. Consequently, African men and African, Indian, and Coloured women and children sought better-paying wartime jobs in city factories, which included the refurbishing and repairing of tanks, ships, and airplanes in Cape Town, Durban, and Pt. Elizabeth. The munitions industry, a by-product of the mining industry, supplied bomb casings, gun and tank parts, and other military goods.[91] The diversification of the economy reflected the diversification of the workforce. With many white South African men away at war, employers seized the opportunity to deskill their positions and replace them with lower-paid non-European and white female workers. Despite the racially divided workforce there were enough examples of multiracial protests to raise concerns within the governing class and Afrikaner politicians. But victories proved elusive and living conditions remained grim.

Municipalities refused to build housing for African workers, who were reduced to living in shantytowns or in open fields with little or no shelter. Housing became a pivot of collective action through a series of squatter movements formed to pressure municipalities to build housing. One of the most famous was led by James "Sofasoke" Mpanza, called the "Father of Soweto."[92] His movement was composed largely of women whom he led to occupy vacant lands where they built "Hessian Houses" (houses of burlap). Although he ran the camps as a despot, he succeeded in forcing the

---

[90] Peter Alexander, *Workers, War and the Origins of Apartheid: Labour and Politics in South Africa 1939–48*, 64–66. For more on the activism of South African women, see Iris Berger, *Threads of Solidarity: Women in South African Industry, 1900–1980* (Bloomington: Indiana University Press, 1992).

[91] Dumett, "Africa's strategic minerals."

[92] Baruch Hirson, *Yours for the Union: Class and Community Struggles in South Africa* (London: Zed Press, 1990); A. W. Stadler, "Birds in the cornfield: Squatter movements in Johannesburg, 1944–1947," *Journal of Southern African Studies*, 6 (1979), 93–123; Phillip Bonner, "The politics of black squatter movements on the Rand, 1944–1952," *Radical History Review*, 46–47 (1990), 89–115. See also Chetty, Chapter 16, this volume.

Johannesburg Municipal Government to establish the South West Township (SOWETO).

Workers in South Africa's large, diversified mining sector shared little of the profits acquired through the sale of industrial diamonds, uranium, and other strategic minerals, all prime exports for the war effort.[93] Miners confronted more stringent barriers in organizing collective action and were unsuccessful in securing gains during the war. But after the war, gold miners, supported by the South African Communist Party, led a massive strike in 1946 for better wages. This was a pyrrhic victory, for subsequent repression was so effective that it destroyed the non-European union movement for several decades. Scholars argue that the 1946 strike, the relaxation of influx control, and other racially motivated labor practices so frightened white voters that it strengthened the position of the Nationalist Party that came to power on the platform of apartheid after the war.[94] Not until the 1970s Durban strikes did non-European workers organize effective unions that were recognized by the state.[95]

Conclusion: The Postwar Impact: Commonalities and Divergences in the War Story of Labor

The impact of the war on labor became glaringly obvious after the armistice was signed. Pent-up grievances and heightened political consciousness exploded in a series of massive general strikes that continued throughout the decade and into the 1950s. These collective protests reflected workers' assessments of their ongoing importance, implicit in the colonies' role in the reconstruction of a devastated Europe. They drew upon the threads of solidarity and the commonalities of suffering under unjust political and economic policies.[96] While the war brought colonialism more deeply into African lives, the harsh realities of their experiences gave them the political and economic weapons to destroy it. Workers organized massive general strikes in Lagos, Zanzibar, Mombasa, and elsewhere.[97] In most of the continent these achieved some notable successes; however, South African mineworkers were unable to protect themselves from the rise of the

---

[93] Dummett, "Africa's strategic minerals."

[94] Dunbar Moodie, "The moral economy of the black miners' strike of 1946," *Journal of Southern African Studies* 13 (1986), 1–35.

[95] One of the first studies was Steven Friedman, *Building Tomorrow Today: African Workers in Trade Unions, 1970–1984*, South Africa, 1987. Johann Maree (ed.), "The Independent Trade Unions 1974–1984: Ten Years of the South African Labour Bulletin," *Ravan Labour Studies* 2, Bramfontein (South Africa: Ravan Press, 1987).

[96] Timothy Oberst, "Cost of living and strikes in British Africa c. 1939–1949: Imperial policy and the impact of the Second World War," PhD thesis, Columbia University (1991).

[97] Frederick Cooper, *On the African Waterfront*.

Nationalist Party and the implementation of apartheid.[98] In FWA thousands of railway workers went out in a protest, immortalized by Sembene's *God's Bits of Wood*, to demand work security, family allowances, and an end to job discrimination.[99] In Enugu workers in the coal industry, linked closely to the railway, were massacred during a peaceful mine occupation.[100]

Certain commonalities in these strikes deserve consideration. First, transport workers played a critical role in many of them. Oberst argues that transport workers became the catalyst because their position in the export economy made them aware of the volume and value of exports coming from their countries.[101] We argue that propaganda also facilitated their appreciation of the value of their country's wealth for the war and the very survival of their mother country. Moreover, the war demystified European workers, convincing colonial workers that they deserved the same treatment as their metropolitan counterparts. After the war the thrust of Colonial Office labor policy was to cede the existence of colonial unions but to drive a wedge between them and the nationalist movement. Thus "depoliticized" unions ironically became the cornerstone of the Labor Party's labor policy.[102] While colonial officials still held stereotyped views of African labor, African contribution to the war could not be denied and their demands for better conditions and political autonomy had to be recognized. Within fifteen years of the armistice, virtually all of Africa was independent. Workers played a seminal role in this reality.

---

[98] Moodie, "The 1946 mineworkers strike."

[99] Ousmane Sembene, God's Bits of Wood (Heineman, 1970). Fred Cooper, "'Our strike': Equality, anticolonial politics and the 1947–48 railway strike in French West Africa," *Journal of African History*, 36 (1996), 81–118.

[100] See Carolyn Brown, Chapter 15, this volume.

[101] Timothy Oberst, "Transport workers, strikes and the 'imperial response': Africa and the post-World War II conjuncture," *African Studies Review*, 31 (1988), 117–34.

[102] Weiler, "Forming responsible trade unions."

TWO

COLONIAL SUBJECTS AND IMPERIAL ARMIES

4

The Military, Race, and Resistance

The Conundrums of Recruiting Black South African Men during the Second World War

Louis Grundlingh

Introduction

At the outbreak of the Second World War, South Africa joined the Allied forces; however, South Africa was ill-prepared for war. The Union Defence Force (UDF) had a small cohort of permanent staff of 260 officers and 4,600 men and was similarly ill-equipped with weapons. A drastic reorganization took place, with emphasis on recruitment. Race determined the focus of the initial recruitment drives: Recruitment of white male soldiers received immediate attention. White men who volunteered for service were deployed as frontline combatants serving in East Africa, North Africa, and eventually Italy. These men were involved in two important battles: The first was the defeat of the Allies at Tobruk, where a South African division had to surrender to the German Afrika Korps under General Erwin Rommel in June 1942, and at El Alamein, where the Afrika Korps was forced to retreat. As a result, the South African military command realized the urgency of expanding its forces, as had been the case in the First World War.

The expediencies of the war forced the government into mental gymnastics: it temporarily waived aspects of its racial policy of segregation, opening its recruitment drive to include black men, Indian men, and men of color. The Native Military Corps (NMC), under the control and command of the newly established Directorate of Non-European Army Services (DNEAS), was created under the command of Colonel Ernest Thomas Stubbs as a military unit specifically for black recruits. About 500 of the recruited black soldiers eventually served in North Africa.

The historiography on the participation of Africans in the Second World War has been quite extensive, with the latest book by David Killingray, *Fighting for Britain: African Soldiers in the Second World War* (2010), adding to the list. Academic works focusing specifically on recruitment of African soldiers during the Second World War are limited. The most important publications directly related to this chapter are those of Robert J. Gordon, Hamilton S. Simelane, and Ashley Jackson, all of them touching on aspects of recruitment.[1] Their studies focus on the South Africa's bordering countries: Namibia (formerly South West Africa) and the High Commission Territories (HTCs) of Lesotho (formerly Basutoland), Botswana (formerly Bechuanaland), and Swaziland.

Gordon investigated the establishment of a system for recruiting black volunteers to serve in the UDF and the operation of this recruitment system. While Simelane's article concentrates on the postwar experience of the Swazi, he nevertheless touches on recruitment among the Swazi. Jackson contrasts the recruitment methods of troops from the HCTs with that of Africans from other British territories. A major issue he explores is why the use of traditional authority to recruit soldiers was so marked in the HCTs, while civil authorities were responsible for recruitment in East Africa. Gordon and Jackson's articles especially informed this chapter, both contextually and comparatively, as the policies and approaches to recruitment of South African blacks and Africans of the HCTs corresponded in a number of ways.

This chapter addresses two main issues. First is the nature and content of the government recruitment drive. Why were specific methods of recruitment used? To what extent did a patriarchal colonial mentality determine both their nature and their content? What was its relative effectiveness? Second, Africans' perceptions and responses to the official recruiting propaganda receive attention. What were their main considerations as they debated whether to enlist or to refuse and how did they experience the recruitment campaign? Drawing on military records, the chapter documents the inherent contradictions as the South African state, with its long history of segregation and black disenfranchisement, tried to recruit black men to fight for democracy. This study also shows the ways in which racial stereotypes about "martial races" shaped white South African expectations and disappointment. Equally important, the chapter demonstrates that those who did enlist to fight in World War II were not convinced by the recruitment drive. Rather, stark and desperate circumstances informed their decision. Further, this chapter examines the interplay of government handling of a crisis of this nature, South African black reaction toward the war, and the dynamics of South African involvement.

---

[1] Robert J. Gordon, "The impact of the Second World War on Namibia," *Journal of Southern African Studies*, 19 (1993), 147–65; Hamilton Sipho Simelane, "Labor Mobilization for the War Effort in Swaziland, 1940–1942," *International Journal of African Historical Studies*, 26 (1993), 541–74; Ashley Jackson, "Supplying the war: The High Commission Territories' military-logistical contribution in the Second World War," *Journal of Military History*, 66 (2002), 719–60.

Recruitment Methods

Roughly 600,000 black men of military age (between 18 and 45) were unemployed[2] at the beginning of the War.[3] In light of this apparently large untapped labor force, the military authorities believed that the UDF would have little difficulty in obtaining recruits without interfering with the labor supply to the mines, industries, farms, or other employers in the Union of South Africa.[4] Due to uncertainty about the ultimate aim of the NMC and the changing requirements of the war, the precise number of recruits required varied constantly.[5] By April 1942, the authorities randomly fixed the ceiling at 60,000 men.[6] This remained the goal until recruitment ceased in February 1943. The methods of recruitment used before 1942 were rather ad hoc; however, the DNEAS realized that a cogent recruitment strategy must be devised to improve the efficiency of its recruitment efforts.[7] The first two changes were to improve and expand the existing communication media and to follow a personal approach by means of recruitment tours undertaken by specially selected recruitment staff. Both methods were shaped by the stereotypical official view that blacks were particularly impressed by ostentatiousness and therefore special recruitment marches were held in large centers. Lt. J. B. Bruce put a racial spin on this arguing that "color" appealed to blacks: "While a blaze of color might offend the susceptibilities of Europeans . . . almost any colorful reproduction will appeal to natives."[8] It certainly succeeded in drawing the crowds, but the majority of blacks enjoyed the spectacle but remained unmoved by its message. On most of

---

[2] A case in point was the unemployment situation in the building trade where at least 50% of black employees were retrenched. Quarter-master general (hereafter QMG) to chief of general staff (hereafter CGS), May 19, 1940, NMC NAS o (M) 14/1 A 5, box 63, Archive of the Native Military Corps (hereafter ANMC), South African National Defence Force Archives (hereafter SANDFA), Pretoria.

[3] W. Martin to QMG, May 15, 1940, NMC NAS o (M) 14/1 A 5, box 63B, ANMC, SANDFA, Pretoria; R. Hallack, "Record of the NEAS, 1939–1945," unpublished typescript, n.d., 3–4, Union War Histories Group, MS 50, box 90, Military Information Bureau, National Archive and Record Services (hereafter NARS), Pretoria.

[4] CGS to secretary for defence, July 25, 1940, Union War Histories Group, MS 50, box 90, Military Information Bureau, NARS, Pretoria.

[5] The perceived demand changed as follows: Initial estimate: 4,000; two months later: 8,000; November 1940: 25,000; December 1940: 100,000; March 1941: 500,000; May 1941: 540,000 men. C. H. Blaine to Authorities Committee, June 27, 1940, NMC NAS 3P/4/1 B 7, box 1, ANMC, SANDFA, Pretoria.

[6] D. L. Smit to R. Fyfe King, May 30, 1941, NMC NAS 3/4/13 B 10, box 4, ANMC, SANDFA, Pretoria; Deputy adjutant-general (DAG) to DNEAS, January 23, 1943, (3)154/667, box 504, Archive of the Adjutant-General (hereafter AAG), SANDFA, Pretoria.

[7] DNEAS to AG, July 1, 1942, NMC NAS 3/4/1 B 4, box 2, ANMC, SANDFA, Pretoria.

[8] 2/Lt. J. B. Bruce, "Notes on native recruiting propaganda," n.d., NMC NAS 3/4/1 B 5, box 1, ANMC, SANDFA, Pretoria.

these occasions it was particularly conspicuous that only women, children and elderly men were present.[9] Eventually, fewer demonstrations were held because of the limited results they yielded and because whites balked at such brazen displays of military "power" to blacks.

The military also engaged mobile recruitment films that presented the NMC in a favorable light and were designed with their propaganda value in mind.[10] They were, however, informed by white perceptions of what constituted "genuine" soldiers.[11] Hence, the anachronistic depiction of black soldiers wearing modern uniforms but armed with assegais was considered a happy and unproblematic combination between the warriors of the nineteenth century and modern soldiers.[12] K. Maxwell remarked: "Now this is a soldier of today. See how differently but how well he is dressed. . . . You will notice that he still carries an assegai."[13]

The recruitment attempts were specifically geared to net young men; however, most of them were conspicuous in their absence. Those who did attend were not interested in enlisting. An area commandant of the NMC wrote that some young men confronted the officials with challenging questions such as "What had the government done for them? Where is the land you promised us? You do not tell us the truth. The Europeans are cheating us."[14] These blunt questions and charges prompted officials to report that the blacks were "hostile" and "insolent."[15] Despite the hostility, the government continued its recruitment effort and tried to counter the hostility by focusing on information it thought would allay any fears about soldiers' welfare in the army. It provided descriptions of the high level of care soldiers would receive and the adequate family allowances in published materials,

[9] W. M. Seymour, "Report on recruiting," enclosure in letter from magistrate Matatiele to chief magistrate Umtata, September 22, 1942, file 69/363, Secretary of Native Affairs (hereafter NTS) box 9130; E. H. Brookes to secretary of native affairs (hereafter NTS), June 17, 1941, file 68/363/19, NTS box 9127, National Archive and Record Services (hereafter NARS), Pretoria.

[10] Bruce, "Notes on native recruiting propaganda."

[11] Notes on a draft synopsis of a film, December 31, 1941, NMC NAS 3/21 A 5, box 15, ANMC, SANDFA, Pretoria.

[12] A light spear or lance, especially one with a short shaft and long blade for close combat, used by Bantu peoples of southern Africa.

[13] K. Maxwell to T. Gutsche (film adviser), May 7, 1942, NMC NAS 3/21 A 5, box 12; and Lt. Hall, Report on the film "A Five Cup Matter," issued by the Tea Market Expansion Board, enclosure to letter from DNEAS to deputy director military intelligence, March 5, 1942, NMC NAS 3/21 A 5, box 12, ANMC, SANDFA, Pretoria.

[14] Area commandant NMC training areas, Welgedacht, to DNEAS, May 23, 1942, NMC NAS 3/4/1 B 5, box 2, ANMC, SANDFA, Pretoria; Acting Assistant Native Commissioner G. V. Essery (Pinetown), report on visit by Chief Mshiyeni to Pinetown, September 5, 1940, file 69/363, NTS box 9130, NARS, Pretoria.

[15] S/Sgt R. E. Symons, F Coy., 2nd Bn, NMC to officer commanding (hereafter OC), 2nd Bn NMC, report on recruiting tour, August 13, 1942, file 69/363, NTS box 9130, NARS, Pretoria.

recruitment speeches, and recruitment films.[16] Propaganda emphasized the radical changes that the army made to a man's life. One film showed the arrival of recruits in torn clothes and how they changed into smart uniforms.

These films were shown in townships, hospitals, beer halls, and reserves, where they attracted much attention and were well attended. Although this was officially interpreted as proof of success, it is a moot point whether blacks attended the shows because of their contents or because of their sheer novelty.[17] In all likelihood the entertainment value was the main draw card.

The government also created recruitment posters in the local vernaculars. Many of these accentuated the danger of a German victory and the need for recruits. A poster with the slogan "Your country needs you" called upon blacks to rally to the flag.[18] It was soon realized that this approach was too general and it was replaced by a more direct and immediate message – the pay of an enlisted sergeant.[19] In addition, arrangements were made with the Bantu press to publish articles dealing with life in the Army.[20] It was believed that these advertisements and two weekly columns in the newspapers, "Soldiers' Gossip Column" and the "Soldier's Friend Column," would encourage men to enlist.[21] This is another example of how unaware the recruiters were of the reality of black peoples' lives.[22]

Despite these propaganda campaigns, recruitment numbers remained poor in some areas. For example, only three blacks actually enlisted at the Eshowe camp in Zululand per month.[23] To boost recruitment in the areas

[16] Recruiting address, presumably by H. S. Mockford, n.d., NMC NAS 3/4/1 A 1, box 3; descriptions of soldiers who had enlisted, enclosure to letter from DNEAS to managing director, Bantu Press, July 16, 1942, file 3/21 B 3, box 18, ANMC, SANDFA, Pretoria.

[17] DNEAS to recruiting officer, Non-European Army Services, January 13, 1943; 8/21, box 34; Report by Lt. S. Horwitz on a recruiting tour, November 26, 1942, file 3/4/13, box 6; S/Sgt. M. H. du Plessis to DNEAS, December 21, 1942, file 3/4/13, box 6, all in the Archives of the Director Non-European Army Services (hereafter ADNEAS), Pretoria. See also additional native commissioner (hereafter ANC) Bushbuckridge to secretary of native affairs (hereafter SNA), July 9, 1942, file 68/363/18, NTS box 9127, NARS, Pretoria.

[18] File 3/21 (A) A 4, box 14; and NMC NAS 3/21 A 4, box 12, ANMC, SANDFA, Pretoria.

[19] Officer commanding (OC) recruiting Natal and Zululand to DNEAS, August 17, 1942, NMC NAS3/4/1 B 2, box 2. ANMC, SANDFA, Pretoria.

[20] A budget of 500 pounds was also allocated for advertisements in the black newspapers circulating in the Union.

[21] Stubbs to deputy chief of staff (DCS), August 20, 1942, NMC NAS3/21 A 6, box 12, ANMC, SANDFA, Pretoria; general circular no. 24 of 1942 issued by Acting SNA H. Rodgers, August 10, 1942, file 68/363, NTS box 9115, NARS, Pretoria.

[22] Notes on a meeting held in the Drill Hall, Durban, March 2, 1942, file 69/363, NTS box 9130, NARS, Pretoria; and J. H. Dugard (inspector of schools Engcobo) to director of information, July 25, 1942, NMC NAS 3/4/1 B 4, box 2 – Non-European Section, ANMC, SANDFA, Pretoria.

[23] Report on visit of NMC detachment to Nongoma, July 7, 1942, NMC NAS 3/4/1 B 8, box I, ANMC, SANDFA, Pretoria.

that attracted few recruits, the military established a few military training camps and depots. The objective was to overcome fears that they would be sent to the Witwatersrand and housed in compounds after enlisting, which happened to mine recruits; and to generate local interest in the war and to make the military more visible and attractive to African communities.[24] Despite this expensive undertaking, the training camps evidently did not meet expectations.[25]

Chiefs and the Recruitment Drive

Perhaps one of the most important methods of recruitment entailed employing chiefs and headmen as recruitment agents as the authorities assumed that they had considerable influence among their people.[26] They argued that "tribal instincts are still strong among the Natives and if chiefs could be made to feel that they... were regarded as being responsible for producing recruits, such an increase in interest would possibly result."[27] By adopting this attitude the authorities, of course, waived their formal policy of only enlisting volunteers and simultaneously proclaimed that they were respecting tribal traditions. The chiefs, however, were by no means unanimous in helping the government with the recruitment campaign. Because of prior maltreatment, some carried a long history of hostility toward the government and did not hesitate to oppose the recruitment campaign openly. Their hostility seriously jeopardized this recruitment method on which the authorities placed such a high premium.

Some chiefs objected that they were not consulted about the conditions of enlistment beforehand. They considered this such a serious matter that they boycotted recruitment meetings, which can be construed as proof that some chiefs and influential leaders were not prepared to act as government collaborators. They clung to their only bargaining power: their freedom to render or withhold their labor. The chief magistrate of the Transkeian territories, R. Fyfe King, regarded the chiefs' response as utter insolence and noted "that they have in fact placed the dignity of their positions before the needs of the country."[28] Thus, the chiefs' unenthusiastic attitude can be

---

[24] "Recruiting conference held at the director's office," June 25, 1941, NMC NAS 3/16/4 A 11, box 40; H. C. Lugg to D. L. Smit, March 3, 1941; and T. G. Schmidt and N. C. Mtunzini to chief native commissioner (hereafter CNC), Pietermaritzburg, October 23, 1941, file 3/4/1 B 9, box 1, ANMC, SANDFA, Pretoria.

[25] DNEAS to SNA, August 3, 1942, NMC NAS 3/4/1 B 4, box 2, ANMC, SANDFA, Pretoria.

[26] C. H. Malcomess to director of information, July 16, 1942, NMC NAS 3/4/1A 1 box 3; Chief Moroka to DNEAS, November 25, 1942, NMC NAS3/4/1 A 1, box 3, ANMC, SANDFA, Pretoria.

[27] OC 3rd Bn. NMC to DNEAS, June 15, 1942, NMC NAS 3/4/1 B 5, box 2, ANMC, SANDFA, Pretoria.

[28] R. Fyfe King to D. L. Smit, August 12, 1940, file 68/363, NTS box 9114, NARS, Pretoria.

considered one of the reasons for the poor recruitment results.[29] Conversely, there were chiefs who were staunch supporters of the war effort, such as Chief Kaka from the Matatiele district. W. H. Seymour, native commissioner of Matatiele, observed that "His [Kaka's] sentiments about getting natives into the army were far in advance of the people among whom he was living and like all men of advanced ideas, he suffered for them."[30] The possibility that his followers might have had "advanced ideas" themselves by not following the government line apparently did not occur to the commissioner.

As in most wartime recruitment campaigns in Africa, the borders between voluntary and compulsory recruitment were often very vague.[31] Officially the government disapproved of any form of coercive action to increase the number of recruits; nevertheless, some chiefs ordered their men to enlist.[32] Zoutpansberg blacks complained that recruiting officers, in collusion the chiefs, rounded up men without giving them any explanation why they should join up, forcing them to choose between enlisting or paying a fine in cattle and goats.[33] Some officials found this practice quite acceptable. They argued that it was not an African custom to ask for volunteers to go to war.[34] The magistrate of Vryheid, a recruitment officer, bluntly stated: "It

---

[29] Clipping from *Territorial News*, August 13, 1942, enclosure to letter, Sen. W. T. Welsh to D. L. Smit, August 17, 1942, file 68/363/20, NTS box 9128; S. Young to SNA, November 1, 1940, file 68/363, NTS box 9114, NARS, Pretoria. See also Sgt. D. A. R. Ndongo to Maj. C. C. Stubbs, October 25, 1941, NMC NAS 3/1/7 A3, box 28; L/Cpl. M. Mqali to OC 3rd Bn. NMC, n.d., enclosure to letter from C. C. Stubbs to DNEAS, September 16, NMC NAS 3/1/7 A 3 box 28; and résumé of a meeting called by Brig. Daniel to afford Col. Stubbs an opportunity to discuss with leading influential men the problems in connection with native recruiting in Natal, March 2, 1942, AG (3) 154/667, box 504, ANMC, SANDFA, Pretoria.

[30] W. M. Seymour to magistrate Matatiele, August 26, 1946, file 68/363/36, NTS box 9129, NARS, Pretoria.

[31] D. Killingray, "Repercussions of World War I in the Gold Coast," *Journal of African History*, 19 (1978), 50–51; D. Kiyaga-Mulindwa, "The Bechuanaland Protectorate and the Second World War," *Journal of Imperial and Commonwealth History*, 12 (1984), 38, 40; M. E. Page, "The War of Thangata: Nyasaland and the East African Campaign, 1914–1918," *Journal of African History*, 19 (1978), 89; R. Rathbone, "World War I and Africa: Introduction," *Journal of African History*, 19 (1978), 5; B. P Willan, "The South African Native Labour Contingent, 1916–1918," *Journal of African History*, 19 (1978), 67; M. Crowder, "The 1939–1945 War and West Africa," in J. F. A. Ajayi and M. Crowder (eds.), *History of West Africa*, vol. II (London: Longman, 1987), 598; K. Vickery, "Wars and rumours of wars: Southern Rhodesian Africans and the Second World War," paper presented at School of Oriental and African Studies Conference on *Africa and the Second World War*, May 1984.

[32] SNA to DNEAS, April 30, 1942, NMC NAS 3/4/1 B 5, box 5, ANMC, SANDFA, Pretoria.

[33] M. B. Mulandzi to M. Ballinger, March 21, 1944, B2.14.14, file 3, A410, Ballinger Papers, Historical Papers, University of the Witwatersrand, Johannesburg.

[34] NTS Box 6813 File 28/318, Minutes of a quarterly meeting held at Moshedi, 10 December 10, 1940, file 28/318, NTS box 6813, NARS, Pretoria; and "NNMC NAS 3/16/4 A 11 Box 40, Nootes of a meeting held in regard to recruiting for the NMC," June 10, 1941, NMC NAS 3/16/4 A 11, box 40, ANMC, MADSANDFA, Pretoria.

is useless to ask a native whether he will kindly join the Forces, he should be compelled to do so by his Paramount Chief in the interest of their Country and not by the government."[35] This appeal to former customs was of course a convenient pretext to mask the racist assumption that black men had no right of choice in these matters. Recruits obtained in this way could not be described as authentic volunteers but rather as "conscripted volunteers."

Even though some chiefs did not increase recruitment substantially, others did. For example, the weekly average of recruits from Natal rose from 27 to 65 after the chiefs had been appointed.[36] It must also be noted that conditions varied greatly in the different areas. In the northern areas of the country, chiefs were responsible for only 16 percent of the recruits.[37] It is therefore difficult to estimate the actual value of the chiefs by merely looking at the number of recruits who enlisted as a result of their efforts. When the chiefs approached the Department of Native Affairs after the war and claimed "small gifts" in recognition of their services as had been given in the previous war, the chief native commissioners did not regard the chiefs' contribution as worthy of any special recognition or gift.[38] After the First World War, rifles had been issued in some deserving cases, but the minister of native affairs thought that this was impolitic after the Second World War, as there were many white farmers whose rifles had been commandeered and who had not received reissues. The commissioners' refusal can, of course, also be attributed to the fact that the war was over by then and the authorities could therefore easily afford to dismiss their claims.

Rendering the War and Participating Therein Relevant

It was no easy task to convince potential black soldiers that their participation was crucial to the Allies' war effort; however, some recruiters tried by claiming that "they [were] fighting together with the three greatest liberty-loving nations of the world – Britain, Soviet Union and America."[39] This attempted to rally them to the cry "Defend Democracy" and to convince them that democracy held rights and privileges for them too. Clearly, this was propagandistic and implied that it was in the blacks' best interest to assist the government against the perceived menace from Germany, Italy, and Japan. Considering the discrepancy between the lofty ideals of freedom

---

[35] Magistrate Vryheid to CNC, Pietermaritzburg, September 19, 1942, file 69/363, NTS box 9130. NARS, Pretoria.

[36] SNA to secretary for finance, June 9, 1943, file 68/363/22, NTS box 9126, NARS, Pretoria.

[37] Schedule of blacks recruited by chiefs of the northern Areas, enclosure to letter from CNC northern areas to SNA, September 13, 1946, file 68/363/36, NTS box 9129, NARS, Pretoria.

[38] Memorandum by D. L. Smit, November 19, 1946. file 68/363/36, NTS box 9129, NARS, Pretoria.

[39] W. O. H. Menge to Magistrate Zeerust, August 13, 1941, file 68/363/27, NTS box 9127, NARS, Pretoria.

and democracy and their abject political, social, and economic reality, it was a crude attempt to ignore the divisions of class and race existing in South Africa.

Despite strict instructions to the contrary, some enterprising recruitment agents deliberately made false promises to induce black men to enlist.[40] Some blacks were therefore under the impression that they would not serve longer than six months, they would be given grants of land, and they would be armed when sent to North Africa.[41] Influential politicians also made vague promises about the postwar position of blacks. Thus Minister of Native Affairs Colonel Deneys Reitz indicated that he was "proud of the part our Native soldiers played in the war and of their loyalty.... In plans for reconstruction after the war, steps will be taken to ensure that the Native people are included."[42] The unfortunate reality is that these promises were not carried out after the war, clearly demonstrating the state's opportunism.

Reasons for Not Enlisting

Even with the use of propaganda and coercion, the recruitment campaign met with such a poor response that the authorities were extremely disappointed and concerned.[43] Recruitment officials consistently complained that blacks were "not interested," "lukewarm," "complacent," and "lacking in enthusiasm."[44] Blacks were deterred from enlisting for numerous reasons. The oppressive ideological milieu and structural constraints of the South

---

[40] DNEAS to DCS, July 15, 1942, CGS (2) G 137/1 Vol. IV, box 69; and Minutes of recruiting conference, June 10, 1941, file 68/363/20, NTS box 9127, NARS, Pretoria.

[41] W. M. Seymour to D. L. Smit, June 25, 1943, 3/4/1 A 3, box 4; B. W. Martin to DNEAS, October 1, 1940, NMC NAS3P/4/1 Vol. II B 6 box 1; Lt Col. B. Nicholson OC 4th Bn. NMC to DNEAS, December 24, 1941, NMC NAS3/4/1 B 9, box 1; and DNEAS to OC Natal Command, October 21, 1941, NMC NAS3/4/1 B 9, box 1, ANMC, SANDFA, Pretoria; interview with J. Lesiba, April 27, 1981.

[42] Speech to the General Council, n.d., minister's tour to Transkei and Ciskei, 1943, file 94/378, NTS box 9326; Draft of speech for the Governor-General for a tour of the Transkei, enclosure to letter from R. Fyfe King to D. L. Smit, May 3, 1941, file 6/378, NTS box 9309, NARS, Pretoria.

[43] Notes of a meeting in regard to recruiting for NMC, June 10, 1941, NMC NAS 3/16/4 A 11, box 40; D. L. Smit to E. T. Stubbs, November 25, 1940, NMC NAS3/16/4 A 11, box 40; *The Natal Witness*, October 4, 1940, NMC NAS3P/4/1, Vol. II B 6, box 1, all in ANMC, SANDFA, Pretoria. See also, clippings from *Rand Daily Mail*, August 5, 1941 and *The Bantu World*, August 9, 1941, file 68/363/21, NTS box 9126, NARS, Pretoria; and minutes of a meeting of the executive committee of the National Advisory Council on Government Publicity, December 5, 1941, file A 11, Part IV, Vol. 15, Archives of the Department of Labour (ARB), NARS, Pretoria.

[44] Capt. H. B. Myburgh, OC 'D' Coy. 8th Bn. NMC to OC 8th Bn. NMC, August 17, 1942, NMC NAS 3/4/1 B 9 box 1; recruiting officer NEAS to area commandant NMC training areas Welgedacht, November 1, 1941, NMC NAS 3/4/1 B 3 box 2, ANMC, SANDFA, Pretoria.

African society in which recruitment took place loomed large in an evalua-
tion of the reasons why blacks refused to enlist. Under these circumstances
black men saw no reason to show their allegiance to "democracy." Members
of the black intellectual elite, such as Z. K. Matthews and D. D. T. Jabavu,
argued that if the blacks participated, they would only be fighting to maintain the status quo of the present policy toward them.[45] As it was clearly
a "white man's war," they did not see why they should defend a country
where "everything worthwhile is a privilege of the white man" and the ultimate result of the war would not be to their advantage.[46] Thus, a growing
mistrust of whites in general and the government in particular shaped black
apathy to recruitment campaigns.

For some blacks, the real and immediate war was not in Europe or North
Africa, but much closer to home in South Africa.[47] Many argued that as
far as their own position and struggles were concerned, there had never
been "any peace."[48] They had to wage a continuous war to alleviate their
hardships and improve their circumstances. There was a strong desire to
know what they were letting themselves in for, what benefit they would
derive by joining up, and what benefits they would receive after the war.[49]
This was understandable, as the idea of entering the military was a totally
strange and new experience for many of these men and it may have filled
them with apprehension, if not trepidation. They therefore expected the
government to indicate specifically what steps it was prepared to carry out
to alleviate their circumstances.[50] Although the government did not commit

[45] Zachariah Keodirelang "ZK" Matthews became professor of Fort Hare's Department of
African Studies in 1944 and the provincial president of the ANC in the Cape in 1949.
Davidson Don Tengo Jabavu became the editor of the first black-owned newspaper, *Imvo
Zabantsundu* (*Black Opinion*), in 1884 and later the first black professor at the University
of Fort Hare. He was also president of the All-Africa Convention (AAC), an umbrella
organization that consisted of several organizations opposed to the segregation legislation
passed by the Hertzog government in 1936. For their views on the war, see Jabavu and
Matthews, "Africans and the War," enclosure in letter from controller of censorship to Col.
Werdmuller, June 30, 1942, NMC NAS 3/4/1 B 3, box 2; S/Sgt. R. E. Symons to OC 2nd
Bn. NMC, July 20, 1942, NMC NAS 3/21 A 7, box 12, ANMC, SANDFA, Pretoria.

[46] N. C. Umzinto to CNC (Natal), September 17, 1942, file 69/363, NTS box 9130, NARS,
Pretoria.

[47] Black South African attitudes were similar to those of African Americans in the United
States; see Hutchinson, Chapter 21, this volume.

[48] Manuscript titled "Africans and the war" by Z. K. Matthews for publication in *Common-
sense*, 1942, BZA 78/9–78/13 B 4.34, Z. K. Matthews Papers, Africana and Special Collections Department, University of Cape Town.

[49] Report on recruiting meetings held at Bloemfontein Location, March 30, 1942, Kimberley
Location, March 31, 1942, and Green Point Location, Beaconsfield, April 1, 1942, NMC
NAS 3/4/1 B 2, box 2; and draft of "The Bantu and the war," enclosure to letter, OC (NMC
Recruiting Natal and Zululand) to DNEAS, September 21, 1942, NMC NAS 3/4/1 B 5 box
2, ANMC, SANDFA, Pretoria.

[50] Jabavu and Matthews, "Africans and the war," enclosure to letter from controller of censorship to Col. Werdmuller, June 30, 1942, NMC NAS 3/4/1 B 3, box 2; C. H. Malcomess to

itself at all on this score, low expectations regarding benefits probably guided some blacks' decisions not to enlist. The decision to arm black soldiers with assegais and knobkerries was a major insult and alienated many blacks who felt that, as they were not fully trusted, there was little sense in joining the army. Noncombatant service simply did not appeal to them.[51] Blacks considered the hazardous duty of guarding military property and facing rifle fire and the destructive power of airplanes with primitive and outdated "weapons" to be sheer folly.

Some officials acknowledged the detrimental effect that not arming blacks had on recruitment. The following remark emphasized this: "How was it possible to work up the spirit of the offensive among natives if the only training given to them was that of watchdogs, patrolling a fence with assegais and at the sign of danger being ordered to withdraw?"[52] They openly stated that recruitment would be brisk if permission was granted to properly arm blacks.[53] Others were clearly unaware of the importance of this and insensitively dismissed the objection as a superficial excuse not to enlist.[54]

Potential recruits also called attention to unequal rates of pay. The basic pay was one shilling and six pence [1/6] per day for recruits without dependants and two shillings three pence [2/3] for recruits with dependants. The remuneration for the whites was five shillings [5/-] a day. L. M. Sediela complained:

> If you can pay me eight pounds and ten shillings in the military service I will join. But there is always a cloud before me – three pounds seven shillings six pence for a month – I fint [sic] it a very meagre subsidy to a man with a family. This worries my mind every time but I wish to defend our country and our things – this I find as my bounden duty.[55]

To a large extent, the success or failure of recruitment hinged on economics. This was a particularly important factor since many blacks did not want to

---

director of information, July 16, 1942, NMC NAS 3/21/A A 4, box 14; Gen. F. H. Theron to DNEAS, January 10, 1942, NMC NAS 3/4/1 A 1, box 3, ANMC, SANDFA, Pretoria.

[51] N. C. Ingwavuma to C. Alport, September 28, 1942, file 69/363, NTS box 9130, NARS, Pretoria.

[52] Extract from MP's conference no. 11 of November 18, 1942, file 1640, CGS 32/3 V I, NARS, Pretoria.

[53] Capt. R. H. Reynolds to D. Reitz, August 19, 1942, NMC NAS 3/4/1 B 5 box 2; OC 3rd Bn. NMC to DNEAS, June 15, 1942, NMC NAS 3/26/15 A 1 box 48, ANMC, SANDFA, Pretoria.

[54] J. Erasmus, NC Bergville to CNC, September 26, 1942, file 69/363, NTS box 9130, NARS, Pretoria.

[55] L. M. Sediela to J. D. R. Jones, December 14, 1941, box 109, J. D. R. Jones Collection, O: World War II, AD 843, South African Institute of Race Relations (SAIRR) Papers, Historical Papers, William Cullen Library, University of the Witwatersrand, Johannesburg

jeopardize the welfare of their families because of inadequate remuneration. Dr. Alfred Bitini Xuma[56] was completely justified when he wrote that

> It is the consensus of opinion among African people... both urban and rural, that the conditions of service for the African soldiers... tend to discourage the African people from joining the Native Military Corps. We cannot maintain these peacetime discriminations in the army and expect the victims of such discriminations or their friends and relatives to rush in their thousands to the army to defend them.[57]

Despite this realization among high-ranking army officials that soldiers' pay was indeed inadequate, Col. Stubbs emphasized that their remuneration package also included free quarters, rations, clothing, medical services, leave privileges, and free rail warrants once a year.[58] As head of the DNEAS and with no prospect of increasing the pay, he was compelled to defend the rates of pay, thus simultaneously dismissing insufficient pay as a reason for the poor response. This contradicts overwhelming evidence to the contrary.

Administrative red tape also played a role. Those without passes were not accepted and ordered to return to their homes to obtain the relevant documents. In most cases they were penniless and had no train fare to return home. This treatment had far-reaching ramifications, for it reinforced blacks' perception that the government did not really need them and further exacerbated their mistrust of the government. Of course, they spread the news of their humiliating experiences.[59] In addition, when some prospective recruits, sometimes after arduous journeys, eventually reached the recruitment office, large numbers were rejected for sometimes trivial medical defects. By then many had already given up their previous employment and received no compensation from the government.[60] This was an obvious reason for not enlisting, as Staff Sergeant Symonds remarked: "They ask what good it is to try and join up when strong strapping young men are sent back as unfit."[61]

Fear and apprehension also played a part in black men's reluctance to enlist. Blacks still retained vivid memories of the sinking of the *S. S. Mendi*

---

[56] Xuma was president-general of the African National Congress (ANC) from 1940 to 1949.

[57] ANC deputation at Cape, March 4, 1942, ABX 420304b, A. B. Xuma Papers, Africana and Special Collections Department, University of Cape Town.

[58] For the authorities, the soldiers' remuneration package, together with free quarters, rations, clothing, medical service, leave privileges, and free rail warrants once a year, was a challenge to other employers and therefore sufficiently attractive. DNEAS to SNA, February 10, 1943, NMC NAS 3/1/1 A 4 box 39, ANMC, SANDFA, Pretoria.

[59] Hon. secretary, Communist Party of South Africa, to SNA, June 19, 1942, file 69/363, NTS box 9130; N. C. Verulam to C. Alport, September 16, 1942, file 68/363, NTS box 9115, NARS, Pretoria.

[60] This anomalous position was only remedied as late as June 1942. Memorandum of a meeting held in the office of the Financial Adviser, June 30, 1942, CGS 32/14, NARS, Pretoria.

[61] S/Sgt. R.E. Symons to OC 2nd Bn. NMC, July 27, 1942, NMC NAS3/21 A 7, box 12, ANMC, SANDFA, Pretoria.

during the First World War in which 616 people (including 607 South African blacks) lost their lives. Consequently, when told that they would be required to travel by sea, many refused to enlist. Their fears seemed justified when the *Nova Scotia* sank off the Natal coast on December 18, 1942. Nearly 300 badly mutilated bodies washed ashore.[62] This fear was aggravated by descriptions of enemy torture if blacks fell into their hands.[63] Moreover, some blacks who might have considered enlisting feared possible harassment and reprisals from a section of the white population that did not support the war effort.[64]

Poor response from the Zulu particularly disappointed and confounded the authorities. In keeping with colonial thinking in the rest of Africa,[65] the Zulu were regarded as an outstanding "martial race" and likely to enlist.[66] They were therefore not totally out of sync with the stereotyped notion in most African colonies whereby only ethnic groups regarded as possessing martial qualities were recruited. Examples are plentiful. In Kenya, the Maasai were preferred recruits to the Kikuyu, while the Kalenjin, Kamba, Nandi, Elgeyo, Luo, and Kakwa were recruited into the King's African Rifles. In Uganda, the Acholi, Langi, Nubi, and Teso were believed to possess martial characteristics, and in Tanganyika, the Nyamwezi, Luo, Kina, Sukuma Ngoni, and Hehe were the most popular ethnic groups being recruited. In the Congo, Lingala speakers were recruited into the Force Publique. In Nigeria, the Hausa/Fulani were preferred to the Igbo, Yoruba, Bini, or other

---

[62] OC NMC Recruiting Natal and Zululand to DNEAS, December 18, 1942, NMC NAS3/4/20/1 B 9, box 5, ANMC, SANDFA, Pretoria.

[63] Because of the possible fear airplanes could generate, it was omitted from any pictorial, photographic, or visual propaganda. J. Keeft, deputy director of military intelligence to secretary for defence, February 13, 1942, NMC NAS 3/21 A 5, box 12; magistrate (Greytown) to CNC (Natal), September 15, 1942, NMC NAS 3/4/20 B 8, ANMC, SANDFA, Pretoria. See also, extract from a report by S/Sgt. R. E. Symons, recruiting in Nkandhla, Zululand, n.d. and J. O. Cornell, magistrate Qumbu to chief magistrate Umtata, November 25, 1941, file 68/363, NTS box 9115, NARS, Pretoria.

[64] Report on Seymour, accompanying letter, Magistrate Matatiele to chief magistrate Umtata, September 22, 1942, file 68/363/19, NTS box 9127, NARS, Pretoria.

[65] The discourse on the idea of a "martial race" has been extensively addressed during the past few years. See C. Hamilton, *Terrific Majesty: The Powers of Shaka Zulu and the Limits of Historical Invention* (Cambridge, MA: Harvard University Press, 1998); T. H. Parsons, "'Wakamba warriors are soldiers of the Queen': The evolution of the Kamba as a martial race, 1890–1970," *Ethnohistory*, 46 (1999), 671–702; G. Rand, "'Martial races' and 'imperial subjects': Violence and governance in colonial India, 1857–1914," *European Review of History*, 13, 2006, 1–20; K. Roy, "The construction of regiments in the Indian Army: 1859–1913," *War in History*, 8 (2001), 127–48; H. Streets, *Martial Races: The Military, Race and Masculinity in British Imperial Culture, 1857–1914* (Manchester: Manchester University Press, 2004).

[66] Speech by D. L. Smit to the Zulu of Pietermaritzburg, June 14, 1941, file 69/363, NTS box 9130; draft speech by the minister of native affairs, Nongoma, June 19, 1941, file 80/37/8, NTS box 9323, NARS, Pretoria.

groups in Nigeria; in the Gold Coast, the Gurusi were believed more suitable for the military than the Mossi, Fante, or Ga. In Southern Rhodesia (now Zimbabwe), the Ndebele were also regarded as a "martial" group.[67]

The validity of this popular notion was suspect because judgments about martial worth, loyalty and disloyalty, and the amenability of one group of people rather than another to military discipline were often subjective and superficial. Popular white superracist ideas from the nineteenth century, as well as the rationalization of Darwin's notion of the "survival of the fittest," spilled over into the twentieth century and persisted in many a military mind.[68] Throughout most of the recruitment campaign, the notions persisted that the Zulu was a race of fighters, disciplined and well equipped both physically and temperamentally for military service, and that they were proud of their heritage and traditions.[69] These assumptions might partially have been based on the somewhat subjective observance "that the average raw Zulu . . . is full of martial ardor and takes naturally to soldiering, as anyone can testify who has witnessed tribal fights or attended large war dances in the Reserves."[70] The minister of native affairs conveniently invoked history out of context to substantiate this claim: "This district [Nongoma] bred many of the old Zulu warriors who, years ago, overran a great portion of South Africa, subduing other Native tribes and making a brave stand against the Europeans in the country."[71] Not surprisingly,

---

[67] A. H. M. Kirk-Greene, "'Damnosa hereditas': Ethnic ranking and the martial races imperative in Africa," *Ethnic and Racial Studies,* 3 (1980), 393–414; J. Bayo Adekson, "Ethnicity and army recruitment in colonial plural societies," *Ethnic and Racial Studies,* 2 (1979), 151–56; D. Killingray, "The colonial army in the Gold Coast: Official policy and local response, 1890–1947," PhD thesis, University of London (1982); N. J. Westcott, "The impact of the Second World War on Tanganyika, 1939–1949," PhD thesis, University of Cambridge (1982); E. A. Schleh, "Post-service careers of African World War II veterans: British East and West Africa with particular reference to Ghana and Uganda," PhD thesis, Yale University (1968); L. J. Greenstein, "Africans in a European war: The First World War in East Africa with special reference to the Nandi of Kenya," PhD thesis, Indiana University (1975); C. M. Andrew and A. S. Kanya-Forstner, "France, Africa and the First World War," *Journal of African History,* 19 (1978), 14.

[68] During the First World War, the authorities had the same view about the Zulu's assumed martial character, which made them ideal candidates to join the South African Native Labour Corps. Adekson, "Ethnicity and army recruitment," 156; A. M. Grundlingh, *Fighting Their Own War: South African Blacks and the First World War* (Johannesburg: Ravan Press, 1987), 65.

[69] Director of information's remarks during a meeting at Eshowe, February 5, 1941, NMC NAS 3/28/15 A 5, box 56, ANMC, SANDFA, Pretoria. See also, clipping from *The Natal Mercury,* June 21, 1941, file 80/378, NTS box 9323, NARS, Pretoria.

[70] "Some views on the recruiting of natives" by Sgt. B. G. Tranchell, n.d., NMC NAS 3/4/1 B 2, box 2, ANMC, SANDFA, Pretoria.

[71] Draft speech by the minister of native affairs Nongoma, June 19, 1941, file 80/378, NTS box 9323, NARS, Pretoria; letter No. 22 by Ndabazabantu, June 27, 1942, NMC NAS 3/21 B 3 box 18, ANMC, SANDFA, Pretoria.

recruitment policy immediately and eagerly targeted the Zulus.[72] However, the "martial race" bubble burst when the anticipated rallying of thousands of Zulus to the flag failed to materialize. The authorities were greatly disillusioned by the "disgustingly poor response."[73] This may have prompted Col. Stubbs to remark that "Native Administrators have found to their sorrow that they have been completely misled and have failed to understand the Zulu mentality and psychological reactions."[74] After two and a half years of intensive recruitment only 803 had enlisted.[75] The "martial race" idea was indeed in the minds of the European recruiters rather than an inherent quality of the men they attempted to recruit.

The general reasons why blacks refrained from enlisting are also applicable to the Zulu. In addition, some Zulu did not trust many officials of the Native Affairs Department responsible for recruitment. Others, especially those who partook in or remembered the Bambatha Rebellion of 1906, were openly disloyal and eschewed any efforts to enlist them. Their apathy can also be explained by the fact that they had been deprived of large parts of Zululand through European settlement. Therefore, as long as this encroachment process continued, they refrained from enlisting.[76]

Even the attempt to flatter and bribe the Acting Paramount Chief of the Zulus, Chief Mshiyeni ka Dinizulu, to gain his assistance with recruitment failed on this score.[77] Although Mshiyeni agreed to cooperate, the expected

---

[72] CGS 32/4 V I; General P. van Ryneveld to DCGS, AG, QMG and DGMS, June 25, 1940, box 1, June 25, 1940, G2/1/9/1, CGS Group 2, NARS, Pretoria. See also D. L. Smit to H. C. Lugg, June 26, 1940, NMC NAS 3/21 C 7 box 54; and director of non-European labour to QMG, June 21, 1940, CGS 32/4/ V I, ANMC, SANDFA, Pretoria.

[73] N. C. Umbumbulu to C. Alport, September 16, 1942, file 69/363, NTS box 9130; SNA to DNEAS, March 11, 1941, "Resume of department's activities," file 68/363, NTS box 9115; draft speech by the minister of native affairs to be delivered at the chiefs' conference Nongoma, November 3, 1943, file 98/276, NTS box 1796; H. C. Lugg to D. L. Smit, November 4, 1940, file 69/363, NTS box 9130; Sen. E. H. Brookes to SNA, June 17, 1941, file 69/363, NTS box 9130, all in NARS, Pretoria.

[74] E. T. Stubbs to AG, May 14, 1941, file 69/363, NTS box 9130, NARS, Pretoria.

[75] DNEAS to SNA, November 11, 1942, NMC NAS3/4/1 B 2, box 2, ANMC, SANDFA, Pretoria.

[76] The Bambatha Uprising was a Zulu revolt against British rule and taxation in Natal, South Africa, in 1906. N. C. Nkandhla to CNC (Pietermaritzburg), November 25, 1940, file 69/363, NTS box 9130, NARS, Pretoria; D. G. Shepstone to E. T. Stubbs, April 16, 1942, NMC NAS 3/20/1/C A 4 box 31, ANMC, SANDFA, Pretoria.

[77] They pampered him by providing him with an ornate uniform, complete with a Sam Browne belt, gloves, and all accoutrements, as well as a monthly allowance. Mshiyeni admitted that he did not wield as much influence over the Zulus as the authorities assumed. His authority extended as far as Nongoma and if he entered another chief's territory he had no jurisdiction there. He was merely the acting chief of the Usutu tribe, and as such, did not differ from the approximately 300 other chiefs. H. C. Lugg to D. L. Smit, May 10, 1942, file 69/363, NTS box 9130, NARS, Pretoria. It was noted that Mshiyeni received a hostile reception at one of the recruitment meetings from the crowd of about 2,000; this did not augur well for

rush to enlist was not forthcoming.[78] Somewhat scornfully, a certain Maj. Franklin commented:

> I am very skeptical of Mshiyeni's airy promises to provide "thousands" ... and in spite of having been lavishly entertained by Defence ... the Acting Paramount Chief has been unable to implement his grandiloquent promises to provide Zulus by the "thousands" for the NMC.[79]

In some quarters it eventually dawned on the authorities that their idea of the Zulus as a "martial race," who would ipso facto enlist, was misplaced. They were compelled to consider other places such as Basutoland for recruitment.[80]

The Enlisted

If there were so many factors discouraging blacks from enlisting, the question arises: why did 74,679 eventually enlist?[81] Was it pressure or cajoling from their chiefs who hoped to win favors from the authorities? Was it simply a spirit of adventure combined with a desire to acquire a steady income? Was it loyalty to the South African and the British governments or was it an awareness of the issues involved? While all these issues played a role, it seems clear that the primary reason for enlisting was economic. Therefore, it is appropriate to examine the participation of blacks in the UDF in terms of economic "push/pull" factors, which are not dissimilar from those pertaining to migratory labor. As Kenneth W. Grundy notes:

his stand in the Zulu community. H. C. Lugg to D. L. Smit, September 5, 1940, file 69/363, NTS box 9130, NARS, Pretoria.

[78] G. Welsh to Capt. Lindsay, August 3, 1942, NMC NAS 3/21 A 7 box 12, W.O. II; Statement No. 123, *News of the War*, week ending June 27, 1942, 3/21/A A 5 box 14, ANMC, SANDFA, Pretoria. See also H. C. Lugg to D. L. Smit, September 4, 1940, file 69/363, NTS box 9130; report of G. V. Essery, NC Pinetown of Chief Mshiyeni's visit to Pinetown, September 4, 1940, file 69/363, NTS box 9130, NARS, Pretoria.

[79] E. T. Stubbs to AG, May 14, 1941, NMC 3/28/15 A 5, box 56, ANMC, SANDFA, Pretoria.

[80] The total number of Zulus recruited from Zululand by November 1942 was a mere 803. DNEAS to SNA, November 11, 1942, NMC NAS 3/4/1 B 2, box 2, ANMC, SANDFA, Pretoria. See also, H. Rogers to E. T. Stubbs, March 11, 1941, file 67/363, NTS box 9114, NARS, Pretoria.

[81] The following figures indicate how the number of recruits who enlisted in the different provinces compares with the approximate number of blacks available for labor.

Recruits	Province	Available Labour
53,037	Transvaal	409,000
9,355	Cape	522,000
7,766	Natal	340,000
5,648	OFS	133,000

AG to Dechief, February 5, 1946, AG (3)154/X/1235/7 box 139, NARS, Pretoria.

A decision to enlist is always a product of a highly personal perception of one's overall career and social prospects in the context of a particular set of situational determinants. Black recruitment is a two-way process involving the absence of opportunity in civil society and the attraction of the armed forces.[82]

This becomes clear when one specifically considers the position of those in the Limpopo Province (formerly Northern Transvaal) who enlisted.[83] During this period the mealie (corn) crop was extremely poor due to a severe infestation of "streak disease" and a plague of so-called "army-worms," leading to economic hardship. In addition, the northern parts of the country were stricken by a devastating drought during 1941–1943, resulting in large-scale crop failures.

This deprived many of a livelihood and led to extreme privation and famine.[84] A further consequence of the drought was that many farmers summarily dismissed their black employees, which added to the number of unemployed.[85] Moreover, the general trend toward the proletarianization of labor tenants and squatters continued, forcing large numbers off the land. It is little wonder that R. Fyfe King callously remarked that "the best recruiting districts both for the Army and the Mines, are those which reap little."[86] These harsh economic conditions were exacerbated by the higher prices of the necessities of life, mainly brought about by the war and the fact that many could not find employment. The upshot was that many blacks were forced to join the army in order to alleviate their desperate situation. Although totally inadequate, the army at least provided a regular income, food, clothing, housing, medical care, and allotments to soldiers' dependants.[87] Because

---

[82] K. W. Grundy, *Soldiers without Politics: Blacks in the South African Armed Forces* (Berkeley: University of California Press, 1983), 28–29.

[83] They constituted more than half of the total number of recruits.

[84] South Africa and C. Lansdown, *Report of the Witwatersrand Mine Natives' Wages Commission on the Remuneration and Conditions of Employment of Natives on Witwatersrand Gold Mines and Regulation and Conditions of Employment of Natives at Transvaal Undertakings of Victoria Falls and Transvaal Power Company, Limited* (Pretoria: Government Printer, 1944).

[85] Secretary for agriculture and forestry to SNA, January 24, 1942, file 53/336, NTS box 7852, NARS, Pretoria.

[86] R. Fyfe King to DNEAS, September 28, 1942, NMC NAS 3/4/1 B 2 box 2, ANMC, SANDFA, Pretoria.

[87] A recruit in the Northern Transvaal received a monthly wage of 15s. plus mealie meal, and his wife worked for the farmer's household at 6s. per month plus food. It seemed only natural that he joined the army where he could earn £3.7s.6d. with food, clothing, etc. W. O. H. Menge, Assistant N. C. Zeerust to Magistrate, Zeerust, August 13, 1941, file 68/363/27, NTS box 9127, NARS, Pretoria. See also, address by urban and rural natives of the Bultfontein Area to J. D. R. Jones, November 17, 1940, S. 2 Senatorial Correspondence box 4, J. D. R. Jones Collection, SAIRR Papers, Historical Papers, William Cullen Library, University of the Witwatersrand. See also, author's interviews with S. Koza, D. Masuku, J. Kgabo, and F. Sexwale, February 6, 1986, Johannesburg.

some farmers were unwilling and others unable to improve their laborers' conditions of service, they left them with little choice but to enlist.

Conclusion

White authorities and blacks often had contradictory views, attitudes, and responses concerning recruitment and enlisting. Consequently, recruitment efforts were not always plain sailing. The authorities continued to exhibit colonial, patriarchal, and racist attitudes and assumptions regarding black people. Within this context, white perspectives of what a black soldier should be were formed. Not only did this dictate recruitment methods but it also shaped their stereotypical views about the types of content that would appeal to black people. As a result, the outcome was not commensurate with their efforts. Black people noticed the contradiction inherent in the need for more recruits that took place within a prejudiced political framework. They were quite aware how this manifested itself – for example, the inequality between black and white service conditions. In light of South Africa's social, political, and economic structure, it proved very difficult to persuade black people to enlist. Their response boiled down to their feeling that they were not regarded as proper soldiers, that it was a "white man's war," and that whites had not treated them fairly in the past.

Contrary to white expectations and rhetoric, the main reason for enlisting was unrelated to notions of patriotism, loyalty, and assumptions of martial races – some of the crucial characteristic of the recruitment campaign. The blacks who enlisted were more concerned about survival in a hostile world than "lofty" considerations. For them, military life, even with its attendant dangers and hardships, provided a temporary shelter. It can thus be concluded that blacks joined the army *despite* the recruitment campaign.

5

The Moroccan "Effort de Guerre" in World War II

Driss Maghraoui

Introduction

In the dramatic accounts of the history of the Second World War in North Africa, it is often the famous meeting of Charles de Gaulle, Franklin D. Roosevelt, Winston Churchill, General Henri Giraud, and Mohammed V at Casablanca that takes the central stage in the memory. Continual reference to the meeting of the major European leaders in Casablanca is indicative of a major historiographical lacuna related to how the war is written about and generally remembered. Very often the history of the empire, its peoples, and how the war affected them has been outside the lens of European historians of World War Two. The important *effort de guerre*, as French colonial authorities called the contributions made by Moroccan colonial troops, has been largely ignored. Beyond the troops, little attention has been given to how the war altered the everyday lives of the popular classes and, more specifically, the peasants who formed the backbone of the colonial army. How the war affected the overall political, economic, and social conditions in Morocco remains unexplored. Unfortunately, "conventional" Moroccan nationalist historiography has also left these kinds of questions unanswered, because the story of the colonial soldiers does not fit neatly within the dominant narrative of resistance to French colonialism.

This chapter examines the war in the context of Moroccan colonial history and illustrates the place of empire and its peoples in the remembrance of war. My goal is to unpack the different layers of the story of World War II in Morocco. First, the surrender of French forces to Nazi Germany and the armistice agreement in June 1940 represented a major blow to the prestige of the French nation and the glory of the French military. As a result, the empire and its colonial troops became a major symbol for the rejuvenation

All the translations from Arabic and French into English are made by the author.

of the French army and its nation.[1] Colonial troops became the embodiment of the French nation and of *la France combattante*. Second, World War II intersected with the heated dynamics of local colonial politics, monarchical symbolic power and nationalism. The Moroccan monarchy played an important role in the gathering momentum of support for the French war effort. Politically, this was a strategic move for the king vis-à-vis the powerful Moroccan *qaids*[2] and local elite that had worked closely with the French since the beginning of the protectorate; however, the war also provided the nationalist movement with new political leverage. On December 10, 1943, the nationalist party (*hizb al-Istiqlal*) was officially established and on January 11, 1944, it presented the king and the representatives of Allied forces with a document that demanded "the independence of Morocco in its territorial integrity." Third, the war had a specific economic impact on different parts of Morocco. In Moroccan popular memory, the war years are often referred to as "*a'm al-boun*" (years of the coupon) as a result of the new wartime economic policies, especially rationing. Finally, the war created a context in which the British, the French, and the Germans engaged in major propaganda campaigns in which the battle of words and radio waves played an important role in trying to win the hearts and minds of Moroccans specifically and North Africans generally. Particularly for the French, the war had to be packaged in very particular ways to make it relevant to Moroccans calibrating the anti-Nazi propaganda campaign within North African sociocultural colonial contexts. Here I will focus on the military aspects of the war in Morocco and how they change our thinking about the place of empire and colonial soldiers in the place of World War II in French and European metropolitan history, for when we consider imperial relationships with the war, geographical, social, and cultural boundaries no longer seem fixed. The case of Moroccan colonial soldiers is one example among many of what historian Marc Michel calls "*la puissance par l'empire*," which meant relying on human and economic mobilization in the

---

[1] Since the 1980s there has been a growing interest in the subject of colonial troops in the French empire. See, for example, Marc Michel, *L'Appel à l'Afrique: Contributions et Réactionsà l'Effort de Guerre en AOF* (Paris: Publications de la Sorbonne, 1982); Myron Echenberg, *Colonial Conscripts: The Tirailleurs Senegalais in French West Africa* (Portsmouth, NH: Heinemann, 1991); Charles John Balesi, *From Adversaries to Comrades-in-Arms: West Africans and the French Military* (Waltham, MA: Cross Roads Press, 1979); Nancy Lawler, *Soldiers of Misfortune: Ivorien Tirailleurs of World War Two* (Athens: Ohio University Press, 1992); Nancy Lawler, *Soldiers, Airmen, Spies and Whisperers: The Gold Coast in World War Two* (Athens: Ohio State University, 2002); Gregory Mann, *Native Sons: West Africa Veterans and France in the Twentieth Century* (Durham, NC: Duke University Press, 2006).

[2] The qaids were the traditional tribal leaders in Morocco. The qaids were used by French colonial authorities as intermediaries and instruments of colonial policies known in general as "*la politique des grands qaids*."

empire to keep the French nation powerful.[3] Here I limit my discussion to the multiple ways in which Moroccan troops were organized to support the Vichy and Free French governments and the critical role of propaganda in securing Moroccan support.

World War II and Empire: Manpower and Symbol

Reports that the greater part of the French metropolitan army was taken prisoner after the German invasion of France came as a devastating blow to the French military, especially colonial officers serving overseas. The prowess of French soldiery was the cornerstone of French imperial power: Gallic imperial pride had always had a strongly military overtone.[4] Even after France's defeat, the empire remained the symbol of the independence of France. The empire became even more symbolically important to both the Vichy regime and to Free France. Preservation of control over the colonies helped the Vichy government to withstand German pressure for concessions in metropolitan France. At the same time, it represented the embodiment of an enduring nation and not a defeated one. The supporters of Marshal Pétain adhered to the idea of a national revolution, which made more symbolic sense in the imperial context than in the metropole. Because the armistice disarmament agreement distinguished between metropolitan France and Vichy's overseas territories, the Armée d'Afrique in North Africa and colonial units elsewhere were considered the backbone of a Vichy military force as well as a symbol of what was believed to be national and colonial renewal. For the Free France government led by General Charles de Gaulle, the empire had also a political and symbolic significance because of its abundant resources.[5] The success of de Gaulle's call for colonial *ralliement* (support) was at the center of his claim to legitimacy. At the same time, the colonies provided an important source of income and the core of Free French military forces. While Vichy-controlled territories were meant to symbolize the ideal of a loyal service to the defeated nation, for the Free French, the colonies were pivotal to the idea of resistance.

Morocco, theoretically also subordinate to the Quai d'Orsay, was in reality controlled by the Ministry of War. For the army – Vichyite or Gaullist – the empire both before and after the armistice was mainly considered as an important manpower reserve for the defense of metropolitan France. French military authorities generally represented colonial forces

---

[3] Marc Michel, "La puissance par l'empire: Note sur la perception du facteur impérial dans l'élaboration de la défense nationale," *Revue Française d'Histoire d'Outre-Mer*, 69 (1982), 35–46.

[4] Martin Thomas, *The French Empire at War: 1940–45* (Manchester: Manchester University Press, 1998).

[5] See Raymond Dumett, "Africa's strategic minerals during the Second World War," *Journal of African History*, 26 (1985), 381–408.

and subject peoples as loyal partners of France and its national defense, viewing the empire in terms reminiscent of the First World War when Morocco was part of French global strategy in which French colonies would balance out the disproportionate advantage that Germany had in population. Resident-General Hubert Lyautey regarded France's colonial empire as a sort of "nursery of men," vital for the war effort. Lieutenant-Colonel Charles Mangin was also a leading proponent of the idea of empire as a "reservoir of men,"[6] again emphasizing the idea that colonial manpower represented a major contribution to a European war.[7] By September 1939, North Africa provided 53 percent of the total number of soldiers provided by the empire.[8]

World War II and the Moroccan Case

French colonial military authorities often prided themselves on the fact that colonial North Africa was policed mainly by indigenous troops, which numbered some 245,000 by the time of the armistice in 1940, but the French defeat in Europe created new problems for imperial control because of the emergence of Maghreb nationalism. The army was especially alert to the danger of popular unrest in North Africa in the event of a French military defeat in Europe. A report by the Vichy regime in 1940 noted, "there are new and infinitely dangerous ferments – nationalism, communism or anti-Semitism – which may produce serious urban agitation within a short period. One may be sure that from now on riots are most likely to begin within the towns."[9] By October 1940, despite the defeat of French armies, the French authorities were able to ensure order throughout North Africa, which quickly contained limited unrest.

In Morocco, the involvement of France in the war did not lead to much nationalist upheaval. Sultan Mohammed V gave his full support to French authorities. As in the First World War, the sultan's declaration of support was read in the mosques and published in *L'Echo du Maroc* in September 5, 1939. He called on his subjects to join the French in the defense of their country, declaring that

---

[6] The idea of a "reservoir of men" was in vogue among most colonial officers in the French empire after the publication of Lieutenant-Colonel Charles Mangin's book, *La Force Noire* (Paris: Hachette, 1910).

[7] Martin Thomas, *The French Empire at War: 1940–45* (Manchester: Manchester University Press, 1998), 12. "Between 1939 and June 1940, about 300,000 colonial troops were recruited in North Africa, 197,300 across Afrique Occidentale Française (AOF) and 116,000 within the Indochina federation. When the armistice agreements were signed in June, a further 313,750 colonial troops had been scheduled for recruitment between 1940 and 1944."

[8] Christine Levisse-Touzé, "L'Afrique du Nord et la Défense Nationale Française," Doctorat de 3eme cycle, Le Mans, Université du Maine (1980), 48.

[9] Quoted in Martin Thomas, *The French Empire at War: 1940–45* (Manchester: Manchester University Press, 1998), 39.

after the protectorate treaty, peace was guaranteed in our homes, in our cities, and in our countryside; our honor as well as our sacred religion were protected. Now that France takes up arms to defend its land, its honor, its dignity, its future and ours, we are ourselves loyal to the principles of honoring our race, our history and our religion. It is our absolute duty to show our support and recognition to the French government for what it has done for us. Any transgression of this duty would be unworthy of our history and contrary to the orders of God who imposes on us the duty of gratitude. From this day on we must give our full support and be ready for any sacrifice.[10]

A few days later, the sultan attended a religious festival in the holy city of Moulay Idriss where he gave another speech calling on Moroccan Muslims to join the Christian French in a unified crusade for the common goal of safeguarding civilization.[11]

As in World War I, the Moroccan elites, including qaids, *ulama*, and religious brotherhoods, supported the French cause.[12] The emergency powers that were enacted immediately after the war began curbed nationalist reactions in Algeria, Tunisia, and Morocco.[13] Only moderate nationalist leaders were left to voice their concerns. In Morocco, the leadership of the nationalist Comité d'action marocaine was detained. The "state of siege" invoked in 1939 was used to curb "radical" nationalist activity; therefore, it was up to the sultanate to assume its role as the defender of nationalist aspirations. Large nationalist demonstrations took place January 1944 in the major cities of Morocco, but nationalism did not have much influence on rural Moroccans who enlisted as *goumiers*.[14]

With weakened support for Moroccan nationalism, the sultan and the local elite provided a more convenient context for facilitating the recruitment of large numbers of Moroccans after the outbreak of the war. Before the armistice, colonial troops were already deployed in France. By May 1940, there were twelve regiments in France totaling more than 90,000 men, 83,000 of whom were Moroccans.[15] Because of the potential threat of a Spanish military force estimated at 100,000 men, more colonial troops were being prepared for the defense of Morocco, although the priority still

---

[10] See the printed declaration in *L'Echo du Maroc*, September 1939.

[11] As in World War I, reference to religious symbolism had always been the main part of the sultan's discourse in support of the French, but the historical context was now much less complicated since the enemy was now limited to Nazi Germany, without the support of the Muslim Turks.

[12] See Driss Maghraoui "The 'Grande Guerre Sainte': Moroccan colonial troops and workers in the First World War," *Journal of North African Studies*, 9 (2004), 1–21.

[13] See Charles-Robert Ageron, "Vichy, les français et l'empire," in Jean-Pierre Azéma and François Bedarida (eds.), *Le Régime de Vichy et les Français* (Paris: Fayard, 1992), 122–34.

[14] The goumiers were Moroccan auxiliaries within the French colonial army. They were organized into regiments known as tabors. The goumiers were used within Morocco for French colonial expansion but also more extensively during the Second World War.

[15] Moshe Gershovich, *French Military Policy in Morocco and the Origins of an Arab Army* (Cambridge, MA: Harvard University, 1995), 375.

remained the defense of France. When the Germans invaded in September 1940, Moroccan regiments were involved in the battles along the Franco-Belgian borders. They were crushed by German armored columns and heavy air raids. Moroccan troops were unable to evacuate from Dunkirk to England: more than 2,100 were killed and 18,000 were taken prisoners in the initial hostilities.[16]

The Armistice and Its Effect

After the signing of the armistice, the Germans compelled the French to reduce the number of North African troops to 120,000 men. In order to guarantee the internal security of North Africa, the Vichy regime requested 150,000 men as part of its colonial troops, but the Germans opposed the request because of Italian pressure to reduce the number to 30,000. After long negotiations, General Charles Huntziger, the head of the French delegation in Wiesbaden (the center of German armistice commission), convinced Germany to allow France to retain 115,000 men in North Africa.[17] Until spring 1941, the Italian commission controlled the implementation of the armistice agreement. Soon thereafter the Germans also became involved through the establishment of the German Inspection Control (KIA) that worked closely with the Wiesbaden German Commission (OKW).

In Morocco the OKW, under the leadership of General Paul Schultheiss, was established in Casablanca, for the control of the navy and the air force, and in Fedala, for the control of the regular army. The Germans became increasingly concerned with Morocco and did not believe the Italian team could handle the task, so they gradually took exclusive control of the inspection commission. By October 1942, the French colonial army in Morocco was officially limited by the terms of the armistice to 21,598 Europeans and 22,676 Moroccans, but after July 1940, French colonial military officials began secretly organizing indigenous troops for an eventual war in Europe.[18] So the conditions of the armistice in Morocco led to the transformation of the *goums* into a secret underground army that became far more important to France than its resistance movement or the Forces Françaises de l'Intérieur (FFI). Resistance in France developed slowly – by the beginning of 1944, the various resistance groups throughout France did not number more than 30,000 men and women.[19]

The Vichyite General Emile Bethouart headed the German commission. He was vaguely aware of the clandestine organization of the *goums*. A report

---

[16] Christine Levisse-Touze, *L'Afrique du Nord, Recours au Secours: Septembre 1939–Juin 1943* (Paris: Panthéon-Sorbonne, 1991).

[17] Christine Levisse-Touze, *L'Afrique du Nord et la Défense Nationale Française*, 50.

[18] Augustin-Léon Guillaume, *Homme de Guerre* (Paris: Editions France-Empire, 1977), 12.

[19] Roger Price, *A Concise History of France* (Cambridge: Cambridge University Press, 1993), 265.

by a German official of the commission found in the German archives in Fedala stated that: "We have controlled almost all the *cherifian* goums. We have the feeling that the French are hiding something, but it's not very important because the goums have no military value and will never be a threat. It is impossible to transfer these uncivilized Berber peasants into combat units."[20] Thus, Germans had a racist view of the *goumiers* and did not take them very seriously. Under German commission restrictions, the French were able to have 26,000 men in eighteen different *tabors* (military units). The *goumiers* represented one of the most promising military forces for the future of French resistance.

French colonial authorities dissociated the *goumiers* from the Troupes d'Occupation du Maroc (TOM). One way of doing so was to place them, along with the *travailleurs coloniaux* and other colonial units, under the fictional authority of the protectorate. Such Moroccan colonial formations assumed the name of *mehallas cherifiennes*, which was the traditional title of *makhzan* troops levied for the Moroccan sultan. Even though they were aware that the French had a secret agenda, the Germans neither paid much attention to the rural areas in Morocco nor provide the commission with the necessary logistical organization to verify independently French military capabilities.[21] As a result, the French were able to secretly organize a military based on the *goumiers*. Commonly known among French colonial officers as the *"periode du camouflage des goums,"* this clandestine organization was able to provide about 50,000 men to the Free French after the allied landings in November 1942.[22]

The architect of the military organization of colonial troops in Morocco was Resident-General Charles Hippolyte Nogues. He personified the blurred character of political allegiance and the split that occurred within the colonial military establishment. Originally, he maintained contact with Philippe Pétain, who replaced Admiral Jean-Francois Darlan after he repudiated the Vichy regime; however, Pétain became gradually less enthusiastic about collaborating with the Vichy regime and on November 10 of the same year, he opposed Pierre Laval's government. For Nogues, North Africa represented France's only hope to organize an army that would eventually liberate the homeland. He wanted to maintain internal order in Morocco and recuperate the military prestige that France had lost in the metropole.

Faced with the armistice agreement, Nogues wanted to build up as much military capacity as possible. He had four main objectives.[23] First, he wanted to reconstitute regular units authorized by the German armistice convention.

---

[20] Quoted in Jacques Augarde, *La Longue Route des Tabors* (Paris: Editions France-Empire, 1983), 47.

[21] Gershovich, *French Military Policy in Morocco*, 380.

[22] The camouflage of the goums is well documented in Yves Jouin, "Le camouflage des Goums marocains pendant la période d'armistice," *Revue Historique de l'Armée*, 2 (1972).

[23] These objectives are spelled out in Salkin, *Histoire des Goums marocains*, 45–47.

These units would be responsible for the internal security of Morocco and for the mobilization of its resources. Second, he desired to create a new military force under the guise of an auxiliary police force, but which did not fall under the quotas imposed by the armistice agreement. Secretly this force would be trained for operations in modern warfare to a high level of operational capability. The third element of Nogues' strategy was the organization of covert depots for munitions and weaponry to be used ultimately for the liberation of France. Finally, he sought to dissimulate the maximum number of military personnel in Morocco within the civil bureaucracy of the protectorate. The implementation of these objectives was carried out by Colonel Augustin-Léon Guillaume, the head of the Direction des Affaires Politiques in Morocco after May 1941. Before the German commission could effectively impose its control, artillery and motorized vehicles were hidden in remote areas, farms, and caves in the Atlas Mountains. According to Colonel Yves Jouin "some 20,000 individual arms, 4,000 automatic weapons, 60 cannons, 200 mortars, 150 cars, 250 trucks, and 50 tanks were hidden in different parts of the Moroccan countryside."[24]

The *goumiers*, together with segments of former *tirailleurs marocains*, were involved in this secret military organizing. On the eve of the armistice, the *forces suppletives marocaines* were made of disparate units including the *goums*, *mokhaznis*, *fezzas*, and *harkas*, all of which comprised an irregular army to be deployed on a need-be basis. In August 1940, the DAP of the protectorate created the *mehallas cherifiennes*, new "police units whose main role is to guarantee the order and security of the tribes. These irregular troops are under the authority of the Resident General who is responsible for their organization and use."[25] The *mehallas cherifiennes* included 268 French officers, 868 noncommissioned officers, 19,700 *goumiers*, and 4,700 *mokhaznis*. Under the pressure of the German commission, the Vichy government disarmed the *mehallas* and put them under the protectorate budget, which was managed by the Ministry of Foreign Affairs. This created an ideal condition for more secret organizing since the Ministry of Foreign Affairs was not under the rigid control of the Germans.

One way of thinking about the camouflage of the *goums* in Morocco is to see it as part of the history of French resistance to Nazi Germany as well as a part of Moroccan history. Further, the Moroccan elite and general popular continually performed their "loyalty" to France as a colonial power. The association of the *goumiers* and the Berber community with the French cause reinforced the notion of comradeship that French colonial officers praised so much as a sign of the common bond between them and Berber society. As Moshe Gershovich points out, "even though the seeds of the 'good Berber' myth which would dominate French native strategy in the

[24] Jouin, "Le camouflage des Goums marocains," 112.
[25] Quoted in Jouin, "Le camouflage des Goums marocains," 103.

postwar era had been planted prior to the armistice era, the camouflage episode certainly contributed to the crystallization of that myth in the minds of contemporary French colonial officers."[26] Of course, there were many ambiguities involved in the perceptions of "comradeship" and "common bonds" by French officers.

Throughout the period of the *"camouflage des goums,"* the French military authorities designated the *goumiers* as a solid force, especially for mountain warfare. They were organized in battalion-size *tabors* consisting of three *goums* each. Each *goum* comprised between 180 and 200 men. The *tabors* were then reassembled into *groupements de tabors marocains* (GTM) of three *tabors* each. The first GTM was organized in Khenifra in February 1941, the second in Azilal in June 1941, the third in Sefrou in January 1942, and the fourth in Rabat in April 1942. Following the armistice, seven additional *tabors* were organized for combat without the knowledge of the German commissions. On November 10, 1942, German troops moved into the previously unoccupied zone of southern France. General Alphonse Juin, the commanding officer of French forces in North Africa, deemed the occupation of southern France as nullification of the Franco-German armistice agreement. From then on, the Moroccan troops fought for the Allied forces against Nazi Germany. Of the 20,000 Armée d'Afrique casualties in the 1943 Tunisian campaign, 8,267 were North Africans.

From a broader perspective, it can be argued that the gradual strengthening of de Gaulle's position was largely due to his reliance on a colonial army throughout the French empire. The comité français de libération nationale (CFLN), formed under his leadership in June 1943, commanded the allegiance of a regular army of 500,000 men formed in North Africa.[27]

Propaganda at Home and at the Front: The Second *guerre sainte*

From a strategic point of view, Morocco was always on Hitler's lens.[28] German propaganda had spread in Morocco since the 1930s, but not very successfully. Yet during the course of the war, it was reinforced thanks to the role played by the German armistice commission. Meanwhile, French and British propaganda reverted to undermining the image of the Vichy government in the eyes of Moroccans. Since the 1930s, the Germans had attracted a small group of Arab nationalists who believed that Germany would be an asset in their anticolonial struggle against the British and the French. Nationalist leaders such as Chakib Arsalan from Syria, Rachid al-Kilani

---

[26] Gershovich, *French Military Policy in Morocco*, 381.

[27] Price, *Concise History of France*, 266.

[28] Norman J. W. Goda, "Hitler's demand for Casablanca in 1940: Incident or policy?," *International History Review*, 16 (1994), 491–510.

from Iraq, and Ahmed Balafrej and Abdelkhalek Torres from Morocco went occasionally to Berlin in search of support.[29] To pursue their propaganda goals in Morocco, the Germans capitalized on these previous relationships with intellectuals and other important groups. One group was related to the social networks around the Grande Mosque established in Berlin since 1927. Another group mobilized around the fact that the mufti of al-Quds was received by Hitler on November 28, 1941, which enabled Germany to present itself as a sympathizer of Islam and Arabs against British and French colonialism.

In 1943, the so-called Bureau du Maghreb Arabe (BMA) was established in Berlin and started to publish a journal known as *al-maghrib al-arabi*.[30] Headed by the Tunisian Youssef Rouissi, the BMA was instrumental in facilitating Nazi propaganda schemes in North Africa. Through these networks, the German propaganda machine functioned, with radio broadcasting as one of the most important communication tools. Since September 1939, Radio-Berlin and Radio-Stuttgart started to broadcast programs in Arabic and French throughout Morocco and the rest of North Africa. From the start, German radio assigned a large part of its broadcast schedule to Muslim preachers and religious programs. Other parts of the schedule related the news about the war and promoted the idea that Germany supported Islam and Muslims. The programs featured a number of Arab speakers, including the Iraqi Younes Bahri and the Moroccan Tkieddine al-Hilali. The Germans contributed articles on the defense of Islam, the glorification of Hitler and the army to newspapers and journals such as *al-maghrib al arabi*, *nashrat al-akhbar*, and *al-jahir*. Anti-Semitic language was part of the general discourse.

To counter German propaganda, the British and the French prepared their own propaganda for radio broadcasts and the newspapers. They focused on religious discourse and the close similarities between Islam and Christianity. The British Broadcasting Corporation (BBC), founded in 1922, broadcast news to the Middle East in general, and after 1939, to Morocco because of its proximity to Gibraltar.[31] Following the split between Britain and the Vichy regime on July 3, 1940, Radio London became more active. British broadcast propaganda utilized Muslims with strong religious and literary credentials. For example, on August 29, 1940, the famous

---

[29] Jamaâ Baida, "Le Maroc et la propagande du IIIème Reich," *Hespéris-Tamuda*, 28 (1990), 91–106.

[30] See Jamaâ Baida, "Perception de la période Nazie au Maroc: quelques indices de l'impact de la propagande allemande sur l'état d'esprit des marocains," in A. Bendaoud and M. Berriane (eds.), *Marocains et Allemands: la perception de l'Autre* (Rabat: Faculté des Lettres et des Sciences Humaines, Série colloques et séminaires no. 44, 1995), 13–19.

[31] Seth Arsenian, "Wartime propaganda in the Middle East," *Middle East Journal*, 2 (1948), 417–29.

Egyptian scholar and journalist, Taha Husein, featured in a program high-lighting "courage and Arabic literature." During the week following the Allied landing in North Africa, Radio London concentrated on the Britain's friendly relationship with its colonies as well as its respect for Muslim tra-ditions. Initially, most speakers came from Egyptian backgrounds, not a very well-conceived strategy when compared to how Germans used speak-ers of local dialects and more varied backgrounds. But starting in November 1942, the British began to broadcast programs in Moroccan dialects as well.

In addition to the radio, the British utilized newspapers such as *al Mus-tami' al-Arabi* or the weekly *Akhbar al ousbou*. Both newspapers used clas-sical Arabic as medium of communication, concentrating on themes related to victory, friendly relationships with Arab countries, and the glorification of the British army; however, the impact of the British newspapers was very limited.

French Propaganda Made for Soldiers

For Moroccan colonial soldiers, French propaganda during the Second World War was packaged in an appropriate cultural form employing their symbolic field of reference. French propagandist discourse sought to bring them into the same mental framework as the French focused on fear and hatred of the Germans, and, more importantly, revenge. After Germany's defeat of France in 1870 and the German occupation of the Alsace in 1914, the defeat of 1940 was even more devastating to the French psyche and military prestige. The armistice triggered a paroxysm of French defensive patriotism and catalyzed an obsessive will to resist.

An analysis of what information was "fed" to the colonial soldiers between 1939 and 1945 also reveals the state of mind of the French colo-nial officers. Its goal was to integrate them psychologically into the French/European conflict. Beyond the French nation, this propagandist discourse projected the idea that human civilization was threatened by Nazi Ger-many. Colonial troops were implicated in a "totalization" of war in which the sacrifice of the colonial subjects became a sacrosanct obligation to save "humanity," which included the colonial subjects themselves. The language and symbols of war propaganda in print form show how ideological pack-aging aimed to integrate colonial subjects in the conflict.

In this final section, I explore how the war was integrated in the everyday life of the soldiers. To do this, I turn to a quick analysis of the propaganda discourse utilized by the French authority in three propaganda newspapers: *Ila al-Amam*, *Bulletin des Armées d'Outre-Mer*, and *Annasr*. This type of French propaganda was intended to persuade colonial soldiers to support a cause that was not necessarily theirs and integrate them into the war effort.

Ila-Amam: Hitler asal-Kafir

Given the importance that the French gave to the role of the North African troops, the central command of the First Armée française created an information cell specifically geared to them. It is this cell that published the first edition of a very short weekly known as *Ila-alamam*, which first appeared on January 14, 1944, and continued publication until May 25, 1945. The front page of the newspaper declared that intended to "remind the fighting men about their victories and to incite them to achieve other." Frequent reference to Islam and Koranic verses was integral to this discourse. "Ila al-mam" in Arabic means literally "let's go forward" and is the phrase that an army officer would use to order subordinates to advance in the battlefield. The newspaper was written in semiclassical Arabic but also included a few translations of Kabyle meant to address non-Arabic speaking soldiers from Algeria. Verse 169 from Surat *āl 'im'rān* in the Koran appeared on the front page of its November 6, 1944, issue: "Do not consider those who were killed in God's path as dead, but rather alive, receiving their livelihood from their almighty." This clearly refers to the notion of jihad that was intended to give a religious overtone to this propaganda, reinforced by the fact that the newspaper appeared on Friday, the Muslim holy day. Additional references to *aid al-fitr* and *aid al-adha* also appear in the paper. Throughout its pages, Hitler is referred to as *kafir*, a word with the strong religious connotation of "infidel."

The *Bulletin des Armées d'Outre-Mer*: Jacques Dubois à Mon Cher Tirailleur

The *Bulletin des Armées d'Outre-Mer* launched its publication at the beginning of the war. The editor was Edward Warren, the Chef de la Mission du Commissariat Général à l'Information auprès des Militaires et Ouvriers d'Outre-Mer. The Bulletin was distinct from the other newspaper, Annasr (discussed later in this section), in the sense that it was directed toward more literate soldiers. As opposed to Annasr, the Bulletin was written primarily in French and addressed three main ethnic groups from "North Africa, Black Africa, Madagascar and Indochina." The Bulletin printed different editions specific to each region. Hence the use of religious symbolism for propaganda purposes changed according to whom the Bulletin was addressed; however, the universalistic idea of sacrifice was appropriate for all. In its February 1940 edition, de Warren incorporated quotations from the letters of colonial soldiers, but did not include the authors' names, which might indicate that these letters were inauthentic. The editor wrote: "all the letters brought me the great joy of noticing how much all of you faithfully love France. You understand what she has done for you. You are ready to sacrifice yourself for her until the last drop of human blood." Perhaps De Warren intentionally stresses the idea of human blood ("*sang humain*") as part of a language of universal sacrifice for the ideals of the French nation because "we will show everybody how much we are all part of the same large French family.[32]

In the same edition of the *Bulletin des Armées d'Outre-Mer* there appeared a well-written letter apparently by a young high school student, Jacques Dubois, to his great friend, the Tirailleur, whose name and ethnic origin are not specified (Figure 5.1). The context in which a Tirailleur came into contact with Jacques Dubois is not clear either, which makes the letter more likely fictive. Since the *Bulletin* was addressed to a wide variety of readers from different ethnic backgrounds, the letter adopts a generic language. It seeks to reach any Tirailleur, whether from North Africa, Senegal, or Indochina. Our school boy, Jacques Dubois, wants to describe l'Arc de triomphe to his Tirailleur friend:

> I am sure that you have already heard about the great arc under which a nameless soldier is buried. He is a soldier from the Great War that people from all over the world come to salute. He is the unknown soldier. We don't know who this soldier is since he is unknown: he might be white, he might be yellow, or he might be black. Only God knows. But he is a soldier of France. It is upon his tomb that the French government has ordered to light a flame animated each night by a group of *anciens combattants*, so that the flame remains eternal as a sigh of gratitude towards those who died for France.

The letter of the school boy ends in the following way: "think hard, my friend, about this monument. On the day of victory, if you fight well for France, maybe your officers will reward you by letting you march under this glorious arch." What is of interest to us is that this propagandist discourse transcends race in order to associate colonial troops in a mythical way with the most symbolic icon of French military "glory."

To integrate colonial soldiers into the psychology of a war that was not theirs required also their integration into the prospect of peace. The language of war was therefore constructed to provide a feeling of hope for a peaceful future for all: "Patience and courage! You should have an absolute confidence in your officers. Victory will bring a fertile peace to all of us once our territories are liberated from the German threat." The ideological ploy of this discourse was meant to inculcate the idea of a universal sacrifice for a universal peace in which the colonial troops would ultimately partake even though their very presence in the theater of war was the result of their condition as subjugated subaltern people. The objective of this form of propaganda was the mythical construction of justice and a new future that was worth the sacrifice of colonial troops:

> with our brothers from overseas, victory will prevail. The moment of an eminent justice is getting close to victory of liberty against tyranny. A day will come

---

[32] See the *Bulletin des armées d'Outre-Mer*, Edition Arabe, Avril 30, 1940, 1.

FIGURE 5.1. The supposed letter of the young high school student Jacques Dubois.

when you enter your *douars* and villages, proud for what you have accomplished for your little countries and of our great common country, the French empire, and for all the nations of the world. Your courage and exploits will contribute to the safeguard of civilization and liberty for all people including yourself in order to live free in this free land.

This rapprochement of humanity in a new era of fraternity was clearly part of a newly created myth of equality between the French and their colonial subjects. This discourse contrasted sharply with the racialized discourse of French colonial officers in the 1920s and 1930s. The nationalist ferment of the 1920s in Morocco, Tunisia, and Egypt were interpreted by colonial military officers as none other than "the revolt of oriental anarchy against the moral, industrial and scientific work of European civilization."[33] Meanwhile, French opposition to any form of immigration during peacetime was often explained in terms of a racist discourse that was very much in contrast with the discourse of fraternity and universality.

Annasr was a newspaper published in Alger and distributed in North Africa throughout the war. It addressed different sections of the North African troops. Written in very simple language, *Annasr* was conceived as a newspaper more likely addressed to children rather than to an adult population. The paper can be seen as part of a moral and psychological mobilization of illiterate colonial soldiers who came from a peasant background. While the French respected them for their courage and sacrifice, they often considered colonial troops as having childlike qualities. Thus, the propagandist discourse of *Annasr* perceives the colonial soldier as a naive "big child."

Annasr, which means victory, was established in 1940 by French military authorities as a way of diverting and "educating" Muslim soldiers from North Africa. As stated in its December 1943 issue, "this journal is conceived of as a form of diversion for the Muslim soldiers who are fighting with the French army and the allied forces. This journal will modestly contribute to our effort, and to our only goal, victory." *Annasr* was not, in fact, the first newspaper addressed to the Muslim soldier. In December 1939, French authorities published a short-lived newspaper known as *Yallah* (a religious call to God) in Arabic, but after the fall of France in June 1940, it stopped publication.

The French defeat was a major blow to French military honor and glory, especially in the colonies. Thus, the rapid creation of another newspaper, *Annasr*, can be seen as part of an effort to rebuild confidence in the French army via its colonial troops. For example, the 1943 issue stated: "France has returned to its field of glory in North Africa and its soldiers have returned

---

[33] Neil MacMaster, *Colonial Migrants and Racism: Algerians in France, 1900–62* (New York: St. Martin's Press, 1997), 142.

to the battlefield. At the forefront, you find the Muslim sons (*fils de l'Islam*) of France who gave the best example of loyalty that history will ever record. It is hoped that *Annasr* will bring some happiness to the Muslim soldiers by providing him with news from his family and tribes."

Of course, *Annasr* was far from containing news from home for France's *fils de l'Islam*. Its main goal was to distract and divert soldiers' attention from the realities of war by printing stories and anecdotes with which they could associate. The "news" from home was always broad, rosy, and carefully managed. Under the rubric of "*situation agricole*" in North Africa (Figure 5.2), the following lines summarized the conditions in Morocco in 1943:

> in the region of Oujda, Guerssif, Ouerrha, Sefrou and Tafilalt, abundant rains have ameliorated the conditions of agriculture which has suffered from drought, while in the Houz of Marrakech and around Agadir, there is no more drought. In all of Morocco, the hope this year is that a good harvest will be satisfying for the peasants.

Since most illiterate colonial soldiers were from peasant backgrounds, the "news" about rain and harvest was deemed important, meant to reassure soldiers about the normalcy and abundance at home. The hand-drawn pictures of the four corners of the rubric on the "*situation agricole*" show peasants going on their work in an abundant harvest, but the harvest can be disrupted if we look more closely at a "story without words."

The title of Figure 5.3 is "Hikaya Bila Kalam," which means in Arabic "a story without words." Here it speaks of the fabricated normalcy of life to a soldier who might be facing death in the battlefront. The image may be interpreted as counterproductive because it might trigger nostalgia for the peaceful life of the countryside at home. Parallel to these images of peacefulness and abundance, we find other images hand-drawn by the same French artist and juxtaposed to them in order to disrupt the normalcy and daily activities of the peasant's life.

The first illustration (top left) shows a woman engaged in her daily work, happily absorbed by the harvest of her field. Behind this woman, her daughter is helping with the task. The appearance of both a woman and her daughter in the image is very significant because it gives a gender dimension to the threat that is symbolized by the Nazi swastika in the form of poisonous snakes. In these illustrations, Nazi Germany is a threat not only to France, but also to life in the home country of the Moroccan colonial soldiers. Furthermore, there is a threat to the soldiers' wives and children. The snake heads in picture two (top right) are not drawn in a haphazard way. Their biting mouths directly face the woman whose face is no longer as serene and happy as in picture one, but threatened and scared. The little girl in the background is no longer carrying a bundle of wheat, but raising her hands to warn her mother of a threat that has more symbolic meaning

La Situation Agricole

TUNISIE

Région Nord. — Les emblavures ont été diminuées par les opérations de guerre, malgré la ténacité des colons qui ont effectué leurs travaux parfois très près de la ligne de feu.

En général, la récolte de blé s'annonce bonne, mais il y aura des difficultés pour la moisson et les battages (transports, carburants, sacherie, pièces de rechange).

Les pluies de printemps ont été satisfaisantes. Des vents très froids ont causé quelques dégâts dans la région de Teboursouk, Le Krib.

Région Centre. — Ensemencements en orge assez réduits, mais récolte de bonne venue.

Région Sud. — Ensemencements en orge normaux ; bonne pluie d'automne et de printemps. Récolte de belle venue, mais la moisson sera gênée par les champs de mines extrêmement nombreux.

La floraison dans la forêt d'oliviers de Sfax est plutôt médiocre. On ne peut espérer une récolte abondante, pour la prochaine campagne, d'autant plus que la récolte précédente a été belle.

L'état du troupeau est satisfaisant sur les Hauts Plateaux et dans

les régions Nord, mais le cheptel a souffert des pillages zone occupée et du fait de la guerre dans toute la zone combat.

ALGÉRIE

Dans la Mitidja et en Kabylie les céréales s'annonce fort belles. Sur les Hauts Plateaux, le cheptel qui avait bea coup souffert à l'automne reprend partout ; les pâturages so en bon état.

De Sétif, Batna, Guelma, Bône, Aïn-Témouchent, Bel-Abbé Mostaganem et Tlemcen, on apprend que les céréales, un me ment compromises, sont suffisamment avancées pour l'époqu et qu'on peut prévoir une soudure facile.

MAROC

Dans les régions d'Oujda, Guercif, Haut-Ouerrha, Sefro et Tafilalet, les pluies abondantes sont venues améliorer l'éta des cultures qui avaient souffert de la sécheresse au début d l'hiver.

Dans le Haouz de Marrakec et autour d'Agadir, la sécheress persistante a pris fin.

Dans tout le Maroc, l'espoi d'une bonne récolte pour cett année récompense les fellahs.

À nos Lecteurs

Nous ne pouvons rien sans vous.

Si vous nous aidez, « AN-NAṢR » sera le trait d'union entre le combattant et les siens restés au pays.

Faites-nous part de vos critiques (langue, illustration, etc...), exprimez vos désirs ou suggestions, envoyez-nous dessins, contes ou poésies susceptibles d'intéresser les camarades.

Nous répondrons à tout envoi ou demande de renseignements adressés à :

Journal « AN-NAṢR », 2, rue de Normandie, Alger, et portant votre adresse exacte.

Les auteurs des meilleurs envois recevront une récompense.

FIGURE 5.2. *Annasr*: "La Situation Agricole"

FIGURE 5.3. "Hikaya Bila Kalam": A Story Without Words

to soldiers at the front than to Berber women, who were probably unaware of the association between the swastika and Nazi Germany. It therefore conveys a direct message to the soldier to defend his family by defending France from a common enemy.

Paradoxically, picture three (bottom right) shows the French army, symbolized by French soldiers in their uniforms, coming to the rescue of both the woman and her child. At the symbolic level, it is France and French soldiers who are presented as the protectors of their colonial subjects at home. In picture four (bottom left), life goes back to normal, thanks to French intervention. For French colonial authorities, the articulation of this propagandist discourse in the form of pictures and silence (at the top of the drawing the Arabic title reads: "a story without words") is meant to associate the soldiers with the common cause of the war. The war against Nazi Germany was fundamental for national honor and the defense of France. It was part of a defensive patriotism against one of the major threats to the nation. Beyond the nation, Nazi Germany was presented as a threat to human civilization and hence to colonial subjects. French war propaganda directed toward illiterate colonial troops had to introduce the idea that Germany was not simply a threat to the French nation but to Moroccans (including their women) as well. The Moroccan colonial soldier had to sacrifice his life not for France alone, but for his family and humanity in general.

Conclusion

By examining the Moroccan colonial context, this chapter demonstrates that our understanding of the history of the Second World War is incomplete if it does not take into consideration the place of empire in general and the role played by colonial subjects who ultimately became soldiers of France without actually being citizens. The history of the French empire and its people, and how European wars affected them, ought to become an integral part of European history. The war was a critical moment of political, economic, and social reverberations between colony and metropole. As Ann Stoler and Frederick Cooper point out, "Europe was made by its imperial projects, as much as colonial encounters were shaped by conflicts within Europe."[34] The important contributions made by colonial troops from Africa, the Middle East, and Asia in general, and the Moroccan colonial troops in particular, are only now starting to be more fully explored in order to understand the broader world dimensions of the war. What united all these regions was not only their role in European colonial empires as major reservoirs of men and warriors. Similar propagandist strategies for securing people's support in Morocco were exercised in other North African and Middle Eastern countries. The Moroccan colonial context provides a specific example,

---

[34] See Fred Cooper and Ann Stoler, "Between metropole and colony: Rethinking a research agenda," in F. Cooper and A. Stoler (eds.), *Tensions of Empire: Colonial Cultures in a Bourgeois World* (Berkeley: University of California Press, 1997), 1.

among many others in Africa, the Middle East, and Asia, that ought to stimulate further scholarship on the place of empire and its people in thinking about European wars and disrupt the Eurocentric historical narratives about the two world wars that witnessed their own *effort de guerre* from the colonies.

6

Free to Coerce

Forced Labor during and after the Vichy Years in French West Africa

Catherine Bogosian Ash

Shortly after the end of the Second World War, administrators in the French Soudan began complaining about numerous incidents of African men deserting their worksites and going to military bases to enlist, boarding trains without authorization, and in other ways causing disruptions. When asked why they demanded free passage on trains or why they wanted to sign up for the army, the men expressed a desire to be treated with the same respect as that given soldiers who had returned from the war. Their complaints came at a time when most West Africans had reason to celebrate major changes in colonial rule. By 1946, new laws brought about an end to forced labor and a separate legal code for colonial subjects; many considered these an overdue reward for the significant contributions Africans had made to the war. But not everyone enjoyed the fruits of these recent political changes. African members of a quasimilitary service known as the *deuxième portion du contingent militaire* (second portion of the military contingent) found that little had changed for them. Since its origins in 1926, men recruited into the *deuxième portion* had considered it to be a form of forced labor. Their distaste for the service only increased during the war, particularly during the Vichy period, when colonial administrators were freer than they had been in decades to coerce Africans. While the war years had been difficult for everyone, the postwar years seemed to hold promise for many, but when the men in the *deuxième portion* realized that the changing political order did not apply to them, they found new ways to express their anger.

Initially, French colonial administrators began recruiting men into the *deuxième portion* to provide cheap labor to the Dakar-Niger Railroad, the Office du Niger, and other public works projects, primarily in the French Soudan. The men who designed this service argued that the conditions in the worksites and campsites were well regulated and that, therefore, the *deuxième portion* was somehow different from previous forms of coercion. By the late 1930s, the *deuxième portion* was well established and administrators at both the Office du Niger and the Dakar-Niger railroad had come to rely heavily upon the hundreds, sometimes thousands, of men sent to work for them every year as part of this service.

Between 1936 and 1946, both administrators and *deuxième portion* workers experienced the side effects of the political pendulum in France. Attempts at serious labor reforms during the Popular Front period gave way under the weight first of other political priorities, and then of outright approval of coercive labor policies in the Vichy period. During the Vichy period, the workers' frustrations rose as Vichy colonial administrators ignored any previous calls to bring about reforms in the *deuxième portion* and instead dramatically increased the number of men called to fulfill this service. In turn, the Vichy period lost favor among administrators in French West Africa (FWA). The latter half of the war brought some modest improvements, but workers continued to feel the neglect and lack of dignity associated with their service. Many began to assert their equality with regular soldiers; some even tried to transfer directly into the army. Following the end of the war, a new wave of political and labor reforms swept through the French African colonies. Even though France abolished forced labor in its colonies, it did not abolish the *deuxième portion*. In response, *deuxième portion* workers stepped up their complaints. This chapter explores the ways in which *deuxième portion* workers reacted to the changing colonial labor policies during and just after World War II. It argues that the intensification of recruitment into the labor army during the Vichy years helped to create a greater awareness among the workers of their position in relation to the French colonial government and in relation to the regular army. As a result, workers' critiques of their conditions in the last years of the war, and in the first years after the war, became increasingly articulate and effective.

The Prewar Period and the Possibility of Reform

While the Second World War would prove to be a period of regression in French colonial labor policies, in the years leading up to the war genuine labor reforms seemed possible. Many colonial administrators actively sought not only to propose improved working conditions, but also to follow through on such promises. Ultimately, the pressures stemming from metropolitan economic difficulties curtailed whatever serious commitment there was for such reforms. Such efforts as did exist, and the workers' awareness that change might be possible laid the groundwork for later postwar debates.

Perhaps the most significant difference during this brief window of attempted labor reforms was a renewed attempt to inspect labor camps and to take seriously the findings of such inspections. The idea of inspecting work camps was not new; since the creation of the *deuxième portion* in 1926, regulations required that the camps and worksites undergo regular inspections. Project directors overseeing the worksites made little real effort to carry out stringent inspections on any kind of regular basis, considering the inspections to be a nuisance that interrupted productivity. This began to change in 1935 when the Service de la Main d'Œuvre, the administrative body that oversaw work inspections, came under the authority of the lieutenant governor. Previously, it had been delegated to the employing services that were understandably less interested in critiquing their own labor practices. By 1935, reports of abuse had become so common that the government deemed it necessary to take control. Finally, the system of inspections was regularized and, backed by the lieutenant governor, inspectors were given more weight.[1] Following this shift, inspections became more common. More important, the inspection reports were not neglected in a filing cabinet, but actually led (albeit briefly) to some significant changes. This process began not long before the Popular Front came into power in 1936, when the support of certain Popular Front administrators then gave it an impetus it would not have otherwise had.

While it was metropolitan concerns that brought the Popular Front to power, the new minister of colonies, Marius Moutet, Governor-General Jules Marcel de Coppet, and Lieutenant Governor Ferdinand Jacques Louis Rougier were devoted to applying the ideals of the Popular Front to France's African colonies. De Coppet and Rougier were among the most committed and effective administrators appointed during the Popular Front period.[2] Several scholars have noted that the Popular Front was not overly concerned with the colonies; economic difficulties and the rise of Fascism were all consuming for the metropolitan government.[3] What reforms the Popular Front administration did try to carry out generally ended up as nothing more than empty promises, largely because of the very limited amount of time they were in power. In particular, FWA was not, in the larger scheme of things, of high-ranking interest, but for de Coppet and Rougier, at least initially, the Popular Front vision of the workers and the common people included African colonized workers.[4] Nevertheless, colonial policy was never a

---

[1] "Rapport sur les travailleurs de la 2ème portion du contingent, année 1938" [Annual Report on 2ème portion 1938], May 6, 1939, K/47, Archives Nationales du Sénégal (hereafter ANS), Dakar.

[2] William Cohen, "The colonial policy of the Popular Front," *French Historical Studies*, 7 (1972), 377; Tony Chafer and Amada Sackur, eds. *French Colonial Empire and the Popular Front: Hope and Disillusion* (New York: St. Martin's Press, 1999), 22.

[3] Jackson states that the "Popular Front lacked a clear colonial policy." Julian Jackson, *The Popular Front in France Defending Democracy, 1934–38* (Cambridge: Cambridge University Press, 1988), 154. See also, Chafer and Sackur, *French Colonial Empire and the Popular Front*; Cohen, "The colonial policy of the Popular Front," 368–94. Cohen remarks that though all three parties that made up the Popular Front were associated with reformism, none was "unconditionally anticolonial." Rather, they accepted the colonies and focused on reform to assure the strength of France's international position.

[4] Nicole Bernard-Duquenet, "Le Front populaire et le problème des prestations en AOF," *Cahiers d'etudes africaines*, 16 (1976), 159.

priority for the Popular Front, and even committed socialists pushed colonial labor issues to the side in favor of the more pressing concerns over
combating fascism at home and, above all, maintaining France's international standing. People of all political viewpoints considered it essential that
France remain politically and economically strong. Instead of moving away
from economic exploitation of the colonies, there was a felt need for the
colonies to provide even more support to France in the form of taxes, natural resources, cash crops, and public works.[5] Thus, while there was increased
sympathy for the workers, a continued desire to benefit from reliable, cheap
labor kept the *deuxième portion* alive even as it continued to be unfavorably
evaluated as a labor system. The demands for manpower and the pressure
to make the colonies economically profitable were incompatible with ending
the *deuxième portion* or even drastically revamping it.

Within the colonies, there was a limit to the extent to which even the most
liberal administrators were willing to reform the *deuxième portion*.[6] Forced
labor remained warranted under particular circumstances. De Coppet, for
example, thought that forced labor was admissible if the men were fed
and paid in an appropriate manner. He stated that "forced labor does not
shock me except when it is gratis, otherwise it is a social necessity imposed
by human solidarity."[7] The colonial government continued to wrap forced
labor in layers of justifications and exceptions. For example, an August 1937
decree again excluded forced or obligatory labor, except in the name of taxes.
Some reforms did go into effect. In 1938, the annual report on *deuxième
portion* labor stated that the employing services observed the regulations
pertaining to this group of workers "in a more satisfactory manner than [in]
previous years and the workers' condition was very noticeably improved."
Changes noted in the report included small, but symbolic, measures such as
the workers finally getting khaki-colored clothing instead of the blue outfits
they disliked and receiving more utensils for eating. Workers despised the
blue uniforms that were reminiscent of prisoners' outfits; they preferred
the khaki outfits that were more evocative of what regular soldiers wore.
Concerning the khaki-colored uniforms, the report noted that the "men were
particularly happy with this last measure, having seen the blue uniforms as
degrading due to the fact of their resemblance to the standard uniform of
prisoners."[8] In addition, administrators made some effort to reduce the

---

[5] Jackson, *The Popular Front*, 154–58; Cohen, "Colonial policy of the Popular Front," 375.

[6] De Coppet made a concerted effort to end *prestations*, but repeatedly came up against European planters and administrators who depended on this form of labor. Bernard-Duquenet
concludes that despite its short tenure and constant resistance, the Popular Front government
brought about a clear improvement in how *prestations* were carried out. These changes,
however, did not endure beyond de Coppet's removal from office in October 1938, following the railroad workers' strike and the fall of the Popular Front government in France.
Bernard-Duquenet, "Le Front populaire," 160, 168–69.

[7] Quoted in Bernard-Duquenet, "Le Front populaire," 164.

[8] Annual Report on 2ème portion 1938, K/47, ANS, Dakar.

numbers of men recruited; however, every time they conscripted a small class of *deuxième portion* workers, they ended up recruiting a much larger class the following year.[9]

Close attention to the *deuxième portion* also provoked a renewed debate about the merits of its existence. For the first time since the 1920s, the colonial government seriously questioned the value of the *deuxième portion*. Ultimately, other priorities ensured the continuance of the *deuxième portion*, despite general acknowledgement that it was neither an economic nor an efficient source of labor. Yet even while the merits of the *deuxième portion* were debated, the constant necessity of finding enough cheap labor, combined with the ambiguity of the *deuxième portion*'s military status, made it difficult to relinquish the annual supply of labor this service provided. Over the course of the 1930s, a constant and reliable source of labor for the most difficult work proved repeatedly to be too valuable to give up. The fall of the Popular Front in 1938 brought an end to this period of open discussion, and when de Coppet and Rougier were removed from their posts after the fall of the Popular Front, the enthusiasm for reform was abruptly curtailed.[10] Thus on the eve of the Second World War, the downfall of the Popular Front and crises in metropolitan France allowed a return to harsh labor practices in the colonies. The Service de la Main d'Œuvre continued to do its work, but without the influence that it had had during the Popular Front administration. Indecision about colonial labor practices remained. During the war, not only did the colonial administration put the effort to improve labor conditions on hold, they also gave employers free reign to use increased coercion. This was particularly true during the brief, but significant, Vichy period.[11]

Vichy Labor Policies

The German occupation of France in 1940 had an immediate and direct impact on Africans who were conscripted both into the colonial army and into the *deuxième portion*. From 1940 to 1942, French West African administrators gave their support to the Vichy government, and, accordingly, stopped sending contingents of Tirailleurs Sénégalais to help fight against the Germans. Vichy rule did not, however, lighten the burden placed upon young West African men. To the contrary, administrators abandoned the modest social reforms made during the Popular Front period and were more willing to rely on coercive labor strategies. Any effective discussion of ending

---

[9] There were unusually small numbers of *deuxième portion* workers conscripted; e.g., 700 in 1933, 600 in 1935, and 1,000 in 1937. However, each of these years was followed by a year of much higher recruitment: 3,100 men in 1934; 3,000 in 1936, and 2,975 men in 1938. Annual Report on 2ème portion 1938, K/47, ANS, Dakar.

[10] Bernard-Duquenet, "Le Front populaire," 169; Chafer and Sackur, *French Colonial Empire*, 12.

[11] Chafer and Sackur, *French Colonial Empire*, 3.

the *deuxième portion* did not occur again until after the end of the Second World War.

Even outside the context of colonial labor needs, Vichy administrators were more inclined to consider work as an obligation. The Vichy government expressed a corporatist philosophy for all its citizens and subjects: Every man had a duty to contribute to the whole, however he was best suited. All men were obligated to work, but in return should be "guaranteed decent wages, working conditions, and a family life at the place of work." In 1942, a French law imposed the *obligation du travail* that required all French men between the ages of 16 and 40 to work. Those who could not prove that they had a valid occupation were to be employed in public works. If compulsion was acceptable for French men, then it was equally so for African men: African men who were not employed in recognizable jobs were not fulfilling their duty. Yet, as Cooper states, in Africa "people had other ways to live than what Vivier du Streel considered to be work: '*obligation au travail*' was in practice nothing but forced labor."[12]

For the *deuxième portion*, this translated into unprecedented levels of recruitment. Before 1940, recruitment for this labor force had averaged 1,900 men per year, but during the Vichy period, this recruitment jumped dramatically. Between 1941 and 1943, every year the *deuxième portion* recruitment averaged 6,000 men a year, peaking at 8,000 men sent to the Office du Niger in 1943.[13] In the last years of the war, recruitment fell again; in 1944 there were 3,604 *deuxième portion* recruits.[14] Thus while there was a ban on further recruitment for the Tirailleurs Sénégalais, those in the *deuxième portion* felt the burden of Vichy's increased reliance on forced labor. This surge in recruitment forced many more men to participate in this labor service and ultimately led to a more organized and articulate critique of the service.

The impact of Vichy rule was more apparent at the Office du Niger than at the Dakar-Niger railroad worksites. Among the strong supporters of the Vichy government was a man named Emile Bélime for whom the Office du Niger had begun essentially as a pet project. Over the years, he had been lukewarm about *deuxième portion* workers. While he relished the labor they provided, he resented fiercely any interference of the colonial administration into a domain he considered to be his own and which he felt should not be subject to the scrutiny of colonial inspectors. The Popular Front years, with their numerous labor reforms, had been particularly difficult for Bélime, who regularly challenged and protested the authority of inspectors who came from Bamako. During those years, he had often asserted that he could

---

[12] Frederick Cooper, *Decolonization and African Society: The Labor Question in French and British Africa* (Cambridge: Cambridge University Press, 1996), 142, 145.

[13] See annual reports on 2ème portion workers, Series K, ANS, Dakar.

[14] Ibid., and annual labor reports, Series G, ANS, Dakar.

do very well without the thousands of *deuxième portion* men who arrived at the Office du Niger each year.

When Vichy rule loosened the restrictions on using forced labor, Bélime happily accepted double and triple the amount of *deuxième portion* labor. When French West African administrators switched their loyalty away from the Vichy government, there was a renewed effort at improving colonial conditions, but few, if any, of these efforts were aimed at reforming the *deuxième portion*. One significant side effect of the political shift was its impact on the Office du Niger. Bélime's support for Vichy rule had been so outspoken that it brought about the end to his two-decade-long career in the French Soudan. When French West African administrators withdrew their support from the Vichy government, his influence shrunk dramatically and he returned to France in 1943. The Vichy period had allowed Bélime to conduct business with virtually no restraints, but this ultimately led to his downfall.

The Dakar-Niger railroad never had a single director as powerful and opinionated as Emile Bélime. Nor was it ever as rigid an environment to work in. Unlike the strictly controlled state-within-a-state atmosphere of the Office du Niger, the Dakar-Niger railroad was, by its very nature, an environment through which a large number and variety of people passed. *Deuxième portion* workers assigned to the railroad were constantly exposed to soldiers, merchants, and other travelers. Ideas and external influences flowed more readily along the railroad than at the Office du Niger. Thus, while the Dakar-Niger railroad continued to use *deuxième portion* labor during the Vichy period, the change was not quite as dramatic.

At both the Office du Niger and the Dakar-Niger railway, the Inspection du Travail and the Service de la Main d'Œuvre continued to supervise and inspect *deuxième portion* worksites and camps, but the commitment to carry out significant reforms was no longer there. The director of the Service de la Main d'Œuvre assigned to the Office du Niger was described as "old and rather tired, not fulfilling his role." He was hesitant to trouble the Office du Niger administrators, who were primarily concerned with output and for whom "anything that is not work does not count, and especially the normal well-being [of the workers] to which, however, the men in the *deuxième portion* have the right."[15] This generation of inspectors was unlikely to rein in the demands of a man like Emile Bélime or to create much trouble about abusive supervisors. Inspection reports from the Vichy period and just after reveal that conditions had not improved a great deal; if anything, the camps, many of which by then were at least ten years old, were in even worse shape. Visiting camps and worksites at the Office du Niger in 1943, an inspector reported numerous faults in the condition of the workers' houses, the state of their clothing, and their sanitary facilities. The ratio of supervisors to

[15] Rapport annuel sur le Travail, 1943, 2G43-24, ANS, Dakar.

workers was at an all time low: There were only ten French supervisors and 167 African supervisors for more than 12,000 *deuxième portion* workers. In some of the larger camps there had been epidemics of dysentery and other diseases, resulting in unusually high death rates at these camps.[16] Unwilling to recruit fewer men and unable to attract enough supervisors, the Office du Niger was at an impasse in terms of improving the situation for the *deuxième portion* workers.

As more and more men joined the *deuxième portion* service during the war years, they became ever more aware of the sharp differences between their work conditions and lack of benefits when compared with the rewards for the more honorable and prestigious work of soldiers. At the beginning of World War II, administrators were already complaining that men preferred to volunteer for the army to avoid possible recruitment into the *deuxième portion*.[17] Whatever dangers soldiers might face, theirs was a more highly regarded status than that of the *deuxième portion* men. Soldiers had more dignity and earned better wages. By the end of the war, *deuxième portion* workers earned only a third of what soldiers earned (even soldiers not stationed abroad), despite earlier declarations that they would get the same pay.[18] In addition, soldiers had access to better resources.[19] After their service, soldiers also had better connections for future opportunities. Increasingly frustrated by the discrepancy between the *deuxième portion* and the regular army, workers often attempted to desert.

Desertion had always been a key way in which *deuxième portion* workers resisted their recruitment, but during the war men began deserting in new ways. Instead of escaping the camps and then hiding out in rural areas, trying to cross the colonial border, or attempting to go home, numerous men fled their work camps and attempted to enlist in the regular army. Several groups of men who left the work camps found their way to the central military training base in Kati, about 250 kilometers away from the Office du Niger, and even farther away from many of the railroad worksites. Once there, they argued that if they had been recruited for military service,

---

[16] Inspection du Travail to the directeur général de l'Office du Niger, August 13, 1943; Gouverneur Soudan Français to Gouverneur-général, report of the inspection du travail au sujet des conditions d'existence de la main d'œuvre employé par l'Office du Niger, October 13, 1943, FN 3N1433, Archives Nationales du Mali (hereafter ANM), Bamako. See also Rapport annuel sur le Travail, 1943. 2G43–24, ANS, Dakar.

[17] Letter, 2/5/39, Bafoulabé. FRS 109, ANM, Bamako.

[18] Letter from GSF to DG ON, Director DN, other services, 23/1/46, FN S2745, ANM, Bamako.

[19] Workers were keenly aware of the shortage of supplies. Men recruited in Ouahigouya in the fall of 1944 had to make the journey to Markala without any blankets or mats. By the time the recruits arrived in Markala, 21 of the original 196 men had fallen sick, mostly due to pneumonia or other respiratory diseases. Such incidents were more common than not. Note from Contrôleur Regional de la Main d'Œuvre à Markala to Chef du Service de la Main d'Œuvre du Soudan, Markala, 2/1/45, FN 4D3111, ANM, Bamako.

they should have the option to complete this service as regular soldiers and not as *deuxième portion*. French officials consistently rebuffed such efforts. In April 1943, a group of five men who left their *deuxième portion* camps at the Office du Niger and traveled to Kati were promptly escorted back; this response awaited anyone else who made a similar attempt.[20] Despite the fact that this never succeeded as a strategy, workers continued to attempt desertion and/or enlistment in the army throughout, and even after, the war. In doing so, they forced administrators to address the theoretically military status of the *deuxième portion*.

For their part, *deuxième portion* workers had always considered their service to be a form of forced labor and had always found ways to contest and challenge it. Nevertheless, three factors during the Vichy period further focused and strengthened the workers' resistance: First, the vast increase in recruitment levels meant that many more people were drawn into the *deuxième portion* every year, and consequently, there were larger groups at the camps and worksites. Not only did this lead to overcrowding and a general degradation of conditions, but it also led to greater communication and awareness about labor conditions and other aspects of colonial life. Second, Vichy's approval of increased coercion exacerbated bad feelings in an already unhappy group of workers. Finally, while recruitment for the Tirailleurs Sénégalais was momentarily on hold, greater exposure to soldiers during the war years further emphasized the differences between the real army and the labor army. *Deuxième portion* workers were well aware that both were difficult services, but also that only one came with the possibility of adventure and honor.

After the War

With the end of World War II, returning African veterans and a new generation of African politicians increased the pressure against the colonial government for greater freedoms and rights; *deuxième portion* workers also continued their protests against their unique service. A renewed debate over the issue of forced labor emerged after the Brazzaville conference in 1944. There Charles de Gaulle declared that there would be changes in France's colonies in exchange for the colonies' support during the war. Without making any specific promises, he spoke of the necessity for all inhabitants of French colonies to participate "in their own country, in the management of their own affairs." He also spoke of France's responsibility to ensure that this came to pass, albeit within the context of remaining part of the French empire.[21] Participants in the Brazzaville conference pledged to give

---

[20] Report, 1/4/43, FN S2745, ANM, Bamako.
[21] Jean Suret-Canale, *French Colonialism in Tropical Africa, 1900–1945* (New York: Pica Press, 1971), 485.

African colonies direct representation in Paris and to work toward freedom of labor within five years. Following the conference, the African deputies who were elected to the National Assembly embraced the task of obtaining real changes from de Gaulle's vague promises. Unwilling to wait five years, they demanded an immediate end to forced labor.

In February 1946, several African deputies, including Félix Houphouët-Boigny, Lamine Guèye, Léopold Senghor, and Fily Dabo Sissoko, wrote a letter of complaint to Marius Moutet, who was once again the colonial minister. In their letter, they spoke against forced labor, using the word "slavery" and calling those who participated in this activity "traitors to France and her noble civilizing mission."[22] This kind of language, combining both references to slavery and to paternalism, would become common in the postwar years, not just in political documents, but from the workers as well. The deputies' efforts were successful. The *indigénat* and *prestations*, two of the most reviled aspects of colonial rule, ended with the passage of two key laws on April 11 and May 7. The April 11 law, named after Félix Houphouët-Boigny, made any form of forced labor, including *prestations* and other labor taxes, illegal in all of the French African colonies.[23] The May 7 law, named after the Senegalese politician Lamine Guèye, abolished the *indigénat*, the system of customary law in French African colonies that had allowed for arbitrary arrest, labor taxes, and other burdens on colonial subjects. The two laws should have made the *deuxième portion* obsolete, but they did not. While the French government was willing to entertain the idea of a complete and immediate abolition of forced labor, the plan to end forced labor excluded, as other debates had in the past, the *deuxième portion*. Yet the deputies had demanded the abolition of all forms of forced labor. They expected the *deuxième portion* to be eliminated, along with *prestations, corvées*, and other forms of coerced and requisitioned labor. Africans throughout FWA rejoiced with the passage of the Houphouët-Boigny law; everyone imagined that it was a definitive end to forced labor. Instead, as before, the *deuxième portion* was categorized as equivalent to military service, and thus an exception, although this was not immediately clear either to those who had campaigned for the law or to those who worked in the *deuxième portion*. Meanwhile, the Office du Niger and several departments of the railway administration still depended heavily on *deuxième portion* labor. In his annual report for 1946, Governor Louveau commented briefly on the impact of the suppression of requisitions. He complained that the African population had not stepped in to volunteer and that they confused

---

[22] The other deputies who signed the letter were Felix Tchicaya, Tacine Diallo, and Sourou Migan Apithy. Cooper, *Decolonization*, 187.

[23] Houphouët-Boigny was a successful coffee and cocoa planter and the president of the Syndicat agricole africain, a planters' association that promoted the interests of African planters. He was also the deputy of the Ivory Coast to the French government.

the "liberty of work with the option to never work again at all, especially for the Administration."[24] Faced with the reality of expensive labor costs and a possible labor shortage, the French administrators declared the *deuxième portion* outside the provisions of the Houphouët-Boigny law.

The first year after the end of the war, 6,084 men actively served in the *deuxième portion* in the Soudan. Half of them worked in some capacity for the Office du Niger, as had always been the case. The other half were spread among the Service Spéciale des Travaux Neufs (SST–DN) and the Société des Dragages in Toukoto and Kita; the MerNiger road project in Gao; cutting wood in the Eaux and Forêt Department in southern French Soudan; and on a bridge-building project in Bougouni.[25] In 1947, more men were recruited into the *deuxième portion*, and those who had not yet completed their service were expected to fulfill their two-year duty. Also during this period, men were recruited in and assigned to new posts in Guinea, Senegal, and Mauritania. With forced labor no longer an option, even in its most disguised forms, the government-approved *deuxième portion* was the only guaranteed labor resource left for numerous public works projects. Of course, there was always the option to pay workers a high enough wage to attract them voluntarily, but the services that relied on *deuxième portion* workers were, as always, faced with a limited budget, undesirable back-breaking work, or in remote and unpleasant locations.

As civilians gained new rights and returning soldiers became increasingly politically active, the young men in the *deuxième portion* must have wondered anew why they were excluded from these changes. In the aftermath of the war, *deuxième portion* workers could not help but be reminded of the stark differences between themselves and the soldiers. Workers began to ask, more bluntly than ever before, whether they were soldiers and if they too were entitled to the benefits of citizenship. Laborers began to demand better treatment, and, at the very least, equality with regular soldiers. Some of the most dramatic protests occurred at several railroad sites, including those near Toukoto and Kita.[26]

A year before the renowned French West African railroad strike of 1947–1948, *deuxième portion* workers assigned to the railroad had already lodged their own complaints against the railroad administration through a number

---

[24] Governor Louveau, Rapport politique annuel, 1946, 2G46–21, ANS, Dakar.

[25] Ibid. The SST was the central administrative body employing *deuxième portion* workers at the railway sites, but they were not the only administrative body. Several different government and private societies combined managed the railway operations, maintenance, and new construction. In addition to the SST, *deuxième portion* workers also worked for the *Service de la Voie* (Tracks Service) and the *Service des Dragages* (Dredging Service).

[26] While the Office du Niger depended on *deuxième portion* labor more heavily than the Dakar-Niger railroad, the Office du Niger was a much more restrictive environment. Even after Bélime's departure, there were fewer dramatic protests at the Office du Niger; however, individual resistance was significant.

of acts of sabotage and disruptive behavior on trains. One of their demands was that they be given the same rights as regular soldiers to ride for free on the trains. Through their actions, the *deuxième portion* workers forced the colonial government to turn its attention to their situation. Their protests drew the notice not only of colonial officials but also of African politicians. In June 1946, a group of *deuxième portion* workers assigned to the Service des Dragages sent a four-page letter to the commandant of Kita, which deserves lengthy analysis.[27] They opened their letter with a question: "Are we soldiers or not? If yes, then we must not in any way be [responsible] to you." The authors complained of the torture, suffering, and degradation that they had experienced while fulfilling their military obligations:

> Believing that never having been more closely in the French union, being French in spirit, in body and in soul, we were astonished to see the following irregularities. Recruited to satisfy our military obligations we were abandoned to works that one would spare even for a convict.

At the end of the letter, the workers posed the same question with which they had begun: "Are we soldiers or not?" They asked either to be incorporated into the army or liberated, for "if it is to serve under the folds of the union flag, [they were] all volunteers," but they could no longer perform any more forced labor. The workers sent this letter to the commandant in early June. The authors of the Kita letter were well aware of the new laws abolishing forced labor and ending the *indigénat* and cited these laws in their letter. What the workers in the Kita district had come to realize in June 1946 was that the new laws granting the rights of French citizenship and abolishing forced labor did not seem to apply to them. In response, the workers intended to claim these rights by corresponding directly with the local representative of the French government. In this striking letter, the authors bring together the issues of civic duty, citizenship, and mutual obligation and contrast them with slavery, coercion, and neglect. Thus, in the aftermath of World War II, as men and women throughout FWA began to demand and to receive more rights and privileges, *deuxième portion* workers refused to be left behind. After 1946, *deuxième portion* workers negotiated their place in a significantly changed environment. Not only had forced labor been abolished, but workers outside of the *deuxième portion* were also beginning to join labor unions and lead strikes against the disparities in the salaries and benefits enjoyed by African and European workers. As workers throughout FWA became increasingly organized in the aftermath of World War II and as African politicians succeeded in obtaining judicial changes to the status of Africans, the continued existence of the *deuxième portion* became ever more unjustifiable in the colonial state.

[27] "2me portions mis à la disposition des Dragages," letter to the commandante de cercle, Kita, certified copy dated June 11, 1946, K/360, ANS, Dakar.

After their opening question, "Are we soldiers or not?," the workers explained their conditions to the commandant who, they offered, might not be fully aware of the situation at hand. Reiterating the often-voiced complaints of bad food, overwork, and lack of appropriate clothing, the authors of the letter make strong emotional declaration to the commandant:

> And for all these atrocities all we have for food is millet boiled in water and sometimes rice and for all clothing as you have seen, Mr. Administrator, a single cotton blouse and shorts completely in rags.... Thus, ignoring what we have done to suffer to such an oppression we resign ourselves to being under the crushing baskets, the overpowering sun.

But the comments go beyond emotion; the workers also cited the recent change in French colonial law. Their letter continues, "All this Mr. Administrator is to show you that we are slaves, while we should be enjoying [the benefits of] the law of May 7 like any other French person of the union." Though it was the April 11 law that abolished forced labor, the authors here base their claim to better treatment on the May 7 law that granted French citizenship to all people in the French union. This reference to the May 7 law was not accidental. Later the authors refer to the April 11 law, demonstrating full awareness of its purpose. Through this comment, in which slavery and neglect are juxtaposed against the rights of citizens, the authors demonstrate a subtle appreciation of the various legal changes taking place in FWA. By suggesting that the commandant of Kita might not be fully aware of the situation at hand, the workers leave him the chance to demonstrate his capacity to act as a protector.

Even as they emphasize their legal rights as citizens, the workers also demand that administrators recognize their moral obligations. Throughout the letter the authors insist that the government representatives have neglected the nation's children. This paternal disregard is put forth as more problematic than the material concerns of food, clothing, and overwork. In one place, the authors present the example of a mother forced to ignore her child while at work:

> One fact even more heart-wrenching: the chief of the Dragages Mr. Jean Purrey had told the wife of a deuxième portion Dembele Deni, spouse of mle. 1077, to go and keep her kid calmly in the hut and to work without concern in the kitchen, because the little one would die between now and tomorrow and this response: all simply because the nurse Robert Drabo begged the purchase of milk for the baby, the mother not possessing a drop (witness Mariko Tiefing and Robert). And we permit ourselves to say not only he has forgotten to put himself in the place of the parents, out of contempt, but further he is not concerned about the representation of France in the union.

The authors of this letter explicitly position themselves as citizens and not as subjects when they cite the May 7 law, but they also point to the paternal duties of the colonial government toward their African workers.

After evoking the image of a desperate mother doing anything possible to save the life of her starving child, they contrast her maternal care with the administrator's lack of paternalism. Moreover, by using the image of a mother forced to abandon her child, the authors direct attention to the fact that the *deuxième portion* was an institution that affected a wider circle of people than just the young men laboring at the worksite. Workers were not isolated individuals, but fathers, sons, and brothers. In just four pages, the issue of an employer's social responsibility appears repeatedly. Earlier in the letter, the authors had evoked slavery, also in conjunction with the blatant neglect by the head of Dragages of his paternalistic duties. The authors accuse him of telling them repeatedly of their servile condition:

> have you forgotten that you were bought by the Société des Dragages (witness Sekou who posed the question to which he refused to respond. That you all die too bad for the thousands of blacks who would come to replace you the next day – witness Sory – Sekou and Boubakar).

Not only in life and work, but also in death, Dragages was negligent. The men who had died at Dragages were wrapped up in their woolen garments because the camp chiefs "always repeat that they cannot find the cloth for the shrouds" and at Dragages, they "bury [the dead] like dogs." Yet again this letter stakes a claim for the social duties that have been neglected.

Deliberately drawing on notions of their own duty to the French union and France's obligation to its citizens, the men who authored this letter present a compelling situation that its audience could not easily ignore. They also put forth the problem of civil versus military systems of discipline and justice; they ask the question, if they are soldiers, for what reason are they subject to the judgment of the native courts of Kita. To emphasize their point, they mention a coworker who had recently been sentenced to six months by the Kita court (they do not mention the reason for this coworker's punishment). At the end of the long letter, the workers restated the question that they had asked at the beginning:

> Are we soldiers or not? You said "you are free deuxième portions." Thus we all ask to be incorporated in the infantry or to be liberated; because if it is to serve under the folds of the union's flag, we would all volunteer. But we do not want any longer to do forced labor.... In a word, Mr. Administrator we ask you simply to be liberated or to be incorporated in the true army of the French union.

The letter is a remarkable piece of testimony; it illustrates that its authors were well aware of the ambiguity of their legal status and that they were also able to carefully manipulate the rhetoric of free labor, slavery, citizenship, civic duty, and the responsibility of a paternalistic nation to its citizens.

A few shorter letters accompanied this four-page letter from the workers to the Commandant of Kita. In one of these letters, the language echoes that of the longer letter: The authors claim that they thought they were "accomplishing their military obligation" and "complied as it is the duty of each French man." Nevertheless, they had come to the realization that they were in the employment of a private service and that they were subject to the judgment of a civil court, among other things. Having concluded that they were no more than forced laborers, they had decided to complete their military service as "all French of the Union" and no longer remain as forced laborers.[28] These men clearly distinguished between the obligation to work for little pay and no status and the obligation to join the army. All these letters, in combination with a series of disruptive actions by *deuxième portion* workers, brought the *deuxième portion* workers to the attention of government officials.

These letters provoked a series of responses from the Bamako-based administration, including several visits to worksites and efforts to root out suspected leaders of the various protests. General Rocafort, a military commander, was one of the officials who visited the Toukoto camps in July. After his visit he described a calmer, improved situation, with the men in the *deuxième portion* placated by better management and materials. Having spoken with those he described as *evolués*, and who he deemed to have led the strike, Rocafort reported that they declared:

> We grant [that there should be] military service and even work service for the works of national interest, but we do not wish, under pretense of recruitment, to be surrendered to private enterprises that seek money, exploit us and where, most of the time, we are mistreated as in the Coastal plantations.
>
> We wish to be soldiers with the same rules and the same rights as the 1st Portion. We have confidence in your Officers and in your non-commissioned officers but the current solution cannot be anything but transitory.
>
> All this is sufficiently justified.[29]

Rocafort's opinion of the *deuxième portion* was like that of so many of his colleagues; it was fundamentally a perfectly good organization, if only it could be well managed. As it was, he conceded, the reality sometimes approached "a sort of state slavery" that had a "disastrous" impact on morale.[30] Still, with more military supervision and training, the *deuxième portion* could become an effective institution. Rocafort's report focused on the few literate members of the *deuxième portion* whom he suspected were leading otherwise unproblematic workers into these protests. Yet at the end of his report in which he detailed the improvements in the Dragages' camps, he added a note about an incident about 250 woodcutters for the Eaux and Forêts Service who had just boarded a train headed for Kati, declaring their

[28] Ibid.
[29] Report no. 3/168/S of Gen. Rocafort, commandante de la 3ème Brigade, July 19, 1946, K/360, ANS, Dakar.
[30] Ibid.

wish to be soldiers. All the workers were returned to the Eaux and Forêts worksites. Despite Rocafort's and other administrators' complaints about educated workers, the kind of incident Rocafort notes at the end of his report was as common and as important as any letters the literate workers could write.

Events at Toukoto drew the attention not only of colonial officials, but also of African politicians. Among the important people who visited Toukoto was Fily Dabo Sissoko, one of the newly appointed African deputies to the French National Assembly. He went to Toukoto in January 1947, after which he sent a scathing telegram to multiple bureaus of the government general in Dakar. In the telegram, Sissoko reported that he had observed workers who were "completely destitute, physiologically deficient, and sick because of insufficient medical care" and that in response to his concerns, the director responsible for the workers replied with "specious reasoning proving his casual attitude" regarding the workers.[31] During his visit, Sissoko echoed the sentiments of the workers themselves, chiding the project director and reminding him that "besides rules there was humanity" to consider. In the conditions in which the men were working, they suffered "from feelings of shame and inferiority."[32] The director responded in his report that the project administration had its own disappointments, considering that "if it had obligations vis-à-vis its *deuxième portion* workers, the latter also had one [an obligation], and this primordial, to furnish a minimum of work." Arguing that Sissoko was asking that the worksites become "philanthropic organizations" or "rest centers," he accused the deputy of not knowing what he was seeing and of breezing through the camps as a political statement.[33] Indeed, Sissoko's visit was short and politically motivated, occurring in the wake of the workers' protests; nevertheless, his visit heightened attention to the workers' situation and sparked the involvement of the high commissioner in Dakar and the colonial minister in Paris.

Events at *deuxième portion* camps and worksites all along the railroad got worse before they got better. Regularly workers refused their pay and deserted en masse and forcibly boarded trains without authorization. In November 1947, the chief of police for the Dakar-Niger wrote a letter to the director of the Sûreté Général stating that he had become aware that "the *deuxième portion* workers do not take into consideration at all the regulations in effect and that they continue to travel in the trains, without paying." He added that he personally had stopped a group of about twenty

---

[31] Telegram from Fily Dabo Sissoko to Haussaire, Dakar, January 3, 1947, K/360, ANS, Dakar.

[32] Cited in letter from directeur, Société de Dragages to directeur du reseau du Dakar-Niger, January 8, 1947, K/360, ANS, Dakar.

[33] Ibid.

workers heading to Bamako, but he needed the help of two policeman to enforce his order. The workers refused to pay, he reported, "on the pretext that 'since the Government makes them work they had the right to travel without paying.' They took up the attack underway, I ascertained that it was the same in all of the stations as far as Kita."[34] According to the chief of police, the workers involved in these incidents were numerous, threatening, and "ready to provoke incidents, serious if necessary, if there is any opposition to their acts." Such a situation required an armed response, the chief added, concluding, "on all the line it is a question of nothing but these workers who make their own law everywhere they are found."[35]

Bertrand believed that at least one of the incidents at Toukoto was provoked by a group of fifteen new workers from Koulikoro district, all of whom had been soldiers who were reassigned to the *deuxième portion* as part of a "disciplinary measure." Considering the consistent evidence of animosity between soldiers and *deuxième portion* workers, one can only imagine the internal dynamics and tensions in a camp with a group of such "punished" workers. One of the benefits granted to African soldiers was free transportation on the railway; wage-laborers working for the Dakar-Niger/Thiès-Niger also had certain train privileges. Men who had been used to this privilege as soldiers, but who had been demoted to the *deuxième portion*, would have quickly learned that *deuxième portion* workers did not enjoy free rail passage. Workers at the Dragages and SST–DN worksites were clearly asserting their equality with the First Portion soldiers, and when that could not be obtained, claimed benefits equivalent to those the soldiers enjoyed.

As workers throughout FWA became increasingly organized in the aftermath of World War II and as African politicians succeeded in obtaining judicial changes to the status of Africans, the continued existence of the *deuxième portion* presented an ever more unjustifiable position for colonial administrators. The experience of these workers during and after the war pushed them to become more assertive and articulate in their demands. They insisted on the rights of citizens and incorporated a language of obligation into their complaints that drew upon both local and French ideas about slavery, duty, service, and an individual's role within the state.

Conclusion

Despite the efforts of such workers as those who wrote the Kita letter, and despite the enactment of the Houphouët-Boigny law, the *deuxième portion* continued to exist. New men were recruited into the service despite the

---

[34] Letter no. 2.257/PS from chef de la police spéciale du Dakar Niger (Divay) to directeur de la Sûreté Générale au Dakar, November 25, 1946, K/360, ANS, Dakar.
[35] Ibid.

fact that it had been one of the institutions the men who designed that law had hoped to attack. It took four more years after the passing of the Houphouët-Boigny law before the release of the last men working for the *deuxième portion*. These years were filled with a continuous debate on the nature of the *deuxième portion* workers, whether or not they were, in fact, affected by the April 11 law, and on how to cope with the potential shift in the labor situation in FWA. West African politicians, particularly those from the French Soudan, campaigned vigorously against the maintenance of the *deuxième portion*, while French colonial administrators fretted over the potential loss of a regular supply of laborers. African and French politicians alike debated the possibility of transforming the *deuxième portion* into something approaching a corps of military engineers. African *deuxième portion* workers asked, as they had in the past, to be made into true soldiers or to be let go. Yet with all of this debate, the end of the *deuxième portion* in 1950 came, as Echenberg and Filipovich have written, "with a whimper" and without contention.[36]

In their attempts to join a military unit or demand the right to free train travel, *deuxième portion* workers protested work that endangered their health and their dignity. Such protests are common from coerced workers in a colonial setting, and indeed, such protests abound in the history of the *deuxième portion*. Yet consistently, the *deuxième portion* workers articulated a critique of their condition that was more profound than a simple condemnation of being forced to work. Ultimately these workers insisted on the reform and/or the eradication of an unjust labor army and the larger system of the *indigénat* through combining the rhetoric of civic duty with the local rhetoric of patronage and mutual obligation. In so doing, these workers engaged in a dynamic exchange about the very meaning of work, duty, and citizenship. While some administrators and many workers had questioned the nature and the future of the *deuxième portion* more than a decade before it ended, it was the intensity of forced labor practices during World War II that pushed those questions to a point where they could no longer be ignored.

---

[36] Myron Echenberg and Jean Filipovich, "African military labour and the building of the Office du Niger installations, 1925–1950," *Journal of African History*, 27 (1986), 550.

7

No Country Fit for Heroes

The Plight of Disabled Kenyan Veterans

Timothy Parsons

In May 1942, former Private A. K. (G2722)[1] turned up on crutches outside the North Kavirondo district commissioner's office. Having lost his right leg serving with the Second (EA) Pioneer battalion earlier in the war, he rejected the simple peg leg offered by the Kenyan medical authorities and refused to budge until they gave him a more advanced mechanical leg and what the district commissioner termed a "great deal of money" as compensation for his sacrifice. The former *askari* (African soldier) was so convincing that he influenced two other similarly disabled ex-servicemen to refuse to be fitted for their peg legs. Kenya's director of medical services (DMS), however, dismissed Private A. K. summarily: "this man is a subversive type and a bad influence and quite undeserving of any sympathy from the [district commissioner] or other civil authorities."[2] Yet the disabled veteran's insubordination was hardly unprecedented. Three years later, Lance Corporal P. K. (KML 14589), who lost a leg to a land mine in the Middle East, similarly refused even to try on a peg leg and rejected appeals to take part in the government rehabilitation program with what the commander of the surgical division of the No. 1 (East Africa) General Hospital termed "mule-like stupidity."

From a broad historical perspective, the plight of Private A. K. and Lance Corporal P. K. was sadly typical of most men who suffered permanent physical or mental impairment as a result of military service. While governments often invest heavily in the means of waging war, most considered impaired former soldiers expendable and disposable. Even the best-intentioned states

---

[1] Initials and military service numbers (when available) protect the privacy of disabled Kenyan ex-servicemen.

[2] District commissioner North Kavirondo to chief secretary Kenya, May 10, 1942, MD 4/5/81/8; E. A. Sutton, director of medical services (DMS), report on G.2722 Andala Kutoyi, June 9, 1942, MD/4/5/81/12a, both in Kenya National Archives (hereafter KNA), Nairobi.

usually lacked the resources and political will to fulfill promises they made to the men who risked their lives in their service.

This was even true in the twentieth century. Indeed, Western governments considered the hundreds of thousands of Europeans and Americans who were disabled during the First World War potential subversives and kept them under close surveillance. These concerns reflected an almost universal fear that soldiers, disabled or otherwise, would not respect civil authority. While all the major powers instituted compensation and rehabilitation programs after the war, it took collective action in the form of unionization, political mobilization, and mass public protests such as the "bonus marches" of the early 1930s for western First World War veterans to win substantial rights and concessions.

Drawing on the collective experience of permanent injury suffered in national service, powerful ex-servicemen's lobbies in Great Britain and the United States ensured that the men who fought in the Second World War won substantially better benefits and services than earlier generations of veterans. Their governments acknowledged that citizen soldiers were entitled to full compensation for sacrifices for the nation-state. Consequently, the British Disabled Person's (Employment Act) of 1944 required that disabled persons had to constitute 3 percent of the workforce in companies employing more than twenty people. In the United States, the result was comprehensive medical care and the package of educational benefits known as the G. I. Bill. David Gerber makes the case that these successful demands for better treatment, vocational training, and compensation laid the groundwork for the modern welfare state.[3]

Conversely, Kenyan *askaris* who served in World War II were subjects of the British empire. Although the metropolitan Labour government promised that the end of the war would usher in a new progressive era in the African colonies, the Africans who fought for the empire were almost entirely missing from its ambitious development plans. According to paternalistic imperial rhetoric they were backwards "protected persons" not yet capable of assuming the responsibilities of citizenship in a western nation-state. Pretending that Africans were simple tribesmen allowed the Kenyan authorities to deny them the dignity and privileges that the metropolitan government accorded soldiers serving in the regular British forces. The Kenyan regime thus reconciled the inherent tyranny of imperial rule with Britain's commitment to democratic liberalism by upholding the collective rights of tribes rather than the human rights of individuals.

In practice, this meant that there was a fundamental tension between the British military strategists who recruited African soldiers in large numbers during the Second World War and the Kenyan civil authorities who sought

---

[3] David Gerber, "Disabled veterans, the state and the experience of disability in western societies, 1914–1950," *Journal of Social History*, 36 (2003), 899.

to ensure that mass mobilization did not undermine the tribal nature of colonial society or threaten the privileged position of the local settler community. More specifically, they wanted to make it clear that imperial military service would not be a path to full citizenship or equal rights in the Colony and Protectorate of Kenya. The Kenyan authorities therefore insisted that African veterans had to return to tribal societies and opposed any concession or privilege that might set them apart from men who had not served. To use the language of the time, they sought to "reabsorb" and "retribalize" Kenyan ex-servicemen.

These self-serving and churlish policies even applied to the men who suffered permanent impairment serving Great Britain and its empire. Although the Kenyan authorities drew up comprehensive plans to treat and demobilize injured askaris in the final years of World War II, they assumed that the ultimate cost of caring for impaired ex-servicemen would be borne by their larger tribal communities. They expected African women to take primary responsibility for mitigating the disabilities of their fellow "tribesmen." This was both their "natural" role in tribal society and a small price to pay for escaping the tyranny and oppression of an Axis victory in the Second World War.

It was small wonder that Private A. K. and Lance Corporal P. K. felt so aggrieved. The trauma of their life-changing injuries was compounded by the inherent injustice and hypocrisy of imperial rule. In the west, civil authorities granted disabled soldiers compensation based on standardized ratings schedules that compared their productivity with that of an imaginary healthy worker. These numerical tables determined the degree of impairment resulting from amputations, crippling injuries, chronic diseases, and mental disorders incurred during military service. For example, in post-WWI Great Britain the loss of a single leg below the knee brought a disability rating of 50 percent, while an above the knee amputation constituted a 60 percent disability.[4]

These ratings determined the amount and length of a man's pension. While they had the appearance of medical objectivity, in reality they represented the prevailing assumption of what it meant to be "normal" and "able bodied." In other words, disability is a form of identity that is "at once both biologically grounded and socially parsed, an umbrella term that denotes different things in different places and at different times."[5] Consequently, British and American veterans often challenged their disability ratings on the grounds that an assigned classification did not reflect that in western industrial society a "normal" man was the autonomous head of a

---

4 Edgar Jones, Ian Palmer, and Simon Wessley, "War pensions (1900–1945): Changing models of psychological understanding," *British Journal of Psychiatry*, 100 (2002), 375.
5 Julie Livingston, *Debility and the Moral Imagination in Botswana* (Bloomington: Indiana University Press, 2005), 7.

household and primary wage earner responsible for supporting a wife and family.[6]

The Kenyan government based its disability ratings system on the tables for metropolitan British troops, but it had an entirely different conception of what it meant to be "able" in tribal society. Where a legless veteran might need considerable support and assistance to support himself and his family in more advanced western economies, a similarly disabled African theoretically could draw on the labor of his female relatives and fellow tribesmen. Therefore there was no need for Private A. K. and Lance Corporal P. K. to receive the expensive and harder to maintain mechanical legs because they would not have to do more than supervise their male juniors and female relatives. According to official Kenyan thinking, a peg leg was sufficient for the average tribesmen. In the west, rehabilitation aimed to promote and facilitate autonomous individualism. The imperial Kenyan state made demobilization and reabsorption a token part of its postwar development program, but its implicit aim was to ensure that rehabilitation did not disrupt the fundamental fabric of tribal society.[7] In Kenya, as in other British African colonies, rehabilitation meant retribalization.

This stemmed from the reality of colonial military service. From the British standpoint, there was an essential distinction between the regular army and a colonial military unit. African regiments like the King's African Rifles (KAR) were not up to Western standards, but they allowed Britain to rule its African empire without drawing directly on metropolitan resources. Viewing African soldiers as cheap and expendable, colonial governments believed their only obligation to disabled "native" ex-servicemen in terms of rehabilitation and compensation was to provide the basic means to function as patriarchal household heads in subsistence rural societies.

These policies had tragic consequences in the First World War when the East and Central African colonies used coercive tactics to recruit 31,000 infantrymen for the KAR and conscripted 120,000 more as porters in the Carrier Corps. Serving primarily in the invasion and occupation of German East Africa, the KAR battalions lost almost 5,000 *askaris* to disease and combat, while at least 40,000 carriers perished from sickness, overwork, and malnutrition.[8]

---

[6] K. Walter Hickel, "Medicine, bureaucracy, and social welfare: The politics of disability compensation for the American veterans of World War I," in Paul Longmore and Laurie Umansky (eds.), *The New Disability History: American Perspectives* (New York: New York University Press, 2001), 252–53.

[7] Livingston, *Debility and the Moral Imagination in Botswana*, 203.

[8] Hubert Moyse-Bartlett, *The King's African Rifles* (Aldershot: Gale & Polden, 1956), 701; Geoffrey Hodges, *The Carrier Corps: Military Labor in the East African Campaign, 1914–1918* (Westport, CT: Greenwood Press, 1986), 110–11, 209; report by Lieutenant Colonel O. F. Watkins, director of military labour (Nairobi: n.p., n.d.).

There are no reliable figures as to how many men suffered permanent disability during World War I because the military and civil authorities did not keep accurate records. In December 1918, army medical officials calculated that they had approximately 1,400 sick and injured *askaris* in their care who could not be discharged until the army passed them medically fit to travel.[9] This figure was unrealistically low and definitely did not include the enormous numbers of carriers left permanently impaired by disease and mistreatment. Although Kenya maintained a "War Relief Fund," throughout most of the war, the government argued that there was no need to provide cash compensation to disabled African ex-servicemen because they did not need it and would waste it. In 1916, John Ainsworth, the colony's first chief native commissioner, baldly asserted that East African tribesmen did not need government pensions because: "They have a home and land to go to and a government war bonus may meet all that is necessary in their case."[10]

Despite Ainsworth's biased view, the Kenyan government had an obligation to compensate injured *askaris* under the terms of the 1908 KAR regulations. Carrying the weight of law, these regulations included disability ratings tables that awarded permanently disabled soldiers or "followers" who lost two limbs or both eyes a lump payment of twelve pounds and a pension equal to one-third of their pay. The army classified the loss of a single limb or eye as "permanent partial disablement," which brought a smaller gratuity and pension. The regulations made no provision for permanent impairment resulting from disease or combat related stress, but they did require the Kenyan authorities to pay compensation to disabled combat veterans.[11]

Yet, recordkeeping in the colonial forces was so bad, particularly in the Carrier Corps, that it was virtually impossible for many African ex-servicemen (or their heirs) to collect back pay or disability payments. The burden of proof was on the claimant, and civil officials argued that unclaimed monies owed to non-Christian carriers had to go to "the tribe as a whole" until the metropolitan British government overruled this as an illegal use of imperial funds.[12] Nevertheless, in the early 1930s, the Kenyan authorities still held more than £50,000 belonging to African veterans of the

[9] Lt. Col. Tilbury-Brown, assistant director of medical services, "Medical arrangements in connection with demobilization of KAR," December 24, 1918, PC/CST/1/13/118/886, KNA, Nairobi.

[10] Minute by John Ainsworth, January 8, 1916, PC/CST/1/11/68/2, KNA, Nairobi.

[11] Great Britain, Colonial Office, *Regulations for the King's African Rifles* (London: Waterlow and Sons, 1908); section 232; GRO no. 764, "Compensation," September 14, 1915, KNA, Nairobi; "Pensions and gratuities, native ranks, King's African Rifles, Nairobi," c1918, PC/CST/1/13/135/185, NSB/3/9/1, National Archives of Malawi (hereafter NAM), Zomba.

[12] The Military Labour Corps Distribution of Pay and Personal Property Ordinance, 1918, AG/5/1356, KNA, Nairobi.

First World War. After considerable bureaucratic debate, the government followed the Carter Land Commission's recommendation to use the windfall to purchase marginal land from white settlers to expand the "native reserves" where the imperial regime segregated the bulk of the African population. Apart from an Inspector General's Trust Fund that paid small pensions to just four "deserving" former KAR *askaris*, there was virtually no further official support for the thousands of disabled African ex-servicemen in interwar Kenya.[13]

By comparison, British veterans of the First World War were much better off. In 1916, the metropolitan government created a Ministry of Pensions to standardize and streamline military benefit payments. By 1921, the Treasury was paying a total of £105.7 million per year in pensions. The British government also guaranteed each of the 41,000 military amputees a free artificial limb made of the most advanced lightweight materials. Although parliament refused to require employers to hire disabled ex-servicemen, a voluntary program known as the King's National Roll Scheme found jobs for tens of thousands of them during the interwar era.[14]

Even the Kenyan government, which balked at caring for its own African soldiers, provided 25,000 acres for fifty-seven disabled metropolitan British officers to grow flax in the "white highlands." The Kipsigis community, which supplied large numbers of young men to the KAR, had to surrender some 4,000 acres of its reserve for this purpose. The members of the British East Africa Disabled Officers' Colony were supposedly men of the public school sort who would maintain their gentlemanly status by supervising African laborers.[15] Clearly, a physical impairment was no bar to exercising the perquisites of racial privilege in a colonial settler society.

To some degree, the metropolitan government's comparatively generous treatment of its disabled ex-servicemen reflected its concern that Bolshevik agents or other subversive elements might exploit their bitterness and discontent. Yet, the primary reason that British veterans of the First World War fared better than their Kenyan counterparts was that they were citizens of a liberal democracy. Consequently, they had the political means to demand better compensation for their sacrifices. The British Legion, the premier ex-servicemen's organization in the United Kingdom, emerged

---

[13] *Kenya Land Commission Report: Summary of Conclusions Reached by His Majesty's Government*, Command Paper 4580, WO 32/4129; and inspector general KAR to commanders of the northern and southern brigades, October 24, 1932, Colonial Office (hereafter CO)/820/16/12, The National Archives (hereafter TNA). Kew.

[14] Jones, Palmer, and Wessley, "War pensions," 376; Mary Guyatt, "Better legs: artificial limbs for British veterans of the First World War," *Journal of Design History*, 14 (2001), 311–12; Meaghan Kowalsky, "'This honourable obligation': The National Roll Scheme for Disabled Ex-Servicemen, 1915–1944," *European Review of History*, 14 (2007), 571, 575.

[15] C. J. D. Duder, "BEADOC – the British East Africa Disabled Officers' Colony and the white frontier in Kenya," *Agricultural History Review*, 40 (1992), 142–45.

from the war as a powerful advocate of veterans' interests. Additionally, influential politicians such as Sir Jack Benn Brunel-Cohen, himself a veteran and double amputee, championed their cause in Parliament.[16] In Kenya, there was no counterpart to the British Legion and the imperial regime refused to recognize groups such as the Kavirondo Taxpayers Association and the Kikuyu Central Association as legitimate political organizations. Therefore a petition by these bodies to spend the £50,000 in uncollected African military benefits on education, agricultural training, and healthcare fell on deaf ears in Nairobi and London.[17]

By the late 1930s, however, even the most ardent imperial partisans had to admit that the Kenyan government had done a disgracefully poor job of looking after the Africans who fought for the British empire in the last war. Pushed by the need to counter Nazi propaganda and make imperial rule more productive and rational, officials in the Colonial Office developed a new doctrine of modernization and trusteeship as a legitimizing ideology for the British empire. While the Kenyan authorities still preferred to govern the native reserves through chiefs and clung to the older tribal stereotypes, African experts and imperial propagandists in London now emphasized centralized planning and mutually beneficial development as the central feature of British rule.[18] This meant that the Kenyan government had to pay greater attention to African welfare.

When war broke out in 1939 the military authorities rushed to expand the KAR. Initially seeking to counter the Italian threat in Ethiopia, they steadily expanded the role of East Africa to serve as an imperial manpower reserve. Over the course of the Second World War, roughly 70,000 Kenyan Africans defended British interests in the Horn of Africa, the Middle East, Madagascar, Ceylon, India, and Burma. Consequently, there was no way that the Kenyan imperial regime would be able to discard these "protected persons" who answered the empire's call to arms voluntarily or under some form of compulsion.

Drawing on the lessons of World War I, the military planners of the East Africa Command (EAC) paid much greater attention to the welfare of African soldiers. As in the earlier conflict, the East African colonial governments once again conscripted men for support units such as the East

---

[16] Stephen R. Ward, "Intelligence surveillance of British ex-servicemen, 1918–1920," *The Historical Journal*, 16 (1973), 179–82; Seth Koven, "Remembering and dismemberment: Crippled children, wounded soldiers, and the Great War in Britain," *American Historical Review*, 99 (1994), 1202.

[17] Kavirondo Tax Payers Association and Kikuyu Central Association, memorandum to the Secretary of State for the Colonies on the Native Lands Ordinances, 1938, PC/NZA/3/1/398/201a, KNA, Nairobi.

[18] John Flint, "Planned decolonization and its failure in British Africa," *African Affairs*, 82, (1983), 398–401; R. D. Pearce, "The Colonial Office and planned decolonisation in Africa," *African Affairs*, 83 (1984), 77.

Africa Military Labour Service (EAMLS), but wartime propaganda claimed that service in the KAR and other combat formations was strictly voluntary. In reality, district commissioners, chiefs, and other imperial proxies still used coercive tactics to fill their manpower quotas, but medical officers made sure that only the hardiest recruits able to withstand the rigors of combat became frontline soldiers. Men destined for the KAR, the East Africa Artillery, and the East Africa Army Service Corps had to weigh 120 pounds, stand five feet three inches tall, and possess "normal" eyesight and hearing. It only took a weight of 112 pounds, a height of five feet, and a single good eye or ear to qualify for labor units such as the EAMLS and the African Auxiliary Pioneer Corps. In place of the *posho* (boiled corn meal) that was the staple food of First World War *askaris*, EAC regulations stipulated that African rations had to include daily servings of meat and a variety of starches amounting to at least 3,500 calories. Similarly, the Kenyans who served in combat units during World War II received roughly the same medical care as regular British troops.[19] Despite these reforms, colonial military service remained inherently inequitable and discriminatory. There were still no African officers, pay remained minimal by metropolitan standards, and settler-style racial segregation still shaped East African military culture. Indeed, a visiting metropolitan education expert noted that "any African [soldier] who spoke English to a white man was qualifying for a belting."[20]

The noxious taint of this "colour bar" also influenced the planning for the aftercare, demobilization, and reabsorption of disabled veterans. Beginning in 1942, discussions between the Kenyan government and the EAC covered physical rehabilitation, the provision of artificial limbs, vocational training, and limited disability pensions. Their plans were born of a sincere sense of paternal obligation, a desire not to repeat the politically embarrassing mistreatment of African soldiers and carriers after the First World War, inherent fiscal conservatism, and the Kenyan imperial regime's unwavering commitment to defending the color bar and chiefly rule in the native reserves. The postwar planners realized that in the era of the Atlantic Charter, which affirmed that the Allies waged a war against tyranny, failure to take proper care of subject African soldiers would result in a public scandal. Consequently, the Kenyan government acknowledged the need to ensure that the most "pitiful" cases did not "remain a burden, not only to their wives and families, but to themselves." Some officials in the metropolitan Colonial Office even envisioned that wartime measures to rehabilitate

---

[19] "Physical standards and medical examination of African recruits," July 8, 1942, DEF/15/12/1b; "1939 units on active service, daily rations," DEF/9/34/6; letter from medical research laboratory to DMS, April 5, 1939, BY/49/25/2, all in KNA, Nairobi.

[20] George (Lord) Wigg, *George Wigg* (London: Michael Joseph, 1972), 110–11.

disabled soldiers might be expanded to include civilian victims of industrial accidents.[21]

Predictably, civil and military authorities disagreed sharply over how to actually rehabilitate and compensate disabled African soldiers. Just as American Veterans Bureau officials and doctors in the segregated south worried that disability payments to African American veterans of the First World War would undermine the Jim Crow social order, Kenyan authorities and settler leaders strove to ensure that military benefits did not detribalize African ex-servicemen by giving them the resources to escape the bonds of chiefly authority and subsistence agriculture in the reserves.[22] E. M. Hyde-Clark, an African labor specialist in the colonial administration, emphasized that rehabilitation had to be geared towards life in the reserves because it "would be a pity to break down Tribal custom by which the Tribe accepts responsibility for their own indigent people."[23] Kenyan officials also sought to ensure that more worldly veterans did not challenge the authority of the elite elder men who were the imperial regime's primary allies in the countryside. Similarly, they opposed proposals to create an advanced rehabilitation center in Nairobi on the grounds that it was too expensive and that it would discourage discharged African soldiers from returning to the reserves.[24]

The EAC, which consisted largely of professional metropolitan officers, was entirely unconcerned with the messy intricacies of imperial rule in Kenya. Focused entirely on the economy and pragmatic needs of the war, the War Office and its representatives in East Africa wanted nothing more than access to tens of thousands of African recruits and expected them to return to civil authority for demobilization and rehabilitation (if necessary) when they were done with them. As the EAC's DMS put it: "when a man was no longer of any value to the Army he must be got rid of."[25]

The result was a fractious wartime debate over who would shoulder the primary financial burden of caring for disabled soldiers. Under the metropolitan British system, the civilian Ministry of Pensions provided surgical treatment and remedial training for members of the regular armed forces, but wartime policy made "coloured personnel" the responsibility of the War Office. However, while East African military hospitals tended to the immediate medical needs of injured *askaris*, the EAC maintained that it did not have the resources to offer long-term care or rehabilitation for the

---

[21] A. R. Paterson, memorandum on physical rehabilitation and training of African soldiers, DMS, June 17, 1941; A. G. H. Smart (CO), to Dr. W. Howard, January 8, 1942, CO/820/48/25, TNA, Kew.

[22] Hickel, "Medicine, bureaucracy, and social welfare," 256.

[23] Hyde-Clark to Nyasaland Labour Department, December 8, 1944, DEF 10/59/41, KNA, Nairobi.

[24] Chief secretary, East African Governors Conference to, CO, June 28, 1944, DEF/10/25/109a, KNA, Nairobi.

[25] "Repatriation and disabled askaris," September 27, 1943, DEF 10/25/4a, KNA, Nairobi.

permanently disabled.[26] Civil officials, in turn, insisted that the army was responsible for the costs of rehabilitation, including the supply, fitting, and maintenance of artificial limbs. Put another way, they insisted on the right to draft the demobilization and rehabilitation plans, but they wanted the EAC to pay for them.

Ultimately, civil and military officials agreed to cooperate in the care of disabled African soldiers. Theoretically, the No. 1 (East African) Military Hospital in Nairobi was the primary collection center for all soldiers requiring rehabilitative care. African army education instructors assigned to the hospital's convalescent wing provided patients with information on their treatment and occupational therapy options. When an *askari*'s condition stabilized to the point where he was able to care for himself, the medical authorities passed him on to the nearby Langata Discharge Centre for three to four months of outpatient treatment. These "medically boarded cases" then received their discharge on the assumption that they would proceed to civilian facilities for further rehabilitation.[27] The Kenyan government arranged to have the Salvation Army provide therapy for blinded veterans and directed its Central Employment Bureau to help disabled ex-servicemen find jobs and vocational training.[28]

The actual discharge and rehabilitation process never ran smoothly. Many *askaris* desperately wanted to return to their families and had little interest in remaining in the army to receive additional therapy. This was particularly true at the Langata base where a senior medical officer found conditions cramped and uncomfortable:

> My impression of the Centre was of a small area, enclosed in a wooden fence, containing about 12 long huts, closely spaced, with a door at each end, no windows, and a small open space between the top of the wall and the roof.... The huts are constructed of a wooden framework covered by a poor type of ... walling. There are earth floors. Beds consist of planks raised a short distance off the ground.[29]

Consequently, army doctors in Nairobi estimated that 90 percent of the outpatients at Langata exercised their right to demand immediate discharge from the army and left for home on their own. With the exception of tuberculosis patients at the No. 3 EAC Chest Centre at Nyeri, there was little the

[26] War pensions officer to Hyde-Clark, November 22, 1943, DEF 10/25/8, KNA, Nairobi.
[27] EAC circular letter, African rehabilitation, June 9, 1944, DEF 10/25/103, KNA, Nairobi; quarterly report, convalescent wing, April–June 1944, WO 222/1827, TNA, Kew.
[28] Precise on rehabilitation, 1945, DEF 10/26/31; and director of manpower to accountant general, June 15, 1946, DEF 10/26/3, KNA, Nairobi.
[29] Chief medical officer (Rehabilitation Centre) to DMS, May 29, 1944, DEF 10/25/100, KNA, Nairobi.

medical authorities could do to stop them.[30] This explains why many men did not receive the treatment and benefits that were due them.

This problem became acute after the war, when in the rush to wind down the colonial forces, the EAC discharged thousands of *askaris* each month in 1945 and 1946. Hyde-Clark, who was now the government's principal civil reabsorption officer, worried that unless the government found a way to keep disabled veterans at the rehabilitation centers "for years to come [there will be] cripples tucked away in all the villages of East Africa, living on their relations when their wives have died or become too old for work, half-starved, and believing that they have been badly treated by the Army and by the Government."[31] While these concerns were legitimate, the Kenyan regime's refusal to devote the proper resources to caring for and rehabilitating its injured African soldiers was the real reason that these men abandoned Langata and the rest of the similarly chaotic and uncomfortable rehabilitation centers.

This mass exodus makes it difficult to determine the extent to which Hyde-Clark's fears came to pass. Even though military recordkeeping in East Africa was much better during World War II, it is still not possible to know precisely how many men suffered a permanent disability while wearing a British uniform. While conditions in the East African forces were markedly improved in comparison to the First World War, service in the colonial military was still fraught with considerable risk. In addition to the obvious dangers of conventional combat, Africans in support units faced grueling and hazardous physical labor. Highly contagious and debilitating diseases such as malaria and tuberculosis were additional threats. Moreover, it seems likely that seriously injured *askaris* were less likely to survive their wounds than their western counterparts. The East African units had relatively good medical support and the EAC's military hospital system was largely up to western standards, but the civilian health care system for "natives" in Kenya was not equipped to deal with serious disabilities beyond the loss of limb. For example, where antibiotics improved the survival rates of paralyzed western veterans markedly, similarly injured Africans probably still died from bladder infections. These sorts of casualties probably helped account for the surprisingly low official disability records.

What is certain is that 76,000 Kenyans served in the military during the war. Official sources record that 2,476 of them died from combat wounds, accident, and disease, but there are no reliable disability statistics. Remarkably, postwar rehabilitation records list only fifty-three men as having lost a limb or eyesight in the army. This undercount was probably due to the

---

[30] EAC circular letter, "African rehabilitation," June 9, 1944, DEF 10/25/103; and principal civil dispersal officer to provincial commissioner (Nyanza), February 28, 1945, DEF/10/28/38, KNA, Nairobi.

[31] Memorandum on rehabilitation, April 17, 1945, DEF 10/26/9, KNA, Nairobi.

tendency of injured men to shun the unpleasant and inadequate rehabilitation centers. The EAC war pensions officer's 1943 estimate that the military
would discharge 170 combat and 200 noncombat casualties per month over
the course of the next two years provides a more realistic sense of the Kenyan
disability figures. In 1951, officials in Central Nyanza reported there were
over 1,000 disabled ex-servicemen in their district alone; therefore, it is
likely that the numbers of Kenyans permanently impaired by wounds and
accidental injury during the war actually numbered in the thousands.[32]

While amputees probably constituted only a relatively small percentage
of this number, their obvious wounds made them the most visible of the
disabled African veteran cohort. Moreover, the discriminatory treatment
suffered by Private A. K. and Lance Corporal P. K. illustrates starkly how
the Kenyan imperial regime was more concerned with economy, segregation,
and "retribalization" than with helping impaired ex-*askaris*. In contrast to
the United States, where a congressional committee kept close watch on the
efforts of the "nation's top engineering and surgical talent" to develop the
best possible artificial limbs for some 14,000 American veterans, the Kenyan
government decided that African ex-servicemen would have to get by with
peg or rocker legs unless they were double amputees or could demonstrate
that they were accustomed to wearing shoes in civil life.[33]

Responding to pension officials who pointed out that peg legs were
hardly compatible with agricultural labor, rehabilitation planners insisted
that wartime Kenya lacked the equipment and proper materials to give
African amputees better prosthetics. Indeed, Italian prisoners of war working with equipment captured in Ethiopia produced the only significant source
of advanced artificial legs in the colony, and most of these went to Europeans. The supply only increased very late in the war with the arrival of
a specialist from South Africa who began to train African assistants in the
more advanced techniques. Australian veterans of the First World War also
had to make do with inferior artificial legs because their government lacked
the financial resources and inclination to provide them with the advanced
limbs that were the right of amputees in metropolitan Britain. Nevertheless,
it is remarkable that in 1945 African ex-servicemen still faced such blatant
discrimination, particularly since the lifelike articulated Anglesey leg (named
for the Marquees of Anglesey who lost a leg at Waterloo) had been available
since the early nineteenth century.[34]

[32] War pensions officer to Hyde-Clark, November 22, 1943, DEF 10/25/8; East Africa Governor's Conference estimates, 1945, DEF 15/29/88a; Kenyan casualty estimates, September
   30, 1946, DEF 10/24/76; K. J. A. Hunt to welfare officer (African), November 13, 1951,
   DC KSM 1/22/67/233, all in KNA, Nairobi.
[33] Anonymous, "Better artificial limbs," *The Science News – Letter*, 47 (May 1945; November
   1945); Kenya Medical Department policy, July 25, 1944, DEM 18/I/131, KNA, Nairobi.
[34] Draft report, African War Pensions Committee, AG 5/2823; minutes of conference between
   West and East African Authorities on rehabilitation, May 22, 1944, DEF 10/39/30, KNA,

It was little wonder that African amputees angrily rejected peg legs. The government's refusal to provide higher quality limbs limited their mobility and earning power. Fatuous declarations that "the tribe" would look after them had absolutely no resonance with veterans who hoped to use their military training and accumulated savings to start businesses or invest in land and cattle. In 1947, the Colonial Office's declared intention to elim-inate racial discrimination in the empire meant that the Kenyan authori-ties could no longer justify the inequity of providing articulated legs only to Europeans, particularly when Uganda and Tanganyika supplied them to their ex-servicemen. Brushing aside warnings that giving former *askaris* advanced limbs would set an expensive precedent for similarly disabled African civilians, the Kenyan government grudgingly made advanced limbs available to Africans willing to pay the roughly one hundred shilling dif-ference in the cost of a peg and articulated prosthetic. Those who could not come up with this considerable sum still had to make do peg or rocker legs.[35]

This was disgraceful, but the large number of *askaris* suffering from posttraumatic stress received even less attention from the imperial regime because they did not display obvious physical wounds. While the metropoli-tan British military had recognized "shell shock" and other forms of combat-induced mental illness as pensionable disabilities since the First World War, colonial officials and medical authorities tended to attribute such ailments among Africans to primitive superstition. During the 1944 campaign in Burma, African troops experienced a condition that one army psychiatrist termed "running amok." "The picture is one of a man quite suddenly seiz-ing a machete or a tommy-gun or a rifle and rushing around slaying all he meets."[36] The jungle fighting in Burma was intense and brutal, and it is little wonder that when exacerbated by the inherent discrimination of colonial military service, the stress of combat led a few men to snap and attack their officers.[37] Colonial experts in African psychiatry blamed these incidents on the inability of primitive minds to cope with the pressures of modernity, but the Tswana veteran who told Julie Livingston that "fighting destroys the

Nairobi. See also Joanna Bourke, "The battle of the limbs: Amputation, artificial limbs and the Great War in Australia," *Australian Historical Studies*, 29 (1998); Guyatt, "Better legs," 308–09.

[35] Great Britain, Colonial Office, *Summer Conference on African Administration: African Local Government, First Session* (London: His Majesty's Stationery Office, 1947); Report of Group VI on Race Relations; DMS to accountant general, April 3, 1947, DEF 10/28/94b; and Secretariat circular on artificial limbs supplied to Africans, January 10, 1950, DC MLE 2/12/6/8, KNA, Nairobi.

[36] N. Dembovitz, "Psychiatry amongst West African troops," *Journal of the Royal Army Medical Corps*, 84 (1944), 73.

[37] For a detailed discussion, see Timothy Parsons, *The African Rank-and-File: Social Implica-tions of Colonial Service in the King's African Rifles, 1902–1964* (Portsmouth: Heinemann, 1999), 258.

mind" offered an elegantly simple and more convincing explanation for the mental injuries that afflicted African combat veterans.[38]

While civil and military rehabilitation planners made no long-term provision for *askaris* with disabling mental illnesses, EAC medical records make it clear that psychological trauma was just as much a threat to African soldiers as it was to their European counterparts. On average, military hospitals admitted roughly one hundred new African "psychiatric cases" each month between 1944 and 1946. Some of the most common diagnoses were schizophrenia, hysteria, "manic depression," and "temperamental instability." Military psychiatrists believed that the simplicity of the African mind made "native troops" more resistant to combat stress, but the doctors treating African troops in Burma noted a substantial increase in the number of psychiatric hospitalizations as the intensity of the fighting increased in late 1944 and early 1945.[39] On the other hand, a Kenyan veteran of the East African Army Medical Corps confirms that African soldiers also understood that a finding of mental incapacity was a way to escape the army and often asked to be discharged as mentally incapacitated. Doctors in Ceylon diagnosed a "miserable petulant little askari" assigned to the East African Engineers with numbing hysterical paralysis and returned him home to Kenya even though he flinched when poked with a pin. Similarly, the No. 1 Military Hospital in Nairobi treated a private suffering from spasms in his left arm and face that only seemed to appear in the presence of Europeans.[40]

It seems certain, however, that significant numbers of African soldiers suffered debilitating combat or disease induced mental illnesses during their wartime service. Military doctors in India claimed good results in treating them, along with similarly incapacitated British troops, with "insulin shock" and "electrical convulsion" therapies. But the military authorities made no long-term provision for their care apart from suggesting that the EAC might contribute to the expansion of Nairobi's civilian Mathere Valley mental hospital.[41] This never came to pass, and the official postwar rehabilitation plans made scant allowance for African ex-servicemen suffering from posttraumatic stress and other service-related mental disorders. Just

[38] Psychiatric report, No. 1 General Hospital, July–September 1943, WO 222/1827, TNA, Kew; Livingston, *Debility and the Moral Imagination in Botswana*, 176–77.

[39] Analysis of psychoneurotic cases, January–March 1944, WO 222/1827; quarterly report, Psychiatry, July 11, 1945, WO/222/1325; quarterly reports, No. 1 General Hospital, 1944–1946, WO/222/1827; quarterly report to DMS ALFSEA by Lt. Col. R. F. Tredgold, advisor in psychiatry, January 1946, WO 222/1319, all in TNA, Kew. See also African service personnel, mental disorders, n.d., DEF 10/162, KNA, Nairobi.

[40] Quarterly reports, No. 1 General Hospital, 1944, WO/222/1827, TNA, Kew; interview with Tom Mzungu, Sergeant EAAMC, June 1994.

[41] Brigadier Knott, DA and CMG to chief secretary, East African Governors Conference, May 2, 1943, BY/49/16/56a, KNA, Nairobi. See also "Analysis of psychoneurotic cases, January–March 1944," WO 222/1827; quarterly report, psychiatry, July 11, 1945, WO/222/1325, TNA, Kew.

as Hyde-Clark predicted, most appear to have become the responsibility of their wives and families, thereby sparing the government any additional expense.

While Kenyan authorities did not specifically set out to deny disabled African ex-servicemen proper care or benefits, they were adamantly unwilling to accept the fiscal and political consequences of treating them like western veterans. This was particularly true in the case of compensation. Throughout most of the colonial era, *askaris* suffering permanent impairment as a result of their service were the only class of veterans entitled to a pension in addition to a cash award. Healthy men received a lump-sum gratuity based on their rank and years of service, thereby sparing the government the much more considerable expense of lifetime support payments. After World War II, Kenyan officials brushed aside appeals by senior officers such as General Sir William Slim, who commanded the African divisions attached to the Fourteenth Army in the Burma campaign, by continuing to maintain that pension payments were unnecessary for "natives" and would disrupt egalitarian tribal societies by creating an unmanageable and lazy class of privileged veterans.[42]

There was, however, no denying that disabled African veterans were entitled to some form of regular state support. An official in the Colonial Office made this clear with the pragmatic observation that:

> It is not improbable that a totally or severely disabled recipient of a lump sum gratuity would spend his award very quickly, whether by way of gifts to his numerous relatives or in some less commendable manner. He would then be destitute, dependent on his relatives.... Moreover, he would provide excellent material for the agitator and those who are always out to harass the Government, who would no doubt be accused of using these men as cannon fodder and then casting them off with a paltry lump sum payment and no pension.[43]

If for political reasons alone, Kenyan officials had to accept the necessity of disability pensions.

Under the terms of the updated 1942 His Majesty's Forces Pension Ordinance, a Pensions Assessment Board consisting of a private doctor and a military representative of the accountant general compared a claimant's "condition as disabled with the condition of a normal healthy person at the same age." There was no provision for skills or earning power in determining the degree of disability. The regulations stipulated men more than 80 percent disabled received a pension of one-third their basic pay at discharge not to exceed 28s per month. Ratings between 20 and 80 percent brought a

---

[42] General Sir William Slim to Nyasaland governor, February 27, 1946, S41/1/8/5/70, NAM, Zomba; Joint Civil and Military Committee on Pensions, September 12 and 13, 1946, DEF/1/26/27B, KNA, Nairobi.

[43] Minute by C. Lambert, July 27, 1940, CO 820/43/18, TNA, Kew.

pension of one-quarter base pay and were capped at 16s, Veterans classified as more than 50 percent disabled qualified for a lifetime hut or poll tax exemption, and all medically boarded ex-*askaris* received an additional one-time gratuity ranging from 160s to 1,000s. Ominously, a qualifying veteran had only three months to claim his pension, and the Pensions Assessment Board tended to deny the appeals of ex-*askaris* suffering from psychological trauma on the convenient grounds that they could not prove it was due to military service.[44] Given these strict limitations, many disabled ex-servicemen, particularly those who gave up on the rehabilitation centers, never received their pensions or else had their cases and petitions drag on for years. Equally serious, the Kenyan government proved stubbornly slow in adjusting pension awards to keep up with postwar inflation. The omission of the provision for a cost of living increase in the regulations rendered most World War II era pensions essentially worthless by the 1950s.[45]

It was hardly surprising that many disabled veterans became so bitter. Corporal B. M., whose leg was shot off in North Africa while he was serving with the African Auxiliary Pioneer Corps, was one of the men who did not receive a pension. Similarly, Private K. N. never won any form of compensation for a leg maimed by a bomb blast in Burma in 1944. Both men blamed the colonial authorities for failing to make good on their promises of support and treatment, and K. N. was so embittered that he joined the banned Kenya African Union. When an ex-serviceman who was fortunate to receive a pension complained that it no longer reflected the cost of living in 1952, the authorities told him that the award was never intended to cover all his expenses.[46]

While politically influential groups such as the British Legion and the Veterans of Foreign Wars and Blind Veterans Association in the United States protected the interests of western veterans of the Second World War, there was no one in Kenya to speak for disabled former *askaris*. Unlike the much more numerous West African veterans of the French colonial military who possessed the vote and were consequently courted by imperial authorities and African politicians, Kenyan ex-servicemen had no recognized political influence beyond "local native councils." In 1945, the Kenyan government sponsored an African Section of the British Legion (ASBL), but this state-controlled institution's primary purpose was to ensure that African ex-servicemen did not join more radical organizations. As a member of the

---

[44] H. M. Forces Pension Ordinance 1942, AG/5/2823; chief secretary (Kenya) to chief secretary (East African Governors Conference), August 24, 1942, MD/4/5/73/88; East Africa Command Military Records to DC Central Kavirondo, March 16, 1944, DC KSM 1/22/52/17, KNA, Nairobi.

[45] Financial secretary to attorney general (Kenya), July 26, 1948, AG/5/1530/3, KNA, Nairobi.

[46] Interviews with Corporal B. M. (African Auxiliary Pioneer Corps), March 1994; Private K. N. (East African Armoured Car Squadron), April 1994. See also Harrison Comba Kimoku to DC (Fort Hall), March 11, 1952, DC FH 3/12/21/31-2, KNA, Nairobi.

ASBL sponsoring committee explained: "Serving askaris were now tending to form all sorts of societies among themselves, many of them trading or political or both. We wish to divert this tendency into safe channels by providing for the ex-askari an organisation which would compete successfully with the spontaneous societies now appearing."[47] The ASBL promised that it would help deserving former *askaris*, but its motto of "service not self" sent the clear message that they should not expect too much from the government or military.[48]

Lacking a viable political voice, disabled veterans had to make their case for better treatment and equitable compensation on their own. This meant that the Kenyan imperial regime could essentially ignore them. Ultimately, government concerns about detribalization and unflinching commitment to maintaining settler preeminence in the colony trumped its responsibility to its disabled African soldiers. Postwar efforts to reabsorb these men into tribal society by making them the responsibility of their wives, mothers, and fellow tribeswomen exposed the highly gendered nature of rehabilitation in particular and African military service in general. The lived experiences of disabled Kenyan veterans of the Second World War peeled back the legitimizing humanitarian rhetoric of British rule to expose the underlying abusive realities of African military service, the empty promises of Britain's elaborate plans for the postwar development of its African empire, and the fundamentally exploitive nature of imperial subjecthood. The permanently impaired former *askaris'* indifferent and often discriminatory treatment brings into sharper focus Britain's attempts to defend the ethnic foundations of imperial rule in the postwar era of increasing social differentiation, urban migration, and ultimately political activism. Unfortunately, the postcolonial Kenyan government paid little attention to their plight on the grounds that the veterans of the Second World War had been disabled in the service of the British empire, not the new Kenyan nation-state.

---

[47] R. Tatton Brown to chief native commissioner, October 2, 1945, DEF 10/24/5, KNA, Nairobi.

[48] Secretariat circular, ASBL Appeal Fund, January 21, 1946, OP EST 1/7/20, KNA, Nairobi.

THREE

MOBILIZING COMMUNITIES AND RESOURCES FOR THE WAR EFFORT

8

Women, Rice, and War

Political and Economic Crisis in Wartime Abeokuta (Nigeria)

Judith A. Byfield

Introduction

Italy's invasion of Ethiopia in 1935 brought about a swift response from residents in Abeokuta and across Nigeria. In meetings in churches, schools, and gathering spaces groups met to decry the invasion, sign petitions to the governor of Nigeria, and collect funds for Ethiopian relief.[1] This activism continued in bursts throughout the remainder of the decade and inspired discussions about Fascism, European intentions, and nationalism.[2] Thus for some Nigerians the beginning of war in Europe on September 3, 1939, was a continuation of military and ideological struggles begun in Ethiopia in 1935.

---

[1] S. K. B. Asante, "The Italo-Ethiopian conflict: A case study in British West African response to crisis diplomacy in the 1930s," *Journal of African History*, 15 (1974), 295–96; letter from G. Schakelford, June 10, 1936, Ake 2/1 #29, National Archives of Nigeria (hereafter NAN), Abeokuta. The Shacklefords, originally from Jamaica, played a prominent role in the local branch of Marcus Garvey's Universal Negro Improvement Association; Programme, "Women's meeting on the Abyssinian question," Ake 2/2, File 29, NAN, Abeokuta. The subscription list of the women who donated money is dated June 16, 1936, suggesting that the meeting occurred on this date.

[2] N. Ayele, "The Horn of Africa and eastern Africa in the World War decade (1935–45)," in *Africa and the Second World War* (Paris: UNESCO, 1980), 77–90. The idea of the world war decade is compelling, for it integrates the link between Italy's invasion of Ethiopia in 1935 and the expanded conflict that began in 1939 more directly. In addition, analyses that begin with 1939 limit our understanding of Africa's engagement with the larger ideological issues behind the war.

The research for the paper was supported by grants from the National Endowment of the Humanities (FB-38725) and a Fulbright Fellowship. Fellowships from the National Humanities Center, the Fund for Historical Studies at the Institute for Advanced Studies (Princeton), and a Professional Development Grant from Cornell University provided the luxury of time to complete it. An earlier version of this chapter appears in "Feeding the troops: Abeokuta (Nigeria) and World War II," *African Economic History* 35 (2007): 77–87.

Officials in Europe anticipated that except for Ethiopia, Africa would be tangentially affected by the war; however, the fall of France in 1940 and the loss of Britain's Far Eastern colonies after 1942 transformed Africa's engagement in this increasingly consuming conflict and brought changes to all levels of society. The colonial state had to transform established practices as it lost European officials to the war front at the same time that it had to reach deeper into the social and economic fabric of African societies to meet demands for food, manpower, and other resources in multiple theaters. The main resources demanded from Abeokuta were manpower and food-stuffs. This chapter examines the consequences of these resource demands specifically on women. It argues that as the colonial state extracted food-stuffs and tried to control prices, the combined actions created particular tensions and economic distress for women in Abeokuta. This distress ulti-mately exploded in a tax revolt in 1947 during which women demanded an end to the Sole Native Authority system, the bedrock of indirect rule, the abolition of taxes on women and the removal of the traditional king – the Alake – Ademola II. Its goal is to illuminate the ways in which the war shaped political and economic conditions that contributed to the women's tax revolt in the immediate postwar era.

Prologue to War

Abeokuta, a Yoruba town in western Nigeria, lies about sixty miles north of Lagos, the former capital of colonial Nigeria. Founded in 1830 in the wake of the collapse of the Oyo empire, Abeokuta was a city of refugees. It provided security to different Yoruba subgroups – primarily Egbas and Owus – as well as those rescued from the slave ships and apprenticed in Sierra Leone – the Saros. Within decades of its establishment, the town and its rural districts were well integrated into the international economy exporting cotton and cocoa to Europe.[3] Abeokuta's economic significance compelled the architects of the railway line between Lagos and Kano, the major economic emporium in northern Nigeria, to place the line through its territory. In 1902, the completed railway line to Abeokuta brought British trading companies en masse to the outskirts of the town. The most profitable economic sectors were cocoa and cloth. Men produced cocoa while male and

[3] See Jacob F. Ajayi, *Christian Missions in Nigeria, 1841–1891: The Making of a New Elite* (London: Longman, 1965); E. A. Ayandele, *The Missionary Impact on Modern Nigeria, 1842–1914: A Political and Social Analysis* (London: Longmans, 1966); Sara Berry, *Cocoa, Custom, and Socio-Economic Change in Rural Western Nigeria* (Oxford: Clarendon Press, 1975); Oluwatoyin B. Oduntan, "Elite identity and power: A study of social change and leadership among the Egba of Western Nigeria, 1860–1950," PhD thesis, Dalhousie University (2010); Adrian M. Deese, "Making Sense of the Past: Ajayi Kolawole Ajisafe and the (Re)Making of Modern Abeokuta (Nigeria)," MA thesis, Cornell University (2013).

female traders bulked and traded the commodity as demand for chocolate grew exponentially. Women dominated the trade in local foodstuffs as well as the retail end of the cloth trade. Women also dominated the production and sale of the lucrative indigo-dyed cloth industry, *adire*. The profitability of the industry depended heavily on cash crops, for its largest markets were in western Nigeria, the Gold Coast, and Senegal, regions that produced cocoa and peanuts.[4]

Abeokuta did not become a formal part of the protectorate until 1914 when the British used a revolt against the government of Alake Gbadebo I, as a ready excuse to abrogate the 1893 treaty in which Great Britain had recognized its independence.[5] Following Abeokuta's integration into the protectorate, the former city-state became the capital of Abeokuta Province and the center of colonial administration. Officials imposed an income tax and a poll tax in 1916, ensuring that producers and traders fulfilled the demands of the colonial economy. Abeokuta's tax structure stood out because it was one of the few places where women were considered individual taxpayers, independent of their husbands. Men and women who earned more than £40 annually paid an income tax while those with lower incomes paid a poll tax. Women who paid the poll tax paid two and a half shillings (2s 6p) while men paid five shillings (5s).[6] When the economy thrived, more people paid their taxes in full and on time; however, the precipitous decline of agricultural prices during the interwar depression, the overall dampening of consumer spending on items such as cloth, and an unchanging tax bill meant that men and women experienced tremendous economic distress before 1939.[7]

Imperial Strategies, Local Actions

Planning for the war began before hostilities actually broke out. By July 1939, Britain already had in place secret plans to restrict imports and exports. The goal was to conserve foreign exchange, secure access to certain

---

[4] Judith Byfield, *The Bluest Hands: A Social and Economic History of Women Dyers in Abeokuta (Nigeria), 1980–1940* (Portsmouth, NH: Heinemann Press, 2002), 48–53, 87–125.

[5] See Harry Gailey, *Lugard and the Abeokuta Uprising: The Demise of Egba Independence* (London: Frank Cass, 1982); Agneta Pallinder-Law, "Aborted modernization in West Africa? The case of Abeokuta," *Journal of African History*, 15 (1974), 65–82.

[6] Judith Byfield, "Taxation, women and the colonial state: Egba women's tax revolt" *Meridians*, 3 (2003), 250–277.

[7] Tax rates could not be reduced, in part, because the colonial government took an extra 10% of the tax revenue collected by the Native Administrations. Robert Pearce, "The colonial economy: Nigeria and the Second World War," in Barbara Ingham and Colin Simmons (eds.), *Development Studies and Colonial Policy* (Totowa, NJ: Frank Cass, 1987), 268.

commodities required by Britain and the Allied Powers, and restrict enemy access to those goods.[8] To coordinate these plans, the government established a central purchasing organization in London, the Ministry of Food and Supply,[9] while the Nigerian colonial government established the Nigeria Supply Board to control trade and coordinate production.[10] In addition, the Nigerian Defense Regulations of 1939 conferred tremendous power to the Supply Board and officials such as the food controller to regulate the distribution of imports as well as local foodstuffs.[11]

When Germany invaded Poland on September 3, officials remained confident that the war would not have a great impact on Africa. On September 15, 1939, the secretary of state communicated to colonial governors that he wanted social services and development activities to continue with little disruption and to avoid personnel retrenchment. Nine months later, his successor sent a circular in a much more grim tone, noting that the German blitzkrieg had transformed their thinking. They now concluded that the war would require a supreme effort from all people in the empire in the "next few months." That effort included maintaining production of materials needed for the war effort, substantially reducing demand for nonessential imports from sterling and nonsterling sources, maximum development of foodstuffs to meet local demand, curtailment of existing social and other services, postponement of plans in the Colonial Development Bill, and the imposition or increase of direct taxation.[12]

The blitzkrieg that led to the surrender of Norway, Belgium, and France transformed Nigeria's engagement in this growing conflict, for Britain was essentially fighting alone.[13] The administrative machinery put in place now had to deliver manpower and resources to meet the needs of this empire-wide effort. The Nigerian Supply Board directed food production in Nigeria and played an instrumental role in ensuring that food also reached other parts of West Africa. Representatives of the Supply Board participated in meetings with representatives from the other West African colonies during

---

[8] Ayodeji Olukoju, "'Buy British, sell foreign': External trade control policies in Nigeria during World War II and its aftermath, 1939–1950," *International Journal of African Historical Studies*, 35 (2002), 364–65.

[9] A. Olorunfemi, "Effects of war-time trade controls on Nigerian cocoa traders and producers, 1939–45: A case-study of the hazards of a dependent economy," *International Journal of African Historical Studies*, 13 (1980), 676.

[10] Olukoju, "Buy British, sell foreign," 366–67.

[11] Toyin Falola, "'Salt is gold': The management of salt scarcity in Nigeria during World War II," *Canadian Journal of African Studies*, 26 (1992), 415–16. For example, firms had to obtain a license from the Supply Board to import salt. Towns and villages were limited to varying amounts of salt based on a formula of six ounces per person per month.

[12] Circular telegram no. 82, secretary of state for the colonies (SSC), London, to governor, Lagos, June 5. 1940, ABP 1631, NAN, Ibadan.

[13] Antony Beevor, *The Second World War* (New York: Little, Brown and Company), especially chapters 3, 5–7.

which they debated the quantities of foodstuffs that would be exported from one colony to another to meet civilian and military requirements.

Rice was high on the agenda, for it was in great demand: Troops in the Gold Coast and the Gambia alone required 3,000 tons. The Gold Coast representative noted that they needed rice to feed workers in the mines and "boat boys." While they had taken steps to increase local production, they could not become self-sufficient in rice. Similarly, the Gambia could not meet the demand for rice for civilians and the military. Sierra Leone produced a significant amount of rice, but since rice was the main staple of its population and the colony also had to satisfy military requirements, it restricted rice exports. Therefore it fell largely to Nigeria to supply rice to the Gold Coast and Gambia.[14] In addition to rice, Nigeria supplied salt, groundnut (peanut) oil, egusi oil, ghee, gari, potatoes, and onions.[15]

Colonial officials also undertook military recruitment. They enlisted technicians into the Royal West African Frontier Force (RWFF), though potential recruits were disappointed that the colonial government did not want them for the regular fighting forces. The 1941 annual report noted that recruitment was steady and they had successfully enlisted 883 men from across the province for the signal corps, for transport duties, as mechanics, and in other noncombat roles. The report also noted that it was impossible to fill the quota allotted to the province by the military authorities. Recruitment posed a challenge because the province was in the midst of a labor shortage since many men had migrated to work on the extensive military construction projects in Lagos. Furthermore, it was particularly difficult to recruit educated men.[16]

Colonial officials tried to encourage recruitment by creating a recruitment circus, a group of seventeen specially selected soldier/tradesmen who toured the provinces for six weeks, demonstrating their trades, and giving physical training, as well as exhibits of drills and unarmed combat. The recruitment circus did have a slight effect on the enlistments in Abeokuta town and some of the rural villages; however, its impact was not sustained, as borne out in the recruitment figures.[17] The total number of recruits declined in

---

[14] "Rice," letter from deputy chairman, West African Governors' Conference, Lagos, to the chief secretary (CS), Lagos, August 23, 1941, Department of Commerce and Industries (hereafter DCI) 1/1 38787/S.20; draft minutes of second meeting of Committee of Supply Center held at Accra, June, 10–11, 1942, pp. 1–2, Chief Secretary's Office (hereafter CSO) 26/38717, NAN, Ibadan.

[15] Draft minutes of second meeting of Committee of Supply Center held at Accra, June, 10–11, 1942, p. 3; and letter about "Food supplies to other colonies" from chief marketing officer to food controller, July 14, 1942, CSO 26/38717, NAN, Ibadan. Nigeria promised to provide 300 tons of salt to Sierra Leone each month. Egusi oil was made from the seed of the egusi melon; ghee is made from clarified butter; and gari is processed cassava.

[16] Annual Report, Abeokuta Province, 1941, 9–10, CSO 26/2/11875, vol. XV.

[17] Savingram from the resident, Abeokuta Province to the secretary, Western Provinces, April 15, 1944, ABP 1401/23, NAN, Ibadan.

1943 to 305, but the pressure to recruit eased after 1943 because the army discontinued recruitment in certain categories.[18] The total number of recruits fell from 176 in 1944 to 61 in 1945.[19] Abeokuta did not contribute much in the way of manpower to the prosecution of the war. Its greatest contribution was in the production of agricultural products needed for the war effort and foodstuffs needed for the civilian and military populations in Lagos and Abeokuta.

Economically, the Second World War was a period of both continuity and change. Nigerians had experienced a prolonged economic crisis due to the worldwide depression in commodity prices and credit markets. The crisis deepened during the war; Pearce argues that the terms of trade were worse during the war than in the worst years of the depression.[20] This was most obvious when you examine the fate of cocoa prices. The government purchased the entire cocoa crop in 1939 and set the price below 1938 levels. Before the outbreak of the war, cocoa sold for £22.50/ton, but the ministry set the price at £16.50/ton and by September 1940 it fell further to £11.00/ton.[21] The government justified the low prices because the German market was closed and the U.S. market had contracted. The low price of cocoa contradicted official claims that the first few months of the war, characterized as the phony war, did not have a significant impact on the colonies.[22] The impact of the war was uneven; therefore, generalizations about its effects were misleading. Anderson and Throup argue that in Kenya the "phoney war" situation was only transformed in 1941 following the Japanese advances and U.S. entry into the war. In those first two years of the war, settler agriculture remained at the same level as in the late 1930s.[23] While the time lag of the "phoney war" may apply in Kenya, Nigerian producers of cocoa felt the consequences of the war immediately.

France's collapse was a major turning point, for it "imposed new burdens and some drastic changes in the economic life" of Abeokuta.[24] The Gambia, the Gold Coast, and Nigeria shared borders with French colonies and once France surrendered, Britain closed the borders between French and British colonies.[25] Residents of the western section of Abeokuta Province felt the

---

[18] Annual report, Abeokuta Province, 1944, 11.

[19] Annual report, Abeokuta Province, 1945, 11, CSO 26/2/11875, vol. XV, NAN, Ibadan.

[20] Pearce, "The colonial economy," 272.

[21] Ibid; see also, Olukoju, "Buy British, sell foreign," 367.

[22] The phony war refers to the period after the occupation of Poland and before the invasion of France when life in England and France seemed to go back to normal. Beevor, *The Second World War*, 40.

[23] David Anderson and David Throup, "Africans and agriculture in colonial Kenya: The myth of the war as a watershed," *Journal of African History*, 26 (1985), 335.

[24] Annual report, Abeokuta Province, 1940, p. 1, CSO 26/2/11875, vol. XV, NAN, Ibadan.

[25] Nancy E. Lawler, *Soldiers, Airmen, Spies and Whisperers: The Gold Coast in World War II* (Athens: Ohio University Press, 2002), 19.

changes most acutely, for they bordered Dahomey. In addition to closing the border between Nigeria and Dahomey, troops from the Gold Coast, Britain, and Belgium were stationed in Ilaro Division (western Abeokuta Province).[26] The most significant turning point came after the fall of the Far East colonies in 1942. It was then that the "Resident Minister took over the supreme direction of West Africa's war effort," creating, "for the first time in its history, a regional machinery, for the administration, control and direction of economic affairs directly associated with His Majesty's Government in Great Britain."[27] Britain's experience over the progression of the war required corresponding shifts and different phases in the restructuring of West African economies.

Experiencing the War

For many people in Abeokuta, scarcity of food items dominated their recollection of the main years of fighting (1939–1945). For the late Justice Adewale Thompson, the shortage of butter stood out most, but for many other people the scarcity of salt was especially difficult.[28] Chief Emanuel Sorunke recalled that "during that war, there was scarcity of salt and I had to travel because salt was being supplied through John Holt and UAC which are located at Ibara and my parents are in the district."[29] Items such as tinned milk, flour, and butter were rationed and one needed a ration card to obtain them. Rationing remained in force as late as 1948.[30]

The war brought privations as well as rumors about Britain's impending defeat. The Alake and colonial officials worked diligently to limit the spread of rumors and took advantage of new technologies in this effort. The 1940 annual report noted "the Alake set a splendid example not only by the outspokenness of his public declarations but by his prompt action in preventing the spreading of false defeatist rumours."[31] The Egba Native Administration (ENA) issued weekly news bulletins that they distributed to all districts and especially to schools. When touring, the administrative officers informed people of the latest developments in the war, and the information officers

---

[26] Annual report, Abeokuta Province, 1942, p. 2, Abeokuta Provincial Office Papers (hereafter Abe Prof) 1/ABP 1543, vol. IV; and Annual report, Abeokuta Province, 1943, p. 2, CSO 26/2/1875, vol. XV, NAN, Ibadan.

[27] M. Fortes, "The impact of the war on British West Africa," *International Affairs*, 21 (1945), 213.

[28] Interview with Justice Thompson, August 14, 2003, Jericho, Ibadan.

[29] Interview with Chief Emanuel Sorunke, August 19, 2003, Abeokuta.

[30] Letter from M. S. Ogunbisi to the resident, Abeokuta Province, March 22, 1948, ABP 1497E: Prof 2: 2nd Accession, NAN, Ibadan. Mr. Ogunbisi was single when he first received his ration card, but he had recently married and needed a new card increasing the amount of milk, sugar, flour, and butter he could buy from the firms.

[31] Annual report, Abeokuta Province, 1940, p. 3, CSO 26/2/11875, vol. XV, NAN, Ibadan.

provided illustrated pamphlets that were very popular. Without elaborating, the reporter noted that the propaganda films were disappointing. While the films were a disappointment, radio was a success. On June 1, 1943, a local radio diffusion service opened in Abeokuta. It was highly popular, but its reach was limited by the fact that the town had only 150 sets.[32] Over the course of the war the number of sets increased dramatically. By 1946 there were 589 sets and a waiting list of 100 subscribers.[33] Radio, which offered programing in both Yoruba and English, became an important tool for disseminating information about the war and assisting recruitment. The station played BBC programs for ten hours daily, produced local programs for broadcast between 6:00 and 7:00 P.M. weekdays and provided a Yoruba version of the news each day.[34]

Newspapers also carried information about the war and tried to boost support for the Allied Forces. *The Yoruba News* included a box with the statement "V – Allies Victory over Axis Forces is Inevitable" in many issues. An editorial on August 11, 1942, argued that Germany, Japan, and Italy were fighting to enslave the people in the rest of the world. It implored people in rousing language to give the government money to make guns and airplanes and to produce the commodities needed by the Allied armies: palm oil, palm kernels, rubber:

> Go into the bush with your wives and your children, and remember that every bunch of palm nuts that you cut down is like cutting down a German soldier; every tin of oil and kernels that you make will help to spoil a German or a German aeroplane.[35]

To be ready in case fighting did come to Nigeria, residents organized defense measures. In June 1940, colonial officials organized a Local Defense Volunteer Force while the Abeokuta Union of Teachers, led by Rev. Israel Oludoton Ransome-Kuti, developed plans for an air raid precaution scheme. Individuals demonstrated their support of the war effort in multiple ways. Oladipo Somoye launched the "Roosevelt-Churchill Club," which hoped to foster equality, fraternity, and mutual understanding.[36] Several fundraising schemes emerged as well. Capt. Mason of the United Africa Company took the lead in organizing the "Win-the-War Fund," and within six months it had collected £2,756. The Alake alone contributed £500 and much of the remainder came from the rural districts, including Ilaro Division, which donated £456. The residents of Abeokuta Province also contributed £392 to

---

[32] Annual report, Abeokuta Province, 1943, p. 13, CSO 26/2/11875, vol. XV.
[33] Annual report, Abeokuta Province, 1946, p. 9, CSO 26/2 11875, vol. XV.
[34] Annual report, Abeokuta Province, 1944, p. 11, CSO 26/2/11875, vol. XV.
[35] "To the chiefs and people of the western provinces of Nigeria," *The Yoruba News*, August 11, 1942.
[36] Letter from Oladipo Somoye to President Roosevelt and Mr. Winston Churchill, August 26, 1943, APB 1631 – War General Correspondence, NAN, Ibadan.

the Nigeria War Relief Fund and £74 to the Comforts for Nigerian Troops Fund. These monetary contributions continued throughout the war. The 1943 annual report noted that since the beginning of the war in 1939, the Egba Division alone contributed £8,307.[37] Abeokuta also contributed to the purchase of a Spitfire that was named *Nigeria* and cost £105,000.[38] The archival records do not disaggregate the information by gender, but it is safe to assume that women contributed to these fundraising campaigns just as they contributed to the fundraising campaigns for Ethiopia.

Women and the Wartime Economy

Women's critical role within the economies of Abeokuta and the other Yoruba provinces meant that very few economic decisions failed to impact their livelihood. Yoruba women not only processed cassava into gari, palm fruit into palm oil, and palm kernels into palm kernel oil, but they also dominated the retail sale of all these products. Although they did not process cocoa, women played a critical role in bulking each year's cocoa crop as they moved through the rural areas purchasing cocoa.[39] Women dominated the retail trade of imports such as salt, matches, and textiles. As mentioned earlier, they controlled the manufacturing of indigo-dyed cloths, one of the Abeokuta's major economic activities, and an industry heavily dependent on imports of cheap textiles, caustic soda, and synthetic dye.[40] As a result of their varied economic activities, many women traders were connected to the international markets through the import or exports of commodities. This meant that women traders were hit hard by the loss of international markets as well as the limited availability of shipping space.

The outbreak of war immediately led to the loss of the German market for cocoa and palm products. All exports to Germany were banned since the British wanted to deprive Germany of war materials and "strangle German trade as a war measure." Although the government purchased the entire crop, officials used the decline in demand, the acute shortage of cocoa storage in Lagos, and the shortage in shipping space to London to justify the prices. Low prices meant that farmers were producing at a loss, and agricultural officers noted that many farmers abandoned their cocoa farms. The storage crisis was so acute that the government destroyed part of the 1940–1941 crop after it was purchased. Low prices also meant that profit margins for women traders who collected cocoa from the farms were equally small.

---

[37] Annual report, Abeokuta Province, 1943, p. 1, CSO 26/2/11875, vol. XV, NAN, Ibadan.

[38] Letter from secretary, western provinces, to resident, Abeokuta Province, February 3, 1942, Abeokuta Provincial Papers 1631. NAN, Ibadan.

[39] See Julian Clarke, "Households and the political economy of small-scale cash crop production in south-western Nigeria," *Africa*, 51 (1981), 7–23.

[40] See Byfield, *The Bluest Hands*.

Cocoa was £11 in September 1940. It increased to £13.10 in October 1940 and fell precipitously to £10 in May 1941. It rose to £14.10 in 1941–1942, declined to £12.10 in October 1942 and hit another low of £10 in 1943.[41]

Difficulties with storage and shipping contributed to the state's decisions on palm products. In August 1940, the government announced that it would not purchase palm kernels on its previous large scale because all the "continental sources...had passed into enemy hands."[42] Nonetheless, palm kernels were a high priority item and had priority for available storage space. To discourage a glut of palm kernel on the market, the government banned the export trade in palm kernels from the cocoa-producing areas in western Nigeria. Although some people "did not fully appreciate the reason behind the prohibition," officials argued that this regional ban was fair since producers in Yorubaland already benefited from government's purchase of the cocoa crop.[43] To help offset the impact of the ban, the government encouraged the expansion of the domestic palm oil market by increasing rail shipments to northern Nigeria.[44] The export ban on palm kernels did not last very long. In fact, the government reversed itself after the Japanese occupation of British colonies in Southeast Asia in 1942 and launched a production drive instead.[45]

The policies on cocoa and palm kernels hurt some women, but others benefited substantially from the state's decision to create an export market in cassava starch.[46] Since the war made it difficult to obtain starch from Java and Brazil, the two major sources for the British market, Britain looked to the colonies as alternatives. In Yorubaland, where starch was used for laundry purposes, women dominated its production. Starch production increased substantially in Abeokuta, Oyo, and Ibadan provinces as producers responded to the government's promotional efforts as well as the higher price offered for starch. Increasing starch production seemed to correlate with declining attention to palm products. In response, the Nigerian government reduced the price of starch in February 1943 and prohibited

---

[41] Olorunfemi, "Effects of war-time trade controls," 676, 683–84; Olukoju, "Buy British, sell foreign," 367, 369.

[42] Olorunfemi, "Effects of war-time trade controls," 684.

[43] Annual report, 1940. Egba Council Records 1/1/12, NAN, Abeokuta; Olorunfemi, "Effects of War-Time Trade Controls," 684.

[44] Allister Hinds, "Government policy and the Nigerian palm oil export industry, 1939–49," *Journal of African History*, 38 (1997), 452.

[45] Olukoju, "Buy British, sell foreign," 370.

[46] Starch was used to make industrial adhesives as well as in the preparation of dextrin, a product used for stiffening cloth goods, thickening colors in calico prints and in the making of surgical bandages. For more information, see N. J. Tonukari, "Cassava and the future of starch," *Electronic Journal of Biotechnology*, 7 (2004), www.ejbiotechnology.info/content/vol7/issue1/issues/2/index.html.

its export the following month. After May 1943, the purchase of starch for export ceased.[47] Consequently, women traders involved in the export sector experienced tremendous ups and downs as the colonial government directed the economy.

The state was equally, if not more, concerned with food. The government had to ensure that there was sufficient food for the civilian and military populations, especially in and around Lagos, and that the food was available at affordable prices for consumers. To meet these requirements the government attempted to control the movement of foodstuffs between provinces in addition to controlling prices. Regulations restricted the movement of gari and rice from Abeokuta to the colony of Lagos and created a license system that by definition greatly restricted those who could take advantage of the more profitable bulk sales between these two cities. The ban did not end the efforts by unlicensed traders to move gari and rice to Ibadan or points beyond, but it made those efforts illegal. Traders caught smuggling were tried in the criminal courts and sentenced to either a substantial fine or imprisonment with hard labor. For example, a survey of criminal court records between 1939 and 1946 shows fourteen cases of smuggling rice and forty-two cases of gari smuggling. Most of the rice cases were tried in 1943, while the majority of gari cases clustered around 1946.

Officials also tried to enforce price controls by prosecuting some traders for profiteering by selling items above the control prices. A trader from one of the rural villages of Abeokuta, Feyisitan, was charged with selling two tins of palm oil at 14s instead of 11s, the control price. For making a profit of 3s, the judge sentenced him to a fine of £2 or one month in prison with hard labor.[48] The enforcement of profiteering appeared to be more rigorous than that of smuggling, for between 1939 and 1946, the Ake courts heard 478 profiteering cases. The higher volume of profiteering cases suggests that colonial officials were most concerned about ensuring abundant and affordable food. Without doubt some people did try to take advantage of the circumstances; nonetheless, profiteering has to be considered against the economic pressures that faced many Nigerians. Limited shipping space increased the cost of imports substantially and contributed to inflationary pressures across the entire economy; however, neither wage nor price freezes took inflation into consideration. As a result, food became a site of tremendous political contention and in Abeokuta the most contentious food item was rice.

---

[47] Toyin Falola, "Cassava starch for export in Nigeria during the Second World War," *African Economic History*, 18 (1989), 76, 78, 92. In other regions starch was a food staple. It was a food item among the Isoko, Urhobo, and Itshekiri of Benin and Warri provinces.

[48] ENA v. Feyisitan, May 4, 1944, Ake Native Court, Grade A, Criminal Record Book, vol. 61, 1944, p. 174, Obafemi Awolowo University Library, Ile-Ife.

The Struggle for Rice

The documentation from this period shows that there was tremendous demand and competition for foodstuffs. Different actors with competing loyalties jostled each other for food to feed the expanded population in Lagos and in Abeokuta Province. Correspondence from the chief secretary's office shows that demand for foodstuffs became increasingly critical since the entire requirements of the armed forces had to be met in full in West Africa.[49] Moreover, Nigerian officials looked to Abeokuta to play a central role in food production. The resident noted in the 1942 annual report, "the main war effort in the province is... food production for the military." In addition to increased military personnel in Lagos, there was a substantial military presence in Abeokuta Province, partly due to the fact that Ilaro Division shared a border with Dahomey. Troops from Britain, the Gold Coast, and Belgium were stationed in Abeokuta, Ilaro, Ajilete, and Meko.[50] A large number of military units were all around Egba division specifically.[51]

In a secret report, officials noted, "rice is going to play an important part as a Nigerian food reserve to meet War requirements." "Rice," the report declared, "is our emergency reserve," and the agriculture department was tasked to increase production at "the earliest possible moment."[52] Within a short time, the principal agricultural officer who happened to be an expert on rice growing, R. R. Glanville, visited the rice-producing areas in Abeokuta Province and recommended plans to experiment with the three varieties of upland rice he identified. As a result of this interest, the 1940 Abeokuta annual report noted that rice cultivation was proving increasingly popular.[53] Historically, Abeokuta was not one of the main rice-producing regions in Nigeria. Officials claimed that the province produced approximately 300 tons of rice annually before the war.[54] By 1943, however, agricultural officers estimated that the province could easily harvest 3,000 tons.[55]

The 1941 season appeared to have been a bumper year: A food production report stated that Abeokuta's production "exceeded local requirement by some 2,000 tons, of which 1,200 tons were supplied to the Army."[56] Despite

---

[49] Letter from A. E. V. Walwyn to chief secretary, January 29, 1942, pp. 1–2, CSO 26/37909/ S.14, NAN, Ibadan.

[50] Annual report, Abeokuta Province 1942, pp. 2–3, Abe Prof 1/ABP 1543 vol. IV; annual report, Abeokuta Province, 1942, p. 2; Abe Prof 1/ABP 1543 vol. IV; annual report, Abeokuta Province, 1943, p. 2, CSO 26/2/11875, vol. XV, NAN, Ibadan.

[51] Egba division report, 1943, p. 12, Abe Dist1 ED 32, NAN, Ibadan.

[52] Dr. G. Bryce (director, Agriculture Department), "War organisation production of rice," September 13, 1939, pp. 1, 6, CSO 26/36378/S.10, vol. I, NAN, Ibadan.

[53] Annual report, Abeokuta Province, 1940, p. 15, CSO 26/2/11875, vol. XV, NAN, Ibadan.

[54] Annual report, Abeokuta Province, 1943, p. 9, CSO 26/2/11875, vol. XV, NAN, Ibadan.

[55] Annual report, Egba division, 1943, p. 7. Abe Prof 1/ABP 1543, vol. IV, NAN, Ibadan.

[56] Report on food production and supply, October 1941–March 1942, p. 3, CSO 26/36378/ S.24, vol. II NAN, Ibadan.

increased production, the availability of rice, especially at the control prices, was a major concern and officials took increasingly extreme measures to address the situation. Orders prohibited the export of rice from the province except by special permit.[57] By October 1943, the resident of Abeokuta Province, Captain A. R. A. Dickins, signed an order under the General Defense Regulations requisitioning rice from farmers. The order created a system of forced cultivation because it gave officials the authority to assign production quotas to villages and prosecute bales (village heads) if the quotas were not met.[58]

Officials also contemplated sending the army to physically requisition the rice.[59] Captain Pullen, in particular, supported these measures because Abeokuta's rice was central to the bulk-marketing scheme he oversaw in Lagos. This system was part of a larger strategy to control the price of food during the war. Pullen and a team of price control officials established prices for foodstuffs in the Lagos markets, but Lagos prices were predicated on obtaining sufficient quantities of foodstuffs at the control purchase price.[60] Abeokuta Province clearly loomed large in Pullen's plans for feeding Lagos because he argued that "the whole scheme of bulk marketing will break down at the outset unless he can secure adequate supplies" from Abeokuta.[61] Native Authority police and certain chiefs applied additional pressure on farmers and women traders by confiscating their rice. In a letter to the district officer, A. M. Salami charged that two Nigerian police confiscated his rice, sold it to the G. B. Ollivant store, and then pocketed the funds.[62]

Despite these efforts, officials still had difficulty obtaining sufficient rice at control prices. Some officials recognized as early as 1941 that the military presence contributed to the difficulty. That year's annual report stated that the "military have caused the prices of agricultural products to soar to a ridiculous level by placing contracts in Lagos instead of in the producing areas, no regard being paid to Food Price Control Order."[63] The military bureaucracy as well as individual soldiers flouted price control measures. In 1943, the resident reported that military personnel with "healthy stomachs

---

[57] Annual report, Abeokuta Province, 1941, p. 10, Abe Prof 1/ABP 1543, vol. IV, NAN, Ibadan.

[58] Letter from acting secretary, western provinces, to chief secretary, November 11, 1943, DCI 1/1/4041/S20/C1, NAN, Ibadan.

[59] Memo from Deputy Food Controller A. Pullen to chief secretary, October 15, 1943, pp. 5–6, DCI 1/1/4041/S.20/C1; extract from letter from P. F. Brandt to the director of supplies, January 12, 1944, p. 65. DCI 1/1/4041/S.20/C1, NAN, Ibadan.

[60] Wale Oyemakinde, "The Pullen marketing scheme: A trial in food price control in Nigeria, 1941–1947," *Journal of the Historical Society of Nigeria*, 6 (1973), 416.

[61] Continuation sheet 3, October 8, 1943, DCI 1/1/4041/S.20/C1, NAN, Ibadan.

[62] Letter from A. M. Salami to district officer, Abeokuta, September 1, 1945, Abe Prof 1/ABP 2060, NAN, Ibadan.

[63] Annual report, Abeokuta Province, 1941, p. 6, CSO 26/2/11875, vol. XV, NAN, Ibadan.

and long purses provided a constant temptation to break the rule."[64] Primarily, colonial officials blamed the "black market" and farmers' resistance to producing rice as the main factors behind the difficulty they faced getting sufficient rice in a timely manner.

Indeed, a substantial unofficial market existed in Lagos. In 1943, 3,000 tons of rice "disappeared" from Abeokuta.[65] The low official price played a significant role in these developments. Farmers complained that the price did not cover their cost of production, but the state used requisition orders to compel them to continue to produce rice rather than switching to other crops.[66] Officials insisted that low prices were necessary to counter inflation. They would not acknowledge that inflation grew nonetheless, or that the increasing price of imports contributed to it. This was seen most clearly in the case of salt. The European firms sold salt at the control price, leaving no room for retailers to gain any profit and stay within the law. Multiple charges were made against a group of women salt traders who were arrested and charged with trying to bribe the chief of the Native Authority police to ignore their illegal actions. In addition, they were accused of reducing the amount of salt they sold at the control price.[67]

Jostling between rice buyers compounded market tensions as well. The Association of West African Merchants (AWAM), which represented the European trading companies, competed with licensed local merchants for the purchase of rice for the military and the Lagos market. The records identify the main local purchaser as a Mr. Shodipo. Harneit-Sievers argues that Shodipo and his counterpart, Timothy Adeola Odutola, in Ijebu flourished in the food procurement business because they had much lower overhead costs than the AWAM firms; however, residents in Abeokuta offered other reasons for Shodipo's success.[68] Farmers, women traders, and AWAM agents alleged that Shodipo had extremely close ties to the Alake, who put the Native Authority police at his disposal. The produce secretary of AWAM, J. C. Graham, suggested that Shodipo's relationship with the Alake gave him an unfair advantage. Graham reported that when he tried to buy rice at 10s above the control price from the Ifo Farmers' Association, the association refused to sell the rice to him. He was told that the rice was being "forwarded to Shodipo and Co., on the instruction of the Alake."[69] AWAM

---

[64] Annual report, Abeokuta Province, 1943, p. 5, CSO 26/2/11875, vol. XV, NAN, Ibadan.

[65] Letter from acting chief secretary to secretary, western provinces, October 16, 1943, p. 7. DCI 1/1/4041/S.20/C.2, NAN, Ibadan.

[66] "Sympathy for farmers," *Daily Service* (Lagos), May 20, 1944, located in DCI 1/1/4041/ S.20/C1, NAN, Ibadan.

[67] Letter to the district officer, August 13, 1944, ABP 1497B, vol. III, NAN, Ibadan.

[68] Axel Harneit-Sievers, "African business, "economic nationalism" and British colonial policy: southern Nigeria, 1935–1954," *African Economic History*, 23 (1995), 102.

[69] Confidential letter from J. C. Graham to the AWAM delegate, Lagos, November 25, 1943. DCI 1/1/4041/S.20/C1, NAN, Ibadan.

agents also insisted that Shodipo had "one foot in the black market and one foot in the government scheme."[70] The AWAM agents did not present any concrete evidence of these charges, but farmers reported that Native Authority police warned them that they had to sell their rice to Shodipo and not to the AWAM agents.[71]

These allegations about Shodipo implicated the Alake and they found sympathetic ears among some colonial officials. Capt. Pullen, for example, insisted on several occasions that the Alake was not doing all that he could to assist the rice effort.[72] Accusations about the Alake using his political power for personal profit also cropped up in relation to other commodities. Traders charged that his store was profiteering on salt.[73] In many people's minds war profiteering and the Alake became linked. Although the governor did not believe that the Alake was obstructing the purchase of rice, he felt "there is little evidence of support from the Alake in the past in this matter of rice."[74] As a result, communication from the top level of the colonial government and supported by the secretary of the western provinces conveyed to the Alake that it was "his personal responsibility" to see that rice reached the appropriate organization at the control price and was "not diverted to other clandestine and undesirable channels."[75] The pressure placed on the Alake bore fruit, for at the end of the 1943 harvest, Abeokuta supplied a total of 2,095 tons of rice. It was below the target of 3,000 tons, but "in consideration of the fact that last year we obtained only 188 tons against the same target figure, the position is not unsatisfactory."[76]

Politics and Rice

The Allied Forces celebrated victory over Germany on May 8, 1945. Nonetheless, the conflicts around rice in Abeokuta did not subside; in fact, they seemed to escalate. On September 11, 1945, the chief secretary to the government, George Beresford Stooke, wrote to the secretary of the western provinces about the poor collection results in Abeokuta. In thinly veiled language he urged the secretary of the western provinces to apply pressure on the Alake.

I am directed by His Excellency to request therefore that subject to His Honour's concurrence, the Alake should be informed that His Excellency

---

[70] Continuation sheet 41, November 23, 1943, DCI 1/1/4041/S20/C1, NAN, Ibadan.
[71] J. F. Winter to Mr. Booth, November 27, 1943, DCI 1/1/4041/S20/C1, NAN, Ibadan.
[72] Continuation sheet 21, DCI 1/1/4041/S20/C1, NAN, Ibadan.
[73] Letter to the resident, July 3, 1943, APB 1497B, vol. III, NAN, Ibadan.
[74] Letter from acting chief secretary of government to secretary, Western Provinces, October 16, 1943, DCI 1/1/4041/S.20/C1, NAN, Ibadan.
[75] Letter from acting secretary, western provinces, to the chief secretary to the government, November 16, 1943, DCI 1/1/4041/S.20/C1, NAN, Ibadan.
[76] Continuation sheet 69, March 17, 1944, DCI 1/1/4041/S.20/C1, NAN, Ibadan.

hopes that he will use his personal influence to ensure that the maximum amount of rice is offered for sale to the Government buying agents.[77]

Colonial officials put in place additional measures to obtain the rice. For example, police were given license to seize rice; in addition, a circular distributed on November 6, 1945, stated that any ENA police officer on rice work would be held responsible for any district that failed to produce its quota of rice unless he was "prepared to give a detailed account of his activities to show that he has exerted all efforts and energy to get the particular district to produce its quota."[78] Officials also put pressure on lorry (truck) owners. An order was put into effect on October 20, 1945, which compelled lorry owners to carry specific amounts of rice depending on the roads they travelled to reach Abeokuta. If they did not have the required amount of rice, the trucks would not be allowed to enter Abeokuta town.[79] Meanwhile, the transport of rice outside of Abeokuta Province by anyone other than a licensed government contractor remained illegal.

The records are full of letters of complaint about rice during and after 1945. Letters came from women traders, farmers, and lorry drivers about police confiscating rice without any compensation to the owner. Despite the order that only the police could seize rice, complainants identified individuals who took their rice as well. In one complaint to the district officer, market women charged a Mr. Alao, who held the chiefly title Otun of Ijaiye Obirinti, as a main culprit. They charged that he and his assistants had taken more than five tons of rice from them.[80] In spite of the complaints, Alao continued to operate without censure.

In November 1945, the ENA issued an ordinance that revoked the rice production order that had been in place since 1943; however, this order did not end complaints about rice.[81] A letter to the *Daily Service* published on November 26, 1948, noted that quotas were still in place and farmers were prosecuted for not filling their quotas. The author also acknowledged the work of the Abeokuta Ladies Club (ALC) in calling attention to the duress women traders of rice experienced. Not only was rice confiscated

[77] Abe Prof 1/ABP 2060, NAN, Ibadan.

[78] Re: seizure of rice, instructions," from officer i/c ENA police, No. E.P.87/101, September 24, 1945; Abe Prof 1/ABP 2060; circular from officer i/c, ENA police, No. E.P. 87/111/ANC, November 6, 1945, Abe Prof 1/ABP 2060, NAN, Ibadan.

[79] Letter to managers, United Africa Company, Ltd., and Patterson Zochonis, Ltd, from S. A. Fajembola, secretary, Local Merchants Committee, Abe Prof 1/ABP 2060, NAN, Ibadan. The district officer shared this information with Fajembola the day before the order went into effect. Lorries entering Abeokuta on the Ijebu Ode road had to carry ten bags of rice, while those along the Asha road had to carry three bags of rice.

[80] Letter from Eleti Ofe to the district officer, Abeokuta, September 19, 1945, Abe Prof 1/ABP 2060, NAN, Ibadan.

[81] The Native Authority Rice Production Revocation Order (1945), issued by the Alake of Abeokuta, November 20, 1945, Abe Prof 1/ABP 2060, NAN, Ibadan.

from traders, but some farmers were forced to purchase rice above the control price and resell it to the government at the control price in order to avoid prosecution.[82] Omo Agbe outlined a number of wrongs perpetrated on the farmers. Farmers insisted that they could not grow large quantities of rice for less than 2s 6d per Olodo measure (approximately 3 lbs), but the government imposed a price of 1s 2d. Following this blow, the Alake imposed a quota of 1,800 tons on several districts without any consultation and

> without reference to their ability, landed possessions, means of buying the necessary implements, food etc.... Many of those who were called upon to supply rice in their areas were not even farmers.[83]

He also hinted that individuals associated with the rice purchase exercised a monopoly and were connected to the black market. Omo Agbe expressed quite clearly that the colonial government and the Alake acted against the best interest of the people of Abeokuta.

The attacks on women traders galvanized them into action. They appealed to influential members of the community to advocate on their behalf. A group of thirty rice traders appealed to Rev. Israel Ransome-Kuti, the principal of the Abeokuta Grammar School, to use his influence on their behalf, for their rice had been confiscated and the Alake had ignored them. The author of the letter, J. A. Ladipo, a school headmaster, used the imagery of the war to great effect, "I beg you to use your good influence for their freedom from want, freedom from fear, freedom of trade and freedom from exploitation for which we have fought the German Nazism, the Italian Fascism and the Japanese atrocity."[84] Women traders also appealed to Ransome-Kuti's wife, Funmilayo Ransome-Kuti, the president of the ALC. She reported to the ALC members during their meeting on February 8, 1946, that she had tried to assist rice traders.[85] In the midst of the continued harassment of market women, the Alake announced an impending tax increase.

In many ways, the impending tax increase was the final straw. It became the catalyst that galvanized concerted political action against the Alake.

---

[82] Omo Agbe, "More about rice trouble in Abeokuta," *Daily Service* (Lagos), November 26, 1948. Omo Agbe is like a pen name adopted by the author. It has multiple meanings, including "child of a farmer" and "child of a beggar."

[83] Ibid. Traders use the small evaporated milk cans (5 oz) as a measuring cup. The commonest Olodo measure used for apportion yam flour, rice and other small grains is 12 milk can "cups." E-mail communication, Joseph Ayodokun (September 30, 2013).

[84] Letter to Rev. I. O. Ransome-Kuti, principal, Abeokuta Grammar School, from J. A. Ladipo, headmaster, Oke-Ona United School, September 19, 1945, Ransome-Kuti Papers, box labeled "Reign of Oba Ademola," Kenneth Dike Memorial Library (hereafter KDML), University of Ibadan. Police seized rice from both Mr. Ladipo and his sister, a rice trader. He also claimed that the police who seized the rice were Mr. Alao's messengers.

[85] Minutes of the Abeokuta Ladies Club, February 8, 1946, Ransome-Kuti Papers, Box 87/1, KDML, University of Ibadan.

The ALC subsequently merged with market women's associations to become the Abeokuta Women's Union (AWU), the organization that led the women's tax revolt. With Mrs. Ransome-Kuti at the helm, AWU protests and effective use of the media made the town ungovernable.[86] At its conclusion, Alake Ademola abdicated and went into exile and the Egba Council removed the poll tax on women.

The tax increase could only have happened with the blessing of colonial officials; however, the Alake as the intermediary between the colonial state and the women bore the full brunt of their anger. Their anger coalesced around several issues. Foremost, given the economic distress of the interwar depression, the war, and the postwar period, most women genuinely could not afford a tax increase. Moreover, they saw the Alake's unwillingness to advocate on their behalf as well as numerous instances of self-enrichment as equally compelling issues. The Alake received a salary from the colonial government; nonetheless, he was a businessman. He was involved in numerous business ventures and land transactions and had weathered many charges of corrupt practices from his earliest days in office.[87] Therefore the women's tax revolt represented an opportunity to address both their perceived political and economic grievances.

Conclusion

World War II reshaped the economic and agricultural landscapes of Abeokuta. More importantly, the war sharpened political tensions in Abeokuta town as men and women struggled to dominate or defend themselves in the grim economic climate. The struggle over foodstuffs during the war made the market an extremely contested space. In the process it exposed struggles between the state and local producers as officials tried to obtain commodities below the cost of production and producers tried to resist this exploitation. The struggle over foodstuffs also exposed tensions between distributors. European trading companies with the support of the colonial state maintained their hegemonic position in trade; however, they had to strategize against local African authorities who supported African traders. In Abeokuta, it is clear that small traders were caught between these two power blocks. Market women were vulnerable to the demands of the military and the food controller in Lagos and equally vulnerable to the Alake and his agents, especially the Native Authority police.

The Alake was a central figure in this unfolding drama. Despite his best efforts to manage his public role as the father of Abeokuta, the Alake became

---

[86] P. Ratclifffe, cadet, in Annual report, Egba division, 1948, p. 3, Abe Prof 1/ABP 1543, vol. IV, NAN, Ibadan.

[87] Ake Palace Papers 4/1/2, NAN, Abeokuta. The file supplied information about loans he had extended.

increasingly associated with duplicitous economic activities in the minds of women traders. No doubt these activities contributed significantly to the market women's demand for his removal from office in the postwar period. Yet, these events make clear that his power was not supreme. As a functionary within the colonial bureaucracy, pressure could be brought to bear on him to ensure that he privileged the state's priorities. The dramatic increase of rice for the government coffers in 1943, nonetheless, raised questions about how it was achieved. Did the Alake and his agents redirect rice from the illegal market to government agents or did the Alake and his agents bring more coercive pressure to bear on farmers and traders? We may never know the full answer, but it is clear that the colonial government gave the Alake and the police license to use whatever methods they had at their disposal to collect rice. The women's anger at the Alake was not misplaced; ultimately, it reflected their continuing critique of broader colonial policy as well as the specific ways in which Ademola used his power.

9

Africa's "Battle for Rubber" in the Second World War

William G. Clarence-Smith

Introduction: A Revolution in Africa's Production of Rubber

Africa accounted for only a little over 1 percent of the global output natural rubber when the Second World War broke out. Production had fallen drastically from the early 1910s, when Africa produced about 13 percent of the world's rubber. Most of this came from wild plants, but Africans had planted rubber during the great boom that ended in 1913, often "encouraged" by officials. In wetter areas, they usually grew indigenous *Funtumia elastica*, or American *Hevea brasiliensis* and *Castilla elastica*, sometimes called the Panama rubber tree. In drier areas, they planted Brazilian *Manihot glaziovii*, also known as the Ceará rubber tree.[1]

These African rubber resources proved unable to compete with *Hevea brasiliensis* planted in Asia, initially on estates and later on smallholdings. Attempts to replicate the success of large Asian rubber plantations were most successful in Liberia, where the American Firestone tire company doggedly pursued a dream of freeing itself from European colonial suppliers in Asia; however, large planters everywhere in Africa complained about the scarcity, the high cost and low productivity of workers, and the difficulties involved in securing concessions of suitable land.[2]

For African smallholders, rubber recalled unpleasant memories, as collection from the wild had been tainted by scandals in the Congo Basin, associated with King Leopold of the Belgians.[3] Smallholder rubber maintained itself most successfully in midwestern Nigeria, where communal plantings of

---

[1] H. N. Whitford and A. Anthony, *Rubber Production in Africa* (Washington, D.C.: U.S. Department of Commerce and Trade, 1926).

[2] William G. Clarence-Smith, "Grands et petits planteurs de caoutchouc en Afrique, 1934–1973," *Économie Rurale: Agricultures, Alimentations, Territoires*, 330–31, 88–102.

[3] Adam Hochschild, *King Leopold's Ghost: A Story of Greed, Terror, and Heroism in Colonial Africa* (Boston: Houghton Mifflin, 1998); Robert Harms, "The end of red rubber: a reassessment," *Journal of African History*, 16 (1975), 73–88.

Funtumia elastica had existed since the late 1890s. The colonial authorities distributed *Hevea brasiliensis* seedlings from 1911, and plots were gradually privatized. Cocoa did not grow well in this area, and rubber yielded incomes not too different from those obtained from palm oil.[4]

Nigeria and Liberia were thus the main beneficiaries of Africa's gently rising exports from 1934, as an international cartel gradually pushed up the world price by restricting both supplies and new planting. Africa was able to act as a "free rider" in this process, as no production quotas were imposed on the continent.[5] The outbreak of war in September 1939 did not immediately transform this situation, but the Japanese conquest of Southeast Asia from late 1941 catapulted Africa to the forefront of the global scene.

African Rubber 1939 to 1941: Modest Growth

After war broke out in Europe in September 1939, demand for African rubber increased slowly and unevenly up to late 1941, even though this commodity had become a crucial strategic resource for the world's increasingly mechanized armed forces.[6] A host of different vehicles ran on pneumatic tires with inner tubes, which accounted for about three quarters of global rubber consumption. Rubber also entered into a bewildering diversity of final and intermediary products. Moreover, virgin natural rubber remained essential for tires with large cross-sections, because they generated too much heat to be manufactured with reclaimed or ersatz materials.[7] Cable insulation also required natural rubber.[8]

However, the Allies blocked Axis access to Africa, while initially drawing mainly on their own supplies in Asia. After declaring war, Britain moved quickly to control prices on the London market and to deny rubber to its

---

[4] R. E. Bradbury and P. C. Lloyd, *The Benin Kingdom and the Edo-Speaking Peoples of South-western Nigeria, Together with a Section on the Itsekiri* (London: International African Institute, 1957), 45, 63, 76–77; Philip A. Igbafe, *Benin under British Administration: The Impact of Colonial Rule on an African Kingdom, 1897–1938* (London: Longman, 1979), 298–99, 342–47, 370–72; K. M. Buchanan and J. C. Pugh, *Land and People in Nigeria: The Human Geography of Nigeria and the Environmental Background* (London: University of London Press, 1955), 152–53.

[5] Andrew McFadyean, *The History of Rubber Regulation, 1934–1943* (London: George Allen and Unwin, 1944); E. O. Egboh, "The Nigerian rubber industry, 1939–1945," *The Nigerian Field*, 44 (1979), 2–4.

[6] Jonathan Marshall, *To Have and Have Not: Southeast Asian Raw Materials and the Origins of the Pacific War* (Berkeley: University of California Press, 1995).

[7] Hugh Allen, *The House of Goodyear: Fifty Years of Men and Industry* (Cleveland, OH: Goodyear, 1949), ch. 15–16.

[8] Peter J. T. Morris, "The development of acetylene chemistry and synthetic rubber by I. G. Farbenindustrie Aktiengesellschaft, 1926–1945," DPhil thesis, Oxford University (1982), 275–76.

enemies.[9] Preventive purchases were thus partly responsible for the upward trend in Africa's output. Average exports for 1934 to 1938 were some 10,000 metric tons a year, which reached nearly 13,000 in 1939, over 16,000 in 1940, and over 18,000 in 1941.[10]

Axis Europe, militarily hobbled by scarcities of raw materials, would gladly have purchased all of Africa's natural rubber. Despite the impressive growth of German synthetic rubber production, shortages of natural rubber contributed to preventing the Nazis from mounting a true *blitzkrieg*.[11] The Wehrmacht was a "poor army," much more heavily reliant on horses than its Western adversaries.[12] Axis designs on African raw materials, however, were frustrated by a tight Allied naval blockade, with rubber as one of the four main commodities involved.[13]

After the fall of France in June 1940, the Germans hoped to obtain rubber from the French West African colonial federation, which remained loyal to the Vichy regime.[14] Vichy earmarked West Africa's rubber output for France itself, however, in return for a promise to supply Germany with any Indochinese rubber that made it through the British blockade.[15] British naval forces soon prevented Vichy ships from rounding the Cape of Good Hope with rubber from Indochina, but the British policed French West Africa more lightly. As they feared pushing the Vichy regime into the war on the Axis side, they allowed neutral vessels to supply essential goods to Vichy, as long as there were no reexports to Axis zones.[16] Indeed, imports of rubber were well below France's needs, proving inadequate to meet contracts that the Germans had placed with French tire factories.[17] That said, by late 1941, Vichy France was bartering a little natural rubber for German synthetic rubber.[18]

---

[9] McFadyean, *History of Rubber Regulation*.

[10] *Rubber Statistical Bulletin*, passim; and Food and Agriculture Organization (FAO), *Yearbook of Food and Agricultural Statistics* (Washington, D.C.: FAO, 1947), Table 43.

[11] Rolf-Dieter Müller, "Albert Speer and armaments policy in total war," in Militärgeschichtliches Forschungsamt, ed., *Germany and the Second World War*, vol. 2, part II (Oxford: Clarendon Press, 2003), 477–78. For synthetic rubber, see Morris, "The development of acetylene chemistry and synthetic rubber"; Diarmuid Jeffreys, *Hell's Cartel: IG Farben and the Making of Hitler's War Machine* (London: Bloomsbury, 2008).

[12] Adam Tooze, *The Wages of Destruction: The Making and Breaking of the Nazi Economy* (New York: Viking, 2007), 164, 454–55.

[13] William N. Medlicott, *The Economic Blockade* (London: HMSO, 1952–59), vol. 1, 61.

[14] Susanne Heim, *Plant Breeding and Agrarian Research in Kaiser-Wilhelm-Institutes, 1933–1945: Calories, Caoutchouc, Careers* (New York: Springer, 2008), 101n115.

[15] Chantal Metzger, *L'empire colonial français dans la stratégie du troisième reich, 1936–45* (Bern: Peter Lang, 2002), vol. 1, 495.

[16] Richard E. Osborne, *World War II in Colonial Africa: The Death Knell of Colonialism* (Indianapolis, IN: Riebel-Roque, 2001), 83–84, 97, 10–14, 117–19, 142, 217–18; Medlicott, *The Economic Blockade*, vol. 1, 561–64, and vol. 2, 670.

[17] Alan S. Milward, *The New Order and the French Economy* (Oxford: Clarendon Press, 1970), 93.

[18] Annie Lacroix-Riz, *Industriels et banquiers français sous l'occupation: la collaboration économique avec le Reich et Vichy* (Paris: A. Colin, 1999), 305.

This loophole in the British blockade sufficed to give a modest boost to exports of rubber from French West Africa which had fallen to a mere 121 tonnes in 1933, but which stood at around 1,850 by 1941, all destined for France.[19] Some 825 tonnes came from Guinea-Conakry in 1941, 725 from Senegal and Mali, and 300 from Ivory Coast.[20] The French had completed a third all-weather road across the Sahara in 1939, maintained air communications, and pushed their Algerian railway a little further south from September 1941.[21] Vichy thus received some tropical produce from French West Africa by the Sahara route, even if Algerian ports found it hard to cope.[22] Rubber also arrived in Marseilles on French vessels slipping through the blockade, or brought by American ships to Morocco for transshipment into the Mediterranean.[23]

Italy's Fascist regime, acutely aware of East Africa's isolation and vulnerability to blockade, placed great hopes in local rubber, whether from *Hevea brasiliensis* plantations in southwestern Ethiopia, or in the form of latex from wild trees and bushes. Nothing appears to have come of either of these schemes, in part because Italian control of rural areas was so shaky.[24] Italian plans to develop a rubber goods industry in East Africa thus floundered.[25] As a result, the Italian armed forces there were chronically short on tires.[26] Indeed, when reviewing the shortages that contributed to the humiliating Italian military collapse in East Africa in 1941, the British referred "above all" to tires.[27]

It was the United States, neutral until December 1941, that did the most to boost Africa's output of natural rubber. The Americans lacked significant Southeast Asian supplies, were pessimistic about Britain's ability to defend Malaya and Indonesia against Japan, and sought to accumulate large natural rubber stocks after the fall of France in June 1940.[28] Washington thus encouraged more planting of *Hevea brasiliensis* in Firestone's estates in

[19] A. Aubréville, "Les forêts," in Eugène Guernier (ed.), *Afrique Occidentale Française* (Paris: Encyclopédie Coloniale et Maritime, 1949) vol. 1, 380.

[20] Afrique Occidentale Française, *Annuaire statistique de l'Afrique Occidentale Française, édition 1949* (Paris: Imprimerie Nationale, 1950), 300–09.

[21] Jean Suret-Canale, *French Colonialism in Tropical Africa, 1900–1945* (London: Hurst, 1971), 489n36; Osborne, *World War II in Colonial Africa*, 64, 83, 176.

[22] Maxime de Cassan-Floyrac, "Blocus et ravitaillement," *Revue des Deux Mondes*, 62 (1941), 81–83.

[23] Osborne, *World War II in Colonial Africa*, 101–04, 117–19, 142, 217–18.

[24] E. W. Polson Newman, *The New Abyssinia* (London: Rich and Cowan Ltd., 1938), 183; Haile Miriam Larebo, *The Building of an Empire: Italian Land Policy and Practice in Ethiopia, 1935–1941* (Oxford: Oxford University Press, 1994), 182, 237.

[25] Ferdinando Quaranta, *Ethiopia, an Empire in the Making* (London: P. S. King and Son, 1939), 72.

[26] Osborne, *World War II in Colonial Africa*, 90–91.

[27] I. S. O. Playfair, *The Mediterranean and the Middle East*, Vol. 1: *The Early Successes against Italy, to May 1941* (London: HMSO, 1954), 167.

[28] Marshall, *To Have and Have Not*, 12–16, 37–38, 50.

Liberia, Africa's most extensive rubber plantations.[29] In 1940 Firestone built the largest factory in the world to prepare latex for export in liquid form.[30] Liberia increased its overall output from some 5,500 tonnes in 1939 to around 8,500 tonnes in 1941.[31]

Rubber exports from the Free French and Belgian possessions in Equatorial Africa scarcely rose in 1940–1941.[32] General de Gaulle's forces secured Cameroon and French Equatorial Africa by November 1940, while the Belgian Congo declared for the exiled Belgian government in London. Both regimes wished to improve their profile in London and Washington, and thus placed rubber alongside minerals in a program of increased production;[33] however, the British were not keen on importing rubber from Equatorial Africa in 1940.[34] They did agree to buy rubber from French Equatorial Africa in 1941, mainly as a means of keeping the colonial federation economically and financially afloat.[35]

Indeed, Britain neglected Africa as a source of rubber during this initial phase of the war, as part of a more general process of allocating scarce shipping to Asia and the Americas.[36] Given the seven years that it took for a newly planted *Hevea* tree to be tapped, the British exploited Asian trees that had been neglected because of the Great Depression, and drew on rubber stocks there.[37] The booming South African tire industry, supplying Allied forces in the Middle East, imported Asian raw rubber.[38] Nigeria, the largest producer in British Africa, even saw its exports of rubber fall slightly, from some 2,800 tonnes in 1939 to 2,000 in 1941.[39] Uganda was in a similar position, with exports declining from around 800 to 550 tonnes over the same period.[40] The custodian of enemy property, in charge of confiscated

[29] Alfred Lief, *The Firestone Story: A History of the Firestone Tire and Rubber Company* (New York: McGraw-Hill, 1951), 205–07, 253–54.

[30] Wayne C. Taylor, *The Firestone Operations in Liberia* (Washington, D.C.: National Planning Association, 1956), 61.

[31] *Rubber Statistical Bulletin*; FAO, *Yearbook*, 1947, Table 43.

[32] Ibid.

[33] Osborne, *World War II in Colonial Africa*, 113–15, 121–22, 174; Jean-Baptiste Serier, *Histoire du caoutchouc* (Paris: Desjonquères, 1993), 199.

[34] André-Hubert Onana-Mfege, *Les Camerounais et le Général de Gaulle* (Paris: L'Harmattan, 2006), 38–39; J.-C. Willame, "Le Congo dans la guerre: la coopération économique belgo-alliée de 1940 à 1944," in *Le Congo belge durant la deuxième guerre mondiale* (Brussels: Académie Royale des Sciences d'Outre-Mer, 1983), 219.

[35] Virginia Thompson and Richard Adloff, *The Emerging States of French Equatorial Africa* (Stanford, CA: Stanford University Press, 1960), 195, 217.

[36] Michael Cowen and Nicholas Westcott, "British imperial economic policy during the war," in David Killingray and Richard Rathbone (eds.), *Africa and the Second World War* (Basingstoke: Macmillan, 1986), 25, 41–44.

[37] McFadyean, *History of Rubber Regulation*.

[38] Lief, *The Firestone Story*, 209, 262–63, 367–68, 413; Ronald Storrs, *Dunlop in War and Peace* (London: Hutchinson & Co, 1946), 85–86.

[39] Egboh, "Nigerian Rubber Industry," 11.

[40] Uganda, Department of Agriculture, Annual Reports, 1944–48, tables.

German-owned estates in British Cameroon, cut back on production and pared down the labor force, although "nonessential" crops suffered most, notably bananas, coffee, and cocoa.[41]

Japanese Expansion and the Scramble for African Rubber, 1942–1945

The situation was transformed by Japan's lightning campaign to seize Southeast Asia between December 1941 and March 1942, so that Africa was producing nearly 30 percent of the world's total output of natural rubber by 1944–1945.[42] The loss of over 90 percent of the world's cultivated *Hevea brasiliensis* trees brought the Allies to the brink of military catastrophe and turned Africa and Latin America into saviors of their cause. Although Allied output of synthetic and recycled rubber soared, aircraft, armored cars, trucks, earth-moving equipment, and buses still depended on natural rubber for their large tires.[43] It was estimated that an American battleship incorporated more than 75 tons of rubber, a tank almost a ton, and a "flying fortress" aircraft about half a ton, though some of this was synthetic or reclaim rubber.[44]

When the armies of the Rising Sun streamed through Southeast Asia, Germany and Italy briefly believed that their Japanese allies would be able to remedy their worsening shortage of natural rubber. However, they had lost the vital lifeline of the Trans-Siberian Railway in June 1941, when Germany's invasion of the Soviet Union put an end to special rubber trains; additionally, blockade-running ships and converted submarines were unable to carry more than a small and declining fraction of Asian natural rubber to Axis Europe.[45]

Even if the Axis powers could not benefit much, Japan's conquest of Southeast Asia fatally threatened to undermine the Allied war effort, offsetting the entry of the United States into the war. The Allies' stocks of natural rubber were only equivalent to about a year's consumption. Latin

[41] Simon J. Epale, *Plantations and Development in Western Cameroon, 1885–1975* (New York: Vantage Press, 1985), 118; Anthony Ndi, "The Second World War in southern Cameroon and its impact on mission-state relations," in David Killingray and Richard Rathbone (eds.), *Africa and the Second World War* (Basingstoke: Macmillan, 1986), 204, 210. For fluctuating rubber output figures, see FAO, *Yearbook*, 1947, Table 43.

[42] My calculations are based mainly on *Rubber Statistical Bulletin*, and FAO, *Yearbook of Food and Agricultural Statistics*, 1947, Table 43.

[43] Peter J. T. Morris, *The American Synthetic Rubber Research Program* (Philadelphia: University of Pennsylvania Press, 1989), 41; Loren G. Polhamus, *Rubber: Botany, Cultivation and Utilization* (London: Leonard Hill, 1962), 380.

[44] Glenn D. Babcock, *History of the U.S. Rubber Company: A Case Study in Corporation Management* (Muncie: Indiana University, 1966), 391.

[45] Medlicott, *Economic Blockade*, vol. 1, 404–05, 428–29, 649–51, 657, 669; vol. 2, 170–71, 44752; and Morris, "The development of acetylene chemistry and synthetic rubber," 273–76.

American cultivation was crippled by leaf blight and produced little from wild *Hevea* trees, India hardly produced more than it consumed, and the South Pacific exported very limited amounts. Ceylon (Sri Lanka) delivered significant quantities, but the island was on the frontline, and subject to devastating Japanese raids and submarine warfare.[46] As for temperate rubber-yielding plants in North America and Europe, they failed to provide more than a trickle of latex.[47] In the space of a few short months, Africa therefore became a vital source of this highly strategic raw material.[48]

Given the time it took for newly planted *Hevea brasiliensis* trees to be ready for tapping, the Allies resorted to emergency measures, squeezing as much as possible out of existing trees, both *Hevea* and non-*Hevea*.[49] Nevertheless, the Allies still encouraged the planting of *Hevea*, as nobody knew how long the war might last, and whether the Japanese might destroy Southeast Asia's stands.[50] For immediate needs, the Allies revived the collection of latex from indigenous wild plants, notably *Funtumia elastica* trees and lianas of the *Landolphia* genus, with rubber extracted from both stems and roots of the latter, but manufacturers complained about the poor quality of wild rubber.[51]

Africa's output of rubber, which had reached a little more than 18,000 tonnes in 1941, jumped to nearly 34,000 in 1942, more than 50,000 in 1943, and 60,000 a year in 1944–1945.[52] Nevertheless, the continent's production remained below that of Ceylon, which was on a plateau of around 100,000 tonnes a year.[53] Liberia and Nigeria were the largest African producers, together accounting for around half of the continent's output. However, their share of the total slipped somewhat, as did that of French and British Cameroon combined, whereas the Belgian Congo witnessed a rise in

---

[46] Peter T. Bauer, *The Rubber Industry, a Study in Competition and Monopoly* (London: Longmans Green & Co., 1948), 303–06; Warren Dean, *Brazil and the Struggle for Rubber, a Study in Environmental History* (Cambridge: Cambridge University Press, 1987), ch. 6; Ceylon, *Report of the Commission on the Rubber Industry in Ceylon, October 1947* (Colombo: Government Press, 1947); Osborne, *World War II in Colonial Africa*, 234, 236–37.

[47] William G. Clarence-Smith, "Synthetic and temperate rubber in the interwar years and during World War II," *Journal of Global History*, 5 (2010), 171–76.

[48] Cowen and Westcott, "British imperial economic policy," 52–53; J. Hurstfield, *The Control of Raw Materials* (London: HMSO, 1953), 168, 293–94, 369–70.

[49] Egboh, "Nigerian Rubber Industry," 4, 12.

[50] William G. Clarence-Smith, "The battle for rubber in the Second World War: cooperation and resistance," Commodities of Empire Working Paper No. 14, 2009.

[51] S. A. Brazier, "The rubber industry in the 1939–45 war," in P. Schidrowitz and T. R. Dawson (eds.), *History of the Rubber Industry* (Cambridge: W. Heffer & Sons Ltd., 1952), 324.

[52] My own calculations, based mainly on *Rubber Statistical Bulletin*, and FAO, *Yearbook*, 1947, Table 43.

[53] Bauer, *Rubber Industry*, 306. Bauer's figures for Africa need to be raised by about 10%. For stagnation in Sri Lanka, see Ceylon, *Report*.

its share. A host of opportunistic or coerced African producers appeared briefly in the statistics between 1942 and 1945, each accounting for small amounts.[54]

The rubber goods industry received a boost from 1942, although the growth of the tire industry continued to be limited to South Africa, where Dunlop began to make aircraft tires.[55] At the same time, Dunlop profited from heightened security anxieties to replace expensive Indian workers with cheaper black operatives, with official backing.[56] To substitute for Asian raw rubber, South Africa was allocated the output of East and Central Africa, including part of the Belgian Congo.[57]

Elsewhere in Africa, import substitution industrialization in the rubber goods sector was less significant. Indeed, the Anglo-American Economic Mission to Equatorial Africa was dismissive about local industries in 1942, and did not mention rubber goods in this context.[58] However, Bata, the Czechoslovak company that had relocated in Canada, already had shoe factories in Nigeria and the Congo, in part drawing on local rubber. The company opened a new plant in Southern Rhodesia (Zimbabwe) in 1943.[59] In Mozambique, a production of rubber-soled shoes, fan belts, and washers for the local market sprang up after 1942.[60] Angola witnessed the rise of another shoe industry reliant on rubber, from 1941.[61] Used tires were reconditioned on a small scale, and new tires were at times available from South Africa.[62]

The small Axis market for African natural rubber withered away after 1942, although Adolf Hitler became personally interested in this question early in that year.[63] The Vichy authorities responded by bartering a small amount of African rubber for manufactured goods.[64] However, the Allied landings in North Africa in November 1942, and the subsequent transfer of

[54] *Rubber Statistical Bulletin*; FAO, *Yearbook*, 1947, Table 43.

[55] Storrs, *Dunlop*, 85–86.

[56] Peter Alexander, *Workers, War and the Origins of Apartheid: Labour and Politics in South Africa, 1939–1948* (Oxford: James Currey, 2000), 48–49.

[57] *India-Rubber Journal*, January 9, 1943.

[58] Anglo-American Economic Mission, 1942, John Cadbury Papers (kindly made available to me by Professor David Birmingham).

[59] Peter Kilby, "Manufacturing in colonial Africa," in Peter Duignan and L. H. Gann, eds., *Colonialism in Africa*, Volume 4: *The Economics of Colonialism* (Cambridge: Cambridge University Press, 1975), 480–81, 485, 515; *Encyclopédie du Congo Belge* (Brussels: Éditions Bieleveld 1949–52), vol. 3, 408–09.

[60] C. F. Spence, *The Portuguese Colony of Mozambique; an Economic Survey* (Cape Town: A. A. Balkema, 1951), 80.

[61] Angola, *Anuário estatístico* (Luanda: Direccão dos Serviços de Economia e Estatística Geral), various years; Carlos Rocha Dilolwa, *Contribuição à história económica de Angola* (Luanda: [no publisher], 1978), 55.

[62] *India-Rubber Journal*, January 9, 1943; Dilolwa, *Contribuição*, 48, 55.

[63] Morris, "The development of acetylene chemistry and synthetic rubber," 273.

[64] Metzger, *L'empire colonial français*, vol. 1, 409.

French West Africa from Vichy to the Free French spelled an end to these deals.[65] In addition, the noose of the Allied blockade was further tightened.

Wild Rubber: King Leopold's Ghost

R. W. Johnson has decried the revival of the collection of rubber from the wild during the war as a return to the scandals associated with King Leopold's regime in the Congo Free State.[66] Logic, however, argued against repression, and the historical record is mixed. Thinly spread collectors in underpopulated regions were hard to control, and harsh pressures provoked rebellions at a time when colonial armed forces were tied up in far-flung theatres of war. As it was difficult, if not impossible, to motivate African collectors in terms of patriotism or similar ideologies, the price offered for raw rubber, and the availability of affordable trade goods, were crucial to obtaining wild rubber from savannas and forests.

After the fall of France in June 1940, the Vichy authorities ordered the African colonies remaining under their control to supply rubber, and the Institut Français du Caoutchouc sent its director to West Africa in early 1941, in part to survey the distribution of stands of wild rubber.[67] Guinea-Conakry emerged as a major focus of compulsory rubber collection, which was said to have endangered the rice harvest in one area in 1941, by draining away male workers.[68] Meanwhile, the British blockade, for all its leaks, made it pointless for Vichy officials to extract too much rubber. Moreover, British officials in Nigeria judged that it was high prices that boosted output in the northern reaches of Guinea-Conakry.[69]

After the fall of Southeast Asia, the Free French are held to have become more coercive than Vichy, thereby endangering the well-being of their African wards.[70] They set unrealistically high targets in West Africa, even when there was no historical record that an area had ever yielded any "liana rubber" during the great boom.[71] In 1944, Gaullist forces destroyed a village in Guinea-Conakry, because "people fled rather than supply rubber." A year later, the governor of Ivory Coast protested that rubber collectors were poorly remunerated, and that they risked contracting sleeping sickness in the forests.[72]

---

[65] *India-Rubber Journal*, January 16, 1943.
[66] R. W. Johnson, "French imperialism in Guinea," in Roger Owen and Bob Sutcliffe, eds., *Studies in the Theory of Imperialism* (London: Longman, 1972), 241.
[67] Raymond de Padirac, *L'Institut de Recherches sur le Caoutchouc, 1936–1984* (Montpellier: CIRAD, 1993), 15.
[68] Suret–Canale, *French Colonialism*, 479–80.
[69] Egboh, "Nigerian Rubber Industry," 6.
[70] Johnson, "French imperialism," 240–41.
[71] Michael Crowder, *West Africa under Colonial Rule* (London: Hutchinson, 1982), 497.
[72] Suret-Canale, *French Colonialism*, 479–80.

Much the same picture has been painted for FEA, for example in the southeastern forests of French Cameroon.[73] Pierre Kalck, an official in Oubangui-Chari (later the Central African Republic) during the war, denounced abuses in rubber collection "that discredited Free France in the eyes of the peasant masses."[74] Gathering wild rubber, whether from *Funtumia* trees or from *Landolphia* vines, was an "inadmissible waste of labor."[75] Félix Éboué, the black Guyanese governor-general of French Equatorial Africa, was unhappy about returning to this "barbaric system," but saw it as necessary to raise production to 4,000 tonnes a year.[76]

A different portrait emerges from the confidential correspondence of the Anglo-American Economic Mission of late 1942, which never mentions administrative coercion. Rather, the mission noted that prices for wild rubber had been raised substantially, and therefore recommended that cloth, clothing, bicycles, sewing machines, and hardware should all be imported in greater quantities than before the war. The report warned that "local authorities have underestimated the future purchasing power of the natives after the rubber program gets under way."[77] The Commission du Caoutchouc, set up in Libreville in 1942, similarly stressed the need to make imported goods available to those who sold rubber.[78] In Berberati, western Oubangui-Chari, John Cadbury remarked in a private letter that rubber was the only thing that Africans could sell to obtain imported goods, while fretting that they might collect less rubber if prices of manufactures were set too low.[79]

This relatively benign version of events is bolstered by oral testimonies recorded in southwestern Oubangui-Chari. Although remembering "abuses," local Africans were more impressed by the fact that the collection of wild rubber was the key to "ready access to consumer goods," in an area where there were no alternative commodities to sell. Indeed, they lamented the passing of the system after 1945. As one informant put it, "Africa had to close the road of rubber.... A law was passed ... America didn't need rubber anymore."[80]

---

73 Eugène Guernier and René Briat, eds., *Cameroun, Togo* (Paris: Encyclopédie de l'Afrique Française, 1951), 217–21.

74 Pierre Kalck, *Réalités oubanguiennes* (Paris: Berger-Levrault, 1959), 159.

75 Ange Franzini, "La forêt," in Eugène Guernier (ed.), *Afrique Équatoriale Française* (Paris: Encyclopédie Coloniale et Maritime, 1950), 356.

76 Daniel Crubilé, "Le caoutchouc," in Eugène Guernier (ed.), *Afrique Équatoriale Française* (Paris: Encyclopédie Coloniale et Maritime, 1950), 317.

77 "Import requirements for French Equatorial Africa for the year 1943," November 19, 1942, John Cadbury Papers, University of Birmingham Information Services, Special Collections Department (hereafter UBIS-SCD).

78 Serier, *Histoire du caoutchouc*, 198.

79 Letter No. 6, October 20, 1942, John Cadbury Papers, UBIS-SCD.

80 Tamara Giles-Vernick, *Cutting the Vines of the Past: Environmental Histories of the Central African Rain Forest* (Charlottesville: University Press of Virginia, 2002), 166.

It is equally difficult to determine whether carrot or stick was more significant in the Belgian Congo, where exports of wild rubber shot up, going from
15 percent of all rubber exported in 1942 to 85 percent in 1944.[81] Decrees
of March and April 1942 added another sixty days of obligatory labor for
war work, on top of the sixty days already owed, and gathering rubber
was a top priority;[82] however, the authorities also sought to set attractive
prices for collectors, and to stock stores with cloth and other trade goods.[83]
The Anglo-American Economic Mission of 1942 estimated that a "native"
would need to collect about half a ton of rubber to purchase a bicycle.[84]

These contradictions are illustrated by the experience of the Congolese
province of Équateur. From May 1942, African men were ordered to collect
either lengths of rubber-bearing vines or latex from wild trees. Women and
children had to beat the vines in the village, and all were told to transport
rubber to river ports. Quotas were set, and slackers were threatened with
a month in prison. Missionaries distanced themselves from the authorities,
reporting that local Africans well remembered the excesses of King Leopold's
regime. In 1944, a few "police operations" were deemed necessary to bring
in rubber, as people were tired of collecting it, and the absence of men in the
bush was interfering with growing food crops. An official report for 1944
also noted that opposition to the program was diminishing. Some Africans,
flush with cash earned from rubber, were judged to be better off than their
counterparts in cities, even if there was a shortage of goods to buy with the
money.[85]

In British and British-occupied parts of Africa, material incentives generally predominated. London sought to set the remuneration for different
qualities of wild rubber at levels that stimulated Africans to seek out latex-
bearing plants in forests and savannas.[86] Nigerian officials slashed wild

---

[81] A. Becquet, "Le caoutchouc," in *Congo Belge 1944* (Léopoldville: Imprimerie du Gouverne-
ment-Général. [1945]), 72–73; Serier, *Histoire du caoutchouc*, 199; *Encyclopédie du Congo
Belge*, vol. 3, 392.

[82] J.-M. Henry, "L'INEAC en Afrique pendant la seconde guerre mondiale," in *Le Congo Belge
durant la deuxième guerre mondiale* (Brussels: Académie Royale des Sciences d'Outre-Mer,
1983), 396n47; *Bulletin Agricole du Congo Belge et du Ruanda-Urundi, volume jubilaire,
1910–1960* (Brussels: Ministère du Congo Belge et du Ruanda-Urundi, 1961), 102; Osborne,
World War II in Colonial Africa, 108.

[83] H. A. A. Cornelis, "Belgisch Congo en Ruanda-Urundi tijdens de Tweede Wereldoorlog: de
economische en financiële situatie," in *Le Congo Belge durant la deuxième guerre mondiale*
(Brussels: Académie Royale des Sciences d'Outre-Mer, 1983), 60–61, 70, 86; Becquet, "Le
caoutchouc," 72–73.

[84] "Civilian consumption requirements of the Belgian Congo," September 24, 1942, John
Cadbury Papers, UBIS-SCD.

[85] Honoré Vinck, "La guerre de 1940–45 vécue à Coquilhatville (Mbandaka, R. D. du
Congo)," *Annales Aequatoria*, 22 (2001), 65–72, 79–91.

[86] *India-Rubber Journal*, July 4, 1942, citing Harold Macmillan, undersecretary of state for
colonies.

rubber tapping fees, raised rubber prices twice, discriminated more carefully between various grades, and accepted the worst kinds of rubber, which generally came from vines of the *Carpodinus* genus, or species of *Ficus* (fig) trees. They also fixed trading margins for private buyers, subsidized inputs needed for tapping and primary processing, obtained consumer goods from America reserved for collectors, and put out a barrage of propaganda.[87] In the Gold Coast (Ghana), there were no reports of force being employed.[88] In their attempts to extract wild rubber from Ethiopia, the British occupation authorities paid well above the world price, but only to obtain a paltry twenty-five tons of rubber between 1942 and 1945.[89]

That said, the British did at times apply compulsion for the war effort. A poor response to an initial appeal for collection in British Cameroon led to the promulgation of the Wild Rubber Order in 1943, whereby all able-bodied men were to deliver three pounds per month.[90] A year later, the report for Bamenda district noted that Africans were sometimes "known to trek eight days to and from their homes in the futile search for wild rubber," and that Native Authorities "quite often" employed force to fulfill rubber quotas.[91] Nigeria's Government Defence Regulations authorized compulsion, and some school children were mobilized to gather wild rubber.[92] In Tanganyika, the British declared in 1942 that, "no price is uneconomic for rubber," while tacitly condoning force in obliging Africans to collect it.[93]

The example of the Luvale, inhabiting a poor area in northwest Northern Rhodesia (modern Zambia), illuminates the complexities of extracting wild rubber in a British colonial context. Raising the local producer price to 2/6d per pound in late 1942 had limited effects, and "the combined exertions of Government officials and traders" were required for a positive outcome.[94] Luvale informants recalled the British telling them that "King George was in trouble with Hitler" and needed their help to obtain rubber; however, they refused to do anything until a chief led the way into the bush, at which point they followed him. Documents from the period reveal that local Africans held out for better compensation, and objected to paying taxes in rubber. The British raised prices again in 1944, in a context of rampant inflation,

[87] Egboh, "Nigerian Rubber Industry," 5–10.
[88] Wendell P. Holbrook, "The impact of the Second World War on the Gold Coast, 1939–1945," PhD thesis, Princeton University (1978), 272–73.
[89] Hurstfield, *Control of Raw Materials*, 168, 370.
[90] Epale, *Plantations*, 125–27.
[91] Ndi, "Second World War in Southern Cameroon," 214.
[92] Egboh, "Nigerian rubber industry," 9.
[93] Nicholas Westcott, "The impact of the Second World War on Tanganyika, 1939–51," PhD thesis, Cambridge University (1982), 84.
[94] R. H. Hobson, *Rubber: A Footnote to Northern Rhodesian History* (Livingstone: Rhodes-Livingstone Museum, 1960), 39.

but simultaneously passed a Compulsory Production Order, ordering Native Authorities to deliver twenty-four pounds per year from every taxpayer.[95]

Smallholdings: Unrecognized and Poorly Developed

Colonial regimes found it hard to distinguish between the exploitation of wild plants and the tapping of trees neglected or abandoned when the world rubber price had reached its nadir in 1932; however, trees that had "gone to bush" actually produced more latex after being rested, and an uncertain quantity of "wild rubber" from 1942 thus came from renewed peasant tapping of planted trees.[96] For example, from 1940, the majority of Oubangui-Chari (Central African Republic) rubber probably came from old *Manihot glaziovii* groves.[97] Between 1916 and 1929, the French authorities had imposed the planting of more than two million *Manihot* trees, with forced planting shading into free cultivation for peasants who lacked alternative cash crops. Although neglected in places, and even uprooted or destroyed by fire, many of these trees were tapped again as rubber prices rose.[98]

During the war, the French switched their attention to *Hevea brasiliensis*, maintaining a significant dose of administrative compulsion. An experimental station was set up in northern Gabon in 1941 for technical support, and estates in Cameroon supplied seeds.[99] After taking over Ivory Coast from Vichy in November 1942, the Free French put pressure on smallholders to switch from cocoa and coffee to rubber and oil palms.[100] The Belgians had already extended the compulsory cultivation of *Hevea brasiliensis* from 1933, especially along newly built dirt roads in the central Congo basin.[101] When they added an extra sixty labor days for the war effort in March 1942, planting rubber was included.[102] The 2,000 hectares of "native plantations" of *Hevea* in 1941 rose to more than 28,000 by the end of the war.[103]

---

[95] My thanks are due to Achim von Oppen for kindly making available his notes on oral interviews, and on documents from the National Archives of Zambia.

[96] Becquet, "Le caoutchouc," 72–73; William G. Clarence-Smith, "The Portuguese empire and the 'battle for rubber' in the Second World War," *Portuguese Studies Review*, 19 (2011), 177–96.

[97] Brian Weinstein, *Éboué* (London: Oxford University Press, 1972), 268.

[98] Catherine Coquery-Vidrovitch, *Le Congo au temps des grandes compagnies concessionnaires, 1898–1930* (Paris: Mouton, 1972), 430–31, 435–36; Pierre Kalck, *Historical Dictionary of the Central African Republic* (Lanham, MD: Scarecrow Press, 2005), 167; Great Britain, Naval Intelligence Division, *French Equatorial Africa and Cameroons* (Oxford: HMSO, 1942), 410.

[99] Thompson and Adloff, *Emerging States of French Equatorial Africa*, 195–96; Serier, *Histoire du caoutchouc*, 199; Crubilé, "Le caoutchouc," 317–18.

[100] Crowder, *West Africa under Colonial Rule*, 497.

[101] Samuel H. Nelson, *Colonialism in the Congo Basin, 1880–1940* (Athens: Ohio University, 1994), 153, 168–69, 171–74.

[102] Osborne, *World War II in Colonial Africa*, 108.

[103] *Bulletin Agricole du Congo Belge et du Ruanda-Urundi, volume jubilaire*, 102.

The only region where truly free rubber farming emerged on any scale was midwestern Nigeria.[104] A wave of enthusiasm greeted higher prices from 1942, and Edo farmers planted *Hevea* wherever they could, although some officials worried about food shortages. *Hevea* invaded forest reserves, some of which were declassified to facilitate the boom.[105] The government subsidized inputs and allowed communal lands to be transferred to private ownership, while stressing that it was not officially encouraging new planting.[106] Estates provided additional seeds as necessary.[107] The war thus consolidated the Benin (Edo) region of Nigeria as Africa's premier center of rubber smallholdings in Africa.

The Liberian government appeared to encourage a similar process, but Firestone mainly extended support to members of the Americo-Liberian elite. These absentee landowners had already created small plantations along roads in the interwar years, and this process accelerated from 1941. These small plantations only produced about 100 tonnes of rubber a year by the end of the war.[108]

Estates and Technology

Both Europeans and Americans placed greater faith in "scientific" western estates for the future of rubber in Africa. In reality, estates suffered from an excessive reliance on borrowed capital, high unskilled labor costs, and stratospheric skilled labor expenditures. They enjoyed no economies of scale in growing *Hevea brasiliensis*, tapping trees, or most forms of preparing raw rubber. Moreover, they often engaged in expensive and counterproductive agricultural strategies, such as clean weeding.[109] Nevertheless, plantation companies held an initial advantage in Africa. They could access effective practices developed in Asia, such as selected *Hevea* seeds, bud-grafted clones, and various tapping and primary processing techniques. Smallholders easily adopted all these methods, once their value had been demonstrated. The

---

[104] Gerald K. Helleiner, *Peasant Agriculture, Government, and Economic Growth in Nigeria* (Homewood, IL: Richard D. Irwin, 1966), 120–22.

[105] Pauline von Hellerman, "Things fall apart? A political ecology of twentieth-century forest management in Edo state, southern Nigeria," PhD thesis, University of Sussex (2006), 112–15, 128; Pauline von Hellerman and Uyilawa Usuanlele, "The owner of the land: The Benin obas and colonial forest reservation in the Benin Division, southern Nigeria," *Journal of African History*, 50 (2009), 244.

[106] Egboh, "Nigerian Rubber Industry," 4, 9, 12.

[107] J. A. S. Edington, *Rubber in West Africa* (London: Rex Collings, 1991), 5.

[108] Willi Schulze, *Liberia: länderkundliche Dominanten und regionale Strukturen* (Darmstadt: Buch Gesellschaft, 1973), 106–07; Paulette Salles, "Plantations au Libéria," in C. Cauvin et al., *Plantations industrielles et productions paysannes: Côte d'Ivoire, Libéria, Cambodge, Indonésie* (Talence: Centre d'Études de Géographie Tropicale, 1979), 167; Lief, *Firestone Story*, 325, 327.

[109] Bauer, *Rubber Industry*.

one exception was producing liquid latex for export, which demanded both much capital and sophisticated technical expertise.

Three rather different plantation groups dominated the cultivation of *Hevea* in West and Equatorial Africa by the late 1930s. Socfin (Groupe Rivaud) was a Franco-Belgian plantation company. Possessing immense rubber estates in Southeast Asia, Socfin developed concessions in French Cameroon and the Belgian Congo from the late 1920s.[110] Firestone, one of the four big American tire producers, hired skilled personnel from Sumatra for its Liberian properties.[111] Anglo-Dutch Unilever concentrated on vegetable oils, but two subsidiaries grew some rubber after 1929, Pamol in Nigeria and British Cameroon, and the Huileries du Congo Belge.[112]

From 1942, the Allies called on estate managers to radically increase their production in unorthodox ways. They "slaughter tapped" existing trees, and laid out new plantations with more than 4,000 trees to a hectare for precocious tapping at two years of age. Companies rarely went so far as to bleed *Hevea* trees to death, however, and ultradense planting failed to supply much rubber.[113] More significant for the future was a surge in the regular planting of *Hevea*. Firestone's estates went from some 7,700 hectares in 1936 to 23,100 in 1945.[114] In French Cameroon, there were around 5,000 hectares in rubber in 1938, and just over 8,000 by the end of 1944.[115] The Belgian Congo's rubber estates went from some 7,000 to 55,000 hectares from 1938 to 1948.[116]

The state itself became a planter, as with the Belgian Congo's agriculture department, which took over rubber estates abandoned during the Great Depression.[117] The British administered confiscated German

[110] William G. Clarence-Smith, "The Rivaud-Hallet plantation group in the economic crises of the inter-war years," in Pierre Lanthier and Hubert Watelet, eds., *Private Enterprises during Economic Crises: Tactics and Strategies* (Ottawa: Legas, 1997), 117–32.

[111] Lief, *Firestone Story*; Taylor, *Firestone Operations in Liberia*.

[112] D. K. Fieldhouse, *Unilever Overseas, the Anatomy of a Multinational, 1895–1965* (London: Croom Helm, 1978), 205–09; Edington, *Rubber in West Africa*, 10–11.

[113] Serier, *Histoire du caoutchouc*, 199; Salles, "Plantations au Libéria," 167; Lief, *Firestone Story*, 326–27; Taylor, *Firestone Operations in Liberia*, 59–60; William G. Clarence-Smith, "La Socfin (Groupe Rivaud) entre l'Axe et les Alliés," in Hubert Bonin, Christophe Bouneau, and Hervé Joly, eds., *Les enterprises et l'outre-mer pendant la Seconde Guerre Mondiale* (Pessac: Maison des Sciences de l'Homme d'Aquitaine, 2010), 111–12; Sanford H. Bedermann, *The Cameroons Development Corporation, Partner in National Growth* (Bota: Cameroons Development Corporation, 1968), 45; Henry, "L'INEAC," 396n47; Vinck, "La guerre," 89; *Bulletin Agricole du Congo Belge et du Ruanda-Urundi, volume jubilaire*, 102.

[114] Schulze, *Liberia*, 103.

[115] *Recueil Financier 1940* (Brussels), vol. 3, 699; France, Ministère de la France d'Outre-Mer, *Annuaire statistique du Cameroun, vol. I, 1938–1945* (Paris: Imprimerie Nationale, 1947), 66.

[116] *Encyclopédie du Congo Belge*, vol. 1, 589.

[117] *India-Rubber Journal*, July 4, 1942.

properties in Cameroon and Tanganyika, employing skilled technicians who had fled from Southeast Asia. From March 1942, nearly 6,000 hectares of derelict plantations of *Manihot glaziovii* in Usambara were brought back into production, producing nearly 5,500 tonnes of rubber for South Africa as a temporary wartime measure.[118] Existing *Funtumia elastica* and *Hevea brasiliensis* trees were intensively tapped in British Cameroon, and the newly formed Cameroons Development Corporation continued with *Hevea* after the war.[119]

It is hard to be sure how much forced labor underpinned these activities. Despite Firestone's protestations that its labor was free, the Liberian authorities applied pressure to ensure that sufficient workers were available.[120] In French and Belgian Africa, "natives" had long owed labor duties to the state. Although such workers were not to be transferred to private employers, conditions of war blurred such distinctions in French Cameroon, albeit seemingly less so in the Belgian Congo.[121] In Tanganyika, the British conscripted men, mainly those who were Gogo by ethnicity, in Central Province. Although many of these workers died or deserted in the difficult early months, some Gogo bought cattle with their wages, and went on to voluntarily sign new contracts.[122] The Nigerian government made strikes illegal in rubber production from 1942, but there is no indication that forced labor as such was employed.[123]

Conclusion

Africans saved the Allied cause in the Second World War by providing enough virgin natural rubber to keep the wheels of the war machine turning, but they received precious little gratitude for this remarkable feat. In his general survey of Africa in the conflict, Richard Osborne mentions rubber quite often, but there is no index entry for the commodity, and no overarching recognition of its significance.[124]

Wild rubber played the most obvious part in boosting output, and the jury remains out on how constraining collection was. Nevertheless, there is enough evidence to show that there was no simple turning of the clock back

---

[118] Nicholas Westcott, "The impact of the Second World War on Tanganyika, 1939–49," in David Killingray and Richard Rathbone (eds.), *Africa and the Second World War* (Basingstoke: Macmillan, 1986), 146, 151; Westcott, "The impact of the Second World War on Tanganyika," PhD thesis, 84–86.

[119] Bedermann, *The Cameroons Development Corporation*.

[120] F. P. M. van der Kraaij, *The Open Door Policy of Liberia: An Economic History of Modern Liberia* (Bremen: Übersee-Museum, 1983), vol. 1, 441–46.

[121] Onana-Mfege, *Les Camerounais*, 59; Cornelis, "Belgisch Congo," 60–61.

[122] Westcott, "The impact of the Second World War on Tanganyika," PhD thesis, 85–86.

[123] Egboh, "Nigerian rubber industry," 5.

[124] Osborne, *World War II in Colonial Africa*.

to the bad old days of King Leopold. Indeed, when the authorities ceased to purchase wild rubber, this entailed hardship for some poor areas.

Similarly, the extent of coercion applied for the obligatory cultivation of rubber, whether by smallholders or on estates, remains to be precisely determined. *Hevea* planted from 1942 did not mature in time to contribute to the war effort, but the long-term consequences for Africa were significant, as this is a long-lived tree. British policies of sustaining peasant dynamism had positive long-term consequences in Nigeria, whereas French and Belgian authoritarianism led to smallholders rejecting the commodity as soon as they could. The abolition of forced labor in French and Belgian Africa after the war also appears to have hampered the expansion of estates[125]

Overall, Africa failed to capitalize on its wartime boom. Despite receiving a second boost from the Korean War and political upheavals in Southeast Asia, Africa's rubber cultivation and manufacturing progressed only modestly, before falling victim to the continent's chaotic process of decolonization and economic mismanagement.[126] Nevertheless, the war demonstrated the continent's potential as a rubber producer, and West Africa may at last be coming into its own in the twenty-first century.[127]

---

[125] Clarence-Smith, "Grands et petits planteurs."

[126] Ibid.

[127] François Ruf, "L'adoption de l'hévéa en Côte d'Ivoire: prix, mimétisme, changement écologique et social" in *Économie Rurale: Agricultures, Alimentations, Territoires*, 330–331 (2012), 103–24.

10

Freetown and World War II

Strategic Militarization, Accommodation, and Resistance

Allen M. Howard

Though its contribution is little known, Freetown, the capital of the colony of Sierra Leone, was central to Allied strategy for several years, primarily as a convoy station.[1] The British started preparing the city for war in 1938, and the next year set in motion a comprehensive militarization. In 1942 and 1943, the United States joined Britain with military installations, officers, and troops stationed there, and the two powers carried out joint construction of port facilities. During the peak period, up to 200 cargo and military vessels might be moored in Freetown's wide, well-protected harbor: Hundreds of convoys formed there, mostly Europe-bound, and many thousands of soldiers and sailors passed through the port. Freetown residents took on a wide variety of skilled and semiskilled jobs related to the war, and tens of thousands of migrants flowed in from the protectorate to load and unload ships, build infrastructure, and handle many other tasks.[2] In the face of arduous work conditions, rising food prices, and low wages, laborers staged strikes and other actions, while residents challenged imperial and Allied designs in other ways. Sierra Leone was also affected by the large numbers of whites and Africans from other colonies who were stationed in or passed through Freetown and nearby bases. Racial, ethnic, and class tensions marked the war era, resulting in tussles on the street, fights, and even deaths. While most of those mobilized for civilian and military service

---

[1] "Sierra Leone" and "colony" often are confusing terms. Historically, the Colony (upper case) of Sierra Leone refers to an area, mainly comprising the Sierra Leone peninsula where Freetown is located, that had a special legal and administrative status with Great Britain. Most of what made up the colony (lower case) of Sierra Leone was the much larger Protectorate, which was administratively separate from the Colony. Britain ruled both and Freetown was the capital of both; here colony (lower case) refers to both. I would like to thank Laura Tabili for her insightful comments on an earlier version of this chapter and the editors, particularly Carolyn Brown and Judith Byfield, for their valuable suggestions on this project and chapter. Annalise Kinkel and, especially, Benjamin Twagira provided excellent research assistance.

[2] *Annual Report of the Colony of Sierra Leone*, 1946, 3.

were men, African women were also deeply affected by the war and acted to protect their interests. All in all, colonial and military officers sought to gain the compliance of Freetown's populace with extraordinary wartime measures through both coercive and subtle techniques, including propaganda. Africans accommodated in various ways and professed their loyalty, but also challenged demands and controls. Many issues were bargained out, and authorities often had to give ground.

Freetown's militarization and subsequent demilitarization followed one time arc that reflected the place of the harbor and city in the overall Allied strategy and also another time arc that involved the British administration's desire to manage the population, the war-distorted economy, and African challenges to policies and practices.[3] Britain established a West African War Council, which met regularly in Freetown and other West African cities to make strategic plans, set production goals, and issue directives for Sierra Leone, the Gold Coast, Nigeria, and the Gambia, all of which supplied commodities deemed essential for military and civilian use. In 1942, Great Britain and the United States signed an agreement based on a study for and the decisions of the Combined Chiefs of Staff (as set out in C.C.S. 63), in which Americans stationed personnel and provided materiel for port development. They created a joint staff arrangement for coordinating operations in and around the city. Freetown was frequently on the agenda of the highest-level war planners of the two powers. In mid-1943, however, the United States ended its participation in port development, having decided that new strategic realities had reduced the importance of Freetown.

Military and civilian authorities generally worked together to realize major strategic goals. They negotiated particular policies and the means for putting them into effect. British commanders oversaw bases in Freetown and elsewhere, drew heavily on the colony's human and natural resources, and instituted measures to safeguard troops. They shared authority in certain sectors with the governor and other colonial officials, who continued handling administrative, tax, and police functions. Since the interests and outlooks of colonial and military officers differed in certain ways, they were at times divided over particular practices in Freetown and policies toward Africans. Although they shared control over the recruitment, control, and application of African labor related to the war effort, colonial officials were much more concerned than the military with the larger implications of wage rates and residents' struggles to meet daily needs. While both responded to racial and ethnic tensions that arose as people interacted in a highly diverse city, civil authorities were worried about the long-term effects of those encounters and the recruitment of Sierra Leoneans into the armed

---

[3] Great Britain had military installations in and around Freetown from the origins of the Colony of Sierra Leone in 1808 and throughout the colonial era. Some of the existing bases were expanded and upgraded during World War II.

forces. Moreover, in contrast with the military, colonial authorities had to plan for postwar economic and political change. Freetown politics were thorny, especially since the city council retained some authority and complex questions about African governance remained unresolved during the war. Starting in 1943, the military command gradually turned sites back to full civilian control, but ranking officers on the spot and War Office representatives still exercised prerogatives during the next two years. Colonial officials maintained wartime controls over prices, wages, movement of people, and political expression through the war and, in some matters, well beyond.

Africans living in Freetown had different chronologies and experiences of the war depending on their gender, ethnicity, class, work and other aspects of their lives, identities, and social positions. Every resident was affected to a greater or lesser degree by militarization of the city and other upheavals of the war era. Yet, even as imperial and global forces transformed Freetown, residents continued to shape the city. Earning an income and obtaining food and other necessities, including housing and education, took ingenuity and great effort in a novel environment. People joined a wide variety of labor, ethnic, and religious associations; managed schools; volunteered for many war-related tasks; published newspapers that shaped opinion; and ran businesses that delivered many commodities, all under stringent and often unpredictable conditions. For Freetown dwellers, demilitarization was a drawn-out multisided process that lasted well beyond the Axis defeat.

Freetown felt some of the same forces as cities elsewhere in Africa, which this book amply demonstrates, but there were also similarities between Freetown and European and American cities. No major German attack came, but authorities expected it, as did Freetown dwellers, who were subjected to years of air raid drills, blackouts, and controls over their movements. Despite parallels with other places, Freetown and its residents experienced the era in unique ways. No other African port matched its role in assembling convoys, and its militarization exceeded that of other capitals in colonial Africa outside the war zones. According to Behrens' semiofficial history of merchant shipping, it was not only the total volume of shipping that made Freetown a unique port, but the great variety of ships as well as the unusually high number that might enter the harbor in a short period of time. On a single day in 1941, over fifty vessels steamed into port. While troop ships were typically oil fired, cargo ships were propelled by coal, which had to be replenished for the trip up the west coast or the return voyage. Freetown became one of the most important bunkering sites in the Atlantic theater of war.

Perhaps what distinguishes Freetown most was the rapidity and scale of its population growth and the severity of the resulting problems. Immediately following the declaration of war, numbers expanded slowly, but after the fall of France and the Allied loss of the port of Dakar, combined with the start of convoying and major infrastructure projects, the jump was phenomenal.

In the first half of 1940, an average of about 10,000 people were formally employed in the Colony (mainly in and around Freetown) by firms, the military, and the civil authorities. Between August and December 1940, the number rose from 15,500 to 25,700, an increase of two-and-a-half times; by November 1942, it had climbed to over 50,000.[4] It stayed near that level for another year before beginning to decline. Beyond those paid wages and salaries, many thousands more long-term residents and immigrants, especially women, worked in the informal sector. Some officials estimated that by mid-1941 Freetown's population, including military personnel, had nearly doubled (it was tallied at 55,000 in the 1931 census). Although the number may have been exaggerated, a contemporary report of a fairly comprehensive registration of workers in 1942 estimated there were 100,000 males between the ages of 18 and 55 in the Colony as a whole, with the overwhelming bulk of them living in Freetown.[5] In addition to the huge flow of immigrants from the interior, the European population of Sierra Leone multiplied from about 400 to 6,000 to 7,000, with most of them living in Freetown and its environs.[6] Seabees and other U.S. forces were stationed in and around Freetown. Their presence added to the city's remarkable heterogeneity and flux, and affected the chronology of militarization and demilitarization.

In official British thinking, constructing massive works, defending the port and its facilities, and controlling its large and growing population required that Freetown, especially certain sites, be militarized. Militarization involved actions by the civilian authorities, the West African War Council, and the Ministry of War Transport. A resident minister of the Ministry of War was appointed for West Africa. He chaired meetings of the West African War Council on which governors, generals, air marshals, and admirals sat. High-ranking military officers and the resident minister negotiated directly with both the Colonial Office and the governor of Sierra Leone, who retained authority over many matters and whose local expertise and staff capabilities were needed by the War Office. British civilian and military authorities also had to negotiate sensitive issues with American officers because of the

---

[4] The figures were based on reports by employers with "not less than ten" Africans employees, who were the large-scale hirers. *Sierra Leone Labour Report*, 1939–1940, 1, 1941–1942, 2.

[5] Extract from the 3rd meeting of the West African War Council, October 6, 1942, appendix B, "Report on the progress of registration and conscription," Colonial Office (hereafter CO) 267/682, The National Archives (hereafter TNA), Kew. The 1963 Census recorded about 128,000 people in Freetown. For Freetown censuses, see Barbara E. Harrell-Bond, Allen M. Howard, and David E. Skinner, *Community Leadership and the Transformation of Freetown (1801–1976)* (Paris: The Hague; New York: Mouton, 1976), 34.

[6] Minute, July 30, 1941, CO/267/682/2, TNA, Kew; acting governor (Sierra Leone) to Secretary of State for the Colonies (hereafter SSC), confidential dispatch, August 8, 1941, and governor to SSC, confidential dispatch, September 26, 1941, both in CO 267/683/4 (Economic and social conditions), TNA, Kew.

United States bases, materiel supplied, and personnel residing in Sierra Leone or passing through the port.

Historians have tended to view Africa's involvement in the war in terms of battles on its soil, contributions by its soldiers, and political changes induced by Allied policy or ideology. Many feel that the war weakened European colonial hegemony and roused African nationalism. Yet, economic and social changes were also of great importance, in both the short and the long run. In a pioneering article on Sierra Leone's war era economy, Gilbert A. Sekgoma demonstrates how Britain extracted resources from the Colony, including direct monetary transfers derived from taxes on subjects, while shelving many health and other development programs. He argues that the war further integrated Sierra Leone into a peripheral relationship with the metropole.[7] That is correct in certain respects, although the process was less mechanical and more contradictory and negotiated than Sekgoma allows. As important as it was, however, the colonial relationship was one component of a complex set of wartime changes. Freetown was part of a worldwide human, economic, and military mobilization that involved multiplying the output of food, other crops, and minerals; coordinating production among various colonies and states; and serving the strategic goals of Britain and its allies. A. G. Hopkins and others historians maintain that the Second World War marked the last stages of "modern" globalization: Freetown certainly shared in that. Yet, the city and its residents also experienced many qualities typically associated with postcolonial globalization: massive urbanization; the worldwide circulation of people, commodities, and ideas; and the severe impact of universal forces on local conditions.[8]

Building Civilian Defense and a Wartime Mentality in Freetown

Until 1943, authorities and residents were genuinely apprehensive of a German assault by sea or air, given Freetown's importance in convoying and U-Boat activities off the West African coast. Officials implemented civil defense plans similar to those in English cities. In mid-1939, an air raid precautionary officer was appointed and emergency response measures were initiated that militarized many places in the city. Expecting that the main government hospital (Connaught) would be unable to handle all the injuries

---

[7] Gilbert A. Sekgoma, "The Second World War and the Sierra Leone economy: Labour employment and utilisation, 1939–45," in David Killingray and Richard Rathbone (eds.), *Africa and the Second World War* (New York: St. Martin's Press, 1968), 233ff.

[8] A. G. Hopkins, "Globalization: An agenda for historians," in A. G. Hopkins (ed.), *Globalization in World History* (New York and London: W. W. Norton and Company, 2002), 1–11. For an examination of the relationship of the local, the regional, and the global in the history of African cities, see Allen M. Howard, "Actors, places, regions, and global forces: An essay on the spatial history of Africa since 1700," in U. Engel and P. Nugent (eds.), *Respacing Africa* (Leiden: Brill Academic Publishers, 2009), 11–44.

from an attack, officials designated schools, a missionary hospital, dispensaries, other government buildings and even the Kroo "Tribal" Court as first aid stations – and equipped them. African sanitary officers and first aid nurses were trained to treat casualties.[9] Other civilian defense measures disturbed daily life and helped create a feeling among residents of a city at war. Air raid and fire drills were held, and authorities recruited, primarily among Krio, wardens responsible for handling emergencies and educating neighbors about how to respond.[10] Drills were announced with sirens, church bells, and drums. Blackouts were initiated by early 1939, and for a period, total blackouts were enforced every night.[11] Violators were subject to fines. Most volunteers were Krio men, but they also included a few Africans of other backgrounds, Europeans, and women, apparently all Krio.[12]

Through various public dramas, the media, and organized propaganda campaigns, officials tried to generate a wartime mentality and win support among Freetownians. Many of their efforts were aimed at the educated Krio community that dominated certain aspects of Freetown life. Officials also had to reach as many city dwellers as possible, including recent immigrants, because of the need to militarize the city, mobilize people, and gain compliance with wartime measures. African elites – Christian and Muslim; Krio and members of other communities – professed their support for the war, and many individuals and organizations joined collection drives.

Newspapers were allowed to publish during the war, but under controls. All papers agreed to submit manuscripts for review, and the more conservative ones regularly provided a voice to officials and carried a great number of articles that, in sum, conveyed a sense that Sierra Leone was an integral part of a dangerous and costly, but noble, war effort. *The African Standard*, the official voice of the radical West African Youth League (WAYL), was the

---

[9] *Sierra Leone Weekly News* (hereafter *SLWN*) September 30, 1939.

[10] CO 267/677/1; and CO 267/677/1 1940, TNA, Kew. The historical and contemporary use and meaning of the terms Krio and Creole have been heavily debated. They refer to (a) the residents of the Colony who had an Atlantic origin, including people of African descent repatriated from Nova Scotia and Jamaica, and, especially, Liberated Africans and their descendants, all of whom mixed with local people; and (b) the language of those people. Repatriated and Liberated Africans had a unique legal status vis-à-vis Great Britain, as they were declared in 1854 to be subjects of the crown. Britain also governed the Colony under different laws and administrative procedures than the Protectorate, which was established in 1898. See Mac Dixon-Fyle and Gibril Cole (eds.), *New Perspectives on the Sierra Leone Krio* (New York: Peter Lang, 2006); Akintola J. G. Wyse, *The Krio of Sierra Leone: An Interpretive History* (Freetown: W. D. Okrafo-Smart and Company, 1989).

[11] Blackout rules changed over the war years, see *SLWN*, January 28, 1939; *Daily Guardian* (hereafter *DG*) March 17, and June 9, 1941; May 4, 1942.

[12] *SLWN*, February 25, 1939. It appears that at first women were not assigned duties, but later they were given civil defense roles. The Sierra Leone Defense Corps was ended by mid-1943, if not earlier. Minutes of the tenth meeting of the West Africa War Council, Achimota, October 26, 1943, CO 554/133/22 (Secret West Africa, Resident Minister, War Council Minutes, 1942–1943), TNA, Kew.

only paper that challenged the initial rules, leading to new regulations that enabled the governor to block publication of material deemed "prejudicial to defense or the efficient prosecution of the war."[13] The newspaper-reading public was informed on a daily basis about fighting in Europe, Asia, and Africa, often in heroic or threatening tones. Officials worried about the need to counter German propaganda, and Germany was depicted in numerous accounts as a racist country that practiced slavery and forced labor.[14]

Sierra Leone authorities were quick to see the value of radio diffusion, a closed circuit with broadcasts transmitted by wire to speakers mounted around the city and in some homes. The colonial government appointed A. B. Matthews as information officer in 1939; he gave talks and coordinated sessions by others.[15] Governors made rousing speeches and also presented mundane details of legislation and policy. Lesser officials and Freetown residents, chosen for their expertise, reputations, and of course, loyalty, also addressed the public on a wide variety of issues.[16] Freetown residents however, did not passively receive British propaganda efforts. Sierra Leoneans regularly criticized Matthews in the local press, through correspondence, and in conversation for not including sufficient African content in broadcasts, having too narrow a range of opinion and "voices," and even being boring. He acknowledged some of these shortcomings and made adjustments, while trying rather paternalistically to suggest that he, himself, was a Sierra Leonean because of his long residence and understanding of the Krio language, Freetown, and the Colony.[17]

Militarizing Freetown

Great quantities of capital and labor were devoted to making Freetown a well-protected convoy harbor. Figure 10.1 shows the location of various war-related sites. A number of military installations in and around the port and on the peninsula were built or upgraded, including artillery batteries and airstrips. Among those were the heavy gun emplacements on Cockerill Point, Aberdeen Hill, and other sites. From those points, most of the expansive harbor was within artillery range. Large-scale infrastructure projects were carried out so that Freetown could supply the essential needs of convoy vessels and other ships: coal and water. Improvements in the main wharf in downtown Freetown and new facilities at Cline Town were very important for the war effort and the colony's commercial future. Great Britain,

---

[13] Acting Governor Blood to Lord Moyne, C.O., January 10, 1941, CO 267/681/1 (Activities of West African Youth League), TNA, Kew.

[14] For an example, *DG*, June 3, 4, 6, 9, 10, and 24, 1941.

[15] For some background on Matthews, see Harrell-Bond, Howard, and Skinner, *Community Leadership and the Transformation of Freetown*, 142–52ff.

[16] *Sierra Leone Daily Mail* (hereafter *SLDM*) January 28, and February 25, 1939.

[17] I wish to thank Benjamin Twagira for his research on A. B. Matthews.

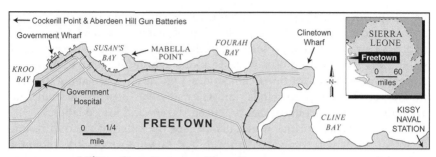

FIGURE 10.1. Military Sites, Freetown, Sierra Leone

and, to a lesser degree, the United States, financed and directed war construction. Private corporations also provided facilities and manpower, for which they were compensated. Africans paid with their bodies, skills, and resources.

Coal was delivered to Freetown from Nigeria and elsewhere for offloading and storage on shore or barges. Except for some burned on the railroad and in machinery and power stations, the coal was reloaded onto ships calling at the port. Turning ships around rapidly and meeting convoy departure schedules had the highest strategic priority. When coal shortages held up convoying or when labor stoppages interfered with strategic goals, the top levels of the Ministry of War Transport demanded improvements.[18] African laborers were caught in a mechanism that, particularly in 1940 and 1941, was chaotic, dangerous, and extremely stress ridden.

Already by the end of 1941, each day an average of 1,700 tons of fresh water were required to supply the ships in the harbor. Moreover, the needs of 40–50,000 new residents, plus war personnel, greatly boosted demand. Civilian and military officials organized a massive water gathering and delivering project. The main dam and piping alone required thousands of laborers, and took years. Despite such efforts, city dwellers experienced shortages – sometimes severe – for drinking, cooking, laundry, and hygiene throughout the war and beyond.[19]

A crisis was reached by the dry season of 1941–1942. In February 1942, water rationing began earlier in the year than previously in order to "meet the essential demands of shipping."[20] Not only were supplies often less than half the estimated per capita needs, but also the water was sometimes

---

[18] Minute, January 31, 1941; and Ministry of War Transport (hereafter MT), May 8, 1942, both in MT 59/115 (Bunkering at Freetown, 1940–1943), TNA, Kew.

[19] Enclosure to memo of the director of public works (hereafter DPW), July 17, 1942; Secret memo from G. H. Barrington Chance, Treasury, to A. C. T. Edwards, Colonial Office, February 17, 1942; and Colonial Office, minute, September 19, 1942, CO 267/680/6 (Freetown Water Supply, 1942), TNA, Kew.

[20] People were asked to accept sacrifices as part of their contribution to the war effort. Notice by president, Freetown City Council, dated January 31, 1942, *DG*, February 3, 1942.

polluted.[21] Even after improvements, rationing was common year after year. In 1944, for instance, beginning on March 15, Freetown water was liable to be shut off at noon; later in the month, taps went dry at 9:00 A.M. Residents then had only four hours to obtain the day's needs. Children missed school as they stood in water lines, and extra stress fell on women, who generally were responsible for household tasks requiring water.[22] Moreover, housing was crowded and sanitation inadequate for many Freetown dwellers. Officials expressed concern about the "appalling" conditions under which the poor lived, which they considered a possible source of social unrest and an embarrassment. Fires leveled densely settled areas and raised fear.[23]

City health policies were also militarized, with gains for some but detrimental impacts on many residents. From the perspective of strategically minded high-ranking military officers, Freetown posed a health problem that superseded all others: malaria. By mid-1940, reports showed a high incidence of malarial symptoms among military personnel whose ships had anchored in Freetown harbor. A worried Colonial Office commissioned an investigation led by Professor D. B. Blacklock from the Liverpool School of Tropical Medicine. Blacklock drew an arc on the map of Freetown and surroundings, with its center near the port: parts of the Colony within that zone received comprehensive eradication treatment, areas outside relatively little. Africans benefited in direct relationship to their proximity to places of strategic significance. Best off were city residents within the arc, people living near troop installations, or those actually in the military. Despite such schemes, fairly high rates of malaria continued to be reported among service personnel who passed through the harbor. After the acting governor protested that the city's population was bearing a heavy burden of disease, the Colonial Office agreed to additional funding through the Colonial Development and Welfare Act.[24]

Clashes in Freetown over Prices, Wages, Race, and Nationality

Colonial and imperial officials were very apprehensive that economic conditions would lead to urban upheavals, making the city difficult to govern and interfering with convoying and other strategic goals. A 1939 Act established

---

[21] Enclosure to memo of DPW, July 17, 1942, CO 267/680/6 (Freetown Water Supply, 1942), TNA, Kew.

[22] *DG*, March 15 and 31, and April 5, 1944.

[23] In December 1940, a fire on a major thoroughfare reportedly leveled 50 houses and left over 600 people homeless. *DG*, January 18, 1941.

[24] Acting Gov. Blood to Lord Moyne, C.O., March 19, 1941 and C. G. Spears, Treasury, to O. G. R. Williams, C.O., June 7, 1941, CO 267/681/7 (Malaria in Freetown Harbor: The Blacklock – Wilson Mission); CO 267/681/9 (Anti-Malarial Measures in Freetown: Schemes Under C. D. & W. Act), TNA, Kew.

a committee that set prices for commodities, legislated against hoarding and profiteering, and criminalized violations. As the population increase ran ahead of supplies, the cost of living index spiraled, reaching 234 in 1942 against a 1939 base of 100.[25] Officials issued even more stringent regulations. Matthews gave many broadcasts on economic subjects, typically mixing pleas for cooperation with threats against those who disobeyed laws.[26] Selling even small quantities of food or nonfood items above approved prices brought harsh punishment.[27] Tension between police and market women could flare.[28] Yet, authorities depended on merchants and traders, most of whom were women, to make food available to the Freetown populace. Some large-scale African traders, especially those with contracts to supply food and building materials, accumulated wealth during the war.[29]

Because food constituted well over half of average household expenditure and residents at the lowest income levels often had a very inadequate diet, officials were intent on addressing questions of supply and price.[30] No commodity was of greater concern to officials and residents alike than rice. Rice had deep significance for most people in Sierra Leone. Because it constituted the basic starch staple, it was at the center of family and ceremonial

[25] After that date, the official number stayed more or less on a plateau, not going above 255 during the war, although workers in 1943 complained of rising prices. In March, 1946, the cost of living index was still 242. *Annual Report of the Colony of Sierra Leone, 1946* (Freetown: Government Printer, 1947), 16.

[26] Matthews and others made at least eight broadcasts on rice, profiteering, and price controls in the second half of 1941, which were reprinted in the *Daily Guardian*.

[27] See, for instance, *DG*, October 1942, and January 4, 1943.

[28] Newspapers did not report any popular attacks on market women, but the elite press criticized women for profiteering, e.g., see *DG*, October 1942. For a history of the clashes between Freetown traders and authorities, see Allen M. Howard, "Contesting commercial space in Freetown, 1860–1930: Traders, merchants, and officials," *Canadian Journal of African Studies/Revue Canadienne des Etudes Africaines*, 37 (2003), 236–68.

[29] Given increased demand, shortages, and higher prices for many commodities, a diverse body of traders saw opportunities to make money. See A. M. Howard's interviews with Teddy Jones, Freetown, December 8, 1968, and with Alhaji Bomporroh Bangura, Port Loko, May 16, 1968; these interviews were deposited at the Center for African Studies, University of Sierra Leone. Alhaji Momodu Allie, who became Fula headman in 1931, ran a lucrative trade in cattle; see Alusine Jalloh, "Alhaji Momodu Allie: Muslim Fula entrepreneur in colonial Sierra Leone," in A. Jalloh and D. E. Skinner (eds.), *Islam and Trade in Sierra Leone* (Trenton, NJ: Africa World Press, 1997), 65–86. Constance Cummings-John profited by supplying stone and materials to those constructing the harbor facilities and airfields; see Constance A. Cummings-John with LaRay Denzer, *Constance Agatha Cummings-John: Memoirs of a Krio Leader* (Ibadan: Humanities Research Center and Sam Bookman Educational and Communication Services, 1995), 57–59. For a longer history of African traders in Freetown, see Allen M. Howard, "Islam and trade in Sierra Leone, 18th–20th centuries," in Jalloh and Skinner (eds.), *Islam and Trade in Sierra Leone*, 21–64.

[30] Sierra Leone Labour Department, *A Report on the Cost of Living Survey, held in Freetown during February, 1941*, Sessional Paper, 1941, no. 9, Freetown, 1941.

life.[31] In 1942, a colonial official wrote, "It is essential that foodstuffs, and rice in particular... should be brought to Freetown regularly in order to sustain the food supplies to the considerable population... which includes a large force of labour employed on essential construction... in addition to considerable number of African personnel of the Services."[32] Authorities dealt harshly with traders accused of hoarding rice or profiteering, and took extraordinary steps to make rice available.[33] A government mill operated long hours, and rice distribution centers were opened for direct sale to the populace.[34] Boosting production also had a high priority.[35] Nonetheless, shortages continued during 1944 and after the war, when price controls remained in effect.

Wartime regulations authorized officials to use involuntary labor for defense purposes; conscripted workers were employed in certain Freetown military projects at rates below what the colonial government paid; however, they constituted only a portion of new arrivals from the protectorate. The majority of migrants came to Freetown seeking money.[36] Although some were pressured by chiefs and district officers, that does not appear to have been a major factor.[37] Like migrant women who went into Freetown's informal sector, men were driven by rural poverty exacerbated by a decline of output and crop prices during the depression and early war years.[38] A 1943 official report estimated "that 23% of the adult male population of the

[31] Richard Fanthorpe, "Limba 'Deep Rural' strategies," *Journal of African History*, 39 (1998). 17–19; Michael Jackson, *The Kuranko: Dimensions of Social Reality in a West African Society* (New York: St. Martin's Press, 1977), 7–8; Paul Richards, *Coping with Hunger: Hazard and Experiment in a West African Farming System* (London: Allen & Unwin, 1986).

[32] Confidential dispatch, Governor Stevenson to SSC, CO, August 5, 1941, CO 267/683/4 (Economic and Social Conditions), TNA, Kew.

[33] For targeting food dealers, see articles in *DG*, June–September 1942, and October 26, 28, and 29, 1942.

[34] Confidential dispatch, acting governor to SSC, August 8, 1941, CO 267/683/4 (Economic and Social Conditions), TNA, Kew.

[35] *SLG*, April 15 and 18, 1944; and report on development and welfare, 1946; CO 267/689/3 (Planning of Development and Welfare), TNA, Kew.

[36] Mining was also a major source of income, particularly the iron mines at Marampa in northwestern Sierra Leone, at least for those in the surrounding region. Ibrahim Abdullah, "Profit versus social reproduction: Labor protests in the Sierra Leonean iron ore mines, 1933–38," *African Studies Review*, 35 (1992), 3.

[37] Without extensive research in Sierra Leone, it is not possible to determine how important pressure from chiefs and other authorities was in generating migration to Freetown as distinct from labor for rural projects. Official records I have read give no indication of coercive devices for transferring rural dwellers to Freetown, other than those who were conscripted.

[38] Governor Stevenson stated in conversations with the Colonial Office that medical examinations for army recruits in the protectorate have "revealed a deplorably low standard of physique, due in part to malnutrition." "Sierra Leone Affairs: A note on points emphasized

Protectorate had left agriculture."[39] Migrants tended to be most numerous as laborers on new construction projects and in certain other sectors. They joined more established workers in challenging conditions.

Freetown had a history of organized unions and of strikes and other actions against private and public employers. During the depression of the 1930s, wages had dropped markedly for both skilled and unskilled workers, work conditions often were abysmal, unemployment was high, and employers were reluctant to negotiate.[40] Immediately before the war, Isaac Theophilus Akunna Wallace-Johnson and the WAYL generated unions more militant and political than the existing ones. Two were in sectors that became central to war mobilization, the All Seaman's Union and the War Department Amalgamated Workers' Union (WDAWU). In early 1939, the WDAWU staged a strike at three sites where preparations for the impending war were going on, and workers also struck the Sierra Leone Coaling Company (SLCC). Colonial authorities ended these strikes with force, intimidation, and legal actions against assemblies, but workers had demonstrated their capacity to disrupt critical sites.[41] After the British began war mobilization, the WAYL and its unions continued organizing, staged strikes in strategic sectors, and demonstrated influence among African troops and police. Backed by the Colonial Office and with the active support of conservative African members, the Legislative Council passed a series of bills aimed at the WAYL. Wallace-Johnson was eventually convicted of criminal libel and detained for the duration of the war. Authorities also arrested other trade unionists and WAYL leaders.[42] Once fighting began, the WAYL, somewhat chastened, professed its loyalty to Britain and support for the war effort. While workers accommodated many of the new regulations, such as the Labor Advisory Board, militants continued to promote more confrontational unionism and organized new unions, such as the Waterfront Workers Union, started in early 1942.

During the war, authorities continued to pursue their prewar goal, aptly described by historian Ibrahim Abdullah, of preventing the "emergence of

by Sir Hubert Stevenson in his talk with the Secretary of State on the 16th of July, 1943," CO 267/683/16 (Sierra Leone Affairs. Notes of talks with Sir H. Stevenson), TNA, Kew.

[39] *Annual Report of the Colony of Sierra Leone, 1946*, appendix: "A review of the years 1939–45," 51–52.

[40] There had been major strikes at Marampa and Pepel, in 1935 and 1938 respectively. Many workers at Pepel were from Freetown, and both strikes influenced workers in the city. Abdullah, "Profit versus social reproduction," 35.

[41] Ibrahim Abdullah, "'Liberty or death': Working class agitation and the labour question in colonial Freetown, 1938–1939," *International Review of Social History*, 40 (1995), 195–221.

[42] Leo Spitzer, *The Creoles of Sierra Leone: Responses to Colonialism, 1870–1945* (Madison: University of Wisconsin Press, 1974), 180–216; Leo Spitzer and LaRay Denzer, "I. T. A. Wallace-Johnson and the West African Youth League," *International Journal of African Historical Studies*, 6 (1973), 413–52 and 561–601.

an independent working-class movement that they could neither control nor predict."[43] But officials now had other pressing concerns that affected their labor policies. As Freetown's port became strategically critical, officials sought to minimize disruptions and find new ways to improve worker output, including raising wages and "stabilizing" work teams. In 1941, authorities introduced a trade union ordinance and took steps to register unions, promote moderate unionism, and channel labor disputes into arbitration or other settlement mechanisms.[44] Laborers in strategic sectors undoubtedly were influenced by unions and the history of organizing, but their strikes and other actions, in their particulars, were responses to the tough realities they faced. Given prices and shortages, making ends meet in Freetown was very difficult for long-term residents and recent migrants alike.

Work conditions often were harsh, especially for those loading coal: coaling operations were a particular site of labor conflict. Gradually, over the course of the war, mechanical loading devices were put in place, but much of the coal, in the words of Behrens, "had to be delivered to ships in canvas bags by native labour."[45] Handling was also done with wicker baskets, each holding "a little more than 3 cwts [336 lbs]... carried by two natives."[46] An improved system employed buckets hoisted by cranes, but the containers still had to be shovel loaded by gangs of eight fillers. Offloading and loading ships went on seven days a week.

Strikes and settlements reveal both the lines of conflicts in Freetown and the ways that strategic concerns influenced officials. The SLCC witnessed a series of strikes. In June 1941, workers walked off the job. The following month, the arbitration panel, which included representatives of workers, arranged an agreement that raised pay for coal haulers to 1/6s per day (with headmen paid more). The SLCC agreed to pay cost-of-living bonuses and to recognize the Mabella Workers Trade Union, which the government hoped would stabilize labor relations in this critical sector.[47] In November 1941, employees on Elder Dempster lighters, tugs, and launches went on strike for higher wages. Officials pressured lightering companies to raise their pay

[43] Abdullah, "Liberty or death," 221.

[44] Governor Douglas Jardine had earlier opposed such recognition, despite the Colonial Office being in favor of it. Once the war was underway, the need for labor stabilization became an overriding concern of officials in Sierra Leone and London. The Labour Advisory Board was an important instrument in stabilizing and moderating labor, CO 267/682/12 (Labor Disputes and Labour Advisory Board), TNA, Kew. For the larger history of colonial labor policy, see Frederick Cooper, *Decolonization and African Society: The Labor Question in French and British Africa* (New York: Cambridge University Press, 1996).

[45] C. B. A. Behrens, *History of the Second World War: Merchant Shipping and the Demands of War* (London: HMSO, 1955), 208.

[46] H. Shoosmith, March 20, 1941, "Particulars of S/S 'Yorkton' and 'Portadoc'" Ministry of War Transport (MWT) 59/145 (1941–1943) (Bunkering at Freetown), TNA, Kew.

[47] Statement of C. H. Newland, arbitrator, June 21, 1941, enclosure II to Sierra Leone dispatch no. 219, July 15, 1941, CO 267/682/12, TNA, Kew.

rates to match those of the government, while threatening workers with new legislation that would designate dock work as essential to the war effort and authorize coercion. Officials also used the opportunity to get both sides to agree to a new plan for "decasualization" supposedly ensuring that a pool of laborers would be available to turn ships around rapidly.[48]

Given their primary goal of supporting the war effort, colonial and military officers were willing to use pay incentives as part of their design to prevent a high turnover rate and reduce upheavals. Administrators increased pay to what became the norm for laborers, 2s per day, with higher rates for more skilled workers, and used leverage to get private firms to offer the same amount. Officials did not, however, want to pay more than what they thought was necessary, so their main strategy became awarding cost-of-living bonuses. Companies typically sought to hold down labor costs, but, under pressure, they accepted some wage increases, up to or equal to the government rate. They also preferred cost-of-living bonuses that did not set precedents for wages in other colonies or for the future in Sierra Leone.

By early 1942, both military and civilian officers decided much stricter controls were needed to ensure speedy handling of ships and completion of strategic construction projects. This led to the Defense (Essential Work) (General Provisions) Order. Core provisions enabled authorities to register all workers, issue them identification cards, and organize them into labor classes that could be matched with work sites. While some laborers objected to registration, most complied. Complaints, short strikes, and other worker actions continued through the war but the high point of labor-management antagonism had passed. Perhaps workers displayed less activism because they were under less stress as the strategic role of Freetown diminished, but certainly antilabor legislation, the procedures of the Labor Board, and government efforts at cooptation stifled workers.

The large foreign military presence led to many clashes of a racial nature, especially from 1941 through 1943. Africans jostled whites on the streets, picked their pockets, took their clothes at swimming beaches, and entered barracks to lift personal property. Many clashes took place around military bases. Organized gangs carried out some of those incidents, while other perpetrators were ordinary urban residents.[49] Some white officers charged that such incidents stemmed from nationalism generated by the WAYL, which may have been true in some cases, but encounters also

---

[48] MWT representative to D. of S. T. (MWT), telegrams (secret), November 10 and 12, 1941, CO 267/267/680/11 (Marampa Iron Ore Mine. Strike and Labour Disturbances), TNA, Kew.

[49] Commander R. N., staff officer (intelligence) to flag officer commanding West Africa, May 18, 1943, Secret, "Molestation and Robbery of Service Personnel by Africans"; Commander, Sierra Leone Area to H. E. the Acting Governor, Sierra Leone 11 July, 1943, CO 267/683/17 (Question of Gangsterism and Lawlessness in Freetown), TNA, Kew.

occurred because whites displayed racist attitudes or were disrespectful to Africans, who refused to accept abuses.[50] Not uncommonly, military and civilian authorities split over how to respond to incidents. The former often called for harsh punishment and the right of white enlisted men to fight back, whereas civilian authorities wanted troops to show greater racial sensitivity and sought to avoid rousing African opinion. The war also witnessed clashes between African troops, especially from Nigeria, and civilians; those incidents had ethnic, territorial, incipient national, and perhaps class connotations. Most were not on Freetown streets but in towns on the peninsula and around bases. In some incidents, Africans were injured or killed.[51]

Demilitarization

The demilitarization of Freetown took place over several years and had different components. Military cooperation between the United States and Britain was based on perceived strategic realities, which by 1943 were changing rapidly as the North Atlantic became much safer for convoys, Allied forces advanced in North Africa, and Dakar again became available for repairs and staging. Acting on recommendations from its staff planners, on May 1, 1943, the United States combined chiefs of staff canceled the arrangement that had been set out in C.S.S. 63. Immediately the United States rechanneled material en route to Freetown, reassigned Seabees engaged in construction there, and began to close down operations and withdraw troops and officers. Extremely upset, the British made a case for the continuing strategic importance of Freetown and asked for a reevaluation. This led to an agreement in which the United States ended its contribution to the construction of the port, but turned over certain facilities and equipment for military and commercial use, and provided some additional assistance. Then in late 1943, British high planners reduced the strategic significance of Freetown's port. The transition went on during 1944 and into 1945. Convoys still were formed in the harbor, but in much smaller numbers. Most of the airports and other military bases in and around Freetown remained in operation, although they lost personnel.

Many large infrastructure projects had been completed by the end of 1943, but still 7,000 laborers were engaged in building a new naval base

---

[50] Secret memo, "Criminal and political conditions in Freetown affecting the services," enclosure to memo by the staff officer (intelligence), Freetown to flag officer commanding West Africa, May 18, 1943, Adm 1/2950, TNA, Kew; "Following extract from Rear Admiral West Africa Orders Paragraph 419 Section IV dated November 1, 1942, Office of US naval observer, November 16, 1942, FA2/Freetown Letters 1941–1942, National Archives and Records Administration (hereafter NARA), College Park, MD.

[51] Enclosures I and II to Sierra Leone confidential dispatch, October 13, 1942, CO 267/680/12 (Temporary File: Strikes and Labour Disturbances), TNA, Kew.

at Kissy in early 1944.[52] Overall, employment by the military and civilian government declined in 1944. During 1945, all service-related projects ended. Some workers returned to the protectorate, but shortages of food, imported commodities, housing, and water remained serious in Freetown. Prices for necessities stayed high and wages remained unsatisfactory in the eyes of most workers. For those and other reasons, colonial authorities were hesitant to demilitarize the city in the economic and administrative senses. Demilitarization continued slowly into 1945 and 1946, as economic and other problems remained. Price controls for imports and local commodities gradually relaxed. Officials and the public remained vigilant against profiteering, but commentators also expressed sympathy for market women who were squeezed.[53] Even though demand from ships dropped off, water shortages still plagued the city.[54]

As early as 1943, authorities had become apprehensive that Freetownians, sensing that victory was certain, would let up on their support for the war and be less willing to accept the stringencies in daily life. This worry lasted into 1945. The Allied advance in Europe, however, gradually brought a reduction in broadcast war coverage, and by early 1945, some issues of the newspapers had no war reporting or only brief articles on the Russian and Western fronts.[55] As the war came to an end, authorities became very concerned with the large number of unemployed former migrants in Freetown, a concern shared by many permanent residents. Authorities took a number of measures to force or induce people to return to the protectorate, but the impact is difficult to assess. In the year or so after the war concluded, perhaps 10,000 to 20,000 left the city.[56] Government attention turned more to discharged soldiers and returning veterans of the Burma campaign, whom officials feared as city dwellers. Nearly 12,000 men, 10,000 of whom had been in the army, were demobilized in 1946. Officials used employment exchanges in Freetown and the protectorate, public works projects, and price supports for cash crops to ease ex-soldiers back into the economy. Although many veterans did resettle, the countryside did not offer the kinds of opportunities they expected, given their wartime training. Even in 1947,

---

[52] Confidential report of U.S. naval observer to director of naval intelligence, February 17, 1944, L-042, NB/EF13–55, NARA, College Park, MD.

[53] *DG*, January 30, 1945.

[54] *SLWN*, January 27, 1945.

[55] *DG*, March 5, 1945.

[56] One scholar estimates the 1947 population of Freetown at about 66,500, which seems unrealistically low because it is only 10,000 above 1931 figures and does not match other figures. See Michael Banton, *West African City: A Study of Tribal Life in Freetown* (London: Oxford University Press, 1957), 24. The government estimated the population of Freetown as "at least 80,000" in 1946, with 150,000 in the Colony. See *Annual Report of the Colony of Sierra Leone, 1946*, 14. The 1963 national census recorded nearly 128,000 in the city.

many Sierra Leoneans and officials alike did not feel a satisfactory transition to peacetime conditions had been made.

During the Second World War, Freetown was caught up in a worldwide maelstrom. As a major convoy port with a significant military presence, the city experienced massive growth and was deeply affected by the global circulation of people, commodities, and ideas. Thousands of ships, loaded with Allied troops and war supplies from throughout the world, were protected and replenished in its harbor. Those who directed the militarization of the city used laws, propaganda, cooptation, threat, and punishment to gain city dwellers' acceptance of wartime controls and exactions. Freetown residents interacted with global forces on their own terms, shaping their lives to whatever degree possible. They endured severe shortages, encountered overseas military personnel who disdained them, and contributed vast amounts of labor as well as a wide range of skills to the war effort. They enabled Freetown to carry out its strategic functions in the global system. City dwellers built huge infrastructure projects, recoaled ships under tight time schedules, and volunteered for civilian and military service. They also went on strike to force up wages and improve conditions, protested what they considered unfair prices, and circumvented controls. By resisting and also by negotiating and adapting, urban residents of many backgrounds obliged authorities to modify their policies, practices, and managing institutions. Thus, global forces were both realized and buffered in Freetown through complex processes of coercion, regulation, confrontation, and accommodation.

11

Extraction and Labor in Equatorial Africa and Cameroon under Free French Rule

Eric T. Jennings

A 1947 documentary entitled "Autour de Brazzaville," filmed partly by avant-garde photographer Germaine Krull, set about informing the French public as to what "FEA had brought Free France" during World War II. By far the largest set of colonies to rally to General Charles de Gaulle's cause in 1940, French Equatorial Africa (FEA) and Cameroon had served as bastions of the Free French movement, as launching points for Free French involvement in North Africa and as sources of international legitimacy. But according to this film, the region's contribution to the allied cause had mostly to do with resources: it "offered" fighting men as well as vital transportation routes, to be sure, but mostly produced massive amounts of rubber, gold, and timber. This focus on extraction constitutes the most captivating aspect of the film today, along with its perhaps more predictable civilizing discourse and condescending tone ("FEA had a hundred years earlier been in the stone age," trumpets the narrator). Frame upon frame focuses on Free French Africa's contribution of natural resources. Free France, one is left thinking, must have bled FEA and Cameroon dry in the span of four years.[1]

Many historians have noted that Free French practices in Africa were no less exploitative than Vichy's. Some contend that the indigenous philosophies and policies of leading Free French officials in Africa, Félix Eboué and Henri Laurentie, shared much with the essentializing and preservationist ethos of Vichy's proconsul to West Africa, Pierre Boisson.[2] And we know,

---

[1] "Autour de Brazzaville," 1947.
[2] Frederick Cooper, *Decolonization and African Society: The Labor Question in French and British Africa* (Cambridge: Cambridge University Press, 1996), 158; Nancy Lawler, "Reform and repression under the Free French: Economic and political transformation in the Côte d'Ivoire, 1942–1945," *Journal of the International African Institute*, 60 (1990), 88–110; James I. Lewis, "Félix Eboué and late French colonial ideology," *Itinerario*, 26 (2002), 127–60.

All quotations and photos by Germaine Krull are copyright of the Folkwang Museum.
Parts of this chapter appeared previously in French in my book *La France libre fut africaine* (Paris: Perrin, 2014). Forthcoming in English with Cambridge University Press under the title: *Free French Africa in World War II*.

thanks to the work of Léon Kaptué, Catherine Coquery Vidrovitch, and others, to what extent FEA had been a site of extraction and coercion since the late nineteenth century, a colony particularly prone to colonial abuses.[3] Indeed, as J. P. Daughton and Jeremy Rich have shown, FEA seemed to draw a disproportionate amount of attention from leagues, reporters, and other groups interested in the question of colonial brutality.[4] There is also a large body of work dealing with the Free/Fighting French in general, as well as with some of the movement's colonial governors, starting with Eboué.[5] Yet, for all of this literature on related topics, there has been scant research conducted on Free French Africa itself.[6] The Free French tapped FEA and Cameroon, the only sizeable territories under their control until the rallying of North and West Africa to de Gaulle in June 1943,[7] funneling natural resources to the allies, redirecting the colony's economy into an Anglo-American sphere, and imposing harsh colonial practices that they justified by invoking the war effort.

This chapter examines the long-neglected question of Africa under the rule of General Charles de Gaulle's Free French movement, focusing on natural resource extraction and labor practices. As "Autour de Brazzaville" suggests, FEA and Cameroun provided much more than territorial legitimacy to the Free French. They served at once to fill the coffers of what was still a small maverick movement and to fuel the British war effort, itself starved for natural resources. The ensuing steep increase in extraction had a massive impact on local populations. Forced labor, already an important phenomenon in the area prior to 1940, was taken to new heights.

---

[3] Catherine Coquery-Vidrovitch, *Le Congo au Temps des grandes compagnies concessionaires, 1898–1930* (Paris: Mouton, 1972); Léon Kaptué, *Travail et main d'oeuvre au Cameroon sous le régime français, 1916–1952* (Paris: L'Harmattan, 1986).

[4] J. P. Daughton, "Behind the imperial curtain: International humanitarian efforts and the critique of French colonialism in the interwar years," *French Historical Studies*, 34 (2011), 503–28; Jeremy Rich, "Gabonese men for French decency: The rise and fall of the Gabonese chapter of the Ligue des Droits de l'Homme," *French Colonial History*, 13 (2012), 23–53.

[5] Jean Crémieux-Brilhac, *La France libre* (Paris: Gallimard, 2001); Jean-François Muracciole, *Les Français libres* (Paris: Tallandier, 2009). The best biography of Eboué remains Brian Weinstein's *Eboué* (Oxford: Oxford University Press, 1972).

[6] With the exception of specialized studies on particular parts of Free French Africa. See Léon Modeste Nnang Ndong, *L'effort de guerre de l'Afrique : Le Gabon dans la deuxième guerre mondiale, 1939–1947* (Paris: L'Harmattan, 2011); Eliane Ebako, *Le ralliement du Gabon à la France libre: une guerre franco-française*, thèse, Université de Paris IV (2004); Léonard Sah, *Le Cameroun sous mandat français dans la deuxième guerre mondiale*, thèse, Université de Provence (1998); Jérôme Ollandet, *Brazzaville, capitale de la France libre: histoire de la résistance française en Afrique, 1940–1944* (Brazzaville: Editions de la Savane, 1980).

[7] French West Africa remained loyal to Marshal Philippe Pétain until November 1942, then to Admiral François Darlan and General Henri Giraud until Pierre Boisson was finally forced to depart in June 1943. Fighting French governor Pierre Cournarie only took over the colony on July 17, 1943.

Time and again, both during and after the war, FEA and Cameroon's authorities repeated the notion that the area "went to work" in 1940, as if it had slumbered before.[8] The work was ultimately undertaken on behalf of the allied war effort. Initial trade assurances given by British representatives in Nigeria to Eboué in August 1940 anticipated much vaster trade protocols between FEA and Great Britain ratified in January and May 1941.[9] By 1941 FEA and Cameroon's authorities were also beginning to make use of the U.S. Lend-Lease act, especially helpful for obtaining trucks and specialized equipment in the forestry sector.[10] Numerous British and American economic missions were dispatched to FEA and Cameroon starting in 1940. The archives reveal that the British Ministry of Supply quickly resorted to telegraphing the Free French when a relevant shortage arose. For instance, in August 1941, René Pleven transmitted an urgent U.S. request for rutile from Cameroon.[11] In September 1942, Eboué conveyed pressing orders to the authorities in Gabon to provide specific pieces of timber for the British navy "for immediate military interest."[12] And in January 1943, de Gaulle's agents relayed an urgent British request for wax and copal.[13]

The economy of Free French Africa entered into lockstep with the British war effort in Nigeria, South Africa, and other British colonies. There, colonial authorities implemented compulsory labor on a wide scale, despite qualms that the step constituted a "regression." As David Killingray has demonstrated, agricultural laborers in Kenya, food producers in Rhodesia, and tin miners in Nigeria were all enrolled by force by virtue of new, admittedly contentious British legislation.[14] Despite René Cassin's insistence on establishing a legal and constitutional framework for his movement, Free France did not need to run forced labor authorizations past any parliament: it streamlined and ramped up forced labor, only to condemn the practice after the war.

Competing Imperatives and the Plight of Workers

This is not to suggest that the Free French were of one mind on matters of recruitment. Already in 1939, tensions had arisen between the dual

---

[8] Clearly, this was not the case. See Christopher Gray and François Ngolet, "Lambaréné, Okoumé and the transformation of labor along the Middle Ogooué (Gabon): 1870–1945," *Journal of African History*, 40 (1999), 87–107.

[9] Eric Jennings, "l'Afrique anglaise et la France libre," in Jean-François Muracciole and François Broche (eds.), *Dictionnaire historique de la France libre* (Paris: Robert Laffont, 2010).

[10] File on Lend-Lease, GGAEF 5D 299, Archives nationales d'outre-mer (hereafter ANOM), Aix-en-Provence.

[11] Pleven to Larminat, August 16, 1941, 3AG1 165, Archives Nationales (hereafter AN), Paris.

[12] Eboué, September 15, 1942, GGAEF 5B 715, ANOM, Aix-en-Provence.

[13] London to Brazzaville, January 6, 1943, GGAEF 5B 715, ANOM, Aix-en-Provence.

[14] David Killingray, "Labour mobilisation in British Colonial Africa for the war effort, 1939–1946," in David Killingray and Richard Rathbone (eds.), *Africa and the Second World War* (London: MacMillan, 1986), 83–88.

necessity to step up production, on the one hand, and recruit soldiers, on the other. In December 1939, the governor of Gabon expressed satisfaction that the colony, already strapped for labor, would "only" have to contribute another 1,540 fighting men and 3,600 workers to the war effort in 1940.[15] This was not the only delicate balancing act. The civilian administration of FEA lamented that vital equipment was being commandeered by the military. Thus, a 1943 report observed that less timber had been exported than the year prior because of a "shortage of means of transport."[16] This particular shortage also flew in the face of attempts in Brazzaville to increase mechanization and guarantee some safeguards for African workers. Indeed in 1942, Henri Laurentie had sought to curtail the practice of portering, replacing it with mechanized transport.[17] But with the shortage of trucks, mine operators, in particular, continued unabashedly to rely extensively on large-scale overland portering. Modern means of transport were all being assigned to General Leclerc's forces.

Goals often proved out of reach. By 1942, local officials openly grumbled that they could not match Gaullist ambitions, given demographic realities. Thus, 150 laborers from well outside Pointe-Noire were urgently dispatched there in August 1942.[18] In October 1942, Eboué requested that Pointe-Noire establish a local "Service de la main d'oeuvre et du travail," in other words, a bureau that would arrange worker supply in this area where "labor is insufficient given the needs."[19] In addition to constituting a critical port and a fertile region, Pointe-Noire was emerging as an important military and air force base for the allies. In 1942, Eboué invoked precisely these different imperatives to justify the creation of a centralized labor bureau for all of FEA. This institution, brought into being by a law signed by General de Gaulle, prioritized and distributed labor throughout the colony.[20] Military and production demands had overcome some of Eboué's own qualms about worker conditions.

Eboué's and Laurentie's overarching objective, though, remained in theory one of social amelioration, indeed social engineering. In particular, they were attached to the idea of creating worker villages within short distances of workplaces, a notion inspired perhaps by similar schemes for worker towns in Europe or America. In August 1942, Laurentie explained: "stabilizing a workforce is to build team spirit, emulation; it means also facilitating the formation and development of veritable worker villages, around worksites."[21]

[15] Masson, Libreville, December 3, 1939, GGAEF 2H 25, ANOM, Aix-en-Provence.
[16] Brazzaville, October 9, 1943, GGAEF 5D 299, ANOM, Aix-en-Provence.
[17] Laurentie, March 7, 1942, GGAEF 126, Archives nationales de la République du Congo (hereafter ANRC), Brazzaville.
[18] Laurentie, August 7, 1942, GGAEF 126, ANRC, Brazzaville.
[19] Eboué to Pointe-Noire, October 31, 1942, GGAEF 126, ANRC, Brazzaville.
[20] Eboué to the head of Kouilou province, September 5, 1942, GGAEF 126, ANRC, Brazzaville.
[21] Laurentie to the head of Kouilou province, August 20, 1942, GGAEF 126, ANRC, Brazzaville.

Gabon is emblematic of the wider stretching of human resources in wartime FEA. In a particularly candid April 1943 message to Free French headquarters, Eboué explained that Gabon could not maintain current gold and wood production if it were also to step up its volume of rubber. He suggested that the gold would still be there after the war, and that the roughly 6,000 gold workers employed in Gabon alone could easily be redirected toward road construction and rubber production. "Do we want gold or rubber?" he asked.[22]

Rubber

The course of the war dictated that FEA suddenly attracted considerable Anglo-American attention in 1942. The fall of British Malaya (January 1942), Singapore (February 1942), and the Dutch East Indies (March 1942) to the Japanese sent London and Washington calling. Although synthetic rubber production was stepped up, it could not compensate entirely for natural rubber, most notably in the production of large tires.[23] According to one estimation: "The total annual production for the year 1941 of the areas remaining [in 1942] to the United Nations in Africa, South America, and Mexico amounted to less than two weeks' current consumption for the United States alone."[24] A desperate plea for latex production went out, which was heeded in Free French Africa.

The United States and Britain formulated several requests to the Free French, aimed at ensuring supply and keeping prices in check. The British would henceforth purchase all FEA's rubber.[25] The Free French initially balked at the idea of a British monopoly, so important were FEA rubber shipments in providing the Free French movement with U.S. dollars.[26] Ultimately, Great Britain issued an assurance to the Fighting French that they could trade pounds for dollars directly if the need arose.[27] The resulting agreements stipulated unambiguously: "All rubber exported from Fighting French Africa shall be at the disposal of the United Nations. It has been agreed that purchases shall be effected by the United Kingdom Ministry of Supply."[28]

---

[22] Eboué to François de Langlade, April 8, 1943, 4B2, Archives de l'Ordre de la Libération (hereafter AOL), Paris.
[23] William G. Clarence-Smith, review of John Andrew Tully, *The Devil's Milk: A Social History of Rubber*, *International Review of Social History*, 56 (2011), 542.
[24] Paul Wendt, "The control of rubber in World War II," *Southern Economic Journal*, 13 (1947), 204.
[25] London to Brazzaville, March 3, 1942, GGAEF 6B 712, ANOM, Aix-en-Provence.
[26] Haut-Commissaire Brazzaville, March 24, 1942, 4B2, AOL, Paris.
[27] London to Brazzaville, January 6, 1943, GGAEF 5D 299, ANOM, Aix-en-Provence.
[28] Memorandum of agreement regarding rubber purchases from Fighting French Africa, 4B2, AOL, Paris.

The United Kingdom also expressed assurances that FEA would be paid a fair rate and that prices would rise if they did in Liberia or in Belgian Congo.[29] The Free French, in turn, agreed to operate through accredited intermediaries: starting in March 1942, all FEA rubber would run through four export companies, approved by the United Kingdom.[30] In an August 1942 telegram to the Free French representative in Washington, Free French colonial "commissaire" to the colonies René Pleven signaled that FEA alone would increase its exports from 1,500 tons in 1941 to 5,000 tons in 1942. This proved an inflated estimate: FEA proper would produce roughly 2,000 tons in 1942, and Cameroon would export 1,055 tons in 1942 and some 3,000 tons the year following. Pleven did express some bitterness, however, that the United States was attempting to foster the creation of massive rubber plantations in FEA and Cameroon, thereby "uprooting workers" when in point of fact it had been U.S. "lack of foresight" that had caused the Americans to lose their supply abruptly, without any backup source.[31]

As a result of these developments, FEA and Cameroon swung full tilt toward rubber production. In effect, they went from being absent on the global list of rubber producers in 1939 to the Allies' sixth largest supplier in 1943, after the loss of Southeast Asia. Indeed, FEA and Cameroon's combined production of 7,000 tons of rubber in 1943 placed them only behind Ceylon, India, and Liberia, on the heels of Brazil and Nigeria.[32]

According to Eboué, beginning in 1942 the rubber crop had become "the natural resource for which our war efforts has an imperious demand."[33] In July of that year, Laurentie ordered all rubber companies to account for their stocks immediately.[34] In the span of a few months, FEA was squarely focused on rubber production. According to calculations of the governor-general's office in Brazzaville, rubber production in the second half of 1942 was 54 percent higher than in the first half.[35] This confirms the responsiveness of FEA officials toward the UK agreements, but it also suggests that the plight and number of African workers in the rubber sector had radically changed in a short span. Indeed, pressure from London was unrelenting. In a March 1943 telegram aimed to congratulate recruiters, buyers, and

[29] Gouverneur Douala, April 2, 1942, 4B2, AOL, Paris.

[30] Laurentie, March 31, 1942, GGAEF, 5B 356, ANOM, Aix-en-Provence.

[31] Pleven to Washington, August 29, 1942. The Cameroon statistics come from Doula, January 14, 1944, 4B2, AOL, Paris; the AEF data comes from Gouverneur Général Brazzaville to Pleven, February 2, 1943, 4B2, AOL, Paris.

[32] The AEF-Cameroon figures are drawn from my forthcoming book, *La France libre fut africaine*. The other data are from B. R. Mitchell (ed.), *International Historical Statistics: Africa, Asia and Oceania, 1750–2000* (London: Palgrave, 2003), 258–59.

[33] Brazzaville to Bangui, October 23, 1942, F22, 17, Archives de la Fondation Charles de Gaulle (hereafter AFCDG), Paris.

[34] Brazzaville to Bangui and Libreville, July 20, 1942, GGAEF 84, ANRC, Brazzaville.

[35] Eboué to Pleven, February 2, 1943, 4B2, AOL, Paris.

plantation owners, Pleven mentioned that FEA would have to maintain rubber production "at the highest possible level" at least until "Indochina is reconquered."[36] This reminds us that in Free French eyes, FEA had abruptly come to replace Vichy and Japanese-controlled Indochina as a source of rubber, while in British eyes, it had come to replace Malaya.

The intensity of wartime demand meant that rubber was sought by all means and from all sources possible. Wild rubber, whose wide-scale colonial exploitation in FEA had dramatically decreased in the 1920s and 1930s, made an officially sanctioned comeback. On August 19, 1942, Brazzaville's economic affairs officer dispatched a telegram authorizing local officials to provide bonuses to "indigenous chiefs" who collected especially large amounts of wild rubber.[37] That same month, Pleven evoked the target of "tripling or even quadrupling" wild rubber collection that same year.[38] By 1943, the governor of Cameroon was reporting that wild rubber was fast growing scarce, so intense was the previous year's campaign.[39] Eboué's team in Brazzaville assuredly showed concern for worker well-being. In a September 15, 1942 telegram, they ordered local rubber collection companies to pay workers in multiples of 25 centimes and to round fractions up systematically.[40] The reality on the ground, however, was often far removed from such good intentions.

Germaine Krull captured the resulting rush on wild rubber in FEA.[41] Her memoirs and photographs reveal little of the brazen confidence in Free French Africa's productivity that permeates "Autour de Brazzaville." Indeed, this volunteer for the Free French information services seems to have taken stock of the growing disjuncture between what her propaganda services stated and the reality on the ground. Her reaction to the rubber market she witnessed at Mayana, outside of Brazzaville, in September 1943, seems worth citing in detail:

> The market at Mayana is a kind of crossroads; a large ceiba tree, a few leaf huts, the hanger of Antonio's [rubber] company, the trucks awaiting the rubber, and that is all. Some hundred women and men crouch under a burning sun. The market runs like cotton markets elsewhere. There is a large scale, across from which are seated two elders, generally the village chiefs, wearing well buttoned uniforms and a helmet.... Next to them is an employee of the

---

[36] Pleven to Eboué, March 15, 1943, 4B2, AOL, Paris.
[37] Telegram, signed Fortune, August 19, 1942, GGAEF 84, ANC, Brazzaville.
[38] Pleven, August 7, 1942, 4B2, AOL, Paris.
[39] Douala to Pleven and de Langlade, April 19, 1943, 4B2, AOL, Paris.
[40] Eboué, Brazzaville, September 15, 1942, 4B2, AOL, Paris.
[41] On Germaine Krull, see Kim Sichel *Germaine Krull, Photographer of Modernity* (Boston: MIT Press, 1999); Kim Sichel, "Germaine Krull and *L'Amitié Noire*: World War II and French colonialist film," in Eleanor M. Hight and Gary D. Sampson (eds.), *Colonialist Photography: Imag(in)ing Race and Place* (London: Routledge, 2002); Kerstein Meincke, "Unter Brüden und Stiefbrüdern: Mythos und Ambivalenz im Afrikabild Germaine Krulls (1942–1944)," Diplomarbeit, Volkwang Hochschule (2010).

company who weighs each parcel; another notes the weight in a large register and a third hands the woman a piece of paper indicating the weight of the rubber she has just deposited. The rubber is then heaved into trucks and the woman goes to join the line of others waiting for their pay. They are given half or a third in cash, and for the rest they are handed merchandise they never asked for: storm lights, shovels, spoons, all sorts of things that are completely useless to them, but which are a way of profitably liquidating stocks in various hangers.... The women leave much as they came: resigned and silent. In fifteen days, the region's commander will once again send militiamen to tell the local people how many kilos of rubber they must bring to the next market. I spend part of the morning taking photos of the market, but the expression of sadness and resignation of these people moves me deeply. There is a *je ne sais quoi* that wounds me.[42]

Krull's camera captured individual expressions. Among the photos she took, but were not utilized by the Free French information services, Figure 11.1 shows an African woman waiting at the Mayana market with her rubber parcels. The picture conveys the woman's fatigue and drawn expression, but it also places a spotlight on the mass of wild rubber at her feet – rubber that is quite literally being brought to the Free French. Another photograph sheds further light on such markets. Taken in 1943 at Lebango in the French Congo by an unknown photographer, this picture (Figure 11.2) shows African women, men and children delivering bundles of rubber to be weighed. A "majordomo" operates the scale, while a colonial official – the only white person in the scene – meticulously records the weights. A wooden rack in the foreground has served to stock and begin processing the rubber. A truck in the background stands at the ready to depart with the precious substance.

Krull's visual and written testimony reveals much about labor practices under Free French rule, but does raise the question of whether rubber collection constituted forced labor per se. Certainly, entire villages were being directed to seek out wild rubber, in the form of roots and vines that needed to be laboriously pulled out. This led to a recrudescence in sleeping sickness and other diseases as well as an abandonment of other crops. Undoubtedly, remuneration in kind, as described earlier by Krull, violated the colonial state's own laws. In March 1943, Pleven wrote Eboué that he would do his utmost to replenish "merchandise necessary for native rubber markets," suggesting that payment in kind was on the rise.[43] It is also true, however, that income from rubber was flowing into Free French Africa. We know from Guillaume Lachenal that in Cameroon latex had yielded one franc a kilo before the war, only to jump to twelve francs a kilo in 1944. And in Carnot (Oubangui) rubber hit a high of 13.40 francs a kilo in 1943; this was the rate at which African providers, rather than chiefs, were directly

---

[42] Germaine Krull manuscript, 125–26, Germaine Krull Archives, Folkwang Museum, Essen.
[43] Pleven to Eboué, March 15, 1943, 4B2, AOL, Paris.

FIGURE II.I. © Estate Germaine Krull (147-657-95-1), Museum Folkwang, Essen
"Mayama, Loukouo. Rubber Market. Native woman waiting her turn for her rubber
to be weighed." September 1943. Germaine Krull, Folkwang Museum, all rights
reserved.

remunerated at the town's rubber market.[44] Tamara Giles-Vernick is correct to suggest that Africans were thereby positioning themselves within
global market networks.[45] Yet, this agency need not stand in opposition to
colonial coercion; in the case of wartime rubber, the two dynamics went
hand in hand. A Congolese man interviewed by Jérôme Ollandet in 1978
remembers rubber collection in the Free French era as follows: "by day,
teams of *miliciens* arrived, called out each name, and one had to present

---

[44] On Carnot, see GGAEF 3Y3, ANOM, Aix-en-Provence; on Cameroon, see Guillaume
   Lachenal, "Le médecin qui voulut être roi: médecine coloniale et utopie au Cameroon,"
   Annales, Histoire, Sciences Sociales (2010), 121–56.
[45] Tamara Giles-Vernick, *Cutting the Vines of the Past: Environmental Histories of the Central
   African Rain Forest* (Charlottesville: University Press of Virginia, 2002), 163.

FIGURE 11.2. "Moyen Congo bush, French Equatorial Africa. The trading activities of Africa. Rubber" Library of Congress, Washington DC. LC-USW33-031073-D.

one's bundles of rubber. Whomever failed to bring the right amount, or brought poorly prepared rubber, was whipped."[46] In the Sanaga Maritime region of Cameroon in 1942, a French administrator set clear per capita quotas on villagers, then additional regional quotas – all in response to insistent, even desperate, calls from London to step up production.[47] In his history of the Central African church, Father Carlo Toso rather diplomatically refers to "practically forced labor" to describe Free France's rubber campaign in Oubangui-Chari.[48]

Gold

In the endless commodities lists the allies dispatched to Brazzaville, gold was conspicuously absent. Yet, de Gaulle and his entourage insisted that extraction of the precious metal be stepped up. The logic was simple. Equatorial African gold, more than any other resource, "contributes to our financial

[46] Cited in Ollandet, *Brazzaville*, 125.
[47] Tournées Eséka, 2AC 21, Archives nationales du Cameroun (hereafter ANC), Yaoundé.
[48] Père Carlo Toso, *Centrafrique, un siècle d'évangélisation* (Bangui: Conférence épiscopale contrafricaine, 1994), 163.

and monetary independence."[49] Indeed, in February 1943, taking stock of the fact that gold rates remained high, and the substance was as precious as ever to the Free French, Free French authorities in London cabled Brazzaville asking them to increase production, close small mines, and concentrate on large mines.[50] On this point, Free French authorities in London and Brazzaville clashed, the latter deeming the reduction of gold mining to be "socially desirable," the former considering gold supply a vital necessity. FEA was torn between multiple imperatives: road construction, gold mining, and military imperatives such as rubber production.[51]

Again, Germaine Krull proved rather more circumspect toward FEA goldmining practices than her 1947 film suggests. In her unpublished manuscript, she described in considerable detail the gold mines at Eteké and N'Djolé in Gabon. In the case of the former, she noted the mine's isolation, which meant that it needed to be supplied by porters. Portering, she estimated, cost hundreds of lives, especially those of women. Work in the mine was perhaps even less enviable. Indeed, she noticed the mines stirred terror among the Gabonese. She spoke at length with a local official and a doctor who tried in vain to reduce the mine's insatiable appetite for African laborers, limiting the number of workers recruited in the villages and removing ill workers from service. Ultimately, they were rebuffed when the mine operators complained to Brazzaville that the war effort was being undermined. The war, it seemed, could be invoked to justify all excesses.[52]

At Armand Vigoureux's operation in N'Djolé, Krull described conditions as follows:

> Here is the mine. Hundreds of blacks dig the ground, collecting it with a shovel and throwing it into small carts. From there, the precious earth is transported to a sluice. This sluice is a kind of wooden conduit in which the blacks throw the earth from the cart. A rudimentary water system runs like a stream through the sluice and washes this earth. This earth cascades down, large stones are caught by the first sieve, smaller ones in a second sieve, then a third, until we reach a very fine sieve that captures the gold... Surveillance of blacks is very strict. Even though they are already nude, except for a kind of cloth around their waist, when they return to the village they are thoroughly searched. Their mouths are examined, their teeth, under their tongues. Some occasionally manage to make off with gold, but when they are caught they are beaten almost to death, therefore theft occurs only very rarely. They work twelve to fifteen hours a day. The work is exhausting. The shovels full of earth are heavy to throw up to the sluice, which is higher than the riverbed. Once the gold is washed, collected and sorted, the powder is blown and collected

---

[49] Free French London to Brazzaville, April 29, 1942, GGAEF 6B 712, ANOM, Aix-en-Provence.
[50] Telegram, February 6, 1943, Cabinet 66, ANOM, Aix-en-Provence.
[51] Douala to Pleven, July 1942, Cabinet 66, 29, ANOM, Aix-en-Provence.
[52] Krull manuscript, 70.

FIGURE 11.3. © Estate Germaine Krull (147-447-95-1), Museum Folkwang, Essen M'Vouti. "Mr Vigoureux's mine." April 1943. Germaine Krull, Folkwang Museum, all rights reserved.

> in boxes, then transported to Brazzaville.... Mortality rates are high among the blacks in the mines. The food is insufficient. They eat only manioc and occasionally dried fish, rarely meat. The administration says meat cannot be found; when in fact the forest is full of game. This human waste is the reason for which the mine's administration must so often renew its labor and call on new recruits. The human waste is terrible.[53]

Once more Krull's camera and words offer overlapping perspectives. Figure 11.3 shows two young African workers throwing earth into the sluice at another locale, the M'Vouti mine in Congo, also belonging to Vigoureux. We know from the archives that in December 1940 and January 1941 alone,

---

[53] Ibid., 96–97.

76 of Vigoureux's 1,764 mine workers had managed to flee his mining operation at M'Vouti.[54] The terror instilled by this mine was no doubt nothing
new; what had changed since 1940 was the owner's ability to circumvent
all rules in the name of the war.

Krull added an interesting detail: She was surprised to see General de
Gaulle's portrait in the offices of the N'Djolé mine's director, finding it
utterly out of place.[55] The photographer had captured in a nutshell the
terrible contradiction between Gaullist ideals – liberating France, fighting
Nazi oppression, taking on the forces of Mussolini and Hitler in the Sahara –
and local reality. Her unbridled enthusiasm for the Gaullist cause, which had
led her to volunteer for the Free French movement in the first place, seemed
momentarily betrayed. Quickly she set about reconciling this experience with
her Gaullist faith, deducing with little evidence that the mine's operators
must in reality have been closet Vichyites.[56] Still, Krull was on the mark
on several scores. FEA's civil administration did indeed attempt on several
occasions to reign in emboldened mine owners, who were using the war as
a pretext to exacerbate already appalling working conditions in their mines.
Brazzaville's political affairs office used precisely such terms in the following
cable to Libreville on April 22, 1942:

> Any evidence of serious infractions to labor laws must be reported, and must
> be brought before trials. Report back to me on guilty verdicts. Yes, production
> must absolutely be maintained but you are to tell mining corporations that we
> are sufficiently informed to know that applying the rules cannot lead to a drop
> in output. Nor can the imperative of maintaining production serve as a pretext
> to flagrantly flout labor laws.[57]

Efforts like these proved largely illusory, but confirm that there was an
ongoing tension in FEA between an administration intent on establishing
some limits and entrepreneurs using the war to extend work hours, harden
practices, and redouble recruitment efforts.

In the mines, 1940 marked a sea change. A 1942 report from Ogooué
province (Gabon) sheds some light on recruitment practices in the gold
sector. Its author lamented the fact that contracts, once iron-clad, meant
strictly nothing to employers since the war had begun. "In theory" he wrote,
"nothing has changed, but in reality nobody, starting with the recruited
worker, has the slightest illusion about the formality of his contract." The
report went on to add: "The native's resignation becomes his consent and the
'volunteer' can consider himself lucky when, once he has signed a contract,
he is told in a few words that he owes two years of work to such and such a
company, and will be paid a salary." Colonial officials were thus under no

---

[54] "Compte-rendu" on labor, February 26, 1941, GGAEF 2 H 25, ANOM, Aix-en-Provence.
[55] Krull manuscript, 96.
[56] Ibid., 110.
[57] Brazzaville to Libreville, April 22, 1942, GGAEF 126, ANRC, Brazzaville.

illusions about the nature of these so-called contracts, signed to placate an administration anxious to follow some semblance of work regulation. The Ogooué report went on to suggest that one white recruiter, in particular, famed for his "empty hands and golden tongue" was capable of persuading villagers to head to the N'Djolé gold mine. He even described the place as a kind of "paradise." Upon arriving at the "pit of despair" that was the mine, however, worker disappointment was all the more bitter, the eagerness to "desert" all the greater.[58]

Runaway workers were also tracked down using wartime logic. On April 17, 1941, the head of Moyen-Congo reminded the chief of the Kouilou department of the range of measures at his disposal for dealing with fugitives. He cited a circular written by Governor-General Eboué in person in December 1940, which read:

> Deserters of mining camps must be tracked down and brought back to the mines, based on the application of disciplinary punishments provided for by the *indigénat* code. I deem that it should apply to desertions and to those unwilling to work. In this sense, gold mines are to be considered to be no different from public works projects.[59]

Although the colonial administration seemed Janus-faced in its attitude toward gold – a social evil at some times, a wartime priority at others – it seems clear that the plight of gold workers discernibly worsened in FEA under Free French rule.

Enforcement in the gold sector was no simple task. A 1942 report on N'Gouiné was quite candid about the difficulties the administration faced in monitoring the condition of gold workers. It reads:

> One mine owner declared to me that workers were numbers to him. Another told me that one could not be sentimental during wartime. It is, however, infinitely delicate and complicated to launch a legal case against a European mine operator or supervisor. The need to collect native testimonies creates an effervescence that can only make an administrator take pause.

The report went on to identify some of the root causes of what was by definition an abusive sector. The main recommendation involved making employers want to keep their workers. This could be achieved by various means: having them recruit workers themselves, as they once had during peacetime, or implementing a system of inquiries into desertions. Gold miners were increasingly voting with their feet. The phenomenon was so widespread as to be described as a "hemorrhaging." Despondent at entrepreneurs' expectation that the administration would do their recruiting for them, and then track down escapees, the author of the report essentially gave up, stating that

[58] Ogooué report, pp. 45–46, GGAEF 4(1) D50, ANOM, Aix-en-Provence.
[59] April 17, 1941, GGAEF 2H25, ANOM, Aix-en-Provence.

it was impractical to "jail 2,000 blacks."[60] Workers were indeed migrating en masse, most notably to neighboring Portuguese and Spanish colonial enclaves, across porous borders, though internal migration was also registered. In October 1942, Eboué wrote to Pointe-Noire to ask the local authorities to investigate a large-scale migration from Kibangou toward Madingo-Kayes on the Congolese coast. Eboué suspected that higher salaries had lured workers, but his chief concern lay elsewhere: that the administration was losing "volunteer" workers to the private sector.[61] In Ogooué, in 1942, a recruiting agent could not raise the fifty workers he needed, despite his appeal to the governor-general in person. Having recruited fifty workers the year before, some of whom subsequently escaped five or even six times, and having gained a reputation for whipping his workforce, his efforts proved unsurprisingly vain.[62]

Road Work

Road construction took place at a particularly brisk pace under Free French rule and required massive numbers of laborers. Thousands of new kilometers of tracks and road were built to support Free France's south-to-north effort (bringing materiel to Colonel Leclerc's forces in Libya), to facilitate the extraction of natural resources, and to integrate Free French Africa into a vast Allied African war effort, spanning the Belgian Congo, Free French territories, and British colonies (the Nigeria–Chad–Sudan axis proved particularly useful to allied supply lines).

Between 1940 and 1942, the road network in N'Gouiné province of Gabon expanded from 276 kilometers to 635, an increase of 77 percent. According to the head of this same province: "Roads should come first, roads above all else."[63] In part, he was reacting to the perception that previous administrations had overemphasized gold at the expense of infrastructure development. What sets the Free French era apart is Pleven's desire to increase output in all sectors: road expansion, military recruitment, gold and rubber extraction, and vast public works projects. Such projects were the fruit of forced labor, mostly in the form of *prestations* and *corvées*. Generally, recruited Africans appear to have considered road construction particularly undesirable, because official remuneration hovered around two francs a day, against roughly six francs a day for portering.[64]

Furthermore, road construction needs to be situated within the framework of a cumulative stretching of resources. The head of the Bas-Chari

---

[60] Report on N'Gouinié, 60–61, F22, 17, AFCDG, Paris.
[61] Eboué to Pointe-Noire, October 19, 1942, GGAEF 126, ANRC, Brazzaville.
[62] Ogoué report for 1942, 46, GGAEF 4(1) D50, ANOM, Aix-en-Provence.
[63] Report on N'Gouinié, 7, 98. F22 17, AFCDG, Paris.
[64] Report on Woleu N'Tem, 31, GGAEF 4(1) D50, ANOM, Aix-en-Provence.

district in Chad reported that in 1940, his region had already provided 450 conscripts for the military and tons of millet. Given this, it would be dangerous, he contended, to significantly raise the number of workers assigned to building roads. Because of its geostrategic importance, Chad was the site of considerable road construction. In Bas-Chari, an early emphasis (August to December 1940) was placed on two roads: the first running between Fort-Lamy (N'Djamena) and Moussoro, the second between Fort-Lamy and Mogroum. Between 1,200 and 1,930 inhabitants of the district were put to work on these roads between the time the colony rallied the Free French in August 1940 and at the end of that year. The region's colonial chief witnessed and reported multiple abuses here too: the recurring problem of low or late wages, routine beatings on construction sites, and significant food and water shortages.[65]

Some African Experiences, Voices, and Strategies

In August 1941, Mr. Tchioula, from Booué, Gabon, wrote to the governor in Libreville and to Governor-General Eboué in Brazzaville to complain of ill treatment on the part of the Booué district chief. His words must have sent a chill down the spine of Gaullist officials. Prior to 1940, previous local administrators, he stated, had been good men, concerned for the plight of Africans; however, "since de Gaulle took over Gabon, the [people] sent here have treated us like beasts." Tchioula proceeded to explain that the new chief routinely whipped Africans for no apparent motive and jailed inhabitants seemingly at random for between eight days and a month. The elderly were also pressed into *prestations*. Tchioula added: "We are forced into *prestations* for one month, on Sundays and on holidays. We are made to work morning through night without rest." On market days, he claimed, twenty to thirty chickens needed to be brought "to the whites." Finally, according to Tchioula, the district head systematically referred to blacks as monkeys.[66]

On more than one occasion, Tchioula deliberately tapped into the administration's discursive register. Booué's blacks were not the only ones to be called monkeys, he noted, the district head had called Félix Eboué in person "a bush monkey." Eboué was a black Guyanese French citizen after all and would become the highest ranking Free French official in Africa in June 1942. Here, Tchioula clearly sought to establish a common ground of racial victimhood. He also warned the administration in the following terms: "if you leave these whites in power in Booué, we will all flee to N'Djolé." Flouting the administration's power to direct population movements was a bold, and no doubt effective menace. Lastly, Tchioula argued that the people

---

[65] Bas-Chari report for 1940, GGAEF 4(4) D 50, ANOM, Aix-en-Provence.
[66] Tchioula to Eboué, 1941, GGAEF 379, ANRC, Brazzaville.

of Booué wanted what the Free French were bringing elsewhere, namely roads. "We want roads like [neighboring districts] where the whites don't just care about eating our chickens, eggs, goats and sheep." The complaint thus struck at the core of Gaullist wartime efficiency: It embraced the Free French language of progress and development, while portraying the local administrator as a counterproductive, bigoted leech.[67]

Complaints from Booué were in fact streaming in. In December 1941, a letter signed "the inhabitants of Booué" reached Eboué's office in Brazzaville. The grievances against administrators Numa Sadoul and Maurice Grandperrin were numerous.[68] They made the dead pay taxes, or rather extracted taxes from living relatives well after a death. They put the "old" to work – those between the ages of 40 and 50 – and beat them and deprived them of food. They collected "taxes" without issuing receipts. And finally, Sadoul and Grandperrin allegedly stated that de Gaulle had made a mistake in appointing Eboué, who was nothing more than a "bush monkey." The marginalia from the governor-general's office in Brazzaville is interesting. The mysterious reader in Brazzaville – perhaps Eboué or Laurentie in person – scrawled next to the racist reference: "I would be surprised if Sadoul expressed himself this way in front of his charges." This left open the possibility that he would do so in private or that he held such beliefs. Again, the inhabitants of Booué had cracked open a contradiction in a Gaullist hierarchy whose alleged color-blindness, embodied by Eboué, was belied by local African realities. To the inhabitants of Booué, Sadoul's and Grandperrin's attitude toward Eboué was inextricably linked to their deeply abusive and exploitative practices toward them. Further along, the petition reveals: "Mr. Sadoul and Mr. Grandperrin tell us that General de Gaulle was wrong to name you, Eboué, as Governor General, and he was also wrong to continue the war against the Germans." Here, the same margin writer fumes: "unacceptable."[69]

In April 1941, roughly eighty inhabitants of the Gabonese town of Lambaréné signed a petition that chronicled their suffering under the reign of another administrator, Pierre Duvergé, who had been at the helm of this subdivision since December 1940. Interestingly, a second version of the text, this one anonymous and more detailed, was also sent to Eboué, probably through different channels. Both documents signed by "the population of Lambaréné" depict a vicious circle. It began with the *prestations*. After twelve days of tough labor, skeletal *prestataires* were then dispatched to

---

[67] Ibid.

[68] Sadoul's personnel file shows him to have been a loyal Free French administrator. He was depicted in April 1941 as having "rallied at the very first hour, and he continues to assert his personality." In October 1943, he was presented as "firm," possessing a "capacity for making decisions," and equipped with "a very good general education." 7230, EEII, ANOM, Aix-en-Provence.

[69] The inhabitants of Booué to Eboué, December 10, 1941, GGAEF 379, ANRC, Brazzaville.

prison, where they were promptly whipped, beaten, and "tortured." The following day, they were sent to work on Mr Casteig's operation – the latter refusing to provide even a pot in which to prepare food. They survived on a few grains of raw rice. Whipped relentlessly and starving, many fled. Those who were caught were jailed for desertion, Duvergé adding for good measure "subdue and kill me those monkeys." In unspeakable conditions, out of either despair or resolve, some jailed women performed abortions on themselves, without receiving any medical attention.

These petitions to Eboué were consciously termed "cries of distress," aiming to rid them of "a pirate commander whose spirit is Hitlerian." In the unsigned version of the document, even more specific arguments are deployed. First of all, Duvergé utilized methods that even armies did not typically employ in conquered territories. Here he was clearly branded a criminal. Next, by using such methods against civilian populations, Duvergé was seeking "his revenge against African Gaullists, because Duvergé had been a Pétainist before."[70] Unfortunately, Duvergé's personnel file does not reveal whether he had indeed sympathized with Vichy, but it does show that during the rallying of FEA on August 26–28, 1940, this thirty-five-year-old official was located at Fort-Archambault, where the swing to de Gaulle did indeed prove arduous.[71] What seems certain is that this represented the multiple aftershocks of the civil war in Gabon between Vichy and Free French forces that raged in the fall of 1940. Local populations, which fully grasped the stakes of the conflict, were now in a position to utilize the language of a panimperial civil war that pitted Free France against Vichy.

The colonial methods described in these touching complaints were nothing new in Gabon or in FEA more generally, which had been the theater of the most ghastly violence since the nineteenth century. Even the form of grievance letters followed well-established lines. What had changed beginning in 1940 was an increased sense of invulnerability on the part of colonials and the determination of victims to seek redress against "torturers" and "Vichyites." The moral landscape of FEA was briskly shifting.

Imperial Reform?

In December 1941, Eboué began his vigorous defense of some sweeping reforms in indigenous policy that he had requested from London. His ideas for reform, he argued, were not new. They drew from Hubert Lyautey in Morocco, from the British and others. If his reforms were not passed, he implied, even the Belgians would seem more progressive than the French in FEA. He added that he had used the "pretext" of the labor question to tackle the topic that was dearest to him: African demography and quality

---

[70] The inhabitants of Lambaréné to Eboué, GGAEF 379, ANRC, Brazzaville.
[71] Duvergé, EEII 6562, ANOM, Aix-en-Provence.

of life in rural Africa.[72] Indeed, Eboué's initial proposal expressed "regret" that in time of war, forced labor could not be suppressed, but he hoped that he could rationalize labor and ensure that villages were constructed near workplaces and families not separated by forced labor practices.[73]

To say that Free French leadership in London was unconvinced would be an understatement. On June 19, 1942, London telegraphed Eboué that his sweeping reform of indigenous policy had been blocked by Free France's justice minister, René Cassin. On the issue of forced labor, Brazzaville was informed: "The main objections were that [your proposals] reinforce the reign of forced labor and end up limiting the administration's powers, by obliging it to accede to any reasonable labor requests from employers."[74] Internal correspondence confirms that Cassin was persuaded that Eboué's measures, far from being liberal, in fact, contravened some of the conventions on forced labor that France had signed between the wars.[75] The Free French were deeply uncomfortable to see forced labor formally codified. This echoes a similar trend in the British imperial context where, as David Killingray has shown, London expressed far greater apprehension about increasing forced labor circa 1942 than did settlers and other colonials on location in Africa.[76]

The law that Free France finally enacted in January 1942 was a compromise between Eboué's original vision and Cassin's qualms. It did, crucially, establish "in each territory of Equatorial French Africa, an Office du Travail et de la main d'oeuvre indigène destined to better ensure the principle of liberty of work, and to control recruitment and the use of indigenous labor."[77] Military efficiency, streamlining of labor fluxes, and administrative control over *prestations* had all been consecrated. Nor was it always necessary to change laws. In the Noun region of Cameroon in May 1941, the *chef de région* requested that administrators cease invoking Africans who "abandoned work sites" in their reports and replace the offense with "vaganbondage."[78] This simple change of wording, the head administrator opined, could achieve the same result in court, without drawing the suspicion of officials from the *affaires politiques*, themselves concerned about Cassin's perceptions. This was especially true in Cameroon, a territory that was not a colony but a mandate.

---

[72] Eboué to London, December 20, 1941, 1Affpol 873, ANOM, Aix-en-Provence.
[73] Décrets présentés par le Gouverneur Général de l'AEF, 1Affpol 873, ANOM, Aix-en-Provence.
[74] London, June 19, 1942, GGAEF 6B 712, ANOM, Aix-en-Provence.
[75] Cassin to Pleven, June 16, 1942, 1Affpol 873, ANOM, Aix-en-Provence.
[76] Killingray, "Labour mobilisation," 70.
[77] *Journal officiel de l'Afrique équatoriale française*, November 1, 1942, 572.
[78] 2AC5940, ANC, Yaoundé.

Conclusion

Remarkably, Free French propaganda made much of its "enlightened" policies in Africa.[79] This was partly the result of a wartime "information" battle that pitted Free France against Vichy, but also a vital piece of the legitimizing process for the one-time fledgling Free French movement. The argument was also rooted in Eboué's and Laurentie's language of reform, one that almost systematically clashed with more pressing wartime production imperatives. This contradiction seems so jarring partly because of an obvious problem with periodization. It seems clear that an era of intense resource extraction occurred in Free French Africa between 1940 and 1943, subsiding somewhat in the second half of 1943 with the arrival of other colonies to the Free French cause: French West Africa and Madagascar, most notably. Another era ensued, marked by the Brazzaville Conference of 1944, an era infused with a greater spirit of colonial reform. It is important, therefore, not to fall prey to the teleological vision of the Brazzaville conference as the logical outcome of some enlightened Gaullist colonial rule, and to see it, for all of its failings, as a break with an era of particularly harsh and demanding colonial rule that preceded it.

Where does this leave us with respect to ruptures and continuities in 1940? The exploitation of FEA and Cameroon was nothing new; neither were outrageous colonial acts that had long triggered complaints from Africans. What was new, however, was Free France's attempt to centralize labor on such a scale, the integration of FEA and Cameroon into an allied economic sphere, the previously unimaginably ambitious production orders received from London, and the attempt to massively expand at once rubber production and road construction, while maintaining gold mining. During the war, FEA and Cameroon were suddenly called upon to serve as stand-ins for colonies such as Indochina, the French empire's largest rubber producer. The capital of Free France, bastion of the French resistance, and springboard for Fighting France's daring raids into North Africa, FEA and Cameroon were also the sites of an unprecedented rush on natural resources, a commodity run that deeply marked local populations. In the words of local administrator Henri de Suremain: "the truth [about Free French Africa] is that we have pressed this orange so hard that we risk not being able to draw juice from it for much longer."[80]

---

[79] André Laguerre, *L'Afrique française libre* (London: Oxford University Press, 1942); and "Native policy in French Africa," *The Forum*, vol. 6, January 29, 1944, 28–30.
[80] Suremain to Vigoureux, May 5, 1942, GGAEF 2H 18, ANOM, Aix-en-Provence.

12

The Portuguese African Colonies during the Second World War

Malyn Newitt

During the First World War, both Angola and Mozambique had become battlefields in the struggle between Germany and the Allies, and in 1940, the authorities in Portugal, Britain, and South Africa feared that history would repeat itself. Both the Allies and the Axis weighed up the advantages and disadvantages of occupying Portuguese territory or of forcing Portugal into the war on their side. German policy was to persuade Franco to enter the war as an Axis ally, a move that would secure Gibraltar and effectively close the Mediterranean to Britain. Portuguese neutrality then would be unsustainable. In the end the Germans settled for Iberian neutrality, satisfied with the willingness of Salazar, the Portuguese prime minister, to provide Germany with the vital strategic mineral, wolfram. Britain, like Germany, preferred Iberian neutrality but with the proviso that "should Spain enter the war against us [it was proposed] to seize and hold both the Cape Verde Islands and the Azores as soon as possible, irrespective of the attitude of the Portuguese."[1]

Salazar was in a delicate situation. If Franco entered the war on the side of Germany, Portugal would face the likelihood of German and Spanish invasion, since he was well aware that elements in both Spain and Germany considered the unification of the Iberian peninsula as a legitimate war aim. However, he knew that, if Portugal tried to save itself by entering the war as an Axis ally, Britain would seize the Portuguese colonies. Accordingly, Portuguese efforts were directed to persuading Spain of the benefits of remaining neutral. In July 1940, a protocol was agreed to by Spain and Portugal, which extended the Treaty of Friendship and Non-Aggression and gave "the belligerents the clear message that the Iberian powers had

---

[1] Foreign Office (hereafter FO) to Lord Lothian, ambassador in Washington, October 9, 1940, C10637, FO 371/24494, The National Archives (hereafter TNA), Kew.

a common preference to remain at peace and to keep the war from the peninsula."[2]

Salazar, however, saw his regime as threatened both by Bolshevik communism and by the predatory liberal democracies of Britain and America. With this perspective he welcomed Germany's attack on the Soviet Union, while at the same time he sought to ward off threats from the western democracies. In March 1940, the British ambassador reported a remarkable conversation he had had with Francisco Vieira Machado, the Portuguese minister for the colonies, in which the latter had expressed great anxiety about "certain ideas which were being ventilated in [Britain] for a European federation on the basis of the pooling of colonial resources as a solution to prevent the repetition of another great war in Europe." The ambassador had reassured him that "Portugal had the absolute guarantee of His Majesty's government as regards her colonies."[3]

Despite the ancient Anglo-Portuguese alliance, it was only in August 1943 that the British were able to turn Portuguese neutrality decisively to their advantage with the lease of the Lajes airbase in the Azores, which provided facilities for trans-Atlantic aircraft and a base for operations against German submarines. Surprisingly, this did not provoke any German response, as Salazar tempered this move by signing a new agreement to continue selling wolfram to the Germans.

Until 1943, the Allies believed that Spain and Portugal might be forced into the war against them. The British believed that a German invasion of Portugal could be countered by the Portuguese government forming a government-in-exile in the Azores or Angola.[4] Otherwise, the British believed that the colonies would break away from a Portugal under German occupation and it was in anticipation of this that so much attention was paid to intelligence gathering in Angola and Mozambique. In their nervousness the British even believed that the African population might act as a German fifth column. In July 1940, the British vice-consul in Beira wrote that

> a possible source of danger lies in the native population among certain sections of whom the Germans appear to have had some success with propaganda. About two weeks ago, a number of natives were found to be wearing grass bracelets and it is claimed that investigation showed that these bracelets were to advertise the pro-German sympathies of the bearers during the German invasion of the colony, which the natives were given to understand was imminent.[5]

[2] Glyn Stone, *The Oldest Ally: Britain and the Portuguese Connection, 1936–1941* (Woodbridge: Boydell Press for the Royal Historical Society, 1994), 133–34.
[3] Sir Walford Selby to Lord Halifax, March 4, 1940, C3718, FO 371/24493, TNA, Kew.
[4] Sir R. Campbell to FO, May 3, 1941, FO 371/26793, TNA, Kew.
[5] C. N. Ezard, vice-consul Beira, to staff officer [intelligence] Cape Town, July 8, 1940, FO 371/24494, TNA, Kew.

Salazar's policy of neutrality saved Portugal from the economic and military disasters that had resulted from the decision to join the Allies in the First World War; however, the Portuguese authorities remained uncertain of British and American intentions, while their deepest suspicions were reserved for General Jan Christiaan Smuts who, they believed, planned to use the German threat to Angola and Mozambique to secure South African influence over the Portuguese colonies. The British shared this suspicion. As the high commissioner in South Africa wrote in December 1940, after contingency plans for taking control of the railways and ports in the Portuguese colonies had been drawn up,

> it will of course be appreciated that behind the attitude of the Union and Southern Rhodesia . . . must lie (a) the desire of the Union to get at least further control of Lourenço Marques (b) the ambition of Southern Rhodesia to obtain an outlet to the sea at Beira; in both cases feeling that here may be the opportunity.[6]

Salazar was also concerned at the apparent growth of subversive movements in the colonies and in 1940 and 1941 the Portuguese authorities carried out a series of arrests in Angola and Mozambique.[7] The British believed that separatist conspiracies had indeed been uncovered[8] The British consul general in Lourenço Marques obtained a copy of a lengthy manifesto from one separatist group, which reads like a reasoned academic essay by an anti-Salazarist economist.[9] The possibility that either Angola or Mozambique might declare its independence, as Brazil did in 1822, continued to be seen as a possible outcome of the war.[10]

The Portuguese government followed the arrests with measures to strengthen their defenses; however, British reports suggest that the quality of the troops left a lot to be desired. After Japan entered the war in 1941, there were fears that the Japanese might link up with the Vichy regime in Madagascar to attack Mozambique. To forestall this possibility, a British force was sent to occupy Madagascar and the Comoro Islands in May 1942. Despite alarmist reports of possible incursions by armed German plantation holders and despite the U-boats torpedoing the occasional merchant ship

---

[6] Telegram from high commissioner South Africa, December 7, 1940, FO 371/26828, TNA, Kew.

[7] Consul general Luanda to high commissioner South Africa, June 25, 1941, July 9, 1941, and July 16, 1941, FO 371/26846, TNA, Kew.

[8] Telegram from Sir Philip Mitchell, governor of Northern Rhodesia, enclosing report of Mr E. K. Scallan, consul general for the Union at Lourenco Marques, to the Internal Security Committee, August 12, 1940, FO 371/24494, TNA, Kew.

[9] Consul general Lourenço Marques to ambassador Lisbon, enclosing copy petition drawn up by the protesters, April 26, 1941, FO 371/26828, TNA, Kew.

[10] Professor Atkinson, "The Political Relations of Angola and Portugal," report from the Royal Institute for International Affairs, April 25, 1942, FO 371/31120, TNA, Kew.

in Portuguese territorial waters, the Portuguese colonies were not directly involved in any military operations.

It was strongly believed in Lisbon that Portugal's economic prosperity and its continued existence as an independent nation depended on its possession of a large colonial empire. The minister of the colonies explained this with disarming frankness in March 1940:

> Portugal was a very poor country industrially and could not possibly hope to compete with countries so magnificently equipped as Great Britain, France, Germany, Belgium, and even Holland. It was only in the preferences that Portugal enjoyed in her old Portuguese Empire that she could at present eke out a difficult existence... and any loss of these privileges would bring about the ruin of the people of Portugal. It is for this reason that there exists this deep Portuguese anxiety as regards her Colonial Empire.[11]

Portugal's policy with regard to its African colonies had been radically revised after the establishment of the New State. A series of enactments, the most important of which was the Colonial Act of 1930, outlined a relationship in which the colonies became an integral part of the Portuguese republic. Economic policy was controlled from Lisbon and the colonies were given the role of producing raw materials and earning foreign exchange to pay for imports of industrial and consumer goods from Portugal; however, it was one thing to outline this relationship, and quite another to make it work. In 1939, only 10 percent of Portugal's imports came from the empire and only 15 percent of its exports went there.

After the outbreak of the war it became clear to Portugal that strengthening the economic ties with its African colonies was the only way it was going to survive. Indeed, the war presented an ideal opportunity for the New State's colonial policy to become a reality.[12] As events unfolded, Portuguese economic policy moved away from the narrow pursuit of autarky outlined in 1930. Increased investment, the growth of the European population, and the pressures of import substitution led to diversification of the colonial economies and the beginnings of rapid economic growth, which was to mark the postwar period. As Clarence Smith wrote, "the economies of the Iberian colonies in some ways became more closely tied to the metropoles, in other ways became more autonomous, and in yet other ways became more dependent on trade with foreign countries"[13]

Although Portugal's colonies escaped the fighting, they did not escape the economic consequences of war. The British economic blockade of the continent of Europe required neutrals to obtain navicerts for their ships and

---

[11] Sir Walford Selby to Lord Halifax, March 4, 1940, FO 371/24493 C3718, TNA, Kew.
[12] Fernando Rosas, *Portugal entre a Paz, e a Guerra 1939–1945* (Lisbon: Editorial Estampa, 1995), 260.
[13] W. G. Clarence-Smith, "The impact of the Spanish Civil War and the Second World War on Portuguese and Spanish Africa," *Journal of African History*, 26 (1985), 310.

to move only goods required for their own internal consumption. This was designed to prevent the Axis being supplied by goods shipped via neutrals. The navicert system caused the Portuguese problems, particularly in supplying their colonies with goods which before the war had been imported from areas now under German occupation. Portuguese reexports of colonial produce were also affected.

As the Allied strategy was to provide economic aid to Spain and Portugal as an incentive for their continued neutrality, the British encouraged the Portuguese to sell colonial produce to Spain. The Spanish Civil War had already allowed the Portuguese to penetrate Spanish markets, particularly in textiles, but now the Portuguese were also allocated quotas for maize, oil seeds, copra, and cotton for reexport to Spain. According to the British consul general in Luanda, "It was hoped [that this] agreement would help the Spanish Government in improving the serious economic situation in Spain caused by the Civil War and that it would help the Portuguese Government by providing a market for a substantial quantity of Portuguese colonial products."[14] The quota system also allowed Portuguese colonies to export to the British empire, exports that were paid for in sterling.[15] As world prices for tropical products rose, the earnings of Portugal's colonies grew with them, earning substantial sums of foreign exchange for Portugal.

Nevertheless, the colonies were, at first, badly hit by the economic blockade as the Portuguese internal market could not absorb the colonial production of cocoa or coffee or other commodities. As the British consul-general in Luanda explained, "one industry, the fishing industry centered at Mossamedes, has been badly hit and is on the verge of complete ruin. If the British authorities could in any way assist in finding an outlet for their fish oil and fish meal, which should be needed by various industries, they would earn [their] undying gratitude." He added that help was also needed to dispose of the castor oil and other oleaginous seeds.[16] The problem was made worse by the lack of shipping,[17] a problem only partly solved when the Germans sold to the Portuguese a number of merchant ships trapped in Portuguese ports.

By 1942, the United States had entered the war, providing a large new market for Portuguese sisal, rubber, and copra,[18] while Japan's conquests in Asia cut off access to Asian rice and created shortages that the Portuguese colonies were able to meet. As new markets opened up, the Portuguese had

---

[14] FO to consul general Luanda, August 12, 1940, FO 371/24493, TNA, Kew.

[15] Consul general Luanda to high commissioner South Africa, September 10, 1941, FO 371/26848, TNA, Kew.

[16] Consul general Luanda to high commissioner South Africa, August 27, 1941, FO 371/26846, TNA, Kew.

[17] V. Cusden to Anthony Eden, enclosing "Short report on economic conditions in Angola," October 22, 1941, FO 371/26846 C13088, TNA, Kew.

[18] Clarence-Smith, "Impact of the Spanish Civil War," 312.

to expand colonial production. Some measures, such as quotas and price controls, had already been planned before the war; prices for key commodities were set in Lisbon and guaranteed against fluctuations in the world market. Concessions were then leased to private companies to organize the production, purchase, and marketing of these commodities. In addition, Juntas de Exportação was established to license exports. The system of quotas and price controls was gradually expanded to cover all the major primary products. Sugar had been subject to quotas before the war, and now the metropolitan demand for hides, tea, and coffee was also met by the colonies. The biggest drive for self-sufficiency, however, was in the production of cotton and rice.

The campaign to increase cotton production began during the Spanish Civil War. In 1938 the Junta de Exportação de Algodão Colonial had been set up, cotton concession areas had been rationalized, and a system of fixed prices for every stage of cotton production and export had been introduced. At that time, the price Portugal paid for colonial cotton was 20 percent above world prices and Salazar believed that price stability was the key to the successful development of the industry. The system involved the African peasants within each concession area being required to grow cotton on their land. Theoretically one hectare had to be planted for every male and half a hectare for every female. The scheme was largely confined to northern Mozambique (with some small concessions in southern Mozambique and Angola). This drive to achieve self-sufficiency in cotton rapidly proved successful. According to Clarence Smith, "in 1938, only a quarter of the raw cotton consumed in Portugal came from the colonies, but by 1942 this proportion had risen to nearly nine-tenths, with imports going from some 2,500 tons to about 18,500 tons."[19] However, the policy was not always well thought out or soundly administered. In much of the area that was leased to concessionaires cotton could not be grown profitably and the returns to both the peasant farmers and the concession companies were low. Unfortunately, the system produced poor quality cotton, as many growers were careless or inexperienced and some of them sabotaged the scheme by damaging plants or by boiling the seed to make it sterile.[20]

The rice concession scheme began in 1941 with the setting up of the Divisão do Fomento Orizícola. Again Mozambique saw most of the rice production, output rising from an initial figure of 100 tons to 1,2000 tons by 1946. The British businessman C. F. Spence described the system in a diary which he kept in Mozambique in 1943:

[19] Ibid.
[20] For African resistance to the cotton growing scheme, see Allen Isaacman, *Cotton Is the Mother of Poverty: Peasants, Work, and Rural Struggle in Colonial Mozambique, 1938–1961* (Westport, CT: Heinemann, 1996).

The system in this country is for the natives to do the growing, whilst hulling and cleaning the rice is in the hands of concessionaires who buy from the native the unhulled rice, hull it, clean it and polish it and then sell it to the traders. Concessions are divided into districts each concession holder having a monopoly in his own district, the natives not being permitted to sell to anyone else. Prices to the natives for unhulled rice, to the traders for ready milled rice and again retail to the natives by the traders are all controlled by the Portuguese government through the price controller.

And he added, "at present controlled prices are high, in fact over three times the cost of prewar imported rice from Burma."[21]

Tea was the other wartime success story. Tea planting had been taken up not only by large companies such as Sena Sugar and the Zambesia Company, but also by settler plantations. War conditions enabled Portuguese tea planters to find new markets, selling officially to the British Ministry of Food after 1942 and unofficially in the contraband market in the Gulf. Tea production rose from 902 long tons in 1939 to 2,231 in 1945.[22] By 1942, 23 percent of all Portugal's imports came from its colonies. Salazar had advanced a long way down the road to autarky.

The New State was not concerned merely to become self-sufficient in primary products; it wanted the colonies to import manufactured goods from Portugal. In 1941, the tariff regime of the colonies was standardized and to prevent countries neighboring Angola and Mozambique from dumping, Portuguese goods enjoyed a 50 percent tariff markdown. Protection was enforced by the Commissões Reguladoras de Importação, created at the beginning of the war, and was focused on areas where Portuguese penetration of the market had been weak. So in Mozambique quotas were set to give Portugal 70 percent of the cotton textile market, 75 percent of the market for beer, and 60 percent of the market for cement.

As the war economy gathered momentum, the populations of the colonies were affected in a number of ways. The Portuguese plantation economy had always been based on the availability of cheap labor. In Mozambique this had traditionally been obtained by devolving the administration of the colony to concession companies. These had been able to collect taxation from the Africans resident in their concessions in the form of labor; however, the abuses connected with this system had led to the government passing a new labor statute in 1928, which ostensibly abolished most forms of forced labor. As a consequence of these measures the plantation companies had had to obtain their labor through recruiting agents without the assistance

---

[21] C. F. Spence, "The diary of a trip through Portuguese East Africa, October and November 1943," 6, typescript in the possession of M. Newitt (the original belongs to the Spence family).

[22] Leroy Vail and Landeg White, *Capitalism and Colonialism in Mozambique* (London: Heinemann, 1980), 265–72.

of the administration, a system that placed them in competition with each other, with urban employers, and with the neighboring British colonies, which were also active in recruiting labor.

The decision to increase the output of peasant-grown cotton and rice and to divide the colony afresh among concession companies meant that the plantations, among them the rapidly expanding tea gardens, were now in direct competition with the cotton concession companies for African labor. To resolve these competing interests some plantation companies took out cotton concessions, enabling them to allocate labor within their concession areas, returning in this way to something very close to the old *prazo* system abolished ten years earlier.[23]

As the demand for labor grew, plantation companies and concessionaires alike were materially helped by the circular 818/D7 issued by Governor-General José Tristão de Bettencourt in October 1942. This once again declared that all Africans had a legal requirement not just to pay taxes, but to work for an employer or to cultivate a certain area of land. Further circulars required the administration to register each individual's contribution in a *cadernete* (pass book) and to assist with the allocation of labor. In 1941, the cotton concession companies had been allowed to appoint *capatazes* to oversee the production of cotton, who "were supposed to remain under the control of the administrator's police [but] from that time beatings, torture, sexual abuse and arbitrary imprisonment... became common methods used for the promotion of cotton production on family *machambas* (fields)."[24] In his 1944 report, the governor of Zambezia explained at length the regulations that now applied to force Africans to fulfill their labor obligations: "by these regulations the workers have the fullest liberty to choose the type of work that best suits them and to carry it out where and in what manner they think best, but this does not give them the right to convert this liberty into a right not to do anything at all."[25] To achieve this mobilization of the labor force, efforts were made to increase the effectiveness of local African *régulos* (chiefs) as agents of the administration. In both Angola and Mozambique chiefs were allocated specific duties in the collection of tax and the recruitment of labor, in return for which they were allowed to keep a proportion of the tax collected and houses were built for them to enhance their prestige.[26] Despite this, Henrique Galvão, one of the most vocal critics of Portuguese

---

[23] Vail and White, *Capitalism and Colonialism*, 278.

[24] David Hedges, Aurélio Rocha, Eduardo Medeiros, Gerhard Liesegang, and Arlindo Chilundo, *História de Moçambique*, Vol. 3: *Moçambique no auge do colonialismo, 1930–1961* (Maputo: Universidade Eduardo Mondlane, Departamento da História, 1993), 92.

[25] "Respostas ao Questionário formulado por Sua Exa o Governador Geral ao Governador da Província da Zambézia, Maio de 1947," 24; typescript in the possession of M. Newitt.

[26] Vail and White, *Capitalism and Colonialism*, 307; Hedges et al., *História de Moçambique*, Vol. 3, 8–9; Linda Heywood, *Contested Power in Angola 1840 to the Present* (Rochester, NY: University of Rochester Press, 2000), 85.

colonial policy, wrote, "it is one of the most serious mistakes in Angolan native policy of recent years to have favoured the destruction (*pulverização*) of the *sobas* (chiefs) and to have hastened the decline in prestige of the native chiefs."[27]

Commenting on this reversal of the trend that marked labor policy since 1928, Governor-General Bettencourt wrote in a confidential circular to district administrators, "at the present moment, when the great nations are occupied with the problems of war, it is natural that a certain arbitrariness practised by us in respect of the system of labour laid down by international agreements, should pass without comment."[28] The colonial administrators, however, were far from happy and in many of their reports they protested strongly at the consequences of this new system of forced labor.[29]

By 1944, nearly 800,000 African peasant farmers were involved in cotton growing in Mozambique and 90,000 in Angola. A further 100,000 were involved in Mozambique's rice-growing schemes. Although no accurate statistics are available, there can be little doubt that this represented a huge increase in numbers involved in cotton growing before the war. Such a commitment of labor led inevitably to a decline in food production. Exports of commodities other than cotton were also hit. Spence noted that traffic using the northern ports had declined since the government had taken over the Niassa Company's concession in 1929: "The implication is that the Niassa Co encouraged production and trading because its own existence depended on trade whereas the Government is more interested in the administration of the native than his productivity. Added to this there is the emphasis put on the production of cotton... the more cotton the native produces, the less he plants of his normal crops."[30] Much labor was wasted in trying to grow cotton on unsuitable land and in 1947, the governor of Zambezia admitted in his report that it was necessary to raise agricultural productivity generally and that mechanization was the only realistic way ahead.[31]

In areas where there were no cotton concessions, small farmers benefited from high prices and food production actually increased.[32] By the end of the war the most important change in rural areas was in the number of Africans growing crops commercially on their own land. The returns from growing cotton varied greatly. Although the average annual income was 85 escudos, the amounts that individuals received varied from 8 to 140 escudos

[27] Henrique Galvão and Carlos Selvagem, *Império Ultramarino Português: Monografia do império*, Vol. 3 (Lisbon: Emprensa Nacional de Publicidade, 1952), 213.
[28] Quoted in Hedges et al., *História de Moçambique*, Vol. 3, 88.
[29] Ibid., 104.
[30] Spence, "Diary," 6.
[31] Respostas ao Questionário... Maio de 1947, 28.
[32] Vail and White, *Capitalism and Colonialism*, 310–11, 317.

according to the suitability of the region for cotton growing.[33] For many this activity brought little wealth and deprived their families of important food crops, but some worked the system to their advantage and the number of Africans becoming commercial farmers increased. Others benefited from the good prices paid for oil-bearing seeds. Along the coast of Mozambique African peasant farmers had taken over many of the coconut trees when the price of copra had fallen in the 1930s. The war led to a sharp rise in copra prices from which African growers were able to benefit. The same was true of cashew nuts, which had been exported to India before the war but were now processed in Mozambique. In Angola, the boom in maize production during the 1930s and the rapid increase in land under coffee also benefited African growers, who grew about a quarter of all coffee produced.[34] Clarence Smith summarized this trend: "African 'kulaks' were responsible for all the production of rubber and wax, and most of the exports of oilseeds, hides, coffee, tobacco, maize, beans and other foodstuffs."[35]

In Angola, the state had created agencies (the Gremio do Milho Colonial and the Junta da Exportação dos Cereais) to increase maize production, distributing improved seed and ploughs to African producers. The result was a great increase in production and in the acreage under cultivation. The years 1936 to 1946 saw annual yields of more than 100,000 tons (with the exception of 1943 and 1944).[36] Total maize production in Angola tripled between 1926 and 1960; however, by the 1940s, Portugal was no longer dependent on Angolan maize as Salazar was pursuing a policy of grain self-sufficiency for metropolitan Portugal. Prices paid for Angolan maize were therefore set artificially low and this coincided with declining productivity of the soil after ten years of expansion.[37] Galvão summed up the effects of twenty years of Salazarist policies in his usual epigrammatic style: "*Angola produz caro e produz mal* (Angola produces expensively and badly)."[38] During the 1940s, internal labor migration in Angola reached unprecedented proportions, with the central highlands providing a pool of labor for the northern coffee farms and coastal fishing businesses as well as for urban-based economic activity.[39] Migration to Northern Rhodesia also gathered pace and during the war the Ovimbundu population residing there was reported to number 300,000.[40] Galvão described the hemorrhage of population in typically dramatic fashion: "the inhabitants of Mozambique

[33] Hedges et al., *História de Moçambique*, Vol. 3, 90.
[34] Clarence-Smith, *Third Portuguese Empire*, 176.
[35] Ibid., 321.
[36] Heywood, *Contested Power*, 90.
[37] Ibid., 83–90.
[38] Galvão and Selvagem, *Império Ultramarino Português*, Vol. 3, 300.
[39] Heywood, *Contested Power*, 75.
[40] Ibid., 78.

emigrate, those of Angola flee,"[41] and later he added the mordant comment, "only the dead are really exempt from contract labour."[42]

Formal opposition to the regime had few opportunities to express itself apart from flight; however, hostile reactions to government policies of a "prepolitical" nature were common. In the northern regions of Angola, where the population shared a common culture with the inhabitants of the Belgian Congo, there was a strong syncretic religious tradition. Kimbanguism had spread in the 1930s. During the war offshoots of the original Kimbanguist movement, of a kind explicitly hostile to colonial rule, appeared in northern Angola. Working through initiation societies, the Tawa movement was described by René Pélissier as "antichristian, antiwhite and accepting the principle of armed struggle against the colonisers. [It believed] that the ancestors would be resurrected and would bring with them the riches of Europe." Another movement was "kakism," founded by Simon Mpadi and also an offshoot of Kimbanguism, which was active in Angola between 1939 and 1941 and is described as "violently anti-Belgian and antimissionary, it adopted a para-military structure ... and spread among the BaKongo the myth of Hitler, protector of the blacks."[43] It was to be among the BaKongo that the first overtly nationalist independence movements emerged in the 1950s.

The general lines of a new colonial policy had been laid down before the war but to make it effective, changes were needed to other core policies of the regime. Since assuming power in Portugal, Salazar had discouraged the settlement in Africa of Portuguese with few resources and no education as they were too often a burden on the colonial exchequers. This, coupled with the effects of the depression and the repatriation of convicts, resulted in the net exodus of settlers from the colonies. During the war, however, attitudes began to change. Vieira Machado produced a new plan for assisted emigration, which did not get beyond the discussion stage during the war but which formed the basis for the *colonatos* (planned agricultural settlements) that featured in the postwar development plans. Net immigration to the colonies began to increase in 1938 and by 1945 was running at around 3,000 a year, a number that rose steeply thereafter as the colonies went through a phase of rapid economic development.[44] Part of the reason for this change was the closing down of other emigrant destinations, but the

[41] Galvão, Henrique, and Carlos Selvagem, *Império ultramarino português: Monografia do Império, Vol. 4: Moçambique. Índia. Macau. Timor* (Lisboa: Emprensa Nacional de Publicidade, 1953), 132.

[42] Henrique Galvão, *The Santa Maria: My Crusade for Portugal* (London: Weidenfeld and Nicolson, 1961), 52.

[43] René Pélissier, *La Colonie du Minotaur: Nationalismes et révoltes en Angola, 1926–1961* (Orgéval, France: Éditions Pélissier, 1978), 167–68.

[44] Cláudia Castello, *Passagens para África: O Povoamento de Angola e Moçambique com Naturais da Metrópole (1920–1974)* (Lisbon: Afrontamento, 2007), 90–98, 189.

wartime influx of Portuguese was also the result of military reinforcements and the expansion of the administration, a notable feature being the relative high level of education and the low rate of illiteracy compared with that of the emigrants who arrived after the war.

Of great significance also was the impetus given by the government to Portuguese investment in Africa. During the war, systematic attempts were made to exploit the mineral resources of the colonies and prospecting licenses were issued for gold, asphalt, manganese, mica, and coal, and for copper in Angola.[45] Major studies were undertaken by hydrographical, botanical, and zoological missions and plans were drawn up for airports in São Tomé, Guiné, Angola, and Cape Verde. Improvements were made to the road systems and the extension of the port of Luanda, begun in 1941, was completed by the end of the war.

Prior to 1940, private Portuguese investment in Africa had been very limited. Some capital had been invested in sugar production and fishing, and in cocoa plantations in São Tomé, but otherwise investment had come almost exclusively from non-Portuguese sources. Foreign companies owned Angolan diamonds and Mozambican sugar as they did the ports and railways. The war presented Salazar with a major opportunity to reverse this trend. As foreign investors became increasingly willing to sell out, Salazar encouraged Portuguese business to take over foreign-owned companies. One example was the German plantations in Angola. Britain had refused to grant navicerts for their products and Germany had responded by providing subsidies to the planters, which increased British and Portuguese suspicion that they were secret agents of Germany. Portugal then proceeded to increase the pressure on them. "As a result of the Governor-General's refusal to help Krueger and other German planters obtain black labour," the British consul-general wrote,

> Krueger is now willing, and possibly anxious, to let his plantations to Portuguese firms until the end of the war.... His plantations produce about half the German sisal in the Colony or approximately one quarter of the colony's total production. Other German planters appear ready to sell right out, amongst them march the German "Governor General of Angola."[46]

Italian-owned timber companies also suffered. Spence mentions in his diary visiting a sawmill

> which had been the property of Italians [who] had found themselves unable to export the timber on that account, so I had made a special trip at the time to Beira to see what I could do to help them, as the timber was badly needed in the Union. I succeeded in arranging for the purchase price to be frozen so

[45] Rosas, *Portugal entre a Paz, e a Guerra*, 262.
[46] Consul general Luanda to high commissioner South Africa, October 7, 1942, FO 371// 31120, C10381, TNA, Kew.

that no funds could pass into Italian hands till after the war, or at any rate till the British Consul, who was given control of them agreed to free them.[47]

Although wartime shortages enabled metropolitan Portuguese industries to obtain a larger share of the colonial market, the most significant development, and the clearest departure from earlier policies, was the decision to allow industrialization in the colonies themselves. In the 1930s, some cheap consumer goods, mostly for the African market, had been manufactured in the colonies and there had been some processing of raw materials. High wartime prices now gave the colonies money to spend and capital to invest. The shortage of shipping made goods from Portugal scarce and expensive, while cotton and other crops often had to be warehoused. One solution was to have the cotton spun and woven in the colonies themselves and pressure began to mount for obstacles to colonial industrialization to be removed. Establishing industries in the colonies was vociferously opposed by many smaller manufacturers in Portugal, but the large business empires (Champalimaud, Companhia União Fabril, Banco Português do Atlântico, and Banco Espirito Santo), which were especially favored by the regime to carry out its industrialization policies, now received licenses to invest in new industries, which included cooking oil, blankets, sacking, paper, rubber, cement, metal tools, tiles, furniture, and varnish.[48] Many other industries were to follow but this policy of limited industrialization remained closely controlled from Lisbon. The 1936 requirement that each application would be considered on a case-by-case basis was maintained and those industries that were established were intended to be for the internal consumption of the colonies and to substitute imports.[49]

The new industrial policy and the intensification of labor recruitment required a more active and engaged administration. During the war, the aspirations of the administration greatly expanded, as can be seen in the extensive report published by Bettencourt, the governor-general of Mozambique.[50] Policies were developed not only for infrastructure projects but also for improvements in agriculture and social welfare, including health and education, although budgetary allocations for these programs were often quite inadequate. As an example, the governor of Zambezia province reported in 1947 on the expansion of health services in his area during the war. The number of health-related establishments in the province rose from 24 in 1941 to 146 in 1946. The number of those treated nearly quadrupled and expenditure rose more than four times; however, this increase was achieved almost entirely through the establishment of what were described

---

[47] Spence, "Diary," 80.
[48] M. Anne Pitcher, *Politics in the Portuguese Empire* (Oxford: Clarendon Press, 1993), 94.
[49] Rosas, *Portugal entre a Paz, e a Guerra*, 269–72.
[50] José Tristão de Bettencourt, *Relatório do Governador Geral de Moçambique*, 2 vols (Lisbon: Agência Geral das Colónias, 1945).

as rudimentary posts, located in wooden huts and in charge of infirmary assistants who had only received basic training in hygiene and asepsis.[51]

The agreements reached with the Catholic church can also be seen as part of the Portuguese response to the war. A concordat and acordo missionário were signed with the Vatican in 1940, while the Estatuto Missionário of 1941 recognized that Portugal had a moral obligation to "promote, by all means, the moral improvement and material life of the population."[52] The statute conferred a monopoly of primary education on the Catholic church. State subsidies to the missions grew by a third during the war.[53] The new education programs were, in part, exercises in trying to limit the influence of the foreign Protestant missions and fit into the more general direction of New State policies designed to "nationalize" the African territories and make them part of a unified Portuguese state.

As well as the mainland colonies, the Portuguese ruled the islands of Cape Verde and São Tomé e Príncipe. The Cape Verde Islands were strategically important for their airfields, bunkering facilities, and submarine cable stations and the British feared a German attempt to seize one or more of the islands. A report by a British naval officer in January 1941 describes these concerns:

> On Christmas Day St Vincent was virtually undefended. The Senior Officer present was the Officer of the Port, [he] is a political exile who will accept little responsibility and who lacks decision, and a lieutenant in charge of the garrison, a man miserable in appearance, who commands fifty native troops, recruited locally. . . . Four to six determined armed men with iron bars and a can of petrol could put the [cable] station out of commission in from five to ten minutes.[54]

Salazar responded to British concerns by sending a warship and dispatching a force of 3,000 men to defend the islands. Despite these measures the British complained that German U-boats operated around the islands and even received aid from the islanders.[55] It was not to be a British or German occupation, however, that brought disaster to wartime Cape Verde, but drought.

The islands were liable to severe and prolonged droughts and the resulting famines could only be ameliorated by imports of food or by emigration. Wartime conditions made the islands particularly vulnerable. In 1939, the rains failed and the islands faced steadily worsening famine conditions over the next three years. The effects of the famine, one of the most severe in the

---

[51] Respostas ao Questionário . . . Maio de 1947, 6.
[52] Heywood, *Contested Power*, 65.
[53] Ibid., 100.
[54] Lt Cumberlege RNR to FO, January 1941, FO 371/26842, TNA, Kew.
[55] Vice-consul St Vincent to British Ambassador Lisbon, October 7, 1941, FO 371/26842, TNA, Kew.

islands' history, were described in the dispatches of the British vice-consul.
In August 1941, he recorded

> from 70% to 80% of the inhabitants of the Cape Verde Islands live within the
> poverty zone, dependent on the annual rainfall for their next year's supplies of
> foods and necessities. A bad year means hunger and shortage, two bad years
> in succession may bring starvation in many islands.... Towards the end of
> 1940 rumours were constant of serious want in many of the islands, as 1941
> advanced food riots due to want were reported from S. Antão and death from
> hunger from S. Nicolau and Fogo.... Children from this island [S. Nicolau]
> are being landed in St Vincent just skin and bone and have to be carried to the
> houses of their friends.[56]

By December the situation was worse. Patrols had turned back people from
the countryside trying to get to one of the towns to find relief. The vice-
counsel observed that, "The starving seem to accept the situation with an
oriental fatalism. They do not press their claims to live, they scarcely beg,
may ask you for alms once or twice, and then simply stare at you as if
resigned to what is to happen." The authorities "are very reticent regarding
information about the famine ... and it is evident the government do not
wish for any outside assistance."[57] The only measures being taken were to
establish relief works but many people were too weak to work. Eventually
some 1,700 starving islanders were sent to São Tomé to work in the cocoa
plantations.

The vice-consul reported that imported foodstuffs continually ran out
because the recently reinforced Portuguese garrison had to be fed and visiting Portuguese ships did not run to schedule or were too full to carry
goods for Cape Verde.[58] Nevertheless, he emphasized that "the Island Government can deal with the situation if they wish to ... [and] Portugal can
also help if required without any inconvenience, it has no war expenditure and is probably at present one of the wealthiest nations in Europe."[59]
António Carreira estimated that during the years 1941–1943, there were
24,643 deaths attributable to the famine.[60] Salazar was very sensitive that
offers of assistance would prove to be excuses for political or military intervention. The Portuguese were aware that drought was a recurring feature of
island life and that the customary survival strategies of the islanders involved
emigration. Because normal emigration routes were closed by the war, the

[56] British vice-consul St Vincent to ambassador Lisbon, August 28, 1941, FO 371/26842,
   TNA, Kew.
[57] British vice-consul St Vincent to ambassador Lisbon, December 3, 1941, FO 371/26842,
   TNA, Kew.
[58] British vice-consul St Vincent to ambassador Lisbon, August 28, 1941, FO 371/26842,
   TNA, Kew.
[59] British vice-consul St Vincent to ambassador Lisbon, December 3, 1941, FO 371/26842,
   TNA, Kew.
[60] António Carreira, *The People of the Cape Verde Islands* (London: Hurst, 1982), 166.

Portuguese encouraged emigration to São Tomé; however, in terms of what was needed to stem deaths from starvation, this measure was too little and too late.

São Tomé and Príncipe had at one time been Portugal's most profitable colonies. Between 1909 had 1919, the islands had exported more than 30,000 tons of cocoa beans every year, with 1919 being a peak year when 55,000 tons had been produced. Thereafter, production went into steep decline until, in 1940, only 6,900 tons were exported and many companies began to produce palm oil as well as cocoa and coffee.[61] While world prices remained low, particularly during the 1930s, the Portuguese companies that owned the plantations (known as *roças*) failed to invest in new fixed capital and saw the cocoa trees ravaged by disease. The *roça* owners, however, believed, almost as an article of faith, that their difficulties were caused by shortage of labor, although the more realistic understood that the problem was actually the very low productivity of the labor they did possess. In the eyes of the more zealous administrators, the problem lay in the appalling conditions on many of the *roças* where the workforce was still treated as virtual slaves.

During the war, a shortage of shipping and a depressed market for cocoa meant that the island economies stagnated. By 1943, cocoa production had fallen to barely 3,000 tons. Although 1,700 starving Cape Verdians had reached the islands in 1942, the next three years saw hardly any newly contracted workers arrive while the labor force continued to suffer attrition through death, desertion, and some repatriation. In 1944–1945, cocoa production began to recover as the world price experienced a modest rise but the contract labor force continued to decline as laborers, who had served their contracts, returned home.[62]

The early years of the war were, therefore, a period of crisis for the *roças*, a crisis that went to the very heart of the colonial system, which is vividly brought out in a report on the *roça* Agua Izé, produced in February 1941 for the Companhia da Ilha de Príncipe that owned the plantation. This confidential report strikingly illuminates Portuguese colonial practice and the slowness in implementing reform. Having discussed in detail the situation on each of the dependencies of the *roças*, the author, Castro Almeida, addressed the delicate matter of relations with the workforce. He pointed out that each laborer cost the *roça* around 700 escudos. Before they could be of any use they needed training but "if brutality and the whip are brought into action unjustly and without any reason the labourers (and particularly the new ones) fled and took refuge in the forest. They remained completely lost to the *roça*, which not only loses the 700 escudos but also a worker who, with

---

[61] Francisco Mantero, *Obras Completas, Vol. 1: A Mão-de-Obra em S. Tomé e Príncipe* (Lisbon: [s.n.], 1954), appendix.
[62] Ibid.

a bit of patience, would become an item of value." It was important that the workforce should be properly fed, for "if we do not feed properly the cattle we need for work, they will not be productive, so why should we adopt other criteria with the labourers?"[63]

"If formerly the workforce on the *roças* was treated as slaves," the report says, "today this cannot be done, not only for reasons of humanity but for legal reasons, seeing that the curators (*curadores*) exercise a strict supervision (more or less, according to which *curador* [is involved])." Complaints made to the *curador* "make a disgraceful impression and damage the prestige of the *roça*." Punishment with the *palmatoria*, which left the laborer unable to work for days, was stupid. Much better was "half a dozen blows administered to each hand daily in front of the other [workers]" rather than punishment, which prevents them from working, administered in private. "I was present at a scene that was not edifying," he wrote. "A young girl of 10 or 12 was given twenty-four blows of the *palmatoria* while Sr Amaro stood behind her with a hippopotamus hide whip to force her to hold out her hand." A halt was called to this scene "when they saw me"; however, he adds for the benefit of his employers, "corporal punishment for the blackman is necessary because it is the only thing he fears."[64]

To achieve a happy workforce, he advises to allow them to cultivate gardens and to hold their *batuques* but "punish without sparing them when it is necessary and they deserve it." As for the administrators of the *roça*,

> morals are of the very worst kind. [The administrator had a girl with whom he sleeps, but he also] has a *moleca* [black girl], a *tonga* [child of a contract labourer born in São Tomé] from the *roça*, who has to sleep on a sofa in the administration office with the result that when I sat down in the office I saw two bedbugs on the sleeve of my coat and the sofa where the girl slept was infested with insects. . . . All this would be less important if the good name of the *roça* was not involved.

Almost all the administrators of the *roças* had relations with young girls, which did not affect their prestige if it was an occasional matter and they paid generously "but what is very bad and prejudices discipline is the selection of one girl who comes to be privileged over the others and is the cause of envy, jealousy and disturbance."[65] Evidently not written *para os inglezes ver* (for the English to see), this report vividly tells its own story.

In February 1945, a new governor, Carlos de Sousa Gorgulho, was appointed to try not only to revive the economy of São Tomé but to deal with the social problems that lay at the root of the island's decline. Gorgulho's

[63] P. L. M. Castro Almeida, "Relatório sobre as condições em que se encontra actualmente a Roça Agua Izé da Companhia da Ilha do Príncipe," 24; typed report in the possession of M. Newitt.

[64] Ibid.

[65] Ibid., 25, 27.

energy, enterprise, and reforming zeal transformed São Tomé but also led to a revolutionary situation, which dramatically challenged the whole postwar colonial system.[66] As de Tocqueville pointed out long ago, the most dangerous moment for any regime is when it begins to reform itself.

---

[66] Gerhard Seibert, *Comrades, Clients and Cousins: Colonialism, Socialism and Democratization in Sao Tome and Principe* (Leiden: Research School of Asian, African, and Amerindian Studies, Leiden University, 1999), 55–75.

13

World War II and the Transformation of the Tanzanian Forests

Thaddeus Sunseri

Historians of World War II in Africa have long recognized that the war acted as "a catalyst for social and economic change" within the continent, creating an extraordinary demand for raw materials and some industry, yet intensifying material deprivations and social stresses that contributed to postwar nationalism.[1] The war sparked a development ethos far beyond that of the Depression years, a prelude to the economic boom of the 1950s.[2] Moreover, after 1941, when the Japanese conquest of Southeast Asia severed the shipment routes of food and primary products previously destined for Allied and colonial territories alike, the war awakened an American interest in Africa as a source of strategic raw materials.[3] Although tropical crops such as rubber, cotton, peanuts, sisal, and rice have been part of economic histories of the war, products of the natural environment, particularly those of the forests, have often escaped attention. Yet demand for timber, firewood, charcoal,

---

[1] David Killingray and Richard Rathbone, "Introduction," in David Killingray and Richard Rathbone (eds.), *Africa and the Second World War* (New York: St. Martin's Press, 1986), 15; Michael Crowder, "The Second World War: Prelude to decolonisation in Africa," in Michael Crowder (ed.), *The Cambridge History of Africa: Volume 8: From c. 1940 to c. 1975* (Cambridge: Cambridge University Press, 1984), 8–51; Michael Cowen and Nicholas Westcott, "British imperial economic policy during the war," in Killingray and Rathbone, *Africa and the Second World War*, 55; Frederick Cooper, *Decolonization and African Society* (Cambridge: Cambridge University Press, 1996), chapter four; Killingray, "Soldiers, ex-servicemen and politics in the Gold Coast, 1939–1950," *Journal of Modern African Studies*, 21 (1983), 523–34; Killingray, *Fighting for Britain: African Soldiers in the Second World War* (Athens: Ohio University Press, 2010), chapter seven.

[2] Joseph Morgan Hodge, *Triumph of the Expert: Agrarian Doctrines of Development and the Legacies of British Colonialism* (Athens: Ohio University Press, 2007), 207–09; Mike Cowen, "Early years of the Colonial Development Corporation: British state enterprise overseas during late colonialism," *African Affairs*, 83 (1984), 63–75.

[3] John Iliffe, *A Modern History of Tanganyika* (Cambridge: Cambridge University Press, 1979), 351–54.

and other tree products, including wild rubber, copal, cellulose, wood alcohol, wood sugar, paper pulp, textiles, and fodder, exploded during the war.[4] German and Japanese total-war planners understood that controlling the forests of occupied territories eased economic quarantines by substituting natural products for industrial raw materials lost from prewar trade linkages, including petroleum, coal, rubber, and chemicals.[5] While historians of the war have often ignored its connections to the natural environment, historians of the environment have rarely incorporated the impact of World War II in their analyses. Just as World War II in Africa launched a "second colonial occupation" following the war, the transformations wrought by the war also sparked an era of conservation and environmentalism.[6]

During the war the British colonial state launched unsustainable encroachment into Tanganyikan forests and woodlands to meet military demands for construction timber, railway ties, mining pit props, building poles, wild rubber, and dyewoods. Although the war created substantial hardships for Africans by curbing imports of food and consumer goods and by military conscription and forcing men to work on plantations, wartime necessity opened forest lands and resources to African exploitation after half a century of colonial forest curtailment. The shortage of European and Asian commercial saw millers and their unwillingness to extract timber in inaccessible landscapes gave African lumbermen opportunity to supply timber and railway ties for military and domestic needs. Shortages of food to feed plantation workers, combined with rationed food imports, periodic famines, and urbanization, created a need to open up new lands in forest reserves to grow food and manufacture charcoal. Some African farmers, often women, responded to this demand by seeking licenses to farm in forest reserves, while others simply pressed into forest lands owing to weak oversight by forest staff. Furthermore, curtailment of Southeast Asian supplies of plantation rubber after 1941 created an unlimited demand for wild rubber, and many African men and women responded by reviving this extractive industry that fifty years previously had been a source of local power and wealth. These activities demonstrate gendered dimensions of wartime forest activities that persisted into the postwar era.

[4] Richard P. Tucker, "The world wars and the globalization of timber cutting," in Richard P. Tucker and Edmund Russell (eds.), *Natural Enemy, Natural Ally: Toward an Environmental History of Warfare* (Corvallis: Oregon State University Press, 2004), 110–41.

[5] Egon Glesinger, *Nazis in the Woodpile* (New York: Bobbs-Merrill, 1942); Raymond L. Bryant, *The Political Ecology of Forestry in Burma 1824–1994* (Honolulu: University of Hawaii Press, 1997), 133–54; Nancy Lee Peluso, *Rich Forests, Poor People: Resource Control and Resistance in Java* (Berkeley: University of California Press, 1992), 93–97; Thaddeus Sunseri, "Exploiting the *urwald*: German post-colonial forestry in Poland and Central Africa, 1900–1960," *Past and Present*, 214 (2012), 305–42.

[6] Roderick P. Neumann, "The postwar conservation boom in British Colonial Africa," *Environmental History*, 7 (2002), 22–47.

Although some Africans gained greater access to forest resources, wartime labor shortages revived colonial proposals for landscape and social engineering that forced thousands of rural people into "closer settlements" to foster development. Ostensibly motivated by outbreaks of sleeping sickness, late colonial closer settlement was a model for rural development during the 1950s and the 1970s period of Ujamaa socialism in independent Tanzania. Moreover, closer wartime settlement foreshadowed early Cold War development schemes that launched Tanzania into a fitful modernity fraught with rural strife. By reviving the value of the Tanzanian landscape to the global economy, World War II empowered state forestry to assume a pivotal role in postwar development schemes.

State Forestry in Tanganyika before the War

All European colonial powers introduced scientific forestry into their colonies, which, they believed, was necessary for resource control and social engineering.[7] Scientific forestry meant claiming tropical forests and woodlands for the state, making them into protected reserves, evicting their peasant and pastoral populations, and imposing managed exploitation of trees and resources. Ideally this meant transforming the tropical landscapes according to a European model, whereby intensive agriculture would be layered with intensive plantation forestry, replacing slow-growing tropical hardwoods with fast-growing exotic softwoods, especially pines and eucalyptus. Peasants evicted from forests would be transformed into forest workers, producing the timber and wood fuel necessary for colonial development, cutting firebreaks around forests, and planting and tending trees on plantations. At the same time, African subsistence agriculture would be transformed into intensive cash crop farming. Colonial foresters saw the East African landscape as devastated by generations of African misuse, and thus regarded fire-using peasants and pastoralists as the chief enemy of scientific forestry.[8]

In Tanzania, German colonizers introduced scientific forestry from the start of colonial rule in 1891. German foresters reserved about 1 percent of the landscape as forest reserves by 1914, which included virtually all the closed-canopy forests and rainforests that protected water catchments and contained concentrations of marketable woods. Many of these forests enclosed rain-making shrines and ancestral graves that Africans used as

---

[7] S. Ravi Rajan, *Modernizing Nature: Forestry and Imperial Eco-Development, 1800–1950* (Oxford: Oxford University Press, 2006); Christopher Conte, *Highland Sanctuary: Environmental History in Tanzania's Usambara Mountains* (Athens: Ohio University Press, 2004); Thaddeus Sunseri, *Wielding the Ax: State Forestry and Social Conflict in Tanzania, 1820–2000* (Athens: Ohio University Press, 2009).

[8] R. S. Troup, *Report on Forestry in Tanganyika Territory* (Dar es Salaam: Government Printer, 1936), 15–16.

social charters and claims to land.[9] These forests were vital resources, including famine foods, medicines, game meat, building poles, fuel, and marketable products such as rubber, copal, beeswax, and mangroves. African extraction of such resources during the nineteenth century had empowered them to purchase imported textiles, currency, and firearms, helping to survive difficult times.[10] Colonial forestry circumscribed these activities, as Germans valued Africans more as growers of cash crops and as plantation and railway workers. Yet German colonizers failed to arrest African shifting cultivation, and failed to introduce meaningful rotational forestry. Most construction timber was imported from Europe and North America because African hardwoods were too difficult to work, were heavy and expensive to transport, and were dispersed in forests and woodlands, far from lines of transport. Scientific forestry was predicated on adequate supplies of labor to do forest work, which East Africa was notably lacking, while sleeping sickness and other livestock diseases killed draft animals.

World War I ruptured scientific forestry in East Africa, as British, Belgian and German forces battled in the recesses of the landscape, and Africans used the forests to escape wartime exactions and forced labor. When the British took over Tanganyika following the war, they largely adopted the German forestry template; however, British reluctance to invest in a colonial periphery and the economic depression of the 1930s weakened colonial forestry, enabling a modest revival of some African forest industries, including beeswax collection and rubber and copal tapping.[11] With East Africa located far from the European industrial heartland, British foresters struggled to find a market for Tanganyikan hardwood, whose names, characteristics, growing patterns, and uses were largely unknown. Britain's ability to rely on Southeast Asian hardwoods, especially teak, meant that there was no incentive to develop East African timber resources.[12]

Although colonial forest departments and timber traders struggled in the interwar years to find markets for timber, in Europe a revolution was taking place in wood use. Owing to raw material shortages during World War I, chemical industries came to see wood as a substitute for products that included textiles, fuel, fodder, sugar, and vinegar, and more tree species were found to be useful for paper pulp and cellulose. Many of these products were distilled from charcoal, making previously little-valued hardwoods

[9] Michael J. Sheridan and Celia Nyamweru (eds.), *African Sacred Groves: Ecological Dynamics and Social Change* (Oxford: James Currey, 2008).

[10] James L. Giblin, "The precolonial politics of disease control in the lowlands of Northeastern Tanzania," in Gregory Maddox, James Giblin, and I. Kimambo (eds.), *Custodians of the Land: Ecology and Culture in the History of Tanzania* (Athens: Ohio University, 1995), 127–51; Sunseri, *Wielding the Ax*, chapter one.

[11] Michael Tuck, "Woodland commodities, global trade, and local struggles: The beeswax trade in British Tanzania," *Journal of Eastern African Studies*, 3 (2009), 259–74.

[12] A. Rule, "East African timber production," *Empire Forestry Journal*, 24 (1945), 47–51.

important for organic chemical industries. With European hardwoods such as oak and beech largely replaced by softwood pine plantations, tropical Africa emerged as a potential supplier of wood for chemicals rather than timber.[13] Although Africa's role as a raw material supplier during World War II is well known, tropical forests have mostly been viewed as sources of products such as rubber and palm oil, and not for timber and wood byproducts.[14]

World War II and the Valuing of Tanganyikan Timbers

The moribund state of Tanganyikan forestry ended in the early stages of World War II, when East Africa became a supply base for the Middle East and northeast Africa. In June 1940, Italy entered the war, launching British military operations in Libya, Ethiopia, Sudan, and Somalia and initial war preparations in Egypt and the Middle East.[15] In December 1940, the Governor's Conference in Nairobi, which coordinated war planning in East Africa, informed the government in Dar es Salaam of the "very urgent military need" for the "greatest possible quantity of timber" for the African and the Middle East theaters of war.[16] An initial order for 300,000 railway ties was quickly curtailed owing to systemic problems of East African forestry, especially the expense of transporting heavy timbers over long distances with poor railway and shipping facilities, and ignorance of how to work unfamiliar East African timbers.[17] Yet India and Burma, despite sophisticated state forestry infrastructures, proved unable to meet timber orders. The East African colonies were directed to supply 2,500 tonnes of timber monthly for Middle East and African operations as well as a further 1,500 tonnes monthly for local military construction. Almost 20,000 cubic tonnes of railway ties were exported from Tanganyika for military purposes in 1941 and 1942, altogether over 300,000 timbers each year, before orders declined in 1943 following the Italian defeat in Ethiopia and Allied victory in North Africa.[18] Many of these ties went for railway construction in Palestine and Egypt, which through the early postwar years demanded Tanganyikan hardwoods. During the North African campaign in 1942, extensions of the

[13] Sunseri, "Exploiting the urwald."

[14] Raymond Dumett, "Africa's strategic minerals during the Second World War," *Journal of African History*, 26 (1985), 381–408; Franz Heske, *Die Wälder Afrikas* (Rome: Reale Accademia D'Italia, 1940); Egon Glesinger, *The Coming Age of Wood* (New York: Simon and Schuster, 1949).

[15] Killingray and Rathbone, "Introduction," 9.

[16] Secretary to the governor's conference to chief secretary, December 27, 1940, 29184, Tanzania National Archives (hereafter TNA), Dar es Salaam.

[17] Timber control meeting of the secretariat, March 15, 1941, 29184, TNA, Dar es Salaam.

[18] Tanganyika Territory, Forest Department. *Annual Reports* (Dar es Salaam: Government Printer, 1941–43).

Palestine Railway connecting Suez to Tel Aviv, Haifa, and Beirut escalated the demand for East African timber.[19] Toward encouraging contractors to supply railway ties, royalties were decreased by 75 percent for military use. As a result, already in 1942 Tanganyikan highland forest reserves were "seriously depleted and impaired" and in need of rehabilitation.[20]

The military demand for timber had significant consequences for Tanganyikan forestry. At the outset of the war, known valuable tree species, including softwoods from the northeast highlands and known workable hardwoods, especially mvule (*Milicia excelsa*), mninga (*Pterocarpus angolensis*), and mahogany (*Khaya spp.*) were used for barracks, bridges, vehicles, tools, and railway ties. Loggers extracted these trees from forest reserves near towns, roads, and railway lines. Although these timber species were still in demand at the end of the war, trees from miombo woodlands, including miombo (*Brachystegia spp.*) and Isoberlina, were deemed suitable for railway ties, and demand for them escalated accordingly. The valuing of these formerly marginal hardwoods challenged foresters to recast the Tanganyikan landscape. Little more than 1 percent of the territory was considered to be proper forest at the outset of the war. With the growing marketability of woodland trees, British foresters redefined the 44 percent of Tanganyika that was woodland as forests suitable for the application of scientific forestry. This became the agenda for the postwar years.

Wartime exploitation of the forests demanded the expansion of the territory's sawmills. At the outset of the war the custodian of enemy property took over many German-owned sawmills on timber concessions.[21] During the war, the timber controller directed the East African governments to lease these sawmills and subsidize new mills by providing machinery to British and South African contractors at favored prices. In 1942, the forest department subsidized eleven new sawmills in Tanganyika, so that by the end of 1943 a total of twenty-five mills operated.[22] Local production was often in the hands of Indian and Greek millers and even mission stations.[23] Most operated in the northeastern highlands – four alone on Mt. Kilimanjaro – where softwoods grew, especially camphor (*Ocotea usambarensis*), cedar (*Juniperus procera*), and podocarpus (*Podocarpus usambarensis*).[24] The Tanganyikan government also provided food subsidies to attract Africans to work in sawmills at a time of food shortages.[25] By war's end, 15,000 workers were

[19] Paul Cotterell, *The Railways of Palestine and Israel* (Oxon: Tourret Publishing, 1984), 67–68.
[20] Chief secretary (Dar es Salaam) October 10, 1942, 29184, TNA, Dar es Salaam.
[21] Forest Department, *Annual Report*, 1939, 2.
[22] Forest Department, *Annual Reports*, 1942, 6; 1943, 9.
[23] Conte, *Highland Sanctuary*, 78, 83–86; Forest Department, *Annual Report*, 1937, 12.
[24] Conte, *Highland Sanctuary*, 74; Forest Department, *Annual Report*, 1944, 10.
[25] Nicholas Westcott, "The impact of the Second World War on Tanganyika, 1939–49," in Killingray and Rathbone (eds.), *Africa and the Second World War*, 147.

FIGURE 13.1. Pitsawing a Mninga log.

employed in sawmills, about 4.4 percent of the total permanent wage labor force.[26] Nevertheless, the timber controller believed that timber output in Tanganyika lagged behind its potential because the shortage of consumer goods in the territory was a disincentive to do wage work.[27]

Because millers focused on closed forests with known workable trees near roads and railways, the Tanganyikan woodlands were left to African lumbermen, known as pitsawyers, to seek out marketable trees dispersed across the landscape. Hardwoods such as mninga, because of their density and weight, had to be sawn into boards before they could be carried to the railways or roadways for collection. Teams of several men (Swahili *vyama*, sing. *chama*) dug a pit below a felled tree supported by crossbeams to saw the log lengthwise into boards or ties (see Figure 13.1). Using a two-handled saw, one man stood in the pit and pulled downward, while his partner stood atop the log and pulled upward, directing the blade into niches calibrated for a uniform cut. Sawyers cut trees to railway-tie size (about 6 cu. ft.) before transporting the timber to roadways. Indian and Greek merchants invested in trucks and contracted sawyers to supply timber and ties, transporting loads of twenty to twenty-five ties to Dar es Salaam, Tanga, and other ports.

[26] Forest Department, *Annual Report*, 1945, 36.
[27] Forest Department, *Annual Report*, 1944, 10.

During the war, some fifty timber contractors paid pitsawing teams two shillings for each tie, each team producing about twenty ties per month.[28] Total earnings might have been about thirteen shillings per man, but may have been supplemented with use of waste wood to make charcoal, construction poles, or other wood products for sale to urban consumers. At a time when sisal plantation wages approached twenty shillings monthly in addition to food rations, it is surprising that pitsawing was considered to be a lucrative business that drew some sisal workers from plantations.[29] Yet isolated in forest locales, unsupervised and unregimented, pitsawing allowed cutters a great deal of autonomy. Although the rainy season often delayed production, during the dry season they supplied about 5,000 ties per month along the Central Railway and 10,000 per month along the Northern Railway to Tanga (owing to denser forests). By 1944, contractors struggled to supply 11,000 ties per month because of labor shortages and difficulty in locating exploitable trees ever farther from roadways and rail lines.

The wartime resurgence of pitsawing was a victory for lumbermen whose way of life was under assault by the forest department in the late 1930s. Compared to mechanized sawing, pitsawing created a good deal of wood waste and ragged cuts that devalued hand-sawn timber on the export market.[30] In 1936, the forest department had complained of pitsawyers:

[They] have little or no capital at stake, operate in remote and widely scattered localities in the bush; mostly produce inaccurately sawn and unseasoned timber and, it is feared, are often not too scrupulous in adhering to the terms of their licenses. They are content with the minimum of profit and become most active when timber prices show a temporary rise. They undercut the capitalized and reputable saw miller, who is finding disposal of his second grade lumber already difficult enough.[31]

Forest department efforts to curtail pitsawing ended with the expansion of gold mines at Geita and Lupa in the late 1930s, then with the World War II timber boom. In cutting railway ties ever farther across the landscape, pitsawyers mapped the territory's woodlands, and taught the forest department to value varieties of miombo that had no prior market value. By war's end, most railway ties, about 80,000 in 1944, came from miombo trees.[32] By then the forest department recognized the market potential of the woodlands, and committed itself to capturing vast tracts of miombo lands as forest reserves after the war.

---

[28] Signature of official illegible, Forest Department to Pike, January 27, 1942, ACC57, TNA, Dar es Salaam.
[29] Iliffe, *Modern History of Tanganyika*, 352–53.
[30] Forest Department, *Annual Report*, 1929, 8.
[31] Forest Department, *Annual Report*, 1936, 12–13.
[32] Forest Department, *Annual Report*, 1944, 17.

Forest Reserves and Forest Farming

The war accelerated the growth of the urban population, increasing consumer demand for food, construction timber, building poles, and wood
fuel. Dar es Salaam's population doubled between 1935 and 1948 to about
70,000 people.[33] Peasant women emerged during the war as forest farmers
producing food for urban consumers and workers, a response to the severing
of rice imports from Japanese-occupied Burma.[34] In addition, food shortages in the Middle East mandated increased supplies from East Africa.[35]
Yet Tanganyika suffered droughts in 1942 and 1943 that impaired crop
production. Moreover, with half of all adult men capable of work absent
from their households as labor migrants or military conscripts, household
food production was undermined. Fear of a disorderly urban population
that lacked adequate food, housing, and fuel at a time of wartime commodity shortages and labor unrest led political officials and foresters alike to
respond favorably to African requests for land in forest reserves near Dar es
Salaam. They adopted a Burmese system of forest farming known as *taungya*
(hill cultivation), which gave farmers permits to clear land and grow food in
forest reserves in exchange for tending fuel-and-pole trees interplanted with
food crops. Forestry officials used *taungya* to anchor a forest work force
to tend exotic fast-growing trees, especially eucalyptus (*Eucalyptus spp.*)
and ironwood (*Cassia siamea*), that would replace slow-growing indigenous hardwoods in forest reserves. Before mid–century, *taungya* plantation
forestry had been frustrated by African access to farm land outside of forest
reserves, where they could farm without taking on the burden of tending
trees that competed with food crops. Peasant refusal of *taungya* in the interwar period led the forest department to recruit landless Kikuyu from Kenya
to work the North Kilimanjaro Forest Reserve;[36] however, by World War
II, as land became scarce in periurban Dar es Salaam, Zaramo farmers of
the region requested *taungya* contracts.

In 1944, farmers and the *wakili* (chief) of Vikindu, ten miles south of
Dar es Salaam, initiated the expansion of *taungya*. For some time they
had sought land in Vikindu Forest, their historical home, once a site of
farms, ancestral shrines, rubber tapping, and copal digging, but since 1904,

---

[33] Thaddeus Sunseri, "'Something else to burn': Forest squatters, conservationists and the
state in modern Tanzania," *Journal of Modern African Studies*, 43 (2005), 609–40; J. E.
G. Sutton, "Dar es Salaam: A sketch of a hundred years," *Tanzania Notes and Records* 71
(1970), 19; Andrew Burton, *African Underclass: Urbanization, Crime and Colonial Order
in Dar es Salaam* (Oxford: James Currey, 2005).

[34] Iliffe, *Modern History of Tanganyika*, 351.

[35] Westcott, "Impact of the Second World War," 147.

[36] Twining to SSC, February 5, 1954, 52–57, CO 822/806, The National Archives, Kew.

a colonial forest reserve.[37] Recognizing a land shortage in the environs of Dar es Salaam, the district forester agreed to allocate ten contiguous plots in Vikindu Forest under Forest Department supervision. There they intended to clear the land, plant food crops, sell waste wood to the Forest Department for wood fuel, and tend saplings provided by the department. The contracts prohibited farmers from growing root crops that competed with saplings for soil moisture, and required the farmers to clear each year an additional acre of forest to extend the tree plantation. Although official correspondence spoke of the farmers as men, extant evidence shows that women were the actual farmers.[38] Most men, after all, were away as labor migrants.

Government foresters assessed the natural forest solely in terms of wood quantity, estimating production of only 500 cu. ft. per acre compared to 2,000 cu. ft. per acre if planted with *Cassia siamea*. Planted and harvested on ten-year rotations, Vikindu would supply Dar es Salaam with charcoal, wood fuel, construction beams, and telephone poles "in perpetuity." Every few years, as planted trees overshadowed food crops and competed for water and soils deteriorated, *taungya* farmers would be compelled to shift to new parcels in the forest and resume the planting process again. Although access to forest land was welcomed, women resented the added burden of tending trees.[39] Prohibitions on root crops, especially a labor-saving crop like cassava, imposed an additional hardship. Land around Dar es Salaam was often marginal, and elders considered cassava as fundamental to rural subsistence, even with its nutritional drawbacks.[40] Despite these hardships, good land near the coast was scarce, and therefore farmers of the region clamored for *taungya* permits.

Besides providing marketable food, the Vikindu scheme supplied charcoal to urban consumers. From the late 1930s to the aftermath of World War II, the housing and fuel shortage in Dar es Salaam was acute.[41] Therefore officials encouraged the trade in construction poles, timber, and fuel wood. While rural farmers obtained adequate fuel from scavenged public lands or as a "free issue" right from the forest department, urban consumers

[37] Senior forester Dar es Salaam to conservator of forests Morogoro, November 15, 1944, ACC57 Ilala, 9/1 Vol. I, TNA, Dar es Salaam. For evidence of the earlier occupation of the forest, see G58/45, TNA, Dar es Salaam.

[38] H. M. Glover, "Soil conservation in parts of Africa and the Middle East," *Empire Forestry Review*, 33 (1954), 39–44, Plates 2 and 3; G. J. Leggat, "A Uganda softwood scheme," *Empire Forestry Review*, 33 (1954), 345–51; Forest Department, *Annual Report*, 1929, 9.

[39] Forest Department, *Annual Report*, 1929, 9.

[40] "The physical background and its influence on settlement," p. 4, Kisarawe District Book, Tanganyika Regional and District Books (hereafter TRDB), MF.30, available through Center for Research Libraries (hereafter CRL), Chicago.

[41] Burton, *African Underclass*, 90, 110; James R. Brennan, *Taifa: Making Nation and Race in Urban Tanzania* (Athens: Ohio University Press, 2012), chapter 3.

depended on the market.[42] The modern Tanzanian reliance on charcoal as
the mainstay of urban fuel was inaugurated during the war, particularly
because kerosene, like other consumer goods, was rationed and prices were
high.[43] In 1943, more than 20,000 tonnes of wood fuel, about a quarter
of which was charcoal, together estimated to be the equivalent of about
1,000 acres of forest, were brought to Dar es Salaam markets. This was
the minimum needed to provide the city's domestic needs, and therefore
forest officials resisted government controls that would cause a "serious
shortfall."[44]

The fuel trade brought together entrepreneurs, woodcutters, farmers, and
urban customers in a complex exchange that was both legal and illegal. Fuel
merchants, often Indians or Greeks, bought licenses and hired workers to
cut trees that were cut into billets or burned into charcoal before being sold
in official markets, where the government imposed a duty and the forest
department collected royalties.[45] In other cases Africans paid two shillings
monthly for licenses to sell wood fuel in the official markets of Vikindu,
Soga, and Pugu surrounding Dar es Salaam. Wood cutters made charcoal in
earthen kilns assembled onsite in forests, which took several weeks and was
confined to the dry season. They stacked billets into a large mound covered
with green branches and earth to prevent the wood from being completely
consumed by fire. The hot-burning charcoal, best made from hardwoods so
as not to pulverize over long distances, was transported in sixty-pound bags
to roadways, and conveyed by trucks, bicycles, or handcarts to urban markets. Sometimes commercial contractors purchased a two-shilling license and
simply bought fuel wood or charcoal from villagers.[46] This illegal method
enabled contractors to avoid hiring labor and farmers to avoid license fees.
Many farmers misused their free-issue right to subsistence wood to sell on
the black market. Women dominated Dar es Salaam's informal charcoal and
wood markets, an important supplement to otherwise meager incomes. In
1932, an estimated 20 percent of African households in Dar es Salaam sold
charcoal and firewood, and by the 1940s, the figure was much higher.[47]
Despite official awareness of the black market, the need for timber and

[42] Roderick Neumann, "Forest rights, privileges and prohibitions: Contextualizing state
forestry policy in colonial Tanganyika," *Environment and History*, 3 (1997), 45–68; Sunseri,
Wielding the Ax, Chapter 4.

[43] Forester Dar es Salaam to district commissioner Dar es Salaam, May 25, 1944, ACC57 Ilala,
9/1 Vol. I, TNA, Dar es Salaam.

[44] Scantling (senior forester) to district commissioner Dar es Salaam, April 17, 1945,
ACC57/9/1, TNA, Dar es Salaam.

[45] Political Kisarawe to political DSM, July 20, 1944, ACC57/9/1, TNA, Dar es Salaam.

[46] Political Kisarawe to senior forester (DSM), March 10, 1945, ACC57/9/1, TNA, Dar es
Salaam.

[47] Burton, *African Underclass*, 67.

fuel to supply urban consumers led most to turn a blind eye. The escalating urban demand for food and fuel following the war made the Vikindu scheme a model for *taungya* farming in all forest reserves within a fifty-mile radius of Dar es Salaam.

Wild Rubber and Wartime Forest Exploitation

Even before Japan's conquest of Southeast Asia, events in the early stages of the war in North Africa and the Horn from 1940 to 1942 threatened the main rubber supply routes to Europe and the United States through Suez, creating shortages well before American entry into the war.[48] Then in the first months of 1942, Japan took control of 90 percent of world rubber supplies, and 97 percent of American sources: more than 75 percent of all raw rubber came from the plantations of British Malaya, Indochina, and the Dutch East Indies. This attack on the "most vulnerable spot" of the American economy created an immediate demand for alternative supplies of wild and plantation rubber, while expediting experimentation with temperate plant sources of rubber and promoting the production of synthetic rubber from petroleum.[49]

As in other parts of tropical Africa, the wartime demand for wild rubber was a major feature of the return to the forests in Tanganyika.[50] Wild rubber had a decades-old history in East Africa. Between 1880 and 1900, wild rubber was the mainstay of the Tanzanian economy of extraction and trade. Dozens of East African vines, shrubs, and trees on varied landscapes, including rainforests, coastal forests, and savanna woodlands, produced latex suitable for rubber production (see Figure 13.2). This market collapsed suddenly after 1910 as European settlers in East Africa opened up rubber plantations growing ceara rubber from South America, and as Southeast Asian rubber plantations came into production.[51] During the 1930s Depression, British officials encouraged Africans to tap wild rubber again to pay taxes and provide the state some export revenues. Tanzanians of the coastal forests

---

[48] William M. Tuttle, Jr., "The birth of an industry: The synthetic rubber 'mess' in World War II," *Technology and Culture*, 22 (1981), 37–38; John Tully, *The Devil's Milk: A Social History of Rubber* (New York: Monthly Review Press, 2011), 294–95, 320–21.

[49] Mark Finlay, *Growing American Rubber: Strategic Plants and the Politics of National Security* (New Brunswick, NJ: Rutgers University Press, 2009), chapter 5; Ernest P. Imle, "Hevea rubber: Past and future," *Economic Botany*, 32 (1978), 269–72.

[50] Elizabeth Schmidt, *Mobilizing the Masses: Gender, Ethnicity, and Class in the Nationalist Movement in Guinea, 1939–1958* (Portsmouth, NH: Heinemann, 2005), 92–102; R. J. Harrison Church, "The Firestone rubber plantations in Liberia," *Geography*, 54 (1969), 430–37.

[51] J. Forbes Munro, "British rubber companies in East Africa before the First World War," *Journal of African History*, 24 (1983), 369–79.

FIGURE 13.2. Tapping a wild rubber vine.

near Kilwa remember the 1930s and 1940s as a time of some prosperity as a result of the revived rubber trade, which enabled them to pay taxes and clothe their families.[52] Colonial foresters decried prewar rubber extraction as destructive of forests, but readily assented to tapping once World War II made rubber a high priority.

In early 1942, with the Japanese occupation of Malaya and the Dutch East Indies, the wild rubber question came to East Africa.[53] Although some government skeptics doubted that the quantity and quality of wild rubber in Tanganyika was worth the destruction it would cause to forests, the matter was deemed urgent. The Ministry of Supply set the price for wild rubber for each territory, which in Tanganyika was one shilling per pound.[54] Because rubber became a wartime priority, a representative from Firestone in South Africa urged payment of whatever sum was necessary to get Africans to tap rubber.[55] As in the late nineteenth century, varieties of *Landolphia* from

[52] Interview with the author, Kinjumbi, Tanzania, July 24, 2004.
[53] Paul Wendt, "The control of rubber in World War II," *Southern Economic Journal*, 13 (1947), 203–27.
[54] Chief secretary to secretary, governor's conference, March 19, 1942, 30512, TNA, Dar es Salaam.
[55] Extract from notes of a discussion on the possible exploitation of rubber with Mr. Mitchell of the Firestone Co. (South Africa), n.d. [1942], 30512, TNA, Dar es Salaam.

savanna woodlands were most promising, with the added advantage that they grew relatively close to coastal ports.[56]

To encourage villagers to take up rubber tapping, the forest department suspended the need for permits to enter forest reserves, royalties, and other fees, and removed rubber from the list of "protected produce."[57] The conservator of forests expressly targeted forest reserves for tapping, rather than public lands, believing them to be the best potential sources of rubber, because fifty years of limited access had enabled some rubber-bearing trees to recover from past exploitation.[58] Rubber tapping endangered reserves because tappers built fires in the forests, and overtapping damaged bark and killed trees. Close oversight of tappers was not feasible during the war, even though foresters feared the increase of illegal wood and game poaching. The rubber shortage trumped these considerations. In April 1942, the British government in London mandated that production of rubber took precedence over every other commodity because "of all strategic war materials it is in the shortest supply" and therefore must have priority for manpower, materials, and transport.[59] At the turn of the century, rubber extractors had often adulterated rubber with sand and gravel to inflate its weight and increase its price, and often cut down whole trees and dug up the roots of shrubs to extract as much latex as possible. Foresters hoped to prevent similar destructive practices during the war by teaching sustainable methods of latex collection.

Figures on quantities of wild rubber exported during the war are fragmentary. The Forest Department listed 12.6 tonnes exported in 1940 and less than four tonnes in 1941, before the wartime prioritization of rubber.[60] This climbed from 120 tonnes in 1944 to 170 tonnes in 1945, far below the 350 tonnes that Tanganyika's forests were estimated to produce.[61] In 1944, the £173,077 of wild rubber made up 44 percent of all forest exports.[62] This figure suggests that either far more rubber was produced than recorded or exporters received ten times the value paid to tappers. Often rubber collection was stymied by the unavailability of purchasing agents in rural regions. The Tanganyika government contracted the Indian firm Kassum Virji and Sons to purchase rubber west of Dar es Salaam, but its subagent

[56] Jamie Monson, "From commerce to colonization: A history of the rubber trade in the Kilombero Valley of Tanzania, 1890–1914," *African Economic History*, 21 (1993), 113–30.

[57] Collection of wild rubber in forest reserves, file minutes, February 23, 1942, 30511, TNA, Dar es Salaam.

[58] Acting chief secretary, April 22, 1942, 30511, TNA, Dar es Salaam.

[59] Extracts from S/S, telegram no. 210, April 16, [1942], 30512, TNA, Dar es Salaam.

[60] Forest Department, *Annual Reports*, 1941–1945.

[61] Secretary of state for the colonies (hereafter SSC) (London), April 13, 1942, 30512, TNA, Dar es Salaam.

[62] Forest Department, *Annual Report*, 1944, 10.

was frequently absent when rubber tappers arrived with their loads.[63] At Vikindu, the political officer issued permits for twenty-five people to collect rubber in the forest reserve, unsure whether wartime rules allowed this activity.[64] In Liwale district, once the most lucrative rubber-producing region of Tanzania, the Indian trader Jaffer Somji was the chief buyer.[65] Somji also controlled a derelict German rubber plantation in Liwale that was brought back under production.[66] As it turned out, derelict pre-WWI German plantations, mostly in the northeastern Tanganyika highlands, produced far more rubber than did wild trees, although they also suffered from labor shortages that limited their output. In 1944, they produced about 1,500 tonnes, a figure that doubled in 1945 to 2,700 tonnes.[67]

Forced Resettlement and the Creation of Labor Reserves

Wartime rubber tapping was frustrated by contradictory British policies during the war that relocated virtually the entire population of Liwale district to the coast as a labor pool liable for wartime production of raw materials. With about 30,000 people, Liwale district was sparsely populated for a region of 13,400 square miles. Its semiarid woodlands made it a prime region for rubber extraction in the late nineteenth century, but since early colonial rule the district had been considered difficult to administer because it was "secluded from civilizing influences."[68] It was also a region where sleeping sickness was endemic, which became the excuse during the war to round up the entire population and concentrate it into "closer settlements" where the people could be more easily taxed and administered and their labor could be controlled.[69] As the dispersed rural population was relocated, the Selous Game Reserve, founded in 1896 as a hunting reserve under German rule, was vastly expanded from the north in a contiguous block, dominating the region.[70] Expanding Selous also expanded the wildlife vector of sleeping

---

[63] Administrative officer (Kisarawe) to Messrs. Kassum Virji and Sons, December 18, 1943, ACC57 Ilala, 9/1, Vol. I, TNA, Dar es Salaam.

[64] Political (Kisarawe) to Forester (Dar es Salaam), December 15, 1942, ACC57 Ilala, 9/1, Vol. I, TNA, Dar es Salaam.

[65] E. E. Hulley, sleeping sickness surveyor (Tabora) to chief secretary, June 15, 1942, 30512, TNA, Dar es Salaam.

[66] Nachingwea District Book, Vol. I: Miscellaneous – Forestry, Sheet 3 [n.d.], TRDB, MF.38, CRL, Chicago.

[67] Forest Department, *Annual Reports*, 1944 and 1945.

[68] Notes to SSC, n.d. [1948], 31796, TNA, Dar es Salaam.

[69] Helge Kjekshus, *Ecology Control and Economic Development in East African History* (Berkeley: University of California, 1977), chapter 8; Kirk Hoppe, *Lords of the Fly: Sleeping Sickness Control in British East Africa, 1900–1960* (Westport, CT: Praeger, 2003), chapter 5; Sunseri, *Wielding the Ax*, Chapter 5.

[70] Roderick Neumann, "Africa's 'last wilderness': Reordering space for political and economic control in colonial Tanzania," *Africa*, 71 (2001), 641–65; Gordon Matzke "The development of the Selous Game Reserve," *Tanzania Notes and Records*, 79 & 80 (1976), 37–48.

sickness, and intentionally exacerbated wildlife depredations in people's fields, making the region uninhabitable.

On the eve of World War II, forestry officials concluded that the time was ripe to expand Tanganyika's forest reserves dramatically, targeting *miombo* woodlands that characterized almost half the territory. The Selous Reserve and sleeping sickness itself aided forest policy by putting the region "in cold storage," limiting its human and livestock populations, so when funds were available for demarcation and policing more land could be taken over as reserves with minimal opposition from peasants targeted for eviction.[71] Assenting to the Liwale relocations in late 1943, Governor Wilfred Edward Francis Jackson used the Latin phrase "*delenda est* Liwale" ("Liwale must be eliminated"), words associated with the complete destruction of Carthage by the Romans.[72]

Initially administrators moved Liwale people to inland sites at Madaba and Ngarambe, but when these settlements proved unviable in 1944, trucks arrived to transport people forcibly to Njinjo near the coastal headquarters at Kilwa.[73] South of Kilwa were the Kiswere sisal estates, which needed labor for production of a vital war product after the Japanese occupation of the Philippines cut off access to Manila hemp (*abacá*) needed for cordage. The United States demanded that sisal be prioritized over all other raw materials from East Africa, and even provided shipping to take sisal directly to America.[74] Wartime rules allowed labor conscription for sisal work, overwhelmingly in the plantation north. The 17,000 workers on the Kiswere estates, one-fifth of all sisal workers, received lower wages than in the north, with no food rations and especially poor conditions.[75] Unable to compete with the better-capitalized north, Kiswere had favored access to Njinjo labor created by the Liwale evictions.

Njinjo workers also went to the coastal mangroves south of Kilwa and in the Rufiji River delta. Mangroves were ideal for railway ties and dye bark. For centuries, Arab dhows had sailed to East Africa to take mangrove rafters back to the Arabian peninsula, an activity that continued during the war on a small scale.[76] Mangroves were suitable as military timber owing to density, durability, and resistance to insects, and their coastal location

[71] R. S. Troup, *Report on Forestry in Tanganyika Territory* (Dar es Salaam: Government Printer, 1936); Forest Department, *Annual Report*, 1944, 1–2.

[72] "Liwale Closer Settlement Scheme," September 1948, MF.38, Nachingwea District Books, TRDB, MF.38, CRL, Chicago.

[73] Rooke Johnston, acting provincial commissioner Southern province to chief secretary, Dar es Salaam, September 13, 1944, 31796, TNA, Dar es Salaam.

[74] Nicholas Westcott, "The East African sisal industry, 1929–1949: The marketing of a colonial commodity during depression and war," *Journal of African History*, 25 (1984), 452.

[75] Southern Province Report, 1944–45, CO1018/72, The National Archives, Kew.

[76] Erik Gilbert, *Dhows and the Colonial Economy of Zanzibar, 1860–1970* (Athens: Ohio University Press); D. K. S. Grant, "Mangrove woods of Tanganyika Territory, their silviculture and dependent industries," *Tanganyika Notes and Records*, 5 (1939), 5–16.

saved time and the expense of transport, which was a drawback of inland hardwoods. In 1943, more than 58,000 railway ties from southern coastal mangroves were produced for the war, altogether 1.3 million cubic feet of the mshinzi (*Bruguiera gymnorhiza*) species. The use of mangroves for ties continued after the war, as the British sought to remain a Middle East power and expand their network of African railways from southern Africa to East African ports.[77]

The most important twentieth-century commercial use of mangroves was for dye bark for leather. Historically, dye bark had been dominated by a Southeast Asia commodity known as cutch, from the *Acacia catechu* tree.[78] The loss of this source during the war gave new momentum to mangrove exploitation. The bark of four East African mangrove species have an unusually high tannin content, well suited for the leather dye needed to supply soldiers and civilian workers with shoes, boots, and belts.[79] The United States was the chief buyer, thus the industry brought in needed dollars at a time of price controls. A gender division of labor existed, whereby men cut mangroves for ties and rafters while women and children stripped bark. This was done by standing on the exposed roots of mangrove trees and cutting bark as high as the worker could reach, before it was packed in sacks or baskets and carried to collection sites. This method often killed the tree, but was faster and cheaper than cutting down the tree before stripping the bark. In 1942 and 1943, the Ghaui concession produced 2,633 and 2,511 tonnes of bark, respectively. In the last two years of the war, Tanganyika exported about 10,000 tonnes of bark.[80] The Njinjo closer settlement eased longstanding labor bottlenecks that had frustrated the development of the mangrove stands before the war.

Conclusion

World War II ended with intense colonial and international focus on African and other tropical forests, and an equally intense scrutiny of Africans in the forests.[81] Before the war, Europe's own forests supplied most of its consumer and industrial needs, but the war ended with a devastated Europe in need

[77] Ronald Hyam (ed.), *The Labour Government and the End of Empire 1945–1951* (London: HMSO, 1992), 213; David R. Devereux, "Britain, the Commonwealth and the defence of the Middle East 1948–56," *Journal of Contemporary History*, 24 (1989), 327–45.
[78] Bryant, *Political Ecology of Forestry*, 92–95.
[79] Grant, "Mangrove Woods," 11–13; Thaddeus Sunseri, "Working in the mangroves and beyond: Scientific forestry and the labour question in early colonial Tanzania," *Environment and History*, 11 (2005), 365–94.
[80] Forest Department, *Annual Report*, 1945, 25.
[81] For Southeast Asia, see Peter Vandergeest and Nancy Lee Peluso, "Empires of forestry: Professional forestry and state power in Southeast Asia," Part 2, *Environment and History*, 12 (2006), 359–93.

of reconstruction.[82] Some 100 million Europeans lacked adequate housing, while European forests had been overexploited during the war. In light of the European wood shortage, which some observers feared would produce "a major social, economic and political crisis," European foresters sought an international response.[83] The newly founded United Nations Food and Agricultural Organization (FAO) called on the colonial powers to apply scientific forestry to Africa to draw its timber products into the global economy. This emergent valuing of African forests claimed that African farmers and pastoralists misused their forests owing to population pressure, overgrazing, and shifting agriculture.[84] With the urging of the FAO, the colonial powers aimed to replace African hardwoods with exotic softwoods to supply Europe's timber and pulp market and chemical industries.[85] This meant stepping up forest reservation and curtailing perceived African destruction of forests and woodlands.[86] The postwar "second colonial occupation" that was characterized by intense efforts to develop the colonies to delay independence thus had its counterpart in forestry.

This revival of state forestry had important consequences for Tanganyika. With funding from the Colonial Development and Welfare Corporation, the forest department emerged as a major player in late-colonial development. The wartime valuing of previously marginal woodlands led to the first major push to expand the forest reserves since German colonial times. Between war's end and independence in 1961, British officials extended the extent of Tanganyikan forest reserves by fourteen times, from just over 1 percent of the landscape to just over 15 percent. This meant demarcating vast tracts of woodland and evicting African farmers and pastoralists. In many respects, the Liwale population removals of the war foreshadowed ambitious rural restructuring that characterized Tanzania well into the 1970s.

With economic development high on the agenda in postwar Tanganyika, the colonial state remained committed to increasing supplies of food, charcoal, construction timber, and railway ties. Price controls and import restrictions remained in place until the late 1940s, meaning that for Africans the war did not end in 1945. Under these circumstances, most forest reserves near Dar es Salaam were brought under *taungya* forest farming schemes, easing some land shortages that accompanied postwar urban expansion.

---

[82] Franz Heske, "Der tropenwald als Rohstoffsquelle Europas," *Zeitschrift für Weltforstwirtschaft*, 12 (1948), 61–89.

[83] Marcel Leloup, "The world's dilemma: More timber, more conservation," and "International timber crisis," both in *Unasylva*, 1 (1947), www.fao.org/docrep/x5340e/x5340e00.htm.

[84] André Marie A. Aubréville, "The disappearance of the tropical forests of Africa," *Unasylva*, 1 (1947), www.fao.org/docrep/x5340e/x5340e00.htm; Heske, "Tropenwald," 67.

[85] Glesinger, *Coming Age of Wood*.

[86] "Plans for the development of timber production in the tropical French territories," *Unasylva*, 1 (1947), www.fao.org/docrep/x5340e/x5340e00.htm.

Taungya farmers came to see this as a time when they obtained legal rights to reside in forest reserves indefinitely.

In contrast, the postwar decade was not friendly to African pitsawyers. With the independence of British colonies in Asia, notably Burma in 1948, and anticolonial insurgencies in Malaya and the Dutch East Indies, hardwood shortages continued, especially of teak, and many British timber corporations relocated to more quiescent regions, including Tanganyika. British colonial foresters favored commercial saw millers as harvesters of the most valuable teak-like timber, relegating African pitsawyers once again to cutting marginal miombo hardwoods. After the war, African rubber tapping was superseded by the revival of Asian plantations and the emergence of synthetic rubber. By 1947, only one ton of wild rubber was exported from Tanganyika, and after 1949 the rubber export market vanished completely.

World War II put Tanganyikan and other African forests irreversibly on the international map. Teak-like hardwoods found a steady market for railway ties and construction timber, much going to the Middle East, while East Asian economic development made Tanzania into an Indian Ocean timber reserve. European corporations maintained an interest in Tanzanian hardwood charcoal for its chemical properties, while Persian Gulf nations sought charcoal for cooking fuel, even as the domestic African urban demand for forest resources exploded. Late colonial and early postcolonial forestry encouraged these activities, launching tensions over access to forests and their resources that continue today.

FOUR

RACE, GENDER, AND SOCIAL CHANGE
IN A TIME OF WAR

14

Wrestling with Race on the Eve of Human Rights

The British Management of the Color Line in Post-Fascist Eritrea

Giulia Barrera

Introduction

In 1944, the British government published a propaganda booklet on the British Military Administration (BMA) of Eritrea and Somalia titled "The First to Be Freed."[1] British troops had entered Eritrea's capital, Asmara, as early as April 1, 1941. A few weeks later, the governor-general of the Africa Orientale Italiana (AOI) surrendered to British forces, formally ending Mussolini's rule over the Horn of Africa. What did it mean for a colony to be freed from Axis rule? In European countries such as Italy or France, liberation from Fascism and Nazism meant, among other things, the end of foreign occupation, the return to democracy, and an immediate stop to racial persecutions. Did the liberation from Fascist rule mean anything similar in the Horn of Africa?

Soon after the Italian defeat, Emperor Haile Selassie returned to his throne in Ethiopia. But Eritrea had been an Italian colony since 1890, long before Fascism, and no Western power had ever questioned the legitimacy of Italian rule on Eritrea. Thus, when the British army took control of Eritrea, it administrated the territory as an occupied enemy territory, which would presumably be returned to Italy at the end of the war. At this early stage of the war, no one forecast that ultimately Italy would be forced to renounce all of its colonial possessions. In other words, Eritrea, "the first to be freed," was not actually freed from alien rule. Was it at least freed from the most heinous forms of racial discrimination introduced by Fascist legislation?

British military authorities were firmly committed to respecting international law and, under the 1907 Hague Convention (IV) Respecting the Laws and Customs of War on Land, military occupants were supposed to

---

[1] K. C. Gandar Dower, *The First to Be Freed: The Record of British Military Administration in Eritrea and Somalia, 1941–1943* (London: H. M. Stationery Office, 1944).

respect the laws of the occupied country.[2] Did that mean that the BMA in
Eritrea was bound to respect Fascist race laws that discriminated against
both Africans and Jews?[3] The issue was discussed at length within the BMA
and with the general headquarters of the Occupied Enemy Territory Administration (OETA), Middle East (ME), in Cairo, but it was never fully solved.[4]
(There was also an OETA East Africa, based in Nairobi, which administered
Eritrea for a short period between October 1941 and February 1942, when
it was transferred from Middle East to East Africa Command.)

Analyzing the BMA officers' debate about Fascist race laws, one can see
that they held ambivalent attitudes regarding race, similar to those recorded
by scholars who examined British interaction with black U.S. soldiers in the
United Kingdom during World War II. From 1942 onward, the United States
posted 130,000 African American soldiers to Britain: "many British soldiers
and civilians felt outraged on behalf of black GIs" and stigmatized white
American soldiers' aggressive racism and their attempts to impose Jim Crow
standards on British soil.[5] As Sonya O. Rose points out, the British defended
their self-image of "a democratic, benign and paternalistic imperial nation"
and "Nazi racial policy made British racial tolerance a particularly salient
aspect of national identity during the war."[6] At the same time, long-held
beliefs on racial difference and black inferiority were widely shared. For
example, most Britons abhorred the idea of interracial sex between white
British women and black GIs.[7]

In Eritrea, relationships between Italian men and Eritrean women and
their mixed-race children were one of the main sources of legal disputes
among British officers. Under Italian rule, the incidence of interracial

---

[2] Convention (IV) Respecting the Laws and Customs of War on Land and Its Annex: Regulations Concerning the Laws and Customs of War on Land (The Hague, October 18, 1907),
www.icrc.org.

[3] Eritrea was under British administration until 1952 when, upon UN decision, it was federated
to Ethiopia. The only general history of this period remains G. K. N. Trevaskis, *Eritrea. A
Colony in Transition: 1941–52* (London: Oxford University Press, 1960). On Eritrean political history, see Ruth Iyob, *The Eritrean Struggle for Independence: Domination, Resistance,
Nationalism, 1941–1993* (Cambridge: Cambridge University Press, 1995).

[4] Richard Pankhurst describes the slow demise of fascist race laws in Eritrea in his excellent
work "The legal question of racism in Eritrea during the British military administration: A
study of colonial attitudes and responses, 1941–1945," *Northeast African Studies*, new series,
2 (1995), 25–70. His study is based on the documents preserved by the National Archives
(hereafter TNA) at Kew (he did not have the opportunity to consult the documents preserved
in Asmara).

[5] Gavin Schaffer, "Fighting racism: Black soldiers and workers in Britain during the Second
World War," *Immigrants and Minorities*, 28 (2010), 246–65; Graham Smith, *When Jim
Crow Met John Bull* (London: I. B. Tauris, 1987).

[6] Sonya O. Rose, "Race, empire and British wartime national identity, 1939–45," *Historical
Research*, 74 (2001), 220, 222.

[7] Besides the studies already cited, see: S. O. Rose, "Sex, citizenship, and the nation in World
War II Britain," *American Historical Review*, 103 (1998), 1147–76.

concubinage and mixed-race children had always been significant.[8] Italy's invasion of Ethiopia (1935–1936) and the subsequent creation of the AOI had brought to the Horn thousands of Italian male newcomers, who were the likely candidates for interracial unions. Mussolini launched a virulent campaign against racial mixing. The Italian government declared interracial concubinage a crime and made it legally impossible for Italian fathers to recognize the children they had by African women.[9] The measures that Mussolini took to prevent racial mixing (metropolitan criminal laws, propaganda, mail and press censorship, etc.) were peculiar to a fascist regime; but in colonial Africa during the 1930s discouraging interracial concubinage was quite standard practice. Interracial concubinage and mixed-race children, in fact, were seen as dangerous to the colonial edifice by liberal democracies as well.[10]

The officers who served in the BMA of Eritrea generally came from the colonial service, so racial subordination of the Africans was deeply engrained in their mindset.[11] Their decision to uphold the Fascist ban on interracial concubinage presumably replicated attitudes they had already developed during their previous colonial experience; however, they pursued this policy in the context of a war that the Allies increasingly characterized as a war against Nazi racism. World War II marked a watershed in the history of European public discourse about race.[12] In the interwar years, some scholars and political activists had begun to challenge the notion that cultural differences among "races" were rooted in biology.[13] But the disclosure of the

---

[8] Giulia Barrera, "Colonial affairs: Italian men, Eritrean women, and the construction of racial hierarchies in colonial Eritrea," PhD thesis, Northwestern University (2002); Barrera, "Patrilinearity, race, and identity: The upbringing of Italo-Eritreans during Italian colonialism (1885–1934)," in Ruth Ben-Ghiat and Mia Fuller (eds.), *Italian Colonialism* (New York: Palgrave Macmillan, 2005), 97–108; Ruth Iyob "Madamismo and beyond: The construction of Eritrean women," *Italian Colonialism*, 233–44.

[9] On fascist race laws for the colonies, see Richard Pankhurst, "Fascist racial policies in Ethiopia, 1922–1941," *Ethiopia Observer*, 12 (1969), 270–85; Alberto Sbacchi, *Ethiopia under Mussolini Fascism and the Colonial Experience* (London: Zed Press, 1985); Giulia Barrera, "Mussolini's colonial race laws and state-settlers relations in AOI (1935–41)," *Journal of Modern Italian Studies*, 8 (2003), 425–43; Barbara Sòrgoni, "Racial policies," in P. Poddar, R. S. Patke, and L. Jensen (eds.), *A Historical Companion to Postcolonial Literatures in Continental Europe and its Empires* (Edinburgh: Edinburgh University Press, 2008), 306–08. There is also a substantial scholarship on this subject in Italian.

[10] Ann L. Stoler, "Carnal knowledge and imperial power: Gender, race, and morality in colonial Asia," in Micaela di Leonardo (ed.), *Gender at the Crossroads of Knowledge: Feminist Anthropology in the Postmodern Era* (Berkeley: University of California Press, 1991), 51–101.

[11] Joseph P. Harris, "Selection and training of civil affairs officers," *Public Opinion Quarterly* 7 (1943), 701; Pankhurst, "The legal question."

[12] George M. Fredrickson, *Racism: A Short History* (Princeton, NJ: Princeton University Press, 2002), 127–29.

[13] Robert Miles, *Racism* (London/New York: Routledge, 1989), 42–43.

horrors of the Shoah (Holocaust) at the end of the war marked the turning point: "After the murderous genocide of European Jewry committed in the name of racial purity, it became commonplace among Western democracies to reject the language of race."[14] However, as Neil MacMaster has pointed out, in the eyes of most Europeans, Nazi racism became associated with anti-Jewish persecutions (even if it also targeted blacks, Slavs, Romani people, etc.). As a consequence, in Western public opinion Nazi racism aroused revulsion mostly against "a particular brand of racism (anti-Semitism)," while leaving relatively unaffected antiblack and colonial racism.[15]

British officers started to make decisions about racial policies in Eritrea when this turn in European attitudes to race was still in the making: When the British army took over Eritrea, the extermination of the Jews had not even started. The Eritrean case thus provides us with an opportunity to see how the war against Nazism and Fascism increasingly influenced the way in which British officers talked about race and encouraged them to take a stance against Fascist racism. At the same time, the Eritrean case shows some of the limits and contradictions of the Allies' reaction against Nazi and Fascist racism, and lends support to MacMaster's point: British officers' revulsion was against anti-Semitism, not against the racial subordination of the colonized people.

British Management of the Color Bar in a Post-Fascist Colony

In Eritrea, the 1940s was a period of growing racial tensions between Eritreans and Italians that had economic and political roots. When the British defeated the Italians, the first consequence for Eritreans was mass unemployment. Italy had exploited Eritrea primarily as a source for colonial soldiers.[16] When the Italian Empire collapsed, tens of thousands of Eritrean soldiers found themselves without any source of income.[17] Moreover, under the AOI many Eritreans had been employed in public works. Mussolini intended to make the AOI a showcase of the Fascist regime and invested lavishly in public works. By contrast, the BMA was on a tight budget and – with Rommel advancing in North Africa – the "primary administrative objective" was "to put Eritrea in the position of making the greatest possible contribution to the British war effort," as the British military administrator of Eritrea

---

[14] Rita Chin and Heide Fehrenbach, "What's race got to do with it? Postwar German history in context," in R. Chin, H. Fehrenbach, Geoff Eley, and Atina Grossmann, *After the Nazi Racial State: Difference and Democracy in Germany and Europe: An Investigation of the Concept of "Race" in Post-Nazi Germany* (Ann Arbor: University of Michigan Press, 2009), 13.

[15] Neil MacMaster, Racism in Europe, 1870–2000 (Hampshire, NY: Palgrave, 2001), 173.

[16] Tekeste Negash, *Italian Colonialism in Eritrea, 1882–1941: Policies, Praxis and Impact* (Uppsala: Uppsala University, 1987), 51.

[17] Duncan C. Cumming, "British stewardship of the Italian colonies: An account rendered," *International Affairs*, 29 (1953), 11; Trevaskis, *Eritrea*, 52–53.

explained.[18] So the British drastically reduced personnel in the civil service and stopped the construction of new infrastructures.[19] Unemployment fostered anti-British feelings among Eritreans, since previous colonial inequalities in the labor market persisted despite the end of Italian rule. Worsening living conditions also fueled Eritrean resentment against the BMA.

Eritrean ill feelings against British authorities had political roots as well. During the war, British propaganda had encouraged Eritreans to rise up against their colonial masters and had promised them freedom.[20] But after the military victory in 1941, the priority of the BMA was to restore law and order, which was by definition colonial. Right after the Italian defeat, anti-Italian protests took place as well as some looting.[21] "Stern repressive measures were therefore taken immediately against all anti-Italian outbreaks and seem to have had the desired effect," reported the military administrator.[22] While repression might have seemed to be effective, Eritrean expectations for a change remained.[23] A few months later, a BMA official laconically recorded: "Considerable unrest among Eritreans and other coloured residents of Massawa reported Dec. '41. These people were hoping that under British rule colour laws would elapse."[24]

Among other things, the Eritreans bitterly resented that the BMA had kept most of the former Italian administration in place.[25] In April 1941, the staff of OETA of Eritrea consisted of only a handful of British officers and Sudanese policemen. As a consequence, the military administrator wrote, "for some months we had no choice but to keep the Italian administrative machine going with very little supervision."[26] Even afterwards, the BMA,

---

[18] The Military Administrator, *Report on Eritrea covering the period July to December 1941*, p. 1, British Military Administration of Eritrea (hereafter BMA), box (hereafter b.) 14, file (hereafter f.) 10102, sub f. "I/H/2 Reports (CA's). Report no. 2," nos. 1–47, in Research and Documentation Center (hereafter RDC), Asmara; see also Cumming, "British stewardship," 14–15; Tekeste Negash, *Eritrea and Ethiopia: The Federal Experience* (Uppsala: Nordiska Afrikainstitutet, 1997), 24.

[19] Military Administrator, *Report on Eritrea*, 5.

[20] Trevaskis, *Eritrea*, 59; see also Alazar Tesfa Michael, *Eritrea To-day: Fascist Oppression under Nose of British Military* (Woodford, Essex: New Times Books Department, 1945), 28; S. Longrigg, *Half-yearly Report by the Military Administrator on the Occupied Enemy Territory of Eritrea, for the Period 1st January to 30th June, 1942* (Asmara: OETA Government Press, 1942?), located in War Office (hereafter WO) 230/106, TNA, Kew.

[21] *Lettera aperta dall'AOI* (Asmara: s.n., 1942).

[22] Military Administrator, *Report on Eritrea*, 41.

[23] Alazar, *Eritrea To-day*.

[24] No author, no. 267, /GEN, b. 62, f. 10694, no. 1, BMA, RDC, Asmara.

[25] In February 1944, there was a strike by the Eritrean policemen in Asmara. They demanded "the removal of Italian police from the force, the annulment of Italian laws and the dismissal of Italian judges." Trevaskis, *Eritrea*, 49–50, 52, 65; Alazar, *Eritrea To-day*; Military Administrator, *Report on Eritrea*, 40.

[26] Military Administrator, *Report on Eritrea*, 40–41. See also F. J. Rennell of Rodd, *British Military Administration of Occupied Territories in Africa during the Years 1941–1947* (London: HMSO, 1948), 102; Trevaskis, *Eritrea*, 21.

pushed by the need to economize personnel, continued to use Italian officials. Only the very highest political authorities, together with Fascist Party leaders and Italian military men, were detained as prisoners of war.[27] Yet some persons in key positions, such as the secretary general of the government, the district commissioner for the region of Asmara,[28] and the public prosecutor, remained in place.[29]

The incorporation of Eritrea into the British empire was never an option. Moreover, "eradicating Fascism from the Italian State apparatus" was hardly a priority on Churchill's agenda in Eritrea and Italy. After the Allies landed in Sicily in July 1943 and started their slow march northbound, Churchill was willing "to offer immunity in return for obedience." Although Churchill wanted Italy to become a democratic country, he considered that the monarchy and Marshal Pietro Badoglio, who became Italy's prime minister after Mussolini was overthrown on July 25, 1943, were the best guarantors of the traditional social order and instrumental for the collaboration of the state apparatus in running occupied Italy, not the anti-Fascists.[30]

In Eritrea, the BMA seemed to consider the anti-Fascists mostly as troublemakers. For the BMA, the top priority was to avoid disorder in order to economize troops.[31] Thus, the administration did not involve the anti-Fascists in the government, but even placed obstacles to their activities, "in accordance to accepted policy of avoiding occasions for bitter political controversy," as Military Administrator Stephen H. Longrigg explained in 1942.[32] The point is that the BMA deemed "the Italian population [to] have remained, for the most part, Fascist,"[33] and it was likely to be right.[34] In Italy, the traumatic experience of war and Nazi occupation played a key role in making many Italians change their minds about Fascism, but Italians in Eritrea did not experience anything comparable.

[27] Military Administrator, *Report on Eritrea*, 5–6, 40–41; F. Guazzini, "De-Fascistizzare l'Eritrea e il vissuto dei vinti, 1941–1945," in M. B. Carcangiu e Tekeste Negash (eds.), *L'Africa orientale italiana nel dibattito storico contemporaneo* (Roma: Carocci, 2008), 51–86.

[28] J. T. Crawford (senior civil affairs officer [hereafter SCAO]), Asmara and Hamasien), weekly notes to chief secretary, no. S/10/A, January 6, 1945, b. 14, f. 10105, p.53, BMA, RDC, Asmara.

[29] Longrigg, *Half-yearly Report*, 8.

[30] Paul Ginsborg, *A History of Contemporary Italy: Society and Politics, 1943–1988* (London: Penguin Books, 1990), 40; David W. Ellwood. *L'alleato nemico: la politica dell'occupazione anglo-americana in Italia, 1943–1946* (Milano: Feltrinelli, 1977).

[31] Francis James Rennell of Rodd, "Allied military government in occupied territory," *International Affairs*, 20 (1944), 307.

[32] Longrigg, *Half-yearly report*, 7, 48.

[33] Ibid., 7.

[34] A. Del Boca, *Gli italiani in Africa Orientale* (Roma: Laterza, 1976), vol. 3, 547–550; Guazzini, "De-fascistizzare l'Eritrea."

There was a thin line between encouraging Italian civil servants to cooperate with the new government and having unduly friendly attitudes with the enemy, a line that OETA officials in Cairo thought that BMA repeatedly crossed. Apparently, one reason why the first military administrator of Eritrea, Brian Kennedy-Cooke, was removed from office in May 1942 was that he "had encouraged British Officers to be friendly with Italians."[35] Under his tenure, "boxing and football matches were organized between British and Italian teams" and "British officers and Italians met in the congenial surrounding of an officially sponsored tennis club."[36] In February 1943, his successor, Longrigg, was also reprimanded for excessive fraternization with the Italians by the chief political officer in Cairo, Herbert Ralph Hone: "You must all constantly remind yourself that the war with Italy is still raging."[37] British officers in Europe would have hardly needed such a reminder, but in Africa things were different: the Italians and the British were enemies, but at the same time they were fellow Europeans in a colonial situation. Such shows of friendly relations between British officers and some members of the Italian elite hardly helped to mitigate Eritreans' frustration and disillusionment with British failed promises.

In September 1941, the Fascist-appointed district commissioner for the region of Asmara, Angelo Lauro, complained that "people of color" now frequented Asmara's cinemas, previously reserved for Italian clients.[38] His complaint found sympathetic ears among British officers. The issue, however, was difficult to tackle, given that the "natives" in question were often "Indians, Sudanese, South Africans of colour or other Allied natives."[39] While the BMA found no objection in excluding the Eritreans from cinemas or from restaurants, coffee shops, bars, and other public places, could members of the imperial armed forces also be placed in a subordinate position vis-à-vis a defeated enemy? Moreover, troops stationed in Eritrea came from different parts of the British empire and the color bar was not the

[35] Sir Gerald Kennedy Trevaskis, *Diary*, April 25–May 5, 1942, The Kennedy Trevaskis Papers, GB 162 MSS. Brit. Emp. s. 546, Bodleian Library of Commonwealth and African Studies at Rhodes House, Oxford.

[36] Trevaskis, *Eritrea*, 23.

[37] Hone to the military administrator, Eritrea, February 22, 1943, WO 230/145, TNA, Kew. The commander-in-chief delegated the administration of occupied territory to a chief political officer (hereafter CPO) (after March 1943 known as the chief civil affairs officer [hereafter CCAO]). Trevaskis, *Eritrea*, 25,

[38] Lauro to the Ispettore di sanità civile, Asmara, September 29, 1941; Lauro's complaint was forwarded to the R. H. Bland (PMO), OETA, Asmara, who forwarded it to the senior political officer (hereafter SPO) of Asmara and Hamasien, who forwarded it to the assistant secretary to the administrator. b. 62, f. 10691, pp. 1–7, "10/E/1 Cinemas. Attendance of natives in cinemas," BMA, RDC, Asmara.

[39] Capt. M. Setton (assistant legal adviser) to A. A. Baerlein (legal adviser Asmara), October 13, 1941, b. 62, f. 10691, pp. 9–10, 10/E/1 [Cinemas. Attendance of natives in cinemas], BMA, RDC, Asmara.

same everywhere. In Khartoum, the Sudanese were "admitted to the bars, hotels and places of amusement as Europeans."[40] Could they be excluded from such places in Asmara? The issue was discussed for more than a year both in Eritrea and in Cairo headquarters. Officers and rank and file of the Sudanese Defense Force vigorously complained about the discriminatory practices they suffered at the hands of the Italians.[41] Initially, the general officer commanding favored maintaining the color bar against "troops in whose countries of origin similar rules existed."[42] But in September 1942, a new military commander took a strong stance in favor of military pre-rogatives: "On my opinion all HM's Forces of whatever race, colour or rank must receive similar treatment, rank by rank."[43] Ultimately, this line prevailed: military status won over race. In October 1942, the BMA issued a public notice granting the same privileges enjoyed by European military men, according to rank, to all uniformed members of the Imperial Armed Forces and the Eritrean police.[44] Unfortunately for the civilians, the color bar remained fully in place, and so did racial zoning in Asmara.[45] Among the factors that made the BMA hesitate before taking such a line of action was the fear of possible incidents with white American servicemen. Lieutenant R. B. Witt, a BMA Intelligence officer, observed that "Some Americans at home feel strongly about the colour bar, and it is possible that irresponsible elements among American civilians may create incidents in cafés, etc. should coloured troops be allowed access."[46] Similar concerns were raised on other occasions as well.[47]

For its part, the BMA was very worried about having African-American troops on Eritrean soil. In September 1942, when the transfer of contingents

[40] Memo signed "G. W.," September 16, 1942?, b. 62, f. 10694, p. 8, 10/E/1 [Cinemas. Attendance of natives in cinemas], BMA, RDC, Asmara.

[41] Miralai (officer commanding no. 3 Infantry [hereafter Inf.] (Frontier) Battalion [hereafter Bn.]) to HQ, Inf. (Frontier) Bns., September 6, 1942 and attachment, "Incidents of Italian behaviour in Eritrea to native officers and other ranks of 3 Inf. Frontier Bn, Sudan Defense Force," b. 62, f. 10694, pp. 5, 6, 7, BMA, RDC, Asmara.

[42] Brig. B. Kennedy-Cooke (MA) to SPO, Asmara, October 14, 1941, b. 62, f. 10691, no. 8. BMA, RDC, Asmara. In 1941, the general officer commanding Eritrea was Lt. Gen. Reginald Arthur Savory; his opinion was cited in Kennedy-Cooke's letter.

[43] Brig. Cyrus Greenslade (commanding officer, HQ 19 Area) to MA Eritrea, September 28, 1942, WO 230/157, TNA, Kew.

[44] Col. F. R. W. Jameson (chief secretary), *Avviso*, Asmara, October 14, 1942, b. 62, f. 10964, p. 34, BMA, RDC, Asmara; also published in *Eritrean Daily News* on October 18, 1942.

[45] Pankhurst, "The legal question"; Lt.-Col. A. Stanley Parker (SCAO Asmara & Hamasien) to president, Rent Commission, April 1, 1944, b. 62, f. 11795, p. 78, BMA, RDC, Asmara.

[46] Lt. R. B. Witt (political officer intelligence) to MA Eritrea, September 28, 1942, WO 230/157, TNA, Kew.

[47] Parker (SCAO Asmara and Hamasien) to chief secretary, BMA, Eritrea, Asmara, August 15, 1955 (sic; should probably be 1944) and police commissioner to chief secretary, August 20, 1944, b. 62, f. 10694, pp. 69 and 75, BMA, RDC.

of African American soldiers was announced, Longrigg did his best to prevent their arrival, warning about possible dangers. The presence of a "contingent of black (that is, negro) troops," he explained, was in itself problematic "in view of their Western education, standard of living and pretensions; they would form a striking contrast to the local coloured peoples of Eritrea." Longrigg was particularly worried because of "the presence in Asmara of thousands of white women, in the position of a conquered people."[48] If "there were assaults by American black troops on Italian women, or any violence done to the Italian population by such troops," Longrigg further warned, the Italians might stop cooperating with the BMA.[49] Eritrea had never experienced outbreaks of "black peril" hysteria; anxieties about black men sexually assaulting white women were a British import product. To make things worse, replied the chief political officer from Cairo, there was "the disparity between the pay of British white and American black troops."[50] U.S. soldiers received a higher pay.[51] Similar concerns were also raised about the stationing of African American troops in the United Kingdom during World War II.[52]

Heide Fehrenbach emphasizes the irony that U.S. troops stationed in Germany after World War II to enforce the de-Nazification and democratization of the country came from a segregated army and from a nation with "a host of anti-miscegenation laws at home."[53] In Eritrea, liberation came at the hands of an imperial army worried about any subversion of racial hierarchy, allied with a segregated army haunted by fears of racial mixing. The tensions and contradictions of BMA's racial policy emerged even more clearly during internal discussions on fascist race laws against interracial concubinage and mixed-race children.

British Ruling on Interracial Concubinage and Italo-Eritrean Children

Sources agree on the high incidence of interracial concubinage in the 1940s and on an equally high level of birth of Italo-Eritrean children. The birth of

[48] Longrigg (MA) to Col. J. N. Hodges (CO, U.S. service command), Asmara, September 28, 1942, WO 230/157, TNA, Kew. See also Pankhurst, "The legal question," 44–45.

[49] Longrigg (MA) to Col. M. G. Babington-Smith (acting CPO), GHQ, OETA, ME, September 28, 1942, no. 6, WO 230/157, TNA, Kew.

[50] Lt. Col. R. M. Arundell (Ag. CPO, Political Branch, GHQ, OETA, ME), to Sir Arthur Rucker, minister of state's office, Cairo, October 6, 1942, WO 230/157, TNA, Kew.

[51] At the end, only two small units of black U.S. troops were sent to Eritrea (one to be deployed at the port of Massawa and another one to run a laundry in Dekemhare). Col. J. N. Hodges (HQ, Eritrea Service Command, U.S. Army forces in the Middle East), Asmara, October 6, 1942, WO 230/157, TNA, Kew.

[52] Smith, *When Jim Crow met John Bull*, 37–96.

[53] The desegregation of the U.S. army only started in 1948. Heide Fehrenbach, *Race after Hitler: Black Occupation Children in Postwar Germany and America* (Princeton, NJ: Princeton University Press, 2005), 2.

3,500 Italo-Eritrean children was recorded in Asmara municipality records, but Bishop G. Marinoni thought that their number was actually many more.[54] In February 1942, the BMA opened discussions with OETA authorities about policy regarding laws on interracial concubinage and mixed-race children in the context of a broader discussion on the possible suspension of Fascist race laws.[55] Everybody agreed that the BMA should abide by the Hague convention on war laws. Alterations to existing legislation were considered acceptable only if justified by war needs. At the same time, it was embarrassing for British authorities to enforce Fascist race laws, which discriminated not only against Africans, but also against Jews; "one can imagine the line which might be taken in Parliament if it comes to someone's notice that the British Military Administration in Eritrea is maintaining discriminating legislation against the Jews," Brigadier Hone (chief political officer in Cairo) commented.[56] The conclusion, reached in April 1942, was that "no action should be taken to suspend the laws in question, but that no proceedings should be instituted by Administration to enforce them."[57]

The Asmara and Hamasien senior political officer, however, was not happy with this solution, and in February 1943, he suggested resuming prosecution of interracial concubinage; "the evils which result from it, notably the propagation of half-castes and the spread of venereal disease, are sufficiently obvious."[58] Interestingly enough, Italian military authorities used to conceive of concubinage as an instrument to *prevent* the spread of sexually transmitted diseases, which they blamed on unlicensed prostitution.[59]

---

[54] Gino Cerbella, *Eritrea 1959: La collettività italiana nelle sue attività economiche, sociali e culturali* (Asmara: Consolato generale d'Italia, 1960); G. Marinoni, *Promemoria*, Asmara, September 24, 1948, 84/3/6, and 84/1/19, Archivio del Vicariato Apostolico, Asmara.

[55] A. A. Baerlein (LA) to CPO, ME, Asmara, February 9, 1942, b. 154, f. 11795, p. 10, BMA, RDC, Asmara.

[56] Hone (CPO, OETA), Italian laws enforced in Eritrea relating to racial questions, September 14, 1942, b. 154, f. 11795, no. 13, BMA, RDC, Asmara.

[57] Lt.-Col. E. F. M. Maxwell (ALA, police branch, GHQ) to military administrator (Asmara), April 17, 1942, b. 154, f. 11795, p. 12, BMA, RDC, Asmara. For the enforcement of such directives in Eritrea, see Major Maxwell Setton, deputy legal adviser (hereafter DLA), circular letter no. 25/10: Suspension of Penal Proceedings under Italian Laws incompatible with present circumstances, April 25, 1942, in b. 154, f. 11795, p. 122, BMA, RDC, Asmara. The laws under scrutiny were: RDL.1728/1938 (Measures for the Defense of the Italian Race); l.1004/1939 (Penal Sanctions for the Defense of Racial Prestige against the Natives of Italian Africa); l.822/1940 (Norms Regarding the Mixed-Race) and r.d.1480/1939 (Police Code for the Italian East Africa) and some articles of the Italian penal code.

[58] Lt.-Col. G. Wellesley (SPO Asmara and Hamasien) to LA, HQ, OETA, Asmara, February 2, 1943, b. 154, f. 11795, p. 15, BMA, RDC, Asmara.

[59] Colonial Eritrea had a system of licensed prostitution similar to that in many British colonies. See Giulia Barrera, "Sex, citizenship and the state: The construction of the public and private spheres in colonial Eritrea," in Perry Willson (ed.), *Gender, Family and Sexuality: The Private Sphere in Italy 1860–1945* (New York: Palgrave Macmillan, 2004), 157–72; Ead, Colonial

Brigadier Hone in Cairo readily agreed and ordered the resumption of prosecution of concubinage between Italian men and Eritrean women.[60] The problem that immediately emerged was that the Italian law applied only to "Aryan" Italians. The implication, explained Longrigg, was that "the Jews were an inferior race and the pollution of their blood was a matter of no concern."[61] Were British officers supposed to use Fascist legislation to sort out who was a Jew and who was an "Aryan?" Or should they modify the law to extend the ban against concubinage to Jews as well? In July 1943, after months of discussions, the new chief civil affairs officer, Sir Arthur Parsons, replaced Major-General Hone (promoted in March 1943) and decided that it was better to suspend prosecutions altogether once again.[62] On July 19, the same day of the Allies' first bombing on Rome, the Asmara and Hamasien senior civil affairs officer protested that such a suspension was "not only disastrous to the prestige of the European race, but cannot fail to intensify the half-castes problem" and insisted that this piece of Italian law "be maintained inflexibly during the British occupation."[63] But Parsons opined that the law 1004/1939 "should be suspended altogether, as having a Fascist complexion."[64]

This exchange of views about the Italian law against interracial concubinage reveals the different political idioms that circulated among the OETA officers in the middle of the war. The notion of a "European race" whose "prestige" deserved protection, articulated by the Asmara senior civil affairs officer, was a long-established topos in colonial discourse, which World War II was stripping bare: The Shoah made expressions such as "European prestige" look like a bad-taste joke. To prove the impracticability of the law, Longrigg chose a line of argument that, paradoxically, stigmatized racial discrimination against the Jews by using the notion "pollution of blood," derived from scientific racism. In post-World War II Europe, expressions of this kind were formerly associated with Nazism and thus expunged from the politically acceptable vocabulary. Sir Arthur Parsons, the chief civil affairs officer, foreshadowed what would be the prevailing attitude in post-World War II Europe. He did so by using a European political category, Fascism, which sounded somehow incongruous in colonial Africa: Race laws were

Affairs; Philippa Levine, *Prostitution, Race, and Politics: Policing Venereal Disease in the British Empire* (New York: Routledge, 2003).

[60] Hone to MA, Eritrea, February 11, 1943, in b. 154, f. 11795, p. 18, BMA, RDC, Asmara.

[61] Longrigg to CCAO, GHQ, Middle East Forces (hereafter MEF), June 26, 1943, b. 154, f. 11795, p. 34, BMA, RDC, Asmara.

[62] Setton (DLA), circular letter to all SPOs, public prosecutor, president of the court, etc., Asmara, July 14, 1943, b. 154, f. 11795, p. 40, BMA, RDC, Asmara.

[63] Lt.-Col. John de Salis (SCAO Asmara and Hamasien) to chief secretary, July 19, 1943; b. 154, f. 11795, p. 41, BMA, RDC, Asmara.

[64] CCAO (GHQ), to chief administrator (hereafter CA), BMA Eritrea, received July 29, 1943), b. 154, f. 11795, p. 42, BMA, RDC, Asmara.

fascist in Europe, but in Africa they were the ordinary instruments of colonial rule, as the legal advisor later observed. This mixing and clashing among different political idioms continued through the following months, with the legal advisor of the OETA taking center stage.

Not enforcing penal sanctions against Italians who violated race laws was by no means tantamount to repealing such laws. The laws affecting personal status (citizenship, marriage, etc.) remained in place, and so did the norms that prevented Jews from performing all sorts of economic activities. In 1942, a case arose in Asmara of "an Italian Aryan girl who wanted to marry an Italian Jew." The Bishop and others strongly pressed the BMA to allow such a marriage, but to no avail. As Brigadier Hone (chief political officer, Cairo GHQ) explained, even if British authorities authorized mixed marriages, they would "be held by the Metropolitan Italian courts to be invalid with the result that the parties would find themselves in a most unenviable situation, married but not married, children illegitimate."[65]

Initially, there was wide agreement among British officers on this line of action because until El Alamein, and possibly until the spring 1943, the BMA took it for granted that after the war Eritrea would revert to Italy and that Italy would keep its race laws.[66] But by the summer of 1943, it was clear that this was not going to happen. On July 10, the Allies landed in Sicily and after a fortnight, Mussolini was deposed and replaced as prime minister by Marshall Badoglio who, on September 3, signed an armistice with the Allies that, among other things, dictated that: "All Italian laws involving discrimination on grounds of race, color, creed or political opinions will... be rescinded."[67] The armistice's clauses were not made public, but the British government was well aware of them.

Even more relevant to the present discussion is the fact that General Harold Alexander, commander of Allied Forces in Italy, took an altogether different line of action from the legalistic approach followed by the OETA, ME. Soon after successfully invading Sicily, in fact, he proclaimed that "the Chief Civil Affairs Officer will by order annul, amend or render inoperative... any laws which discriminated against any person or persons on the basis of race, colour or creed."[68] General Alexander's proclamation heralded official European postwar policy and public discourse about racism.

[65] Hone, "Italian laws enforced in Eritrea relating to racial questions," to the MA, Eritrea, September 14, 1942, b. 154, f. 11795, p. 13, BMA, RDC, Asmara.

[66] Kennedy-Cooke (MA) to CPO, OETA, GHQ, ME, February 12, 1942, in b. 154, f. 11795, p. 11, BMA, RDC, Asmara.

[67] Additional instrument of armistice and surrender of the Italian forces to the commander-in-chief of the Allied Forces, signed by General Dwight D. Eisenhower, Malta, September 29, 1943, article 31.

[68] Article 4, proclamation no. 7: Allied Military Government of Occupied Territories, *Sicily Gazette*, no. 1, July 1943.

The legal adviser of OETA, ME, Colonel E. F. M. Maxwell, strongly disagreed with Sir Arthur Parsons and found that General Alexander's proclamation was illegitimate, since it violated the Hague convention on war laws, which specified that the occupying power must respect the laws in force in the country. Maxwell was a staunch advocate of a legalistic approach, which presumably derived from a belief in the legitimacy of British rule and moral superiority that rested on a scrupulous observance of the rule of law.[69] Maxwell seemed to belong to the ranks of "those professional jurists who had for the past half-century seen international law as the key instrument for promoting its [European civilization] values."[70] Maxwell probably believed that Nazi disregard for international law made scrupulous respect for the rule of law all the more valuable. The legalistic approach he advocated had many followers in OETA. Their legalism could border on the surreal. In September 1945, the BMA was still discussing whether it was legitimate to suspend by proclamation a 1937 gubernatorial decree prohibiting Italian taxi drivers from carrying African passengers. Surprisingly, the answer was "no." One administrator wrote that "The fact that we disagree with racial discrimination is not in my opinion sufficient excuse for an interference with the occupied territories' domestic law."[71] In 1943, replying to those in favor of suspending Fascist race laws in order to allow marriages between "Aryan" and Jewish Italians, Maxwell argued that "a much more important principle [than freedom of marriages] for which the war is being fought is the principle that laws are made and unmade by Parliaments and not by dictators, whether civil or military."[72] He seemed to forget that Fascist race laws were the product of a dictatorship; but one should also notice how his words echoed the deep-rooted British idea that a sovereign parliament was a bulwark against tyranny. Maxwell's argument against repealing race laws deserves to be considered as the expression of the colonial attitude that saw nothing particularly objectionable in racial discrimination as well as that of a diligent, unimaginative lawyer who acted within an international legal framework that considered colonial rule to be legitimate and that lacked a legal instrument qualifying race laws as per se illegitimate. The Universal Declaration, the European Convention on Human Rights, and the UN Covenant on Civil and Political Rights were still distant. In 1919, "Japan's suggestion to insert a clause affirming racial equality in the League of Nations covenant" had been rebuffed by liberal

---

[69] Simpson, *Human Rights*, 18.

[70] Mark Mazower, *No Enchanted Palace: The End of Empire and the Ideological Origins of the United Nations* (Princeton, NJ, and Oxford: Princeton University Press, 2009), 123.

[71] Handwritten note (illegible initials) September 8, [1945], replying to a question by the LA and to previous notes on the matter. Lt.-Col. H.S.S. for chief secretary to SCAO, Asmara, September 10, 1945, b. 62, f. 10694, pp. 100–102, BMA, RDC, Asmara.

[72] Maxwell, chief legal advisor to GSO I (P), WO 230/147, TNA, Kew.

powers.[73] In 1943, race laws could be considered illegitimate only by using political arguments (as the War Office later did), not legal arguments.

In October 1943, an Eritrean weekly paper published news that the king of Italy had abrogated fascist race laws, but this was a rumor, for the Italian government did not actually do this until January 1944. Longrigg wrote to the GHQ in Cairo asking whether the BMA could do the same in Eritrea. "At present," he explained, "our devotion to the letter of international law seems to have the effect of perpetuating the worst features of Fascism."[74] Similar questions were raised in Libya as well, where, in February 1943, General Montgomery had been "dissuaded from issuing a proclamation suspending anti-Jews laws."[75] In November 1943, the legal advisor in Cairo still maintained that no war need justified the suspension of race laws, even if the new version of the *Military Manual of Civil Affairs in the Field* had been published and it dictated that "it will be necessary to suspend the operation of laws such as anti-Jews legislation, which are repugnant to the principles for which the war is being fought."[76]

In Libya, the issue of Fascist race laws was particularly sensitive because there was a substantial population of local Jews and a minority of European Jews; in Eritrea, by contrast, there were only a handful of Jews. When the local legal adviser asked the GHQ in Cairo to suspend the race laws in Tripolitania (Libya), he made it clear that he was talking only of "laws which discriminate against Jews." There were, he argued, also many laws which discriminated against Africans, but "some of these are really most salutary and necessary and are concerned with upholding the dignity of the white man."[77] Such a double standard found advocates at the GHQ of OETA ME as well.

In November 1943, Sir Arthur Parsons asked the War Office in London whether OETA, ME, could "annul or suspend" the laws discriminating against Jews "throughout our occupied territories"; in his opinion, race laws were "the epitome of what we are fighting to destroy."[78] The War Office's reply was strongly worded: "Fascist discriminatory laws are considered to be contrary to fundamental principles.... In view of His Majesty's Government such legislation is covered neither by the Hague convention nor by international law," and went to declare, "the respect of a military

---

73 Mark Mazower. *Dark Continent: Europe's Twentieth Century* (London: Penguin Books, 1999), 57; see also Paul Gordon Lauren, *The Evolution of International Human Rights: Visions Seen* (Philadelphia: University of Pennsylvania Press, 1998), 100–01.

74 Longrigg (CA) to CCAO, GHQ, ME, November 13, 1943, WO 230/157, TNA, Kew.

75 Lt.-Col. P. A. Macrory (deputy chief legal adviser) to CCAO, through GSO I (P), November 9, 1943, WO 230/147, TNA, Kew.

76 *Military Manual of Civil Affairs in the Field*, 15, para 2.

77 Major D. Renton (ALA) to GSO I (P), November 13, 1943, no. 126, WO 230/147, TNA, Kew.

78 Parsons to director of civil affairs, WO, November 16, 1943, WO 230/147, TNA, Kew.

occupant for the laws in force in the country does not legally prohibit him from suspending the operation of laws of an oppressive character."[79]

Legal Adviser Maxwell took it for granted that the War Office ruling applied only to anti-Jewish laws. The problem in giving effect to the War Office instructions, he explained, was that Fascist discriminatory laws often targeted "natives" or "non Aryan persons and only occasionally [were] Jews specifically referred to." He explained, "Many of the laws in themselves would not be objectable if properly applied and, indeed, there is hardly one of them which is not represented in the laws of our own Empire or of the Empire of one or other of our Allies."[80] Thus the objective was to suspend discrimination against Jews, while leaving in force that against the "natives." Things were made particularly difficult, in Maxwell's eyes, by the presence in former Italian colonies of both European and local Jews, the latter "properly treated as natives." Carefully crafted proclamations were thus needed, so that the suspension of race laws could benefit in some cases all Jews, in others "European Jews only."[81]

In January 1944, the Italian government issued a law that repealed law 1728/1938, "Measures for the Defense of the Italian Race" (the law that had forbidden mixed marriages), and "any other disposition or law" that mentioned race or had "a racial character (*carattere razziale*)."[82] The letter of the law was very clear. Nonetheless, in Eritrea the Fascist-appointed Public Prosecutor Emanuele Montefusco stated that the law intended to repeal only racial legislation against Jews and did not apply to colonial race laws.[83] British authorities fully agreed. At this point, any legal impediment against mixed marriages had fallen, including marriages with Africans, much to the legal adviser's surprise.[84] By contrast, the law that discriminated against mixed-race children (822/1940) remained in place. In 1947, Italy passed a law exclusively dedicated to the "mixed-race" of the former AOI.[85] This legislation not only explicitly repealed law 822/1940 that prohibited paternal recognition, but also introduced a special, relatively easy channel for Italo-Eritreans not recognized by their fathers to obtain Italian citizenship.

Despite appearances, the purpose of the law was not to repair damage done by law 822/1940 but to use the Italo-Eritreans for political goals.

---

[79] G. W. Labert, assistant undersecretary of state, WO, to CCAO, GHQ, MEF, London, December 29, 1943, WO 230/147, TNA, Kew.

[80] Maxwell to CCAO, January 6, 1944, WO 230/147, TNA, Kew.

[81] Ibid.

[82] *Regio decreto legge*, January 20, 1944, n. 25.

[83] Procura del re dell'Eritrea (Montefusco) to commissario straordinario presso l'amm.ne municipale di Asmara, Asmara, June 17, 1944, no. 668/4, b. 154, f. 11795, no. 100, BMA, RDC, Asmara.

[84] Macrory (deputy chief LA), to CCAO through GSO I (P), n.d., WO 230/157, TNA, Kew.

[85] *Decreto legislativo del capo provvisorio dello Stato*, August 3, 1947, no. 1096, "Abrogazione della legge 13 maggio 1940, n. 822 contenente norme relative ai meticci."

The law was approved only a few months before the visit in Eritrea of the Four Power Commission of Investigation for the Former Italian Colonies. Political conflicts were raging over the future of Eritrea. The Italian government was intervening forcefully in the dispute and through covert channels it poured substantial amounts of money into buying the support of Eritrean political leaders.[86] Within this context, the Italo-Eritreans could become assets. An Italian intelligence officer made this point explicitly when he reported on the political situation in Eritrea in January 1947: "The race laws, which in the colony were totally appropriate, estranged such youngsters [the Italo-Eritreans] from our community . . . they now aspire to Italian citizenship . . . If their desires could be met in one way or another, they could become a valuable instrument to advance the Italian cause in the native milieu."[87] Martino Mario Moreno, the director general of political affairs of the Ministry of Italian Africa, a position he held since 1938, liked the idea and soon suggested that government repeal law 822/1940. To be valid in Eritrea, the BMA had to issue a proclamation endorsing any particular Italian law. Revealing his real goal, Moreno argued that if the British authorities failed to apply the law in Eritrea, "they will not destroy but rather strengthen the political effect that we intend to achieve with this law."[88] This is exactly what happened. Only in 1952 did the BMA issue a proclamation that repealed law 822/1940.[89] At that point, most Italian men who had fathered Italo-Eritrean children had already left; the Italian population shrunk by 75 percent from 1941 to 1952. Italo-Eritreans born in the 1940s grew up without paternal recognition and this left them with indelible scars.[90]

Conclusion

The British debate about Fascist race laws in Eritrea reminds us what it was to have a world without any international legal instrument that declared racial discrimination to be illegitimate. Law-abiding officers could legitimately consider the repealing of Fascist race laws as a violation of

[86] Tekeste Negash, "Italy and its relations with Eritrean political parties, 1948–1950," *Africa* (Roma), 59 (2004), 417–52.

[87] Stato Maggiore della Marina, II reparto, sez. C/h3, no. 17, Promemoria: La situazione politica dell'Eritrea al 1 gennaio 1947, 17 gen. 1947, Archivio storico diplomatico del Ministero affari esteri, Archivio storico del Ministero Africa Italiana, II Direzione Africa Orientale, b. 1. f. sf. 1947: "Notizie politiche Eritrea. Informazioni dall'Eritrea. Stato Maggiore Esercito. Stato Maggiore Marina."

[88] Moreno to Ministero dell'interno, Ministero di grazia e giustizia e Presidenza del Consiglio dei ministri, February 27, 1947, no. 187432, Presidenza del Consiglio dei Ministri, Provvedimenti legislativi, 1947, Ministero Africa Italiana, no. 6, Archivio centrale dello Stato, Roma.

[89] Proclamation no. 125, March 21, 1952.

[90] Barrera, "Patrilinearity."

international law. By today's international legal standards, it looks like the world upside down.

The British military officers who were in charge of administering Eritrea during World War II did not have an easy task. They had to rule over a country inhabited by a large white enemy population, ruled by a comprehensive body of Fascist race laws, plagued by economic crisis and soaring racial tensions. As far as racial policies were concerned, they were guided by their own experience as colonial administrators who considered the racial subordination of the colonized as part of the natural order of things. They also felt obliged to comply with the Hague convention on war laws, which required the respect of the laws of the occupied country, regardless of their colonial nature or their violation of fundamental human rights. British officers continued to partially enforce Fascist race laws, thus increasingly exposing themselves to political contradictions.

In fact, in the early 1940s, the Allies started to construct the war itself as a struggle against Nazi racism. Such a narrative became prominent after the war, when the horrors of the Shoah became common knowledge. This process did not happen in a day: the Eritrean case shows how in the course of the war, British officers started debating what the war was about and whether racial discrimination was acceptable. They did it in the absence of international legal instruments that declared racial discrimination as illegitimate. And they did it without perceiving the contradiction of considering Fascist race laws as "the epitome of what we are fighting to destroy" when they applied to the Jews, but considered them acceptable when they were applied to Africans. The Allies' antiracist stance was intended to be confined to Europe: it was not supposed to spill over into Africa.

15

To Be Treated as a Man

Wartime Struggles over Masculinity, Race, and Honor in the Nigerian Coal Industry

Carolyn A. Brown

When defeat and colonial rule fragmented African notions of honour, elements were absorbed not only into the ethics of colonial armies and respectable Christians but also into a working-class ethic designed to ensure survival and dignity in towns and workplaces.

John Iliffe, *Honour in African History*, 281

Then Isiah [sic] started to laugh so I told him that it was not a laughing matter, he persisted on laughing so I warned him a second time that he need not laugh about it. He still laughed so I *slapped him across the mouth* with the back of my hand. He laughed again so I slapped him again, then he seemed to go mad at the thought that he had been struck and went and called two hewers to witness the fact that I had severely flogged him when all the time the only witness was my cloth boy.

Thomas Yates, Underground Manager, August 21, 1945[1]

Introduction

Late summer 1945, in the twilight of empire, an incident occurred in the Enugu Government Colliery, southeastern Nigeria, which was emblematic of the new ways that the changing political context of the war encouraged African workers to contest imperial power. Thomas Yates, one of the British underground managers, twice slapped Isaiah Ojiyi, general secretary of the Colliery Workers Union (CWU), for refusing his orders and laughing at him. From Yates' description, it appears that Ojiyi goaded him into this performance to provide an opportunity for him to demonstrate his defiance of white managerial power. What followed, however, was unusual. Rather than fight back, Ojiyi took Yates to court and won. The slap itself was not unusual, as such assaults were customary in the colonial workplace, but

---

[1] Mr. Yates to colliery manager, August 21, 1945, Nigerian Colliery Files, (hereafter NCF) P.2/1/1, National Archives of Nigeria (hereafter NAN), Enugu.

Ojiyi was manipulating the situation to display his defiance and heroism in challenging a figure of white power who exerted such extreme control over the miners.

Ojiyi, a rather flamboyant orator and iconoclastic leader, was the type of Nigerian trade unionist who relished the opportunity to "display defiance" against racial insult and draw upon the "heroic honor" traditions of his people, the Igbo, by his willingness to push the boundaries of the state's timid attempts to eliminate racial insults.[2] By winning the court case Ojiyi showed his legal sophistication in understanding the new forms of seeking redress that were successful during the war. With this act he became one of the first Africans to successfully challenge the brutal forms of industrial discipline in the white man's court. This act of defiance drew upon heroic indigenous traditions in which strong leaders had the audacity to do what others feared. Immediately, it raised Ojiyi's stature to that of hero in the eyes of the hundreds of coal miners who had themselves been subjected to these severe forms of abuse. To the men in his union, the CWU, he was a knowledgeable, brave figure, a person they could trust to represent their interests in the new form of worker representation – the trade union. As the colonial government pushed workers to resolve their grievances in labor unions and complex negotiating processes, workers adapted these new inventions – the unions – as a means of reclaiming their honor. But their faith in these institutions was conditioned upon the success of these unions and leaders in successfully addressing their grievances.

In many ways the Yates-Ojiyi incident and its resolution exposed the sharpened racial contradictions that erupted in workplaces with increased frequency during the war throughout the colony. Workers' leaders evoked ancient honor codes, often challenging European bosses whose behavior followed the time-honored principles of imperial arrogance. The trade union, introduced by the state as a method of control, became the vehicle that workers used to challenge the arrogance and racist insults of the white boss. Racial abuses were quite normal in colonial industries, but during the war Britain could ill afford to alienate its African subjects, especially those living adjacent to Vichy's large West African empire and working in a crucial energy industry. Yates, like other white bosses, was caught off guard by the state's willingness to rule for Africans in the judicial challenge. Like many colonial managers during this period, Yates felt abandoned by a state that had never before called him to task for "tossing around" African workers. Yes, the war had changed workers' attitudes and the willingness of the colonial state to defend British bosses. This was only one example of how the political realities of wartime West Africa filtered into the workplace. This was all because Britain desperately needed the support of its colonies

---

[2] John Iliffe, *Honour in African History* (Cambridge: Cambridge University Press, 2005), 308.

during the war. Especially with the Japanese victories in Southeast Asia and in February 1942 Britain lost Singapore while the United States lost its major source of tin, and Britain lost its access to the agricultural and mineral wealth of the region. Nigeria[3] and the entirety of West Africa was revved up to substitute for this lost supply. The need was so dire that even tepid reformers such as Orde-Brown countenanced a massive project of conscription to bring in over 200,000 local men.[4] This enhanced the colonial importance of Nigerian coal making working conditions of the miners a matter of strategic importance. Enugu coal was necessary to transfer the tons of tin to the coast. Additionally, Enugu miners were called upon to compensate for the crisis in the British coal fields where worker protest, manpower shortages, and absenteeism exacerbated fuel shortages.[5]

In this context, the managers' ability to evoke the privileges of *imperial masculinity* over the *subordinate masculinity* of the "native man" caved in under the weight of this reality. Colliery workers developed a class identity that was not only shaped by the underground workplace but by the social and political roles they played in their homes, in the city and in the regional economy during the war. Their reputation as progressive young men in the village and urban locations mediated the humiliating experiences of the colonial workplace, as did their recognition of their coal's role in the war-time economy. These levels of consciousness would lead them to lodge protests during the war. Enugu coal fueled the Nigerian railway that brought the tin from the northern minefields, even more crucial after the fall of Singapore, Britain's major source, in 1942. Table 15.1 notes the major consumers of Enugu coal in the last two years of the war. Enugu coal supplied the ships at the ports of Takoradi and Lagos and the convoys stopping weekly at Freetown for fuel and water.[6] After the liberation of France in 1944, over 80,000 tons of coal were shipped to Free France colonies, slightly less than the nearly 90,000 tons sent to the Gold Coast.[7] Thus, Enugu coal and its workers were at the nucleus of the regional economy facilitating the transport of valuable minerals and tropical exports, within the imperial economy. British propaganda emphasized this role as a mutual dependence of imperial "master" and "subject" and the importance of their role in saving England. Further, productivity campaigns underscored the coal miners' important role in saving England. Like Nigerian workers elsewhere, they

[3] Bill Freund, *Capital and Labour in the Nigerian Tin Mines* (Atlantic Highlands, NJ: Humanities Press, 1981), 137.

[4] Ibid.

[5] For a historical summary of the proverbial crises in the British coal industry, see Barry Supple, *The History of the British Coal Industry*, Vol. 4: *1913–1946* (Oxford: Clarendon Press, 1986).

[6] See Howard, Chapter 10, this volume.

[7] Nigeria, *Report on the Accounts and Finances for the Years 1944/45 and 1945/46* (Lagos: Government Printer, 1947).

TABLE 15.1. *Sales of Coal to African Colonies,*
1944/45 to 1945/46

Colony	1944/45 Sales	1945/46 Sales
Gold Coast	89,403	84,510
South Africa	6,149	–
Belgium	17,156	–
Sierra Leone	14,882	17,020
Gambia	602	1,502
Dahomey	541	–
Free France	83,033	46,341
Spanish Gov.	6,559	785
TOTAL	218,325	150,158

Source: Nigeria, *Report on the Accounts and Finances
for the Years 1944/45 and 1945/46* (Lagos: Government
Printer, 1947).

began to throw their support behind nationalists whose critiques of colonial rule often linked discriminatory workplace treatment to the "racial contempt" to which they were subjected. Iliffe argues that "racial insult" was a formative experience for many nationalist leaders and became "a primary source of nationalist thought and action."[8]

The global scale of the war and coordination of production regimes made colonial workers aware of the conditions of their counterparts in the metropole and encouraged Nigerian miners to compare their sacrifices and conditions of service with those of expatriate government staff as well as European and American coal miners. Enugu miners shaped their expectations for treatment and remuneration with an awareness of the discrepancies of their working lives when compared with those of their counterparts in the metropole. Coal mining followed common technological patterns and these encouraged miners to feel membership in a type of international brotherhood, a brotherhood of the "country of coal."[9] They shared with coal miners in England a gendered occupational "life-world," which celebrated masculine values of bravery, a warm but rough male camaraderie on and off the job, and an awareness of the special intuitive skill that allowed them to survive the danger, psychological strain, and exhaustive work regime of mining. Enugu miners also constructed a proud self-identity as "coal men" that gave them prestige in their villages and led them to expect far more

[8] Iliffe, *Honour in African History*, 306.
[9] See David Frank, "The county of coal," *Labour/Le Travail*, 21 (1988), 239–48; this review essay of several coal mining studies considers the universalizing characteristics of coal mining.

political power than was then granted by the Nigerian state.[10] Their demands also reflected a racialized class consciousness that drew upon the nationalist discourse of the period which raised issues of dignity, social justice, and racial parity that were condemnations of the dehumanizing and abusive systems of industrial discipline. Moreover, they complained of the state's unwillingness to give them the wages that supported the lifestyle they and their families deserved. Their demands expressed a confrontation of workers' self-perception as modern, industrial men with the colonialists' disdain for an imaginary "African worker" whom managers debased and reviled.

At the same time, wartime propaganda sharpened the contradictions in the work place and encouraged Enugu miners to add their concerns to the generalized critique of colonial rule. As working men, they brought humiliating industrial practices into the public eye by using the nationalist press, particularly popular in Enugu. As a regional capital, Enugu had hundreds of discontented African clerks for whom the nationalist press expressed their interests. Miners appropriated the discourse of the male breadwinner norm to emphasize their need for more money, which they used with considerable opportunism to underscore demands.[11] They argued that as men whose labor supported the very survival of Britain they should be able to provide their families with the lifestyle of a responsible, respectable man and could protect their families from the indignity and humiliation of poverty. In 1937, two years before war broke out, they had launched a series of strikes in which they explicitly articulated the moral violations that their paltry wages created. The "pick boys" (miners) resented the degradation of substandard overcrowded housing and escalating inflation that prevented them from investing in their future – the education of their children. They were especially outraged by the violations of home conventions as they were being forced to board a single "pick boy" with their family or to share a room with another family. In the rough-hewn language of workers they demanded

> new construction of quarters with more accommodative rooms that the present ones enough to live in, that is to say, quarters of providency [sic]of sufficient rooms each of which may be able to accommodate a workman and his wife alone meaning either a pick boy coupled or a coupled tub – boy without to be tampered with, by an uncoupled workman or without two couples to occupy or share one room without a party wall or partition as this mode of living is often unbecoming.[12]

---

[10] Lisa Lindsay, "Domesticity and difference: Male breadwinners, working women and colonial citizenship in the 1945 Nigerian General Strike," *American Historical Review*, 104 (1999), 783–812.

[11] Ibid.

[12] Letter from Colliery Department, Iva Valley, to general manager, Railway, Lagos, July 12, 1937, NIGCOAL 2/1/94, NAN, Enugu.

Enugu, popularly known as "Coal City," was a bustling city of 40,000 inhabitants during the war.[13] The city's role as the administrative capital of southeast Nigeria and an industrial center gave it a social composition that was politically volatile. With its hundreds of discontented clerical workers, unsatisfied with the pace of political change and thousands of strategically placed industrial workers trying to scrape together a living with wages that had deteriorated since the Depression, the city was a hotbed of nationalist activity. The clerks were the foundation of the nationalist movement. They dominated the leadership of the radical Zikist movement, which attracted many impatient young men and women. The ideologies of the movement's leadership were a broad representation of political radicalism, which included several prominent Marxist Leninists.[14] Additionally during the North African campaign (June 10, 1940–May 13, 1943) some 7,500 soldiers from the West African Frontier Force[15] were stationed in Enugu, giving an added dimension to the forms of masculinity incorporated into the culture of the city. Here, as elsewhere in Nigeria, workers raised demands that articulated a blending of British working-class notions of masculinity and reformulated indigenous rural norms based on fatherhood and elite status.[16] This reconceptualization of their role as men in the household, workplace, and community was expressed in demands, petitions, and grievances that they raised during the war.

Until the war, neither the French nor the British could reconcile their responsibility for the social reproduction of the working class with the assumptions they made about the backwardness of African societies. For most policy makers the term "African worker" wedded two contradictory concepts – "African" and "worker." They persisted in believing that the men who constructed and ran their railways, mines, and ports were in essence "peasants" and "temporary sojourners" in the workforce. It was not necessary to pay them a living wage because these men were still rural inhabitants whose extended families, on the farm, could help them to subsist. Most, officials felt they entered the workforce as "target workers," most often only working for enough money to marry or to join a title society. For many decades mine management had assumed that the men could best be handled using "traditional" rural authorities rather than applying techniques of industrial relations and social engineering used with their mine workers

---

[13] Local authority to resident, March 20, 1945, NIGCOAL 2/1/38, NAN, Enugu.
[14] Ehiedu E. G. Iweriebor, *Radical Politics in Nigeria, 1945–1950: The Significance of the Zikist Movement* (Zaria: Ahmadu Bello University Press, 1996).
[15] "Local Authority Census of Enugu" para. 32, CO 522/B NIGCOAL 2/1/138, The National Archives (hereafter TNA), Kew.
[16] This is the central argument in Lisa Lindsay, "Domesticity and difference," esp. 801–03. See also Lisa Lindsay, "Money, marriage, and masculinity on the colonial Nigerian railway," in Lisa Lindsay and Stephen Meischer (eds.), *Men and Masculinities in Africa* (Portsmouth, NH: Heinemann Press, 2003), 150–51.

at home in Europe. But the war empowered young male workers to assert that their concerns were too specialized and "modern" to be addressed by "native authorities," the elder men in the village. These fluid contentions all played out in the politicized environment of wartime West Africa, in which nationalists articulated a gendered discourse that linked the goal of responsible government with the restitution of African men's lost honor and dignity. This perspective was implicit in the ways nationalist leaders framed the case for independence and the ways that the "masses" understood the daily humiliations of British rule.

During the war several workers' protests in the Nigerian coal industry indicate how the desire to fulfil gender norms, both "traditional" and "evolving," of masculinity led men to organize protests at the Enugu colliery. This chapter underscores the existence of African "labor" as a social category embedded in villages, urban communities, and voluntary associations, all important spaces for the expression of masculinity. By examining the expressions and transformations of gender ideologies and practices in this industry, we can develop a deeper understanding of the causes of labor activism during World War II. This chapter outlines some of the issues that informed workers' behavior and speaks to the transformative process of the war as it shaped and reshaped the gender ideologies of working men. While the study is restricted to Nigerian coal miners, many of the policies and worker responses are characteristic of the working class in the entire colonial continent.

Fathers, "Big Men," Slaves, and Boys circa World War II: "Young" Workers Challenge Senior Masculinity

Scholars of Africa have noted how wage labor and urbanization undermined the authority of senior men, enabled young men to "redefine previous notions of masculinity," and reshaped "the parameters of masculinity."[17] Colonialism presented young men with a multiplicity of masculine models that related to age, economic power, ritual authority, and social status. Some models were beyond the reach of the young men – age – while others, especially those based on fatherhood and wealth, were made accessible by the colonial economy.[18] Men could not escape the impact of wage labor, the new economy, and the exercise of colonial state power. To some extent, colonial conditions – both economic and political – empowered younger men while reducing the power and authority of elders. The influence of Enugu and its coal miners on the adjacent villages gave rural masculinity a complexity and instability that concerned political officials and the "traditional" village authorities they created to insure rural stability. These concerns reached a

---

[17] "Introduction," in Lindsay and Miescher, eds., *Men and Masculinities.*
[18] Ibid., 7.

peak during the war when those coal miners who commuted from local villages became the "mouthpieces" of a radical nationalism emerging among the educated clerks in Enugu.[19]

Most coal miners were Igbo, the major ethnolinguistic group in southeastern Nigeria and lived in villages organized in autonomous kin-based settlements, with neither chiefs nor forms of political collaboration above the village-group, that is, a cluster of villages claiming descent from a common ancestor. Colonial rule changed this and officials introduced a system of indirect rule with colonially appointed chiefs, which was so hated it collapsed with the Women's War of 1929.[20] The subsequent system was of village councils composed of mostly senior men. By the twentieth century, there were status differences rooted in wealth from the centuries of involvement in slave and palm oil trades, all of which affected the types of masculine models accessible to junior men.

The mines were located in the Udi district in northern Igboland on land occupied by two groups of local villages, both of which became the largest constituent group in the mines' labor force. One, the Agbaja, lived on an overcrowded escarpment and flocked to colliery jobs that replaced enslavement and the outmigration of young men to work on farms elsewhere.[21] The other group, the Nkanu, had historically used slaves in farming their rich, fertile plateau, and preferred farming to feed Enugu to mining jobs. They refused to work underground, arguing to do so, "A man might as well be buried alive."[22] The few Nkanu at the colliery would only take less-dangerous surface jobs, while the Agbaja worked underground, making work an important factor in fostering a regional identity. However, one group of men in Nkanu had little choice over their participation in the mine workforce: the descendants of slaves still called *ohu*, a twentieth-century

---

[19] For more on these political discussions, see Carolyn A. Brown, *"We Were All Slaves": African Miners, Culture and Resistance at the Enugu Government Colliery* (Portsmouth, NH: Heinemann Press, 2003).

[20] The Women's War of 1929 has generated a vast literature, including commissions of enquiry, contemporary newspaper commentary, anthropology and history studies, a novel, and a play. Two recent studies are Susan Kingsley Kenty, Misty L. Bastian, and Marc Matera, *The Women's War of 1929: Gender and Violence in Colonial Nigeria* (New York: Palgrave Macmillan, 2011); and Toyin Falola and Adam Paddock, *The Women's War of 1929: A History of Anti-Colonial Resistance in Eastern Nigeria* (Durham, NC: Carolina Academic Press, 2011). The best short analysis is chapter 3 in Nina Emma Mba, *Nigerian Women Mobilized: Women's Political Activity in Southern Nigeria, 1900–1965* (Berkeley: Institute of International Studies, University of California, 1982).

[21] G. I. Jones, "Igbo land tenure," *Africa*, 19 (1949), 309–23. For a discussion of the importance of slavery in this region, see Carolyn A. Brown, "Testing the boundaries of marginality: Twentieth century slavery and emancipation struggles in Nkanu, northern Igboland, 1920–1929," *Journal of African History*, 37 (1996), 51–80.

[22] P. E. H. Hair, "Enugu: A West African industrial town," mimeograph, n. d., located in NAN, Enugu.

legacy of the area's intensive involvement in the Atlantic slave trade.[23] They were locked in a position of permanent subordination to the freeborn who continued to discriminate against them in the twentieth century. Mine work allowed many of them to secure the resources needed to found their own lineages and eventually establish their own settlements.[24]

The transformative process of becoming a worker is expressed by Anyionovo Nwodo, an *ohu* from Ugbawka, a large militant slave population. He was drafted to work in the new economy during World War I. He recalled:

> I was among those sent by the chief to work in the construction of railway line from Otakpa, now in Imo State. Chief Agunweru Mba was our chief and via his agents, he appointed those both Amadu [freeborn] and Awbia [descended from slaves] were to be sent out to work either at the coal mine or at the railway construction. All payment... was directed to the chief. We were left with nothing but at a later date, the chief started giving us small amount of what each of us realized. This was after we had realized from the Europeans that we were paid for the job we had been doing for long.[25]

Just as wages from mine jobs undermined the power of *ohu* owners they similarly enabled young men to "redefine previous notions of masculinity."[26] Wage labor sharpened intergenerational conflict as young men reduced their dependence on their fathers or village elders for resources necessary to become socially mature. After suffering from lower commodity prices during the Depression communities were now, in wartime, benefiting from miners' income and a progressive outlook. The largesse that these young men displayed earned for them a position of influence within the village hierarchy which differed significantly from the "traditional" reliance on age as a marker of leadership. Further, as the coal mines expanded their workforce to meet the demand of the war, these young men were the key facilitators for securing a mining job. Thus their being influential without the imprimatur of age or marriage redefined the basis of political prestige, freeing it from the usual parameters of age and fatherhood. District officers called them "coal gentlemen," who were recognizable by their flashy clothes,

---

[23] In the initial years of the mines, they were victimized by chiefs who were commissioned to provide forced labor for the mines. While work in the coal mines and on the railway eroded the masters' control over their slaves, the rapid growth of Enugu during World War I challenged slavery in a contradictory way. On the one hand, the growing urban market encouraged slave owners to intensify the use of slaves to grow produce, while on the other hand, living in Enugu encouraged slaves to become independent farmers.

[24] Brown, "Testing the boundaries of marginality."

[25] *Awbia* and *amadi* were the words used to refer to slaves and freeborn respectively after a tumultuous revolt in the 1920s when the *ohu* had partial success in securing state support for a new identity. Interview with Anyionovo Nwodo, Obiofia, Akegbe-Ugwu, August 5, 1986. See also, Brown, "Testing the boundaries of marginality."

[26] Brown, "Testing the boundaries of marginality."

their bicycles (a prestigious symbol of modernity), and their articulation of new ideologies of "freedom," "democracy," and antiauthoritarianism. They inserted new prestigious commodities (e.g., bicycles, sewing machines) into village life and financed massive development projects in their natal villages. As the war raged on and shortages caused by import controls raised the prices of all imported goods, many of these projects were beyond the reach of those with lower salaries. In their assessments of their wages coal miners took into account their ability to fulfill their development goals: provide potable water; build roads, stone churches, and maternity hospitals; and put zinc roofs on their homes. This was the metric that they used to valorize their labor. They also brought a new politics to the village – the radical nationalism of the disgruntled urban clerical class.

In the freeborn community there were two dominant forms of masculinity, one based on fatherhood, the other on elite status.[27] The war caused adjustments in both. Most men fulfilled the former, as fathers and elders who held power over the kinship group. As patriarchs they could appropriate the labor of their wives and children for farming and of their sons for clearing fields, construction, and contributing to communal village projects. The core of paternal power was the control that fathers had over young men's ability to move through the life stages to increased maturity. A son depended on his father's capacity (and willingness) to finance the series of rituals and obligations accompanying his initiation into manhood. Of all these life passages, marriage was the defining feature of male social maturity. So important was marriage in defining masculinity that the gender of an unmarried man was suspect, as indicated by the term *oke okporo* (male woman).[28] The war played havoc with these life passages largely because of inflation, which reached 200 percent by 1943, putting bride price (the goods and services that the groom had to pay to a woman's family to replace her value) beyond the reach of many young men. This relegated them to an extended period of political exclusion and social subordination.[29] Sons would normally need the father's assistance to help them pay the bride price and to acquire land for their own homesteads.[30] Young women's fathers also determined other

---

[27] Meredith McKittrick, "Forsaking their fathers? Colonialism, Christianity, and coming of age in Ovamboland, northern Namibia," in L. Lindsay and S. Meischer (eds.), *Men and Masculinities in Modern Africa*, 34.

[28] This is especially suggestive as the word for an unmarried woman is only descriptive: *"j-onwegh di"* (she has no husband). Victor Uchendu, *The Igbo of Southeast Nigeria* (New York: Holt, Rinehart and Winston, 1965), 86.

[29] This was not uncontested. Young unmarried men, both employed and unemployed, experimented with new identities in the city during the war and created youth gangs, such as the "Cowboys," who created a new and prestigious identity that emulated a figure of American masculinity, the American cowboy. See P. E. H. Hair, "The Cowboys: A acculturative institution in Nigeria, ca. 1950," *History in Africa*, 28 (2001), 83–93.

[30] The *obi*, or compound, was the basic unit of production.

young men's access to their daughters in marriage. Men in the bride's family negotiated with the men in the prospective grooms family to determine the bride price. This intergenerational relationship of dependence and eventual autonomy was a powerful source of tension between senior and junior men as well as fathers and son, but a source that was eventually resolved through age.

But the war introduced new systems of marriage negotiation and bride-wealth calculations initiated by Igbo soldiers abroad. The absence of prospective grooms caused significant transformations in the marriage system and the ability of local men to negotiate it. First, as young soldiers abroad desperately tried to participate in the contracting of marriages they introduced a program called "Send Me a Wife," which created a new form of marriage "marriage by photograph."[31] In this case men abroad exchanged pictures with prospective brides and decided if their relatives should begin marriage negotiations. Soldiers would send remittances to trusted relatives who acted as surrogates in arranging these marriages. In so doing the soldier abroad both raised the cost of the bride price and competed with local men over eligible wives. It is unclear the extent to which coal miners felt disenfranchised by the escalating bride price, but they may well have been among the local men seeking to undermine the power of the absent soldiers. The vulnerability of the absent military man was suggested in letters written to the district officer complaining about the abuse of relatives who failed to allocate funds to existing wives or to use these remittances for bridewealth payments for future wives.[32] Additionally, there were numerous complaints of adultery, which could mean that the bride absconded with another man before the payments were completed. For local men this may have been as a favored strategy to "level the playing field" with absent servicemen. Nonetheless, bride price inflation continued to escalate and put pressure on wages that became an important stimulus to worker unrest.

Missionaries also attacked the power of senior and elite men, for they saw them as impediments to the conversion of the young. Their preoccupation with the alleged hypersexuality of "deviant" African customs, such as polygyny, was partially an attack on the extended family as a barrier to the individuality that assisted them with conversions. Similarly, they attacked the institutions that represented elite masculinity: the prestigious title societies, especially the Ozo.[33] (The Ozo society was a male association to which members paid an increasing scale of fees to rise through its ranks. They were an exalted group, with privileges and a sacred aura that protected them from

---

[31] Uchendu, *The Igbo*, 51.

[32] While the letters in the Enugu Archives were not from the local area there is some evidence – in the number of adultery cases – that a similar process occurred. See a collection of these letters in file 1810, Ikotdist 13/1/533, NAN, Enugu.

[33] Ifi Amadiume, *Male Daughters and Female Husbands: Gender and Sex in an African Society* (London: Zed Press, 1987), 44.

the dangers of the period.) Missionaries used education to promote an alternative "respectable" Christian masculinity, rooted in the ideology of female domesticity, the male breadwinner, companiate marriage, independence, hard work, and self-control.[34]

Despite these attacks, the second type of masculinity, based on elite status, proved especially resilient to western intervention and was accessible to young men who earned wages. The public symbol of elite masculinity was the Igbo "big man" (*ogaranyan*), a status that originated among the wealthy merchants whose origins were rooted in the centuries of slave and palm trades. These men headed a "big compound," an expansive polygamous household of many wives, children, clients, and slaves.[35]

In the twentieth century some of these wealthy men shifted from slave dealing into labor recruitment, trading, and real estate.[36] In fact, several of them, especially Chief Chukwuani of Nkanu, benefited from the increased urban population of the war and built houses in "Coal Town," the former labor camp of the city. In Igboland these "Big Men" constituted a merchant capitalist class who expressed their wealth in typically conspicuous ways. They had special ritual prestige, danced exclusive dances, were buried with exorbitant ceremony and expense, and dressed in conspicuously symbolic ways.[37] Often they incorporated foreign clothing to signify their familiarity with the exotic culture of the "modern" world. Import restrictions during the war had a stifling impact on elite male display; however, they retained their title societies, in which the payment of an escalating level of fees elevated a man to higher rungs of status and power.

The Ogaranyan's leadership of large households of many wives, children, and free and unfree dependents gave them power in village council deliberations over the important allocation of communal lands that augmented their economic power.[38] By appropriating family labor-power, an elite man was entitled to large farmland allotments and could produce surpluses for sale in Enugu and to the West Africa Frontier Force (WAFF) soldiers housed in barracks outside Enugu. For these reasons the acquisition of an Ozo title was a compelling desire for many miners and figured into their calculation of the appropriate value of their remuneration. Regular wages opened this possibility to young aspirants who, in imitating this model, transformed it

---

[34] For a discussion of marriage, see Kristin Mann, *Marrying Well: Marriage, Status and Social Change among the Educated Elite in Colonial Lagos* (Cambridge and New York: Cambridge University Press, 1985).

[35] See C. Brown, *We Were All Slaves*, 69–76.

[36] Since internal slave trading continued into the twentieth century, there was at least one local *ogaranyan*, Chief Onyeama, who began as a slave trader in the nineteenth century. He committed suicide in the 1930s, when it appeared he would be arrested for the murder of a woman. See Dillibe Onyeama, *Chief Onyeama: The Story of an African God* (Enugu, Nigeria: Delta Publishers 1982), 121.

[37] Amadiume, *Male Daughters and Female Husbands*, 31.

[38] Uchendu, *The Igbo of Southeast Nigeria*, 51.

into a symbol of modernity linked with wage labor. Coal mining allowed one miner, Samuel Onoh, to incorporate both "traditional" and "modern" symbols of male prestige. He noted:

> The development of [the] coal industry did a lot to my village. But for coal industry civilization would have not reached us as early as it had reached us. The coal industry initiated me into Ozo title. Now I am Ozo Samuel N. Onoh. I was able to train up my children, build good houses. We contributed money and build schools and churches.[39]

By World War II, coal mining had been fully integrated into the social strategies of local men, most especially the Agbaja, as they advanced into senior manhood amidst the economic crisis of the war. This was the complexity of masculinity and causes of intergenerational conflict in the Nkanu and Agbaja regions during the war. The mine workforce, which reached a high of 7,000 during the war, retained its presence in village political and social life and became an important avenue for urban ideas to reach the rural village. Within Enugu, coal miners held pride of place as the men who made it possible for the city to function as an important part of the Nigerian wartime economy.

In these ways this generation of young men challenged older forms of senior rural masculinity. These were the men who worked in colonial mines, on the railways, on the docks, and in construction. They understood the complexities of the colonial economy and the war further underscored their importance in the colony and to the very survival of the metropolitan state. These were the men who would prove most challenging to the colonial state, for their coalition with nationalist politicians would clarify the untenable nature of British rule. As industrial workers, their location in the imperial political economy strengthened their consciousness and ability to act in their interests.

The War Crisis and Colonial Policy Initiatives

Until shaken by the West Indies riots, the Colonial Office was unable to escape their assumptions about the inherent "backwardness" of African labor. These assumptions were undermined when colonial workers elsewhere began to *act like* industrial workers. In 1934–1935 and 1937–1938, thousands of workers in Britain's Caribbean colonies and the Zambian Copperbelt launched strikes that focused on industrial concerns, and expanded into critiques of colonial rule. All these protests spilled into the streets where colonial workers were joined by the unpredictable masses of urban poor.

---

[39] Onoh began work in 1915 as a "tub boy" and worked up through the ranks until he became an underground foreman after World War II. Interview with Samuel Onoh, Ngwo Etiti, August 9, 1974.

The strikes quickly evolved into popular insurrections that shook the very foundations of colonial order.[40] Having weathered this experience before the war, the Colonial Office reexamined their policies about the best ways of controlling colonial labor. The result was a period of reform that pushed colonial governments into new ways of responding to the social and economic dimensions of African labor. This process was barely underway when war was declared.

The war accelerated the socioeconomic crises that were rooted in the Depression, calling into question whether local colonial authorities could control, let alone recognize, the threat this posed to the war effort. Rapid urbanization, severe inflation, and food and housing shortages deepened the horrible conditions of most urban dwellers. Enugu's two eyesore areas and expansive slums – Ogui Overside and Abakpa – grew exponentially, as the city's population increased to about 40,000.[41] Nor was it clear that authorities could keep "economic" conflicts such as strikes from feeding into political movements. The Nigerian state and the Colonial Office reconceptualized colonial labor within an existing context of improved social welfare, increased worker productivity, and controlled systems of representation. The Colonial Office embarked upon a multipronged process of preemptive reform, which, for the first time, acknowledged that there was, indeed, a nascent colonial working class. Elements of the process appeared in Enugu, most notably in the form of the state apparatus to monitor the social welfare of the workers and the regulation of the interminable labor conflicts. In London structural changes in the Colonial Office produced a more professional labor policy that recognized that it could not leave labor issues to myopic colonial administrators who were unaware of the more sophisticated systems of control. The Colonial Office Labor Committee, a group of officials with an interest in "native" labor, had included, since 1938, Major Granville Orde-Browne, a labor officer in East Africa, who became the first official labor adviser.[42] In 1942 the Committee was restructured to include, for the first time, the British Trades Union Congress (TUC) and was renamed the

---

[40] Peter Weiler, "Forming responsible trade unions: The Colonial Office, colonial labor and the Trades Union Congress," *Radical History Review*, 28–30 (1984), 367–92.

[41] It wasn't until after the war that these areas were brought under the jurisdiction of the Local Authority, "Enugu township: Annual report January–August 1948," file 1865, vol. XI [Annual Reports], Onprof 8/1/14906, NAN, Enugu.

[42] Orde Browne's visit in 1940 corroborated the Colonial Office's worst suspicions. Management neglect, poor labor practices, deplorable underground conditions, the lack of a labor consultative system, and few amenities (e.g., housing, medical care) led to the disruptions. His report became the foundation for reforms begun during the war. He represented a "progressive" and "enlightened" direction in labor policy and he suggested some system of worker representation; however, he considered the miners "too primitive and uneducated" to be trusted to form trade unions. See Major Granville St. G. Orde-Browne, *Labour Conditions in West Africa*, Cmd. 6277 (London: HMSO, 1941).

Colonial Labor Advisory Committee. The inclusion of TUC members, formerly rejected by the members of the committee, represented a co-optation and they accepted the position of partners to promote "responsible" trade union activity in the colonies.[43] Thus the TUC and overseas employers' federations collaborated to supervise and formulate labor policy throughout the empire.[44]

In West Africa, the Colonial Office created the post of resident West African commissioner to coordinate all wartime policies in the region. Additionally for the first time, officials from Britain's four colonies (i.e., Sierra Leone, Nigeria, the Gold Coast, and Gambia) met to synchronize labor policy through a series of West African Labor Conferences. They designed strategies to contain worker protest, set production targets, and developed economic policies to facilitate the deployment of colonial resources, both human and material, to the war effort. Escalating prices of essential goods led to largely unsuccessful experiments with controlled market schemes, which were ineffective and only succeeded in mobilizing market women against the state.[45] Farmers who supplied Enugu proved effective in evading all the restrictions to control food prices, and controlled articles usually disappeared to appear later in the black market.[46]

The Colonial Office recognized that African workers could not survive with fixed wages and rampant inflation and proposed a series of reforms that replicated, in colonially modified form, those industrial strategies Great Britain developed to contain Britain's own restive working class. The key challenge was to get colonial governments to implement the most "modern" forms of labor regulation and industrial relations practices, which required the legalization of trade unions.[47] Although proposed as institutions of state-initiated labor management, the Colonial Office had difficulty convincing

---

[43] For an attack from the left, see Jack Woodis, *The Mask is Off! An Examination of the Activities of Trade Union Advisers in the British Colonies* (Ilford: Thames Publications, 1954).

[44] Documentation regarding colonial labor policy is located in file series CO 323/1117, CO 888/1 and CO 888/2–11, TNA, Kew.

[45] Market women were angered by conditional sales, in which they were required to sell slow-moving goods with more desirable products. During the war, the government initiated the Pullen Marketing Scheme in which the state attempted to restrict price gouging by setting price ceilings, distributing consumer items to market women, and prohibiting high profits. See Wale Oyemakinde, "The Pullen marketing scheme: A trial in food price control in Nigeria 1941–47," *Journal of the Historical Society of Nigeria*, 6 (1973), 413–23.

[46] Annual report for Udi District, 1943, UDDIST 1942, NAN, Enugu.

[47] Manpower shortages during the war made it difficult to deploy experienced trade unionists to teach colonial workers the "correct" way to organize and lead trade unions. The realization, however, that without such "tutelage" unions might become vehicles for class radicalization, led the Colonial Office to suspend its distrust of the British TUC and bring them into the Colonial Labor Advisory Committee. Weiler, "Forming responsible trade unions," 372.

local administrators that these institutions and industrial procedures, could, in effect, be quite useful to the state. Unions were part of a broader process to make industrial conflict more predictable and less militant, but local administrators saw them as concessions to militant worker action.

But war conditions were severe and demonstrated the need for some type of worker representation. In Enugu a reluctant colliery management acceded to the Colonial Office demand that it establish the coal industry's first trade unions. In 1939 the Colonial Office had pushed colonial governments to create unions as "the surest means of securing industrial stability and the removal of extremist tendencies."[48] But African unions were never given the full equality of their sister institutions in Britain, especially in times of economic duress, such as the war. African unions had compulsory registration, which could be revoked at will, and were forced to give the state access to their financial and other records. Despite these restrictions workers throughout Nigeria formed unions and immediately pressed their grievances to keep pace with inflation that had reached 200 percent in cities such as Lagos. In Enugu, unions were launched by the most hated men, the "Boss Boys" or "native" managers, who were the eyes and ears of management and the rural political elite. One was the Colliery Surface Improvement Union (CSIU) and the other was the underground Colliery Workers Union. Neither was initially popular with the workers. Not until 1943, when Isaiah Ojiyi, the militant unionist, became the general secretary, did the CWU garner support from the several thousand underground workers.[49] With unions as established representatives of workers, the Colonial Office felt that it could filter pent-up grievances through a cumbersome system of collective bargaining and postpone eruptions and work stoppages. It did not quite work this way.

The growing population of Enugu led officials to raise questions about the mine's system of daily labor deployment, which kept hundreds of surplus workers on the books, and consequently, in the city where they were engaged daily on the spot. In 1938 rather than terminate redundant workers, the industry began a system of shared jobs, in which the mines employed workers far in excess of requirements but allowed them to share jobs. With so many redundant workers sharing work few men were able to work more than eleven days a month, earning far too little to meet wartime inflation.[50]

[48] Great Britain, *West India Royal Commission Report*, Cmd. 6608 (London: HMSO, 1945); Weiler, "Forming responsible trade unions," 372.

[49] For a discussion of the turbulent period of Ojiyi's tenure, see Brown, "*We Were All Slaves*," chapter 6.

[50] The system was called "rostering" after the daily list or roster of workers posted to work each day. This allowed management to have, at hand, a stable "pool" of eligible workers who could be employed depending on the daily requirements. The system was rife with corruption, with many timekeepers, those controlling the list, demanding bribes to put a worker on the list. The war did help, however, because the expansion of the workforce

As far as the colonial administration was concerned, these workers filled the dangerous slums, immersed in the culture of the "dangerous" classes, the "lumpenproletariat" of thieves, prostitutes, gamblers, and "ne'er-do-wells." Officials realized that they needed to segregate the "committed" workers, who were both indispensable to the economy and habituated to the industrial habits of a "proper" working class, from the group of casual workers, lest they encourage the type of broad-based coalitions that threatened political order. This policy neglected conditions for the vast majority but offered meager amenities to skilled workers deemed more "responsible" and essential. Many employers preferred "casual" workers hired on a daily basis, which gave them flexibility in deploying and firing workers at will; but this group posed a political problem for the state.[51] By granting differential privileges to the essential workers and applying an elaborate grading system, officials hoped to prevent the type of huge, political general strikes that shook the West Indies and Zambian Copperbelt. This required some modifications of the color bar, a new initiative that frightened expatriate workers who had come to the colony to enjoy special privileges. Now the state proposed admitting some Africans to the senior service as part of a broader Africanization in response to nationalist demands for more equality. In 1943, the mines began "Africanization," training a small number of men to fill posts formerly held by Europeans. It was in this context that Ojiyi entered the Junior Technical Service, a specialized training program to put Africans into the "pipeline" for supervisory positions. Although aimed at creating collaborative African managers, it often had the opposite effect of training men on the intricacies of labor law who often went into the forefront of the labor movement.[52]

The Colonial Office recognized that, in wartime, disputes were inevitable, but they felt that the first challenge was to determine which conflicts were politically motivated and which were economic/industrial. This would then allow political disputes to be handled by government officials and industrial by labor experts. The problem, however, was how to make this distinction in an economy in which most workers were state employees and were accustomed to politicizing their protests and negotiating with the state. But the Colonial Office felt that there was a "correct way" to handle labor disputes and an "incorrect way." The "correct" way was to acknowledge that workers had grievances, recognize a system of labor representation,

---

helped to absorb many of the superfluous workers. For a discussion of this, see Brown, "We Were All Slaves," 218, 242–43.

[51] For a discussion of the use of casual labor in dock works, see Frederick Cooper, On the African Waterfront: Urban Disorder and the Transformation of Work in Colonial Mombasa (New Haven, CT: Yale University Press, 1987).

[52] For examples, see petitions submitted to Orde Browne on his visit to Enugu, located in NIGCOAL 2/1/126 [Boss Boys – Colliery], NAN, Enugu.

and prevent those grievances from seriously jeopardizing the production process. To mediate conflicts and delay strikes, the colonial administration introduced trades' disputes machinery with mandatory arbitration, conciliation, and the adoption of a series of industrial relations bodies imported from England.[53] However, these bodies could work in England but Nigeria lacked the sociopolitical preconditions for collective bargaining to succeed. Neither employers nor the state *recognized* African men as "true" employees who could sit across the table from them in collective bargaining sessions *as equals*. Few colonial governors, officials, or employers were prepared to make this assumption so rooted in the racialized ideologies about African working men and society.[54]

Predictably, the entire structure of labor reform unfolded against the backdrop of coercion and authoritarianism and threatened violence. Even Colonial Office reformers were not prepared to treat African workers as the equals of British workers. Policies that appeared on the surface to replicate those of the metropole were, upon closer inspection, stifled by the brutal realities of colonial rule. African trade union legislation had compulsory registration, a prerequisite for the binding nature of collective agreements. When the state revoked registration, all agreements between employees and the then "illegal union" were abrogated. Additionally, in 1942 the draconian arm of the state came out and introduced the Essential Works Orders, which restricted the right to strike of all workers in industries deemed "essential" for the war effort. Although this law resembled its counterpart in England, in the colonies the definition of "essential" industry was so liberally applied that it included virtually the majority of the small working class. Thus, the Nigerian working class was so small and located in such narrow areas of the economy, with a large percentage being state employees, that the law effectively eliminated the possibility of strike for the majority of workers. Militant trade unions leaders, such as Michael Imoudu[55] of the powerful Railway Workers' Union, were imprisoned for violating vague restrictions evoked by the colonial government. Thus, labor reforms actually stimulated the very unrest that officials sought to prevent.[56]

---

[53] As part of the standardization process in operation during the war the Colonial Office used a set model of trades disputes law and sent it throughout the colonies. The most popular model was the Trinidad Trades Disputes Law which was drafted with the help of Sir Granville Orde Browne by the Colonial Labor Committee.

[54] An excellent example of this problem is captured in fiction in Ousmane Sembène's *God's Bits of Wood* (1960) when Dejeune, the railway administrator, slapped Bakayoko in the midst of a negotiation session, considering him to be an arrogant "native."

[55] Robin Cohen, "Nigeria's Labour Leader No. 1: Notes for a Biographical Study of M.A.O. Imoudu," *Journal of the Historical Society of Nigeria*, 5,2 (1970), 303–8.

[56] Carolyn A. Brown, "Race and the construction of working-class masculinity in the Nigerian coal industry: The initial phase, 1914–1930," *International Labor and Working Class History*, 69 (2006), 35–56.

It was no coincidence that workers chose educated men to be union leaders. The complexity of trade union laws and systems of disputes management led workers to select leaders who were educated or had been trained for managerial positions in the industry. These were the same types of men who were both frustrated with the meager political reforms being proposed by wartime Nigerian government and, given their training, well positioned to manipulate the legislation. Most, like Ojiyi, a former school teacher, were charismatic leaders, especially eager to challenge the humiliating racial practices in the work place. They recognized that these practices were a powerful motivator for labor agitation and they used a discourse of "masculine honor denied" in their petitions, speeches, and demands. How can an honorable man fulfill his role in his household, workplace, and community when he is slapped around in the workplace? When he is repeatedly called "boy"? When he cannot exercise political power?[57] These questions were raised many times over by nationalist figures and they resonated with the workplace experiences of workers.

Finally, both nationalist politicians and trade union leaders refused to accept the Colonial Office distinction between "industrial" and "political" disputes. This was especially clear in Enugu, where industrial workers and government clerks created a hotbed of political activism fed by the vibrant nationalist press of Nnamdi Azikiwe. As an administrative center Enugu had a "'new middle class' of government employees and men of initiative in the professional, business and service fields, drawn from all parts of the region, settled in the burgeoning city."[58] These men were outraged by the disparity between their wages and conditions of service and that of their white co-workers. They supported the radical nationalist press and financed political movements. They had formed village improvement unions that provided a space for interchange with the city's two important groups of industrial workers – the miners and Nigerian Railway employees. The proximity of a large, discontented population to the commercial and administration agencies in Enugu created an explosive formula that had already proven disruptive in the British Caribbean. In February 1939 before the beginning of the war officials noted the political sophistication of the miners:

> I have some fears. The miners are very agitated and under influential leadership. We must not assume that they are docile and [un]willing to take risks which might result in unemployment for a prolonged period. While a sense of determination is not widespread, the fact remains that enough of them are

---

[57] John Iliffe is one of the few historians to recognize the role of honor and humiliation in shaping African men's behavior; see *Honour in African History*.

[58] Richard Sklar, *Nigerian Political Parties* (Princeton, NJ: Princeton University Press, 1963), 208.

prepared to go on strike. It must be recognized that *as miners* [author's emphasis] they have developed an aggressive turn of mind which some of them are able to convert in to political protest. The days seemed to have passed when we can assume that fair but firm negotiations with the natives will produce honourable results. I see no way of avoiding the observation that these men are far from politically naive.[59]

African Worker Protest during World War II

In addition to the economic hardship noted earlier, imperial fiscal policy retained sterling and dollar reserves earned from these exports in England to finance the war effort.[60] These policies, in addition to failed price controls, import shortages, meager wages and high inflation rates had drastic implications for the standards of living of colonial workers.

By 1942 West African workers struggled to sustain their families while rural communities faced famine. Economic conditions deteriorated between 1942 and 1943, causing inflation rates of 200 percent in Lagos, and the cities exploded with rural immigrants unable to survive the price restrictions, on the one hand, and purchasing combines, on the other.[61] The Nigerian working class was the largest and most militant in British West Africa and it was they who led the most threatening protests. By 1942, they had responded rapidly to union legalization by establishing dozens of unions. National agitation began in Lagos and emanated outward to the major urban centers. Enugu and Port Harcourt, the two industrial cities of coal miners and railway workers in southeastern Nigeria, usually reflected Lagos protests. Between 1941 and 1943, the unions challenged fiscal policies that restricted imports, fixed depressed prices of agroexports, created food shortages, and froze wages. The state responded aggressively with legislation that circumscribed workers' rights to strike, persecuted workers' leaders, and burdened trade union functioning. These laws, collectively known as the Nigerian Defense Regulations, rapidly provoked resistance by the most organized sectors of the nation's working class. Restricted in their rights to strike, railway workers and government employees nonetheless engaged in several

---

[59] District Commissioner, Enugu to Provincial Commissioner, February 21,1939, Nigerian Archives, Enugu 314/39/PE476, as quoted in P. Gutkind, "The emergent African urban proletariat," Center for Developing-Area Studies, Occasional Paper Series, No. 8, (Montreal: McGill University, 1974), 32.

[60] Michael Cowen and Nicholas Westcott, "British imperial economic policy during the war," in David Killingray and Richard Rathbone (eds.), *Africa and the Second World War* (London: MacMillan, 1986), 20–21.

[61] In 1942 The Combined Food Board established group purchasing agreements. Through this the major purchasing firms had privileged access to colonial crops. The farmers, on the other hand, were unable to bargain with buyers for the best price.

agitations between 1941 and 1943, which led the government to form commissions and grant wage increases. But the most serious protest followed the war. From June 22 to August 6, 1945, the Lagos unions launched a general strike that brought the economy to its knees and succeeded in securing wage increases. The political power of this industrial action implicitly defeated Britain's attempt to depoliticize trade unions.[62] One of the striking features of workers' protest during the war was the frequency with which accusations of racial discrimination and unequal treatment were mentioned in petitions and demands. Racial discrimination became an important issue underlining the inherent undemocratic nature of imperial rule, which the state sought to eliminate.[63] In the colonial workplace, white bosses were under increased pressure to end the abusive forms of colonial discipline as workers challenged racist traditions. As shown in the incident between Ojiyi and Yates, noted earlier, the more the workers tested the new reality, the more white bosses assaulted workers. British bosses found it very difficult to adjust to the changing racial reality and their outbursts were the last expressions of a dying racial work culture incompatible with the realities of the war.

The mines were fundamentally a "colonial workplace" in which racism was "the organizing principle" of power within the labor process. As is often the case with racial or class hierarchies the subordination of men was represented as weakness or effeminacy.[64] Thus European bosses considered African miners to be immature and irresponsible "boys" who had to be brutalized to ensure that they performed their jobs. This created a discourse of infantalization reflected in the job titles: pick boys (hewers) undercut coal and loaded the tubs, tub boys hooked the tubs to the central haulage system in the main roads, rail boys laid tracks, and timber boys reinforced the roof with timber. A retired tub man angrily recalled these offensive forms of address: "Then all African workers were titled boy.... Everything, boy, boy! Only the Europeans were called overman and foreman."[65] Further, racism was expressed in a series of rituals in the mines. One especially offensive ritual was the "hammock tradition" which continued during World War II. Workers were forced to transport expatriate underground foremen and overmen to work in hammocks. A second racialized ritual was the extensive use of corporeal punishment and degrading racial epithets to intimidate

---

[62] For the 1945 general strike, see L. Lindsay, "Domesticity and Difference"; see also Weiler, "Forming responsible trade unions."

[63] When colonial subjects failed to protect Singapore and Malaysia during the Japanese invasion, Margery Perham argued that the policies of racial discrimination were responsible for the failure of the "subjects" to identify with the British. See Rosaleen Smyth, "Britain's African colonies and British propaganda during the Second World War," *Journal of Imperial and Commonwealth History*, 14 (1985), 65–82.

[64] Andrea Cornwall and Nancy Lindsfarne, *Dislocating Masculinity: Comparative Ethnographies* (London: Routledge, 1994), 20.

[65] Interview with Eze Ozogwu, Amankwo-Ngwo, June 2, 1975.

workers.[66] A third was management's neglect of dangerous and unhealthy underground conditions, which were considered "appropriate" for African workers, most of whom worked barefoot, wearing only a loincloth, and sustained numerous injuries. Poor ventilation standards reflected racist stereotypes about African tolerance of heat and humidity, which caused oxygen deficiency.[67] Humidity levels of 80 percent to 100 percent saturation and temperatures of 85 to 90 degrees Fahrenheit degrees were common and debilitating.

But workers developed ways of mediating these conditions. Despite the deprecating way that management referred to colliery miners, the work nonetheless encouraged a strong masculine identity and pride. The skills required, the danger involved, and the crucial role played by their coal in the political economy of Nigeria led miners to understand their power in the economy in gendered ways. For male manual workers, the possession of mining skills and "the aggressive celebration of physical strength" were key contributing factors to the masculine ethos that developed in coal mining. Historically in Europe hewers ("pit men")[68] had a self-identity as skilled workers and were proud, independent, self-improving men who were resentful of supervision. In Britain, these values defined a social hierarchy within mining communities that coincided with the ranking in production. Similarly, these same work conditions fostered a proud occupational identity among hewers in Enugu, an identity that defied humiliating racial names.

The nationalist discourse about race, the global dimensions of the war, and the shared hardship of metropolitan and colonial workers encouraged African workers to compare their sacrifices and conditions of service with those of expatriate civil servants in the colonies and with coal workers in Europe and America. Implicit in their comparison was the rejection of the notion, fundamental to colonialism, that they were not equal to or deserving of the treatment, privileges, and pay of Europeans. This was one of the myths that collapsed when the colonies rescued Britain during the war. The nationalist press publicized instances of discriminatory treatment that helped

[66] Iliffe, "Urbanisation and masculinity," *Honour in African History*, 281–305, especially 291.
[67] For a "scientific" study based on the alleged "heat tolerance" of West African miners, see W. S. S. Ladell, "Some physiological observations on West African coal miners," *British Journal of Industrial Medicine*, 5 (1948), 16–20. See also, Powell Duffryn Technical Services, *First report to the under-secretary of state for the colonies, Colonial Office, Dover House, Whitehall, S. W.1, on the Government Colliery, Enugu: The characteristics of the coal produced and the investigation into the other coal and lignite resources* (London, mimeograph, 1948), section D, part IV, "Ventilation," D66–D67.
[68] Robert Colls explains the distinction between "pit man" and "collier." "The word 'pit man' carried with it meanings of social bearing; other men were 'colliers' compared to 'pit men', and others again were labourers compared to colliers." *The Pitmen of the Northern Coalfield: Work, Culture and Protest 1790–1850* (Manchester: Manchester University Press, 1987), 12.

to shape their discourse of antidiscrimination. Nnamdi Azikiwe, national-ist politician and the owner of the Zik Group of nationalist papers, was especially receptive to publicizing these racial infractions because of his own experiences with racism during his student days in the United States.[69] Yet, despite the nationalist campaigns in May 1942, the government nonetheless continued discriminatory practices and increased "separation allowances" to expatriate men whose wives were not in Nigeria, followed by additional increments in November 1943 for other dependents.[70] African men whose wives lived in another colony or another area of Nigeria had no such relief. Thus, while implicitly recognizing the financial responsibilities of white men to their families, officials ignored those of African working men who were barely able to meet their individual, let alone family, obligations. Incredu-lously in October 1942, Governor Bernard Bourdillon, oblivious of workers' attention to discriminatory work conditions, naively reported to the West African War Council that he doubted that these increases would incite "the more highly paid African grades who did not receive this allowance at present."[71] He was wrong. Within weeks the CWU had raised the issue as an example of the discriminatory nature of colonial labor policies.

Enugu miners also used the conditions of British and American coal min-ers to determine their own complaints about treatment and wages.[72] Under Ojiyi's leadership the CWU demanded improved conditions and wages. These claims were especially salient when, in 1943, Enugu miners were called upon to supply the Allies' West African railways made vulnerable by the crisis in the British coal industry.[73] Ojiyi also argued that their mea-ger wages made it possible for his men to live and work with dignity. The struggles he waged to articulate and secure the demands of his workers were difficult and protracted as the government erected one barrier after another to block the effectiveness of the union. Finally in late 1943, the government withdrew the union's registration and decided to recognize village elders rather than the union, as representatives of the workers. The workers were insulted by this rejection of their union and the "modern" institutions of representation. Local elders, they felt, were too "backward" to understand

---

[69] Nnamdi Azikiwe, _My Odyssey_ (London: C. Hurst, 1970).

[70] Robin Cohen, _Labour and Politics in Nigeria_ (New York: Africana Publishing Corporation, 1974) 159; Wogu Ananaba, _The Trade Union Movement in Nigeria_ (New York: Africana Publishing Corporation, 1969), 47–48.

[71] Secretary of state for the colonies to O. A. G. Nigeria, July 10, 1942; and extract of minutes of the West African War Council (47), October 17, 1942, CO. 554/129, TNA, Kew.

[72] In at least one case, a protest referenced the conditions of U.S. miners who struck during the war for an underground allowance. Throughout the war most of Britain's coal workforce was on strike, leading eventually to the use of _forced labor_ in the mines themselves. Barry Supple, _The History of the British Coal Industry_, Vol. 4: _1913–1946: The Political Economy of Decline_ (Oxford: Clarendon Press, 1987), 558.

[73] Ibid.

the nature of their job and to represent them in discussions with management and they campaigned to restore their union and its leadership.

Ojiyi was the type of leader who illiterate workers selected to interpret the complicated disputes and industrial systems of colonial industries. He was educated, able to understand the complex laws and regulations, and sufficiently bold to challenge racial and wage discrimination, whatever the personal cost. The incident with Yates was but an indication of his daring to confront powerful white bosses who abused him. As noted earlier, he became a hero when he won the court case.[74] The men became more conscious of the colliery's discriminatory practices when they heard a "wireless" report that the American miners, like the colliery British staff, had been awarded underground allowances.[75] Discriminatory wages and racist practices contrasted significantly with the prestigious position the men held in their rural villages. But the economic crisis of the war threatened their role as modernizers in their village and as patriarchs in their homes. The self identity of Enugu coal miners was very dependant upon the progressive role that they played in improving their communities. Thus wages squeezed by inflation hindered their ability to fund village "development" projects and to continue the extraordinary sacrifices they made to build schools, educate their children, and improve health care in their villages. They were preparing for a future of political independence; however, to build this future, they had to struggle for the income to invest in its foundation. These types of expenditures were never included in any of the government assessments of the "cost of living" but they "implicitly challenged British assumptions that Africans were incapable of conceptualizing, let alone executing, their own model of development."[76] Although authorities saw that the workers were putting a tremendous amount of energy into "improvement" – both self and community – they felt that only the colonial government had a coherent plan for the future.

These projects and the ways in which industrial workers behaved in the villages and cities of West Africa indicated changes in the ways that manhood was being constructed during the war. The complexities of this construction – borrowing foreign models and melding them with indigenous rural models – demonstrates the importance of considering how changes in gender norms are reflected in the protests of working men. Often, their perceptions of what constituted a "just wage" or "just treatment" were not only developed through workplace experiences but through the way

[74] Mr. Yates to colliery manager, August 21, 1945, NCF P.2/1/1, NAN, Enugu.
[75] O. A. G. Grantham to colonial secretary, November 30, 1943, CO 583/261/30425, TNA, Kew.
[76] Fred Cooper notes that even the Labour Party could not conceive of African society being able to generate its own plan for the future. Cooper, *Decolonization and African Society*, 176–77.

that they, *as men*, saw themselves participating in the broader society. Lisa Lindsay identifies the role of played by these new gender constructions in the behavior of Lagos railway workers during the 1945 Nigerian general strike.[77] While astutely using the male breadwinner norm to articulate a discourse demanding family wages, these men reshaped this concept to match the realities of their own households, where there was more reciprocity in the contributions of both husband and wife to the household income. Because of the differences between European and African marital systems some of the most difficult struggles between labor and employer, both during and after the war, focused on the nature of the African family.

One grievance in the 1947–1948 French West African railway workers strike, immortalized by Sembène's *God's Bits of Wood*, was the definition of the African family. Were women in polygynous families actually wives or were these women concubines? In Enugu the nature of the African family created a conflict over the occupancy rates in a new workers' housing project developed as part of the strategy to segment the labor force. The core issue of the conflict was the size and composition of the African household. Salaries allowed government workers to reproduce a family model reflective of elite rural masculinity in their urban households. We have noted how wealthy men for many centuries had replicated the model of elite masculinity. They created the "big compound," a household of many wives, children, and dependents. While wages permitted some coal miners to fulfill this ideal, it clashed with British ideas of suitable occupancy rates. Officials argued that only three and a half people were allowed per room in the largest camp, Garden City. These projects were designed to regulate the home life of a sector of the work force and conditioned their residency on allowing interventions of social workers and medical officers into their home lives. Predictably, this would become a flashpoint of conflict between workers and the state. At a meeting with the senior resident and acting manager, the workers complained that under these occupancy limits residents would have to leave part of their family "behind or throw them away."[78]

The men resisted the most invasive aspects of the project. Those with polygynous families insisted on adequate housing for their families and servants as well. The union organized a boycott of the estates and fined people who agreed to occupy them. When only one hundred people consented to live in the houses, the Colonial Secretary complained: "no one had apparently attempted to find out the sort of accommodation which, while satisfactory from the health point of view, would be acceptable to the Africans."[79] It was one thing to design the physical space that workers and their families

---

[77] Lindsay, *Working with Gender*.
[78] "Enugu colliery workers and the new housing scheme," UDDIST 3/1/104, NAN, Enugu.
[79] "Notes on points arising in discussions with the secretary of state on Wednesday, 27 October and Thursday, 28 October 1943," CO 583/261/30425, TNA, Kew.

occupied. It was quite another to make them occupy them according to the abstract standards developed by remote colonial labor experts.

Conclusion

By World War II, the Enugu coal miners were among the most militant members of the Nigerian working class. This chapter has used their words and collective action to reveal a preoccupation with their stature as men, a stature that, while challenged by racism in the work place, was reinforced by the prominent role these men played in the village and the city and by the inherent skill and bravery required for their underground work. Mining has a masculinized work culture whose risk and danger contribute to an "oppositional work culture" that challenges authority and encourages a solidarity that, in the case of Enugu, propelled the colliery workers into the concerns of the Colonial Office.[80] By using race and gender, specifically masculinity, as prisms to analyze the issues that generated resistance and worker protest during World War II we have moved beyond the technocratic calculations officials used to determine a living wage, calculations that failed to satisfy workers during and immediately after the war. By focusing on a limited but crucial period in the industry's history, we can access the importance of affronts to personal identity and status in generating collective action during the war. Workers were sensitized to issues of race by the treatment they endured in the racialized work place. These ideas were further reinforced by the public discourse fueled by the nationalist press, which framed discussions of national integrity in a gendered idiom.

Men could not be men if they could not govern their own affairs, if they could not gain respect at work, and if they could not create, through marriage, their own households. Working class masculinity was new in Enugu and it was introduced by the opening of the mines during World War I. Now, during World War II, this identity had become an important expression of the tensions between "modernity" and "traditionalism," a dichotomy with generational dimensions. By launching protests to reinforce their role as "providers," they appropriated the discourse of the "male breadwinner norm," even though the women in their households hardly conformed to the model of domesticity promoted through this model. The narrative of the Enugu coal miners' wartime protests suggests that a deeper analysis of the nature and demands of worker protests could reveal important changes in the ways that gender is being transformed by the socioeconomic turmoil of the war. This focus would also enable us to determine the interesting new ways in which power is consolidated and expressed in late colonial

---

[80] Paul M. Klubock, *Contested Communities: Class, Gender, and Politics in Chile's El Teniente Copper Mine, 1904–1951* (Durham, NC: Duke University Press, 1998), 138, 151–53.

Carolyn A. Brown

Africa. The war provided a crucial conjuncture in the development of working men's consciousness of themselves and their role both in the empire and in their own communities. After the war these new lessons would become clear in the rash of general strikes in Nigeria, Zanzibar, and elsewhere and at the colliery, in the tragic shooting of Enugu's coal miners in 1949.[81]

---

[81] Carolyn A. Brown, "The Iva Valley shooting at Enugu Colliery, Nigeria: African workers' aspirations and the failure of colonial labor reform," in Toyin Falola and Salah M. Hassan (eds.), *Power and Nationalism in Modern Africa* (Durham, NC: Carolina Academic Press, 2008), 187–212.

16

"A White Man's War"

Settler Masculinity in the Union Defense Force, 1939–1945

Suryakanthie Chetty

In December 1940 and January 1941, respectively, two recruiting posters appeared in the South African magazine *Libertas*, both carrying the slogan "Join the Springbok Army of Sportsmen." The name, "Springbok Army of Sportsmen," carried a clear association of the link between war, sport, and nationalism; it also created a particular kind of white masculine identity. This chapter focuses on the construction of white masculine identity in the Union Defence Force (UDF) during the Second World War as soldiers enlisted, underwent training, and were sent to the various fields of combat. This study uses a variety of sources – visual images, oral interviews, written memoirs, and archival sources. These sources complement each other and allow a multiplicity of voices and experiences of the Second World War. These voices represent different facets of South African society, signifying ideas and ideologies of wartime experience that may have been in harmony at various points and contradictory in others, but are necessary for a coherent understanding of South African identity at this key historical juncture.

Enlistment

The outbreak of war on September 3, 1939, had a mixed reception in the South African parliament. Prime Minister James Barry Munnik Hertzog desired neutrality, believing that joining the war on the side of the Allies would divide the country, suggesting that some South Africans had greater loyalty for Britain, which would ultimately "destroy South African unity." In contrast, Jan Christiaan Smuts, who became prime minister two days later, supported Britain, arguing that if Hitler turned his attention to regaining South West Africa, he would present a real threat to South Africa, which could only be countered with Allied backing.[1] Ultimately it was the Smuts'

[1] W. K. Hancock, *Smuts*: Vol. 2: *The Fields of Force, 1919–1950* (Cambridge: Cambridge University Press, 1968), 322.

Sluit aan by die Springbok-leër van Sportmanne

Jy moet dapper wees om 'n jagluiperd mak te kan maak, maar dis alles
deel van die veldtog in die Noorde. Vir die Suid-Afrikaanse soldaat is dit sommer 'n brekfis.

Daar is 'n plek vir u in die Leër van Sportmanne

| South African airmen of a bomber squadron with their mascots—two baby cheetahs. | Suid-Afrikaanse vliegeniers van 'n bomwerpereska-drielje met hul gelukbringers—twee klein jagluiperds. |

Join the Springbok Army of Sportsmen

You need to be tough to tame a cheetah, but it is all part of the
campaign up north. The South African soldier to-day takes it all
in his stride.

There is a place for you in this Sportsmen's Army.

FIGURE 16.1. Image from *Libertas* January 1941, p. 13.

coalition that held sway with a narrow victory, marking South Africa's entry
into the war.

The main fighting force was drawn from the almost 200,000 white men
who volunteered for active duty.[2] South African troops served in three

[2] *South Africa's Yesterdays* (Cape Town: Readers' Digest Association of South Africa, 1981),
302.

Sluit aan by die Springbok-leër van Sportmanne

Majoor Danie Craven, Direkteur van Liggaamsoefening, en beroemde Springbok-skrumskakel, het die ou formele oefeninge vervang deur mededingende spele vir die opleiding van die Unie se nuwe leër. Die Suid-Afrikaanse soldaat van vandag is liggaamlik geskik, gesond en gelukkig.

Daar is 'n plek vir u in die geledere van die Sportmansleër.

"Legs Over": One of the many training games played in the army.

„Bene Oor": Een van die baie opleidingspele wat in die leër gespeel word.

Inset: Major Danie Craven.   By-portret: Majoor Danie Craven.

Join the Springbok Army of Sportsmen

Major Danie Craven, Director of Physical Training, and famous Springbok scrum-half, has replaced the old formal exercises with competitive games for the training of the new Union army. The South African soldier of to-day is fit, vigorous and happy.

There is a place for you in the ranks of the Sportsmen's Army.

FIGURE 16.2. Image from *Libertas* December 1940, p. 19.

theatres of war. Initially, they were based in Kenya in East Africa, where they faced the Italian forces in Abyssinia and Somaliland. They went on to form part of an Allied contingent that opposed the combined German and Italian forces in the North African desert of Egypt and Libya, which inflicted a devastating defeat at Tobruk. Finally, with Axis forces in retreat, South African troops were stationed in Italy. Due to the political tensions aroused by South Africa's participation in the war, only white men were allowed combat roles, as the right wing opposition vehemently opposed arming black men.

Since the South African military force in the war was composed entirely of volunteers, the support of these white men for the war effort was clearly necessary. Perhaps the most common factor here for English-speaking South Africans, still strong loyal of Britain, was the rallying cry of "For King and Country." There was little debate about participation. Quentin Smythe, presented as the archetypal war hero in official state films due to his winning the Victoria Cross, was motivated by loyalty to the empire: "Several of us got together and decided we would definitely volunteer for service. We had heard a hell of a lot about the Nazis, and we still had strong feelings for Britain. Natal was the last outpost."[3] He made specific reference to the notion of Natal as a British colony, "the last outpost" of the empire.

Many Afrikaner men, however, were ambiguous in their attitude toward Britain. They had either participated in the South African War (1899–1902) or were descendants of those who had fought Britain or had experienced the ravages of the war carried out by the British against the Afrikaner population. Yet, they also enlisted in large numbers.[4] Afrikaner liberals in the Smuts camp, Leo Marquard and Ernst Gideon Malherbe, were prominent members of the war effort. Malherbe, director of military intelligence, recalled Marquard's rationale for supporting the war effort: "Our fathers were fighting for their freedom against British imperialism. Now we are fighting against a worse imperialism, namely Hitler's. History is the story of one man's eternal struggle for freedom." With these words Marquard epitomized the feelings of many Afrikaner volunteers to serve against Nazism.[5] In Marquard's view, serving in the Second World War was linked to a past of imperial exploitation and struggle against oppression. In this way, these men reconciled the sense of the British as historic oppressors of the Afrikaners with their role as allies. There were also economic reasons for enlistment: the majority of Afrikaans-speaking men who enlisted had been adversely affected by the financial distress of the 1930s.[6]

---

[3] Terry McElligott and Keith Ross, "Remembering the declaration of World War 2," Independent Newspapers Archives, September 2, 1989, Durban. The Independent Newspaper Archives are a private archives located at Independent Newspapers in Greyville, Durban, and consist of articles drawn from the various publications of Independent Newspapers and, with regards to KwaZulu-Natal in particular, consisting of *The Daily News, The Post, The Mercury, The Sunday Tribune* and the *Independent on Saturday*. Archived articles are filed according to subject matter and date and not according to newspaper, however, for the purposes of this paper, the articles used were obtained from publications in KwaZulu-Natal.

[4] During the South African War, Smuts played a significant role fighting the British and General Pienaar spent part of his childhood with his mother and siblings in a concentration camp.

[5] E. G. Malherbe, *Never a Dull Moment* (Cape Town: Howard Timmins Publishers, 1981), 217.

[6] Neil Roos, *Ordinary Springboks: White Servicemen and Social Justice in South Africa, 1939–1961* (Aldershot: Ashgate Publishing, 2005), 30.

Besides the framework of duty and the fight against Nazism, other reasons influenced South African white men's participation in the war. Schools played a significant role in shaping white masculinity and the importance of military service. According to Major Allan Ryan, a product of the system, "The groundwork for the militarism of the volunteer regiments was laid in the schools and on the sports fields. There, the notion of teamwork, was entrenched and the importance of bravery and self-sacrifice underlined."[7] For the individual, the war presented the opportunity for adventure and escape. An English-speaking veteran recalled that "We were so thrilled that we jumped up and shook hands and said that at last we were going to get a bit of adventure."[8] The glamour of being in uniform related in no small measure to how women would perceive these men: "Feminine attention from the young and not so young was focused on the heroic and manly appearance of the chaps in uniform."[9] The flip side of the coin was the pressure brought to bear on men who did not conform. Ryan experienced an inkling of this when, classified as a "key man," he was unable to enlist immediately upon the outbreak of war; he had a feeling of disquiet when he appeared in public in civilian dress.[10] The voluntary status of enlistment combined with ambiguous support for the war meant that overt pressure could not be brought to bear on men who did not enlist; however, a form of coercion linked to masculinity, duty, and patriotism was present – not necessarily overt but internalized – in the decision to volunteer. Women were the imagined audience, and thus a raison d'être for men to don the masculine persona of the soldier. The nature of volunteerism itself came under the spotlight with the passing of a law requiring men willing to serve anywhere in the world to take a further oath. Their compliance was signified by the addition of a red patch to their epaulettes – contemptuously viewed as "imperialist" by the parliamentary opposition – that distinguished them from soldiers who had not taken the oath.[11]

According to Major Arthur Elton Blamey, a decorated veteran who was stationed in both East and North Africa, volunteerism itself and the sense that men in the military wanted to be there, as opposed to coerced conscripts, contributed to the strong camaraderie felt by those in the military: "with conscripted men we would not have the same wonderful spirit of comradeship and esprit de corps which officers and men in our regiment ... were

---

[7] Robert Morrell, *From Boys to Gentlemen: Settler Masculinity in Colonial Natal, 1880–1920* (Pretoria: University of South Africa, 2001), 142.

[8] Terry McElligott, "Clive was probably the first to volunteer for active service," Durban September 9, 1989, Independent Newspapers Archive.

[9] Major Allan Ryan, *Thru Times and Places* (Johannesburg: Wakely-Smith, 1977), 27–28.

[10] Ibid., 28.

[11] Translation of "die rooi eed" in Guy Butler, *Bursting World: An Autobiography, 1936–1945* (Claremont: David Philip Publisher, 1983), 163.

so privileged to enjoy."[12] Still, volunteerism was not without coercion in any form; peer pressure and a sense of duty and obligation were recalled as important motivations to enlist.

Recruitment

The recruiting advertisements appearing in the photo magazine *Libertas*, with which I began this chapter, bear further study. In Figure 16.1, two airmen are depicted with cheetah cubs, the mascots of their squadron. The advertisement itself makes explicit reference to the task of rendering the animals docile: "You need to be tough to tame a cheetah, but it is all part of the campaign up north. The South African soldier to-day takes it all in his stride."[13] These advertisements drew on and fed into already existing ideas of settler masculinity, evident in their similarity to the personal photographs taken by servicemen in East Africa. Moreover, there are clear parallels between these images and those taken in the South African mandate, South West Africa, where colonial officials posed with guns and hunting trophies in full safari gear. This made these advertisements part of an established visual tradition.[14]

Both advertisements use the slogan "Join the Springbok Army of Sportsmen: There is a place for you in the ranks of the Sportsmen's Army," although Figure 16.2 is more overtly concerned with sport. It is titled "Legs Over" and depicts two men engaged in sprinting over the legs of their prone comrades, along with an inset of Major Danie Craven, a South African rugby legend and the director of physical training during the war.[15] The emphasis is on competitive physical activity with the ultimate aim of making these young men "fit, vigorous and happy."[16] Equating the Union Army with a "Sportsmen's Army" suggests the link between military activity and sport. War is reimagined as a sport and the term "sportsmen" evokes sportsman-like behavior: rules of honor and fair play on the gaming field, evident of a kind of etiquette in the Union Army.[17]

---

[12] Major A. E. Blamey, *A Company Commander Remembers; From El Yibo to El Alamein* (Pietermaritzburg: The Natal Witness, 1963), 2.

[13] Copies of *Libertas* are located in Killie Campbell Africana Library (hereafter KCAL), University of KwaZulu-Natal.

[14] Cf. Paul S. Landau, "Hunting with gun and camera: a commentary"; and Wolfram Hartmann, "Performing gender, staging colonialism: Camping it up/acting it out in Ovamboland," in W. Hartmann, J. Silvester, and P. Hayes (eds.), *The Colonising Camera: Photographs in the Making of Namibian History* (Cape Town: University of Cape Town Press, 2001); Suryakanthie Chetty, "All the news that's fit to print": The print media of the Second World War and its portrayal of the gendered and racial identities of the war's participants," *South African Historical Journal*, 54 (2005), 31–32.

[15] *Libertas*, December 1940, 19, KCAL, University of KwaZulu-Natal.

[16] Ibid., 19.

[17] Chetty, "All the news," 32–33.

Simultaneously, both advertisements draw on a tradition of equating masculinity with hunting, a sport with a long history in Europe, North America, and South Africa. Private schools, with their emphasis on sport, allowed the application of the sporting metaphor to military service itself.[18] To a large extent, sport was perceived as helping men to prepare for a life in the military. Besides fostering male camaraderie, blood sports, such as hunting, accustomed men to killing; the greater the number of hunting trophies, the greater the physical prowess and masculinity of the individual. Men, in turn, equated war with a game and the killing of the enemy with hunting, which desensitized them to death.[19]

The symbol of sport also led to a perception of the enemy being reduced to that of an opposing team: it diminished the reality of war, giving it the status of a game. Simultaneously, the enemy was dehumanized. The metaphor of the team was effective in creating a simple dichotomy of "us" against "them." This essentialized the two groups, making unlikely any interaction beyond that of conflict and hostility. Within the colonial context, the process of "othering" was even more pronounced. For instance, in Natal, faced with people who appeared different socially, culturally, and even physically, the settlers demonized the Zulu, making the categories of "us" and "them" even more rigid.[20]

UDF recruiting drives, in which Malherbe was involved, attempted to mobilize Afrikaans support for the war. To do this, they drew on symbolic moments in Afrikaner nationalism, such as the commemoration of the Great Trek in 1938. Further attempts to garner Afrikaner support were evident in the use of the "Steel Commando" and "Air Commando" recruiting units traveling the platteland. The use of "Commando" was significant, along with Malherbe's use of the Trek image, as these were based on an already existing "martial and social tradition."[21] Afrikaners eventually comprised approximately fifty percent of white recruits.[22]

Training

After enlistment came training and drill instruction. Training created a disciplined cohesive force, where individual men functioned as a unit,

---

[18] S. Chetty, "Gender under fire: Interrogating war in South Africa, 1939–1945," MA thesis, University of Natal Durban (2001), 13–14.

[19] Michael C. C. Adams, *The Great Adventure: Male Desire and the Coming of World War I* (Bloomington: Indiana University Press, 1990), 43.

[20] Robert Morrell, "White farmers, social institutions and settler masculinity in the Natal Midlands, 1880–1920," MEd thesis, University of KwaZulu-Natal (1996), 133.

[21] Neil Roos, "From war to workplace: Class, race and gender amongst white volunteers, 1939–1953," PhD dissertation, North-West University-Mafikeng (2001), 96.

[22] Albert Grundlingh, "The king's Afrikaners? Enlistment and ethnic identity in the Union of South Africa's defence force during the Second World War, 1939–45," *Journal of African History*, 40 (1999), 354.

obedient to authority and deferring their personal concerns to that of the group. For Allan Ryan, the hard physical training and the near brutality of the drill instructors presented the recruits with a means of proving themselves worthy soldiers: "It was the accepted theme of the course that we were here to be tested and 'broken' – or otherwise make the grade!"[23] He observed that military training, while serving to create the disciplined, capable soldier, had the additional function of "weeding out" those without the physical and psychological stamina for war. Making the grade involved pride in being part of an elite.

The ties among men who had come through training together and then shared the experiences of war were enduring.[24] According to Quentin Smythe, their camaraderie was forged by their common experiences of living together, in training and in battle and, more significantly, the necessity for each man to be wholly dependent on the support of his comrades, particularly in battle. It was the war that provided the direction for this camaraderie – the coming together of men from diverse walks of life in a spirit of volunteerism with the common goal of fighting Nazism.[25] One of the few positive aspects in a destructive war was the strong bond that positively colored their memories of war. These experiences became some of the defining memories of the war that veterans were most likely to relate.

The Great White Hunter: Masculinity in East Africa

The East African campaign was the first in which South African troops engaged. The Italian invasion of Abyssinia in 1935 created fears of a strong Axis presence in the region. As Italy continued its plans to create an East African empire, British Somaliland was increasingly threatened, fears that proved well founded when the Italians attacked in August 1940. The First South Africa Brigade, led by Major General Daniel Hermanus Pienaar, had left for Kenya two months earlier – and had already begun air raids into Abyssinia – and was later joined by the rest of the First South Africa Division.[26] In January 1941 South African forces crossed into Abyssinia using armored cars. Over the succeeding months they were immensely successful, taking control over Mogadishu and reaching Addis Ababa, which subsequently surrendered to the South Africans in April 1941. The remaining Italian forces were defeated in mountainous Amba Alagi and the East African campaign formally concluded in November 1941.[27]

---

[23] Ryan, *Thru Times and Places*, 72.

[24] McElligott and Ross, "Remembering the declaration of World War 2."

[25] Rusty Bernstein, *Memory against Forgetting: Memoirs from a Life in South African Politics, 1938–1964* (London: Viking, 1999), 81.

[26] Ian Gleeson, *The Unknown Force: Black, Indian and Coloured Soldiers through Two World Wars* (Rivonia: Ashanti Publishing, 1994), 106–07.

[27] Jennifer Crwys-Williams, *A Country at War, 1939–1945: The Mood of a Nation* (Rivonia: Ashanti Publishing, 1992), 123–24.

Figure 16.3 shows three images of soldiers in East Africa. Figure 16.3a is of two men standing in the bush, one holding a rifle. The pith helmet bears strong overtones of the conventional nineteenth-century image of white men on safari. The portrait of a soldier standing in front of his tent (Figure 16.3b), pipe in hand, presents a romanticized, dashing, heroic figure, reminiscent of popular characters in "boy's own" adventures such as H. Rider Haggard's *King Solomon's Mines*. In Figure 16.3c, the image of a soldier squatting with his hunting trophies, posing with rifle in hand, the parallels between war and hunting are emphasized. In conjunction with the recruiting advertisements, they demonstrate that the experiences of service sustained the recruiting promise of adventure. A common element is of the colonial mindset of white adventurers on safari, dominating the natural landscape. It creates a restricted world of male camaraderie on the basis of gender as well as race – neither women nor black men are present in the images. These photographs drew on an already existing genre of colonial officials depicting themselves on safari, posing with guns over their kills.[28] Through the use of writing and personal photographs, these men were able to construct a specific kind of masculine identity based on their war experiences.

"Up North": The Experiences of White Men in North Africa

Part of this war experience was the opportunity for these men, many for the first time, to travel abroad. While the East African campaign had been an unqualified success for South African forces, they faced a far more difficult prospect in North Africa. South African troops had already been deployed to North Africa and were joined by the troops from the East Africa campaign. The First South Africa Division was stationed at Mersa Matruh and the Second Division at El Alamein. Both were part of a combination of Allied forces drawn from all over the globe. In November 1941 their first action was in Operation Crusader at Sidi Rezegh where 2,000 men were taken prisoner. The Second Division had greater success, capturing Bardia, Sollum, and Halfaya. Therefore the first year of South African troops in North Africa was one of mixed fortunes during which they experienced cultures very different from their own.[29]

The images in Figure 16.4 were taken by soldiers in North Africa, in particular Egypt. They are drawn from photo albums with few captions, yet they function as a means of ordering the experience of travel, providing a visual record of these experiences as well as providing a context of travel, tourism, and empire, of which masculinity is a significant part. The depiction of Egypt appears strongly influenced by postcard images of

---

[28] Cf. Landau, "Hunting with gun and camera," 151–55; Hartmann, "Performing gender, staging colonialism," 156–63.

[29] Gleeson, *The Unknown Force*, 134, 140–41, 144.

FIGURE 16.3. Images taken from Photo Album 2 of Donald Murray, 11 Motor Ambulance Company (courtesy of Documentation Centre, Department of Defence Archives, Pretoria).

FIGURE 16.4. Images taken from private collection of May Kirkman.

the country, which themselves mirrored the vision of Egypt in European popular imagination. In the photo album, postcards often stood in for direct representations of what the soldier had seen, placed alongside photographs taken of similar scenes. The similarity between postcards and photographs suggests that the photographer already had in mind a vision of the mythical Egypt that his images merely reaffirmed.[30]

Yet these images of Egypt are ones that are easily identifiable today: Egypt evokes the ancient past of the pharaohs, the Sphinx, and the pyramids. The similarity of images taken by men and women visiting the country is due to the already existing place held by Egypt in the tourist imagination.[31]

The photographs in Figure 16.4 are evocative of the adventurer/soldier T. E. Lawrence, the intrepid explorer who united the Arabs in a fight for freedom. They recalled the same "boy's own" adventure stories evidenced in the East African images. Similarities across albums suggest that this vision was shared.

In the descriptions of contemporary Egypt, however, an element of the "other" was introduced. The perception of the country and its people as

[30] Peter D. Osborne, *Travelling Light: Photography, Travel and Visual Culture* (Manchester: Manchester University Press, 2000), 22, 83.
[31] James Duncan and Derek Gregory, "Introduction," *Writes of Passage: Reading Travel Writing* (London: Routledge, 1999), 6.

a contrast to the "civilized" West is also evident in written memoirs. For example, Major Blamey's colorful and compelling descriptions of crime, vice, and poverty were a common feature of soldiers' narratives, as was the use of derogatory language when describing the Egyptians:

> The continual "peep, peep" and "clonk, clonk" of motor klaxons in the streets, together with the shrill cries of the shoe shine boys loudly advertising their business, at practically every street corner, combined to make a babel of noise.... We were repelled by the numerous beggars in the streets and in the slums, as well as by the loathsome sight of diseased people and the awful squalor.[32]

Two contrasting images of Egypt dominated these narratives: the chaos and "squalor" of the city streets and the remnants of a glorious past and heritage.

Combat

Key to white masculinity was combat in warfare, as this distinguished them from the other official participants in the UDF – white women and black men.[33] Yet the combatants were defined in relation to these other participants. Because of vehement opposition to arming black men with modern rifles during the war, black South Africans were compelled to use assegais (shortened spears). It was common to see men on sentry duty armed with little more than this. Figure 16.5b depicts men of the Non-European Army Services (NEAS) training with assegais and gas masks, an absurd juxtaposition of the "modern" and the "traditional." Thus the assegais symbolized the disempowerment of South African black men, emphasizing their secondary status in the war effort. While the assegai greatly resembles the bayonet fixed on the rifle of the white soldier in Figure 16.5a, here it signifies the courageous masculinity of close combat. The masculine identity of the combatant is defined against the enforced helplessness of the NEAS soldier. This relationship is reflected in the caption of the bayonet charge image: "In the present push up north the deeds of our fighters, who charge with fixed bayonets singing and shouting native war-cries as they go, have astonished their friends and terrified their foes."[34] Ironically, it was the appropriated war cries of the historical settler enemy that were used to assert white male prowess on the battlefield.[35]

---

[32] Blamey, *A Company Commander Remembers*, 85.
[33] Section 7 of the Defence Act of 1912 allowed for the recruitment of black South Africans in a solely noncombatant capacity. This would be the legislation cited to prevent black participation in combat on equal terms with white soldiers. Cf. Ian Gleeson, *The Unknown Force: Black, Indian and Coloured Soldiers through Two World Wars* (Rivonia: Ashanti Publishing, 1994), 104.
[34] "Steady," *Libertas*, December 1941, 18, KCAL.
[35] Chetty, "All the news," 35.

FIGURE 16.5. Photos from *Libertas* December 1941, 18 (courtesy of Documentation Centre and Department of Defence Archives, Pretoria, respectively).

The historical identity of white military regiments had origins in colonial conflict between settlers and "natives." A *Libertas* article entitled "Gunners Were Everywhere" begins with the history of the artillery within the settler context: "More than one hundred years ago, on December 16, a few hundred 'Sannas' and one solitary brass cannon blazed away with crazy fits and starts at Zulu hordes trying to wipe out a small Voortrekker laager in Natal,"[36] a reference to the Battle of Blood River between the Dutch Afrikaans Trekkers and the Zulu army, which ended in the decisive defeat of the Zulu due to the crucial role played by modern weaponry. The fighting tradition of white soldiers therefore defined itself against the indigenous people with whom their forebears came into conflict. The exclusion of black men from the UDF fighting tradition was an inherent feature of the very identity of white combat regiments.[37]

Another aspect of the frontlines was the perception of the enemy. The impression of the Germans was inevitably colored by hindsight, integral to the personal narratives related so many years later. When white soldiers were enlisting, the Nazis were generally regarded as a threat to democracy, but later knowledge of atrocities and the Holocaust played a significant factor in soldiers' memories of the Germans. According to Godfrey Herbert, an English-speaking volunteer, who was taken prisoner at Tobruk:

> they hated Jews for instance, imagine what they'd be like with Blacks and Indians . . . they were a very evil, dreadful people when you think of the Holocaust, what they did to those millions of Jews, I mean, the very thought of it makes you sick and weak all over, and we just knew they were evil.[38]

[36] "Gunners were everywhere," *Libertas*, December 1941, 44, KCAL, University of KwaZulu-Natal.
[37] Chetty, "All the news," 35.
[38] Interview with Godfrey Herbert, conducted by S. Chetty and S. Sparks, June 9, 2004, Durban, South Africa.

Important in these written and oral narratives is the way in which memory functions. Distant from the events itself, it incorporates subsequent occurrences that become the lens through which participation in the war was perceived, with the past and later life experiences working together to create coherence. For Herbert, the racial oppression symbolized by the Nazis outweighed that of the apartheid state. In this way, white soldiers may have seen themselves – with hindsight – as fighting against racial oppression.

The nature of modern warfare meant that little personal interaction could take place between South Africans and Axis soldiers. Prominent South African activist and Communist Party member Rusty Bernstein recalls the way in which modern warfare took on an alienating, dehumanizing face. No longer were these the days of charging into battle and meeting the enemy face-to-face, the idealized hallmark of battle:

> If war is ever totally pointless and pursued purely out of habit, this must have been it.... In the mindless nature of the game, we were obliged to show that we were there.... We would fire off our own ration of shells at odd hours of day or night at targets we could not see, working only from map references[39]

At this abstracted level no real strong emotion existed, either positive or negative, for the enemy. Emphasis on the cruelty – evident across accounts – of the Japanese far outweighed that of the Germans, at least until news of the Holocaust spread. A large part of this was related to race: unlike the Germans and the Italians, the Japanese were the "other." Yet this did not preclude them from being viewed as exemplifying the notion of the "noble warrior." While relating stories of Japanese atrocities, Ryan simultaneously suggested that it was in fact their idea of honor that was partially responsible for their treatment of prisoners where surrender was considered "dishonorable" and those who allowed themselves to be captured were treated with "contempt."[40] Several themes are apparent in how these men remember and relate the experiences of combat. There is the reticence, the silences and self-censorship in their descriptions of death and destruction, evident across accounts and in images of war. These experiences of war were impossible to describe to an outsider. They were also in line with an overall censoring of combat evident in official and public sources that personal accounts and images drew on conventions of what was "proper" to show. Where combat was described and remembered, there was often a sense of distance from the events. Combatants appeared to function automatically, leaving analysis of their experiences for later. Combat became relegated to the mundane, a normal part of the existence of the soldier. Nevertheless combat exerted some form of attraction for participants torn between the perpetuation of stereotypical ideas of glory and sacrifice in war and experiences that stood

---

39 Bernstein, *Memory against Forgetting*, 73.
40 Ryan, *Thru Times and Places*, 189.

in stark contrast to this. As the defining event of war, it became politicized as an obligation of citizenship and was important in policies of inclusion and exclusion. Black men were excluded from combat, which mirrored their exclusion from citizenship.

The prominent poet, Guy Butler, compromising his pacifism to enter the war, was determined to retain some elements of his pacifist upbringing, joining the engineers rather than one of the more combative corps.[41] Principled pacifist or not, Butler nevertheless found himself envious of his younger brother Jeffrey, who had come under intense fire: "Two days before Jeffrey had got the fright of his life. Shelling had compelled them to lie flat on mother earth. . . . I envied my younger brother. I felt out of it, prosaic, unheroic, almost a base wallah."[42] Thus combat had appeal even for one as opposed to it as Butler. This attraction was based on the notion of heroism under fire, of proving oneself under pressure and the romanticism of achieving glory.

Like many individual experiences of war, combat itself was perceived differently by the men involved. For Rusty Bernstein – initially neutral about participation in the war due to the position adopted by the Communist Party and thus less likely than Blamey, for instance, to be "gung ho" – the predictability and routine of his experience was a far cry from the stereotypes of heroism and glory: "the familiarity of it all make it feel more like theatre than war – lots of suspense but little blood. When the day's ammunition had been expended . . . the performance was over for the day."[43] This was compounded by the periods of inactivity and boredom.

More conventional visions of combat were apparent as well. On hearing distant firing for the first time, Blamey was torn between concern for his comrades facing the Germans as well as apprehension and nervous tension. He found it difficult to describe his emotional reaction. While he condemned the war and the killing of men, he still felt a desire to experience what was happening. When, eventually he found himself under fire for the first time, he experienced a detachment from the fear of being injured or killed and instead a concentration on duty:

> it was a strange feeling to be at the receiving end of the machine-gun bullets which were whizzing past us, mostly over our heads. This was my baptism of fire, but strangely enough I was not afraid, for no doubt my mind was too occupied with my responsibilities to think about anything else.[44]

His detachment existed even during the most horrific incidents. When his driver was killed by a mine, he felt compelled to analyze his own reaction,

[41] Butler, *Bursting World*, 125.
[42] Ibid., 220.
[43] Bernstein, *Memory against Forgetting*, 73.
[44] Blamey, *A Company Commander Remembers*, 21–22.

the reasons behind his calm and detached façade in the face of a gruesome and brutal experience. He recalled that this ultimately served as a means of allowing the soldier to continue to fight even when confronted with the worst aspects of war: "If the normal connections between stimulus and response, between pain and pity, between danger and fear continued intact among soldiers, no war would last for long."[45]

Meanwhile, war and death became incorporated into everyday life. "A fatal Wimpie crash today – whole crew killed – machine burnt out completely. Broke out in some kind of rash – not getting enough grub," wrote Kevin Aloysius Kelly in his diary on November 17, 1943.[46] The disturbing death of comrades, at whose funeral young Kelly was later to be a pallbearer, was juxtaposed with his more mundane experiences and personal concerns in Egypt. His diary conveys a sense of immediacy, allowing the historian to see the juxtaposition of the extraordinary and the mundane or the way in which the extraordinary became the mundane. It captures the way in which the combatant experienced the war. Kelly had no qualms about the possibility of being killed in combat, as evidenced in his entry on December 31, 1943: "I shall never regret joining the SAAF and learning to fly even if it costs my life in the near future – it has been well worth it and I'd sooner 'Go' in an aeroplane than anywhere else." This entry was one of his last prior to his death, aged just 22, when his parachute failed to open after his plane was shot down.[47]

Yet for some soldiers the extreme nature of combat forced its way past detachment and pragmatism. While antiapartheid activist, Mary Benson, was stationed in Egypt, she received news of men's combat experiences secondhand:

> When I visited the wounded men in hospital, a South African had news of another friend, Brewer – tall, blond and cheerful. After killing four Italians as he single-handedly captured a machine-gun post, he had been badly wounded, his leg would have to be amputated; he'd just sat there, *laughing*, until he was captured by the Italians.[48]

She evoked a poignant image, capturing both the complexity and horror of war and perhaps something of its reality, a far cry from the simple stereotypes employed in propaganda. But this image is a rare one and thus the stoic image of masculinity is kept intact.

Soldiers in combat found themselves confronted with two very different and even conflicting perceptions of the war and combat. The first was the

[45] Butler, *Bursting World*, 249.
[46] Diary of Kevin Aloysius Kelly, November 17, 1943, KCM 55127–55129, KCAL, University of KwaZulu-Natal.
[47] Ibid., December 31, 1943.
[48] Mary Benson, A Far Cry (London: Viking, 1989), 28.

ideal of honor and duty, the desire for glory, which was a strong motivation for enlistment and integral to their understanding of war. Second, however, was the actual experience of war on the frontlines where the loss of comrades belied this belief. Nonetheless, they continued to fight, understanding and abhorring the nature of warfare, yet remaining duty-bound. In many instances this resulted in an inability to give voice to their experiences. Quentin Smythe, whose exploits were used by the state to create and maintain support for the war, was himself unwilling to describe those same experiences: "I never even told my own parents what I did in that thing.... Can one ever really tell people what it was like? You know your mind rejects things that were nasty; you can read up the citation if you like, but you'll get nothing from me." He was awarded the Victoria Cross for bravery and personally congratulated by Smuts. Information films detailed his exploits. He had achieved military glory, yet the price, both psychological and physical, was high. It was an experience that he preferred not to relive through the recounting of it. Instead he defined his war experiences in terms of the camaraderie, the humor, and the loyalty of those alongside whom he had fought.[49]

Combat was an intense, life-changing experience. It confronted these men with war in its awful reality, ending its schoolboy idealization. They witnessed horrendous sights. Godfrey Herbert expressed dismay that:

> I've seen tanks, burnt tanks, rotting bodies.... I don't know, people make a romance out of war now, it's not romantic at all, I mean it's not very nice – bloody bombs going off and shells... and some... great friends of mine were in one little dugout near me and a Stuka bomb went straight in and took the whole lot of them – finished.[50]

In his descriptions of combat there is little sense of agency in terms of what he had actually done as a combatant; instead the emphasis focuses on the violence done to those around him. Bombs and shells are given agency as inanimate objects and the actual violence committed by men on both sides is rendered invisible, subordinated to the artillery. Moreover, his hesitations in his descriptions not only suggest the difficulty of recounting these experiences but also indicate their hold on his memory so many years after the event.

Sporting POWs

Combat was not the only defining feature of war. The Allies held off German and Italian forces under the command of Lieutenant-General Erwin Rommel for most of 1941, but the Allied forces were defeated at Tobruk in 1942.

---

[49] Sam Sole, "The war to end all wars," Sunday Tribune (KwaZulu-Natal), September 3, 1989.
[50] Interview with G. Herbert.

Tobruk, with its harbor and significant supplies, was a strategically valuable position. The Second South African Division was moved there under the command of Major-General Hendrik Bakzazar Klopper. Cut off from Allied assistance, Tobruk was attacked by Rommel's army on June 20, 1942, which captured the airfield and, subsequently, the harbor.[51] The inability of Allied troops to evacuate the area due to the German capture of their transport vehicles led to a huge number being taken prisoner of war (POW) when Klopper eventually surrendered to Axis forces. Of the approximately 30,000 men taken prisoner, South African soldiers formed one-third, almost the entire Second South African Division.[52] Confinement as prisoners of war was the defining experience in their recollections. In an interview Godfrey Herbert observed:

> we didn't have enough to eat, we were very, very hungry the whole time – 18 months, I can honestly say that we were hungry most of the time there. And the water came on at midnight and, you know, in dribs and drabs and there were terrible stinking latrines and, you know, it wasn't very nice.[53]

Despite the adverse conditions and desperate hunger that reduced these men to a shadow of their former selves, sport nonetheless made its ubiquitous appearance. In the German POW camp, Stalag IVB, South African men competed with their Allied counterparts from Australia, New Zealand, England, France, and Wales in "international" rugby matches. The preparation that went into these matches included the conversion of Italian long underwear into shorts dyed yellow with dye obtained from antimalarial tablets. Uniforms came at great cost: "Five precious cigarettes, which would buy a tin of sardines, were needed to buy a vest and so one rugger jersey could cost a man a third of his weekly ration." The physical exertion when many were on the brink of starvation, suggested that playing rugby was more than mere recreation.[54] For Ross Hinds, it was both an act of defiance and a "morale booster" in the face of tremendous odds, as well as an assertion of patriotism: "The mere staging of rugby 'internationals' by prisoners who were suffering incredible privation was a triumph of diplomacy and endurance."[55]

Sport, and in particular rugby, also served as a process of inclusion and exclusion. In late nineteenth- and early twentieth-century in South Africa, playing sports such as cricket and rugby symbolized the contempt of English-speaking white South Africans for Afrikaners due to the perception of the

---

[51] Crys-Williams, *A Country at War*, 229–30.

[52] Nigel Cawthorne, *Turning the Tide: Decisive Battles of the Second World War* (London: Arcturus Publishing, 2002), 51–56.

[53] Interview with G. Herbert.

[54] Bob Frean, "Memories of Rugby 'Boks' in German camp," Durban, June 26, 1991, Independent Newspapers Archive.

[55] Frean, "Memories of Rugby 'Boks.'"

latter's lack of idealized sportsmanlike behavior. While test cricket was considered "Anglo-Saxon," rugby became a defiant assertion of Afrikaner identity: "The Springboks may have been playing an 'imperial' game but they were playing it to assert themselves as a proud and independent people, whose attitude to the British Crown was ambiguous to say the least."[56] Yet the South African national rugby team, the Springboks, also functioned as a means of reconciliation between English and Afrikaner after the South African War and a means of propagating a particularly white masculine identity. Through the twentieth century both groups "were united in their support of the Springboks and in their identification with Springbok success."[57] Representing the country in sport, however, was an honor given only to white sportsmen and women. The privileged few were allowed to wear the "national sporting colours and the Springbok emblem."[58] By designating the UDF combatants as "Springboks," there was a sense that rugby, like combat, served as a process of racial exclusion.[59] In the POW camps, rugby also became an assertion of masculinity, which was sorely needed as the lack of food and the will to survive reduced these men to an almost subhuman level. This is evident in a poem in the diary of a South African prisoner:

> Of all the places in the world,
> At least it seems to me,
> A prison camp is not a place
> For women's eyes to see...
> The saddest thing of all to see,
> Is virile manhood brave,
> Reduced to fleshless skin and bone,
> Like those due for the grave.... [60]

A key theme in this poem is the way in which being a POW was perceived in stark contrast to the notion of "virile" masculinity, making these men an unfit sight for women still holding onto idealized visions of men in uniform. The poem suggests that life as a POW robbed them of this masculinity, of their "manhood," reducing them to a desperate existence. There is a sense of helplessness, which does not fit into the conventions of honor and duty that are such a strong component of accounts appearing years later, when their authors had incorporated their war experiences into public and official narratives. In these accounts, a dominant theme was the way in which some

---

[56] R. Holt, *Sport and the British: A Modern History* (Oxford: Oxford University Press, 1990), 228.

[57] John Nauright, *Sport, Cultures and Identities in South Africa* (Claremont: David Philip Publishers, 1998), 83.

[58] Ibid., 11.

[59] Ibid., 87.

[60] "Prison camp II," in Diary of Gert Spencer Dreyer, KCM 65263, KCAL, University of KwaZulu-Natal.

of these men asserted themselves. There were numerous escape attempts, a means of holding true to a notion of duty in an almost impossible situation. The escape attempt became yet another trial and men felt compelled to try to escape even if their hearts were not in it. Colonel Arthur Clive Martin derided one such attempt:

> Chesney... and MacDonald staged an *"escape effort."* They chose a foggy afternoon and walked with their suitcases to the wire... the Italians had no difficulty in discovering the two *"heroes."* They were picked up with their suit-cases at the wire. A more ridiculous *"attempt"* could not be imagined. I think it was phony from the word go. [Emphasis in the original.][61]

Clearly he had a highly contemptuous attitude of the two men. His statement suggests that these men were fundamentally flawed and not imbued with the military ethic of honor and duty. Still it raises the consideration of the pressure on these men to prove their masculinity and carry out their duty, compelling them to attempt to escape, even if it was a somewhat desultory effort.

Conclusion

During the war, the Smuts government walked a tightrope between the vociferous demands of black South Africans for equal participation and the vehement conservative opposition agitating against South African partic-ipation in an "imperialist" war. In this context white men were deemed to be the key figures in the war effort, yet state propaganda as well as their own understanding of war service suggested that their identity was defined against both white women and black men. The portrayal of black men in the war, when it was acknowledged, was placed within an existing warrior tradition, justifying the decision not to arm them. This tradition was invoked as a means of acknowledging the noncombatant and auxil-iary roles of black men. White men's notion of combat allowed them to strengthen their own fighting roles as inextricably linked with masculin-ity and citizenship. Training and war provided the means by which white combatants forged strong bonds of solidarity and camaraderie, creating an all-male world. Each experience became an assertion of masculinity through successfully overcoming the challenge presented by it: basic training weeded out the physically unsuited; combat presented opportunities for doing one's duty and defending one's comrades; and even being taken prisoner entailed the assertion of agency through escape attempts and acts of sabotage.

Nevertheless women were always present. They were the imagined and the actual audience of a censored experience of war. This was evident in the reticence of men to share their experiences despite the fact that women

[61] Memoirs of Colonel A. C. Martin, 145, KCM 97/2, KCAL, University of KwaZulu-Natal.

apparently provided the motivation to fight. This silence allowed men to embody the idealized masculine image of the soldier. In situations where that was impossible and masculinity itself was perceived to be under threat, such as the experiences of POWs or even the extremes of combat, the silences helped cement this all-male world where women had little place. Although the propagandistic notions of the idealized soldier were belied by their actual experiences of war, soldiers themselves were complicit in the promulgation of these notions through their silences. Despite the ultimate dashing of these hopes for a new South Africa, the legacy of the war itself was not extinguished but took its place in both individual and public memory. It not only affected those taking part, but also achieved a kind of immortality in the public imagination which was reinforced by the various media of popular culture.

17

African Soldiers, French Women, and Colonial Fears during and after World War II

Ruth Ginio

Introduction

World War II brought the European conflict into the African continent and carried Africans into the battlefields in Europe and Asia. Of all the allied powers France was the one that took full advantage of the manpower its colonies offered. It was also the only European power to deploy African soldiers on metropolitan soil.[1] This had already been done in World War I, but the grim circumstances of France in the second global conflict as well as the timing of the war made the participation of Africans in it especially problematic for France as a colonial power.

Two colonial divisions, both consisting of a large number of African troops, stood on the Aisne and the Argonne in May 1940 and were hit by the full force of the Panzer invasion. Two other colonial divisions faced German attacks on the Somme from May 23 onward and were forced to retreat.[2] Africans who fought in the battles of 1940 witnessed France's defeat and German occupation of its soil. Many of them spent considerable time in German prisoner of war (POW) camps. African soldiers fought on two opposite sides in Syria and Lebanon, and later took part in the liberation of France in the ranks of the Free French forces. Around 120,000 colonial soldiers, many from sub-Saharan Africa, participated in the landing in Provence on August 16, 1944. African soldiers experienced discrimination during the war, which culminated in de Gaulle's decision to "whiten" the

---

[1] According to David Killingray, Britain dispatched Indian colonial troops to the Western front in WWI, but did not employ African troops in Europe. In WWII the British employed African troops in Europe as laborers but not in combat. See David Killingray, "African voices from two world wars," *Historical Research*, 74 (2001), 426–28.

[2] Myron Echenberg, *Colonial Conscripts: The Tirailleurs Sénégalais in French West Africa, 1857–1960* (Portsmouth, NH: Heinnemann, 1991), 92.

The author thanks the Israel Science Foundation (grant no. 822/09) for their support for research leading to this chapter.

forces that marched into Paris in August 1944. Their experiences on and off the battlefields reshaped their views of French colonialism.[3]

This chapter examines French colonial fears regarding the influence of soldiers' experiences during the war on the stability of colonial rule in French West Africa (FWA). These fears had developed during the war and were shared by both Vichy and Free French administrations. They were further aggravated in the postwar years when French colonial rule faced threats first from Indochina and Madagascar and later in Algeria.[4] I begin with an examination of the colonial concerns of the Vichy administration in FWA with regard to the return of African soldiers to the colonies after the fall of France. I then look at a specific kind of colonial fear – perhaps one of the greatest – the concern about interracial relations, which I discuss by exploring cases of French women seeking the return of their African husbands or lovers who had been sent back to West Africa and the administration's responses to these requests. Finally, I analyze the ways in which the war experiences of African soldiers and colonial concerns regarding these experiences influenced postwar colonial policies in FWA, especially regarding African soldiers.

The Vichy Administration in French West Africa and the Returning Soldiers

From the outbreak of war in September 1939 up to the fall of France in 1940, about 100,000 soldiers from FWA were recruited into the French army. Seventy-five percent of them served in Europe. At the time of the signing of the armistice agreement with Germany, as many as 28,000 Africans were declared missing. Of these, almost 16,000 had fallen into German captivity. Exact figures on the number of fatalities among these soldiers are unavailable, but Myron Echenberg estimates that it reached about 17,000.[5] (The overall number of soldiers in the French army who died in the battles of May and June 1940 was some 100,000.)[6]

---

[3] Nancy Lawler, *Soldats d'Infortune: Les tirailleurs Ivoiriens de la IIe guerre mondiale*, trans. François Manchuelle (Paris: L'Harmattan, 1996), 149–57; 176–85; Jean-Yves Le Naour, *La honte noire: L'Allemagne et les troupes coloniales françaises, 1914–1945* (Paris: Hachette Litteratures, 2004), 247–48. According to Le Naour, the whitening process continued during the autumn and winter of 1944. The sixth regiment of the Tirailleurs Sénégalais, for example, which was originally 90 percent black, had no black soldiers at all by October 1944. Lawler, however, questions the assertion that the motives behind the whitening were purely racist and insists that De Gaulle did not doubt the bravery of the African soldiers.

[4] For a detailed military history of the participation of African troops in the battles of WWII, see Anthony Clayton, *France, Soldiers, and Africa* (London: Brassey's Defence Publishers, 1988), 120–52.

[5] Echenberg, *Colonial Conscripts*, 88.

[6] Jean-Pierre Azéma, *De Munich à la Libération, 1938–1944* (Paris: Seuil, 1979), 44. For comparison, the British recruited around 500,000 Africans who served mainly in the Levant,

Shortly after the signing of the armistice in June 1940, the general-governor of the Federation of French Equatorial Africa, Pierre Boisson, stated his loyalty to the new leader of France, Marshal Philippe Pétain, and was consequently transferred to the strategically more important FWA. Until Boisson's departure in July 1943, FWA was under Vichy rule; however, as we shall see, fears regarding demobilized soldiers and their impact on colonial stability characterized both the Vichy administration and that of the Free French that replaced it.[7]

In examining the colonial regime's treatment of African soldiers, it is necessary to distinguish between three groups: soldiers who were discharged after the defeat, those who were German POWs, and those who continued to serve during the Vichy period in the defense forces that were allowed to remain in FWA under the terms of the armistice agreement to support the Vichy regime against attacks by the British and the Gaullists.[8] Here I focus on the first group: the discharged soldiers. The colonial regime's main concern regarding these soldiers was that they return to their everyday lives and reintegrate into their places of residence as rapidly as possible. The colonial administration was aware of the destructive potential of a mass discharge of soldiers who had witnessed France's humiliating defeat and sought to keep this group from becoming excessively embittered.[9]

In 1940, about 35,000 soldiers were sent back to Dakar via North Africa. An additional 27,000 awaited their transfer in North Africa. In 1941, the British began to create obstacles to the transfer of the African soldiers because they regarded FWA as enemy territory. The facilities in Dakar were not adequate for the return of such a large number of soldiers. Grave problems of discipline arose in the transition camps in Africa. The soldiers, who did not understand why they were being delayed, became angry and lost respect for the defeated French; their officers were often replaced and they waited for discharge payments that often did not arrive. This situation brought the soldiers to the verge of mutiny. Even when transportation problems were solved, new hurdles sprang up. Many soldiers lacked identification documents; the authorities had no means of verifying their home villages and whether they belonged to the standing army or the reserves. The graver problem, however, was payment of the discharge grants, which most soldiers insisted that they had been promised that they would receive upon

---

Burma, India, Ceylon, Madagascar, North Africa and Italy. See David Killingray, *Fighting for Britain: African Soldiers in the Second World War* (London: James Curry, 2010), 142.

[7] On the establishment of the Vichy regime in FWA, see Ruth Ginio, *French Colonialism Unmasked: The Vichy Years in French West Africa* (Lincoln: Nebraska University Press, 2006), 3–9.

[8] After the armistice, the number of the African soldiers in FWA was reduced from 118,000 to 25,000. See Nancy Lawler, *Soldiers, Airmen, Spies and Whisperers: The Gold Coast in World War II* (Columbus: Ohio University Press, 2002), 3.

[9] 17G/199 (17), Archives nationales du Sénégal (hereafter ANS), Dakar.

arriving in Dakar. They demanded money, not promises. The French officers assured them that the grants would be awaiting them when they arrived in their villages, and once there, they would receive the money in their circles.[10] When these commitments were not fulfilled, the soldiers became violent.[11]

In November 1940 in the Kindia district of Guinea, a revolt broke out among 450 Tirailleurs who were in the process of being discharged. The governor of Guinea reported that the situation remained extremely grave for two hours, but the Tirailleurs dispersed after they beat many French officers, lightly wounding four of them. According to his report, a rather large group, armed with rifles, cried out for murderous retribution, threw stones at houses, barged into the offices of the administration, assaulted the circle commandant, and subsequently attacked a group of Europeans who escaped to the railway station. After three hours, a European team armed with automatic weapons succeeded in overcoming the rebellious soldiers. Three hundred of them were arrested immediately, and thirty-five additional arrests were made the next day. They received sentences ranging from five to twenty years in prison. The governor stated that while the immediate motive for the violent outburst was indeed the delay in discharge grants, the real reason was communist propaganda disseminated among the soldiers by the British and the Gaullists who urged them to rebel and defect.[12] Despite the conclusion that the delay in the discharge grants was just the spark that ignited the revolt and not its real cause, the administration acknowledged that the delay was a problem. In January 1941, the governor of Senegal advised one of his circle commandants that in light of the grave incident in Guinea special care must be taken to pay the discharge grants. The issue was left in the hands of the circle commandants so as to prevent any unnecessary waste of time. He requested that the circle commandant report the number of discharged soldiers and how many received discharge grants.[13] Even after the first stage of the soldiers' discharge ended, the colonial regime was concerned about the matter of reintegrating them into daily life, which it saw as necessary for preventing unrest among them. The French cautiously discharged the soldiers to their villages gradually.[14]

The colonial administration perceived the soldiers as a menace, especially in the period immediately following their discharge. Even after the soldiers

---

[10] A circle (*cercle*) is the term for an administrative unit in the French colonial system.

[11] Lawler, *Soldats d'infortune*, 131–32.

[12] Aff, Pol. 638/6, Archives Nationales, Centre des Archives d'Outre-Mer, Aix-en-Provence. Also see Myron Echenberg, "Tragedy at Thiaroye: The Senegalese soldiers' uprising of 1944," in Peter Gutkind, Robin Cohen, and Jean Copans (eds.), *African Labor History* (Beverly Hills, CA, and London: Sage Publications, 1978), 113.

[13] On demobilization, the soldiers were supposed to receive 500 francs and, at a later stage, an additional 400 francs, 11D1/869, ANS, Dakar.

[14] Sénégal: Rapport politique annuel,1940, 2G40/2 (200mi/1815), Archives nationales (hereafter AN), Paris.

returned to their villages, the colonial administration did not let up. Most of the disruptive incidents involving discharged soldiers had to do with refusing to pay taxes to the African chief, sometimes including aggression toward the chief and anti-French statements. It appears that France's defeat led the discharged soldiers to scorn the authority of the colonial administration and its African representatives.

In one case, a son of a village chief who was a discharged solider was put on trial. The son and his father, also a former soldier, had refused to participate in the rubber harvest. Beyond the son's refusal to toil physically, in an assembly convened by the canton chief, he claimed that he had seen and heard everything in France and knew that French authority no longer existed. He added that the decrees of the canton chief were meaningless because they did not accord with those of the new authority that was going to replace the French one.[15] In another report on the same case, the governor of Ivory Coast quoted the same former soldier as saying: "The French should not count on me for anything. They took me to fight in a land that is not mine and the English are the ones who returned me to my land and my family. If the English were to ask me to work for them I would." The same report describes additional cases in which former soldiers refused to obey the orders of African representatives of the administration and even behaved violently toward them. One of the circle commandants in Ivory Coast wrote that this was a widespread phenomenon among soldiers who had returned from the European battlefields.[16]

Many colonial administrators complained that the main obstacle to dealing with such incidents was the decree of April 19, 1939, stating that former Tirailleurs were to be tried by European courts.[17] In almost all the reports on incidents involving discharged soldiers, the complaining administrator asked for the annulment of this law so that the soldiers could be punished severely. One Ivory Coast circle commandant explained his demand to cancel the decree by claiming that in most cases a "native court" could give an "appropriate" punishment of fifteen to thirty days in jail for transgressions of this kind.[18] Indeed, an injunction canceling the discharged soldiers' right to be tried in European courts was published on February 5, 1942.[19]

---

[15] 17G/83 (17), ANS, Dakar.

[16] 2D/29 (28), ANS, Dakar.

[17] Two parallel justice systems existed in FWA: one for Europeans and Africans holding French citizenship and the other for African "subjects." In the European courts cases were judged by French judges according to French law, while in the native courts French administrators ruled with the assistance of African assessors. See J. Chabas, "La justice française en Afrique occidentale française," *Annales Africaines* (1955), 79–108; Alice Conklin, *A Mission to Civilize: The Republican Idea of Empire in France and West Africa, 1895–1930* (Stanford, CA: Stanford University Press, 1997), 86–102.

[18] 2D/29 (28), ANS; 2G40/4 (200mi/1815), AN, Paris.

[19] This decree also annulled that of August 22, 1939, which accorded this right to members of the Legion of Honor and to those who were entitled to vote for the local assemblies, Haut

We see that African demobilized soldiers were a great source of worry to the Vichy colonial administration. As the war advanced, these worries became graver. Such concerns, however, were not confined to the Vichy regime. In fact, it was under the Free French that the most serious incident of soldiers' revolt and its brutal repression took place at Camp Thiaroye near Dakar in December 1944.[20]

To understand the colonial fears regarding African demobilized soldiers we have to examine the nature of these soldiers' experiences: What was it that made them so menacing in the eyes of the colonial administration in their home colonies? Various kinds of experiences influenced the soldiers' view of the colonial situation: African soldiers witnessed French defeat and its consequences; they were imprisoned in German camps (see Raffael Scheck's Chapter 22 in this volume) and they actively participated in the liberation of their colonial master from its occupier. There cannot be any doubt that such experiences had an impact on the way that African soldiers perceived French colonial rule. While such experiences were directly related to the military aspect of the war, it was a different experience off the battlefields that was even more worrying: the encounters between African soldiers and French civilian population, especially with French women.

Searching for Lost Lovers: The French Colonial Administration, French Women, and African Soldiers

The presence of a large number of colonial troops, among them many Africans, on French soil during the two world wars inevitably led to various encounters between the soldiers and French civilians, men and women. African soldiers were often surprised to discover the great difference between the treatment they received from metropolitan French and the one they received in the colonies. Soldiers were often invited into French homes during their service in France. African soldiers met French women and formed various kinds of relations with them. Prostitution was one way that allowed African soldiers access to French women, but there were many other more respectable ways in which they could meet French women. During World War I, colonial soldiers spent the winter months of every year in the southern city of Fréjus where they had many opportunities to befriend local women. Soldiers also met French women as nurses who attended to them when they were hospitalized. While in some cases these relations were platonic friendships, in others they led to pregnancies and/or marriages.[21]

Commissariat de l'Afrique française, *La justice indigène en AOF* (Rufisque: Imprimerie du Gouvernement Général, 1942), 419–22.

[20] On the tragic events at camp Thiaroye, see Echenberg, "Tragedy at Thiaroye," 109–27.

[21] Richard Forgarty, *Race and War in France: Colonial Subjects in the French Army, 1914–1918* (Baltimore, MD: The John Hopkins University Press, 2008), 202–29.

Similar encounters took place during World War II, when African soldiers were drafted again in large numbers to save the motherland. Following the defeat in 1940, 120,000 colonial soldiers became POWs. While European prisoners were sent to camps in Germany, colonial ones stayed on French soil in the occupied zone. During their captivity African POWs met French women serving as nurses, drivers of Red Cross trucks that brought food to the camps, and sympathizers who often gathered near the camp's walls, talked to prisoners, and threw food to them. Local organizations arranged a service of young women, called *marraines de guerre*, who, like in WWI, accompanied African soldiers, sent them letters, and invited them to their homes during their leaves. Again, like in WWI, some of these relations remained nonsexual, while in others, soldiers had intimate relations with French women which sometimes led to pregnancies.[22]

If African soldiers involved with French women wanted to establish these relations legally, they had to apply for permission to marry from their commanders. In fact, all marriages of African soldiers, regardless the origin of the intended wife, had to be approved by the military authorities.[23] While at least some of these requests were approved, the military did not allow African soldiers married to French women to stay in France after the war. These soldiers were sent back to their home colonies upon demobilization, leaving behind French girlfriends, wives, and sometimes babies and children. The persistent attempts of the women who were left behind to locate their partners and bring them back to France are recorded in their letters to the colonial administrators, which shed light on the nature of these relationships and on French colonial perceptions of them.

Of all the experiences of African soldiers, their relations with French women were conceived by the colonial authorities as the most dangerous. Sexual relations between African men and French women represented the ultimate blurring of colonial boundaries and therefore menace to the continuity of colonial rule. To understand the deep roots of such anxieties let us now briefly consider the background of the French attitudes to interracial relations. Interracial relations have fired the European imagination since the first encounters with non-European peoples and have formed the subject of many European literary works. Shakespeare's *Othello* is perhaps the most famous example. This play does not convey, of course, a very encouraging way of looking at love across races, and indeed in many later literary texts on this issue, interracial relations came to no good. Celia R. Daileader terms

---

[22] Raffael Scheck, "French colonial soldiers in German prisoners of war camps (1940–1945)," *French History*, 24 (2010), 431–32.

[23] This requirement was based on a law from 1808, which applied to all soldiers. During and after WWII, however, it was mainly applied to colonial soldiers. See Gregory Mann, *Native Sons: West African Veterans and France in the Twentieth Century* (Durham, NC: Duke University Press, 2006), 177–78.

this tendency in literature as Othellophilia, which she defines as "the critical mad cultural fixation on Shakespeare's tragedy of interracial marriage to the exclusion of broader definitions, and more positive visions of interracial erotism." Othellophilia, according to Daileader, focused primarily on white women, with emphasis on punishment of the white woman for falling in love with a black man.[24]

Within the colonial world, the colonizers considered interracial relations as extremely dangerous. Indeed, racism was innate in the colonial discourse that distinguished between different categories of human beings. Colonialism had need of rigid boundaries, of clear distinctions between colonizers and colonized if the colonial project was to run smoothly. Each individual had to know his or her place. Although in practice colonizers soon found this goal impossible to attain, they persisted in their attempts to maintain these boundaries. Ann Stoler speaks of certain groups of colonial subjects who defied colonial categories because they crossed imperial divides. One such group is the *métis*, descendants of interracial relations. According to Stoler, the ways in which colonial authorities handled these groups reflect the tensions of empire: the relationship between the discourses of inclusion, humanitarianism, and equality and exclusionary, discriminatory practices. She shows that in both the Indies and Indochina *métissage* was conceived as a dangerous source of subversion, a threat to white prestige as well as the embodiment of European degeneration and moral decay.[25]

Notwithstanding these fears, interracial relations could not be entirely prohibited in the colonies. In fact, in the French colonies of West Africa they were even institutionalized. In *Children of the French Empire*, Owen White counters French negative views about interracial relations with a practical acceptance of such relations in FWA where French men sought the company of African women from the earliest days of France's presence. West African women and Frenchmen were rarely united in Catholic marriages, but rather in *"marriage à la mode du pays,"* marked by local rites and lasting as long as the French man stayed in the colony.[26]

Temporary unions between French men and African women were thus formally regulated despite the emphatic and sometimes vehement opposition to miscegenation expressed by French racist theoreticians such as Arthur Gobineau and Gustav Le Bon.[27] However, when the mixed couple consisted

[24] Celia R. Daileader, *Racism, Misogyny, and the Othello Myth: Inter-racial Couples from Shakespeare to Spike Lee* (Cambridge: Cambridge University Press, 2005), 6, 8.

[25] Ann L. Stoler, "Sexual affronts and racial frontiers: European identities and the cultural politics of exclusion in colonial Southeast Asia," in Les Back and John Solomos (eds.), *Theories of Race and Racism* (London: Routledge, 1999), 324–25.

[26] Owen White, *Children of the French Empire: Miscegenation and Colonial Society in French West Africa, 1895–1960* (Oxford: Oxford University Press, 1999), 7–11.

[27] Arthur de Gobinau, *Essai sur l'Inegalité des Races humains* (Paris: Firmin-Didot, 1884); Gustave Le Bon, *Lois psychologiques de l'Evolution des Peoples* (Paris: F. Alcan, 1916).

of a black man and a white woman, such tacit acceptance ceased. What was involved here was not only colonial fear of losing control but also a whole set of psychological anxieties – the white man's fear of the ostensibly more powerful sexuality and masculinity of the black man as well as the fear of losing control of both African men and French women. In addition, there was concern that sexual relations with white women would encourage African men to mock French men and women and to feel equal, if not superior, to them. French authorities perceived sexual relations as a terrain in which power was exercised. Hence, while they deemed it natural for the colonizer to conquer colonized women symbolically, the idea that colonized men might do the same to French women was so outrageous that it was totally rejected.

The letters sent by French women after World War II to colonial administrators in FWA prove that many French women ignored white male anxieties regarding interracial relations. They also demonstrate their determination to take control over their destiny and bypass bureaucratic obstacles to bring their husbands and lovers back to them.[28] These women took the initiative of writing to colonial administrators and even to the minister for the colonies to get their husbands or boyfriends back. Most did not give up easily, even when told that their husbands/lovers could not be located, and wrote several letters to attain their goal. This unique source also allows us an indirect access to the voice of African ex-soldiers. As we shall see, not all of these men were anxious to get back to their new French families. Some saw their wartime love affairs as no more than a passing adventure and wished to resume their former lives without further interference. The letters also shed light on the perceptions of interracial relations held by colonial administrators of the time, and how they attempted to reduce the dangers such relations posed to the stability of colonial rule.

Every request made by a woman or on her behalf triggered an administrative procedure that included several stages. After the letter was received by the governor-general or by one of the territorial governors, an attempt was made to locate the ex-soldier in question in the colonies. If found, he was asked whether he was interested in joining the woman in France. In the case of an affirmative answer, the security service produced a report about the ex-Tirailleur, and if positive, he was sent back to France. The process of dealing with such requests was relatively smooth. Considering the relative slowness of communication at the time, most cases were resolved quite efficiently and within a few months.

---

[28] Owen White used this source to demonstrate the readiness of French women to form relationships with black men in spite of the racist theories of the time. See "Miscegenation and the popular imagination," in T. Chafer and A. Sackur (eds.), *Promoting the Colonial Idea: Propaganda and Visions of Empire in France* (New York: Palgrave, 2001).

Basically, the various letters tell similar stories, but the endings are different. A story with a "happy ending" (at least as far as we can tell) is that of Madame J. L.,[29] who wrote to the governor of Senegal on April 15, 1946, requesting that her Senegalese boyfriend, D. S., whom she considered as her husband, be permitted to return to France and share the raising of their ten-month-old son. J. L. explained that she had been an orphan from the age of three months and therefore had no one in the world except D. S.[30] As we shall see, some other women who sought their African lovers came from similar social backgrounds. This suggests that women without relatives found it easier to marry Africans as they did not have to deal with familial objections; however, it should be noted that in several cases it was the mother of the woman in question who wrote the letter on her behalf, which means that some kind of family support existed for these relations, even if this support was extended only after the birth of a child.

Eleven days after J. L.'s letter was sent, D. S.'s response reached the governor. In it he recounted that he had met J. L. when serving as a Tirailleur in her town, Tarascon, and that she had invited him to eat at her home. They later had a child. D. S. wrote that he took care of the mother and son with his meager savings until he was repatriated in December 1945. Since his return to Africa he had regularly sent J. L. coffee, cocoa, rice, and soap, but not money because he had begun working only three months after his discharge. He expressed his wish to join the mother of his son in France and marry her. He intended, so he assured the governor, to send her half of his salary even if he was not allowed to join her in France, but was sure that by being by her side he could help her much more.[31] The security service's report about D. S. was positive, recounting his participation in important battles in the war and stating that he spoke correct French. Following the report, the minister for the colonies approved D. S.'s return to France, saying that this was a better solution than allowing J. L. to join her boyfriend in Dakar.[32]

Not all cases ended, however, in such a manner. In December 1946, Madame N. from Saint Raphael wrote to the governor-general in search of her husband, a Senegalese sergeant who had married her in October 1945 and was repatriated in May 1946. She asked him to ascertain her husband's plans regarding her, adding that she possessed no resources whatsoever. About six weeks later the governor of Senegal reported to the governor-general that he had found the husband who was living in a hut with his uncle and earning very little. The ostensible husband denied being married and told the officials who came to see him that he had met the woman in

[29] The full names are cited in the documents; however, due to the intimate content of the letters I chose to use initials.
[30] April 15, 1946, 4D 61 (89), ANS, Dakar.
[31] April 26, 1946, 4D 61 (89), ANS, Dakar.
[32] April 26 and May 31, 1946, 4D 61 (89), ANS, Dakar.

November 1945 (a month after he supposedly married her) and had some fun with her, but did not wish to see her again. The governor advised vetoing the woman's entry to FWA.[33] Mademoiselle B. from Houille, who was not married to her Tirailleur but pregnant with his child, received a similar response when she searched for him. The father of her child, S. B., declared to the colonial authorities that he was a Muslim and did not want to expose Mademoiselle B. to a life that was too complicated for her. After discussing the matter with his parents, so he said, he reached the conclusion that such a marriage was impossible. When confronted with the information regarding Mademoiselle B.'s pregnancy, he speculated that this was a ploy planned by the woman so she could come to FWA to marry him. He then stated that even if she came, he would not marry her.[34]

A more complicated case that ended in a broken heart was the triangular love story involving Mademoiselle B. from Vittel. In March 1946, she wrote to the commandant of the circle of Porto Novo (Dahomey) asking him to help her locate A. Y., her fiancé since September 19, 1941. She told the commandant that she was now raising their daughter by herself. While they had been preparing to get married, A. Y. had suddenly been sent back to his colony. She was an orphan lacking any family support.[35] A few months later, the governor of Dahomey wrote to the governor-general that the only problem preventing A. Y. from rejoining his fiancée and daughter was the sum of 21,000 metropolitan francs needed for him to return to France. Soon enough a new problem emerged: Another ex-Tirailleur by the name of J. I. sent a letter to the head of the security service claiming that he had been Mademoiselle B's fiancé before A. Y. snatched her away from him. According to him, after he left the German POW camp in Vittel, A. Y. told Mademoiselle B that J. I. was dead. J. I. later came back to France and settled there. He stated that he intended to "take back" his fiancée, marry her, and adopt A. Y.'s child.[36] The colonial administration was at a loss as to how to act. The governor insisted that his intervention in this intimate and complicated case should be limited. He suggested that perhaps marrying J. I., who was living in France and working as a customs official in Meuse, would be the perfect solution for Mademoiselle B who was looking for financial support, but he insisted that she should be allowed to choose which of the two men she preferred.[37]

The case was then transferred to the police in the city of Vittel and on December 3, 1946, the security service of Dahomey received a detailed report on the affair. It stated that the two fiancés were imprisoned in May 1941

[33] January 23, 1947, 4D 61 (89), ANS, Dakar.
[34] After March 1946 (date is not clear), 4D 61 (89), ANS, Dakar.
[35] March 18, 1946, 4D 61 (89), ANS, Dakar.
[36] November 28, 1946, 4D 61 (89), ANS, Dakar.
[37] Ibid.

by the Germans in a POW camp in Vittel designated for British civilians. There they began to receive regular visits from "certain female elements." J. I. and A. Y. both knew Mademoiselle B, but while J. I. left the camp a short time later for an unknown reason, his compatriot stayed on and developed his relationship with the woman and impregnated her. After their release both men were sent back to their colony, but J. I. returned to France and proposed to Mademoiselle B.; however, this "perfect solution" as the governor of Dahomey described it, did not appeal to Mademoiselle B who insisted it was A. Y., the father of her child, she wished to marry.[38]

The way that the colonial administration dealt with this complex love story reflects its relative tolerance towards interracial relations. In all of this long correspondence there was only one negative reference to the character of the women involved in interracial relations – the expression "*certains éléments féminines*" (certain female elements) – but this document was formulated by the local police in Vittel, not by the colonial administration. The correspondence between colonial officials treated the case as a normal, yet complex, love story. It is quite evident that the Dahomey governor's main concern was to help Mademoiselle B. find support for herself and her child. While he believed she should go for the simpler solution and choose the man who was close at hand and who specifically expressed his wish to marry her, even though he was not the father of her child, he accepted that it was up to her to choose. In any case, he was prepared to allow A. Y. to go back to France and even to cover his expenses. Perhaps it would have been better for Mademoiselle B. to follow the administrator's advice. Although A. Y.'s return to France was approved, he did not go back to his fiancé and child, using the pretext that for two years he could not manage to find a place on a ship.[39]

In all the cases I examined, the authorities never objected to the return of the Tirailleur to his girlfriend, wife, or family in France unless, of course, the Tirailleur himself refused to go back. Only in one case the approval of the request was postponed until an inquiry would be performed regarding the ostensible involvement of a certain Tirailleur in the revolt in Thiaroye in December 1944.[40] Otherwise, if the soldier expressed his willingness to return to France to marry the French woman (if they were not already married) and provide for her needs, the authorization was given and occasionally the administration even covered the cost of the journey.

This enthusiasm to send African soldiers away from the colonies to their French wives or girlfriends can also be explained by the colonial administration's fear concerning the impact of such relations if they became visible in

---

[38] December 3, 1946, 4D 61 (89), ANS, Dakar.

[39] August 2, 1947, 4D 61 (89), ANS, Dakar.

[40] February 18, 1946, 4D 61 (89), ANS, Dakar. On the revolt, see Echenberg, "Tragedy at Thiaroye," 109–128.

the colonies. Indeed, although French administrators did not object to the unification of French women with their African lovers on French soil, their tolerance completely disappeared when the French woman suggested joining her husband or lover in the colonies. There was always a fierce objection to this idea. Colonial authorities often referred to the decision to send the soldier back to France as a "lesser evil." To send a French woman to live in the colonies with Africans was unthinkable to them. They explained that they did not consider the colonies as suitable places for white women to live, especially among colonial subjects. Such blurring of boundaries was tolerable when it occurred in France, but utterly unacceptable in the colonies. A letter from the security services regarding the request of a Tirailleur from French Sudan to bring his French wife with him to the colony illustrates this position. The governor of French Sudan was praised in this letter for objecting to the move, because it was obvious that a French woman could not live with a "native" (*indigène*) in the forest. On the other hand, the letter emphasized that it would be relatively simple to allow an African to settle in France; anyone familiar with Marseille knew that the city had a quarter where blacks live. The letter also mentioned an organization that existed in the city, the Association des Noirs de l'AOF, which supported Africans, adding that some Africans who lived in Marseille supported themselves honorably and none died of hunger.[41]

Nevertheless, the ability to prevent this sort of family reunion was limited as can be seen from the case of Madame D., aged fifty-two, who insisted on joining her thirty-year-old husband in Dahomey, in spite of the objections of the governor-general and the minister for the colonies. The administrator objected partly due to the age difference between the two, but especially against the arrival of a French woman in Dahomey, even though the ex-soldier in question was a hero of the French resistance. These objections notwithstanding, the restoration of the freedom of movement of French citizens between France and FWA after the war enabled Madame D. to do as she pleased.[42] Although FWA administrators objected to the arrival of French women in FWA to live with their African husbands and lovers on the grounds of their inability to adjust to the African way of life, it seems clear that their real motive was the fear of the dangerous influence of such mixed couples living among Africans. In France, these couples lived far from the eyes of colonial subjects and therefore were less dangerous.

In an article on colonial POWs during World War II, Armelle Mabon maintains that it was mainly racist attitudes that guided military authorities to oppose intimate relations between African soldiers and French women. She quotes two French generals who warned about the danger of these relations for the future of France and its empire. She also points to the military

---

[41] June 26, 1945, 4D 61 (89), ANS, Dakar.
[42] July 1, July 24, July 25, and August 27, 1946, 4D 61(89), ANS, Dakar.

policy of sending African soldiers back to their colonies, thus forcing them to leave their wives, lovers, and children behind, as proof of this racism.[43] While I do not deny that racist attitudes and negative views about interracial relations abounded among military officers and colonial administrators, I maintain that we should be careful not to explain all policies regarding this issue by racism. While it is impossible to underestimate the extent of concern and anxiety among colonial administrators regarding encounters between African soldiers and French women during the war, this does not mean that the objection to these relations was the result of pure racism based on an abhorrence of racial mixing.

As I have shown, it is obvious that French colonial administrators were not guided by biological anxieties regarding interracial relations, as they treated these affairs as normal love stories between women and liberating soldiers, frequent in wartime. Otherwise, it is impossible to explain the extreme efforts colonial administrators invested in locating African ex-soldiers for the anxious women who wrote to them and their willingness to send these ex-soldiers to France. It is also important to bear in mind that African ex-soldiers were not always interested to return to their French girlfriends or wives. Therefore, the fact that even today children of French women and African soldiers try to trace their fathers, which Mabon points out, does not necessarily mean that these fathers were forcibly kept away from their children.[44] The colonial administrators' main concern was to minimize the threat to the stability of colonial rule, and they certainly feared that such visible relations on African soil might undermine colonial authority. The policy of sending away from the colonies African ex-soldiers who were involved in love affairs with French women reduced the "administrative headaches" these officials already had to handle with regard to problematic demobilized soldiers.

Conclusions: African Soldiers' Experiences in World War II and the Decolonization of French West Africa

In an article on African soldiers from British and French colonies in World War II, Rita Headrick asserts that France succeeded in creating a wide group of supporters from among the soldiers who participated in the war.[45] While this is true, it certainly demanded a great deal of effort and extensive reforms in the colonial army. Relations between African soldiers and the French army in which they had served were at a very low point toward the end of the

---

[43] Armelle Mabon, "La singulière captivité des prisonniers de guerre coloniaux durant la seconde guerre mondiale," *French Colonial History*, 7 (2006), 190–91.

[44] Ibid., 190.

[45] Rita Headrick, "African soldiers in World War II," *Armed Forces and Society*, 4 (1978), 519.

war and the late 1940s. As I have shown in this chapter, the experiences of African colonial soldiers in Europe during World War II transformed the way in which they saw the colonial power they served. Disobedience to the African representatives of the FWA colonial administration, contempt toward the French, and statements about the weakening of France as a nation were the main symptoms of this transformation; they were seen as a serious challenge to both the Vichy and the Free French colonial administrations.

World War II contributed much to the hostility of African soldiers toward France and the army in which they served. Witnessing the fall of France in 1940, the experiences of the soldiers in Europe during the war, discrimination against the soldiers, and violent incidents, most notably the brutal repression of the 1944 Thiaroye revolt, alienated many of the soldiers and loosened their discipline and motivation. Within a few years, however, the French army began to implement measures to render the military service more attractive for African soldiers. The equation of African soldiers' pensions to those of the French in 1950 was the first efficient move in a general campaign to win over African veterans. This was followed by augmenting the percentage of volunteers in the army, improving pay and service conditions, offering professional education to soldiers, encouraging African soldiers to become officers, and perhaps the most symbolic change – replacing the term "*tirailleurs sénégalais*" with the much more respectful "*soldats africains.*"[46]

These extensive reforms contributed, no doubt, to the restoration of the soldiers' trust in the French army and attracted more volunteers after World War II who wanted to take advantage of the social and economic opportunities the "new army" offered them. Thus, African soldiers and veterans presented no obstacle to the continuation of French colonial rule. In fact, alienation between them and France resumed only after the independence of the FWA colonies and the crystallization of their pensions. While it is difficult to assess the impact of the stories soldiers returning from the battlefields of Europe had to tell their relatives, friends, and neighbors, one can imagine that they certainly did not enhance French legitimacy to continue colonial domination over Africans. Stories of warm welcome of French civilians and love affairs with French women were no doubt as influential (or even more) as stories of discrimination and suffering. The possibility of equal relations between Africans and French offered an attractive alternative to repressive colonial reality. In this respect, the experiences African soldiers had gone through during World War II undermined French colonial authority and cracked the foundations of the French empire in Africa.

[46] Mann, *Native Sons*, 110, 171–74.

18

World War II and the Sex Trade in British West Africa

Carina Ray

Introduction

Many of the essays in this volume unequivocally show the manifold ways in which Africans were central to the evolution and outcome of World War II, despite Africa's marginality in the war's historiography. Equally important, contributors to this volume demonstrate how the profound social, political, and economic upheaval spawned by the war significantly shaped Africa's mid-twentieth century history in ways that we now understand more fully. This particular essay argues that World War II was a watershed in the social and legislative history of the sex trade in West Africa. The deployment of large numbers of European and American male military personnel to the Gold Coast during the war, along with the predeployment training of local African troops, swelled the number of single military men in the colony and the demand for commercial sex.

As sex work became an increasingly lucrative form of wartime employment, large numbers of African women, particularly from Nigeria, migrated to the Gold Coast. Others, including young girls, were trafficked into the colony, often under false pretences, and forced into sex work.[1] Open prostitution in the streets of cities reconfigured by the war (e.g., Accra, Sekondi, and Takoradi) became a seemingly uncontrollable nuisance to the police and a public embarrassment. Rising rates of venereal disease among both European and African military personnel began to affect the war effort negatively. In the face of this, colonial administrators were pressured to adopt stricter antiprostitution laws, including legislation designed to curb the traffic in women and children from Nigeria into the Gold Coast for the purpose of prostitution. Although this legislative intervention was not without its opponents in the administration, its eventual success marked a

---

[1] Saheed Aderinto, "'The Problem of Nigeria Is Slavery, Not White Slave Traffic': Globalization and the Politicization of Prostitution in Southern Nigeria, 1921–1955," *Canadian Journal of African Studies*, 46 (2012), 7.

departure from the longstanding refusal of Gold Coast colonial authorities to strengthen antiprostitution laws when safeguarding the health of Africans from venereal disease was a concern.

This chapter contends that racist notions about African sexualities played a decisive role in delaying the introduction of legal measures to curb colonial West Africa's sex trade, while wartime exigencies were largely responsible for the introduction of stricter antiprostitution and sex trafficking legislation in 1942 and 1943, just as West Africa's strategic value to Britain gained new importance when Singapore fell to the Japanese in early 1942.[2] Despite increased demand for Gold Coast troops, as evidenced by the extended reach of the colony's Compulsory Service Ordinance, antiprostitution measures were intended to protect European military personnel, rather than Africans, from the ravages of venereal disease.[3] Thus, even as World War II and the social changes it occasioned ushered in a new legislative era for the sex trade in British West Africa, as in so many other facets of the war, the interests and well-being of Europeans were paramount to those of Africans.

World War II-Era Interracial Prostitution in the Gold Coast

While World War II was a key turning point in the legislative history of West Africa's sex trade, it was not the first time that prostitution in the Gold Coast was the subject of controversy and legal debate. In the decades prior to World War II, the movement of women across West African colonial borders for the purpose of prostitution was already a recognized phenomenon that created anxiety on the part of many Africans and Europeans. On at least two occasions, concern about the epidemiological consequences of prostitution led local African leaders in the Gold Coast to lobby the colonial government to strengthen antiprostitution legislation.[4] In 1911, chiefs from various parts of the Keta district in the Gold Coast's Eastern Province complained to the provincial commissioner that venereal disease rates were on the rise in the province due to an influx of women from neighboring Togoland who were practicing prostitution.[5] Although their concerns gained traction with the district commissioner, the colony's governor, Sir James Jamieson

---

[2] David Killingray, "Military and labour recruitment in the Gold Coast during the Second World War," *Journal of African History*, 23 (1982), 83.

[3] Ibid., 92.

[4] I explore this history in greater detail in Carina Ray, "Sex trafficking, prostitution and the law in colonial British West Africa, 1911–1943," in Benjamin Lawrance and Richard Roberts (eds.), *Trafficking in Slavery's Wake: Law and the Experience of Women and Children in Africa* (Athens: Ohio University Press, 2012), 101–20.

[5] John Maxwell, commissioner (Eastern Province) to acting colonial secretary (Accra), "Prostitution – Unsatisfactory state of the law respecting," April 26, 1911, case no. 86/1911, ADM 11/1/922, Public Records and Archives Administration Department (hereafter PRAAD), Accra.

Thorburn, dismissed them. Justifying his decision not to enact stricter antiprostitution legislation, Thorburn claimed that such measures were fundamentally incompatible with the "customs of the [colony's] natives . . . such that it would be practically impossible to so frame laws as to prevent prostitution and yet safeguard the liberty of the subject in giving reach to his natural – even though excessive possibly – inclinations in this regard." He concluded that "much as one may deplore immorality" it was not possible "to render people moral by virtue of passing ordinances." Instead, Thorburn opted to lend "support" to the concerned chiefs should "they take action themselves for the removal of these undesirable visitors, and to prevent others with similar disqualifications from entering their divisions."[6]

The colonial government continued to stand by this noninterventionist policy fourteen years later when, in 1925, Chief Kadri English, the self-described "tribal ruler of Hausas in Accra and its environs," complained to the district commissioner of Accra that Hausa women from Nigeria were entering into prostitution after arriving in the Gold Coast, compromising their piety and the health of their communities.[7] As historian Emmanuel Akyeampong notes, English "wisely linked his petition to colonial concerns about health and finances" because these were the kinds of issues that typically gained traction with the colonial state.[8] Indeed, many administrators who appreciated the negative effect venereal diseases were having on local populations shared his concerns, but the attorney general and the governor did not.[9] Despite considerable evidence that prostitution was indeed causing the proliferation of venereal diseases among the African population, the colonial administration rejected English's call for a legal remedy in favor of abiding by the policy established in 1911. We can conclude, therefore, that venereal disease among the African population was not regarded as a problem significant enough to warrant new legislation. The colony's laws were not alone in being ill-equipped to deal with prostitution. Its medical infrastructure was also incapable of providing treatment to the vast majority of people infected with sexually transmitted diseases. Indeed, the colony only had one venereal disease clinic, established in 1920 in Accra by a local doctor, Carl E. Reindorf.[10] Reindorf not only ran the clinic, but he also vigorously campaigned for better and more expansive treatment options

---

[6] Acting Governor Thorburn to acting colonial secretary (Accra), May 8, 1911, case no. 86/1911, ADM 11/1/922 [Prostitution], PRAAD, Accra.

[7] Kadri English, Hausa tribal ruler to district commissioner (Accra), May 13, 1925, case no. 25/1925, ADM 11/1/922, PRAAD, Accra.

[8] Emmanuel Akyeampong, "Sexuality and prostitution among the Akan of the Gold Coast, c. 1650–1950," *Past and Present*, 156 (1997), 158.

[9] H. S. Newlands, secretary for native affairs, to colonial secretary, September 1, 1925, case no. 25/1925, ADM 11/1/922, PRAAD, Accra.

[10] K. David Patterson, "Health in urban Ghana: The case of Accra 1900–1940 [1]," *Social Science and Medicine. Part B: Medical Anthropology*, 13 (1979), 257.

for Africans afflicted by venereal diseases throughout his long career.[11] The onset of World War II, however, brought the Gold Coast government's decades-long legislative intransigence on the question of prostitution into sharp relief as the flow of sex workers from Nigeria into the colony increased dramatically to meet the demand for commercial sex by thousands of newly arrived European and American male military personnel, as well as African troops undergoing predeployment training.

In the months preceding the summer of 1941, Accra, the Gold Coast capital, and the coastal town Takoradi, witnessed an influx of European personnel, numbering in the thousands, belonging to the British military and Royal Air Force (RAF). Takoradi's small airport was transformed into a major RAF base to assemble aircraft for the British forces in North Africa and the Middle East. In addition to the European colonial and military personnel resident in Takoradi, there was also an American presence. According to Nancy Lawler, by October 1941, Takoradi became "the base where U.S. planes were overhauled and refueled before joining the ferry route to the Middle East."[12] Yet, it was Accra that became the most significant base of operation for the Americans, with just over 5,000 troops.[13] In 1942, the year after the U.S. Army Air Force opened a base in Accra, it relocated its Air Transport Command from Cairo to the capital, where it established its Africa–Middle East Wing.[14] Unlike the American deployment of some 2,000 African American rank and file troops and a small cadre of white American superiors to Liberia, one of the U.S. Army's first racially integrated units, the American presence on the Gold Coast was entirely white.[15] The Americans established a system of medically regulated prostitution for African American troops in Liberia, which provided them with access to nearly 600 Liberian sex workers who were housed in two "villages" adjacent to their Roberts Field base.[16] African American men,

---

[11] Deborah Pellow, "STDs and AIDS in Ghana," *Genitourinary Medicine*, 70 (1994), 418–20.

[12] Nancy Ellen Lawler, *Soldiers, Airmen, Spies, and Whisperers: The Gold Coast in World War II* (Athens: Ohio University Press, 2001), 54–55. On the logistical and diplomatic history of what became known as the "Takoradi Route," see Deborah Wing Ray, "The Takoradi Route: Roosevelt's prewar venture beyond the western hemisphere," *Journal of American History*, 62 (1975), 340–58.

[13] James Tobias, U.S. Army Center of Military History, e-mail message to author, May 19, 2006.

[14] Lawler, *Soldiers, Airmen*, 56. For more on the British and American presence in the Gold Coast and West Africa more generally, see also Ashley Jackson, *The British Empire and the Second World War* (London: Hambledon Continuum, 2006), 171–268.

[15] Jane Mersky Leder, *Thanks for the Memories: Love, Sex, and World War II* (Westport, CT: Praeger Publishers, 2006), 212; David Killingray, "Soldiers, ex-servicemen, and politics in the Gold Coast, 1939–50," *Journal of Modern African Studies*, 21 (1983), 525.

[16] Leder, *Thanks for the Memories*, 122. For a more sensational account of army-sponsored prostitution in Liberia, see George Abraham, *The Belles of Shangri-La: And Other Stories of Sex, Snakes, and Survival from World War II*, 1st ed. (New York: Vantage Press, 2000). Both

it was assumed, could not remain celibate during their deployment. Thus, like their African counterparts, underlying racist assumptions about African American male sexuality influenced policymaking on the question of prostitution. No such provisions for easily accessible commercial sex were made for their white superiors in Liberia or the all-white American personnel in the Gold Coast. Extant sources do not address the extent to which American troops in the Gold Coast were involved in prostitution, but U.S. Army sources attest to the fact that venereal diseases plagued personnel stationed there.[17] This suggests that alongside their British counterparts, Americans, whether as vectors or recipients of sexually transmitted diseases, were involved in prostitution.

While as early as 1940, police authorities began to notice an increase in the number of women and girls being trafficked into the Gold Coast from Nigeria, it was not until the following year that Police Commissioner Eric Cato Nottingham declared that the sudden rise in the number of foreign military men in the colony was causing an "increase in the number of women who earn their living by prostitution with Europeans." Commensurate with the increase in prostitution was an escalation in the number of European military personnel infected with venereal diseases, which alarmed medical authorities. In Nottingham's view this was "an additional reason why these women who are a danger to health should be removed from the immediate vicinity of the large camps housing European personnel." Not surprisingly he singled out Accra and Takoradi, where the largest populations of military men were stationed, as the towns in which "the conduct of these women is causing embarrassment."[18] Typical of contemporary gendered discourses on prostitution, the behavior of johns were never identified as factors in the prostitution epidemic; nor were their actions considered punishable offenses, constitutive of a public health threat, or cause for "embarrassment."

The war not only brought thousands of European and American men to the colony, but it also drew, voluntarily and by force, close to 70,000 men from all over the Gold Coast into Britain's Royal West Africa Frontier Force for service in West and East Africa, Burma and, to a lesser extent, North Africa.[19] The lengthy predeployment training Gold Coast soldiers received in military camps, along with those soldiers and military laborers manning the home front, ensured that there were always sizeable numbers

---

Leder and Abraham suggest that the women who worked in these brothels were Liberian, but this assertion is not proved.

[17] Charles M. Wiltse, *The Medical Department: Medical Service in the Mediterranean and Minor Theaters* (Washington, D.C.: Office of the Chief of Military History, Department of the Army, 1965), 67.

[18] "Prostitutes – control of by police," memorandum, E. C. Nottingham to colonial secretary (Accra), May 30, 1941, CSO 15/1/222 [Traffic in women and children], PRAAD, Accra.

[19] Killingray, "Military and labour recruitment in the Gold Coast," 84–85, and "Soldiers, ex-servicemen, and politics in the Gold Coast," 529.

of African troops stationed in the colony.[20] For example, large numbers of Gold Coast recruits were stationed in Accra where they helped in the construction of military accommodation, and in Takoradi where they supplied the manpower to build the airfields and facilities for the Middle East supply route.[21]

This, in turn, created further demand for commercial sex and helps to explain why venereal disease rates among this group were also extremely high. Indeed, the war office adviser in venereology, Richard R. Willcox, reported that indigenous troops in the Gold Coast had a 50 percent per annum rate of venereal disease infection between 1943 and 1945. Yet this did not provoke the same outcry for legislative reform from police and medical authorities as did prostitution and venereal diseases involving Europeans. While the army provided medical treatment for European and African soldiers infected with sexually transmitted diseases, the fact that infection rates among Africans remained high, even as European infection rates fell in response to the legislative reforms of 1942–1943, suggests that such reforms were meant to prevent European troops from being infected in the first place, while the best African troops could hope for was remedial care. No comparable care was available for the civilian African population, including sex workers.[22]

With cities and towns like Accra and Takoradi swelled to capacity with both European and African troops, the war introduced new forms of nightlife that fostered greater opportunities for interracial contact, including prostitution. The increased number of dances and other social functions to support wartime charities became fertile places for prostitution; it was even alleged that sexual indecencies were occurring at the functions themselves.[23] The most lucrative of these charities was the Spitfires Fund, established by the Gold Coast government to raise money for the purchase of aircraft for the RAF. In a bid to encourage Gold Coasters to rally behind the war effort with their hard-earned cash, the RAF named two of its squadrons after the colony. The aircraft of choice for the squadron was called the Spitfire, hence the name Spitfires Fund. According to Nancy Lawler, in its first year, 1940, the Gold Coast Spitfires Fund raised £65,000; its goal for 1941 was £100,000, which was quickly raised within the first half of the year. The success of the Spitfires Fund was largely due to the fact that it utilized popular attractions such as dances, contests, and other events throughout the colony

---

[20] David Killingray and Martin Plaut, *Fighting for Britain: African Soldiers in the Second World War* (Woodbridge, Suffolk: James Currey, 2010), 83–84.

[21] Killingray, "Military and labour recruitment in the Gold Coast," 86.

[22] R. R. Willcox, "Venereal disease in British West Africa," *British Journal of Venereal Diseases*, 22 (1946), 65–66.

[23] Nottingham, memorandum on control of prostitutes, May 30, 1941, CSO 15/1/222 [Traffic in women and children], PRAAD, Accra.

to raise money.[24] Promoters of the dances, most likely Lebanese immigrants, who owned the majority of the colony's dance halls, were blamed for encouraging the attendance of sex workers by selling "Single Ladies Tickets" at prices far reduced from the rate charged to single men and couples.[25]

In addition to sex workers, who allegedly conducted their business at wartime charity socials, another group was identified as loitering around dances and clubs and in the streets. So openly practiced was prostitution in wartime Accra that the police reported that "recognized 'stands' have become existent at which women nightly offer themselves for the purpose of prostitution." These women were considered the greatest "nuisance" because they "openly shouted" and molested men in an attempt to attract clients. In explaining why the situation had spiraled out of control Nottingham drew attention to the unsatisfactory state of the law regarding prostitution, which kept the police's hands tied:

> In the Gold Coast, Police have no power to control these women or to proceed against prostitutes – not being Europeans – who behave in such manner and I urge that legislation similar to that which exists in Nigeria may be enacted whereby some measure of control can be obtained over the movements of this class of person. I particularly invite attention to the fact that the Gold Coast Laws (See Section 435(1) of the Criminal Code) provide that any female *not being a native of West Africa* who follows a calling of a common prostitute is liable to imprisonment without hard labor for six months. From the wording of the section it seems that in the Gold Coast the calling of a common prostitute, provided she is a native of West Africa, is recognized and it is remarkable that the words, "brothel," "keeping," "soliciting," "loitering," "importuning" and etc. do not exist in the Gold Coast Laws. [Emphasis in the original.][26]

In short, Nottingham contended that the Gold Coast's wartime prostitution problem resulted from both the increased demand for commercial sex occasioned by the deployment of thousands of European male military personnel and the colony's practically nonexistent laws on prostitution, which made it a prime destination for sex workers.

Intimating that the lax nature of the Criminal Code on prostitution was not simply an oversight, Nottingham concluded that, "It would almost seem that this has been done purposely, a state of affairs which I venture to suggest would not be tolerated elsewhere in the British Empire." His suspicions were

---

[24] Lawler, *Soldiers, Airmen*, 188–91. For more on the mobilization of support in the Gold Coast for Britain's war efforts, see Wendell Holbrook, "British propaganda and the mobilization of the Gold Coast war effort," *Journal of African History*, 26 (1985), 347–61.

[25] Nottingham, memorandum on control of prostitutes, May 30, 1941, CSO 15/1/222 [Traffic in women and children], PRAAD, Accra. On the Lebanese ownership of the colony's dance halls, see R. Bayly Winder, "The Lebanese in West Africa," *Comparative Studies in Society and History*, 4 (1962), 312.

[26] Nottingham, memorandum on control of prostitutes, May 30, 1941, CSO 15/1/222 [Traffic in women and children], PRAAD, Accra.

well founded. As we have already seen, the Gold Coast government twice rejected calls from both African and European authorities to strengthen the colony's antiprostitution laws.[27] As was the case in 1911, racist notions about African sexuality continued to inform wartime resistance to reforming the colony's legal code on prostitution, even as wartime conditions spurred on the demand for commercial sex. It is worth pausing to consider the possibility that these notions found new currency during the war when they could be invoked to forestall the introduction of tougher antiprostitution laws precisely because activities associated with prostitution, such as wartime charity socials, played an important role in raising money for the war effort.

The Wartime Sex Trade: From Nigeria to the Gold Coast

While local police authorities in the Gold Coast lamented their inability to curb wartime interracial prostitution in Accra and Takoradi, others drew attention to the regional traffic in women and children that was feeding the demand for commercial sex in these cities. In March 1941, an exposé on the sex trade between Nigeria and the Gold Coast appeared in the widely read *West Africa* magazine, titled "The social question: A startling disclosure." The exposé's author, Henry Ormston, cited an investigation into the traffic undertaken by Mr. R. K. Floyer, the local authority of Port Harcourt in Nigeria, which found eighty young girls from Owerri Province, alone, practicing prostitution in the Gold Coast, allegedly with the consent of their parents.[28]

Aside from the trade itself, Ormston's "startling disclosure" was his assertion that it was attributable to "two non-African sub-communities" in the Gold Coast. While he never directly named the two groups, his descriptions of them suggest that he held the Lebanese community responsible for orchestrating the sex trade and Europeans responsible for hiring sex workers.[29] While Lebanese owned many of the colony's dance halls, reportedly popular wartime hangouts for sex workers, and evidence suggests that some Lebanese were involved in supplying prostitutes to Europeans, there is simply not enough accurate evidence to judge the extent of their role in the transregional sex trade in colonial West Africa.[30] Available evidence does, however, substantiate the fact that large numbers of Europeans, especially recently deployed military personnel, hired West African sex workers. So too did Gold Coast men. Indeed, observers linked the low number of Gold Coast

---

[27] Cases no. 86/1911 and 25/1925, ADM 11/1/922 [Prostitution – unsatisfactory state of the law respecting], PRAAD, Accra.
[28] Henry Ormston, "The social question: A startling disclosure," *West Africa*, March 15, 1941, 250. Also see Mary Chorlton, "Nigerian 'social question': Pertinent posers that demand official enquiry," *West Africa*, September 13, 1941, 887.
[29] Ormston, "The social question," 250.
[30] Winder, "Lebanese in West Africa," 312.

recruits available for the war effort to the sex trade's role in spreading vene-real diseases.[31] While Ormston acknowledged that African men engaged the services of sex workers, he rejected the idea that Africans were involved in organizing the traffic. He contended, "nobody who has any acquaintance with African ways of life will for a moment believe that this is a business between Africans and Africans." He also rejected the notion that Owerri girls were practicing prostitution with the consent of their parents.[32] To be sure, many Nigerians and Gold Coasters were deeply disturbed by the sex trade and voiced their grievances in local newspapers.[33] In the pages of *The Nigerian Eastern Mail*, one Ibibio author lamented the traffic's potential to ruin "the future women of their [Ibibio] race," citing its adverse effects on population growth and traditional gender hierarchies.[34] Political action against the trade came from the Gold Coast branch of the Nigerian Youth Movement (NYM) and elite Lagosian women who campaigned for greater legislative means and social resources to bring an end to the sex trade in the Gold Coast and in Nigeria, respectively.[35]

Yet ample evidence also indicates that some communities in areas affected by the trade not only sanctioned it, but also actively orchestrated it. Accord-ing to Nigeria's then governor, Sir Bernard Henry Bourdillon, it had become "abundantly clear that migration of women from Nigeria to the Gold Coast for the purposes of prostitution is a profitable, well-organised trade, sup-ported and maintained by the very communities to which the women them-selves belong." Citing the Obubra Division in Ogoja Province of the Cross River Basin, he noted that investigators had found that "there is hardly a family that has not an interest in it, and Elders openly admit that they receive a fee, amounting to some pounds, from every woman who practices this calling." Bourdillon described the elaborate and closely regulated nature of the trade and its profitability as follows:

> The communities principally concerned maintain Societies, which are respon-sible for the management of the trade. These Societies have representatives in the Gold Coast who receive and establish the women on their arrival, and it is

---

[31] Ormston, "Social question," 250. Mary Chorlton cites an article in *The Nigerian Eastern Mail* that linked the traffic's role in spreading venereal diseases to the lower number of Gold Coast recruits available for the war-effort. See Chorlton, "Nigerian 'social question,'" 887.

[32] Ormston, "Social question," 250.

[33] Henry Ormston noted in his exposé that Gold Coast newspapers were awash with public commentary by Africans who were upset by the trade and its adverse effect on wartime recruitment. Indicative of the fact that Nigerians were discussing this question, Mary Chorl-ton also referenced several articles authored by Nigerians that appeared in *The Nigerian Eastern Mail*. Ormston, "Social question," 250; Chorlton, "Nigerian 'social question,'" 887.

[34] Chorlton quotes the Ibibio author in "Nigerian 'social question,'" 887.

[35] For more on the activities of the NYM and elite Lagosian women, see Aderinto, "'The Problem of Nigeria is Slavery, Not White Slave Traffic," 2–3.

even claimed that the fees extracted from the latter have rendered the Societies so affluent that they are able to build houses and provide legal assistance for their clients ... there can be no doubt that the profits from this traffic are considerable, and the case is quoted of one of these harlots who returned recently from the Gold Coast with no less than eighty pounds in her possession.[36]

So great was the revenue generated by women engaged in sex work from the Obubra Division that in 1942 their verifiable remittances, alone, totaled nearly £7,000, almost twice the division's estimated public revenue for the last tallied fiscal year, 1937–1938.[37] While this amount was not remitted solely by sex workers in the Gold Coast, as it included women who were engaged in sex work in other parts of Nigeria as well, it is one indication of how widespread and profitable the traffic had become during the war.[38]

Why were such sizeable numbers of Nigerian women, particularly from the Cross River Basin, entering into prostitution as a profession, both within Nigeria and in the Gold Coast? Benedict Naanen argues that Cross River was economically marginal and underdeveloped in comparison to other areas of Nigeria that had been more centrally integrated into global economic and social networks through colonialism. As a result, many Cross River women found sex work to be "more profitable than the locally available peasant occupations." Sex work offered remuneration in cash, which was significant, given the monetization of the indigenous economy, and in turn provided women with the ability to acquire material wealth, property, and other status symbols hitherto unavailable to them in the local economy.

These push factors toward prostitution, according to Naanen, were exacerbated at the structural level by the fact that the colonial state "eroded the power of indigenous institutions of social control ... or abolished them altogether" and "provided large territorial space, the demand for commercial sex (through urbanization), and security" which in turn "enabled women to travel freely and far away from their indigenous communities to places where they could profitably escape rural patriarchy and commercialize their sexual freedom."[39] Yet the existence of elaborate community-based

---

[36] Bourdillon (Nigeria) to Hodson (Gold Coast), July 29, 1941, CSO 15/1/222 [Traffic in women and children], PRAAD, Accra.

[37] Benedict Naanen, "'Itinerant gold mines': Prostitution in the Cross River Basin of Nigeria, 1930–1950," *African Studies Review*, 34 (1991), 61.

[38] For further details on the revenue these communities derived from women engaged in sex work in the Gold Coast, see Aderinto, "'The Problem of Nigeria Is Slavery,'" 2.

[39] Ibid., 61, 63–66. Studies on prostitution elsewhere in Africa similarly demonstrate that some women succeeded in turning it into a lucrative entrepreneurial enterprise, regardless of how they initially entered the activity. For Kenya, see Janet Bujra, "Production, property and prostitution: 'Sexual politics' in Atu," *Cahiers d'Etudes Africaines*, 65 (1977), 13–39; Bujra, "Women 'Entrepreneurs' of early Nairobi," *Canadian Journal of African Studies*, 9, (1975), 213–234; and Luise White, *The Comforts of Home: Prostitution in Colonial Nairobi* (Chicago, IL: University of Chicago Press, 1990). While documenting a similar pattern in Asia and the Pacific, Linda Bryder warns us of "the danger in pushing agency

systems designed to regulate the sex trade suggests that colonialism did not necessarily erode indigenous institutions of social control altogether, but either created new ones or forced preexisting ones to adapt to the changing socioeconomic imperatives of the time. Regulatory systems to achieve the intended purpose of generating much-needed financial revenue that was otherwise difficult to obtain, while minimizing the trade's negative impact on sex workers even included the predeparture provision of medicinal protection against venereal disease and spiritual and physical ablution upon their return.[40]

Given that economic factors played the largest role in pushing women into prostitution, the negative impact that the worldwide economic depression had on African economies during the 1930s, closely followed by the economic turmoil occasioned by World War II, helps to explain why even centrally located and more fully integrated areas, such as Calabar, were also hard-hit by the sex trade. One of the striking aspects of the sex trade emerging out of Nigeria was that a large percentage of sex workers went to the Gold Coast. While internal migration within Nigeria was a pronounced phenomenon of the sex trade, where external migration was concerned, the Gold Coast greatly surpassed other destinations such as Cameroon and Fernando Po.[41] The very factors that Captain Nottingham had identified during his initial plea for greater police powers to deal with prostitution may explain why this was the case. First, the laxity of the Gold Coast's antiprostitution laws safeguarded sex workers from surveillance and criminal prosecution. Indeed, as far back as 1911 the Gold Coast had emerged as a haven for sex workers fleeing Togoland's German colonial authorities. Second, during the war, sex work in the Gold Coast became incredibly lucrative as the demand for commercial sex skyrocketed, a result of the deployment of thousands of male military personnel. Profitability and possibility combined to make prostitution a viable means of capital accumulation in the Gold Coast during a period when other possibilities were either far less lucrative, unattractive, or simply unavailable.

Racial Ideologies and Legislative Reform

While it is clear that Africans were active participants in the wartime sex trade, the ways in which colonial officials deployed racist notions about African sexuality in service of their arguments against implementing stricter antiprostitution and trafficking laws sheds light on the relationship between

---

too far," given that many women were forced into prostitution against their will and often faced horrific abuses; see Linda Bryder, "Sex, race, and colonialism: An historiographical review," *International History Review*, 20 (1998), 811–12.

[40] Aderinto, "'The Problem of Nigeria Is Slavery,'" 11.

[41] Ibid., 60.

racial thought and legislative history.[42] Long before the start of the war, the Gold Coast colony's Criminal Code on prostitution was already racially coded: West African women were exempt from the law, whereas it was illegal for European women to work as prostitutes in the colony. When police authorities called for legislative reforms that would allow them to prosecute West African sex workers, the colony's attorney general, H. W. D. Blackall, argued in favor of maintaining the Criminal Code's longstanding race-based double standard for two reasons. First, he claimed that the law justifiably criminalized prostitution by nonnatives because, in his words, "in tropical Africa it would not conduce to the prestige of Europeans if white prostitutes were allowed to ply their trade here."[43] Here we see that in practice, when the law referred to "any female not being a native of West Africa who follows a calling of a common prostitute," it meant a "white" prostitute. Blackall further noted that this special provision was in effect in other African colonies.[44] Second, he contended that the exclusion of West African sex workers from the law kept European women safe from the sexual deprivations of African men. If the police were empowered to remove them from areas where there were large numbers of single African men, Blackall ominously warned that "the position of European women in those places might not be as safe as it is at present."[45] The attorney general even went so far as to raise the specter of the "Black Peril" in South Africa to drive his point home. Echoing the very same sentiment expressed by Acting Governor Thorburn in 1911, when he too refused to introduce stricter antiprostitution legislation, Blackall concluded by arguing that "the remedy of making people good by act of parliament is not as easy as he [Commissioner Nottingham] thinks."[46] Blackall's invocation of racist rhetoric about African sexuality was successful: the government rejected Nottingham's call to reform the colony's lax laws on prostitution.

The Gold Coast government was not only impervious to internal calls for legislative reform, it also resisted external calls for developing strategies to

---

[42] I intentionally use sexuality in the singular here because racist colonial ideologies typically presented a monolithic view of African sexualities as hyperlicentious.

[43] Attorney-general to colonial secretary, June 6, 1941, CSO 15/1/222 [Traffic in women and children], PRAAD, Accra.

[44] Racial anxieties about European women working as prostitutes in the colonies were by no means limited to the African colonies. For India and elsewhere in the British Empire, see Philippa Levine, "Venereal disease, prostitution, and the politics of empire: The case of British India," *Journal of the History of Sexuality*, 4 (1994), 579–602; Philippa Levine, Prostitution, Race, and Politics: Policing Venereal Disease in the British Empire (New York: Routledge, 2003), 231–56.

[45] Attorney-general to clerk (executive council), September 19, 1941, CSO 15/1/222 [Traffic in women and children], PRAAD, Accra.

[46] Ibid. For Acting Governor Thorburn, see his memorandum to acting colonial secretary, May 8, 1911, case no. 86/1911, ADM 11/1/922 [Prostitution – Unsatisfactory state of the law respecting], PRAAD, Accra.

stem the traffic of women and children into the colony from Nigeria, where the greatest number of the colony's sex workers originated. In the wake of Ormston's exposé, Lord Moyne, the secretary of state for the colonies, asked Governor Arnold Weinholt Hodson of the Gold Coast for a report on possible measures to combat the traffic.[47] In his role as advisor to Governor Hodson, Attorney-General Blackall once again resorted to racist rhetoric about African sexuality to argue against enacting antitrafficking legislation. This time Blackall insisted that even if the Gold Coast was willing to institute a passport system for West Africans and force them to comply with Immigration Restriction Regulations, these measures would prove ineffective because in his view, Nigerian women, especially those coming from Calabar, simultaneously inhabited licit and illicit social worlds, rendering it nearly impossible for authorities to distinguish between women desiring to enter the colony for legitimate purposes, such as traders, and those entering for illicit purposes, such as sex workers:

> If a Calabar woman makes up her mind to engage in this vocation [prostitution] in the Gold Coast, she will probably put on her passport that she is a petty trader and possibly add that she is a married woman. Both these descriptions will quite likely be correct, as it would appear from C. I. D.'s report that many of the Calabar prostitutes are in fact married women who come here with the consent of their husbands, and it would also seem that the young Calabar girls who come here for this purpose do so with the full knowledge and consent of their parents. If then such a female's bona fides are queried by the Immigration Officer and enquiries are made in Nigeria, I do not see how this will enable the Police to prove that she is a prostitute and as such a prohibited immigrant.[48]

In contrast, it was possible to keep foreign prostitutes from entering the United Kingdom not only because it already had a passport system, argued Blackall, but also because it was visibly possible to distinguish between immoral and moral European women in a way that was not possible with African women. Making his point and animosity toward Captain Nottingham clear, he gibed "it does not take a Sherlock Holmes to spot a French lady of easy virtue when she arrives at Dover. But I doubt whether even the eagle eye of Capt. Nottingham could discern the difference between a Calabar petty trader and a Calabar prostitute." Blackall's remark reveals more about its author's racist attitudes and assumptions, and preconceived notions about sex workers, than it does about the women he presumed to so authoritatively speak about. While increased female prostitution, as

---

[47] Moyne to Hodson, March 29, 1941, CSO 15/1/222 [Traffic in women and children], PRAAD, Accra.

[48] Blackall to colonial secretary (Accra), July 26, 1941, CSO 15/1/222 [Traffic in women and children]. For similar sentiments expressed by British colonial authorities about Indian women, see Levine, *Prostitution, Race, and Politics*, 190.

occurred in the Gold Coast during the war, is a widely acknowledged correlate of significant increases in the number of single or unattached male laborers or soldiers in a given area, there is also substantial evidence that points to the sustained and widespread economic activity of Nigerian female traders in the Gold Coast.[49] While it is certainly possible that some of these women supplemented their incomes as petty traders with money earned from sex work, the idea that all traders were prostitutes and all prostitutes were traders is just what it seems: racist rhetoric. But like earlier iterations of this rhetoric, it was powerful enough to further forestall the introduction of stricter antiprostitution and trafficking legislation in the Gold Coast.

Indeed, major legislative reform would have to wait until Sir Alan Burns and Raymond Browne replaced Governor Hodson and Attorney-General Blackall, respectively. Under this new leadership and with the continued prodding of Captain Nottingham, legislative action was finally taken in 1942 on the question of the traffic in women and children, and prostitution more generally.[50] In the summer of 1942, the Gold Coast executive council met and approved the implementation of legislation to "prevent the entry and provide for the deportation of Nigerian prostitutes and other persons connected with prostitution."[51] After a series of further revisions to expand the purview of both the Criminal Code and the Immigration Restriction Ordinance, the new legislation came into force on May 20, 1943.[52] Ordinance No. 7/43 made it an offense to: "(a) Loiter and solicit passengers [passersby] for the purpose of prostitution; (b) Encourage prostitution of girls under 13 years; (c) Allow persons under 13 years to be in brothels; (d) Trade in prostitution or live on the earnings of prostitutes; (e) Keep brothels."[53] Penalties for these offenses ranged from pecuniary fines to imprisonment for two years; all but the first offense were further punishable by deportation for offenders who were "nonnatives" of the Gold Coast.

One anomaly in the Immigration Ordinance remained, however: West Africans were still exempt from it. Browne's amendments did not address

---

[49] Niara Sudarkasa, "Women and migration in contemporary West Africa," *Signs*, 3 (1997), 182–83; see also, Gloria Ifeoma Chuku, "From petty traders to international merchants: A historical account of three Igbo women of Nigeria in trade and commerce, 1886 to 1970, *African Economic History*, 27 (1999), 1–22.

[50] Burns to Moyne, January 6, 1942, CSO 15/1/222 [Traffic in women and children], PRAAD, Accra.

[51] Executive council memorandum, August 10, 1942, CSO 15/1/222 [Traffic in women and children], PRAAD, Accra.

[52] Acting Attorney-General Raymond Browne to colonial secretary (Accra), September 8, 1942, CSO 15/1/222 [Traffic in women and children], PRAAD, Accra. A copy of the complete set of amendments to both the Criminal Code and the Immigration Ordinance can be found in the dispatch from Burns to Bourdillon, October 11, 1942, CSO 15/1/222 [Traffic in women and children], PRAAD, Accra.

[53] Acting commissioner of police (Accra) to the colonial secretary (Accra), October 1, 1943, CSO 15/1/222 [Traffic in women and children], PRAAD, Accra.

this point and so the letter of the law still technically excluded Nigerians involved in prostitution and trafficking from being defined as "prohibitive immigrants." As of July 1943, however, Nigerians traveling to the Gold Coast were required to hold a national travel document. Subsequently, the Gold Coast government requested that the Nigerian government refuse to issue travel documents to persons who would come under any of the categories specified in the new amendments to the Immigration Ordinance. While it is unclear how successful these measures were in stopping the flow of persons involved in prostitution and trafficking into the Gold Coast, the amendments to the Criminal Code quickly proved effective in allowing police to crack down on prostitution within the colony. The police carried out a series of raids in the summer of 1943, which resulted in the arrest, prosecution, and conviction of 263 people, including the deportation of 94 Nigerian women convicted of prostitution or prostitution-related offenses, such as brothel keeping.[54]

Given that the driving force behind the institution of stricter antiprostitution measures was the escalating rate of venereal diseases among European military personnel, it should come as no surprise that one of the areas raided during the antiprostitution drives was Sekondi-Takoradi, where the largest contingent of RAF personnel was located. In fact, the police had been authorized by the governor to undertake "special drives" in the area precisely because RAF personnel in the twin towns had the highest rate of venereal disease infection along the coast.[55] In addition to the raids conducted in the area, more police were deployed to locate brothels and enforce an "out of bounds" order for prostitution in the hopes that such measures would reduce venereal disease rates in Takoradi, which was described as "the 'Red Lamp' section as far as the RAF is concerned."[56] In effect a *cordon sanitaire* was created around the town. Moreover, a propaganda campaign was vigorously undertaken within the RAF to educate its personnel about the dangers of venereal diseases. While the Western Province's acting senior health officer, E. Daly, described the compulsory medical examination and treatment of women convicted of prostitution as "the next logical step," he doubted the practicality of such measures, given wartime constraints and the lack of clinics within the colony.[57] Nonetheless, statistical evidence shows that the newly instituted antiprostitution measures, alone, were successful in reducing the spread of venereal diseases among Europeans. By September 1943, the officer commanding the RAF reported that infection rates had

[54] Ibid.
[55] Extract from West African War Council meeting: Conclusions, May 27–28, 1943, CSO 11/11/140. [Venereal disease in the Takoradi/Sekondi area, investigation into possibility of special drive in connection with], PRAAD, Accra.
[56] E. Daly, acting senior health officer (Western Province) to deputy director of health service, July 2, 1943, CSO 11/11/140, PRAAD, Accra.
[57] Ibid.

dropped from 77 in 1,000 during the months of March, April, and May to 48 in 1,000 during the months of June, July, and August.[58]

While these new measures were successful in reducing the spread of venereal disease among European military personnel, the level and efficacy of treatment available to infected African troops is lamentable. At the same time that rates of infection dropped precipitously among Europeans, nearly half of the African troops in the colony were said to be infected with venereal diseases. Perhaps this is related to the fact that the use of penicillin, which was introduced during the war and found to be highly effective in the treatment of venereal diseases, was stopped for indigenous troops in the Gold Coast because of an "insufficient supply."[59] Even if treatment was rendered to all soldiers in need, regardless of race, the very fact that civilians, including sex workers, were neither compelled to seek treatment, nor given the resources to do so voluntarily, meant that reinfection rates among African soldiers were bound to be high.[60]

In contrast to Nigeria's implementation of wartime legislation, which made it legal to subject persons suspected of suffering from venereal diseases to compulsory examination and treatment, the Gold Coast government responded pessimistically to the secretary of state's invitation to enact the same legislation. The director of medical services (DMS), James Balfour-Kirk, flatly advised the government "not [to] contemplate the enactment of legislation of this kind."[61] Later that year Balfour-Kirk's successor outlined why medical services found the implementation of such legislation inadvisable. In addition to questioning the ability of the colony to actually provide treatment to all those afflicted by venereal diseases, the DMS also suggested that unlike Europeans, Gold Coasters were not ashamed of having venereal diseases and therefore legislation "compelling" them to seek treatment was unnecessary.[62] While it is difficult to say what kinds of attitudes Africans infected with venereal disease had toward seeking treatment in the Gold Coast, the medical authorities' assumption that they felt no shame in obtaining healthcare was not a positive statement on the willingness of Africans to break free of the morality discourses surrounding venereal diseases that often prevented Europeans from doing the same, but rather an extension of the old racist trope of African immorality and sexual shamelessness.

Thus, the DMS's line of reasoning completed the circle of racist logic, which had consistently underpinned legislative inaction on the interrelated

---

[58] J. Colt Hamilton, officer commanding RAF, West Africa, to governor (Gold Coast), September 15, 1943, CSO 11/11/140, PRAAD, Accra.

[59] Willcox, "Venereal disease," 69.

[60] Ibid., 66.

[61] J. Balfour-Kirk, director of medical service, to colonial secretary, March 5, 1943, CSO 11/10/136 [Venereal diseases], PRAAD, Accra.

[62] DMS to colonial secretary, September 4, 1943, CSO 11/10/136 [Venereal diseases], PRAAD, Accra.

questions of prostitution and venereal diseases. Whereas the alleged hyper-sexuality of Africans had previously formed the basis for arguing that legislative measures to control prostitution would be ineffective, now the supposed lack of shame that Africans possessed around the epidemiological consequences of their sexual behavior became the basis for arguing that legislation compelling infected people to seek treatment was unnecessary. While Gold Coasters had for several decades continually taken the initiative to petition the government to strengthen antiprostitution laws because of the negative effects venereal diseases were having on local populations – which suggests that people were not readily being treated for these diseases – the government only took action when prostitution began to impede the war effort through its adverse effects on the health of European military personnel stationed in the colony. Even wartime exigencies were not enough, however, to compel Governor Hodson and Attorney-General Blackall to introduce stricter antiprostitution laws. Instead the colony had to wait for a change in leadership before it finally achieved legislative parity with its counterparts in British West Africa. This reaffirms the need to integrate more fully the ideological proclivities – in this case racial ideologies – of particular colonial administrators into our analysis of the factors that shaped colonial history and law.

We also know that venereal diseases hampered the war effort among African troops. So why was passage of antiprostitution and antitrafficking legislation linked to the phenomenon of *interracial* prostitution and sexually transmitted diseases among European military men in particular? A partial answer might be found in the fact that the health of European soldiers was always prioritized over that of colonial troops and other colonized subjects.[63] While the British army viewed the available supply of European soldiers as finite, especially for service in places like West Africa, it imagined the colonies as an inexhaustible reservoir of labor that it could tap through either voluntary methods or conscription. And when the British army's own physical standards got in the way of its recruitment efforts, it simply responded by lowering these benchmarks.[64] We should also consider the ways in which the specter of open prostitution between European men and African women in the busy city streets of Accra and Takoradi was simply intolerable. Perhaps it was not just the behavior of West African sex workers that was "causing embarrassment," in the words of Captain Nottingham, to the "respectable European and African inhabitants of Accra and Takoradi,"

---

[63] On the long history of British indifference toward venereal diseases among African soldiers and the privileging of treatment for the Europeans who garrisoned the empire, see Richard Phillips, "Heterogeneous imperialism and the regulation of sexuality in British West Africa," *Journal of the History of Sexuality*, 14 (2005), 295. Bryder makes a similar observation in Bryder, "Sex, race, and colonialism," 818.

[64] Killingray, "Military and labour recruitment in the Gold Coast," 88.

but also the behavior of their European johns.[65] This suggests that we need to rethink the commonly held assumption that "only when prostitutes were white did the imperial authorities ask whether the correct social distance and even the imperial relationship itself were being jeopardized."[66]

Above all else, the foregoing raises unsettling questions about the long-term implications of the Gold Coast government's longstanding intransigence on the question of antiprostitution and sex trafficking legislation. We now know that efforts to dramatically reduce the spread of venereal disease among Africans through legislative action were consistently rejected across the decades of colonial rule in the Gold Coast, while only paltry measures to treat these diseases were funded by the government. Indeed, on the eve of independence in Ghana there was still no department responsible for the treatment of venereal diseases, a state of affairs that continued for almost three decades after independence.[67] Given the well-established fact that sexually transmitted diseases "assist the transmission of the AIDS-causing human immunodeficiency virus (HIV)," we must necessarily ask what the epidemiological consequences of allowing this kind of disease environment to flourish among the colony's African population have been in the post-colonial period.[68] This is no small question given the devastating effect that HIV-AIDS has had not only in Ghana, but also throughout the African continent. This points to the urgent need for more historical research into the relationship between disease and colonial policy and legislation, if we are to better understand the social, economic, ideological, political, and wartime dynamics involved not only in how diseases spread, but also in how treatment regimes or the lack thereof become part and parcel of the proliferation of disease environments.[69]

---

[65] Nottingham, memorandum on control of prostitutes, May 30, 1941, CSO 15/1/222 [Traffic in women and children], PRAAD, Accra.

[66] Bryder, "Sex, race, and colonialism," 822.

[67] Pellow, "STDs and Aids in Ghana," 420.

[68] Pellow, "STDs and Aids in Ghana," 418.

[69] Two notable studies that do historicize this very question are John Iliffe's *The African Aids Epidemic: A History* (Athens: Ohio University Press, 2006) and Megan Vaughan's *Curing Their Ills: Colonial Power and African Illness* (Stanford, CA: Stanford University Press, 1991).

FIVE

EXPERIENCING WAR IN AFRICA AND EUROPE

19

American Missions in Wartime French West Africa

Travails of the Sudan Interior Mission in Niger

Barbara M. Cooper

This chapter explores the implications of World War II for the perception of American missionaries in French colonial Africa both during and after the war. The Sudan Interior Mission (SIM), an interdenominational "faith mission" staffed by British, American, Canadian, and New Zealand citizens, found its work in Niger caught up on the complex dynamics of Vichy Africa. Tagged as "British" by the French colonial administration of Niger, the mission staff was highly suspect in the context of tensions with British Nigeria to the south and territories sympathetic to de Gaulle to the north and east; however, in many respects the religious orientation of the mission in American evangelical fundamentalism meant that in cultural style and philosophy it was rather American. Misunderstandings between the mission and the French administration abounded, leading to the eventual detention of the head of the mission, David Osborne. In the wake of the war the French tagged the mission as "American" and hoped to channel its unruly impulses in directions thought more suitable to French interests in the knowledge that the United States had become a wealthy global force that could no longer be ignored.

In 1940, plans for expanding the mission's stations were afoot, despite the war in Europe. The attitude of the colonial government in Niger appeared to be receptive:

> The Governor of Niger Colony was passing through Maradi and Mr. and Mrs. Osborne were able to have an informal interview with him. The Governor assured Mr. Osborne that the SIM could purchase a certain plot and house in Maradi, put up temporary buildings in Jiratawa, and that he was also willing to let us occupy Diapaga.[1]

There is something surreal in the cheerful reportage of the mission's publications of the early war period, suggesting that the mission staff of North

---

[1] N. A. Kapp, "Station Flash, Tsibiri," *The Sudan Witness*, 16 (1940), 19.

Americans and New Zealanders was more than a little out of synch with the fears and preoccupations of most Europeans and certainly of the French.

The mission's obliviousness to the impact of the war and its implications for continued evangelism was to be short-lived, however. With the fall of France and the Armistice of June 22, 1940, the political landscape in French West Africa (FWA; in French, Afrique occidentale française [AOF]) was thrown into extraordinary confusion. Any effort to recapture France from outside its borders, whether led from Britain or North Africa, would rely heavily upon the overseas territories for soldiers, materiel, food supplies, and moral support. It was entirely within the realm of possibility that Niger, along with the rest of the AOF, would rally to the Free French in support of de Gaulle – certainly at the immediate announcement of the Armistice, some elements of the military in Niger rejected capitulation and envisaged joining Allied forces either in Dakar or Nigeria.[2] By August 1940, Governor-General Felix Éboué had decided to lend the weight of Afrique équatoriale française (AEF) to support de Gaulle. If all of AOF had followed suit, the bloc of African colonies would have become the backbone of the French resistance forces. As it happened, the head of the AOF, Governor-General Pierre Boisson, experienced the rallying of the AEF to de Gaulle as a betrayal. For him the primary duty of France's overseas administrators was to maintain the cohesion of the French empire and to prevent any further erosion of the position of France. Vichy policy toward AOF was to hold Germany at bay while attempting to sustain and cultivate economic links to the US, which was at that point neutral.[3] Anything that might sever metropolitan France from control of the empire, then, was seen as a threat to the very survival of France as a sovereign nation. On July 6, 1940, Boisson decided to back Philippe Pétain and to forestall the emergence of an African bloc.

It was a complex and difficult decision to make, one necessarily tempered by the sense of embattlement that the Allied pressure on the colonial territories fostered. In their haste to forestall Germany and Italy from seizing the French fleet, the Allies attacked the French navy at its base, Mers-el-Kebir, in Algeria on July 3 before the situation had fully crystallized, reinforcing French fears that the British were making a move to seize the French African empire. While many individual soldiers and administrators eventually made their way across the borders into British territory or the AEF to join the Allies, the federation as a whole determined to support the Pétain government at Vichy.

---

[2] Catherine Akpo-Vaché, *L'AOF et la seconde guerre mondiale* (Paris: Karthala, 1996), 28; see also "Mission d'Inspection au Niger," 1941, Affaires Politiques 634 (8), Fonds Ministériels, Archives nationales d'outre-mer (hereafter ANOM), Aix-en-Provence.

[3] Akpo-Vaché, *L'AOF et la seconde guerre mondiale*, 37, 49.

Thus, in the confused political currents of the time, it was the *"britan-niques"* who appeared as the most immediate threat to France's African empire. Despite Boisson's willingness to support Pétain in this approach to the colonial territories, he took advantage of the distance of AOF from France to carve a path of relative autonomy from the excesses of the Vichy regime. Nevertheless, he regarded the liberal partisans of the Front Populaire and supporters of de Gaulle as a threat to the political cohesion of the feder-ation, which made the government of the period increasingly authoritarian and resolutely conservative. Under the circumstances any British subject would have come under heavy scrutiny, but those whose contacts, activities, and institutional ties linked them most closely with British African terri-tories were particularly suspect. British Protestant missionaries, then, were closely watched because they seemed to be natural conduits of informa-tion in likely sympathy with the expansionist interests of Great Britain as a colonial power.

While Boisson himself was neither an avid supporter of Vichy's cultural agenda nor pro-Nazi in orientation, local administrators far from Dakar had tremendous latitude to pursue the discriminatory policies authorized by Vichy if they so chose. The Vichy government (both in France and abroad) advanced a pro-Catholic policy as part of a crusade to renew and purify France in the wake of the perceived failure of the Popular Front. This move-ment simply heightened the contradictions already present in the French colonial claims to republicanism in the context of empire. Niger's gover-nor for much of the war, Maurice Falvy, unlike Boisson, had a reputation for strong pro-German sentiments and collaborated vigorously with Vichy. Thus in Niger, the mistrust of the *britanniques* was compounded with the pro-Catholic policies of the Pétain government, creating a climate particu-larly inauspicious for a Protestant mission such as SIM.

So it was that by November 1942, David Osborne, who as a citizen of New Zealand held a British passport, was under detention in Niamey, and relations between the mission and the colonial regime were at their lowest point ever. Osborne's detention and the subsequent efforts of a French Protestant, Pastor Jean Keller, to act as intermediary on his behalf provide an occasion to consider the unenviable position of Protestant missionaries in this period: If they spoke out against the Vichy government they would lose their ability to continue their missionary work; on the other hand, if they cooperated with the government, they could be branded (as Keller later found) as collaborators with the German occupation.

It was a time of tremendous stress for the mission, but one with intrigu-ing consequences. As potential Gaullists in contest with the colonial regime, the mission may have earned some sympathy from local Africans despite the missionaries' repeated protests that it was entirely apolitical. The mis-sion certainly benefited from the far more tolerant attitude toward Protes-tant missions signaled at the Brazzaville conference, as de Gaulle moved to neutralize the emphasis on Catholicism promoted under Vichy and as highly articulate Protestant missionaries and converts from within AEF capitalized on their support for de Gaulle to critique the status quo ante and to protest their marginalization at the proceedings. In effect, the French colonial government's combative relationship with Protestant missions under Vichy set the stage for a far more sympathetic colonial attitude toward those missions after the Brazzaville conference, giving Protestant converts in colonial French Africa a greater voice than might have been expected in the process of decolonization and enabling non-French missionaries to have a broader scope for action in the postwar period. If the detention of Osborne during the war was the nadir of mission-state relations, the Brazzaville conference opened the way for an unprecedented postwar boom in mission activities, particularly in the realms of education and health work, which was to have a profound effect upon the growth of the Christian community and the perception of Christianity in Niger.

One final issue emerges in a consideration of this period, that of the national and denominational identity of SIM as a mission. SIM had always seen itself as international and nondenominational. While on the whole its staff was made up of Protestants, there was no reason in principle that appropriately evangelical Catholics or orthodox Christians could not become missionaries so long as they passed a doctrinal test. Yet this apparent openness was somewhat illusory, given Andrew Walls' interesting observation that the notion of using such tests as a mark of membership in the fellowship of believers was in itself characteristically American.[4] It was during the Vichy and early postwar period that the Protestantism of the mission became most clearly marked and that the staff was gradually identified not as "European," but as "American." Most importantly, the shifting national inflection of the "international" mission became central to its relations with the French administration in the period leading up to independence.

The Backdrop of the War

The colony of Niger was a particularly vulnerable and sensitive site in Vichy's eyes, surrounded as it was by Chad (which had rallied to de Gaulle and the Free French), Italian Libya, and British Nigeria (see Figure 19.1). It was also a strategically important source of oils, labor, and revenue. According to Finn Fuglestad, Niger's military governor, Brigadier-General Falvy was "dubbed von Falvy for his alleged pro-German sentiments." Falvy closed the border with Nigeria, stationed military units along the border to patrol and build trenches and retooled Niger's state-controlled economy to provision

---

[4] Andrew Walls, "The American dimension in the history of the missionary movement," in Joel Carpenter and Wilbert R. Shenk (eds.), *Earthen Vessels: American Evangelicals and Foreign Missions, 1880–1980* (Grand Rapids, MI: William B. Eerdmans Publishing Company, 1990), 17.

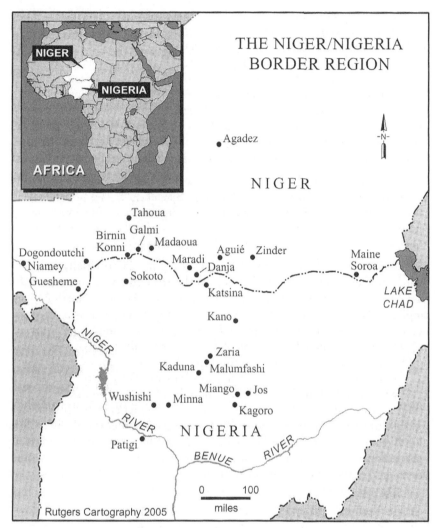

FIGURE 19.1. Niger-Nigeria Borderlands

North Africa and France. Trade with Nigeria was banned and the government made heavy demands on the local population through forced labor on
administrative fields to grow peanuts, through increased taxes, and through
requisitions of crops and animals. Fuglestad notes, "under the Vichy regime
the Nigeriens were for the first time effectively reduced to a state not unlike
slavery as the French organized the systematic plundering and looting of their
country and its meager resources."[5] Upon his initial arrival in Niger Falvy

[5] Finn Fuglestad, *A History of Niger 1850–1960* (Cambridge: Cambridge University Press,
1982), 139, 144.

was concerned about the eighteen SIM missionaries, who had made "little progress in evangelization" and whose numbers "could not be justified simply for evangelism. The unrelenting surveillance they have been subjected to has not enabled us to discern any reprehensible behavior, but it is carried out with all the more care since most of these individuals are British nationals."[6] For the missionaries, this persistent scrutiny was extremely trying and being cut off from mission health facilities in Nigeria was, in several instances, to prove fatal. "Owing to the British blockade and a state of general suspicion and misunderstanding," Osborne reported in December 1940, shortly after the death of his wife Drusille from blood poisoning:

> we with the rest of the workers in the Niger Colony have been almost entirely cut off from contact with Nigeria from last September. We are not allowed to cross the frontier. Supplies of European requirements are getting very low. No mail reaches us from the outside except an occasional letter via Cotonou. These take more than 2 months to reach us from Nigeria.[7]

By November 1942, the status of the Vichy regime as nominally independent from Germany had been shattered with the German occupation of the southern zone of France. With the Allied invasion of France's North African empire on November 8, 1942, the Vichy government moved into a defensive posture that was particularly oppressive to anyone who might be construed as sympathetic to the Allies. It was only with the Gaullist takeover of North and West Africa in June 1943 that this difficult period of colonial rule began to fade. Falvy's successor, Governor Jean-François Toby, lifted the ban on trade with Nigeria and abolished the unpopular *champs administratifs*. Nevertheless, the colonial administration, whose personnel changed little under the shift of regime (as we shall see, Toby had served under the Vichy regime as well), continued to make heavy demands on the economy. Local chiefs were deposed if they failed to meet French demands; indeed, some would argue that France made even heavier demands on the AOF after 1943 to meet the war effort.[8]

Protestant Travails under Vichy

The entire war put tremendous strain on SIM's struggling missionaries, as the death of Drusille Osborne in 1940 suggests; however, the brief period between the allied landing in French North Africa on November 8, 1942, and de Gaulle's actual takeover of the AOF in June 1943 was particularly

---

[6] Falvy, Rapport Politique, 1941, 2G41 (23) (14miom/1829), Affaires politiques: Niger, ANOM, Aix-en-Provence.

[7] October–December Quarterly Report 1940, SR-2/A, Box 188, Tsibiri Station Resumés 1930–45, Sudan Interior Mission Archives, Fort Mill, SC.

[8] Patrick Manning, *Francophone Sub-Saharan Africa, 1880–1985* (Cambridge: Cambridge University Press, 1988), 139.

fraught. With the allied landing, the Falvy administration's suspicions of "foreign" missionaries were heightened. SIM missionaries themselves, cut off as they were from news sources, were baffled by the increased surveillance under which they suddenly found themselves. After 1941, the colonial administration had forced them to move to Maradi, where they could be watched more readily. Further, it forbade any transborder activity linking the missionaries to their coworkers in Nigeria, and prevented them from "itinerating," or traveling in the region to evangelize.[9] The missionaries found themselves permanently cut off from information and medical supplies; a number of children within the mission community died as a consequence.[10]

Mission publications of the period are oddly reticent about the difficulties the Niger mission was having, doubtless to avoid further tensions with the French administration and to reassure potential American donors. In an annual report for 1941, Reverend Gordon Beacham, the director of the mission, remarks obliquely:

> Many have been the difficulties with which we have had to contend. The conflict in Europe, which had spread to Africa during the past year, greatly increased transportation problems. Sinister forces in official circles threatened the very existence of our missionary activities, especially among children. A large part of our field is now amongst Moslems, who steadfastly and unitedly oppose every new effort to win converts from amongst them. We wondered how the war with its economic pressure would affect mission finances. Above all has been the constant "counter-attacks" of Satan himself in the spiritual realm, blinding men's eyes, veiling their hearts, dragging down those who have made profession of faith in Christ, "for we are not ignorant of his devices."[11]

Under Vichy the French administration made a sustained effort to learn something more about the activities of the Protestant missionaries, commissioning a study in 1941 that established that there were four stations in Niger, eighteen missionaries, six *collaborateurs indigènes*, and 250 converts.[12] Until this time the beleaguered administrators of the region had shown little interest in the missionaries beyond expressing skepticism that they would succeed in converting any Muslims. When diplomatic relations between Niger and Nigeria had been good, the regular suspicion expressed in colonial reports that the missionaries must be engaged in intelligence gathering (given the seeming implausibility of converting the local population) simply meant that mission proposals to expand its activities were regularly rebuffed. With the break between France and Britain after the Armistice such harmless information gathering was regarded as a sinister threat to France's

---

[9] Rev. C. Gordon Beacham, "French West Africa," *The Sudan Witness*, 17 (1941), 9.
[10] Interview with Ray de la Haye, Sebring, November 17, 1990.
[11] Rev. C. Gordon Beacham, "1941 Annual Field Report," *The Sudan Witness*, 17 (1941), 1.
[12] Confidential telegram #235, Gouverneur Falvy to Gouverneur Général de l'AOF, Dakar, mai 8, 1941, 17G115 (Missions: divers), Affaires Politiques AOF, ANOM, Aix-en-Provence.

overseas empire. Suddenly the activities of these *"britanniques"* were subject to intense scrutiny that became routine.

African converts to evangelical Christianity played a central role in the survival of the mission, particularly in sustaining contacts with the much larger contingent of SIM missionaries across the border in Nigeria. Martha Wall, stationed in Nigeria at the time, recalls the arrival of a Hausa convert, 'Dan Nana, who was to become an important figure in the Christian community in Niger, on one of his illicit forays across the border to collect and convey news: "Dan Nana, a Hausa Christian . . . had slipped through the lines, his mind crammed with messages to our mission family and with questions from the news-hungry isolated missionaries who valiantly kept at their labors for Christ. He had to memorize all the information that he carried back across that formidable border."[13] Hausa Christians probably played a larger role in the survival of the mission than is generally reflected in the published mission periodicals of the period. Catherine Akpo-Vaché's work on the Vichy period suggests that this may have been typical of a broader pattern; Africans bore much of the brunt of semiillegal or clandestine work, and, when caught, were punished far more severely than Europeans.[14]

Pastor 'Dan Nana's account of that period reveals the high degree of autonomy Africans had relative to the mission by that time but also the ways in which African labor and life were taken for granted. When the missionaries were required to leave Jiratawa for Maradi where they could be watched more closely, the mission had 'Dan Nana return from Hisatau, where he was preaching and teaching, to take over the site and also to carry messages across the border to Nigeria. I asked him whether this was risky. He replied:

> Oh yes! It was dangerous! They had said they wanted to give me a vehicle, a Land Rover, that I could use to act as if I were a trader. They'd give me trade goods, and I'd go over and get the news. So that's what we did, I'd bring it back to Malam Osborne, our leader. He cautioned me, "This is dangerous, if someone is caught in political spying they will kill him."[15]

So long as the information conveyed was not overtly political, one supposes, Osborne could comfort himself that he was not placing 'Dan Nana at unwarranted risk. Despite the closure of the border, clandestine trade continued across the border – indeed, France needed to permit some permeability of the border in order to guarantee supplies of imported goods. While the system proposed by Osborne proved workable for someone who knew the local terrain well, 'Dan Nana adapted the plan to make it safer.

[13] Martha Wall, *Splinters Off an African Log* (Chicago, IL: Moody Press, 1960), 148.

[14] Akpo-Vaché, *L'AOF et la seconde guerre mondiale*, 64, 108, 113, 122.

[15] Interview with Pastor 'Dan Nana, Soura, October 24, 2000.

He became well known to the border guards as an ordinary Hausa trader dealing in traditional medicines, a commodity of no interest to the government. The guards took little notice of him, for, as he put it, "as a black person they weren't at all afraid of me, I wasn't a European."[16] Clearly the mission succeeded through the offices of 'Dan Nana in maintaining occasional links with the mission offices in Nigeria. The French administration, whether out of paranoia or perspicacity, suspected as much, but was not able to prove one way or the other that the mission was maintaining such ties, nor did it understand through what mechanism the information was flowing. So convinced was it that the mission's evangelism was a façade that it seems never to have occurred to the administration that Christian converts might act as couriers.

It is important to underscore the relatively personal and intimate quality of the missives 'Dan Nana memorized and carried. The sole clue within the mission's own publications that any information had made its way out of the French territory came in early 1941, when an announcement of the death of Osborne's wife, Drusille, on October 11, 1940, of complications due to blood poisoning and pneumonia appeared in *The Sudan Witness*. The announcement regretted that there was no word of her illness until after her death and that Osborne's wired message requesting prayer had not arrived in time. The missionaries had to rely on the French doctor rather than the mission's doctors in Nigeria; the doctor was unable to save her. It was only when missionaries in Nigeria received a verbal message through "a Christian man" that the news got through to her friends and relatives outside Niger that Mrs. Osborne had died. Clearly, being cut off from spiritual and moral support was extremely painful to the missionaries, quite aside from the logistical problems presented by their isolation from their primary source of medical expertise, supplies, and finances: "The Mission has lost a noble worker, a French scholar, and one who was her husband's faithful helper in all matters pertaining to Mission and Government. French West Africa has lost one of its greatest benefactors, greater than any soldier who ever fell in battle."[17] Drusille Osborne, a French Canadian, had served as a critical intermediary between the administration and the mission, and it was not long before her absence was to be keenly felt.

Upon the landing of the Allies in North Africa, and in the absence of the mission's most valued intermediary with the French, David Osborne was arrested and detained. Retired missionary Ray de la Haye's account of Osborne's detention highlights his own sense of bewilderment and vulnerability:

---

[16] Ibid.
[17] "Obituary: Mrs. D. M. Osborne," *The Sudan Witness*, 1941, 4.

We didn't know anything about it, because the news that we were receiving
was through Germany and all slanted.... We were in Jiratawa, and south of
the administration, so administrators came down there with some Senegalese
soldiers [*Tirailleurs Sénégalais*, soldiers in the colonial army who were not
necessarily from Senegal] and told us to get out of there in a half an hour!
Leave everything! They took our radio away, they took our Ford.... So, here
we were.... They took Mr. Osborne and that was a sad situation, we didn't
know what they were going to do to him, we didn't know where he went. And
he was away about maybe three or four weeks.[18]

If mistrust of foreign (and in particular English-speaking) missions had a long
and rather complex history, that mistrust seems to have reached its height
under Vichy epitomized in the detention of Pastor Osborne. An extract
from an annual report for the colony of Ivory Coast in 1940 gives a feel
for the AOF administration's sense that under Vichy there was nothing to
be gained in supporting "foreign" missions. In reporting on mission activity the new administrator remarks: "there is reason to fear that British
missionaries will never think like the French while our national interests
run up against those of their own country."[19] Several conscious strategies
emerged from this mistrust. First, non-French missions' requests to enter
into new mission activities were denied throughout the territories, particularly if they involved developing new properties.[20] Second, Catholic missions
were promoted wherever possible (despite the fact that their personnel was
often "foreign," if French-speaking, as well). Vichy's unabashed preference
for Catholic missions during this period was so egregious that it prompted
many an outcry from Protestant mission groups and raised serious questions
about the separation of church and state.[21] Third, French Protestant personnel were encouraged to enter the West African field.[22] Finally, a commission

[18] Interview with Ray de la Haye.
[19] Extract of Annual Report, Côte d'Ivoire, 1940, 17G115 (Missions: divers), Affaires Politiques: AOF, ANOM, Aix-en-Provence.
[20] A terse, but unambiguous, telegram from Governor Falvy to his superiors in Dakar responding to the suggestion that more American missionaries be permitted to enter Niamey captures the tone of the moment: "Absolutely opposed to any new installation this nature
Niger." Confidential telegram #235 from Gouverneur Falvy to Gouverneur Général de
l'AOF, Dakar, mai 8, 1941, 17G115 (Missions: divers), Affaires politiques AOF, ANOM,
Aix-en-Provence.
[21] On the regular subventions of the Vichy government to the Séminaire des Colonies, a
Catholic seminary devoted to training Catholic priests for mission work overseas, see dossier
9, FM 2196 (Subventions divers aux missions), ANOM, Aix-en-Provence. The subventions
ended with the close of the war, although the French government did continue to help
missionaries of all denominations return home after being stranded during the war. For an
extended and nuanced study of the relations between the Catholic church and Vichy, see
W. D. Halls, *Politics, Society and Christianity in Vichy France* (Oxford: Berg Publishers,
1995).
[22] See for example a cable from Vichy to Dakar in 1941 offering safe conduct to a French
protestant in FM 2192, ANOM, Aix-en-Provence.

was created to oversee all Protestant missions under French Protestant leadership. The umbrella commission was known as the Missionary Federation of French West Africa, and was headed by a French pastor named Jean Keller of the Société des Missions Evangeliques de Paris.[23]

According to Virginia Thompson and Richard Adloff in their magisterial 1950s era study of French West Africa:

> In 1942 the Evangelical Mission of Paris took the initiative in organizing a Missionary Federation of French West Africa, which all but two of the Protestant missions in the Federation joined of their own accord shortly after the war. The Paris Mission not only helps its foreign colleagues acquire in France the linguistic and other training still necessitated by the French government's decrees, but one of its members stationed in Dakar represents the whole Missionary Federation in the latter's dealings with the administration. This organization gives unity to the work of Protestantism in French West Africa, smoothes relations between its missionaries and officials there, and, most important of all, imparts to it a supra-national character that has glossed over the many confusing sectarian and national differences which for years have hampered Protestant missionary work among Africans.[24]

This benign picture belies the coercion involved in the French administration's encouragement of a Protestant uniformity to be directed by French interests. It is not at all clear that the federation was initiated by the Paris mission rather than the Vichy government. The French administration commissioned Pastor Keller to make a trip in early 1942 to visit all ten of the foreign Protestant missions in AOF to see whether they would be willing to accept him as liaison with the AOF government in Dakar. He also, of course, submitted a confidential report on what he had discovered about the various missions and their staffs on his tournée. Keller, as Délégué général des missions protestantes en AOF, acted as intermediary between the Vichy government and the "foreign" Protestant missionaries, at times attempting to protect the missionaries' interests, at others subtly advancing Vichy's vision of appropriate Protestant activity. "Foreign" missionaries were therefore presented with an unpleasant quandary. They agreed either to take advantage of Keller's offer to serve as intermediary, despite his unappealing pro-Vichy politics, or to resign themselves for the foreseeable future to harassment that rendered them far less effective as evangelists.

Ultimately, the SIM availed itself of Keller's services in the wake of a series of unpleasant incidents.[25] Such confrontations seem to have led to

---

[23] Letter from Pasteur J. Keller to Monsieur le directeur de la Sureté Générale (Dakar), December 29, 1942, 17G115, Affaires politiques AOF, ANOM, Aix-en-Provence.

[24] Virginia Thompson and Richard Adloff, *French West Africa* (Stanford, CA: Stanford University Press, 1957), 584–85.

[25] The missionaries in Niger seem to have had a number of disagreements with the administration over staffing, but the most serious incident seems to have been the French administration's ire at a publication in Hausa by Edward Morrow, in which he set passages from

the deterioration of relations between the SIM and Falvy such that at the time of Keller's visit to Niamey in May 1942, Keller had been warned in advance that he should be very cautious around Osborne, characterized as "an extremely dangerous suspect."[26] The general impression within the administration that Osborne was not to be trusted was so powerful that when Jean-François Toby succeeded Falvy as governor of Niger late in 1942, he seems to have accepted wholeheartedly the notion that the mission was dangerous and its leader a spy. When Osborne failed to appear before Toby on the new governor's first tournée in the territory, Toby had him arrested.

How had Osborne come to be seen as "an extremely dangerous suspect"? In part suspicions about the mission may have arisen out of the coincidence of the mission's requests to expand its operations in Niger with the outbreak of the war. Prior to the Vichy regime, the activities of the mission during the war were seen as relatively innocuous.[27] Indeed, the mission's shift from its unsuccessful efforts to convince the administration to permit the creation of vernacular language schools to a new approach that would replicate the success of its leprosy work in Nigeria seemed to be bearing fruit. The mission's proposal to build a leprosarium in Maradi had been vetted and approved, its request for a large tract of land and allocations for both patients and medical supplies rather generously granted and its request that its medical personnel be permitted to practice despite their lack of certification in France approved on condition that they confine themselves to leprosy work and that the facility operate under the authority of the colonial medical services. As of June 13, 1940, all that remained was to choose an appropriate site and begin building the facility.[28]

By June 22, however, France had declared an armistice with Germany, and by July 6, Boisson had decided to prevent an African bloc from joining the Allies. From the vantage point of Niger's governor, Jean Rapenne, everything had changed and the situation was too uncertain to move forward with any such proposal. SIM seems, nevertheless, to have envisioned continuing as if nothing had changed. In response to a letter from Osborne

the Koran and the Bible alongside one another in an effort to convince Muslims of the superiority of Christianity.

[26] Letter from Pastor J. Keller, délégué général des Missions Protestantes en AOF in Dakar, to Monsieur le directeur de la Sureté Général, December 29, 1942, 17G115 (Missions: divers), Affaires politiques AOF, ANOM, Aix-en-Provence.

[27] In "Bulletin hebdomadaire de renseignement" of November 13, 1939, marked "secret," Governor Jean Rapenne of Niger reported on both the loyalty of teachers and students to "la France menacée" and upon the favorable response of the Ministry of Foreign Affairs to the SIM's request to expand its operations in Niger; 11G31 (14miom/2208), Affaires politiques diverses; and Rapport Politique Annuel, 1939, 2G39 4 (14miom/1803), Affaires politiques: Niger, both in ANOM, Aix-en-Provence.

[28] Letter from Jean Rapenne to Osborne, 1543/ P/A, sujet "Construction d'une léproserie," June 13, 1940, 1H 73 versement 144, Archives du Sénégal (hereafter AS), Dakar.

dated August 2, 1940 (presumably proposing a suitable plot and a timetable for building), Rapenne gently replied:

> I have the honor of informing you that I most willingly authorize you to choose right away, in cooperation with the Commandant of Maradi, land that would be suitable for the eventual construction of a leprosarium. I nevertheless regret to inform you that I will not be able to make that land available to you without a formal request. The general situation having rather considerably changed since my letter of June 13th, it would be appropriate to postpone the project until the return of more favorable circumstances.[29]

Rapenne's delicate suggestion that the situation was in flux provoked some ire from above as evidenced in the marginalia to the letter, which insisted, "the general situation has now returned to normal." From the point of view of Boisson and Dakar, the backing of Vichy was to be taken as definitive and administrative personnel should not suggest that there was any reason to be uncertain about the future. Shortly thereafter, Rapenne was replaced as governor by Falvy, whose support of Vichy was unambiguous.

To Falvy, the mission's proposed expansion took on an increasingly sinister air; by 1941, the governor characterized the mission's expansion as "abnormal" given the small number of converts and the purported retreat in Islam.[30] The increasing mistrust of the mission resulted in alarmed telegraph correspondence between Governor Falvy and the AOF commanders in Dakar: "Have distinct impression that at Maradi, where I just went, the English are in the process of organizing an intelligence center, particularly by means of the SUDAN MISSION. Indispensable that Zinder research office direct its efforts to this issue immediately."[31] A perception that the mission staff was largely British contributed to the paranoia concerning the mission: "More than ever the maintenance of so many pastors (18) is not justified by evangelism. Permanent surveillance has not enabled us to discover any reprehensible activities, but it continues with the greatest care because most of these persons are British nationals."[32] Falvy did little to disguise his distaste and mistrust for the mission from Osborne.

The correspondence surrounding Osborne's detention in November of 1942 in the wake of the Allied landing in North Africa sheds much light on the mix of personality, cultural obtuseness, and wartime politics that entered into the escalation of mistrust that led to the incident and

[29] Letter from Jean Rapenne to Osborne, 2354/S, sujet "Creation d'une léproserie Maradi," September 17, 1940, 1H73 versement 144, AS, Dakar.
[30] Excerpt from the Rapport Politique, Niger, 1941, 11G21 (14miom/2204), Affaires Politiques: Niger, ANOM, Aix-en-Provence.
[31] Governor Falvy to Genesuper, secret telegram, Dakar no. 101, transmission no. 53, February 28, 1941, 11G32–36 (14 miom/2209), Affaires politiques: divers, ANOM., Aix-en-Provence.
[32] Excerpt from the Rapport Politique, Niger, 1941, 11G21 (14miom/2204), Affaires politiques: divers, ANOM, Aix-en-Provence.

contributed to the tensions between the French administration and Protestant mission groups more generally. The most useful source for understanding the incident is a letter written by Osborne to Governor Toby after his
release protesting his detention and calling for a full investigation so that
he could be exonerated (see the Appendix). The letter, dated December
12, 1942, was written in uncharacteristically polished and formal French,
rather different from the blunt, even presumptuous style of Osborne's earlier request to build a leprosarium. It belies the frequent complaints of the
administration that the foreign missionaries had little skill in French – perhaps Osborne enlisted the assistance of a sympathetic native speaker. The
formal veneer does not disguise, however, the deep anger and resentment
the recently widowed Osborne evidently felt as a result of his detention and
the espionage accusation.

Osborne's letter suggests that relations with the administration were quite
strained well before Toby's arrival and that Falvy attempted to prevent the
missionaries from discovering any information that they could pass along
to the British across the border. The mission was clearly in an awkward
situation. The French administration was hardly welcoming and the mission
personnel, whatever their real feelings about the Vichy government, felt
unappreciated and misunderstood. Nevertheless, the letter also suggests a
certain obtuseness verging on arrogance on the part of Osborne. Osborne
abstained from making an appearance at events organized to introduce
Jean-François Toby as the new governor of the colony. Clearly, with a new
governor making the rounds, it was appropriate for the head of the mission
to introduce himself, whatever Falvy's practice might have been. Newton
Kapp, a SIM missionary resident in Maradi, appears to have sensed this
and made an overture on his own initiative that was accepted.[33] Given
Osborne's poor relations with Falvy, the head of mission's claim that he
hoped to show as much respect to Toby as he has to the preceding governors
was unlikely to assuage Toby's apprehensions. This moment of confusion
and cultural dissonance evidently prompted Toby to detain Osborne shortly
thereafter.

If this scenario had played itself out in Maradi alone, then we could simply
conclude that personality issues had driven the incident and that with more
tact Osborne might have evaded scrutiny, but all across the AOF Protestant missions were in hot water. There seem to have been specific cultural
dynamics and political tensions that contributed to this broader pattern,
well captured by Keller in his study of "foreign" missions. In his report on

---

[33] African Christians I spoke with claimed that the "American" missionaries regarded Newton
Kapp as a potential *German* spy. Kapp, an Armenian born in Georgia, was fluent in several
languages including Arabic. He set up in a Hausa-style rental house in Maradi away from
the mission compound in 1940 and went on to violate the antimaterial ethos of the mission
by conducting trade to stay afloat in wartime. He had friends among the French, Nigerien
evolués, and the Lebanese traders. Interview with Ray de la Haye.

his 1942 *tournée*, Keller suggests that as far as he can tell the "attitude of the missions is correct" and that they do not in fact engage in politics. There were a handful of incidents in which individual missionaries were engaged in activities in support of the Free French, resulting in the expulsion of a few missionary children from Guinea, the imprisonment of an African pastor in Guinea, and imprisonment for one English pastor who helped some French citizens escape to a British colony. Of these incidents Keller remarked coolly, "it doesn't appear that one could argue that these foreigners have conducted themselves any worse than the French themselves."[34] In other words, Keller seemed to argue that foreign missionaries are no more likely to spy than the French who are resident in the colonies. So why, he asked, does the heightened suspicion of them persist?

First, he suggested, they were strangers. Furthermore, their Protestant emphasis on evangelism was unfamiliar to French administrators, who were more comfortable and more familiar with the Catholic emphasis on schooling exemplified in the work of Lavigerie and the White Fathers. The missionaries' evangelical zeal evidently wore thin when combined with relatively weak skills in French. They also, he suggested, had a "characteristically British tenacity" derived from an undeserved sense of entitlement that was irksome to an administration emphasizing hierarchy and acquiescence to authority. I suspect that the "tenacity" referred to in the case of SIM had to do with Osborne's unreasonable expectation that the mission could go forward with the building of the leprosarium, which was to be sited on the road to Nigeria and which would have entailed bringing in more missionary staff, after the fall of France. Keller went on to argue that despite these cultural misunderstandings the missionaries did preach submission to authority "in conformity with biblical teaching" and encouraged the payment of taxes. Despite the slow progress of the missions, given their emphasis on evangelism, their work did tend to support, Keller argued, the kind of moral, personal, and familial development that are of the greatest interest for the civilizing mission of France in these territories. As if to apologize for the Protestant missionaries' misguided emphasis on evangelism, Keller pointed out that the missions appeared to be rethinking whether they have missed out on opportunities to win the sympathy of the indigenous populations, presumably through education and medical work.

Keller intervened on Osborne's behalf, writing in a letter to the director of security in Dakar in December 1942, attesting firsthand to Osborne's sympathy for France, his prayers for Marshal Pétain, and his commitment to a life consecrated to the religious work in French territory for which he felt a particular calling. Of Osborne's missteps, Keller remarked, "perhaps he has committed a few blunders; he does not seem to have understood from the beginning the new situation created by the events of 1940 and has perhaps

---

[34] J. Keller, "Rapport de tournée," January 12–May 26, 1942, 17G115 (Missions: divers), Affaires politiques AOF, ANOM, Aix-en-Provence.

indisposed the administration for this reason. But that is not sufficient to justify his reputation as a dangerous man." In a subtle critique of the local administration that did not go unremarked on high (it was underlined by the reader, presumably the director of security), Keller observed, "The fact that he is both Anglo-Saxon and Protestant is perhaps sufficient for some to justify a prejudicial attitude."[35]

One might wonder whether Keller, as a Protestant interested in advancing the work of Protestant missions, might not have underplayed the Gaullist sympathies of the missionaries he visited. Certainly, French Protestants in France had occasionally criticized Vichy policies and some had entered the resistance movement.[36] Most French Protestants, however, remained loyal to Pétain despite increasing discomfort with Vichy's treatment of the Jewish population and outrage over forced labor. By the time of the German occupation of the southern zone of France, disillusionment with the Vichy regime was high among Protestants. It is not clear that Protestants in Niger were any more inclined toward resistance than their French coreligionists. Akpo-Vaché suggests that no systematic resistance network existed in Niger, although individual Africans in Zinder, Maradi, and Birnin Koni made unauthorized trips to Nigeria to meet with traditional and religious leaders. Even these individuals, who, it might be argued, may more plausibly have resisted the Vichy regime, primarily conveyed only news and information on potential travel routes.[37] Even assuming Pastor 'Dan Nana qualified in this limited sense as a member of the resistance, this would seem rather slender evidence for the participation of the missionaries themselves in a resistance movement.

My interviews, however, suggest that, at least in the case of the SIM, Keller was in fact correct, for the *evangelical* missions so thoroughly placed evangelism before politics that the missionaries engaged in remarkably little activity that might be construed as resistance to Vichy. Unless one takes attempting to maintain information flows with the mission stations in Nigeria as in itself a subversive activity, SIM missionaries in Niger did not really contribute to the resistance movement. Like their evangelical colleagues within France, they espoused a kind of political quietism that distinguished them from the slightly more liberal tradition of Protestants following Pastor Marc Boegner and the Église Réformé de France.[38] A stance of disengagement from politics is, of course, its own kind of political engagement.

---

35 Letter from Pasteur J. Keller to Monsieur le directeur de la Sureté Générale, Dakar, December 29, 1942, 17G115 (Missions: divers), Affaires politiques AOF, ANOM, Aix-en-Provence.

36 Roderick Kedward suggests that the long history of Protestant resistance in the face of religious persecution in some regions of France may have contributed to Maquis outlaw culture; see his article, "The Maquis and the culture of the outlaw (with particular reference to the Cevennes)," in R. Kedward and R. Austin (eds.), *Vichy France and the Resistance: Culture and Ideology* (London: Croom Helm, 1985), 225–32.

37 Akpo-Vaché, *L'AOF et la seconde guerre mondiale*, 122.

38 Halls, *Politics, Society and Christianity in Vichy France*, 103–05, 123–24, 193.

So far as I can tell this was the end of the affair, for before Keller's next visit, the AOF fell to de Gaulle and the entire political landscape changed, once again, overnight. Here is how Ray de la Haye experienced the transition:

> Then suddenly, everything changed. The administration came out and said, "you're free. You can go home, border's opened up." And it had, you see, Eisenhower had been successful in North Africa. And all of French West Africa, as it was known then, was free again, and de Gaulle came down to Dakar. And do you know who they attributed it to? Mr. Osborne. He came back. Of course, they [the local Hausa population] just about worshiped him.[39]

This representation of the innocent and credulous Africans is rather typical of an older generation of missionaries' storytelling style, but is little borne out by my own interviews with local Christians, who tended to underplay Osborne's brief detention and any heroism it might have implied. Nevertheless, a more diffuse perception of the mission as part of the American liberation effort and de Gaulle's liberalizing movement may have served the mission well for a time.

As far as relations with the administration went, after de Gaulle's takeover of AOF, the missionaries experienced near complete reversal in the administration's attitudes toward its activities. While it is clear that the surveillance of the missions continued, the obstruction of their expansion gradually faded until the administration seems even to have consciously relied on the networks, finances, personnel, and energy of the Protestant missions to promote a postwar explosion of educational and medical work. How much of this expansion resulted from the shifts the missions were already considering before the war and how much derived from the interests of the French administration as encouraged by Pastor Keller is hard to determine. SIM had already committed itself to the Maradi leprosarium before Keller's intervention. Certainly, Keller, in his visits to the Protestant missions, did forcefully encourage mission work of a social nature and was happy to attribute the shift in attitude as evidence of the "penetration of our French mentality in the hearts of missions up to now rather closed to our influence."[40]

A Sea Change in French Attitudes toward Protestants: The Brazzaville Conference

The wartime experience punctured France's sense of her own infallibility. For many Africans, both those who served in the war and those who suffered under the repressive policies of the Vichy regime, any remaining myth of

---

[39] Interview with Ray de la Haye.
[40] Pasteur J. Keller, "Note sur la délégation général des missions Protestantes en AOF," October 5, 1943, 17G115 (Missions: divers), Affaires politiques AOF, ANOM, Aix-en-Provence.

French grandeur had dissipated. "In fact, the Vichy regime," as Fuglestad remarks, "by pushing the classic colonial system to its logical extreme so late in the day, had in a sense done the Africans a favour, that of thoroughly discrediting the system."[41] Under the circumstances colonial extraction in the absence of the right to self-government was readily equated with Nazism. The Atlantic Charter as articulated by Roosevelt seemed to augur an entirely new world order, one in which it was not clear that France would have a role alongside the great powers and one in which self-government would become the mark of legitimacy.[42]

If de Gaulle hoped to retain and shore up the support of colonialists within the African territories he had to assuage their fears that he would deliver France's colonial territories up to others on a silver platter. Well before the territory of France had been taken back, de Gaulle had to begin to preempt any American criticism of French colonial rule. Certainly de Gaulle and France already owed the Africans, and in particular the African Tirailleurs, a tremendous debt. De Gaulle convened the famous Brazzaville conference of 1944 to recognize the need for reform and to begin articulating a new colonial policy that, in principle, recognized African agency, input and interests; however "one striking feature of the conference," as William Cohen notes, "was that although it had been called to decide the future of French Africa, no Africans actively participated in its deliberations." The outcome of the conference was highly conservative: France explicitly rejected any plan for autonomy or self-government for African territories while articulating the continuing importance of France's paternalist role in the affairs of its empire. Despite emphasis on the importance of traditional authorities, the conference's unwillingness to entertain Felix Eboué's proposal that indigenous institutions be respected is evident in the paternalist recommendation that polygyny be abolished and the continuing insistence upon an educational policy leading to assimilation to French language and culture.[43]

If the political implications of the Brazzaville proposals were less revolutionary than one might have hoped, the paternalist emphasis on the social welfare of Africans opened the way for advances in the previously neglected realms of education and health. With little financial means of implementing its social welfare proposals, and in view of the embarrassing record of the Vichy regime toward Protestant missions, it is not surprising that after the war Protestant missions found they had more latitude to engage in "social mission" work than they had encountered previously. After decades of near complete neglect of Protestant missions (they were barely in evidence

[41] Fuglestad, *History of Niger*, 145.
[42] Akpo-Vaché, *L'AOF et la seconde guerre mondiale*, 192–93.
[43] William B. Cohen, *Rulers of Empire: The French Colonial Service in Africa* (Stanford, CA: Hoover Institution Press, 1971), 166–67.

in the colonial records prior to 1939),[44] the French administration began systematically collecting information both openly and covertly about their scope, personnel, activities, and potential. Certainly, the impetus for this information gathering was, as we shall see, a need to keep close tabs on "the Americans"; however, it also resulted from the attitude of greater openness toward Protestants and their missions that emerged out of the dynamics of the war. On the one hand, the Vichy regime's harassment of Protestant pastors and preferential treatment of Catholics left the postwar regime with the task of mending fences and restoring the luster of France's republican claims to religious neutrality. On the other hand, de Gaulle owed a particular debt to his fervent (and well-endowed) supporters in the France Forever Association based in the United States, many of whom were Protestant.[45] Certainly in France during the war, Protestant pastors and their congregations, notably under the leadership of Pastor Boegner (head of the Fédération Protestante de France) had often been visible and active critics of the Vichy regime.[46] As the war drew to a close and as American finance and influence was increasingly important in Europe and elsewhere, de Gaulle found himself warily supporting the activities of Protestant missions, many of which had significant ties to the United States. Consequently, as decolonization drew nearer, a larger and more developed network of Protestant converts, students, missionaries, and pastors emerged. While this occasionally fractious network was not particularly visible in the party politics of the decolonization era, the colonial administration took note of its clamorous critiques of colonial policy and systematically investigated mission policy regarding marriage, the separation of church and state, and educational policy. One result, then, of Vichy's pro-Catholic and xenophobic policies was that after the war, "foreign" Protestant missions and their converts had greater influence and a broader scope of activity than prior to the war.

Conclusion: The American Invasion

There was a veritable explosion in studies of the missions by the French colonial administration after 1944 in the wake of the Vichy government's harassment of Protestant missions.[47] These studies ranged broadly in

---

44 When the Foreign Ministry finally began to systematically collect materials on missions in the French African colonies, it had to turn to the Société des Missions Evangeliques de Paris, which itself had only partial data. FM 2192 (Questions religieuses [missions]), ANOM, Aix-en-Provence.

45 S. Beynon John, "Saint-Exupery's *Pilote de Guerre*: Testimony, art and ideology," in Roderick Kedward and Roger Austin (eds.), *Vichy France and the Resistance: Culture and Ideology* (London: Croom Helm, 1984), 94.

46 Halls, *Politics, Society and Christianity in Vichy France*.

47 Among the studies undertaken were the following: "Situation Juridique Comparée des Missions, 1944," Fonds Ministériels (hereafter FM) 2190; "Questions Religieuses: Missions,"

attitude toward Protestant missions, from the suggestion of Christian Merlo that France interpret international treaties in such a way as to promote Catholic (French) missions over Protestant (foreign) missions to the assertion of Guy Monod (from a prominent Protestant family himself) that Protestant missions proved more attentive than Catholic missions to the social needs of Africans. While much of this material retains a tone of skepticism and wariness about American missions, it is clear that on the whole a far more positive, if opportunistic, attitude toward such missions had emerged. The policy that eventually emerged would channel the finances and energies of these well-endowed missions toward more effective social intervention while containing the political influence of the Americans.

As the Foreign Ministry began to gather intelligence on Protestant missions, it increasingly became clear that despite the frequent characterization of, for example, SIM in Niger as "britannique," the staff was in fact heavily made up of Americans.[48] A report to the Foreign Ministry on the staffing of evangelical missions throughout AOF suggested the overwhelming presence of American missionaries among evangelicals. Ten of the thirty mission societies were American, and their 425 missionaries vastly outnumbered the total of 177 French missionaries working there.[49] Reasonably enough, therefore, in the latter part of the war and the early postwar period, the English-speaking missionaries came to be seen as "American" rather than British. Given de Gaulle's occasionally rocky relations with the United States, the presence of so many Americans may have been unsettling. Despite a greater sense of openness toward Protestant missions after the Allied victory in Africa it should be noted that covert surveillance of Protestant missions continued throughout the war, well after the Vichy regime's fall, and indeed intensified under de Gaulle.

The governor thwarted SIM efforts to gain permission to start a school, and as if to find the evidence necessary to convince those on high, seems to have intensified surveillance of the missionaries: In 1946, the commandant of the police in Niger submitted a secret report on missions in Niger in which it appears that his attentions went as far as intercepting the film the

---

FM 2192; Enquête sur les Missions Religieuses" 1945, FM 2190 and 2192; G. Monod, "Influence des Missions Protestantes en Afrique noire," dossier 7, FM 2190; "Aide et Protection aux Missions Religieuses," dossier 1, FM 3369; and Christian Merlo, "Fondement juridique d'une politique missionaire positive," dossier 4, FM 3369; all in ANOM, Aix-en-Provence.

[48] "Enquête sur les Missions Religieuses," FM 2190, ANOM, Aix-en-Provence. Closer scrutiny revealed that SIM's Niger staff included five French citizens, three Canadians, one New Zealander, four "English," and sixteen Americans. More than half of the personnel were from the United States.

[49] Foltz report to the Foreign Ministry, "Société de Mission travaillant dans les Colonies françaises, mai 17, 1946," FM 2192, ANOM, Aix-en-Provence.

American missionaries were having developed.[50] In the face of a renewal of the mission staff after the war, the governor's skepticism concerning the true nature of the mission's activities continued: "The missionary zeal of the American pastors not being particularly active, *this invasion does leave one speculating about the true motives for their action.* They all remain under a discrete, but attentive, surveillance."[51] As late as 1947, the political officer was noting the peculiarities of the mission's typewriter, presumably to be able to track the authors of anticolonial political tracts.[52]

This mistrust abated by 1948, when Governor Jean Colombani remarked that although the Protestant missions seemed to make little progress in converting local populations, their relations with the authorities were always "correct."[53] By 1950, SIM had finally obtained approval to set up the girls' home at Soura and had opened a dispensary in Galmi.[54] The much-discussed leprosarium was finally approved in 1953 under Toby, after consultation with the relevant medical services and negotiation as to the best location within the colony.[55]

Monod had argued in 1945 that France needed to address the critical issue of how to educate the African in order to emancipate him. In this urgent matter, he averred, Christian missions had an important role to play. Rather than oppose the Americans, whose power has been driven home by the course of the war, France should attempt to channel their youthful energy:

[50] After the war and in the context of the rise of political activity as decolonization loomed on the horizon a secret study was done of foreign missions in the AOF. See letter from Lieutenant-Colonel Cases (commandant de détachement de gendarmerie de l'AOF), to Pierre Cournarie (gouverneur-général de l'AOF), December 16, 1946; and Adjudant Fajole (commandant de brigade de gendarmerie du Niger), "Sur l'importance, l'organisation, l'influence, et l'activité des missions religieuses installées au Niger," November 28, 1946, both in 17G141 (14miom/2318), Affaires Politiques AOF, ANOM, Aix-en-Provence. Local administrators seem to have been more suspicious of the mission's activities than their superiors. When, in his 1945 annual report, the governor remarked to his superiors that he suspected that the missionaries were above all agents of the British and American governments, a more highly placed skeptic made the marginal note, "there's nothing to support this"; see Rapport politique annuel 1945, 2G45 17 (14miom/1863), Affaires politiques: Niger, ANOM, Aix-en-Provence.

[51] Confidential report, Affaires Politiques, Niger, juillet 1946, 11 G 21 (14miom/2204), Affaires politiques: divers, ANOM, Aix-en-Provence.

[52] "Renseignement: Origine: Maradi," January 21, 1947: Objet: activité des missions religieuses étrangères, 11G21 (14miom/2204), Affaires politiques: divers, ANOM, Aix-en-Provence.

[53] "Rapport Politique Annuel, 1948" Gouverneur p.i. du Niger Colombani, 2G48 2 (14miom/1887), Affaires politiques: Niger, ANOM, Aix-en-Provence.

[54] Rapport politique annuel 1950, 2G50 30 (14miom/1917), Affaires politiques, ANOM, Aix-en-Provence.

[55] Letter from directeur du service général d'hygiène mobile et de prophylaxie to monsieur le directeur général de la sante publique en AOF, no 1783, mai 4, 1953, 1H73 versement 144, records of the AOF, AS, Dakar.

> There is no question, as we've seen, of attempting to oppose the irresistible force of American messianism. . . . Rather, in working together with this movement, in cooperating with it, it seems that it might be possible to channel its sometimes incoherent flow, to act as guide and open the door so far as our interests will permit, in order to avoid its being broken open.[56]

Indeed, doors did open, although in the end France did not abandon its policy of insisting that schooling in the French territories be conducted in French. Nevertheless, the general climate of support for the Protestant missions enabled missions such as SIM to expand tremendously in the postwar period, opening a new era for both the missions and the populations they served, and enabling the missions to forge close ties with the African elites who eventually replaced the colonial administration.

Let me close, then, with Pastor Osborne's exhilarated description of the mission field after his release, blissfully ignorant, as he was, of the ongoing surveillance and suspicions of "the Americans," happy only that the mission could finally move forward. Free once again to travel; Osborne began to seek out new sites for the mission. In June 1944, he wrote home to call for at least thirty more missionaries for the AOF: "Never have we known the French officials to show a more sympathetic and friendly attitude toward us and our work. God has wonderfully answered the many prayers sent up over a period of at least ten years for the creating of this very attitude and the opening of these very doors."[57] Osborne had gone from being an extremely dangerous suspect to being an irresistible force of change, part of the postwar Africa taking shape, as Monod observed, right before France's wary eyes.

Appendix to Chapter 19

Letter from David M. Osborne, missionnaire in Tibiri (Maradi) to Monsieur le Gouverneur du Niger, Niamey, Décembre, 12, 1942, 17G115, CAOM.

December 12, 1942
Monsieur le Gouverneur:

Allow me the honor of presenting you with this letter pursuant to our conversation of November 30th in your office in Niamey, at which time you expressed your displeasure at my absence during your first visit to Maradi the 15th of June, 1942. I would ask that you permit me to explain in greater detail the circumstances surrounding this matter.

---

[56] G. Monod, "Influence des missions protestantes en Afrique noire," p. 59, dossier 7, FM 2190, ANOM, Aix-en-Provence.
[57] D. M. Osborne, "Prospecting," *The Sudan Witness*, 20 (1944), 6.

Governor Falvy had made a visit prior to your own during which he had evidently conveyed to his administration his desire that the missionaries not be notified of his arrival. Undoubtedly as a result of this the Mission was taken off the list of recipients for the circular announcing that visit. At the time of your aforementioned visit another circular was sent out to the Europeans [sic] but once again neither the Mission nor the name of any missionary was included on the recipients list. As a consequence, and in the knowledge of how General Falvy had handled the matter of his own movements, I came to the conclusion that the presence of the missionaries was not desired, and as a result I considered it an act of discretion to abstain myself from the public reception. On the day of your visit Mr. Kapp [an SIM missionary heading work in Maradi] was in his office in Maradi, and in his conversation with the Commandant de Cercle did ask whether the Commandant thought that the Governor would want to see him. He responded that he would find out at the time of your arrival. That evening, the Commandant de Cercle sent a word to Mr. Kapp informing him that the Governor would see him the following day at 10 o'clock. Mr. Kapp kept that appointment, to which he had personally been invited. At the time of that meeting he conveyed to you how much I, as chief of the mission, lamented not being able to speak with you.

I believe that this explanation will demonstrate that under the circumstances I could not have acted in any other manner. Once again allow me to assure you that I had no intention of behaving disrespectfully. On the contrary, please believe that it is my sincere desire to show you a respect and devotion as deep as I have shown all the governors who have preceded you in the fifteen years of my residence in the colony.

After my arrest in Tibiri the 9th of November and my detention in Niamey, I think that it might be appropriate for me to set out my own attitude regarding the administration and more generally toward the French. I have been accused of spying and anti-French sentiments. I categorically and energetically deny these utterly groundless accusations. I defy anyone to provide proof of such allegations. I have never under any circumstances acted as a spy for Great Britain or any other country. Have I been anti-French? If that were so I would have left this territory, for the mission has neither the desire nor the ability to force me to remain against my will. In the colony I have always attempted to be respectful and amiable toward the French among whom I found myself. On three different occasions I have been to France, where I have spent a year overall. I have always strived to know more about France, its people and its language, as much for myself as for my work as director of our mission in Niger. Until her death in Tibiri in October of 1940 I was married to a French Canadian of purely French origins, and her death was an extraordinary blow to me and to the Sudan Interior Mission. I hope that all these reasons will make it possible for you to see that these accusations of espionage and anti-French feelings are in no way justified. I must protest once again and insist that these allegations are pure lies.

Allow me the honor, Monsieur le Gouverneur, of requesting that you order an investigation of this subject immediately, and as soon as my claims have been verified, as I am sure they will be, may I ask that you take whatever measures necessary to obliterate any traces of these accusations from my files. Far from being anti-French and acting in a manner that is prejudicial to the French Empire, I have the most ardent desire to see France reestablished in her ancient glory and playing an important role among the great powers.

Please accept, Monsieur le Gouverneur, along with my anticipated thanks, the expression of my profound respect.

David Osborne

20

Fighting Fascism

Ethiopian Women Patriots 1935–1941

Hailu Habtu and Judith A. Byfield

I could see him firing behind a growth of tall grass. Suddenly, he waved to me and fell. I went over to his side leaving my position. He was dead. Enemy soldiers were close by on the other side of the river. Before I started to pull away, I fired across the river and killed three men. I then pulled his body and his gun and withdrew. The rest of my men were safe. I went back to camp and the following day I buried him at the church of Dirma Gabriel.[1]

Lekelesh Bayan, who watched her husband get killed, is just one of thousands of women who fought alongside Ethiopian men during the Italian occupation from 1935 to 1941. A decree issued on November 30, 1944, and enacted January 20, 1945, identified the three categories of combatants who contributed to the resistance during the occupation, and the medal each received. These three categories of combatants were the *arbegna, the yewist arbegna,* and *sidetegna.* The *arbegna* was a patriot who received the "Medal of the Campaign 1936–1941" for engaging the enemy in combat. The *yewist arbegna* was an underground patriot who operated in Italian organizational networks and passed on information and supplies to patriots in the field; he or she received the "Medal of the Patriots of the Interior." The *sidetegna* was a refugee, who received the "Medal of the Patriot Refugees," which recognized supporters of the resistance from outside the country.[2] The largest number of refugees fled to Kenya and Sudan, but some of the aristocracy accompanied Emperor Haile Selassie to Britain and others went

[1] Tsehai Berhane Sellasie, "Women guerrilla fighters", *Northeast African Studies*, new series, 1, (1979–1980), 73–83.

[2] Bahru Zewde, *A History of Modern Ethiopia, 1855–1991*, 2nd ed. (Athens: Ohio University Press, 2001), 172.

This paper was completed while I was in residence at the Institute for Advanced Study (IAS), School of Historical Studies, Princeton. I enjoyed the generous support of the IAS Fund for Historical Studies and a Professional Development Grant from Cornell University.

to Jerusalem. The courageous actions of medal recipients listed in the *Book of Honor 1935–1941* had to be verified by fellow combatants.

The significance of women's contribution to the resistance was publicly recognized in the *Book of Honor*. Tsehai Berhane Sellassie estimates that approximately one-third of the names recorded there belong to women.[3] This public acknowledgement of Ethiopian women was important. By comparison, even though thousands of women participated in the French resistance to German occupation, only six women were among the one thousand recipients of the medals distributed by Charles de Gaulle in 1944.[4] Despite the recognition afforded these women following Ethiopia's liberation, most histories of the occupation ignore women combatants. This chapter moves beyond merely acknowledging the role of these women to consider the nature of their participation in the resistance and the ways that gender ideologies informed their wartime experiences.

Fascist Occupation

In his speech to the assembly of the League of Nations on June 30, 1936, Emperor Haile Selassie warned of the threat to the collective security of small states if Italy's use of force was allowed to triumph in Ethiopia.[5] The representatives of three major powers – Anthony Eden of Britain, Léon Blum of France, and Maxim Litvinov of the Soviet Union – ignored his warning and signaled their willingness to reward Italy by calling for an end to sanctions. The invasion and subsequent occupation of Ethiopia temporally falls outside Eurocentric views concerning the beginning of the Second World War in Europe; nonetheless, it is critical to include this conflict in analyses of Africa's engagement in the war and in studies of Fascism.[6] Indeed, the peace treaty concluded after the war acknowledged that for Ethiopia, World War II began with the Italian invasion on October 3, 1935. Thus, the Horn of Africa experienced a decade of war from 1935 to 1945.[7]

---

[3] This ratio is similar to the ratio of female/male guerrilla fighters who later participated in the Tigrai People's Liberation Front and the Eritrean People's Liberation Front (EPLF). For example, women constituted one-third of the 95,000 fighters in the EPLF. Selassie, "Women guerilla fighters," 82; John Young, *Peasant Revolution in Ethiopia: The Tigray People's Liberation Front* (Cambridge: Cambridge University Press, 1997), 179; Victoria Bernal, "From warriors to wives: Contradictions of liberation and development in Eritrea," *Northeast African Studies*, new series, 8 (2001), 132.

[4] Margaret Collins Weitz, *Sisters in the Resistance: How Women Fought to Free France, 1940–1945* (New York: John Wiley and Sons, 1995), 10.

[5] Anthony Mockler, *Haile Selassie's War* (New York: Olive Branch Press, 2003), 151.

[6] Richard Pankhurst, "Italian Fascist war crimes in Ethiopia: A history of their discussion from the League of Nations to the United Nations (1936–1949)," *Northeast African Studies*, new series, 6 (1999), 109–11.

[7] N. Ayele, "The Horn of Africa and Eastern Africa in the world war decade: 1935–45," 77; and A. Eshete, "The Horn of Africa in a decade of world conflict (1935–45)," 91–106; both in *Africa and the Second World War: Report and Papers of the Symposium organized by*

Scholars of Fascism argue that it is only in examining Mussolini's domestic and foreign policies from the 1930s that we can appreciate the evolution of Fascism as well as the similarities between Hitler and Mussolini.[8] Mussolini's appointment as prime minister in 1922 handed him the opportunity to implement his vision of a Fascist state. There were no elections or strikes while political opponents were forced into exile, imprisoned, or banished to geographically distant and inhospitable places. Mockler notes that by 1931, the rules and regulations of the Fascist state had become institutionalized in everyday life. Teachers and civil servants had to wear black shirts, party officials began the day with military-style gymnastics and the party salute had to be given while standing, not sitting. The alternative armed force, the *milizias*, answered directly to Mussolini and only indirectly to the state.[9] As early as 1932, Mussolini began considering plans to conquer Ethiopia and had General Emilio de Bono, the governor of Italy's two North African provinces – Tripolitania and Cyrenaica, (seized in 1911) – conduct several reconnaissance trips to Eritrea.[10] Mussolini's vision for a Fascist state included imperial expansion, but he also hoped to avenge Italy's defeat to Ethiopian forces in 1896 in the battle of Adwa.[11] While Mussolini did not act on these plans, Italian authorities carried out multiple acts of subversion. They sowed discord among the Ethiopian aristocracy in provinces bordering Italian-controlled territories, and sent troops into Ethiopian territory well beyond the border.[12] Mussolini would use one of these border incidents at Walwal as the justification for going to war with Ethiopia.[13]

On October 3, 1935, Italian forces under the command of de Bono invaded Ethiopia from the north (see Figure 20.1). While the emperor explored a number of diplomatic options, a military counteroffensive did not begin until January 20, 1936. Unfortunately by the end of March, the Ethiopian army in the north had been routed. Italian forces under the

UNESCO at Benghazi, Libyan Arab Jamahiriya, 10–13 November 1980 (Paris: UNESCO, 1985).

[8] Anthony Cardoza, "Recasting the Duce for the new century: Recent scholarship on Mussolini and Italian Fascism," *Journal of Modern History*, 77 (2005), 722–37; Alexander de Grand, "Mussolini's follies: Fascism in its imperial and racist phase, 1935–1940," *Contemporary European History*, 13 (2004), 127–47; MacGregor Knox, "The Fascist regime, its foreign policy and its wars: An 'anti-anti-Fascist' orthodoxy?," *Contemporary European History*, 4 (1995), 347–65.

[9] Mockler, *Haile Selassie's War*, 25–26.

[10] Ibid., 41–42.

[11] Italy's defeat at the battle of Adwa in 1896 protected Ethiopia's independence as other European imperial powers divided the rest of the continent.

[12] Zewde, *History of Modern Ethiopia*, 71–78, 152.

[13] Mockler argues that the confrontation began because an Ethiopian soldier tossed a bone at a Somali soldier in the Italian forces. Although this was a very small incident, it escalated, in part, because Italy wanted to use the incident to move the border between Ethiopia and Somalia, and in the process claim more of Ethiopia. Mockler, *Haile Selassie's War*, 37–43.

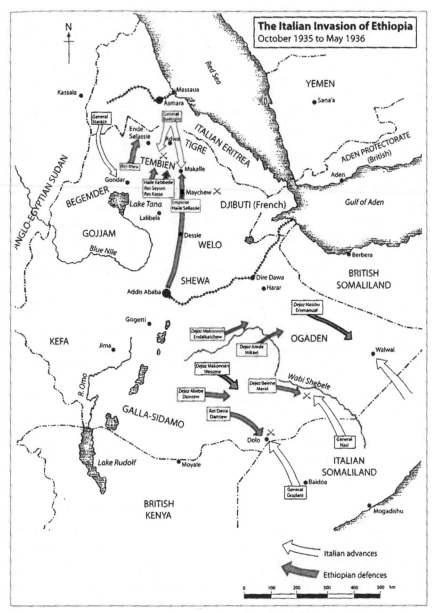

FIGURE 20.1. From: Andrew Hilton (ed.), *The Ethiopian Patriots: Forgotten Voices of the Italo-Abyssinian War 1935–41* (Spellmount, 2007), 47.

command of General Rudolfo Graziani had invaded from the south and southeast. The Italians met stiff resistance; nonetheless, the conclusion remained the same. The Italians marched into Addis Ababa on May 5, 1936, and Emperor Haile Selassie began his journey into exile, reaching England on June 3, 1936, where he would remain for the next five years.

Several factors contributed to Italy's swift conquest of Ethiopia. They included distrust and disunity among the Ethiopian political elite, Italy's larger and more sophisticated weapons systems (tanks, planes, machine guns, bombs, and mustard gas), and much larger ground forces. Italy's ground troops included a Libyan battalion as well as volunteers, two divisions from Eritrea, five divisions from the regular Italian army, and five divisions of Blackshirts (military units composed entirely of Fascist Party members). During combat they were attached to the army, but operated under the direction of the Italian army commanders.[14] Ethiopia could not match Italian military preparedness because it had been encumbered by the arms embargo placed on both parties in 1934.[15] It is estimated that the Ethiopians had between 50,000 and 60,000 modern rifles and twelve airplanes, no match whatsoever for Italy's superior army equipped with the latest weaponry and an air force of 400 airplanes.[16] Historically, the Ethiopian army comprised a collection of soldiers under the control of specific chiefs or members of the aristocracy.[17] Selassie had begun to professionalize the Ethiopian army in 1934 by hiring Belgian officers to train soldiers and Swedish officers who established an officer cadet school, Oletta, in January 1935. Before the fighting began, the Belgians had succeeded in training only three battalions, three machine-gun companies, two batteries, and a horse-mounted squadron. Furthermore, communication between the Ethiopian forces was poor and the Italians often intercepted their radio

---

[14] During combat the Blackshirt units were attached to the army, but operated under the direction of the Italian Army commanders. Zewde, *History of Modern Ethiopia*, 153–59; Mockler, *Haile Selassie's War*, 54; Richard E. Osborne, *World War II in Colonial Africa: The Death Knell of Colonialism* (Indianapolis, IN: Riebel-Roque Publishing Company, 2001), 8.

[15] Although the sanctions hurt Ethiopia, Baer argues that the agreement must be recognized as an important moment of collective action. He further suggests that the sanctions intensified militant statism and strengthened Mussolini. George W. Baer, "Sanctions and security: The League of Nations and the Italian-Ethiopian War, 1935–1936," *International Organization*, 27 (1973), 165–79.

[16] Zewde, *History of Modern Ethiopia*, 159.

[17] In addition to troops raised through the traditional method based on the *dambagna* and the regular army, Ethiopian forces were augmented by international volunteers from the Caribbean and the United States, and hired mercenaries. Sellassie, "Women guerrilla fighters," 73; Osborne, *World War II in Colonial Africa*, 4; William R. Scott, *The Sons of Sheba's Race: African-Americans and the Italo-Ethiopian War, 1935–1941*, 2nd ed. (Hollywood, CA: Tschai Publishers and Distributors, 2006); Fikru Gebrekidan, "In defense of Ethiopia: A comparative assessment of Caribbean and African-American anti-Fascist protests, 1935–1941" *Northeast African Studies*, new series, 2 (1995), 145–73.

communications.[18] In short, Ethiopia did not have the resources to fight a conventional war even though they continued to rely on this strategy. Hockler argues that Haile Selassie recognized the need for alternative tactics and had ordered the Rases (princes) to use guerrilla tactics to harass the Italians instead of confronting them, but they continually disobeyed his orders.[19]

Mussolini and his generals basked in the glow of their victory and moved quickly to annex Ethiopia. On June 1, 1936, a new law reorganized the Horn of Africa – Ethiopia, Eritrea, Italian Somaliland – in a new colonial entity: Africa Orientale Italiana (AOI), with Marshal Pietro Badoglio appointed as viceroy and governor-general. They divided the new colony into five provinces, each under the command of a military governor. Commissars, the equivalent of residents in the British system, oversaw all major towns. Political officers negotiated surrenders with nobles who had to formally submit before the viceroy and take an oath of loyalty to "the King of Italy, Emperor of Ethiopia... and the Duce of Fascism Benito Mussolini." Some members of the aristocracy were also brought into the colonial government. Viceroy Graziani, who succeeded Badoglio, restored authority on conditional terms to Dejaz[20] Gugsa of Tigre and Ras Hailu of Gojjam. Ras Hailu was also allowed to raise a *banda* or a company of 1,000 men, although he could never take them to his home province, Gojjam. Successive viceroys discussed plans to appoint more members of the aristocracy to an advisory council, but that did not materialize until 1939.[21]

While aspects of Italian colonial rule resembled that of other colonial powers, the edifice was also distinguished by its Fascist structure. Like any Italian region, Ethiopia had a federal secretary, "with a position and powers parallel to that of the civil and military authorities, and responsible not to the Ministry of the Colonies, but to the Party Secretary in Rome." Fascist federations and federal secretaries were extended to each of the five provinces, and in Addis Ababa they established a Casa del Fascio, and a militia headquarters. In addition, the Blackshirt battalions were retained in Ethiopia as garrison troops in the large towns. The Italians effectively created parallel structures, one accountable to the government and the other to the Fascist Party.[22]

Periodizing the Resistance

Despite the elaborate administrative structure put in place, it could not mask the weakness of the Italian colonial state, since Italians did not control major

---

[18] Mockler, *Haile Selassie's War*, 47–49, 116.

[19] Ibid., 85.

[20] Abbreviation of Dejazmatch: Commander of the gate, politicomiliatry title below Ras. Sbacchi, *Legacy of Bitterness*, 396.

[21] Ibid., 148, 153, 154; Alberto Sbacchi, *Legacy of Bitterness: Ethiopia and Fascist Italy, 1925–1941* (Lawrence, NJ: Red Sea Press, 1997), 136.

[22] Mockler, *Haile Selassie's War*, 154.

parts of the country. At the time of annexation, Italy occupied only a third of Ethiopia and controlled only a few major routes, specifically the route from Eritrea to Addis Ababa and the roadway from Somalia to Addis Ababa. The occupying army primarily controlled the urban areas and would spend the next five years trying to extend that control across the entire country.[23]

Meanwhile Ethiopian resistance to Italian occupation spread throughout the countryside. Zewde argues that the resistance had two phases. The first phase continued the conventional war and was led primarily by the nobility, who disregarded calls to deploy guerrilla tactics from Bajerond[24] Takla-Yawaryat, Ethiopia's ambassador to France and Switzerland, exiled in Paris.[25] Zewde contends that it was only in the second phase of the resistance, after 1937, that Ethiopian forces, primarily led by lower-ranking nobles, used guerrilla warfare; however, this was not so cut and dry. As early as June 1936, Ethiopian rebel groups attacked the railway line between Addis Ababa and Djibouti, the main supply route to the capital. The Patriots removed rails, blew up bridges, cut telegraph wire and interrupted service for up to a week at a time. In response, the colonial government used tanks and over one hundred airplanes against the resistance fighters, in addition to posting guards every fifty meters along the railway.[26]

The Italians spent the second half of 1936 attempting to subdue those nobles who still controlled armies. They repelled an attack against Addis Ababa in July and spent the rest of the year essentially hunting nobles in the southwest and southeast.[27] The search for nobles such as Ras Desta, the son-in-law of Haile Selassie, was especially brutal. Sbacchi notes that the air force and troops were given a free hand to chase and exterminate the enemy. As a result entire villages were burned to the ground and all male residents above eighteen years old were executed. By the beginning of 1937, the Italians had eliminated all major Ethiopian military leaders.[28]

The attempted assassination of Viceroy Graziani in February 1937 formed the dividing line between the two phases.[29] Aregawi Berhe argues that this event transformed the policy of Italian occupation as officials instituted draconian measures to subdue a growing Ethiopian resistance.[30]

---

[23] Sbacci, *Legacy of Bitterness*, 163.
[24] Court title: Guardian of the Royal Property. Mockler, *Haile Selassie's War*, List of Titles.
[25] Ibid., 165.
[26] Ibid., 171; Mockler, *Haile Selassie's War*, 158.
[27] Mockler, *Haile Selassie's War*, 163–73.
[28] Sbacchi, *Legacy of Bitterness*, 176. Takla-Hawaryat received military training in Russia in the first decade of the twentieth century. Three years before the war he submitted a comprehensive report to the council of ministers recommending the establishment of a regular army with the last arms and a coordinated strategy of attack and defense. See Bahru Zewde, "The Ethiopian Intelligentsia and the Italo-Ethiopian War, 1935–1941" *International Journal of African Historical Studies*, 26 (1993), 275.
[29] Zewde, *History of Modern Ethiopia*, 167.
[30] Aregawi Berhe, "Revisiting Resistance in Italian-occupied Ethiopia: The Patriots' Movement (1936–1941) and the redefinition of post-war Ethiopia," in J. Abbink, Mirjam de Bruign, and

Officials assumed that increased repression would quell the resistance, but instead it had the opposite effect. Salome Egzaiabher noted that following the massacres after the assassination attempt on Graziani many people in Addis Ababa fled to the relative safety of forests around the city to join the resistance.[31] As resistance spread throughout the entire country, its leaders adopted guerrilla warfare tactics as the only effective military option available under the circumstances. The movement also became more democratic, going beyond the aristocracy as men and women from all walks of life, including the *shifta* (bandit or rebel), joined the struggle.[32] Therefore, February 1937 marked the intensification of both Italian repression and Ethiopian resistance.

Women and Armed Resistance

Lekelesh Bayan and the thousands of women who fought in the resistance did not reflect a new development in Ethiopian warfare. Sources from the earliest period of the Ethiopian state discuss queens engaged in warfare.[33] While some royal women led troops, women also participated in combat and numbered among the retainers who provided domestic services for the armies. Each soldier was responsible for his or her provisions, thus enslaved women, peasant women, servants, and concubines formed a significant part of the contingents that followed male and female soldiers into battle.

Arguably the most important factor that contributed to the large number of women involved in military campaigns revolved around land distribution. Theoretically the emperors owned all lands and distributed allotments to churches, government officials, and military office holders. Men and women who resided on *dambagna* (military lands) were expected to provide military service whenever the army was mobilized.[34] Control over military lands over time became hereditary. Although women were not permitted to inherit land, they could control military lands if the heir was a minor or their husbands

---

Klass van Walraven (eds.) *Rethinking Resistance: Revolt and Violence in African History* (Boston, MA: Brill, 2003), 104–08.

[31] Pankhurst, "The Graziani massacre and consequences."

[32] Charles Schaefer, "Serendipitous resistance in Fascist-occupied Ethiopia, 1936–1941," *Northeast African Studies*, new series, 3, (1996), 89. Berhe argues that the translation of *shifta* as "bandit" does not convey its broader meaning for those branded *shifta* were sometimes nobles rebelling against those in power. Emperors Tewodros and Yohannes were at one time considered *shiftas*. Berhe, "Revisiting resistance in Italian-occupied Ethiopia," 95–96.

[33] The best known of these women is Gudit (also known as Yodit, Esato and the Queen of the Baniyal Hamiwiyah) who reportedly rebelled against the southward expansion of the Christian Aksumite state in the tenth century. Belete Bizuneh, "Women in Ethiopian history: A bibliographic review," *Northeast African Studies*, new series, 8 (2001), 14; Sergew Hable Selassie, "The problem of Gudit," *Journal of Ethiopian Studies*, 10 (1972), 113–24.

[34] Sellassie, "Women guerrilla fighters," 73.

were absent, ill, or dead. Weapons, particularly rifles, also passed down from father to son; however, in the absence of male successors, daughters could inherit their father's weapons. Like their male counterparts, women who held military lands or weapons were expected to carry out the duties attached to them.[35]

Exceptions in Ethiopian inheritance laws accounted for many instances in which elite women led troops or served in combat.[36] Nonetheless, Ethiopian emperors tried to reinforce the idea that combat was an exclusively male activity. In 1691, Emperor Iyasu passed a decree prohibiting women who "rode their mules or horses into battle armed with their spears."[37] In the twentieth century, just a few months before the Italian invasion, Haile Selassie also tried to prohibit women from serving in the army. In the country's first written constitution, the parliament approved Article 46, which prohibited a daughter from enlisting during the mobilization of the *dambagna* and from inheriting rifles.[38] Ultimately, the invasion and the course of the war rendered this constitutional provision moot.

Joining the Patriots

In a photograph in the collection, *The Ethiopian Patriots: Forgotten Voices of the Italo-Abyssinian War 1935–41*, 80-year-old Woizero (Lady) Zenebech Woldeyes stands proudly in her military uniform displaying her medals. Her husband fought in the battle in Maichew in which the Italians decisively defeated the northern Ethiopian forces. Although still a teen, she decided to join her husband in the resistance.[39] Like so many other women, Woldeyes joined the resistance to defend their country and because family members who had preceded them inspired them. Regardless of their social background, this pattern held consistently. Woldeyes came from a peasant background, but Princess Romanworq Haille Selassie, wife of the governor of Bale, accompanied her husband from the start of the war in 1935 until his death in 1937. Similarly, Woizero Lakech Demisew, the

---

[35] Minale Adugna, *Women and Warfare in Ethiopia: A Case Study of Their Role During the Campaign of Adwa, 1895/96, and the Italo–Ethiopian War, 1935–41*, Gender Issues Research Report Series, No. 13 (Addis Ababa: Organization for Social Science Research in Eastern and Southern Africa, 2001), 3.

[36] Among the elite women who controlled armies were Empress Menen who rebelled against Tewodros II in nineteenth century Ethiopia, Empress Taytu, wife of Menelik II and Mastawat of Waloo, who supported Menelik's campaigns in the nineteenth century. Sellassie, "Women guerrilla fighters," 75.

[37] Adugna, *Women and Warfare in Ethiopia*, 7.

[38] Sellasie, "Women guerrilla fighters," 75 (mistake in pagination; technically p. 76).

[39] Woizero Zenebech Woldeyes, "Large numbers of people have passed like shedding leaves . . . but after those five years of misery and war, we were able to have a time of peace," in Andrew Hilton (ed.), *The Ethiopian Patriots: Forgotten Voices of the Italo-Abyssinian War 1935–41* (Gloucestershire, UK: Spellmount Ltd., 2007), 178.

great-granddaughter of King Sahle Selassie of Shoa, accompanied her husband, Dejazmach Mengaesh Aboye, to the northern front "holding a rifle and in men's uniform."[40] Some women followed fathers and brothers into battle. Woizero Alemitu Mekonnen watched her grandfather, father, and brothers go off to war. At the age of fifteen she joined the Patriots after having lost sixteen family members.[41] Mekonnen's story is distinctive, for her mother, Woizero Igigayehu, also fought in the resistance. She credits her maternal grandfather, who had fought with Menelik II, as the inspiration that led her mother to take up arms.[42]

Although women may have joined their husbands in the resistance movement, they were not necessarily under their husbands' command. When Dejazmach Habte Mikael hesitated to take the offensive against the Italian army, his wife wore his uniform, mounted a mule, and took 150 soldiers with her to engage the enemy. Her forces killed a number of Italian soldiers and captured much-needed guns and ammunition.[43] Kebedech Seyoum's husband, Dejazmatch Aberra Kassa, surrendered to the Italians despite her pleas that he continue fighting. Even though he surrendered, the Italians killed him. Seyoum, leading a group of forty soldiers or sometimes collaborating with other guerilla units, continued her campaign against the Italians. Olamawarq Terunah faced a similar situation when her husband defected and joined the Italians in 1936. In response she took command of government troops, engaged local communities that supported the Italians, and finally led her troops to exile in Kenya.[44]

Just Another Soldier

From the very outset of the invasion a number of men and women dismissed Haile Selassie's attempt to forbid women from engaging in combat. Minale Adugna suggests that women's participation increased significantly after 1937 for several reasons: alien occupation of the national capital, the attempt to disarm the population by the Italian army, abusive treatment of women who refused to disclose the whereabouts of men in the resistance, and the horror of wholesale aerial bombardment of towns and villages.[45] Women in combat brought a range of skills that supported the resistance effort. Some women already had experience with guns and other critical skills. Mekonnen learned to shoot as a child:

[40] Adugna, *Women and Warfare in Ethiopia*, 24.
[41] Woizero Alemitu Mekonnen, "The emperor encouraged us by sending messages, saying "Be strong!" in Hilton, *The Ethiopian Patriots*, 97.
[42] Mekonnen, "The emperor encouraged us by sending messages," 103.
[43] Her name was not recorded and Adunga references her as the "anonymous wife." Adugna, *Women and Warfare in Ethiopia*, 13.
[44] Sellassie, "Women guerrilla fighters," 81.
[45] Adugna, *Women and Warfare in Ethiopia*, 13.

Our families used to teach us how to shoot and hit a target in our childhood. They instructed us to hit a target, usually a piece of paper or cloth, on a tree trunk. They taught every male and female child over ten. We would be scolded it we missed the target. They used to say, "These lazy people are the ones who will give us to the enemy. If they do not fight with us, they shall die, and so will we."[46]

Woizero Shewareged Gedle, the daughter of a military officer, had learned to fight with swords.[47] Women combatants also learned skills in the field as Mekonnen did: "we would throw grenades from a distance by snatching its fuse with our teeth, as the men had taught us, so as not to get harmed."[48] Some women brought tremendous organizational skills and others medical knowledge. Shewareged helped to organize first-aid and medicine for government troops as they prepared for the invasion, mobilized a league of women patriots, and fought in Shoa. She sold the land her father had left in her care for her brothers and used the proceeds to buy clothes, guns, bullets, and medicine for the guerrillas near the capital. Gedle also played a critical role in gathering intelligence through contacts she had in the office of the chief of security. In 1940, she led an attack on a prison in the process freeing Ethiopian prisoners and capturing ammunition. She was subsequently captured and imprisoned until after the end of the war.[49]

Like their male colleagues, women resistance fighters suffered privations of all kinds. Mekonnen wrote of enduring such thirst that they were "forced to drink filthy water from a pond through which cattle had passed."[50] Although peasants in many areas supplied foodstuffs, resistance fighters faced chronic food shortage. Sellassie suggests that food shortage worsened after 1939, for many villages wearied of the guerrilla fighters and refused to assist them. As a result patriots sometimes looted for food.[51] Guerrillas were also at the mercy of environmental crises such as droughts, crop failures, locusts, and famines, which forced them to survive on wild animals and roots.[52] Combatants also engaged in frontline battle and suffered aerial bombardment and mustard gas.

Despite the fact that Italy had signed and ratified the Geneva protocol banning the use of asphyxiating and poisonous gas, from the inception of planning the war in Northeast Africa, Mussolini's strategy included the use

---

[46] Mekonnen, "The emperor encouraged us," 99.
[47] Adugna, *Women and Warfare in Ethiopia*, 29.
[48] Mekonnen, "The emperor encouraged us," 99.
[49] Adugna, *Women and Warfare in Ethiopia*, 29; Selassie "Women guerrilla fighters," 81–82.
[50] Mekonnen, "The emperor encouraged us," 100.
[51] Sellassie "Women guerrilla fighters," 80.
[52] Kegnazmach Admasu Zeleke, "From the beginning we fought by ambushing," in Andrew Hilton (ed.), *The Ethiopian Patriots: Forgotten Voices of the Italo-Abyssinian War 1935–41*, 2007), 87.

of poison gas.[53] Italian forces used mustard gas against Ethiopian forces, civilians, and Red Cross field hospitals. In film footage collected by Haile Gerima, Woldeyes described one of these incidents: "in a place called Worqu, the Italians dropped barrels of poison gas.... The skin on people's hands peeled off; they lost their sight."[54] Several doctors working with Red Cross hospitals gave poignant descriptions of patients suffering from exposure to the gas. Upon seeing his first victim of mustard gas, John Macfie, a British Red Cross doctor wrote, "He looked as if someone had tried to skin him, clumsily; he had been horribly burned by 'mustard gas' all over his face, the back and the arms." W. S. Empey, also working with the British Red Cross, wrote of seeing long lines of victims who had lost their sight. As they walked to the field hospital for treatment they formed a chain, "those behind clutching the cloaks of those in front."[55]

Both male and female combatants recalled the tremendous odds under which they conducted their struggle. Woldeyes described their weapons as primitive. Afa-Mamber Malak Negatu joined the resistance at the young age of nine, following the example of his mother, father, and brothers. He recounted that

> When the struggle began most of us had only traditional arms such as sticks, spears and swords and occasionally an obsolete Wujigra. Later we started to get American-made guns, which we captured from the enemy soldiers.[56]

Sometimes they faced acute shortages of ammunition and had to make their own. They put "gun powder into the empty cartridge of a fired bullet and then (fit) the bullet missile on to it."[57] Thus, Patriots put a premium on the capture of enemy weapons, ammunition, and even uniforms. During the attack on the prison Shewareged Gedle's forces captured 2,700 rifles and many grenades.[58] Lekelash Bayan once had the special assignment to guard day and night 1,000 rounds of bullets for mauser guns and several machine guns.[59]

Mekonnen also participated in an attack that captured weapons and munitions. She recounted that:

---

[53] Rainer Baudendistel, *Between Bombs and Good Intentions: The Red Cross and the Italo-Ethiopian War, 1935–1936* (New York: Berghahn Books, 2006), 262–64.

[54] Interview with Zenebetch Woldeyes. Footage viewed and transcribed by Hailu Habtu, June 2, 2009, Sankofa Studio, Washington, D.C. Haile Gerima has more than sixty hours of footage of both men and women patriots.

[55] Quoted in Baudendistel, *Between Bombs and Good Intentions*, 276–77.

[56] *Wujigra* is the Ethiopian name for the French rifle, the *Fusil Gras*. Afa-Mamber Malak Negatu, "Many people died walking into unwinnable battles," in Andrew Hilton, ed, *The Ethiopian Patriots: Forgotten Voices of the Italo-Abyssinian War 1935–41*, 110.

[57] Mekonnen, "The emperor encouraged us," 99.

[58] Adugna, *Women and Warfare in Ethiopia*, 13.

[59] Sellassie, "Women guerrilla fighters," 79.

This was near the town of Gondar where the Vincent [aircraft], full of weapons, ammunitions and provisions was shot down while circling around looking for somewhere to land. It was tricked by our fellow Patriots who disguised themselves by wearing enemy uniforms and called for it to land. They then shot the tyres as it landed, and all the supplies it carried fell out as it crashed.[60]

In addition to conveying the challenging conditions under which they fought, accounts by male and female combatants often suggest that on the battlefield they were equals; however, it is important to explore the ways in which gender ideals and expectations still conditioned the experiences of male and female combatants.

Gender in the Field

Haile Gerima, the acclaimed filmmaker and documentarian, collected more than sixty hours of interviews with both men and women patriots.[61] The interviews constitute a critical historical source for scholars, for they capture the recollections, affectations, and demeanor of these ex-combatants as they constructed their own narrative of the occupation and resistance. In one of Haile Gerima's filmed interviews, Zenebetch Woldeyes insisted that "in battle, there was no gender distinction. We, both men and women, were equally on the battle line. We did not wear dresses, but jackets and trousers just like the men."[62] Nonetheless, they continued to perform many tasks primarily associated with women, such as collecting and caring for wounded soldiers, preparing food, making coffee, and fetching water.[63] In another interview Askale Wessin provides a searing account of conducting these tasks while under fire:

> We women would crawl on our bellies and give the fighters water, all day. Those who are hopeless, we leave, but we pull out the wounded and wash and nurse them. On one occasion, twelve women were hit by bullets; another woman and I survived. While pulling out the wounded, we would not duck to dodge the bullets. I remember the names of four of the women who died in such circumstances.... We did not wear dresses; we wore trousers and jackets like the men and we considered and treated each other as equals.[64]

Other women combatants also spoke of the gendered tasks they performed. Lekelesh Bayan recalled that during their spare time women always did

---

[60] The editor believes that her identification of the plane as a Vincent may be mistaken, for the Vicker's Vincent was a British RAF bomber. Mekonnen, "The emperor encouraged us," 99.

[61] Gerima's film credits include: *Bush Mama* (1976); *After Winter: Sterling Brown* (1985); *Sankofa* (1993); *Adwa – An African Victory* (1999) and *Teza* (2009).

[62] Interview with Zenebetch Woldeyes.

[63] Woldeyes, "Large numbers of people have passed like shedding leaves," 181.

[64] Interview with Askale Wessin. Footage viewed and transcribed by Hailu Habtu, June 2, 2009, Sankofa Studio, Washington, D.C.

domestic work. She spun thread and had it woven, and distributed clothes to other leaders. Lekelesh also had her daughter with her. When she was in battle, her five female assistants remained in the camp and tended to her daughter, but she was alone with her daughter when the Italians captured her and both were taken.[65] Kebbedech Seyoun conceived during the war and was pregnant by the time she took command of her husband's army after the Italians beheaded him. She gave birth to a son while she was in the field. Although her fighters maintained respect for her leadership, leading an army while tending to a baby became increasingly difficult. In 1939, she went into exile in Sudan and eventually settled in Jerusalem until Ethiopia's liberation in 1941.[66]

Wearing trousers like the men or being equally respected by one's troops did not dismantle gender ideologies or expectations. The contradictions that this posed is especially clear in the filmed narratives provided by Zenebetch Woldeyes. Her husband died soon after she joined the Patriots. Upon his death she was advised to remarry because a widowed woman would find it hard to protect herself from sexual advances or assault. She took this advice to heart and married a high-ranking military officer. While Woldeyes insisted that men and women were equals on the battlefields, her advised second marriage suggests that male combatants did not perceive women as their social equals off the battlefield. Furthermore, men retained the "right" to compel unattached women to satisfy their sexual desire.

Combat also reinforced notions of masculinity.[67] Kegnaznach Admasu Zeleki joined the resistance as a thirteen-year-old in the spring of 1936. One can sense his glee as he recalled an opportunity during which he and a friend seized several rifles, grenades, and cartridges from an Italian road construction crew:

> One unforgettable and wonderful adventure I can speak about with pride is one in which I captured a number of guns. Obviously, a man who has not captured a weapon and has not performed a dangerous task is not a man.[68]

In this moment of celebrating his daring, Zeleki revealed the strong link between guns and masculinity as well as the social and cultural ambiguity of women in combat. The historical relationship between guns and masculinity was actually encoded in the term for weapons, *"ya wand lej masareya"* (effects of a male person).[69] Whereas shared combat and danger enabled women to imagine themselves equal to men, for men the battlefield reinforced masculinity and its attendant privileges.

[65] Sellassie, "Women guerrilla fighters," 78.

[66] Adugna, *Women and Warfare in Ethiopia*, 28.

[67] Commander of the right wing of the army, Sbacchi, *Legacy of Bitterness*, 397.

[68] Zeleke, "From the beginning we fought by ambushing," 87.

[69] The "effects of a female person" (*"ya set lej maserya"*) consisted of jewelry, clothing, and materials for spinning cotton and making baskets. Sellassie, "Women guerrilla fighters," 73.

Noncombatant Women

The vast majority of women who contributed to the resistance were not in combat roles. Contemporaneous and archaeological records indicate that guerillas had large numbers of female servants with them. They performed the tasks that male guerrilla leaders would have considered debasing – cooking, preparing and serving coffee, brewing beer, preparing butter, winnowing and grinding cereals, spinning cotton, carrying water, and transporting wood. They carried out the critical maintenance activities that are often overlooked by combatants who narrate the history of the occupation. Feminist scholars suggest that historians and archaeologists have also downplayed maintenance: "the set of practices that involve the sustenance, welfare and effective reproduction of all the members of a social group." These activities reflect the routines of social reproduction, continuity, and collectivity instead of "individualism, change and progress which are associated with men and regarded as positive."

Archaeological evidence from the caves of Zeret in the Shoa region of northern Ethiopia exemplifies the concept of maintenance activities, for it shows that residents tried to reproduce their traditional way of life underground. Cooking happened near the mouth of the cave, social activities such as drinking and eating occurred in the front part of the cave, while in the cave's recesses residents built granaries out of mud and straw that could each store 50 kg of cereals. Archaeologists documented eighty-one granaries, indicating that they could store five tons of cereal. It appears that women also produced and stored butter, beer, and cotton. Animal remains reveal that cows, horses, sheep, and goats stayed in the caves as well.[70]

Being away from the battlefield did not protect these women from the invaders. When the Italians discovered the caves, they attacked the main entrance with artillery and machine-gun fire and brought in flamethrowers and mustard gas. Sergeant Major Boaglio, who led the attack on the caves, described the attack in his memoir. At dawn on April 9, he threw a charge near the cave's entrance followed by tear gas shells fired from a 65 mm howitzer. When the surviving Ethiopians ended their resistance two days later, 800 people lay dead outside the cave and its surroundings. Archaeologists have not been able to determine how many people died inside the caves, but skeletal remain show that the dead included women, children, and the elderly. Zeret was just one of many massacres carried out by Italian forces as they tried to impose their control over Ethiopia. Therefore it is one of many places where women who carried out maintenance activities for the resistance paid the same price as those who challenged the occupiers with guns.[71]

---

[70] Alfredo González-Ruibal, Yonatan Sahle and Xurxo Ayán Vila, "A social archaeology of colonial war in Ethiopia," *World Archaeology*, 43 (2011), 47–50, 53.
[71] Ibid., 56.

Conclusion

Critical analytical work remains as we document Ethiopian women's role in the struggle against imperialism and fascism. The extant narratives of Ethiopian women in the resistance movement are relatively small; nonetheless, their stories allow us to begin to craft a more complex and gendered picture of the resistance movement. Their stories also allow us to think comparatively about women in antifascist resistance movements in other theatres of World War II. Some scholars have begun to do comparative work but they focus exclusively on European women. Ingrid Strobl's study of women in antifascist resistance in eastern and western Europe, for example, is an important collection. Strobl identified and interviewed women who belonged to resistance movements in Spain, Yugoslavia, the Netherlands, France, Poland, and Belarus. In *Women of the Resistance: Eight Who Defied the Third Reich* Marc Vargo profiled women from America, Denmark, Germany, Palestine, France, and Poland.[72] Since many studies on women in antifascist movements tend to fall along national lines, Strobl and Vargo help us to see how women's experiences in antifascist movements converged and diverged across multiple national and cultural landscapes.[73]

In narrating their stories European and Ethiopian women illustrated the numerous ways in which gender mattered even though they risked death, capture, and torture like their male colleagues. Pregnancy allowed some to conceal items under their clothing and playing to gender expectations enabled some women to avoid searches and capture. When in positions of authority, women had to confront and eventually overcome male resistance to this gender role reversal.[74] In spite of the resistance some women encountered, many women argue that combat provided experiences that were gender equalizing.

To varying degrees the battlefield was a liminal space where feminine roles were sometimes suspended for some women. Capdevila et al. argue that the

---

[72] Ingrid Strobl, *Partisanas: Women in the Armed Resistance to Fascism and German Occupation (1936–1945)* (Oakland, CA: AK Press, 2008); Marc Vargo, *Women of the Resistance: Eight Who Defied the Third Reich* (Jefferson, NC: McFarland & Co., 2012).

[73] See, for example, Jane Slaughter, *Women and the Italian Resistance 1943–1945* (Denver, CO: Arden Press, 1997); Tom Behan, *Italian Resistance: Fascists, Guerrillas and the Allies* (New York: Pluto Press, 2009); Hanna Diamond and Simon Kitson (eds.), *Vichy, Resistance, Liberation: New Perspectives on Wartime France* (New York: Berg, 2005); Perry Wilson, "Saints and heroines: Re-writing the history of Italian women in the resistance," in Tim Kirk and Anthony McElligott (eds.), *Opposing Fascism: Community, Authority and Resistance in Europe* (Cambridge and New York: Cambridge University Press, 1999), 180–98; Anna Krylova, *Soviet Women in Combat: a History of Violence on the Eastern Front* (New York: Cambridge University Press, 2010) and Roger M. Marwick and Euridice Charon Cardona, *Soviet Women on the Frontline in the Second World War* (New York: Palgrave Macmillan, 2012).

[74] See Vargo, *Women of the Resistance*, 150, and Weitz, *Sisters in the Resistance*, 287.

war with its attendant upheaval in relationships and in daily life, and the intensification of emotions and traumas, created a vast blurring process where the ordinary criteria that structured gender identity norms became confused. The war also generated partial changes and a recomposition in gender identities, some of which were superficial and some deep-seated.[75] The recomposition in gender identity and the impact of these changes were often reflected in common details that emerged across national borders. Women combatants in Spain, Italy, and Ethiopia described wearing pants and carrying their rifles.[76] The significance that women combatants place on these details and on equality alerts us to the importance of these moments for their self-identity as well as their reconstruction of the past and their anticipation of the future. Yet their participation did not radically alter gender relations in the immediate post-war period in many countries. In fact, Slaughter argues, "battlefield experiences, of whatever kind, do not translate automatically into political consciousness, permanent political strategies, or tangible changes in women's status in a civilian world."[77] Therefore, it is important that we refine our understanding of the meanings, changes, and challenges that ensued from these life-altering experiences.

Comparing women's experiences across regional and national boundaries also highlights the ways in which class and educational attainment also shaped their lives in resistance movements. In Ethiopia many of the women in positions of authority came from the country's aristocratic elite. Elite status, educational level, and fluency in multiple languages allowed women in espionage to don a wide variety of costumes and cover stories. Virginia Hall, an American who worked with British and American intelligence services to help organize, arm, and sustain the partisans in France, presented herself as a journalist, elderly stout French woman, and goat herder in order to carry out her tasks.[78] Looking across national boundaries also encourages consideration of the age of participants. Strobl argues that most of the combatants she discussed were very young women, usually single as well. In Ethiopia, more research is necessary to determine the average age of women fighters, however, from the memoirs we know that some women were married and had children.[79]

Experiences of Italian and Ethiopian women inspire special attention since they were both subject to the Mussolini regime. Accounts by Italian

---

[75] Luc Capdevila, François Rouquet, Paula Schwartz, Fabrice Virgili and Danièle Voldman, "'Quite simple, Colonel...': Gender and the Second World War" in Hanna Diamond and Simon Kitson (eds.), *Vichy, Resistance, Liberation: New Perspectives on Wartime France* (New York: Berg, 2005), 53.

[76] For example, see Behan, *Italian Resistance: Fascists, Guerrillas and the Allies* (New York: Pluto Press, 2009), 174, and Strobl, *Partisanas*, 21.

[77] Slaughter, *Women and the Italian Resistance*, 129.

[78] Vargo, *Women of the Resistance*, 148–51.

[79] Strobl, *Partisanas*, 254.

women suggest that combat transformed their sense of self.[80] Was it equally transformative for Ethiopian women who had longer historical experience in combat? The Italian state was very concerned about women's place within Fascist society. Even though the war forced many Italian women out of the house, the Fascist state championed women's domestic role, arguing "The perfect fascist woman was a remarkably new hybrid: she served her family's every need, yet was also zealously responsive to the state's interests."[81] How did the idea of the perfect Fascist woman translate into policies in Italy's African colonies? How did race shape ideas of Fascist womanhood?

We can also explore the relationship between combat and other political identities to which men and women ascribed. How did membership in a communist or anarchist party shape women's experiences in combat and the antifascist movement? Did combat and anti-Fascist politics transform ideas about imperialism, colonialism, or racism? How did the occupation and the resistance movement shape women's national identity and their internationalism? Finally, we can explore the processes and adjustments of European and Ethiopian female combatants as they integrated into postwar society. Did they receive acknowledgement and compensation after the war? Did they experience difficulty reintegrating into their communities socially and culturally? Bernal found that in the wake of recent liberation movements in Ethiopia combat experience lessened women's appeal as potential wives.[82] Did women of the post-World War II period in Ethiopia, France, Italy, and Denmark experience similar dislocations? Explorations of these questions and more will allow us to internationalize and engender our understanding of Fascism and its resistance.

[80] Tom Behan, *Italian Resistance: Fascists, Guerrillas and the Allies*, 161–62, 171.
[81] Victoria De Grazia, *How Fascism Ruled Women: Italy 1922–1945* (Berkeley: University California), 77; quoted in Slaughter, *Women and the Italian Resistance*, 23.
[82] Bernal, "From warriors to wives," 136–39.

21

Defending the Lands of Their Ancestors

The African American Military Experience in Africa during World War II

Daniel Hutchinson

In December 1942, as the outcome of World War II remained uncertain, African American newspapers across the United States focused on West Africa. A contingent of African American soldiers had landed in Liberia to establish an Allied presence in one of the continent's remaining two independent nations; Ethiopia was liberated on January 18, 1941. As the *Pittsburgh Courier* noted, the war had brought African American soldiers "back to the land of their ancestors . . . helping the new Allied partner maintain its freedom and keep out enemy invaders."[1] The soldiers arriving in Liberia were the first of tens of thousands of African American military personnel that served in over a dozen African countries during the war. African American soldiers, sailors, marines, and medical staff interacted with local peoples wherever they served, forming relationships that transcended the barriers of language and culture. These encounters left lasting marks on both African American veterans and Africans that would shape their postwar experiences in the decades ahead. While considerable scholarship has examined the African American contribution to World War II in other combat theatres, the African American military experience in Africa has received little scholarly attention. This chapter provides a preliminary examination of this topic and suggests avenues for future research.

African Americans have served in the U.S. armed forces since the nation's founding. Their sacrifices on the battlefield were means by which African Americans advanced the cause of racial equality, whether to end slavery during the American Civil War or to achieve simultaneous victories over Fascism and Jim Crow during World War II's "Double V" campaign. Jim Crow's malignant influence extended to the American military itself, with the nation's armed forces as segregated as American society.

---

[1] "Brown troops back in land of their ancestors to protect it from invaders," *Pittsburgh Courier*, December 19, 1942.

With few exceptions African Americans fought in segregated units, slept in separate barracks, ate in separate mess halls, and enjoyed leisure time in separate recreational facilities. The American Red Cross even separated African American blood into segregated blood banks. White officers from the American South frequently commanded African American units and vigorously defended any attempt to break down segregation within the military.[2]

Segregation went beyond the separation of physical space between black and white soldiers. African American military personnel disproportionately served in units charged with the most labor-intensive and least desirable responsibilities. The most prestigious military roles were the exclusive domain of white soldiers, such as aviation, tank, and paratrooper units responsible for combat duties on the frontlines. African American soldiers, in contrast, often found themselves delegated to support units in the rear responsible for loading and unloading ships, transporting troops and material, and constructing and maintaining military structures. While these tasks were essential to the war effort, African Americans perceived their restriction to second-class roles in the army as evidence of their second-class citizenship in America. Such a conclusion seemed undeniable when menial duties such serving meals or cleaning latrines became tasks almost exclusively assigned to African American units. Even more limited opportunities existed within the other branches of the American military. The Navy employed African Americans solely in service positions as messmen and cooks, while the Marine Corps did not admit African Americans to its ranks at all until 1942.

Persistent efforts by African American institutions such as the National Association for the Advancement of Colored People (NAACP) and the black press resulted in the creation of exclusive but nonetheless segregated combat units for African Americans. These units represented a far greater range of service opportunities than any previous conflict. Yet the White House and the War Department refused to accommodate the ultimate demand of the African American community for the racial integration of the armed forces, a goal that would not be realized until 1948.[3] Of course, African

---

[2] Benjamin Quarles, *The Negro in the American Revolution* (Chapel Hill: University of North Carolina Press, 1961); John David Smith, *Black Soldiers in Blue: African American Troops in the Civil War Era* (Chapel Hill: University of North Carolina Press, 2003); Chad Louis Williams, *Torchbearers of Democracy: African American Soldiers in the World War I Era* (Chapel Hill: University of North Carolina Press, 2010); Gerald Astor, *The Right To Fight: A History of African Americans in the Military* (Cambridge, MA: Da Capo Press, 2001); Ulysses Lee, *The Employment of Negro Troops* (Washington, D.C.: Center for Military History, 1966).

[3] Lee, *Employment of Negro Troops*; Lawrence D. Riddick, "The Negro in the United States Navy during World War II," *Journal of Negro History*, 32 (1947), 201–19; Melton McLaurin, *The Marines of Montford Point: America's First Black Marines* (Chapel Hill: University of North Carolina Press, 2007); Morris J. MacGregor, *Integration of the Armed Forces, 1940–1965* (Washington, D.C.: Center for Military History, 1985).

soldiers serving in European colonial armies endured similar inequality and segregation within their ranks. Recognition of this shared injustice became an important dynamic shaping interaction between African American and African soldiers during World War II. Understanding the context of segregation within the American military is important in order to appreciate the character of the African American experience in Africa.

Likewise, understanding Africa's strategic significance to the United States during World War II explains the deployment of African American personnel across the continent. Control of Africa represented a crucial objective for both the Axis and the Allied Powers. Africa's human and material contribution to the war meant the difference between victory and defeat. Soldiers from the African colonies of Britain and France served with distinction throughout Europe and Asia (one such soldier included the grandfather of future U.S. president Barack Obama).[4] Not only did Allied war economies depend on Africa's natural resources, but also its geographic position held key strategic significance.[5] If German armies were to seize the Suez Canal, Britain would be denied easy access to its African, East Asian, and Pacific colonies. Further, Axis victory over France in 1940 gave Germany influence in the French West African colonies now administered by the collaborationist Vichy regime. These colonies could serve as a potential base for an invasion of the western hemisphere. These strategic implications resulted in the United States establishing a substantial military presence in Africa during the war.

African American personnel formed the core of the American military presence in Africa. By the war's end, African American military units had served in Algeria, Chad, the Congo, Egypt, Eritrea, Ghana, Kenya, Liberia, Libya, Nigeria, Senegal, Sierra Leone, South Africa, Sudan, and Tunisia.[6] Important qualitative and quantitative differences mark the African American experience in sub-Saharan and North Africa. Over the course of the war approximately 85,000 African Americans served in North Africa while fewer than 10,000 served in sub-Saharan Africa.[7] African American units serving

---

[4] David Killingray with Martin Plaut, *Fighting For Britain: African Soldiers in the Second World War* (Woodbridge, Suffolk: James Currey, 2010); Nancy Ellen Lawler, *Soldiers of Misfortune: Ivorien Tirailluers of World War II* (Athens: Ohio University Press, 1992); Myron Echenberg, "'Morts pour la France': The African soldier in France during the Second World War," *Journal of African History*, 26 (1985), 363–80.

[5] Raymond Dumett, "Africa's strategic minerals during the Second World War," *Journal of African History*, 26 (1985), 381–408; Ashley Jackson, *The British Empire and the Second World War* (London: Hambledon Continuum, 2008), 178–80.

[6] Christopher Paul Moore, *Fighting For America: Black Soldiers – The Unsung Heroes of World War II* (New York: One World Books, 2005), 89; Lee, *Employment of Negro Troops*, 433.

[7] Lee, *Employment of Negro Troops*, 433; Elliott V. Converse III, Daniel K. Gibran, John A. Cash, Robert K. Griffith, and Richard H. Kohn, *The Exclusion of Black Soldiers from the Medal of Honor in World War II* (Jefferson, NC: McFarland & Company, 1997), 93.

in sub-Saharan Africa, however, experienced a far greater degree of interaction with Africans. In North Africa combat conditions and campaigning
in less densely populated areas resulted in fewer opportunities for sustained
contact between soldiers and civilians. Units stationed in sub-Saharan Africa
tended to remain in place for a longer period, as in Liberia, where African
Americans served for the duration of the war.

Typically African American units were tasked with building military bases
and air strips near major African cities, which formed a chain of air fields
across the continent facilitating transport of manpower and supplies from
the Americas to southern Europe and Asia. Permission and access to establish these facilities had been negotiated between American officials and European colonial administrators in exchange for economic aid and Lend-Lease
support.[8] Yet, even in sub-Saharan Africa the African American presence
was often fleeting; most units completed their missions in only a few months
before moving to another location, sometimes across the continent.[9] The
transitory nature of these units' missions pose difficulties in documenting the
historical experiences of their members. The frequency and speed of these
movements partly account for the relative paucity of scholarship addressing
this chapter of African wartime history.

The first major deployment of U.S. soldiers to Africa reveals the diplomatic impact of the African American military presence in Africa. An
African American transport unit, the Twenty-seventh Quartermaster Truck
Regiment, was assigned to the new Central African Service Command that
arrived in the Congolese port city of Matadi in August 1942 to construct
the first military installations to establish an Allied trans-African air supply route. While Belgian colonial administrators welcomed the American
presence in the colony, they voiced strong apprehension concerning the
deployment of African American soldiers to the Congo. The German conquest of Belgium in 1940 had cut off the colonial administration from its
metropolitan leadership, increasing the challenge of sustaining Belgian rule
over an increasingly assertive Congolese population. Some Belgian officials
believed the Congolese would be emboldened by the sight of black soldiers
in positions of authority and possessing a comparatively high level of wealth
relative to local conditions, leading to a demand for greater autonomy and
opportunity. As one Belgian official wrote to Secretary of State Cordell Hull,
"there is no doubt that the appearance in our Colony of negroes having a
standard of living much higher than that of the natives would cause . . . great

---

[8] James P. Hubbard, *The United States and the End of British Colonial Rule in Africa, 1941–
1968* (Jefferson, NC: McFarland, 2001), 15–17; Jonathan F. Helmreich, *United States Relations with Belgium and the Congo, 1940–1960* (Newark, NJ: University of Delaware Press,
1998), 15–26.

[9] John E. Fagg, "The aviation engineers in Africa and Europe," in Wesley Frank Craven and
James Lea Cate, *The Army Air Forces in World War II*, Vol. 7: *Services Around the World*
(Chicago, IL: University of Chicago Press, 1983), 239–75.

difficulties."[10] Diplomatic communiqués soon were sent that demanded the removal of the Twenty-seventh Quartermaster Regiment. Inhospitality was not confined to the Belgian colonial government. The Twenty-seventh discovered the doors to Matadi's restaurants, stores, and social facilities were closed to African Americans, as they were to local Congolese, although white American soldiers enjoyed the full access to a friendly city controlled by a wartime ally.

The soldiers of the Twenty-seventh Regiment soon reciprocated the sentiments of Belgian officials. During their brief tour in the Congo, African American soldiers observed firsthand the brutality and exploitation of Belgium's colonial regime, and collectively requested a transfer from the colony. The commanding officer of the unit observed that "the condition of the [Congolese] population is exciting considerable comment among our men who are rapidly becoming to feel that the things they are fighting for are [a] fallacy." The Twenty-seventh's request for a transfer from the Congo was approved, and the unit moved on to Liberia.[11]

The Twenty-seventh's tour in the Congo encapsulates dynamics that occurred frequently where African Americans served. Despite their second-class status within America's segregated military, the example of a black man possessing military training, social standing, and a degree of wealth relative to local conditions served as stark contrasts to the more severe inequality inherent in Europe's colonial regimes. Colonial regimes feared the disruptive effect caused by the mere presence of African American soldiers. Evidence of this runs through U.S. diplomatic correspondence with colonial officials, which provides a source for future research into this topic.[12]

The Twenty-seventh Quartermaster Truck Regiment's fleeting deployment in Congo provides a vivid example of the African American presence in Africa, which often featured intense, if brief, encounters. Far more lasting, however, was the African American presence in Liberia. Liberia hosted the largest number of African American personnel of any African nation and for the longest period, from June 1942 to the end of the war. This prolonged concentration of American forces resulted from Liberia's special historical relationship to the United States going back to Liberia's founding in the nineteenth century. Cultural, diplomatic, and economic connections remained strong between the United States and the "Americo-Liberian" ruling class.[13]

---

[10] Helmreich, *United States Relations with Belgium and the Congo*, 38.

[11] Lee, *Employment of Negro Troops*, 437–38.

[12] See the following archival collections: Record group 59, Records of the U.S. Department of State, Records of the Division of African Affairs, 1943–1949, National Archives II (hereafter NARA II), College Park, MD.

[13] Tom W. Shick, *Behold the Promised Land: A History of Afro-American Settler Society in Nineteenth Century Liberia* (Baltimore, MD: John Hopkins University Press, 1980); Claude Andrew Clegg, *The Price of Liberty: African Americans and the Making of Liberia* (Chapel Hill: University of North Carolina Press, 2004); Marie-Tyler McGraw, *An African*

After 1926, American economic influence intensified following the arrival of the Firestone Rubber Company and its establishment of sprawling rubber plantations on one million acres of land leased from the Liberian government. Firestone employed thousands of local workers.[14]

Liberia's strategic importance to the United States increased dramatically following Japan's conquests in East Asia, which cut access to 95% of the global rubber supply, robbing the Allies of an essential war commodity. The Allies scrambled to secure alternative sources of rubber to avoid an industrial crisis. Firestone's rubber plantations, combined with Liberia's geographic position, gave the country its strategic value for transcontinental supply routes to North Africa, the Middle East, and East Asia.[15]

Even before Pearl Harbor, in July 1941, the United States negotiated an agreement between the Liberian government, the Firestone Company, and Pan American Airways to establish Roberts Field, a sizeable airfield near Monrovia.[16] In March 1942, the United States negotiated a wartime alliance with Liberia that offered economic aid and Lend-Lease assistance. Franklin Roosevelt even made a surprise visit to Liberia in January 1943 after the Allied war conference in Casablanca, and invited Liberian President Edwin Barclay to a state visit to the White House in May 1943. In exchange for American aid, Liberia permitted American military personnel to operate Roberts Field. American military units responsible for building and running these bases arrived only months later.[17]

Among the first of these units to arrive was the Forty-first Engineer General Service Regiment, which embarked from Charleston, South Carolina, in May 1942 and arrived in Liberia in June after a harrowing journey across seas actively patrolled by U-boats.[18] The deployment of an African American unit to a location with such significant strategic and symbolic value was widely appreciated by the soldiers of the unit and the African American press at home. The *Chicago Defender* reported that the first African American soldier stepping ashore in Liberia, Private Napoleon Edward Taylor of Baltimore, read a carefully prepared speech emphasizing the shared war aims of the United States and Liberia: "Liberians! We are here to join hands

Republic: Black and White Virginians in the Making of Liberia (Chapel Hill: University of North Carolina Press, 2007).

[14] Wayne Chatfield Taylor, *The Firestone Operations in Liberia* (New York: Arno Press, 1956), 52.

[15] Mark R. Finlay, *Growing American Rubber: Strategic Plants and the Politics of National Security* (New Brunswick, NJ: Rutgers University Press, 2009), 140.

[16] R. Earle Anderson, *Liberia: America's African Friend* (Chapel Hill: University of North Carolina Press, 1952), 145.

[17] United States, Department of State, *Foreign Relations of the United States, 1942*. Volume IV: *The Near East and Africa* (Washington, D.C.: Government Printing Office, 1963), 355–438.

[18] Shelby L. Stanton, *World War II Order of Battle* (New York: Galahad Books, 1991), 539.

to fight together until this world is free of tyrannical dictators."[19] The regiment's primary mission in Liberia was to upgrade Roberts Field into a fully functional military airfield fit for large transport planes and heavy bombers. Other African American units soon followed the Forty-first, responsible for tasks as varied as guarding Roberts Field, building highways in Liberia's interior, and training a Liberian national defense force. By December 1942, more than 1,000 African American soldiers were stationed in Liberia, the first of some 5,000 that ultimately composed what became known as the Liberian Task Force.[20]

Among the more noteworthy units belonging to this task force was the Twenty-fifth Station Hospital, which operated a 250-bed hospital near Roberts Field and provided medical care for American soldiers and Liberian workers. The hospital staff consisted of twenty-one medical officers (both white and black, a rare example of military integration at the time), thirty African American nurses, and 180 enlisted medical personnel.[21] Memoirs and oral histories of veterans of the Twenty-fifth describe the African American experience in Liberia. One such account comes from Lieutenant Gertrude Bertram, one of the 479 African American nurses who served in the Army Nurse Corps for the entire war. Born in Clarksville, Georgia, in 1916, Bertram had joined the Army Nurse Corps in May 1941 out of a sense of patriotism and professional advancement: "The Army offered more money, prestige, and a chance to travel. But I only got the chance because the war broke out. They needed nurses no matter what color, so they let us in."[22] Bertram and her fellow nurses arrived in Liberia in March 1943. Theirs was one of the few units of African American women deployed overseas by the American military during the war.[23]

In contrast to the experience of African American personnel in the Congo, the nurses of the Twenty-fifth received a warm welcome in Liberia. Bertram happily recalled the reception given by Liberian citizens upon their arrival. "They loved us," noted Bertram, and "they wanted all of us to come back [after the war]." Part of this encouragement came from the quality of care provided by Bertram and her fellow nurses. Besides working near Roberts Field, the nurses occasionally left the hospital and traveled across the

[19] "Axis doomed, first Yank ashore tells Liberians," *Chicago Defender*, December 12, 1942.

[20] Lee, *Employment of Negro Troops*, 433, 620–21; Anderson, *Liberia: America's African Friend*, 151.

[21] Barbara Brooks Tomblin, *G. I. Nightingales: The Army Nurse Corps in World War II* (Lexington: University of Kentucky Press, 1996), 178.

[22] Yvonne Latty and Ron Tarver, *We Were There: Voices of African American Veterans, from World War II to the War in Iraq* (New York: HarperCollins, 2005), 9.

[23] See Brenda L. Moore, *To Serve My Country, To Serve My Race: The Story of the Only African-American WACs Stationed Overseas During World War II* (New York: New York University Press, 1996).

country, providing medical care in the streets of Monrovia and rural hamlets alike, serving as ambassadors of American goodwill.

As such, the nurses labored under guidelines of proper decorum in dress etiquette and comportment. "We were told to be ladies at all times," recalled Bertram. They were warned against "discussing politics or religion with strange people in the village or anywhere that we were traveling." Strictly off-limits was conversation with Liberians relating to the country's origins as a colony for emancipated slaves. "We were not allowed to discuss politics and slavery with them. They told us that we'd been slaves so we were second-class citizens. So none of us did that, or we did it very discreetly. You could always meet someone that you can talk to and confide in." Nonetheless, the nurses often practiced discretion. They knew that potential mistakes could prove costly. As Bertram noted, "We had to be careful what you did, what you said, and how you act because we know they [the American military were] watching us. They wanted us to fail.... We were sort of like an elite group, and we were going to be watched very closely." Moreover, the nurses knew that their mistakes would impact not just them, but could potentially undermine the African American cause of the "Double V." "[Our community] didn't want to be embarrassed.... We have always been told by our parents of a certain class, that your behavior should always be acceptable to the society. Because you represent everyone else from your race."[24] Bertram's experience informed her perceptions regarding the careful scrutiny her comrades received. From their arrival in March 1943, African American nurses treated numerous cases of malaria and other tropical diseases among American soldiers and Liberian workers. The Liberian government recognized the service of the nurses and inducted the hospital's chief nurse, Susan K. Freeman, into the Liberian Humane Order of African Redemption. Despite this, in November 1943, the army recalled the nurses to the United States. Various explanations were given: health problems among the nurses, overstaffing at the hospital, even low morale among the Twenty-fifth, but a report from an official in the Army Nurses Corps cited misconduct among the nurses, particularly their use in nursing white soldiers and their defiance of army policies regarding segregation.[25] The African-American press vigorously responded to what it considered a slur against the nurses. The War Department denied the substance of the report and fired the official.[26] The army reassigned the former nurses of the Twenty-fifth to hospitals across the United States, to the

---

[24] Interview with Gertrude Margaritte Ivory Bertram by Joan Denman, October 10, 2007, Dayton, OH. Gertrude Margaritte Ivory Bertram Collection, 07.0114. The Institute on World War II and the Human Experience, Florida State University.

[25] Mary T. Sarnecky, *A History of the U.S. Army Nurse Corps* (Philadelphia: University of Pennsylvania Press, 1999), 213–14.

[26] "Anti-nurse propaganda causes official to lose post," *Baltimore Afro-American*, December 11, 1943; Harry McAlpin, "Mystery in return of nurses from Liberia," *Chicago Defender*, December 18, 1943.

China-Burma-India Theatre, and to the Pacific, where they again provided medical care to predominately African American units.[27]

Despite the rumors surrounding her unit's service, Gertrude Bertram's return from Liberia was celebrated in her hometown. In an article in the Atlanta Daily World, published on December 18, 1943, she described conditions for African American personnel overseas. She assured women on the homefront that: "There is [no] need for worry about the boys and girls of the other lands, because from my observation, they just don't appeal to our boys like their girls and wives back home."[28]

Regardless of Bertram's reassurances, frequent interactions occurred between American men and Liberian women. Throughout World War II, American soldiers stationed overseas often found themselves in a new sociosexual landscape, where their wealth and national identity provided them with a valuable form of sexual capital. The war provided new avenues for sexual expression and exploitation both at home and abroad.[29] Just as in England, France, Australia, and the Pacific, Liberia offered American soldiers a new sexual landscape in which to leverage their socioeconomic capital. African American soldiers freely fraternized with Liberian women, with some forming romantic relationships and others using their military pay to purchase sex. These sexual encounters resulted in an increase in the prevalence of venereal disease. When rates of venereal infection among soldiers stationed in Liberia reached extremely high levels in September 1942, American military officials intervened by attempting to regulate sexual contact between American men and Liberian women. After negotiating with officials from the Liberian Health Department and the Firestone Company, the army authorized the establishment of two "women's villages" where American soldiers could visit prostitutes that received regular medical inspections. These two camps were known as "Camp Shangri-La" and "Camp Paradise."

---

[27] Judith Bellafaire, *The Women's Army Corps: A Commemoration of World War II Service* (Washington, D.C.: Center for Military History, 1994), 8–9.

[28] Spike Washington, "Army nurse back from battle zone tells experience," *Atlanta Daily World*, December 18, 1943.

[29] John Hammond Moore, *Over-Sexed, Over-Paid, and Over Here: Americans in Australia, 1941–1945* (New York: University of Queensland Press, 1981); Allan Bérubé, *Coming Out under Fire: The History of Gay Men and Women in World War II* (New York: Free Press, 1990); Beth Baily and David Farber, *The First Strange Place: The Alchemy of Race and Sex in World War II Hawaii* (New York: Free Press, 1992); David Reynolds, *Rich Relations: The American Occupation of Britain, 1942–1945* (New York: Random House, 1995); Sonya Rose, "Sex, citizenship, and the nation in World War II Britain," *American Historical Review*, 103 (1998), 1147–76; Pamela Winfield, *Melancholy Baby: The Unplanned Consequences of the G.I.'s Arrival in Europe for World War II* (Westport, CT: Greenwood Publishing, 2000); Harvey R. Neptune, *Caliban and the Yankees: Trinidad and the United States Occupation* (Chapel Hill: University of North Carolina Press, 2007); Mary Louise Roberts, *What Soldiers Do: Sex and the American G.I. in World War II France* (Chicago, IL: University of Chicago Press, 2013).

Even in this act of regulating illicit behavior, the Army insisted on maintaining segregated facilities: Camp Paradise for African Americans, and Camp Shangri-La for white soldiers.[30] This controlled form of sexual commerce in Liberia was similar to regulations in European colonial regimes throughout the continent.[31]

Before the start of his influential acting career, Ossie Davis served as a surgical technician stationed at the Twenty-fifth Station Hospital in Liberia. His memoir of his experience in Africa profoundly influenced his postwar career. Raised in rural Georgia, Davis's encounters with Jim Crow made him feel like an unwelcome stranger in his own community. His reception in Liberia presented a stark contrast: "It did my heart, my soul, my whole purpose in life a lot of good to find myself in Africa, especially Liberia. The people were open and friendly, and made us feel more than welcome."[32] Nonetheless, this hospitality could be easily compromised by sexual misconduct. Davis recalled two incidents concerning Liberian "women's villages." The first concerned a fellow soldier who established a "line of credit" with one of the women of Camp Paradise. The terms seemed agreeable to all parties involved, but the soldier never returned to the village to pay his debt for services rendered. To his surprise, the woman and her father (a local paramount chief) arrived at Roberts Field demanding compensation. The soldier's commanding officer sided with the chief, and forced the soldier to sheepishly repay the debt. Another soldier established an arrangement that guaranteed him exclusive access to a particular sex worker, but after he lost his money gambling, the agreement ended. Frustrated, the soldier traveled to the village with several comrades (including Davis) in an effort to restore the relationship through intimidation. According to Davis, "Jackson was in trouble. But after a few drinks of cane juice [a potent local concoction], he didn't see it that way. He got boisterous and belligerent, and finally decided to show his woman who was boss." Jackson entered the woman's hut, but when she refused to resume their agreement, he slapped her. To his shock, however, she responded with a vigorous counterattack that involved a head butt to Jackson's jaw, sending him flying through the walls of the hut and into the dirt. The other soldiers dragged the semiconscious Jackson away. He did not return.

Encounters between American soldiers and Liberian women soon became subjects in local performance in nearby villages. Davis recalled that "The songs were sprightly stories told in fun. They dealt with that was happening

---

[30] George "Doc" Abraham, *The Belles of Shangri-La: And Other Stories of Sex, Snakes, and Survival from World War II* (New York: Vantage Press, 2000).

[31] Linda Bryder, "Sex, race, and colonialism: An historiographical review," *International History Review*, 20 (1998), 806–22.

[32] Ossie Davis and Ruby Dee, *With Ossie and Ruby: In This Life Together* (New York: William Morrow, 1998), 129.

in the villages and at [Roberts Field]. Listening to them was almost like reading the gossip column in a racy newspaper." One such song went as follows:

> Airport soldier drowned in the river.
> No more jigjig, no more money.
> Sister Taylor, why do you cry?
> 'Cause your darling boy is dead and
> Gone to hell.[33]

Not every encounter between American soldiers and Liberian women centered on sex. Davis formed a close platonic relationship with an "Americo-Liberian" woman that provided him with insight into the social divisions within Liberian society. The social division among peoples sharing a common racial heritage confounded him. Descendants of African American freedmen who had founded the nation, they formed Liberia's economic and political elite. Their rule over Liberia's indigenous ethnic groups differed little from that practiced by European colonial administrations and social interaction was limited.[34] Davis observed the considerable wealth and social influence enjoyed by his friend and her family, and noted the prevalent practice of Americo-Liberian youth obtaining college educations in American and European universities.

During his time in Liberia, Davis attracted a popular following in the villages for his ability to perform Liberian songs. Davis quickly discovered he had learned more about indigenous culture after just a few months than his Americo-Liberian friend had acquired during her lifetime. He was disturbed by the similarities between Liberian class distinctions and Jim Crow barriers in the United States, commenting that

> For most of my life, I had believed that black folks were in many ways morally superior to white folks, especially in our dealings with each other. . . . I was profoundly disappointed that the Americo-Liberians, the children of slaves themselves, would come to Africa and behave as if they themselves were the slaveholders now.

Far more disturbing to him was the attitude of cultural arrogance among his fellow African American soldiers. He observed that:

> They, too, quite easily took to treating natives, not as brothers and comrades, but like servants, in much the same way white folks treated black folks down in Georgia. . . . I was even more disappointed in much of our behavior, at how easily we became racist and exploiters, treating the natives with that very same

[33] Ibid., 131, 133–34.
[34] M. B. Akpan, "Black imperialism: Americo-Liberian rule over the African peoples of Liberia, 1841–1964," *Canadian Journal of African Studies*, 7 (1973), 217–36; Edward Lama Wonkeryor, "Ethnicity in Liberia and democratic governance," in Santosh C. Saha (ed.), *The Politics of Ethnicity and National Identity* (New York: Peter Lang, 2006), 105–20.

superior disdain and disrespect about which we ourselves were constantly complaining to the company commander. Calling the natives zigaboos and burrheads, some of the soldiers were patronizing, and condescending, treating them, in many instances, as if we were white, and they were niggers.[35]

While some African Americans privileged their nationality and class status over their shared racial identity with Africans, other soldiers established friendships despite these differences. For example, in 1942, Frank James, a native of Charleston, West Virginia, who served as a medic in the 812th Engineer Aviation Battalion in Nairobi, Kenya, formed a close friendship with Nelson Thawi, a Somali serving in the headquarters of the second battalion of the Northern Rhodesian Regiment.[36] According to James, Thawi served as his guide and interpreter to Kenyan culture:

> [Thawi] and I would roam the streets of Nairobi and also the hills into the villages outside of Nairobi. We would go to these villages and he would introduce me to the natives.... We would roam into the Pumwani Villages outside of Nairobi where there were natives that spoke nothing but Swahili. He started to teach me Swahili. When I left Nairobi I could speak it well enough to get around, even walking up and down the streets by myself.[37]

In his memoir, James clearly valued his friendship with Thawi, but their interaction was affected by economic differences. James's military salary dwarfed that of his friend. James used this disparity to his advantage: "[Thawi] used to do my laundry for me. I paid him more to do my laundry than his salary in the British Army." Economic disparities also influenced his relationships with Kenyan women. James formed relationships with two Kikuyu women residing in the Pumwani district, but he did not fully understand traditional customs or how the women viewed their relationship with him. He observed that: "They were fascinated with me because I was a black soldier and they considered themselves to be in love with me.... Because I was an American soldier with the huge grade of sergeant, I was wealthy in their eyes." To secure their relationship, each of the women gave James a metal bracelet, which he failed to realize possessed an important role in Kikuyu courtship rituals. It turned out that he had unwittingly signaled his acceptance of a marriage engagement to two different women, neither of whom he intended on marrying (indeed, he already had a wife back in the United States).[38]

---

35 Davis and Dee, *With Ossie and Ruby*, 133.

36 Fagg, "Aviation engineers in Africa and Europe," 262–63; William Vernon Breisford, *The Story of the Northern Rhodesia Regiment* (Lusaka: Northern Rhodesian Government Printer, 1954).

37 Frank James, *Capers of a Medic* (Bloomington, IN: AuthorHouse, 2007), 22.

38 Ibid., 22–23; John Karanja, "Legal union: Kikuyu sexual relationships," in J. Bryson Arthur, *A Theology of Sexuality and Marriage* (Nairobi: Uzima Press, 2001), 73–91.

It seems clear that African Americans and African forged relationships based on mutual respect during World War II. But mutual respect was more difficult to establish between African Americans and European colonial administrators, especially concerning the segregation and racial discrimination. In November 1942, a shoot-out between members of the 812th Engineer Aviation Battalion and the Nairobi police in November 1942 characterizes a particularly dangerous wartime confrontation over these issues. Before deployment to Africa, the 812th had already experienced tense encounters with police in Tampa, Florida, while training at MacDill Army Air Field. The local sheriff gave a stern lecture to the unit on the consequences of violating the city's segregation laws. Indeed, police violence against African American soldiers for violations of Jim Crow occurred repeatedly. As one soldier recalled, they were "delighted when orders came for us to go.... Anything was better than this hell hole."[39] When the 812th arrived in Kenya, they were at first greeted warmly and treated as Europeans, but this soon changed after intervention the British authorities intervened. The British feared that the sight of African American soldiers enjoying equality with whites would stir unrest among their Kenyan subjects.[40]

Simmering resentment toward the British provides the context for the conflict that occurred between the members of the 812th and the Nairobi police on the night of November 21, 1942. Four soldiers from the 812th visited the Eastleigh district police station to secure the release of a Kenyan woman detained there. The reason for her detention remains unclear, as does the nature of the relationship between the woman and the soldiers. What is known is that in the process of attempting to free the woman, the soldiers and white policemen came to blows. Outnumbered, the soldiers departed the police station and returned to their base where the sight of their bruised and bloodied comrades infuriated their fellow soldiers. Now joined by a larger group, the soldiers took rifles and ammunition from their camp and returned to the police station. There they fired between fifteen to sixty rounds into the structure, causing considerable chaos but fortunately no fatalities. The shootings marked a diplomatically sensitive moment for American military authorities in Kenya. The Army promptly convened a court martial and tried the soldiers involved, with ten soldiers receiving sentences ranging from ten to eighteen years of hard labor at Fort Leavenworth, Kansas (later overturned on the basis of improper judicial procedure).[41] Meanwhile, the army

[39] Gary Mormino, "GI Joe meets Jim Crow: Racial violence and reform in World War II Florida," *Florida Historical Quarterly*, 73 (1994), 23–42.

[40] Mary Penick Motley, *The Invisible Soldier: The Experience of the Black Soldier, World War II* (Detroit, MI: Wayne State University Press, 1975), 252–253.

[41] U.S. Army, Holding by the Board of Review concerning *U.S. v. Herbert C. Abrahams, et. all*, March 29, 1943, *Judge Advocate General's Department Board of Review: Holdings, Opinions, and Reviews* (Washington, D.C.: Office of the Judge Advocate General, 1944), vol. 17, 241–53.

quickly transferred the 812th to Egypt to build airfields and assist in the drive
to expel Axis forces from North Africa.[42] Military investigations and judicial
proceedings, such as those concerning the 812th, provide another potential
archival source documenting the African American experience in Africa.[43]

While African American soldiers in sub-Saharan Africa served far from
the frontlines, they experienced the greatest sustained contact with African
societies. In contrast, African American soldiers serving in the North African
campaign experienced Africa primarily through the hazy and chaotic perspective of combat. Allied forces invaded North Africa in November 1943
during Operation Torch, the massive amphibious assault that succeeded in
removing the Axis from French West Africa. African American units played
a variety of combat roles in the campaign. Ollie Stewart, a reporter for the
Baltimore *Afro-American*, described the dramatic performance of an African
American artillery team against a rival German unit:

> A correspondent can have only a bird's-eye view of a battle such as this
> one, and when I found a field artillery unit blasting the Germans out of the
> mountains. . . . I took a front-row seat for an hour without actually knowing
> the full importance of the action. It was early one morning that I sat on a ridge
> behind big guns manned by colored troops in a wooded area. Every time the
> lads cut loose with a barrage, the earth trembled and my ears roared. . . . The
> show was not one-sided. The enemy found our range with his heavy stuff, and
> I learned what it means to be close to bursting shell fire. . . . During a lull, I lit
> a cigarette and wondered who was winning. There was no way of knowing.
> These colored soldiers firing away throughout the morning never saw their
> target.[44]

Only later did Stewart and the artillery unit learn how effective their performance had been in blasting the Germans out of their mountain strong-hold.
Stewart, whose mission in North Africa was to report on the experience of
African American soldiers, felt vindicated by the efforts of this unit. "This
is a story I have wanted to write since I left America in August – the story
of colored troops in actual combat, exchanging lead with the enemy," he
wrote.[45]

---

[42] Gerald Horne, *Mau Mau in Harlem? The U.S. and the Liberation of Kenya* (New York: Palgrave Macmillan, 2009), 70–72.

[43] Among the most promising collections for this research include the wartime editions of the *Judge Advocate General's Department Board of Review: Holdings, Opinions, and Reviews* (Washington, D.C.: Office of the Judge Advocate General) and the archival collection that contains military police investigations: RG 389, Records of the Provost Marshal General's Office, Military Government Division, 1942–1946, NARA II, College Park, MD.

[44] Ollie Stewart, "Guns shell Rommel," *Baltimore Afro American*, April 10, 1943; Moore, *Fighting For America*, 126–27.

[45] Stewart, "Guns shell Rommel," April 10, 1943.

As Allied armies advanced on retreating Axis forces, the contribution of African American units proved invaluable. The quartermaster and transportation units in which most African American soldiers served provided critical logistical support by supplying ammunition, fuel, and food to the frontlines under grueling conditions, often traveling hundreds of miles across rugged conditions and under enemy fire. Stewart reported on bravery of Corporal Ernest Jones and Private William Jones, both of New Orleans (and unrelated), who left French Morocco in an army transport truck "Equipped with arms, ammunition, rations and orders to get through at any cost, they left December 4 [1943] for the front." They "got on through hundreds of miles of flatland, foothills and mountains, stopping only to refuel the bouncing buggy." They crossed Algeria and survived German dive bombers in Tunisia, finally completing their mission on Christmas morning. The rapid movement of men and supplies over the difficult terrain provided a critical advantage for the American military's successful advance against Axis forces, exemplified by the two Joneses.[46]

Even though African Americans demonstrated bravery and sacrifice on the frontlines, unfortunately they frequently suffered the inequities of segregation behind the lines. Reporting on the existence of Jim Crow in the North Africa campaign was Walter White, chief secretary of the National Association for the Advancement of Colored People and wartime correspondent on race relations overseas for the *New York Post*. He reported on conditions African American soldiers experienced in Europe and the Mediterranean.[47] In North Africa, he observed that the arrival of the American military further complicated existing historical divisions among Muslim, Jewish, and Christian communities. It created a new division: skin color. African American soldiers seeking recreation and female companionship in North African cities often found that white soldiers had advised the locals to avoid them, because "the Negro troops are not clean or healthy; that they are beastly and inhuman and should not be associated with." When local women disregarded this advice, White reported that French authorities in Casablanca often arrested the women and subjected them to mandatory screenings for venereal disease. Even American-run recreational facilities, such as those established by the Red Cross, ran on a segregated basis. While a relieved White noted that segregation did not extend to the city's major military hospital, he nonetheless found that segregation had a toxic effect on African American morale.[48]

---

[46] Ollie Stewart, "Jones boys take a truck to the front," *Baltimore Afro-American*, January 16, 1943.

[47] Thomas Hachey, "Walter White and the American negro soldier in World War II: A diplomatic dilemma for Britain," *Phylon*, 39 (1978), 241–49.

[48] Walter White, *A Rising Wind* (New York: Doubleday, Doran, and Company, 1945), 71–75.

For example, White encountered a demoralized unit of African American cavalrymen stationed in Oran (Algeria). Trained for combat duty, in North Africa this unit was reassigned to unloading American supply ships. Several other African American cavalry units in Oran were also transferred to port duty, including the Fourth and Fifth Cavalry Brigades and the Tenth, Twenty-seventh, and Twenty-eighth Cavalry Regiments.[49] African American soldiers perceived such reassignment as not only robbing them of an opportunity to demonstrate their bravery on the battlefield but also as confirmation of their second-class status in the American military. Their disappointment was palpable to White, who attempted to deliver a morale-boosting speech.

> I was taken to a hillside from whose natural amphitheater one looked upon the blue expanse of the Mediterranean. At the foot of the hill was a microphone to which I was escorted. Seated on the hillside were between five and six thousand Negro soldiers. The late afternoon sun lighted up the thousands of battle helmets. An ominous, brooding, intent silence hung like a pall over them. Little applause, even of the courtesy variety, followed my introduction.... Having steeled themselves to combat and having eagerly anticipated service as fighting men, the sudden transition had driven morale to the vanishing point. A few attempted to rationalize what had happened to them by saying that as service troops they would be less likely to get killed. But that comfort, such as it was, was short-lived.... An army always attacks the supply lines of the enemy. Men handling bulldozers, driving trucks, handling supplies, are unable simultaneously to do those things and man guns. Thus these men knew that, in addition to the humiliation of being reduced from fighting men to manual laborers, the hazard of life was increased.

White felt that his speech did little to raise morale:

> No speech I have ever made before or since was more difficult than the feeble and ineffective one on that occasion. I could only assure them that I knew the reasons for their dejection and that those of us who were in a position to would do all we could.[50]

In May 1943, Allied forces defeated Axis forces in North Africa, setting the stage for the invasion of Sicily, Italy, and ultimately, the beaches of Normandy. As in Africa, African American units proudly served in these theatres. In Italy units such as the "Tuskegee Airmen" and the Ninety-second Infantry Division established an extensive combat record, while in France the Red Ball Express and the 761st Tank Battalion defied expectations with their skill, poise, and bravery. Likewise, African Americans serving in the Pacific, the China-Burma-India, and the Middle East theaters made vital contributions to Allied victory over Japan. The war proved a powerful

[49] Stanton, *World War II Order of Battle*, 305, 314, 316.
[50] White, *A Rising Wind*, 76–77.

experience for the approximately 909,000 African Americans who served in the American military. Their overseas struggle against oppression shaped their postwar efforts to end inequality at home.[51]

World War II brought African Americans into contact with Africa, both physically and symbolically, in ways not experienced since Marcus Garvey's back-to-Africa movement decades earlier. Reports of African American bravery overseas, of Liberian president Edwin Barclay's state visit to Washington, D.C., and of the bravery of African soldiers in British and French colonial armies filled African Americans with pride. As the war progressed, African Americans linked their freedom struggles at home with Africa's postwar destiny.[52] In 1945, Walter White wrote, "World War II has given to the Negro a sense of kinship with other colored – and also oppressed – peoples of the world.... He senses that the struggle of the Negro in the United States is part and parcel of the struggle against imperialism and exploitation."[53] White's prediction proved prophetic. As newly independent nations emerged in Africa, Asia, and the Western Hemisphere in the wake of the decolonization movement, their tactics and strategies to achieve independence were widely adopted in the Civil Rights Movement.[54]

Many foot soldiers in the freedom struggles of the Civil Rights Movement were also veterans of World War II. Their wartime sacrifices provided a powerful claim to assert full equality as American citizens. Among the African American veterans who continued the battle for equality begun during World War II was Ossie Davis, who became a successful film, television, and theater performer. He and his wife Ruby Dee became deeply involved in civil rights activism, helping to organize the March on Washington in 1963.[55] Numerous other veterans marched, sat-in, and endured the punishment meted out for defying Jim Crow. Not all veterans, however, employed techniques of passive resistance against white supremacy. The organizational skills and military training that African American veterans obtained during World War II served as another powerful tool in the freedom struggle. While the nonviolent activism of leaders such as Martin

[51] Brenda Moore, "African Americans in the Military," in Robert Harris Jr. and Rosalyn Terborg-Penn (eds.), *The Columbia Guide to African American History Since 1939* (New York: Columbia University Press, 2006), 122.

[52] Brenda Gayle Plummer, *Rising Wind: Black Americans and U.S. Foreign Relations, 1935–1960* (Chapel Hill: University of North Carolina Press, 1996), 105–18.

[53] White, *A Rising Wind*, 144.

[54] On the influence of de-colonization on the Civil Rights Movement, see Thomas J. Noer, *Cold War and Black Liberation: The United States and White Rule in Africa, 1948–1968* (Columbia: University of Missouri Press, 1985); Mary L. Dudziak, *Cold War Civil Rights: Race and the Image of American Democracy* (Princeton, NJ: Princeton University Press, 2000); Thomas Borstelmann, *Cold War and the Color Line: American Race Relations in the Global Arena* (Cambridge, MA: Harvard University Press, 2001).

[55] Davis and Dee, *With Ossie and Ruby*, 305–307.

Luther King, Jr., has rightly taken a central position in the historical memory of the civil rights movement, scholars have uncovered the important role of African American veterans using armed force to defend their communities from violent reprisal.[56]

More difficult to assess is the impact of the war on African American perceptions of Africa. For some veterans, their service provided a powerful sense of solidarity with other people of African descent. Ossie Davis, for example, returned to Africa repeatedly after the war, including a trip to Nigeria in 1970 to direct a film adaptation of Nobel Prize-winning playwright Wole Soyinka's work *Kongi's Harvest*. Davis noted that: "The movement for freedom on the African continent had had a tremendously inspiring effect on the [Civil Rights] Struggle over here. Some of us were so moved that we changed our hairstyles; we had our dashikis."[57] Davis's interest in Africa helped forge an influential friendship with Malcolm X, whose message of Pan-African unity inspired considerable interest in the continent's culture and history. Nonetheless, Davis recognized the risk of romanticizing Africa. During his visit to Nigeria to film *Kongi's Harvest*, he recalled:

> Initially, Ruby [Dee, Davis's wife] and I were slightly sentimental about Nigeria. We particularly wanted [our] children to see it as we saw it: Africa, the motherland, which we expected would welcome her long lost children with open arms, ending forever the historical trauma of slavery.... The Africans we met had no special sense of kinship. To them we were friends, yes, relatives, yes, but mostly we were Americans who happened to be black.[58]

If Davis retained a sense of connection to Africa because of his service during World War II, other African American veterans felt greater distance to the continent, and even expressed skepticism of the Afrocentrism that emerged out of the Civil Rights Movement. Frank James, for example, possessed a great affinity for Kenya and its people during his service there with the 812th Engineer Aviation Battalion. "I felt particularly close to them at that particular time," he recalled some sixty years later in his memoirs. However, this attachment diminished as the years passed. "I no longer feel like that now. I have come to realize that the Africans are not the same as the

---

[56] Timothy Tyson, *Radio Free Dixie: Robert F. Williams and the Roots of Black Power* (Chapel Hill: University of North Carolina Press, 1999); Lance Hill, *The Deacons of Defense: Armed Resistance and the Civil Rights Movement* (Chapel Hill: University of North Carolina Press, 2002); Steve Estes, *I Am A Man! Race, Manhood, and the Civil Rights Movement* (Chapel Hill: University of North Carolina Press, 2005); Christopher B. Stain, *Pure Fire: Self-Defense as Activism in the Civil Rights Era* (Athens: University of Georgia Press, 2005); Simon Wendt, *The Spirit and the Shotgun: Armed Resistance and the Struggle for Civil Rights* (Gainesville: University Press of Florida, 2007).

[57] Ossie Davis and Ruby Dee, *Life Lit by Some Large Vision: Selected Speeches and Writings* (New York: Atria Books, 2006), 196.

[58] Davis and Dee, *With Ossie and Ruby*, 343.

American blacks."[59] In a newspaper interview in 1994, Gertrude Bertram expressed similar sentiments about her wartime experiences as a nurse in Liberia, observing that "[Africans] are a different people altogether.... So many [American] blacks want to connect with them, but an African would just say be yourself."[60]

African Americans soldiers, sailors, and marines offered their lives to protect Africa from coming under the domination of the Axis Powers. African American construction battalions serving in Africa left behind barracks, airfields, roads, and hospitals. While some of these structures proved short-lived, others are still in use today, such as Roberts Field near Monrovia. More substantial was the influence African American personnel had on local economies, local culture, and especially local politics. The presence of these troops brought wealth, social interaction, and sometimes conflict. But the wartime efforts of African American soldiers to defeat inequality at home and abroad provided a clear parallel for what Africans themselves sought to achieve: freedom and independence.

[59] James, *Capers of a Medic*, 23.
[60] Marisol Bello, "Racism's battleground: Trail-blazing nurse felt first shots of discrimination during World War II," *Dayton Daily News*, February 20, 1994.

22

French African Soldiers in German POW Camps, 1940–1945

Raffael Scheck

World War II scholarship is moving beyond an exclusive focus on the United States, Europe, and Japan to examine the experience of people in Africa, Asia, Latin America, and Australia.[1] The war initiated important economic, social, and ideological changes in their communities as the result of the participation of millions of Africans and Asians as soldiers and laborers. Not least, the ideological aspect of fighting a war for democracy and self-determination against a tyrannical opponent strengthened aspirations for self-determination and independence. The foreign occupation of part of the French empire undermined colonial order and caused widespread administrative disruption. This chapter focuses on one group of people, whose experience connected the African and European sides of the war, including the experience of fighting for France and of being captive of Nazi Germany. How did captivity affect African soldiers, and how might it have shaped their postwar mindset?

After the western campaign in May and June 1940, the German army held nearly 1.8 million French prisoners of war (POWs) including 100,000 soldiers from the French empire, the vast majority of them from Africa.[2] Forty thousand of these POWs were sent to Germany in the summer of

---

[1] The contributions in this volume offer rich perspectives on the impact of the war on Africa. A pioneering work is Birgit Morgenrath and Rheinisches JournalistInnenbüro (Köln), *"Unsere Opfer zählen nicht:" Die Dritte Welt im Zweiten Weltkrieg* (Berlin: Assoziation A, 2005). See also Roger Chickering, Stig Förster, and Bernd Greiner, *A World at Total War: Global Conflict and the Politics of Destruction, 1937–1945* (Washington and Cambridge: German Historical Institute and Cambridge University Press, 2005), and Gerhard L. Weinberg, *A World at Arms: A Global History of World War II*, 2nd ed. (Cambridge: Cambridge University Press, 2005).

[2] North Africans made up around 65%, West Africans around 20%, French Equatorial Africans 5%, and soldiers from Indochina and the Caribbean 10%. For exact numbers and shifts in the proportions, see Raffael Scheck, *French Colonial Soldiers in German Captivity during World War II* (Cambridge and New York: Cambridge University Press, 2014), 26–31.

1940, but almost all returned to camps in occupied France by the end of the year following a decision by Adolf Hitler not to hold nonwhite POWs on German soil.[3] After some escapes and dismissals, there were still more than 70,000 colonial POWs in German-occupied France in July 1941. Their number declined to 30,000 three years later due to dismissals because of disease or political reasons and some 5,000 escapes. By the fall of 1944, the Allies had liberated at least half of the soldiers remaining in captivity, but the German army transferred the remaining 10,000 to 15,000 POWs to Germany. In the literature, these soldiers are usually called "colonial prisoners," whereas documents from the war itself call them "indigenous prisoners," "prisoners of color," or, in official French parlance, "North African *and* colonial prisoners" (because the French North African territories were not considered colonies).

Until recently, the standard works on French POWs focused almost entirely on white French prisoners.[4] A recently published book by Armelle Mabon gives the fullest picture of the captivity experience of colonial soldiers and complements the earlier studies by Belkacem Recham on Algerian soldiers and by Myron Echenberg and Nancy Lawler on West African soldiers. Mabon's study is especially rich with respect to the connections between the prisoners and French civilians, but it does not consider German primary sources and English-language secondary sources.[5] Several recent articles stress specific aspects of the experience of the prisoners from the French

---

3 Georges Scapini, *Mission sans gloire* (Paris: Editions Morgan, 1960), 335; Yves Durand, *La captivité: histoire des prisonniers de guerre français, 1939–1945* (Paris: Fédération nationale des combattants et prisonniers de guerre et combattants d'Algérie, de Tunisie et du Maroc, 1982), 58. The transfer of prisoners of color from Germany to France continued into 1943 because inspection teams repeatedly discovered more colonial POWs in the German camps. These prisoners often requested a transfer to France. See "An Kommandantur stalag IID (Stargard)," September 15, 1942, in Farbige Truppen, Kolonialbeamten, R 67003: F 301d, PAAA, Berlin.

4 Durand, *La captivité*, and *La vie quotidienne des prisonniers de guerre dans les Stalags, les Oflags et les Kommandos, 1939–1945* (Paris: Hachette, 1987); Pierre Gascar, *Histoire de la captivité des Français en Allemagne (1939–1945)* (Paris: Gallimard, 1967). For an excellent overview of the POW problem in World War II, see Rüdiger Overmans, "Die Kriegsgefangenenpolitik des Deutschen Reiches 1939 bis 1945," in Jörg Echternkamp (ed.), *Das Deutsche Reich und der Zweite Weltkrieg* (Munich: Oldenbourg Verlag, 2005), 729–875.

5 Armelle Mabon, *Prisonniers de guerre "indigènes": Visages oubliés de la France occupée* (Paris: La Découverte, 2010). See also Belkacem Recham, *Les musulmans algériens dans l'armée française (1919–1945)* (Paris: L'Harmattan, 1996); Myron Echenberg, *Colonial Conscripts: The Tirailleurs Sénégalais in French West Africa, 1857–1960* (Portsmouth, NH, and London: Heinemann and James Currey, 1991); Nancy Ellen Lawler, *Soldiers of Misfortune: Ivoirien Tirailleurs of World War II* (Athens: Ohio University Press, 1992); Bob Moore and Kent Fedorowich, *Prisoners of War and Their Captors in World War II* (Oxford and Washington, D.C.: Berg, 1996), in particular the articles by Martin Thomas and David Killingray. See also Julien Fargettas, *Les Tirailleurs sénégalais: Les soldats noirs entre légendes et réalité 1939–1945* (Paris: Tallandier, 2012).

empire, but they do not use German materials. A well-documented article by Martin Thomas accuses the Vichy authorities of using colonial prisoners in a racist attempt to restore paternalist order in the empire and depicts German authorities as harsh and abusive. Articles by Thierry Godechot and Julien Fargettas deal with the frustration of African soldiers awaiting repatriation toward the end of the war, but they make little of the connection between the captivity experience of these soldiers and their rebellious mood at the end of the war.[6]

My research leads me to some differentiations and slightly different conclusions. I found that the German treatment of colonial prisoners, after a harsh period with many abuses particularly against blacks, became more humane. By comparing the experiences of white French prisoners in Germany and colonial prisoners in France, I argue that imprisonment in France was an advantage for the colonial prisoners that balanced out the disadvantage of poor communications with home: Prisoners in France had better access to French aid organizations and were surrounded by generally supportive civilians. I also found that the Vichy authorities, though keen on helping the prisoners because of Vichy's interest in maintaining a colonial empire, discredited themselves through their negotiations with the Germans, leaving colonial prisoners increasingly disenchanted with France. Finally, I argue that the provisional government of General Charles de Gaulle was unprepared to address the grievances of ex-prisoners and alienated them further.[7]

A basic problem of research on colonial POWs is that few written records from the prisoners themselves exist because most were illiterate or semiliterate. In the 1980s, Nancy Lawler interviewed veterans from Ivory Coast, among them many ex-prisoners, but very few veterans are still alive today.[8] German archival sources provide evidence about the framework of the camp organization and the labor of the prisoners, but they say little about the experience of captivity. Yet, the Vichy authorities and many French semiofficial and private aid organizations gathered much information about their living conditions and tried to improve shortcomings. The French Diplomatic

---

[6] Martin Thomas, "The Vichy government and French colonial prisoners of war, 1940–1944," *French Historical Studies*, 25 (2002), 657–92; Thierry Godechot, "Prélude aux rebellions en Afrique du Nord: les mutineries de soldats maghrébins, décembre 1944–mai 1945," *Revue historique des Armées*, 4 (2002), 3–6; Julien Fargettas, "La révolte des tirailleurs sénégalais de Thiaroye: entre reconstructions mémorielles et histoire," *Vingtième Siècle, revue d'histoire*, 92 (2006), 117–30; Belkacem Recham, "Les indigènes nord-africains prisonniers de guerre (1940–1945)," *Guerres mondiales et conflits contemporains*, 56 (2006), 109–25.

[7] Scheck, *French Colonial Soldiers*, 8–11. See also Raffael Scheck, "French colonial soldiers in German prisoner of war camps, 1940–1945," *French History*, 24 (2010), 420–46; "The prisoner of war question and the beginnings of collaboration: The Franco-German Agreement of 16 November 1940," *Journal of Contemporary History*, 45 (2010), 364–88.

[8] Lawler, *Soldiers of Misfortune*.

Service for the Prisoners of War under special ambassador Georges Scapini (referred to as the Scapini Mission) conducted numerous camp inspections according to the Geneva Convention on Prisoners of War (1929) beginning in February 1941.[9] Although a German officer always accompanied inspection teams, the reports openly address shortages and abuses.[10] Moreover, the Scapini Mission and other French agencies collected additional material that tends to corroborate inspection reports, such as letters from aid workers and literate prisoners, who often wrote for illiterate prisoners as well. Finally, a rich photographic record exists: guards, farmers, and entrepreneurs took pictures, and some of their collections found their way into the archives.[11]

The initial period of captivity was harsh for all prisoners from the Western European armies. The German army, unprepared for the number of prisoners it captured, assembled them in overcrowded and unsanitary quarters in France, often without adequate shelter and insufficient water and food supplies. Diseases spread rapidly.[12] Guards used excessive violence to maintain order. Several thousand Africans, together with 1.6 million white Frenchmen and 40,000 British prisoners, were forced into extreme marches to Belgium and the Netherlands, where they were packed onto river barges and cattle cars that brought them to camps in Germany. When they returned to France later in the year, however, they found improved conditions because the departure of white prisoners had eased overcrowding and allowed better organization of the physical structure and supply of the camps.

Black prisoners suffered the most in the first months. Under the impression of a hateful propaganda campaign that stigmatized black French soldiers as mutilating savages and illegitimate combatants, German units had executed at least 3,000 black soldiers during the campaign. Often the finding

---

[9] For the work of the Scapini Mission, see Scapini, *Mission sans gloire*; Georges Baud, Louis Devaux, and Jean Poigny, *Mémoire complémentaire sur quelques aspects du Service Diplomatique des Prisonniers de Guerre: SDPG-DFB-Mission Scapini, 1940–1945* (Paris: G. Baud, 1984); Jean Vedrine, *Dossier PG-Rapatriés 1940–1945: recueil de témoignages, d'informations et de commentaires sur les activités, en France, des prisonniers de guerre (PG) évadés, ou rapatriés avant 1945, dans l'administration PG, l'action sociale PG, la résistance PG* (Asnières: Dossier PG-Rapatriés, 1940–1945, 1981). Unfortunately, these works contain very little information on colonial prisoners.

[10] The inspection reports are available in French in the Archives Nationales (hereafter AN), Paris, and in German at the Politisches Archiv des Auswärtigen Amtes (hereafter PAAA), Berlin. The archives of the ICRC, Geneva, hold the reports of the Red Cross, which are less detailed and far less numerous: Dossier CSC, Service des camps, France (hereafter Frontstalags).

[11] See in particular the Collection Belisle in the Archives départementales de la Nièvre (hereafter AND), Nevers; and the Collection Guyon in the Archives départementales de la Mayenne (hereafter ADM), Laval. A German private collector has many pictures likely taken by German guards: see Historicmedia-Verlag Dietrich Klose (www.historicmedia.de).

[12] Durand, *La captivité*, 44–47.

of a mutilated corpse of a German soldier had served officers as justification for separating all black prisoners from "white" French, North African, and Allied prisoners, and for ordering their execution. An investigation into the circumstances under which German soldiers were "mutilated" never occurred, and it was proven that in many cases the wounds of the dead German soldiers were the effects of gunshot wounds and not of deliberate mutilations. The frequency of close combat with French West African troops and their staunch resistance even during the last days of the campaign created a hysterical fear and hatred of black soldiers among German troops. Abuses of German prisoners by French West Africans soldiers are documented, but many German officers and soldiers began to read battle situations in the light of the gruesome racist propaganda about the "mutilating savages" and therefore randomly killed and abused disarmed West African prisoners.[13]

The hatred provoked by this propaganda particularly affected the treatment of the black prisoners during the first weeks of captivity on marches and in POW camps. Nervous German guards interpreted every spontaneous move of a black prisoner as an attack or an attempted escape and responded by randomly shooting prisoners. Often the guards deprived black soldiers of water and food, and denied them medical care.[14] Those black prisoners who arrived in Germany were met with curiosity and abuse from civilians who associated blacks with exotic zoos and circuses. One German witness told me that during the summer of 1940, parents in a little town on the Dutch border took their children to see the famished and desperate blacks crowded into cattle cars passing through the town every evening.[15] A West African noncommissioned officer, Édouard Ouédraogo, reported that German civilians insulted blacks and spat on them as they arrived in the camps. He also recorded the presence of news teams eager to film his facial scars and ordering the blacks to dance in front of the cameras.[16] Many of these films appeared on German weekly newsreels as an example of the perfidy of France, which had allegedly mobilized "savages." In late July 1940, however, Ouédraogo and other black African POWs in both Germany and France experienced a sudden improvement in treatment, which they ascribed to German colonial interests in West Africa.[17]

---

[13] Raffael Scheck, *Hitler's African Victims: The German Army Massacres of Black French Soldiers in 1940* (New York: Cambridge University Press, 2006), 21–41, 45; Lawler, *Soldiers of Misfortune*, 98–105. For cases of documented abuses of German prisoners by West Africans, see Scheck, *Hitler's African Victims*, 126–29; Lawler, *Soldiers of Misfortune*, 96; Fargettas, *Les Tirailleurs sénégalais*, 165–67.

[14] Scheck, *Hitler's African Victims*, 42–44.

[15] Personal e-mail communication, Helmut Schaffrannek to author, January 14, 2006.

[16] Report in Dossier "VIII AOF 1944–45: Mentalité des tirailleurs sénégalais," 5H16, Service Historique de la Défense (hereafter SHD), Vincennes.

[17] Scheck, *Hitler's African Victims*, 46–49; Lawler, *Soldiers of Misfortune*, 104–08.

Until the liberation of France in 1944, the vast majority of Africans in German captivity belonged to work detachments (*Arbeitskommandos*) linked to German camps in occupied France (*Front-Stammlager* or *Frontstalags*). These *Arbeitskommandos* ranged in size from one to one thousand men and worked in public services, industry, and above all in forestry and agriculture. In the *Arbeitskommandos*, North Africans, Senegalese, Madagascans, and Indochinese were usually kept apart. In the main camps and the larger *Arbeitskommandos*, however, prisoners were mixed, although they often occupied different barracks according to their homeland.[18]

The German Military Command in France, worried about detaining enemy soldiers in the midst of the enemy population, passed stern guidelines that were sent to all camp commanders and posted in every guardhouse. Guards had to use their weapons ruthlessly and were forbidden to have their picture taken with prisoners, to mingle casually with them, or to let them have contact with French civilians, especially women.[19] Photos from archives in France and private collections of German soldiers show, however, that the guards were not nearly as distant from the prisoners as they should have been (see Figures 22.1 and 22.2). Many pictures show German soldiers, often without weapons, in the middle of a group of prisoners in a relaxed and friendly atmosphere, leading a German radical right-wing newspaper, which printed such a friendly group picture, to claim that this author had blatantly invented German massacres of black French soldiers in the campaign of 1940.[20] Inspection reports confirm the relatively good treatment of French colonial prisoners, especially in small commandos. Although linguistic barriers limited communication between the guards and the prisoners, relations were often friendly.[21]

There are several reasons for this. German colonial designs did play a role in the improved treatment of black soldiers, as various German agencies began looking for potential collaborators. Moreover, a change of personnel made a difference. After the summer of 1940, the guards were no longer frontline troops but Home Guard Battalions (*Landesschützenbataillone*),

---

[18] This characterization relies on the reading of thousands of camp inspection reports by the French Diplomatic Service for the Prisoners of War in F9:2351–2356, AN, Paris; and R 40987–40992, PAAA, Berlin.

[19] "Merkblatt," Oberbefehlshaber des Heeres, Chef der Militärverwaltung in Frankreich, August 13, 1940, in Bundesarchiv-Militärarchiv, Freiburg im Breisgau (BA-MA), RH 19 II, vol. 295, 24; "Betreffend: Behandlung der Kriegsgefangenen," Oberbefehlshaber des Heeres, Chef der Militärverwaltung in Frankreich, August 13, 1940, in BA-MA, RH 19 II, vol. 295, 17–21. A similar order was issued in January 1943; see "Der deutsche Soldat in der Kriegsgefangenenbewachung," January 16, 1943, in BA–MA, RW 6, vol. 487.

[20] See "Neue Lügen gegen die Wehrmacht," *Deutsche National-Zeitung*, no. 07/06, February 10, 2006. This article was a reaction to my article "Keine Kameraden" in *Die Zeit*, January 12, 2006, which summarized the findings of my book, *Hitler's African Victims*.

[21] Report by Édouard Ouédraogo in Dossier "VIII AOF 1944–45 Mentalité des tirailleurs sénégalais," 5H16, SHD, Vincennes. See also Lawler, *Soldiers of Misfortune*, 106.

FIGURE 22.1. The guard posing with prisoners violated several German orders but exemplified the generally relaxed atmosphere in rural work commandos. Copyright: Archives départementales de la Mayenne.

military formations that included older soldiers and people with slight disabilities. Many of these men were not committed to Nazism.[22] The most important factor, however, was that the living situation of guards and prisoners encouraged companionship between them. In many *Arbeitskommandos*, a small group of prisoners lived on a farm, a forest encampment or in a village together with one or two guards. They ate and slept together and went to town in the evenings and on Sundays. The German army deployed very small forces on guard duty in the French *Frontstalags*.[23] A low ratio of guards to prisoners could encourage excessive violence, as happened during the first weeks of captivity, but the situation in the small *Arbeitskommandos* was built more on trust and companionship than on terror and intimidation.

Even with relatively friendly guards, captivity remained a harsh experience. Prisoners suffered from the lack of news from home, and they often lamented the shortage of clothing, shoes, blankets, and occasionally food. Diseases were widespread, especially pulmonary diseases. Moreover, abuses

---

[22] See Raffael Scheck, "Vom Massaker zur Kameradschaft? Die Behandlung der schwarzen französischen Kriegsgefangenen durch die deutsche Wehrmacht, 1940–1945," in Manuel Menrath, *Afrika im Blick. Afrikabilder im deutschsprachigen Europa, 1870–1970* (Zürich: Chronos Verlag, 2012).

[23] For the reports of the Military Commander in France, see RW 35/8 and 10, BA–MA; and AJ 40/443, AN, Paris (available online at www.ihtp.cnrs.fr/prefets/).

FIGURE 22.2. Doing laundry in a camp near hangars. Copyright: Dietrich Klose (www.historicmedia.de).

continued to happen. In a hospital near Bordeaux, for example, German doctors tested tropical medicine and vaccines on sick black prisoners.[24] Some African prisoners also experienced deliberate brutality from angry guards.[25] Colonial prisoners who were caught after having escaped and joined the French resistance were executed or sent to a concentration camp

---

[24] Report by Édouard Ouédraogo, in Dossier "VIII AOF 1944–45 Mentalité des tirailleurs sénégalais," 5H16, SHD, Vincennes. See also Margrit Berner, "Rassenforschung an kriegsgefangenen Schwarzen," in Peter Martin and Christine Alonzo, *Zwischen Charleston und Stechschritt. Schwarze im Nationalsozialismus* (Hamburg: Dölling und Galitz, 2004), 605–13.

[25] For examples, see Scheck, *French Colonial Soldiers*, 107–09.

in Germany, but this was also the fate of captured white resisters.[26] Those *Frontstalag* prisoners transferred to Germany in late 1944 experienced further hardship during the chaos of the collapsing Reich.

Yet, abuses were, at least after July 1940, the exception. At the insistence of the Scapini Mission, the Germans usually investigated them and sometimes admonished or punished the guards.[27] The German High Command, pressed by the Scapini Mission and the International Committee of the Red Cross (ICRC), began to move West African soldiers to the milder southwest of France, where they would suffer less from disease. Yet, the Germans never completed this transfer because they needed the labor of prisoners in other parts of France, and because the camps in southwestern France quickly became overcrowded.[28] The Germans, however, easily dismissed prisoners on medical grounds, often after falsified diagnoses by French doctors (it seems that the German doctors and camp commanders often closed both eyes).[29] The reduction of the *Frontstalag* population from over 70,000 in July 1941 to just over 30,000 three years later reflected this generous dismissal policy: At least half of the 40,000 "lost" prisoners were dismissed on medical grounds, some on the basis of a simple cold.[30]

French authorities (both Vichyist and Gaullist) worried that German treatment of colonial POWs was part of a propaganda effort to win them over to Germany. This was true for the initial change in the treatment of black prisoners, but it does not explain the continued benign treatment. Usually German propaganda was directed at specific prisoner groups. Some North Africans, for example, were sent to a special camp in Luckenwalde near Berlin (Stalag IIIa), where they received preferential treatment and special liberties. In this camp, German officials and Arabic collaborators sought to discredit French and British imperialism, spread hatred of Jews, and promote an anticolonial jihad against the British.[31] Later the Germans sent these prisoners to *Frontstalags* in France, so that they would spread the message.

---

[26] Maurice Rives, "Die Tirailleurs Sénégalais in der Résistance," in Peter Martin and Christine Alonzo (eds.), *Zwischen Charleston und Stechschritt. Schwarze im Nationalsozialismus* (Hamburg: Dölling und Galitz, 2004), 675–95.

[27] For example, see the inspection report on *Arbeitskommando* Buglose (belonging to Frontstalag 222) by Dr. Bonnaud, July 8, 1941, in F9:2356, AN, Paris.

[28] The reports of the Military Commander in France from August and September 1940 mention plans to move nearly all colonial prisoners to southwest France, RW 35/10, BA-MA, www .ihtp.cnrs.fr/prefets/. See also Scapini to Secrétaire Général du Chef de l'Etat, February 25, 1942, F9:2276, AN, Paris.

[29] Lawler, *Soldiers of Misfortune*, 112.

[30] Hélène de Gobineau, *Noblesse d'Afrique* (Paris: Fasquelles Editeurs, 1946), 13.

[31] Raffael Scheck, "Nazi propaganda toward French Muslim prisoners of war," *Holocaust and Genocide Studies*, 26 (2012), 447–77; Gerhard Höpp, "Der verdrängte Diskurs. Arabische Opfer des Nationalsozialismus," in Gerhard Höpp, Peter Wien, and René Wildangel, *Blind für die Geschichte?: Arabische Begegnungen mit dem Nationalsozialismus* (Berlin: Klaus Schwarz, 2004), 226–27; Klaus Michael Mallmann and Martin Cüppers, *Halbmond und*

The German propaganda ministry also produced a newspaper in Arabic and distributed it in all camps with Arab-speakers. In France, the German military administration supported groups of Algerian, Moroccan, or Tunisian nationalists, and in at least one case (Bordeaux), such a group received access to North African POWs. German propaganda made few converts to the Nazi cause, but it planted seeds of doubt about French colonialism and attracted a select group of collaborators and spies, often among literate prisoners.[32] The Vichy administration was so worried that it set up camps in unoccupied France where secret service agents questioned dismissed North African prisoners and promoted pro-French propaganda before releasing them. Ambassador Scapini even suggested launching a joint Franco-German propaganda campaign aiming to reconcile the North Africans with colonialism by using anti-Jewish messages, an idea that the German embassy in Paris welcomed but did not pursue.[33]

Relations between colonial prisoners and French civilians were generally good. Although the German guards had strict orders to keep prisoners and civilians separated, scores of photos show prisoners in close contact with French civilians (see Figure 22.3). Only rarely did the Germans try to curtail these contacts, although the nature of prisoner work assignments would have made this nearly impossible. Often relationships between farming families and prisoners became cordial, with the atmosphere resembling that of a large family, sometimes including the guards. In factories, prisoners worked on the same machines as French workers, which greatly worried French officials because colonial prisoners in some factories met French workers with communist and anticolonial ideas.[34] Given that prisoners in many *Arbeitskommandos* went to town with minimal surveillance on weekday evenings and Sundays, it does not come as a surprise that amorous liaisons developed. Contacts with women who participated in informal adoption programs for colonial POWs (*marraines de guerre*) or drivers from the French ICRC (almost exclusively young women) could become intimate. Many pregnant women or their mothers asked French military authorities for permission to marry a prisoner (given that the POWs were still mobilized soldiers, they needed the army's permission to marry).[35] Most French civilians appreciated the contribution that the soldiers from the empire had made to the defense of France and treated them with respect.

Hakenkreuz: das Dritte Reich, die Araber und Palästina (Darmstadt: Wissenschaftliche Buchgesellschaft, 2006), 150.

[32] Scheck, "Nazi Propaganda," 447, 468; Mallmann and Cüppers, *Halbmond und Hakenkreuz,* 43–44.

[33] Scheck, "Nazi Propaganda," 462.

[34] "Compte-rendu, octobre 22 & 23, 1943," F9:2177, AN, Paris; Scapini to Chef du Gouvernement, August 12, 1943, 2P78, SHD, Vincennes; Ribillard to Colonel Mermet, May 5, 1943, 3P84, SHD, Vincennes.

[35] A collection of these letters is located in F9:2571, AN, Paris.

FIGURE 22.3. An African prisoner as member of the family. Copyright: Archives départementales de la Mayenne (M. Guyon).

By contrast, colonial prisoners often experienced French officials as alienating and condescending. The prisoners started out with the feeling that they were second-class members of the French army and less important to the French authorities than the white prisoners. In a fatal process that was only partly the responsibility of French officials, this feeling became stronger during captivity.[36] It started with an agreement between Scapini and the German High Command from November 16, 1940, that stipulated that all

---

[36] Martin Thomas puts much emphasis on the Vichy state's own racism in this process. Without wanting to deny that racism, I see the Vichy authorities more as a reacting agent here. Many features of Vichy racism, moreover, were not germane to Vichy but characterized French colonialism (perhaps *any* colonialism) more generally. See Thomas, "Vichy government and French colonial prisoners of war."

fathers of four minor children living in poverty would be dismissed and likewise the oldest brothers of four siblings if the father was deceased. To be dismissed, a prisoner had to provide the birth certificates of minor children and confirmation from the town mayor. The Vichy regime broadcast this agreement as a substantial concession by Germany and as a justification for collaboration.[37] Colonial prisoners soon found out, however, that the Germans, using the difficulties of verification as a pretext, did not intend to apply the agreement to them. Africans in German captivity tended to blame the French authorities for this injustice. They did not know that Scapini repeatedly requested a total release of colonial prisoners.[38] To make this demand more palatable to the Germans, Scapini once even made the dubious proposal to deploy colonial prisoners on work commandos under French command for the trans-Saharan railway in Morocco, but to no avail.[39]

More disappointments followed. In May 1941, the Vichy prime minister negotiated with Hitler an agreement for the release of World War I veterans among the French prisoners. This time, the Germans did not object to the release of colonial soldiers, but colonial prisoners had to wait much longer than white prisoners because the French administration in the empire was slow in providing the necessary documents.[40] More serious was the German decision in July 1941 to release most remaining white soldiers from the *Frontstalags* – approximately 3,000 – in exchange for French military concessions. It is true that the Vichy officials agreed to this measure hoping that it would be the first step toward the release of *all Frontstalag* prisoners, but by doing so, they condoned German categories of race. For Nazi Germany, skin color counted, not French citizenship or membership in the French army. A significant minority among the colonial prisoners *had* French citizenship, for example, some Senegalese, Algerians, and people from the French Antilles.[41] The July 1941 decree, however, applied only to white prisoners, leaving nonwhite French citizens frustrated and questioning the worth of their French citizenship. Even people with mixed family background who were French citizens and lived in France did not qualify for release. The prisoner Christian Rajaobelina, for example, was born in France of a Madagascan father and a

---

37 For background, see Scheck, "The prisoner of war question," 374–77.

38 For example, see "Entretien du mai 20, 1941," F9:2176, AN, Paris; minutes of the Scapini-von Rosenberg meeting of July 30, 1941, F9:2177, AN, Paris; and "Note pour l'OKW" December 11, 1941, F 9, 2276, AN, Paris (requesting the dismissal of all prisoners of color still left in Germany).

39 "Note pour l'ambassadeur," July 22, 1941, in F9, 2276, AN, Paris; and Protocol, Berlin, May 23, 1941, in Box 15, Georges Scapini Papers, Hoover Institution Archives, Stanford University.

40 "Entretien," July 17, 1941, and "Compte-rendu 20 & 21 novembre, 1942," both in F9, 2177, AN, Paris.

41 On citizenship, see Robert Aldrich, *Greater France: A History of French Overseas Empire* (New York: St. Martin's Press, 1996), 212–13.

white French mother, but the Germans rejected his release because they considered him a person of color.[42] Colonial prisoners, regardless of citizenship status, resented that the French authorities condoned distinctions among members of the French army. These soldiers argued that since bullets did not distinguish between white and nonwhite members of the French army, decrees should not do so either.[43] Inspection reports of the Scapini Mission and prisoners' letters reflect the disappointment and outrage of many colonial prisoners caused by the dismissal of the white *Frontstalag* prisoners, as one passage from a prisoner's letter exemplifies: "The French are leaving and the slaves are staying."[44]

At the end of 1941, the German High Command hinted that it was considering the dismissal of 10,000 colonial prisoners in response to the French recall of General Maxime Weygand, the commander-in-chief in North Africa known to be strongly anti-German.[45] Scapini suggested the release of 6,500 North Africans and 3,500 West Africans, which roughly corresponded to the proportions of the North and West Africans in captivity, but the Germans decided to dismiss only North Africans, whom they considered more important for propaganda reasons. This caused much anger among the prisoners who were left behind. Moreover, Scapini found out that the majority of the dismissed soldiers should have been liberated according to earlier agreements (e.g., fathers or oldest brothers of four; World War I veterans).[46] Unaware of the efforts of Scapini and his staff, the colonial prisoners blamed the French authorities for the arbitrary German measure.

Another Franco-German agreement concluded by the Vichy government without consultation of the Scapini Mission, also left a troubling legacy: In January 1943, Vichy accepted a German request that French officers and soldiers with colonial experience replace German guard personnel transferred to the Soviet Union. The change of guards began despite objections from Scapini and his staff, who warned that it would undermine the remaining respect for France among colonial soldiers. In the end, only 6,000 colonial prisoners received French guards because the Germans became worried

---

[42] French Red Cross to Ambassador Scapini, March 31, 1942, F9:2356, AN, Paris.
[43] For one example, see Tebibel Djaffes to Madame la Maréchale, April 1, 1943, F9:2258, AN, Paris.
[44] Excerpt from a prisoner's letter quoted in Contre-Amiral Platon, Secrétaire d'Etat aux colonies to vice-président du conseil, Mr. l'Amiral de la flotte, [Darlan], September 12, 1941, F9:2276, AN, Paris.
[45] Christine Levisse-Touzé, *L'Afrique du Nord dans la guerre, 1939–1945* (Paris: Albin Michel, 1998), 177–78.
[46] "Note pour l'OKW," March 10, 1942, F9:2176, AN, Paris; Desbons to M. l'Amiral de la Flotte, Ministre de la Défense Nationale, Direction des Services de l'Armistice, February 2, 1942, F9:2869, AN, Paris; L'amiral, secretaire d'etat à la marine et aux colonies to Mr. le Général, directeur du service des prisonniers de guerre, August 7, 1943, F9:2966, AN, Paris.

that French-led *Frontstalags* might defect to the resistance. Although some prisoners seem to have appreciated their French guards because they allowed them more freedom than the German guards, other prisoners experienced their French guards as so abusive and exploitative that they asked for the return of the German guards.[47]

Another crucial dimension of the captivity experience was the contact among the prisoners themselves. Typically, prisoners in each camp had a French commander, usually the highest-ranking officer present and almost always a white Frenchman (officers were exempt from the liberation of white *Frontstalag* prisoners in July 1941). The officers did not have to work and received other privileges, such as free passage to nearby towns and extra rations. Some French officers in the *Frontstalags* established cordial relations with German commanders and guards, giving colonial prisoners the impression that the French and Germans were fraternizing. Several African soldiers complained in their letters that French officers spent their time socializing and drinking with German officers and making condescending remarks to prisoners of color.[48]

Much tension and anger arose from allegations of corruption against the most important man for the prisoners: the man of confidence. Each camp and each *Arbeitskommando*, no matter how small, had a man of confidence who was either appointed by the German authorities or chosen by the prisoners themselves. The man of confidence was the prisoners' contact person to the German camp administration, the Scapini Mission, and the ICRC. He was also the designated recipient of parcels from aid organizations and the distributor of their contents. Usually if white French officers or soldiers were present in a camp or *Arbeitskommando*, one of them worked as the man of confidence; however, the few white officers who stayed after the release of white Frontstalag prisoners were mostly stationed in the main camps, so many branch camps and almost all *Arbeitskommandos* had colonial prisoners as men of confidence.[49] In some cases, prisoners accused the man of confidence of corruption, sometimes in conjunction with a German guard or the camp commander. In one typical case, the man of confidence in a big camp near Bordeaux (Camp des As), Mohamed Bel Aïd, was accused of withholding the contents of parcels and of selling them at inflated prices in the camp canteen. The German commander investigated and found 15,000

---

[47] Raffael Scheck, "Des officiers français comme gardiens de leurs propres soldats? Les prisonniers de guerre 'indigènes' sous encadrement français, 1943–1944," in Anne-Marie Pathé and Fabien Théofilakis (eds.), *La captivité de guerre au XXe siècle. Des archives, des histoires, des mémoires* (Paris: Armand Colin/Ministère de la Défense, 2012), 251–62.

[48] Bonko Kambiré to Pétain, no date, and anonymous letter, February 19, 1943, both in F9:2351, AN, Paris.

[49] The camp inspections usually listed the name of the man of confidence. See the reports in F9:2352–2356, AN, Paris.

francs on Bel Aïd, who claimed to have saved this money legally. The outcome of this case is unknown, but according to Édouard Ouédraogo, who was in the same camp, the German commander himself was implicated in the corruption with Bel Aïd his accomplice.[50]

Complaints against corrupt men of confidence were not uncommon in the camps in Germany, too, but what made them special in Frontstalags was that they often brought to the surface prejudices about certain ethnic groups.[51] In camps with a mixed population, prisoners sometimes complained that the man of confidence favored people from the same territory in the distribution of parcel contents. In the camp of Morcenx near Bordeaux, for example, a West African prisoner became the spokesperson of prisoners against a Tunisian man of confidence and his two associates, whom he accused of holding back food parcels, starving five hundred prisoners. An aid organization forwarded his letter to Scapini: "it is not the Germans who are hurting us. We are [badly] treated by your officers and the secretary of the camp.... You should not let us die from hunger. We are your sons. First off, you should know the character of the Arabs: they are all unjust. They are all robbers."[52]

Unequal supplies triggered many tensions among the prisoners. Some private or semiprivate aid organizations existed specifically for people from one region of the French empire, with the result that some prisoners received more plentiful deliveries than the others. Moroccan POWs probably had the best supplies, thanks to the efforts of Madame Noguès, the wife of the French resident general in Morocco. With good connections to the government in Vichy, she directed a well-endowed assistance organization for Moroccan prisoners that provoked much envy.[53] The Scapini Mission asked aid organizations to send more parcels to camps and *Arbeitskommandos* with less well-supplied prisoners, and the Vichy authorities occasionally tried to improve the general level of supply by sending gifts to all prisoners, such as the "*colis du maréchal*" ("parcel of the Marshal [Pétain]"). Despite these efforts, inequities and the resulting animosities persisted.[54]

---

[50] See camp inspection AK Camp des As, February 26, 1942 by Dantan Merlin, F9:2356, AN, Paris, and report by Édouard Ouédraogo, in Dossier "VIII AOF 1944–45 Mentalité des tirailleurs sénégalais," 5H16, SHD, Vincennes.

[51] MacKenzie, *The Colditz Myth*, 132–33.

[52] Anonymous prisoner to Comité Algérien d'Assistance aux Prisonniers de guerre. Morsenx, March 9, 1942, in F9:2356, AN, Paris. The camp of Morsenx belonged to Frontstalag 222 (Bayonne), which at this time held a large number of Tunisian and West African prisoners.

[53] See ICRC inspection report on the camp of Lanniron in Bretagne, part of Frontstalag 135 (Rennes), May 27 and 28, 1941, F (-D) 135 and 135DT, Service des camps, France (Frontstalags) CSC, ICRC Archives, Geneva. See also Dr. Bonnaud to M. Salie (min. des colonies), July 16, 1941, F9:2351, AN, Paris.

[54] "Note: Les remarques suivantes s'imposent pour les 3 camps de: Onesse Laharie, Saint-Médard, Bayonne-Anglet et leurs Arbeits Kommando," F9:2355, AN, Paris.

Differences among prisoners were exacerbated by the location of their home territory and its socioeconomic development, which influenced postal connections. Until the Allied landings in North Africa, many North Africans received letters and packages from home and were able to write to their families, albeit at a very slow pace; but many West Africans, Madagascans, and North Africans from remote regions had no contact with their families for the entire duration of the war. Even if postal connections functioned, the ICRC often found it impossible to deliver prisoners' letters to their families because of insufficient addresses, particularly in West Africa. The Vichy authorities, aware that this problem was sapping the morale of many colonial prisoners, invited them to record radio messages that would be broadcast in the empire, but few prisoners benefited from this program.[55]

General tension existed between the North African and other prisoners. West Africans often perceived North Africans as better supplied and privileged by the French and Germans, as well as prejudiced against them.[56] There probably was some truth to this. Until the Allied invasion in November 1942, the Vichy government considered North Africa as its most important overseas territory and an asset in negotiations with Germany. In addition, North African prisoners were the primary targets of German propaganda, and for this reason Vichy also tended to give special attention to them.[57] Ethnic tensions, created through inequities and exacerbated by allegations of corruption, were a significant part of the prisoner experience. They likely led to crimes against other prisoners, but I was unable to pursue research on judicial cases in the *Frontstalags*, for the French National Archives denied access to files that might contain more material on this topic and offer a fuller picture of ethnic tensions in the camps.[58]

By the time of their liberation, most colonial prisoners probably felt alienated by the Vichy authorities and desperate to go home. Unfortunately, the treatment of colonial soldiers by the new provisional government under de Gaulle further alienated them from the French state. For several months, most former prisoners remained in military camps, sometimes in the same places where they had been under the Germans. Whereas the colonial soldiers had worked for a small salary in the *Frontstalags*, they were now

---

[55] Inspection Frontstalag 194, Camp de Nancy, by Captain Jean Detroyat, January 23, 1942, F9:2354, AN, Paris; Directeur du cabinet to Mr. Paillette, December 7, 1943, F9:2276, AN, Paris.

[56] For a specific case involving Frontstalag 221 (St. Médard), see Dr. Bonnaud to Cmdt. Bouret, Comité d'Assistance aux Troupes Noires, Paris, May 21, 1942, F9:2356, AN, Paris. See also the report by Léopold Sédar Senghor on his captivity experience that I identified and published: "Senghor: Le manuscrit inconnu," *Jeune Afrique*, July 24, 2011, 22–31.

[57] Thomas, "The Vichy government and French colonial prisoners of war," 658.

[58] Martine de Boisdeffre (Direction des Archives de France) to author, September 21, 2006. The files relating to judicial cases are F9:2560 and F9:2561, AN, Paris.

idle and without income. Supplies and hygienic conditions in some camps induced ex-prisoners to compare their postliberation existence negatively to their time under the Germans.[59] Some ex-prisoners began to drink and became unruly and violent. One of the first confrontations happened near Trévé in Brittany in November 1944 when disputes over pay between West African ex-prisoners and state officials turned violent. The police opened fire and severely wounded six soldiers. Then the ex-prisoners had to march to a heavily guarded camp surrounded by barbed wire. A Senegalese corporal wrote to his *marraine de guerre*: "Now it is France that hurts me by locking me up behind this barbed wire and without food.... After four years of suffering at the hands of the Germans, now it is France that makes of us prisoners of war for the second time."[60] A few weeks later, some of these ex-prisoners arrived in the camp of Thiaroye outside Dakar, Senegal, where they rebelled when once again they did not receive the promised payments. The local French commander sent in army units, killing at least thirty-five ex-prisoners. In their analyses of the reasons for the rebellion, the French authorities concluded that ex-prisoners had lost their respect for the French colonial order due to German propaganda as well as their relatively good treatment by the Germans and their close relations with French civilians, in particular women. Many rebels had taunted the officers by mentioning the French defeat of 1940 and by boasting of their "success" with French women.[61]

The situation in the repatriation camps in France remained explosive. On December 15, 1944, a rebellion occurred in Versailles, where nearly 2,000 North African and West African ex-prisoners were stationed. A group of ex-prisoners attacked the local police station, took eighteen hostages, and demanded the release of three comrades who had been arrested by the police during a brawl. After a firefight between ex-prisoners and police reinforcements, the French authorities agreed to free the arrested soldiers. The war ministry rapidly sent the units implicated in the revolt home and ordered strict secrecy about the event.[62] In May 1945, in a typical incident, a drunken Algerian ex-prisoner approached a French woman, which triggered a hostile

---

[59] For example, see Lahsen Ben Mohammed to ministère des PG et déportés, service colonial," November 20, 1944, F9:3815, AN, Paris.

[60] Corporal Charles Poutraka (12 RTS) to Mademoiselle Beauvoir, November 13, 1944, F9:3815, AN, Paris.

[61] "Synthèse concernant la propagande et les influences auxquelles ont été soumis les ex-prisonniers (annexe au rapport du Général de Perier)," 5H16, SHD, Vincennes. See also the reports of Lieutenant Le Berre, chef de batallion Le Treut, and Colonel Le Masle in the same box. For similar concerns about the impact of the defeat of 1940 and relationships with white women on discharged veterans, see Ruth Ginio's contribution in this volume.

[62] "Rapport du Chef d'Escadron Martin-Maurice, Cmdt, la Légion de Seine-et-Oise, sur les incidents qui se sont déroulés à Versailles le 15 décembre 1944 entre les militaires indigènes et la Gendarmerie," R/2 023 443, Archives de la Gendarmerie nationale (hereafter AGN), Vincennes; Lieutenant A. Bouker to Service des PG, December 16, 1944, F9:3815, AN,

intervention by two men. A fistfight broke out in front of a growing crowd of civilians and Algerian soldiers from a repatriation camp. A policeman appeared and tried to hold down the ex-prisoner, which led an Algerian officer to yell at the policeman: "You would not have done this to a *Boche* [derogatory term for German], you dirty Frenchman." A battle between the crowd and the Algerian soldiers was avoided only because the policeman let go of the soldier and the Algerian officer calmed down his comrades who were watching the scene with increasing anger.[63] In August 1945, West African soldiers in the camps of Saint Raphaël and Fréjus became impatient with the slow pace of repatriation and the miserable conditions in the camps. After a brawl between some soldiers and police, between 500 and 600 West Africans occupied several buildings in Saint Raphaël and opened a battle with the police during which four people were killed and many more wounded. Again, the French authorities blamed the riot on the Germans, whose good treatment of the colonial POWs had allegedly undermined their loyalty to France and made their present condition appear unsatisfactory.[64] In short, the repatriation of colonial ex-prisoners was a process full of frustration and conflict that often cast a rosy glaze on the *Frontstalag* experience.

The Free French government may have been overwhelmed by the problem of supporting and repatriating so many ex-prisoners, but it is also clear that it considered the large presence of African soldiers in France as an embarrassment. Free French, British, and American commanders, for example, all agreed that black French troops should stay in the background during the liberation of Paris in August 1944.[65] Moreover, the French war ministry in May 1945 seriously considered a proposal by the director of the Free French colonial troops to deport all mixed-race couples involving colonial ex-prisoners to the highlands of Madagascar so that they would not destabilize French society and "spoil" the French race.[66]

In conclusion, the experience of African POWs in German camps led to a strong disaffection of the prisoners from France. The prisoners did not perceive much difference between Nazi Germany and Vichy with respect to

---

Paris. See also Godechot, "Prélude aux rébellions," and Fargettas, "La révolte des tirailleurs sénégalais."

[63] Testimonies of Bouahadjar Roched, Corporal Ahmed Zeghdoud, Gilbert Bastide, and Jean Le Gall, Brigade de Vernon, 27 E 1955, AGN, Vincennes.

[64] Rapport Lt.-Colonel QUENARD to Mr. le Ministre de la Guerre, Paris, August 31, 1945, 6P6, SHD, Vincennes. See also "Six cents Sénégalais provoquent à Saint-Raphaël des bagarres meurtrières," *Combat*, August 21, 1945, F9:3815, AN, Paris.

[65] BBC 4 broadcast, April 6, 2009; www.bbc.co.uk/programmes/boojhp5d#synopsis (last visited on July 25, 2013). The information is based on Olivier Wieviorka, *Normandy: The Landings to the Liberation of Paris*, trans. M. B. DeBevoise (Cambridge, MA: Belknap Press of Harvard University Press, 2008), 314–15.

[66] Ministère de la guerre, Direction des Troupes coloniales, May 2, 1945, 6P6, SHD, Vincennes.

discrimination or much difference either between Vichy and Gaullist officials. Experiences in the *Frontstalags* and after liberation tended to confirm the feeling of being a second-class soldier and member of the French empire. The Vichy government, hoping to use one concession as a wedge for the next one, accepted to play by the racist categories of Nazi Germany instead of insisting on a color-blind solidarity of French soldiers. Racist discrimination of colonial prisoners with French citizenship cast doubt on the vision of equality promoted by defenders of the French empire and its colonial residents. Moreover, the frustrations that the prisoners experienced with liberation, repatriation, and payments made the time in the *Frontstalags*, or "under the Germans," as the ex-prisoners used to say, appear rosier than it actually had been. The situation in the *Frontstalags* would have been far worse had it not been for the generous support of the Vichy authorities, the many private or semiofficial support organizations, and French civilians, but ex-prisoners did not recognize the contributions of the Vichy authorities, all the more so since the Vichy government was discredited and no longer in power. The experiences of African soldiers with the French authorities appeared more frustrating in light of the relatively friendly and respectful treatment of the colonial prisoners by French civilians.

The disaffection from the French state and the idea of the French empire brought about by the *Frontstalag* experience likely helped to undermine the stability and viability of the French empire.[67] The involvement of former POWs in independence movements makes this connection plausible. Nazi propaganda failed in forging new ties between Muslim North Africans and Nazi Germany, but it helped to discredit the French and British as colonial powers in Africa. Nonetheless, the path from the *Frontstalag* experience to the independence movements was not a straight one. As Gregory Mann has shown with respect to veterans from Mali, returning soldiers did not always receive respect and admiration, particularly from those people who advocated independence and blamed the veterans for having helped the colonial power. Veterans also were somewhat dependent on a network of French state patronage that kept paying their pensions and organized meeting centers and mutual help societies for them. They returned to an ambiguous social space as nationalism came to dominate the post-war period.[68]

---

[67] This is the argument in Echenberg, *Colonial Conscripts*; Lawler, *Soldiers of Misfortune*, Chapter 9; and Thomas, "Vichy government and French colonial prisoners of war."

[68] Gregory Mann, *Native Sons: West African Veterans and France in the Twentieth Century* (Durham, NC, and London: Duke University Press, 2006). David Killingray, in his work on African soldiers in British service during World War II, comes to a similar conclusion. See David Killingray, *Fighting for Britain: African Soldiers in the Second World War* (Woodbridge and Rochester: James Currey, 2010), 2.

SIX

WORLD WAR II AND ANTICOLONIALISM

23

Popular Resistance and Anticolonial Mobilization

The War Effort in French Guinea

Elizabeth Schmidt

This chapter focuses on the Second World War and its impact on the French West African territory of Guinea (Figure 23.1), where the war effort and experiences of war inspired the anticolonial agitation that ultimately led to Guinea's independence in 1958. These events played out in the context of a divided France. Following Germany's invasion of France in May 1940 and its victory on the battlefield in June, three-fifths of France was occupied by the Nazis, while a collaborationist regime headquartered in Vichy controlled the rest. A substantial number of French citizens refused to recognize the legitimacy of the Vichy regime. Some resisted Nazi occupation in a broad-based underground movement; others swore allegiance to the Free French government-in-exile and continued to fight the Axis powers on the battlefield. Throughout the French empire, imperial subjects made enormous contributions to the French war effort serving both Vichy and the Free French. African populations played a critical role, contributing labor, resources, and lives. At the historic January 1944 Brazzaville Conference in the French Congo, Free French president General Charles de Gaulle stressed the importance of Africa in sustaining France during the war: "Up to the present, it has been largely an African war," he declared. "The absolute and relative importance of African resources, communications and contingents has become apparent in the harsh light of the theatres of operations."[1]

---

[1] Quoted in Jean Suret-Canale, *French Colonialism in Tropical Africa: 1900–1945* (New York: Pica Press, 1971), 485. See also Charles de Gaulle, *The War Memoirs of Charles de Gaulle: Unity, 1942–1944* (New York: Simon and Schuster, 1959), 208.

I owe a great debt to participants in various workshops and panels for their invaluable comments on earlier drafts of this chapter: "Re-evaluating Africa and World War II," Rutgers University, March 27–30, 2008; the American Historical Association, January 4, 2009; Cornell University, September 17–19, 2009; and the African History and Anthropology Workshop, University of Michigan, March 26, 2009. I am also grateful to the editors of this volume and to anonymous readers for Cambridge University Press for their insights and suggestions.

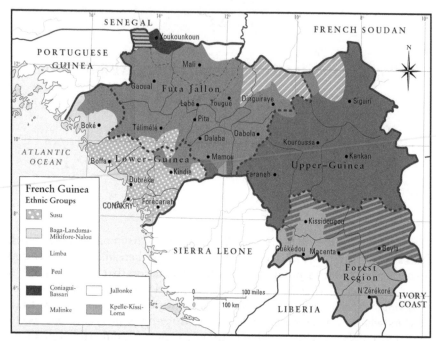

FIGURE 23.1. Map of French Guinea. Cartographer: Malcolm Swanston. Reprinted by permission from *Mobilizing the Masses: Gender, Ethnicity, and Class in the Nationalist Movement in Guinea, 1939–1958,* by Elizabeth Schmidt. Copyright 2005 by Elizabeth Schmidt. Published by Heinemann, a division of Reed Elsevier, Inc., Portsmouth NH. All rights reserved.

Although this claim was made more than a half century ago, there has been surprisingly little investigation of the contributions of African societies to the French war effort, the impact of the Second World War on African populations, and the implications of wartime experiences for postwar anticolonial agitation.[2] Military veterans have been an exception to this generalization. Since the 1960s, many scholars have argued that African soldiers were radicalized by their wartime experiences, were exposed to new

[2] In the war's aftermath, de Gaulle downplayed Africa's critical role in the war effort, convinced that France needed to retain its empire to resume its great power status. His three-volume war memoirs make only passing reference to the presence of sub-Saharan African troops in the war theaters. Their role in the defense and liberation of France and the role of the African home front are not mentioned. See Charles de Gaulle, *War Memoirs: The Call to Honour, 1940–1942* (New York: The Viking Press, 1955), 106–107, 111, 132, 136; *The War Memoirs of Charles de Gaulle: Unity, 1942–1944* (New York: Simon and Schuster, 1959), 35, 110–112, 164, 205–206, 208, 277, 322; *The War Memoirs of Charles de Gaulle: Salvation, 1944–1946* (New York: Simon and Schuster, 1960), 32, 36, 38. An exception to the scholarly neglect of the African home front is David Killingray and Richard Rathbone's edited collection, *Africa and the Second World War* (New York: St. Martin's Press, 1986). Focusing on military conscription, forced labor, and crop requisitions, this collection fills an

ideas, formed relatively egalitarian bonds with European soldiers and civilians, and witnessed the weaknesses of imperial powers. After the war, they demanded compensation for their sacrifices, which they translated into political, economic, and social terms. Some veterans' movements sought colonial reforms; others cast their lot with political parties that ultimately aspired to national independence.[3] More recent scholarship has begun to focus on the African home front. Ruth Ginio has explored the economic impact of Vichy rule on African societies and the wartime protests of religious leaders and demobilized soldiers. Catherine Bogosian Ash has examined French Soudan's conscripted labor army (the second portion of the military contingent) and demonstrated how labor recruits invoked the language of rights and citizenship in the postwar period. Alexandra Jacobs has analyzed popular resistance to canton chiefs in Upper Volta, where rural constituents, often led by military veterans, protested wartime taxes, military recruitment, and labor demands. Nancy Lawler and I have drawn connections between wartime experiences on the home front and postwar anticolonial activities.[4]

important gap in the literature; however, it concentrates almost exclusively on the British colonies.

[3] For British Africa, see Dennis Austin, *Politics in Ghana, 1946–1960* (New York: Oxford University Press, 1964), 73–77; Okete J. E. Shiroya, "The Impact of World War II in Kenya: The role of ex-servicemen in Kenyan nationalism, Ph.D. dissertation, Michigan State University (1968); Eugene P. A. Schleh, "The post-war careers of ex-servicemen in Ghana and Uganda," *Journal of Modern African Studies*, 6 (1968), 203–20; G. O. Olusanya, "The role of ex-servicemen in Nigerian politics," *Journal of Modern African Studies*, 6 (1968), 221–32; David Killingray, "Soldiers, ex-servicemen, and politics in the Gold Coast, 1939–50," *Journal of Modern African Studies*, 21 (1983), 523–34; Adrienne M. Israel, "Measuring the war experience: Ghanaian soldiers in World War II," *Journal of Modern African Studies*, 25 (1987), 159–68; Adrienne M. Israel, "Ex-servicemen at the crossroads: Protest and politics in post-war Ghana," *Journal of Modern African Studies*, 30 (1992), 359–68; Geoffrey I. Nwaka, "Rebellion in Umuahia, 1950–1951: Ex-servicemen and anti-Colonial protest in eastern Nigeria," *Transafrican Journal of History*, 16 (1987), 47–62; Timothy H. Parsons, *The African Rank-and-File: Social Implications of Colonial Military Service in the King's African Rifles, 1902–1964* (Portsmouth, NH: Heinemann, 1999); and David Killingray with Martin Plaut, *Fighting for Britain: African Soldiers in the Second World War* (Woodbridge: James Currey, 2010). For French Africa, see Myron Echenberg, *Colonial Conscripts: The Tirailleurs Sénégalais in French West Africa, 1857–1960* (Portsmouth, NH: Heinemann, 1991); Nancy Ellen Lawler, *Soldiers of Misfortune: Ivoirien Tirailleurs of World War II* (Athens: Ohio University Press, 1992); and Gregory Mann, *Native Sons: West African Veterans and France in the Twentieth Century* (Durham, NC: Duke University Press, 2006).

[4] Ruth Ginio, *French Colonialism Unmasked: The Vichy Years in French West Africa* (Lincoln: University of Nebraska Press, 2006); Catherine Mornane Bogosian, "Forced labor, resistance and memory: The deuxième portion in the French Soudan, 1926–1950," PhD dissertation, University of Pennsylvania (2002), 189–218, and Catherine Bogosian Ash, Chapter 6, this volume; Alexandra Maria Jacobs, "La question des chefs: Canton chiefs, contested authority, and rebellion in colonial Upper Volta, 1934–1946," B.A. honors thesis, Harvard University (2008); Nancy Lawler, "Reform and repression under the Free French: Economic and political transformation in the Côte d'Ivoire, 1942–45," *Africa*, 60 (1990), 88–110; and Elizabeth Schmidt, *Mobilizing the Masses: Gender, Ethnicity, and Class in the Nationalist*

Focusing on Guinea, one of eight French West African territories, this chapter investigates the impact of the war effort on the communities the soldiers left behind. It examines the effects of military conscription, the emergence of widespread resistance to state demands, and the harnessing of local discontent to a broad-based anticolonial movement in the postwar period. In the colonies, mobilization for the war effort was not voluntary. The colonial state imposed stringent demands on the indigenous populations, hitting rural populations especially hard. The wartime burden of military conscription, forced labor, and crop requisitions, compounded by extreme shortages and inflation, generated immense popular hostility toward the colonial state. Rural cultivators, finding it increasingly difficult to provide for their families, resisted the onerous labor and crop exactions. Forced laborers, embittered by poor pay and working conditions, deserted their work sites in droves. Whole villages absconded across territorial boundaries to avoid military and labor recruiters. Military veterans, who returned home with a new sense of confidence and entitlement, took the lead in articulating rural grievances. This chapter demonstrates the ways in which wartime exactions, imposed by government-appointed chiefs, sparked widespread resistance, laying the groundwork for rural rejection of chiefly authority in the postwar period and, by extension, and colonial rule more generally.

This case study makes three contributions toward a new understanding of Africa and the Second World War. First, it reperiodizes the war. In French West Africa (FWA), the war began in 1939, but it did not end in 1945. It continued for another decade, as labor conscripts and military veterans agitated for rights, wages, and benefits resulting from their wartime services. The war finally ended in 1955, when veterans' demands had largely been accommodated. By that time, however, anticolonial protests that began during the war had taken on a life of their own, as new demands and grievances propelled them onward. Moreover, the phases of the war differed for Africans and Europeans. For Africans, the significant events occurred in 1939, when the war effort was launched and intensified demands were made for military and labor conscripts and requisitioned crops; 1940, when African soldiers were demobilized after the fall of France; 1942, when the colonial administration in FWA transferred its allegiance from Vichy to the Free French, and even greater burdens were imposed on the local populations; 1944, when African soldiers were again demobilized following the liberation of France; 1950, when the Equality Law was passed, mandating an unprecedented degree of parity in the treatment of French and African veterans, and the conscripted labor army was officially abolished; and 1955, when veterans' demands were finally met.

Movement in Guinea, 1939–1958 (Portsmouth, NH: Heinemann, 2005). For the home front in British colonies, see John Iliffe, *A Modern History of Tanganyika* (New York: Cambridge University Press, 1979), 436–484; and Ashley Jackson, *Botswana, 1939–1945: An African Country at War* (New York: Oxford University Press, 1999), 121–213.

Second, this study reevaluates the privileging of West African veterans as the instigators of postwar anticolonial protests. Clearly, the veterans' role in political agitation was significant in some colonies; however, returning soldiers also gained special prominence as a result of their greater visibility and emotional appeal.[5] They were war heroes who had given their blood for France, and their cause was quickly embraced by African politicians. They engaged in highly visible urban protests that captured the attention of the public and the administration. They had a public voice and left records in the form of letters, newspaper articles, and testimonies to government commissions. Their stories have been more accessible than those of other participants in anticolonial movements and, as a result, have carried greater weight. In postwar Guinea, military veterans were important actors on the home front. They often assumed leadership roles, but they did not "educate" the rural populace or instigate rural resistance. Rather they took the lead in ongoing protests against the chiefs and the burdens imposed by the war effort. This chapter highlights the roles of the "silent" people on the home front, whose protests during the war laid the groundwork for postwar anticolonial activities.

Third, this study reperiodizes the "postwar" nationalist movements. It argues that the anticolonial agitation from which the independence movements emerged was not a postwar phenomenon. Rather, labor unrest and resistance to the chiefs, who enforced colonial demands for taxes, labor, and military recruits, all began during the war.

Military Conscription

Military conscription and the wartime experiences of African soldiers were important factors in the evolution of Guinea's postwar anticolonial

---

[5] Although scholars generally agree that West African veterans were key players in postwar agitation for social and economic rights, considerable debate surrounds their role in nationalist movements. Olusanya and Killingray argue that veterans, as an identifiable group, did not play a significant role in postwar Nigerian or Gold Coast politics, despite their early protests concerning postwar conditions. Israel, in contrast, contends that Gold Coast ex-servicemen played important roles in postwar anticolonial protests, which ignited nationalist mobilization. Killingray and Plaut maintain that most returning British African veterans, though angered by their poor treatment, were primarily concerned with claiming a better place in colonial society. It was African intellectuals, rather than the military rank-and-file, who attempted to harness soldiers' grievances to the nationalist cause. Lawler, in contrast, describes Ivory Coast veterans joining the Ivorian branch of the RDA in large numbers, while Echenberg shows how the loyalties of French West African veterans changed as the French government strove to win their allegiance. In the French Soudan, Mann argues, African veterans were courted by the RDA, and most were won over by government efforts to meet their demands. Olusanya, "Role of ex-servicemen in Nigerian politics"; Killingray, "Soldiers, ex-servicemen, and politics in the Gold Coast"; Israel, "Ex-servicemen at the crossroads"; Killingray and Plaut, *Fighting for Britain*, 203–35; Lawler, *Soldiers of Misfortune*, 203–30; Echenberg, *Colonial Conscripts*, 146–63; Mann, *Native Sons*, 116–45.

movement. Since the passage of the Conscription Law of 1919, all male subjects of the French empire were obliged to serve three years of military service. Every year from January to March, a mobile draft board moved through each of Guinea's nineteen administrative circles, inspecting and registering recruits. During the Second World War, an estimated 18,000 to 20,000 Guinean men from a population of some two million were forcibly recruited into the French armed forces, while another 38,153 were assigned to the second portion of the military contingent, building and maintaining railroads, airfields, ports, and roads. Under threat of sanctions, canton chiefs were required to provide the stipulated number of conscripts.[6]

Taking their place among hundreds of thousands of recruits from across the empire, French West African soldiers (Tirailleurs Sénégalais) played a major role in the French armed forces. Some 250,000 to 350,000 were drafted during the Second World War, and an estimated 20,000 to 25,000 died. They served France before its fall in 1940 and subsequently fought for both Vichy and the Free French. They were engaged in operations in Europe, North Africa, and the Middle East, and the vast majority served in the infantry. Although the French High Command denied that African troops were put at greater risk to preserve French lives, Africans were often on the front lines and covered the retreat of French soldiers. In 1940, Africans constituted nearly 9 percent of the French army serving in France. In the spring of that year, the forces that attempted to hold the line against the German onslaught included large numbers of French West African troops in five colonial infantry divisions. In the final days of May, French West African troops protected the retreating French and British forces as they made their way to the beaches of Dunkirk for evacuation to Britain. Other Tirailleurs fought on in central France, along the Loire River, and in Lyon. In late June, the Battle of France ended with a French surrender. At least 3,000 French West African soldiers were executed by Germans after their capture; another 48,000 were taken prisoner, including 9,000 from Guinea. Conditions in the prison camps were treacherous, and thousands of African prisoners of war died in captivity. Some were massacred in the camps. Others died of hunger, malnutrition, cold, and disease, especially tuberculosis, pneumonia,

[6] Rapport politique annuel, 1941, 2G41/21; Rapport politique annuel, 1942, 2G42/22; Rapport politique annuel, 1943, 2G43/19; Rapport sur le travail et la main d'œuvre de la Guinée Française pendant l'année 1943, Conakry, July 24, 1944, #994/IT, 2G43/25; Rapport sur le travail et la main d'œuvre de la Guinée française pendant l'année 1944, Conakry, 2G44/30; Rapport politique annuel, 1947, 2G47/22; Rapport général d'activité 1947–1950, présenté par Mamadou Madéïra Kéïta, secrétaire général du PDG au premier congrès territorial du Parti Démocratique de Guinée (section Guinéenne du Rassemblement Démocratique Africain), Conakry, October 15–18, 1950, #271/APA, 17G573, Archives Nationales du Sénégal (hereafter ANS), Dakar; Echenberg, *Colonial Conscripts*, 50–54, 83–84; Sidiki Kobélé Kéïta, *Le P.D.G.: Artisan de l'indépendance nationale en Guinée (1947–1958)* (Conakry: INRDG, Bibliothèque Nationale, 1978), vol. 1, 96.

and other pulmonary illnesses. Thousands of other African soldiers were repatriated. These veterans were among the first to experience, and protest, disparate and discriminatory treatment.[7]

In late 1940, disturbances broke out among military veterans in Kankan and Kindia in Guinea, and in other French West African territories. These incidents foreshadowed others that would follow French liberation, most notably the Thiaroye uprising of December 1944, in which 1,280 demobilized soldiers were harshly repressed by colonial soldiers and police. In the 1940 Kindia case, African soldiers who were not imprisoned after the fall of France were scheduled for repatriation. Before leaving the European mainland, they were informed that they would receive their back pay in metropolitan francs in Dakar as well as any accrued savings and demobilization bonuses. In Dakar, however, Guinean soldiers were told that their money awaited them in Conakry. In Guinea's capital, the governor promised that they would be paid by the circle commandants in their home districts. Not surprisingly, when the men reached the Kindia barracks, a few hours inland from Conakry, they were on edge. When the Kindia circle commandant also failed to pay them, hundreds of angry soldiers attacked him and overran the town. Other colonial troops, as well as civilian police, were called in to put down the disturbance. One Tirailleur died, another was wounded, and 335 were arrested. Thirty-one received prison sentences of five to twenty years "for 'outrages' against a superior officer."[8]

Despite the demobilization of 1940, the war was not over for African soldiers. After the French defeat, General de Gaulle rallied the Free French, assembled an army, and continued the struggle. While French Equatorial Africa (FEA) joined the Free French, French West Africa remained under Vichy authority until the end of 1942, when it switched sides. Military conscription continued under both regimes, although it was significantly heavier under the Free French. From the fall of France in June 1940 until

---

[7] Lawler, *Soldiers of Misfortune*, 28–29, 75–81, 88, 93–114, 118; Echenberg, *Colonial Conscripts*, 88, 96, 97, 193 n. 40; Myron Echenberg, "'Morts pour la France': The African soldier in France during the Second World War," *Journal of African History*, 26 (1985), 364–65, 364 n. 6, 367–72; Alistair Horne, *To Lose a Battle: France 1940* (Boston: Little, Brown and Co., 1969), 549, 551, 554, 557; Raffael Scheck, *Hitler's African Victims: The German Army Massacres of Black French Soldiers in 1940* (New York: Cambridge University Press, 2006), 17–60; and Scheck, Chapter 22, in this volume. Some scholars using French archival materials contend that approximately half of all African prisoners of war died in captivity. Scheck, who has supplemented these sources with German ones, argues that 5% of French colonial prisoners, including Africans, died in the camps. Raffael Scheck, "French Colonial Soldiers in German Prisoner-of-War Camps (1940–1945)," *French History*, vol. 24, no. 3 (2010): 420–46.

[8] Myron J. Echenberg, "Tragedy at Thiaroye: The Senegalese soldiers' uprising of 1944," in Peter C. W. Gutkind, Robin Cohen, and Jean Copans (eds.), *African Labor History* (Beverly Hills, CA: Sage Publications, 1978), 112–13; Ginio, *French Colonialism Unmasked*, 126; Mann, *Native Sons*, 109, 114–15.

its liberation in the summer of 1944, French West and Equatorial African soldiers constituted the most important elements of the Free French forces. Tirailleurs Sénégalais helped to defeat Italian and German troops in North Africa from 1940 to 1943. They joined Allied forces in the invasion of Italy in the summer of 1943 and southern France in August 1944. The 20,000 African soldiers who participated in the landings in southern France constituted 20 percent of Free France's First Army. In the fall of 1944, Tirailleurs helped to liberate Toulon, Marseilles, the Rhone River valley, and Lyon.[9]

By the end of 1944, France had been freed from German occupation. While French soldiers celebrated with their countrymen, tens of thousands of African troops, including recently freed prisoners of war, were herded into prison-like camps in central and southern France. Food, shelter, and clothing were miserably inadequate, and the situation was worsened by the confiscation of uniforms. Whereas French soldiers were given back pay and discharged, African soldiers waited for months in transit camps, where they were denied their wages and subjected to tough military discipline. According to Myron Echenberg, forced labor was routine, with former prisoners exchanging German "stalags for French military camps; hard labor in the German war industry for construction work under French military supervision." Adhering to the stipulations of the 1929 Geneva Convention on the treatment of prisoners of war, the Germans had paid African workers minimal wages, but the French authorities continued to deny them the back pay owed for the period of their imprisonment.[10]

As in 1940, miserable conditions and discriminatory treatment led to a number of incidents, fifteen of which have been recorded. Grievances focused on inadequate food, clothing, and shelter, and failure to receive back pay, demobilization premiums, and prisoner of war hardship bonuses similar to those of their French counterparts. Reports of unrest aboard Africa-bound troop ships deeply concerned French authorities. To avoid a large concentration of indignant soldiers in Dakar, Free French Commissioner for the Colonies René Pleven ordered the French West African governor-general to repatriate the returning troops as quickly as possible, warning that "the [former] prisoners of war may be a factor in stirring up discontent among the people."[11]

---

[9] Lawler, *Soldiers of Misfortune*, 93, 149, 154–55, 168, 171–78; de Gaulle, *War Memoirs*, vol. 1: 83–84, 88–94; vol. 2: 67, 110–11, 152, 322–23; vol. 3: 11–13, 36, 151–52; Echenberg, *Colonial Conscripts*, 87–88, 98; Echenberg, "Morts pour la France," 364, 374; Suret-Canale, *French Colonialism*, 469.

[10] Quote from Echenberg, "Tragedy at Thiaroye," 113–14. See also Echenberg, *Colonial Conscripts*, 97–99; Echenberg, "Morts pour la France," 372–74; Lawler, *Soldiers of Misfortune*, 104, 108, 193–94, 196.

[11] Quoted in Lawler, *Soldiers of Misfortune*, 194.

Indeed, the wartime experiences of the Tirailleurs Sénégalais had a strong impact on the veterans' later political development.[12] Many had their first taste of integration when African and metropolitan companies were combined to form Régiments d'Infanterie Coloniale Mixtes Sénégalais. African soldiers had lived and fought side by side with Frenchmen, experiencing a semblance of equality in combat that was unthinkable at home. Their experience with French civilians had further leveling effects. Accustomed to a highly stratified and segregated colonial society, Africans found that in the metropole, French people were generally hospitable and welcoming. They provided African soldiers with food, clothing, and entertainment and invited them into their homes. African soldiers drank and conversed with Frenchmen in local cafes. Some even found French girlfriends and wives. Many African soldiers believed they had fought more courageously than their French counterparts, and the magnitude of their sacrifices inspired many of their postwar demands for official recognition and just compensation. Despite their sacrifices, African soldiers suffered from degrading and discriminatory treatment on their return home, underscoring the point that while they had fought to liberate France, they themselves were not free. Moreover, having witnessed French defeat, they had learned that the imperial power was indeed vulnerable. These lessons had important ramifications for their subsequent involvement in the postwar anticolonial movement.

Crop Requisitions

Wartime military recruitment had a major impact on life in the rural areas, as well as on the men conscripted from the countryside. The draft removed large numbers of able-bodied young men from the rural areas, seriously affecting economic production. Thousands of conscripts died. Many who returned were severely disabled. Others came home with infectious pulmonary ailments or venereal disease. In conjunction with military conscription, African civilians were subjected to a harsh system of forced labor, working for a united France until its defeat in June 1940, for the Vichy government through November 1942, and for the Free French until the war's official end in 1945. Under all three regimes, civilians were compelled to collect or cultivate crops considered crucial to the war effort. If state-imposed quotas were not met, chiefs were sanctioned with dismissal, imprisonment, or even the abolition of their cantons. As a result, chiefs exerted extreme pressure on their subjects, forcing them to comply with government demands. Providing for the urban populations of Guinea and France as well as the military, men and women in the countryside were forced to intensify their agricultural production. They were taxed in rice, millet, fonio, and maize, as well as

---

[12] The following discussion summarizes the findings of Echenberg, Lawler, and Mann.

beef, potatoes, fruits, vegetables, honey, pepper, coffee, and tobacco. They furnished wild rubber, wax, cotton, sisal, and indigo, as well as vast quantities of oil-producing plants for fuel, lubricants for military and industrial use, cooking, and soap production.[13]

French West Africa's shift in allegiance from Vichy to the Free French in late 1942 brought no relief. To meet the needs of the growing war effort, the Free French governor-general of FWA called for the "intensification of production of vegetable oils, rubber and all products useful for the war."[14] Under Free French authority, quotas for rubber, food crops, and military and civilian labor increased dramatically. Rubber production in Guinea grew from 944 tons in 1942 to 1,323 tons in 1943. Likewise, the production of oil-bearing palm kernels increased from 7,131 tons in 1942 to 17,000 tons in 1943. Rice production rose from 2,000 tons in 1942 to 13,474 tons in 1943. The same year, Guinea shipped 200 tons of sisal for the manufacture of rope and sacks to the Allies. If the desired products were unavailable locally, rural dwellers were forced to meet their quotas with overpriced goods purchased on the black market. In 1941, under Vichy authority, Kissidougou circle furnished nine tons of rubber to the state, most of it purchased outside the circle. The residents of Dialakoro canton rendered 566 kilos of rubber, 476 kilos of which had been purchased elsewhere. Similarly, the people of Tinki canton were forced to buy 345 of 360 kilos of rubber that were delivered to the government.[15] In 1943, under the Free French, Jacques Richard-Molard wrote,

> One *cercle* is required to produce so many tons of liana rubber, even though there is no liana in their territory. The native is therefore forced to travel on foot, sometimes very far, to buy rubber elsewhere, regardless of cost, in order to escape the hand of "justice." He must sell this to the commandant at the official price, which is many times lower than the purchase price. Another *cercle* is

[13] Rapport politique annuel, 1941, 2G41/21; Rapport politique annuel, 1942, 2G42/22; Rapport politique Annuel, 1943, 2G43/19; Rapport politique annuel, 1947, 2G47/22; Rapport général d'activité 1947–1950, PDG, October 15–18, 1950, 17G573, ANS, Dakar; Echenberg, *Colonial Conscripts*, 84, 88; Virginia Thompson and Richard Adloff, *French West Africa* (New York: Greenwood Press, 1969), 227, 314, 316, 386, 388, 390; Frederick Cooper, *Decolonization and African Society: The Labor Question in French and British Africa* (New York: Cambridge University Press, 1996), 159; Jacques Richard-Molard, *Afrique Occidentale Française* (Paris: Éditions Berger-Levrault, 1952), 65–168; Suret-Canale, *French Colonialism*, 462, 477–79, 481–82; Jean Suret-Canale," La fin de la chefferie en Guinée," *Journal of African History*, 7 (1966), 472–75.

[14] FWA Governor-General Pierre Cournarie, quoted in Cooper, *Decolonization and African Society*, 159.

[15] Rapport politique annuel, 1943, 2G43/19, ANS, Dakar; Suret-Canale, *French Colonialism*, 476, 480; Suret-Canale, "Fin de la chefferie en Guinée," 472–73; Kéïta, *P.D.G.*, vol. 1, 144–45; Richard-Molard, *Afrique Occidentale Française*, 166; Lawler, *Soldiers of Misfortune*, 207; Thompson and Adloff, *French West Africa*, 29.

taxed in honey. None is produced there. The commandant is punished for telegraphing his government: "AGREE TO HONEY. STOP. SEND BEES."[16]

Forced to abandon their own fields to produce commodities for the state, rural people suffered nutritional deficits. Food rationing was introduced, and in some regions, famine occurred. During the first year of Free French rule, nearly all the rice produced in Guinea was designated for export. Despite the local shortage of beef, 8,400 head of cattle were exported to Sierra Leone for consumption by Allied soldiers and civilians working in the port of Freetown. Less labor intensive – and less nutritious – crops were consumed locally, while the more desirable crops were requisitioned for the war effort.[17]

Forced Labor

Mandatory crop production was supplemented by other forms of forced labor. With consumer goods in short supply, Africans had little incentive to volunteer for wage labor. Faced with a growing labor crisis in both the public and private sectors, the colonial administration resorted to compulsion. Once again, chiefs were expected to provide the requisite number of "volunteers." During the war years, tens of thousands of able-bodied men and women were taken from their homes and forced to work as the state saw fit. During the last year of Vichy rule (1942), Kouroussa circle provided "490 labourers for the Conakry-Niger railway line (tree-felling at Nono and Tamba); 80 labourers for the Baro plantation (Kankan circle); 80 labourers for the Delsol plantation; 15 labourers for the African Banana plantation; 40 labourers for the Linkeny banana plantations; 200 labourers for public works at Kankan; 100 labourers for charcoal burning at Conakry; 100 labourers for road-repair work – making a total of 1,105."[18]

During the first year of the Free French regime (1943), more than 20,000 Guineans were compelled to engage in forced labor on behalf of European interests. Men were forced to cut and haul wood to fuel the Conakry-Niger railway. Men and women built roads, labored on European-owned coffee and banana plantations, and toiled in the fields of colonial officials, while tens of thousands of Guinean men were sent to work in the peanut fields of Senegal. Thousands of men were substituted for motorized vehicles when severe shortages of coal and gasoline resulted in the reintroduction

[16] Quoted in Ruth Schachter Morgenthau, *Political Parties in French-Speaking West Africa* (Oxford: Clarendon Press, 1964), 9.
[17] Rapport politique annuel, 1941, 2G41/21; Rapport politique annuel, 1943, 2G43/19; Rapport sur le Travail...1944, 2G44/30; Rapport sur le Travail...1945, 2G45/21, ANS, Dakar. For Freetown's role in the war, see Howard, Chapter 10, this volume.
[18] Kouroussa Archives, Political Reports, August 25, 1942, quoted in Suret-Canale, *French Colonialism in Tropical Africa*, 472.

of head portage. The amount of labor needed to transport export goods was enormous. For instance, 600 workers had to walk for twelve days to transport one ton of rice to a railway station 300 kilometers from their home.[19]

Taxed in food, which depleted their own reserves, and labor, which hindered their own productivity, the Guinean population was also required to purchase "voluntary subscriptions" to support the war effort. In 1943, these subscriptions were valued at nearly one hundred million francs. There was little pretense that the subscriptions were freely given. Chiefs pressed their subjects to contribute in cash and kind, and in official reports, such "donations" were grouped with taxes, forced labor, and the obligatory provision of foodstuffs.[20]

Wartime Resistance to Colonial Institutions

Active opposition to the colonial state began during the war. Individual workers resisted intolerable working conditions – and the principle of forced labor – by deserting their workplaces and returning home. In 1943, the inspector of labor reported massive desertions from European-owned plantations in Lower Guinea as a result of low wages and inadequate rations. Woodcutters on the Conakry-Niger railway took advantage of their relative isolation and lax supervision to abandon their work sites. Official documents reported the widespread exodus of rural populations, as whole villages absconded across territorial boundaries to avoid taxes, compulsory rubber collection, forced labor, and military recruitment. Lower Guinea residents fled into Portuguese territory to avoid furnishing rice and rubber. In the forest region, the population evaded military recruiters by crossing the border into Liberia. In 1943, one Futa Jallon subdivision lost more than 8,000 inhabitants to Senegal. By the end of the war, approximately one-tenth of the population of the Upper Guinea subdivision of Faranah had fled. Some 7,000 to 8,000 people had migrated from N'Zérékoré circle in the forest region to Liberia, depopulating all of the frontier cantons. In Forécariah circle (Lower Guinea), 5,000 to 6,000 people abandoned their homes between 1941 and 1946.[21]

---

[19] Rapport politique annuel, 1941, 2G41/21; Rapport politique annuel, 1942, 2G42/22; Rapport politique annuel, 1943, 2G43/19; Rapport sur le travail…1943, 2G43/25; Rapport de tournée effectuée du 27 janvier au 9 février par M. Chopin, Administratuer des Colonies, Inspecteur du Travail, dans les cercles de Conakry-Kindia-Forécariah, April 2, 1943, 2G43/25; Rapport sur le travail…1944, 2G44/30; Rapport sur le travail…1945, 2G45/21; Rapport sur la main d'oeuvre en Guinée, July 13, 1946, 2G46/50, ANS, Dakar.

[20] Rapport politique annuel, 1943, 2G43/19, ANS, Dakar; Rapport politique annuel, 1948, Guinée française, cercle de Gaoual, subdivision centrale, 1E38, Archives de Guinée (hereafter AG), Conakry; Kéïta, *P.D.G.*, vol. 1, 144; Suret-Canale, "Fin de la chefferie," 474–75; Suret-Canale, *French Colonialism*, 483–84, 490 n. 49.

[21] Rapport politique annuel, 1941, 2G41/21; Rapport politique annuel, 1942, 2G42/22; Rapport politique annuel, 1943, 2G43/19; Rapport de tournée…April 2, 1943, 2G43/25;

Colonial authorities worried that local disenchantment might escalate into generalized political discontent. As the war drew to a close, the fear of anticolonial agitation in the countryside increasingly trumped other government concerns. The intensified hardships of the war effort had led to a crisis in chiefly authority. Although rural populations had long resented the chiefs for their role in colonial administration, the war effort brought matters to a head. Since state demands for labor and commodities were enforced by the chiefs, the people held them responsible for their plight. During the war, rural dwellers throughout the territory engaged in widespread resistance to wartime exactions. They refused to pay taxes, perform unpaid labor, and provide crops on demand. Rather than meet their quotas, they sold their crops on the black market and smuggled them into other territories. After the war, rural resistance continued. This time, however, it occurred within the context of the political ferment that gave rise to the anticolonial nationalist movement.[22]

During the first postwar decade, the political scene in Guinea was dominated by the Guinean branch of the Rassemblement Démocratique Africain (RDA), an interterritorial alliance of political parties with affiliates in most of the fourteen territories of FWA, FEA, and the United Nations trusts of Togo and Cameroon. The RDA's success in Guinea was largely due to its focus on groups that had begun to mobilize themselves during the war, particularly military veterans, agricultural producers (both male and female), and workers.[23] The RDA initially captured the loyalty of many veterans by championing their claims; however, the French state battled for the veterans' allegiance and gradually met their demands. By the mid-1950s, African veterans had largely reconciled with the colonial regime and withdrawn from the political scene. When independence came in 1958, military veterans were no longer a significant political force within the RDA.

Military Veterans

Military veterans, who were largely of rural background, were among the first Guineans to join the RDA. They often took the lead in postwar

Rapport sur le travail... 1943, 2G43/25; Rapport sur la main d'œuvre en Guinée, July 13, 1946, 2G46/50; Rapport annuel du travail, 1946, Conakry, February 15, 1947, #66/IT.GV, 2G46/50; Rapport politique annuel, 1946, #284/APA, 2G46/22; Rapport politique annuel, 1947, 2G47/22, ANS, Dakar.

[22] Rapport politique annuel, 1941, 2G41/21; Rapport politique annuel, 1946, 2G46/22; Revues trimestrielles des événements, 1er trimestre 1947, June 17, 1947, #143 APA, 2G47/121, Exposé sommaire de la situation politique de l'Afrique occidentale française et du Togo au 30 mai 1945, June 26, 1945, 2G45/105; Situation politique de l'AOF... mois de février 1945, 2G45/105, ANS, Dakar; interview with Léon Maka, Conakry, February 20, 1991.

[23] Urban women, who were central to postwar political movements, are not considered in this chapter.

agitation against colonial institutions.[24] Although they had long served as the backbone of the colonial administration, African soldiers were politicized by their wartime experiences, as discussed earlier. Paying heed to the French rhetoric of universalism imbibed during their wartime service, and campaigning under the banner "Equal sacrifices = Equal rights," they demanded pay and benefits equal to those of metropolitan soldiers.[25] As one colonial administrator observed, "The African military veterans continue their efforts to benefit from the same rights as metropolitan military veterans. This question, which is taking long to be resolved, especially in that which concerns the payment of different pensions to Africans according to their origin, is creating a malaise in this milieu."[26] According to a police informant in Conakry, Guinean veterans decried "the oblivion in which the military veterans of Guinea find themselves (lack of employment, negligence of the responsible authorities concerning payment of disability and retirement pensions, the granting of decorations and awards, etc.)."[27] Police in Kankan noted that former Tirailleurs were making "energetic demands concerning their pension arrears."[28] The N'Zérékoré circle commandant worried about the continued loyalty of a large group of military veterans in his area who "complain, and for good reason, [about] the incredible delays in the regularization of their pensions."[29]

As long as the parity issue was not resolved, there was the possibility of serious unrest. Returning veterans constituted an influential group within the French West African federation. Five years after the war's end, there were some 16,222 Second World War veterans in Guinea alone. Military veterans were among the few Africans accorded the vote in the postwar political order, and they formed a significant proportion of the African electorate. While some former soldiers migrated to the urban areas and became players in the regional and ethnic associations that formed the nucleus of postwar political parties, the vast majority returned to their rural villages, where they quickly began to challenge local authority structures.[30]

Anxious to move beyond its urban base, the RDA championed veterans' demands in the political arena and followed their lead in the countryside.

---

[24] For further discussion of military veterans' political activities in the postwar period, see Schmidt, *Mobilizing the Masses*, chapter 2.

[25] Echenberg, *Colonial Conscripts*, 104. See also Situation politique de l'AOF... mois de janvier 1945, 2G45/105, ANS, Dakar; Renseignements, situation des anciens combattants, commissariat de police, Kankan, May 22, 1950, #518/PS/I, 1E42, AG, Conakry. For labor's embrace of French universalism, see Cooper, *Decolonization and African Society*, 178, 184, 290.

[26] Gouverneur du Sénégal, Rapport politique, 4ème trimestre, 1949, 21G101, ANS, Dakar.

[27] Renseignements, March 12, 1947, #177/C/PS, 2Z5, 504/2, AG, Conakry.

[28] Rapport mensuel, mois de mars 1950, commissariat de police, Kankan, 1E42, AG, Conakry.

[29] Rapport politique annuel, 1949, cercle de N'Zérékoré, 1E39, AG, Conakry.

[30] Echenberg, *Colonial Conscripts*, 140, 145, 149, 128, 155; Morgenthau, *Political Parties*, 55–56, 401; Thompson and Adloff, *French West Africa*, 58–60.

Veterans' grievances provided fertile ground for political organizing. The soldiers' wartime sacrifices – and the consequent debt owed by France – figured heavily in the party's postwar demands. Building upon preexisting discontent, the RDA called for equality of rights, wages, pensions, and other benefits for all servicemen, no matter what their race, civil status, or national origin. In the overseas territories and in metropolitan France, the RDA rapidly assumed the role of spokesman for the veterans' cause. French army intelligence noted that throughout the French West African federation, veterans were "profoundly influenced" by the RDA and were joining the party in large numbers. In Guinea, veterans were represented on the executives of nearly all local RDA committees, and there was substantial overlap in the membership of RDA and veterans' associations.[31]

The RDA also brought international attention to veterans' grievances. Their claims were frequently discussed in the columns of *Réveil*, the organ of the interterritorial RDA. Its May 13, 1948, issue reprinted a resolution presented in the Assembly of the French Union by RDA councilors, French Communists, and their allies. Recounting the veterans' continuing struggle for equal rights, the resolution urged the government "to put an end to the shocking inequalities existing between the pensions paid to military veterans of metropolitan origin and those paid to [veterans] from the Overseas Territories."[32] In April 1949, RDA deputy from Niger Hamani Diori introduced an amendment in the French National Assembly to guarantee pension equality for all military veterans. Two months later, RDA deputies in the National Assembly proposed a "unified statute" for all soldiers and veterans serving France that would ensure equality for all military veterans in wages, pensions, loans, and all other monetary matters. Although both proposals were defeated, they helped to establish the RDA's reputation as an advocate for veterans' rights.[33]

In Guinea, the RDA's focus on veterans' affairs increased the organization's popularity in all parts of the territory. In July 1947, the police reported that large numbers of veterans were joining the Kindia RDA subsection in Lower Guinea.[34] In Kankan (Upper Guinea), 300 military veterans

---

[31] Quoted in Renseignements objet: groupements politiques, January 13, 1948, Services de Police, Kissidougou, 17G573; Renseignements A/S réunion publique organisée à Kindia le 1er février par le R.D.A., February 2, 1948, #159/55 C, 17G573; Renseignements de Kankan, A/S passage Léon Maka, militant R.D.A., October 13, 1949, #2048, C/PS/I, 17G573; Rapport politique annuel, 1955, #281/APA, 2G55/152, ANS, Dakar. See also, Renseignements A/S réunion publique organisée à Kindia, le 6 Avril 1947 par le R.D.A., ca. April 7, 1947, #320/C, 5B43; Renseignements, March 3, 1947, 2Z5, 504/2, AG, Conakry; Echenberg, *Colonial Conscripts*, 143, 151–53, 157–58; Schmidt, *Mobilizing the Masses*, chapter 2.
[32] "Justice aux anciens combattants," *Réveil*, May 13, 1948.
[33] Echenberg, *Colonial Conscripts*, 152.
[34] Renseignements A/S section R.D.A. Kindia, July 1, 1947, 504 A. #575 G, 17G573, ANS, Dakar.

requested RDA membership cards when RDA militant Léon Maka toured the area in October 1949.[35] In the Futa Jallon, the RDA sought members at the Labé air field and used veterans' organizations as a launching pad for its recruitment drives.[36] The military police in N'Zérékoré reported that military pensions were an important theme in RDA election campaigns. In preparation for the March 1952 Territorial Assembly elections, the RDA had rallied military veterans under the banner, "Equality of military pension rates for Europeans and Africans." The veterans who supported the RDA had once been the epitome of loyalty to France and its institutions, the military police lamented, adding: "If one considers that these same servicemen, in years gone by, formed the reinforcements of the canton and village chieftaincies, it is to fear that in the days to come, the latter will meet with certain difficulties in the exercise of their functions."[37]

Challenging the Chiefs: Military Veterans

Indeed, in the rural areas, military veterans led popular challenges to the chiefs, who had enforced the government's war effort, threatening the very basis of colonial authority in the countryside. They rapidly emerged as a self-styled elite whose worldly experience, access to cash income and consumer goods, and command of the French language gave them a new status. Although many were the descendants of slaves and other low-status groups, they aspired to leadership positions and "big man" stature previously denied to them. They rapidly entered into fierce competition with the traditional aristocracy. Some sought appointments in place of chiefs they deemed corrupt, abusive, or ineffectual.[38] After the war, recalled RDA militant Ibrahima Fofana, "Men from slave families came back home as lieutenants and colonels. And when the opportunity arose, they presented themselves to the colonial administration as candidates for canton chieftaincies. The French, of course, were pleased, considering these men to have served France well. Often, the military veterans were appointed as chiefs."[39]

---

[35] Kankan, A/S passage Léon Maka, October 13, 1949, 17G573, ANS, Dakar.

[36] Renseignements objet: Activité du R.D.A., May 11, 1948, Services de Police, Labé, 17G573; Renseignements objet: groupements politiques, June 10, 1948, 17G573; Renseignements A/S activité politique, July 18, 1951, #1040/490, C/PS.2, 17G573, ANS, Dakar.

[37] Gendarmerie, En Guinée Française, September 12, 1951, 17G573, ANS, Dakar.

[38] Revues trimestrielles, 1er trimestre 1947, 2G47/121; Revues trimestrielles des événements, 2ème trimestre 1947, October 11, 1947, #273 APA, 2G47/121; Revues trimestrielles des événements, 3ème Trimestre 1947, December 5, 1947, #389 APA, 2G47/121; Rapport politique annuel, 1947, #271/APA, 2G47/22, ANS, Dakar; interviews with: Léon Maka, Conakry, February 25, 1991; Ibrahima Fofana, May 5, 1991; Suret–Canale, *French Colonialism*, 374–75, 377, 384, 388; Echenberg, *Colonial Conscripts*, 11–19, 136, 138.

[39] Interview with Ibrahima Fofana, May 5, 1991. See also, Gaoual, Rapport politique annuel, 1948, 1E38, AG, Conakry.

Whereas some veterans aspired to become chiefs in place of existing authorities, others attempted to undermine the chieftaincy as an institution and to install alternative power structures. They helped to organize rural resistance to unpaid compulsory labor – and to the village and canton chiefs who enforced it. When forced labor was abolished in 1946, certain types of involuntary labor, including "customary" dues owed to the chiefs, were specifically excluded from the law's provisions. Although characterized as "traditional" practices, many so-called customary obligations originated in the colonial era. When the administration declined to include unremunerated labor for the chiefs in the forced labor ban, rural Africans simply refused to work. Military veterans often spearheaded this type of resistance.[40]

In other cases, veterans undermined chiefly authority by usurping chiefly functions. In the postwar period, rural resistance to the chiefs frequently focused on their role as tax collectors. According to Maka,

> [the veterans] took the initiative to detach from the chieftaincies. They formed committees to collect taxes and send the taxes directly to the circle commandants, bypassing the chiefs who enriched themselves from these taxes. Instead of giving the taxes to the village chiefs and the canton chiefs, they sent them directly to the circle commandants – in order to undermine the chiefs and to keep some of the money in the area [for local development]. As a result, the influence of the chiefs diminished. It no longer had any importance.

> Military veterans began this process. The RDA thought it was a good idea and decided to have village committees that would make the village chiefs redundant. Why the military veterans? Because they were the people who had traveled, served in France. They had seen how whites acted at home and in the colonies. They saw that there was a difference. They always had a white commander, even if they were competent to do the job for themselves. They understood the system of colonization, and they were angry.

Maka recalled that "former Tirailleurs were usually at the core of RDA actions. They protested before the chiefs, before the circle commandants."[41] As esteemed men in their villages, who did not bow down before chiefs and colonial officials, veterans were in a prime position to mobilize for the RDA.

Although military veterans were early leaders in the anticolonial struggle, they had withdrawn from the political scene by the mid-1950s. The Liger campaign of 1948–1952, which resulted in the registration of tens of thousands of French West African veterans and the settlement of financial demands, the Equality Law of 1950, and subsequent administrative actions largely satisfied veterans' demands. Better off than the majority of

---

[40] Rapport sur la main d'œuvre en Guinée, July 13, 1946, 2G46/50; Rapport politique annuel, 1946, 2G46/22, ANS, Dakar. See also, Macenta, Rapport politique annuel, 1948, 1E38, AG, Conakry; Thompson and Adloff, *French West Africa*, 230, 492.

[41] Interview with Léon Maka, February 25, 1991.

their compatriots, many Guinean veterans retreated from anticolonial agitation and, from the mid-1950s, again became stalwarts of the colonial administration.[42]

Challenging the Chiefs: The RDA

Just as the RDA channeled and articulated veterans' grievances, it also focused on those emanating from the rural war effort. The party threw its support behind agricultural producers who refused to fulfill forced labor demands, pay taxes to the chiefs, and recognize chiefly authority more generally. Responding to rural dwellers' complaints and speaking on their behalf, the RDA expanded beyond its original urban base into the countryside. Like the military veterans, the RDA zeroed in on the chiefs' continued use of involuntary labor. The party charged that since forced labor had been outlawed in 1946, rural residents should no longer have to work for the chiefs without pay. Consequently, the RDA actively encouraged the passive resistance campaign already under way in the rural areas. From the early 1950s, police records are filled with reports of RDA villagers refusing to work in the chiefs' fields, to construct and maintain their huts, or to perform other services. In October 1951, the military police charged that the RDA was establishing alternative authority structures in the rural areas that circumvented village and canton chiefs. RDA village committees collected taxes and usurped other chiefly functions. In response, the chiefs cracked down hard, targeting RDA activists and rigging elections against them. The party's ability to penetrate and hold the populous rural areas was contingent on subverting chiefly power. As a result, the antichief campaigns became the centerpiece of the RDA's rural strategy.[43]

Forced by growing unrest to implement empire-wide reforms in 1956, France introduced local self-government in the overseas territories. In

---

[42] Schmidt, *Mobilizing the Masses*, 52–54.

[43] Rapport Hebdomadaire, September 17–23, 1951, Services de Police; Fiche de Renseignements, ca. October 19, 1951, Gendarmerie nationale, Détachement de l'A.O.F.-Togo, Dakar, #181/4R; Revues trimestrielles, 3ème trimestre 1951, November 24, 1951, Services de Police, Guinée Française; Comité directeur, Parti Démocratique de Guinée, Conakry, à gouverneur (Conakry), February 29, 1952; all in 17G573, ANS, Dakar. See also, PDG, Comité directeur, Conakry, Rapport à la délégation du Comité de coordination et groupe parlementaire RDA, Assemblée Nationale, Paris, #1, January 14, 1952, dos. 7, carton 2143, Centre des Archives d=Outre-Mer, Aix-en-Provence; Gaoual, Rapport politique annuel, 1947, 1E37, AG, Conakry; interview with Léon Maka, February 25, 1991; Sékou Touré, "Contre tout travail forcé," *La Liberté* (March 1, 1955), 3; Claude Gérard, "Incidents en Guinée française, 1954–1955," *Afrique Informations*, 34 (March 15–April 1, 1955), 5–7; "Élections législatives partielles de Guinée," June 17, 1954, in P.D.G.-R.D.A., *Parti Démocratique de Guinée, 1947–1959: Activités – Répression – Élections*, Centre de Recherche et de Documentation Africaine, Paris; Elizabeth Schmidt, *Cold War and Decolonization in Guinea, 1946–1958* (Athens: Ohio University Press, 2007), chapters 2 and 3; Schmidt, *Mobilizing the Masses*, chapter 4.

Guinea, the RDA, which had successfully weakened the chiefs in the rural areas, swept the March 1957 territorial elections and dominated the local government that was established in May. In short order, the new government implemented a number of reforms that both benefited its popular base and diminished the influence of chiefs and notables. Most significantly, in December 1957, it abolished the despised institution of the canton chieftaincy.[44] Although the RDA government had taken charge of the situation, the abolition of the chieftaincy was, in Jean Suret-Canale's words, the "end result of a profound popular movement . . . the legal consecration of a popular revolution."[45] The suppression of this institution, and its replacement by elected local councils that included low-status citizens, had tremendous political ramifications. Throughout the 1950s, the chiefs had used their significant coercive powers to manipulate elections to the RDA's detriment. Had they survived, the canton chiefs could have forced a very different outcome to the September 1958 referendum that led to Guinea's independence.

Worker Mobilization

African workers, like military veterans and agricultural producers, bore the burdens of the war effort. Wartime exactions had provoked general discontent in the rural areas, including widespread desertion from forced labor sites. Disenchanted with low wages and inadequate rations, workers absconded from both European-owned plantations and public works sites. Men cutting wood for the Conakry-Niger railway, who worked in isolated areas with relatively little supervision, were especially prone to flight. When forced labor was abruptly outlawed in 1946, rural workers abandoned their work sites en masse. The circle commandants and administrative heads of service were informed of the new law on April 24. By April 26, rural workers were deserting their stations in droves. According to Inspector of Colonies H. Pruvost, as "the news spread like wildfire into the depths of the bush," local authorities feared the loss of large numbers of laborers from the plantations, mines, and major public and private work sites. Between April 26 and the end of June, more than 20,000 forced laborers in both the public and private sectors deserted their workplaces. In the forest region and parts of Upper Guinea, the inspector of colonies continued, "all the work sites and all the projects, small or large, were immediately abandoned in an explosion of enthusiasm, at the announcement of free labor. . . . In many places, the workers departed en masse, without even waiting for the pay that was due to them."[46] Inspired by the forced laborers' actions, voluntary workers also

---

[44] Kéïta, *P.D.G.*, vol. 2, 66–67; Suret-Canale, "Fin de la chefferie en Guinée," 459, 490.
[45] Suret-Canale, "Fin de la chefferie en Guinée," 460, 490, 493.
[46] Inspecteur des colonies (Pruvost), Mission en Guinée, Rapport sur la main d'œuvre en Guinée, Conakry, July 13, 1946, #116/C, 2G46/50. See also Rapport annuel du travail, 1946, 2G46/50, ANS, Dakar.

broke contract and returned home. When all 1,000 forced laborers quit the Sérédou quinine plantations in the forest region, the administration called out the second portion of the military contingent, which had been explicitly excluded from the forced labor ban, to ensure the continued production of the crop. Second portion draftees provoked a number of incidents and demanded a clarification of their status. If they were military personnel, they should be placed under the command of military officers and treated like their French counterparts, with equal rights and obligations. If they were civilian employees, they should be treated like voluntary workers, their wages and benefits determined by collective bargaining agreements; moreover, since forced labor had been abolished, they should be accorded the right to return to their homes if they chose.[47]

The impositions of the war effort and the continued practice of forced labor in the rural areas had led to massive workplace desertions. Profiting from this ferment, metropolitan-based trade unions, particularly the French Communist Party-affiliated and RDA-associated Confédération Général du Travail (CGT), began to organize urban workers into local branches. While they focused on the urban rather than the rural areas, trade unions attempted to harness the popular discontent unleashed by the war. Promoting the workers' cause as its own, the RDA successfully drew trade unionists into the party.[48]

Conclusion

Although military veterans were early leaders in the anticolonial struggle, they had withdrawn from the political scene by the mid-1950s. Once the government met their major demands, military veterans were better off than most other Guineans. When offered the option of voting for independence in September 1958 or remaining in a French-dominated community, many Guinean veterans opted to stay with France. When Guinea voted overwhelmingly for independence, some Tirailleurs relocated to other territories and joined the French army there.[49] Once the veterans had retreated into the

---

[47] Inspecteur des colonies, Rapport sur la main d'œuvre en Guinée, July 13, 1946, 2G46/50; Rapport annuel du travail, 1946, 2G46/50; Revues trimestrielles, 1er trimestre 1947, 2G47/121, ANS, Dakar. See also Thompson and Adloff, *French West Africa*, 230, 329–30, 492; Babacar Fall, *Le Travail Forcé en Afrique-Occidentale Française (1900–1945)* (Paris: Éditions Karthala, 1993), 283–85; Bogosian Ash, "Forced labor, resistance and memory," 189–218; Bogosian Ash, Chapter 6, this volume.

[48] For a discussion of the RDA and trade union activities in the postwar period, see Schmidt, *Mobilizing the Masses*, chapter 3.

[49] A major concern for veterans was the security of their pensions. Although France continued to pay the veterans' pensions after Guinea voted for independence in 1958, this issue had not yet been resolved at the time of the referendum. Mann, *Native Sons*, 140–42. See also William Attwood, *The Reds and the Blacks: A Personal Adventure* (New York: Harper & Row, 1967), 116.

background, agricultural producers and workers, whose political engagement also began during the war, and urban women, who came to the fore in its aftermath, played increasingly prominent roles.

This chapter makes several contributions to the historiography of Africa and the Second World War. It reperiodizes the war and reevaluates the privileging of veterans in the postwar nationalist movements by highlighting the actions of civilians, whose wartime protests on the home front laid the groundwork for postwar anticolonial activities. It reperiodizes the "postwar" nationalist movements, arguing that the labor unrest and resistance to colonial authorities that culminated in those postwar movements all began during the war. Finally, it shows how the RDA, French West Africa's most powerful political movement during the first postwar decade, rode the wave of discontent resulting from the harsh exactions of the war effort. In Guinea, the RDA was successful largely because it focused on groups that had mobilized themselves in response to the wartime impositions. When this movement took a nationalist turn, however, the alliance began to shred. Once their particular demands were satisfied, African veterans withdrew from a movement that, through the promotion of African independence, threatened their mutually beneficial relationship with France. Other anticolonial activists, including male and female agricultural producers, workers, and urban women, continued the struggle until political independence in 1958.

24

Sudanese Popular Response to World War II

Ahmad Alawad Sikainga

Historians of World War II, particularly non-Africanists, may be intrigued by the way in which Sudan became involved in the war and the role it played in the East and North African campaigns. This was a British colony that was attacked by the Italians who occupied parts of its territories. Situated between Egypt and Libya in the north and Italian-occupied Ethiopia in the east, Sudan's involvement in World War II was inevitable. The country became a major theater of military operations and a pivotal supply center for the Allied Forces in North Africa and the Middle East. Not surprisingly, Sudan became a prime target of Italian forces in Ethiopia whose main goal was to cut off this vital supply line. In addition to launching several air strikes on major Sudanese towns, including the capital city of Khartoum and the railway town of Atbara, the Italians occupied key border towns such as Kassala and Gedarif. Sudan also received a large influx of Ethiopian refugees after the Italian occupation and provided a base for training and organizing Ethiopian resistance. Sudanese troops played a critical role in the liberation of Ethiopia and the North African military campaign.

The few studies that have dealt with the Sudanese experience in World War II were written mainly by British and Sudanese war veterans and have, therefore, focused mainly on military aspects of the story. This chapter explores one of the most neglected dimensions of the narrative, namely the engagement of the Sudanese public with the war. Its main goal is to examine the way in which various segments of Sudanese society responded to the war and the events associated with it. Examining the history of the war through this lens will provide a more nuanced understanding of the impact of the war at the grassroots level and its powerful, transformative role in social change. The Sudanese experience illuminates numerous aspects of Africa's involvement in the war. On one level, the Sudanese story sheds significant light on the local and regional dynamics of the war. Sudan occupied a central place in Italy's grand strategy in East Africa: Capturing this huge territory would have fulfilled the Italian dream of creating an empire stretching from

Somalia in the east to Libya in the northwest, with far-reaching military and geopolitical consequences. While European colonial powers in Africa and Asia often framed the attitude of their subjects toward the war in terms of "loyalty" and "allegiance," this chapter contends that the response of colonized Africans was shaped by myriad factors. Prominent among these was the impact of the war on the daily lives of African communities and individuals. In this regard, it is important to point out that the war affected various segments of African societies in different ways. Residents of major Sudanese towns were subjected to Italian air raids, while the prevailing economic conditions and wartime measures created severe hardships for rural folk, workers, and the urban poor. Moreover, several communities near the border with Ethiopia lived under Italian occupation for several months. At the same time, the war provided the small educated class and nationalist leaders with an opportunity to advance their cause and embrace the emerging trends and discourse on self-determination, equality, and liberty.

The Course of the War in Sudan

The military aspects of Sudanese involvement in the war cannot be understood without reference to the country's strategic location, abundant agricultural resources, and extensive network of rail, river, and land routes, which made Sudan a vital source of food supplies and an important transit point for the Allied forces in the Middle East and North Africa. As the Mediterranean route became increasingly risky, especially after the German occupation of North Africa, the Allies had to reroute their supply lines to West and Central Africa through Sudan by air, river, and road to Egypt and the Middle East. This route became known as the African Line of Communication (AFLOC).[1] Supplies for both military and civilian purposes were transported from Matadi on the Atlantic coast of the Congo to Juba in southern Sudan.[2] From there they were carried by steamers to Kosti on the White Nile, then by rail to Wadi Halfa near the Egyptian border, from where they were taken by steamers to Aswan and then by rail to Cairo. Juba also was a staging post for supplies that came from Mombasa through Kenya and Uganda. Another air route started from Takoradi in West Africa, going through French Equatorial Africa to western Sudan. The city of Al-Fashir in Darfur province became an important post where Allied aircraft was refueled with petrol brought by road from Al-Ubbayyid in Kordofan province. During the war, Sudan refueled some 14,000 aircraft bound for Egypt. Traffic on Sudan Railways (SR) increased sharply: The SR carried

---

[1] Deborah Wing Ray, "The Takoradi Route: Roosevelt's prewar venture beyond the Western hemisphere," *The Journal of American History*, 62 (1975), 340–58.
[2] K. D. D. Henderson, *The Making of the Modern Sudan* (London: Faber, 1953), 267, 271–72.

78,000 troops, 5,000 motor vehicles, and 80,000 pieces of military equipment between Sudanese ports and Eritrea.[3] Not surprisingly, Sudan became a primary target for the Italian military.

As Timothy Parsons points out in Chapter 1 of this volume, the British colonial authorities in Sudan were caught off guard by the Italian invasion of Ethiopia in 1935. For the first time since the scramble for Africa at the end of the nineteenth century, the British were confronted with a well-armed and potentially hostile European power on their colony's borders, against whom they were unprepared. The defense of Sudan depended on three British battalions and the Sudan Defense Force (SDF) of approximately 5,000 men. Established in 1925 to maintain internal security within the Sudan, it was more of a military police force rather than a regular army.[4] Despite the Italian threat, British authorities introduced limited defense measures that increased the size of SDF and created armored mobile companies. Moreover, there were major disagreements among senior British officials in both London and Khartoum regarding what strategy should be adopted toward the Italians. Some officials argued that the Italians had neither the will nor the capability to overrun the Sudan. They argued that attention should be focused on the defense of Port Sudan, the main port, and Khartoum, the capital. Sudan's rulers were finally awakened when war broke out in Europe in 1939. Hurriedly they introduced a series of measures in the summer of 1939, including a declaration of a state of emergency and regulations for the control of basic consumer goods. Despite Sudan's official declaration of war with Germany on September 3, 1939 and with Italy on June 10, 1940, little progress was made in military preparation. By 1940, the British had 85,000 troops in the Middle East and the Horn of Africa, facing 215,000 Italian soldiers in Libya and another 200,000 in the Horn of Africa. The Sudanese army lacked tanks, artillery, and aircraft, with the bulk of the army concentrated in Khartoum, Atbara, and Port Sudan. The 1,200-mile-long border between Sudan and Ethiopia was totally unsecured. This long frontier became the principal theater of military operations in three areas: the Red Sea region, the Blue Nile, and the Upper Nile.[5]

Italy's main goal in northeast Africa was to occupy Sudan and push westward to Libya to cut off this line of supply and encircle the Allied forces in North Africa. Its strategy was to occupy and secure important centers in eastern Sudan and then advance to Khartoum. On July 4, 1940, the Italian army overran the town of Kassala on the Sudan-Eritrea border. Kassala was a small but important market town, originally established in the 1830s as a military camp for the Turco-Egyptian army until its capture by the Mahdist

[3] Ibid.

[4] See Ahmad Alawad Muhammad, *The Sudan Defence Force: Origin and Role, 1925–1955* (Khartoum: Institute of African and Asian Studies, 1980), 33.

[5] M. W. Daly, *Imperial Sudan: The Anglo-Egyptian Condominium, 1934–1956* (Cambridge: Cambridge University Press, 1991), 127–30.

forces in 1884. Eventually, the town was incorporated into Anglo-Egyptian Sudan. Situated in the inland delta of the Gash river, a major producer of fruits and vegetables, it was linked by railway to both Khartoum and Port Sudan. Located just about 270 miles from Khartoum, the town was an obvious gateway to the Sudanese interior.

Intensive air raids that lasted twelve hours preceded the Italian invasion of Kassala. The invading forces consisted of two brigades, four cavalry squadrons, and about twenty-four light and medium tanks and armored vehicles and various artillery batteries. With their superior air power, the Italians could have easily marched to the Sudanese capital, but they lacked accurate information about the strength of the British forces, which they believed was a much larger force than it was. Another factor was Sudan's unbearable summer with its blinding *haboubs* (dust storms) and heavy rains, which made military operations difficult if not impossible.[6] Khartoum and Atbara were of such importance that their capture would have changed the course of the war not only in North Africa but in the entire Middle East. Egypt would have been threatened from the south at a time when the Germans were advancing from the north. The capture of Atbara would have led to Italian control of the whole railway system to Port Sudan, Kassala, and the Egyptian frontier while the capture of Khartoum would have put the Italians in control of the rail route to southern and western Sudan, the line of communications along the Blue and the White Niles, and the rich cotton and grain fields in the Gezira.

Unable to advance into the interior of the Sudan, the Italians embarked on a relentless air campaign against key targets. Their air force raided the railway town of Atbara on July 7, 1940, injuring three people but causing no major damage. On August 23, Khartoum was raided, and the next day Omdurman was bombed, killing three children. Khartoum was attacked again on September 10. Only after the second attack of Khartoum was a warning system established, trenches dug, and blackout regulations introduced. On August 10, Port Sudan was attacked, sustaining heavy casualties.

For six months after the Italian occupation of Kassala, the burden of defending Sudan's eastern frontier fell on small SDF units and irregular forces recruited from the local Beja who lived on both sides of the Sudan-Eritrea border. These irregular troops were recruited through local chiefs and organized into a unit called the Frosty Force, which derived its name from "Frosty Face," the nickname of the white-bearded chief who commanded them.[7] Using their connections with their kinsmen in Eritrea, the Beja acted as guides and spies and provided the British with vital information about Italian troops. During the first few months of the conflict, Beja fighters captured twenty-eight Italian agents who had penetrated the Red Sea region. Other irregular units included Baker Force and the Banda Force,

[6] H. C. Jackson, *The Fighting Sudanese* (London: Macmillan St. Martin's Press, 1945), 60.
[7] Henderson, *The Making of the Modern Sudan*, 571.

which was recruited in Gedarif and Gallabat. Despite their small size and poor equipment, Beja irregulars and SDF soldiers fought gallantly. A British official praised their performance, observing that though they were "inadequately armed and often outnumbered by more than ten to one, they held 1,200 miles of frontier against tanks, aircraft and mechanized artillery."[8]

It took the British authorities several months to launch a counteroffensive. Under the leadership of General William Platt, the British officer who commanded the Allied forces in the region, a campaign was launched at the end of 1940 involving a British brigade and two Indian battalions. On January 18, 1941, after a series of setbacks, the Italians withdrew from Kassala, which the SDF occupied the following day. Two days later, Emperor Haile Selassie entered Ethiopia from Sudan, accompanied by 2,000 Ethiopian fighters who joined the battle for the liberation of Ethiopia.

The retreating Italian forces were pursued by Indian and Sudanese troops whose advance was halted at Keren, a key defensive Italian position and gateway to the Eritrean interior. After two months of fierce fighting, Keren was taken by the Allies and the door was now opened to Asmara and the port of Massawa. On April 5, Addis Ababa fell to the Allied forces and Massawa followed on the following day.[9] Thereafter, the Allied forces advanced to the Amba Alagi mountains, where the Sudanese fought the last battle in this part of the frontier.

Another theater of operations was the long Sudan-Ethiopia borderland along the Blue Nile, which stretched 160 miles between Kurmuk and Roseiris. The defense of this frontier was left in the hands of a police force of about 110 men, who faced 500 Italian troops. In July 1940, the Italians occupied Kurmuk. Three months later they tried to penetrate into the interior, but were repulsed by a unit of Sudanese police. The Italian military also made a serious attempt to take over Roseiris, but met strong resistance from the local people, who were organized into irregular units under the leadership of Shaykh Naiyl, a local chief. As a major gateway to Ethiopia, the Blue Nile region served as a staging ground for Ethiopian resistance fighters to launch attacks against Italian positions. These fighters were recruited from among the thousands of young Ethiopians who had escaped to the Sudan after the Italian occupation. With the support of both British authorities and Sudanese nationalist groups, Ethiopian volunteers organized irregular units such as the Demissi Force and rallied the support of the Sudanese public. They established a training camp in Soba village, south of Khartoum.[10] In early 1941, a mixed force of Ethiopian fighters, Sudanese soldiers and King's African Rifles of Tanganyika began their advance into Ethiopia.[11]

---

[8] Quoted in Daly, *Imperial Sudan*, 131.
[9] Jackson, *The Fighting Sudanese*, 75.
[10] Muhammad Osman Ahmad, *Quwat Dfia al-Sudan: dawraha wa athar ishtrakiha fil al-harb al-'alamiyya al-thaniyya* (Omdurman: Military Press, 1990), 49.
[11] Kennedy Cook, "Kassala at war," *Sudan Pamphlets*, 4 (1942), 2, 54–55.

The third theater of operation was further south in the Upper Nile region, which shared 400 miles of borders with Ethiopia. At the beginning of the war the Italians occupied Gambeila, an Ethiopian trading post administered by the British, as well as other outposts. By October 1940, the British prepared a counteroffensive, which was launched two months later and involved Sudanese soldiers, irregular troops, and a battalion of King's African Rifles. In March 1941, Gambeila was retaken. By May 20, 1941, the Italians were completely defeated and the Abyssinian campaign came to an end. The Allied forces suffered about 4,000 casualties and captured 41,000 prisoners of war, of whom 17,500 were Italians and the rest Eritreans. The Italians were detained in camps in the Red Sea hills until they were sent to South Africa and India. Eritrean captives were held in Sudanese camps in Atbara, Shendi, Wad Medani, and near Khartoum until they were gradually repatriated to Eritrea.[12]

The completion of the Abyssinian campaign did not end Sudan's involvement in the war. In view of the German advance, the British dispatched some SDF units to North Africa in 1942. As a partner in the condominium, the Egyptian government objected to this decision, arguing that the SDF should not be involved in military operations not related to the defense of the Sudan; however, the British dismissed Egyptian objections, arguing that since the SDF had no clear mandate, its sphere of operations was unlimited. They pointed out that Sudan was now threatened from the north as it had previously been threatened from the east.[13] The Egyptian government finally caved in and agreed to use Sudanese troops in Libya so long as they did not operate from Egyptian territory. In reality, Sudanese soldiers fought in the battle of Alamain and carried out police duties in various parts of the region. They were also dispatched to the French colonies in Equatorial Africa to protect that region against possible Italian attacks from Libya. Some of these soldiers were captured as war prisoners, including Sergeant Sulayman, who was transferred to Libya, then to Italy, and later to Germany, where he was eventually freed by the Allied forces.[14]

Sudanese Public Response to the War

Initially, British officials believed that the Sudanese people would be disinterested in the war. Sir Stewart Symes, the governor-general of Sudan, observed that typical Sudanese would be "unmoved" by the war as long as "he is able to provide himself with tea and sugar."[15] His remarks reflected the thinking prevalent among many of his colleagues who remained detached and continued to downplay the Italian threat. From their perspective, the

---

[12] Henderson, *The Making of the Modern Sudan*, 200.
[13] Muhammad, *The Sudan Defence Force*, 95.
[14] Interview with Muhammad Sulayman, *al-Sudan al-Jadid*, July 7, 1944.
[15] Quoted in Daly, *Imperial Sudan*, 128.

most important thing was to ensure that Sudanese people remained calm
and loyal to the British. Their main concern was retaining the allegiance
of this predominantly Muslim society. British anxiety stemmed from the
experience of World War I, when the Ottoman empire supported Germany
and called upon Muslims worldwide to follow its example and launch a
"jihad" against the British, a direct response to European imperial designs
in the Middle East. The British had to make a strenuous effort to persuade
Sudanese religious leaders to reject the Ottoman call.

To ensure Sudanese support during World War II, the British launched
a vigorous propaganda campaign even before the outbreak of the war.
Their strategy involved cultivating close connections with the small class
of Sudanese intelligentsia in the urban centers and to mobilize religious and
tribal leaders. On June 11, 1940, one day after the official declaration of
war with Italy, the governor-general summoned twenty-one notables to his
office, including three religious figures – Sayyid Ali al-Mirghani, Sayyid Abd
al-Rahman al-Mahdi, and Sharif al-Hindi – as well as the *mufti* (grand judge)
of the Sudan, representatives of the *ulama*, retired army officers, merchants
and leaders of the Graduate General Congress (GGC). The governor-general
read his "Proclamation to the People of the Sudan" in which he appealed
for support and loyalty. He read the proclamation in English and an Arabic
translation followed. The religious leaders offered unconditional support
and the GGC representatives expressed their willingness to set aside their
political demands and support the war effort. Writing about this meeting
several years later, Sir Douglas Newbold, the British civil secretary of the
Sudan in the early 1940s, recalled that Saleh Shingeite took him aside and
confided that the Sudanese intelligentsia "regarded the fight against Nazism
and Fascism as much their war as ours." Still Newbold was uncertain, saying, "This was all genuine, I am sure, though how far this fervor will stand
the strain of military setbacks, hope deferred, blackouts, rationing, alarmist
rumors, etc. remains to be seen."[16] However, it was the Italian actions that
galvanized the Sudanese public toward the Allies. Italian occupation drew
Sudanese people directly into the war, especially in a number of Sudanese
towns along the border with Ethiopia. Of these, the most important was
Kassala on the Sudan-Eritrea border. The story of Kassala provides important insights into the way in which ordinary Sudanese experienced the war
and responded to the occupation.

Kassala under Italian Occupation

Kassala's population included Beja-speaking groups, Halenga, and Bani
Amir who lived on both sides of the border. As a result, these borders
remained porous as people moved back and forth as they maintained links

---

[16] Henderson, *The Making of the Modern Sudan*, 151–52.

with their kin. Moreover, Kassala was a major center of the Khatmiyya brotherhood, one of the largest *tariqas* or Sufi orders, in Sudan, Eritrea, and Ethiopia. Its main followers in Sudan reside in the northern part of the country and include the Beja-speaking groups in the Red Sea region. At the time of the war, its leader was Muhammad 'Uthman al-Mirghani, whose family resided in a quarter known as al-Mirghaniyya.

Kassala's fertile land and farming opportunities attracted a large number of immigrants from northern Sudan, including Dangala, Ja'aliyyin, and Shaiqiyya, many of whom were followers of the Khatmiyya. Other immigrants included West Africans such as Hausa, Fulani, and Borno, as well as Rashaida from Arabia, Yemenis, and Ethiopians. These communities engaged in farming, pastoralism, commerce, and other occupations; an extensive trading network thrived along the Sudan-Eritrea border region. Before the outbreak of the war, many Sudanese residents in Kassala and the neighboring areas sought wage employment in Eritrea on Italian infrastructural projects, where they received relatively high wages paid in Italian lire. Initially, these workers were allowed to bring home part of their earnings in Italian currency; however, following the outbreak of hostilities, the Italians prohibited bringing Italian currency to Sudan. Instead, workers were allowed to take Italian-made goods, which they could sell in Kassala at higher prices. The British responded by imposing high customs on imported Italian goods, forcing many workers to either return home or remain in Eritrea.[17]

The Italian occupation of Kassala lasted six months. It was a terrifying period for the city's residents. As mentioned earlier, the invasion was preceded by air strikes, which killed one person and wounded more than a dozen. To calm the local population, Italian planes dropped leaflets telling Kassala's residents about the "mild" Italian administration of Libya, Eritrea, and Somalia and emphasizing Mussolini's love for the "Mohamedans" (Muslims) and his interest in the welfare of the Sudanese by promoting cotton and grain schemes. The leaflets went on to state that Italy's war was against the British, not the Sudanese, but warned that anyone who resisted would be sternly punished.[18] The Italians also made relentless efforts to recruit spies from the local population. Although their attempt mostly failed, they did manage to recruit a few individuals. One of those was 'Abd al-Majid Sultan, who allegedly destroyed several local shops. During the Blue Nile campaign, the British captured several Sudanese spies at al-Roseiris and executed some of them for espionage.[19] When the Italians withdrew from Kassala, Sultan escaped to Asmara, where he was captured and returned to

---

[17] Muhammad 'Uthman Ahmad, *Quwat Difa al – Sudan: Dawraha and Athar Ishtirakiha fi al-Harb al-Almiyya al-Thaniyya* (Omdurman: Military Press, 1990), 86–87.

[18] Henderson, *The Making of Modern Sudan*, 161–63.

[19] Daly, *Empire on the Nile*, 137.

Kassala, and eventually tried and executed at Port Sudan prison in 1942.[20]
British officials reported that the Italians constantly complained about their
inability to recruit Sudanese spies, while the British had no trouble in recruiting a large number for surveillance in Eritrea. Many Kassala residents, however, were angered by what they considered the failure of the British to
protect them against Italian attacks. For instance, Ahmad Jafar, a Beja chief,
wrote to the SDF commander, declaring his people's loyalty to the British,
but deploring government defense measures. He pleaded for the British to
expel the Italians from the town as soon as possible.[21] Yet, despite their
frustration with British inaction, the city's residents and community leaders
displayed strong support for the British.

Before launching their counteroffensive to retake the city, the British
encouraged the residents to evacuate. Meanwhile, the Italians wanted to use
the local population as hostages to prevent a British assault and specifically
targeted Khatmiyya leaders, believing that their presence in the city would
stop the British from attacking. A curfew was imposed and people were not
allowed to leave the city, except farmers who were permitted to work on
their farms to produce food. Despite these measures, many people escaped
and returned to their homes. About 7,000 people remained and took refuge
in the Mirghaniyya neighbourhood. Italian actions terrified and incensed the
population, turning them into a major asset for the British.

Khatimiyya leaders directed their followers among farmers, who were
allowed to move back and forth, to smuggle letters and messages to British
forces outside the city, informing them about the movement of Italian troops.
Farmers reportedly hid clandestine messages in their vegetable sacks. Among
these farmers were Shaykh Ahmad Hasab al-Baggi, a Khatimiyya follower,
and al-Shafi' Khalid al-Rasul. They gave the messages to a woman named
Mastora, a shop owner living in the outskirts of the city, who delivered them
to British officials. These communications provided the British with vital
intelligence information. During the occupation, leaders of the Khatimiyya
provided strong moral support to the besieged population, managed and
distributed the limited supplies, and helped individuals who were targeted
by the Italians to escape from Kassala. After the town's liberation, Katmiyya
and other community leaders were awarded some of the most prestigious
British medals. For instance, Muhammad Uthman al-Mirghani, the supreme
leader of the Khatmiyya, and Shaykh 'Abdalla Bakr were named Officer of
the Most Excellent Order of the British Empire (OBE), while al-Hasan al-
Mirghani and Uthman Ali Kayli were named to the Most Excellent Order of
the British Empire (MBE). Shaykh Muhammad al-Amin Tark, a local Beja
chief, was honored as Commander of the Most Excellent Order of the British

---

[20] Ibid., 210.
[21] Cook, "Kassala at war," 1–5.

Empire (CBE), while Shaykh 'Abdalla Fikri was given a Robe of Honor.[22] It is clear that the Italian occupation of Kassala created a strong sense of communal solidarity during a period of hardship. It also underscored the importance of social networks, religious loyalties, and kinship ties in political mobilization and resistance.

The Sudanese Public and the War

In a letter to Lord Lugard, Sir Douglas Newbold spoke for many of his colleagues when he observed:

> The Sudanese, soldiers and villagers and tribesmen, have been wonderful, patient and trusting in those dark days when we had few troops and planes, no guns and a long unprotected frontier; courageous and helpful when fighting began; they poured in money, men and material to aid Gen. Platt's Army Corps; the Sudan Defense Force won golden opinions from all officers and men of British, Dominion and Indian forces.[23]

Sudanese attitudes toward the war must be considered within the context of the general sociopolitical climate in the country during the 1930s and the 1940 and the forces that created that climate. One of the most important developments during this period was the emergence of a small, politically active Sudanese intelligentsia who spearheaded the nationalist movement and established political organizations such as the GGC. Most were graduates of Gordon Memorial College (GMC) and were employed as junior civil servants, teachers, and professionals. They published journals and magazines and established literary associations and social clubs in Khartoum, Wad Medani, Atbara, and other towns. These periodicals and clubs became important sites of cultural production and activities, including regular public lectures, opinion columns, poetry readings, and theater performances.

The 1930s also witnessed the emergence of an urban popular music culture, including new styles of music such as the *haqiba*, which was performed by individual vocalists accompanied by a chorus backed by the tambourine. The *haqiba* flourished in Omdurman, once capital of the Mahdist state (1884–1898), where it dominated social ceremonies. After the overthrow of the Mahdist state, the Anglo-Egyptian regime moved the seat of government across the river to Khartoum; hence, Omdurman remained a "native" town, a symbol of Sudanese nationalism that became the cultural hub of the country. Among the most prominent haqiba singers of the time were Khalil Farah, a Nubian from northern Sudan who became famous for his patriotic songs, Muhammad Ahmad Sarour, Karoma, and several others.

---

[22] Ahmad, *Quwat Difa al-Sudan*, 98–99.
[23] Quoted in Henderson, *The Making of Modern Sudan*, 217.

The Sudanese public received news of the progress of the war mainly through newspapers and radio broadcasts, which limited circulation among a tiny segment of the urban population. Counting on the prevailing anti-Allies feeling in the Middle East, the Germans and the Italians launched a propaganda campaign targeting Arab Muslims in North Africa and the Middle East. The roots of the anti-British sentiment among some Arab nationalists dated back to the post-World War I arrangements that divided the Arab provinces of the defeated Ottoman empire between Britain and France. Using an Arabic-speaking anchor named Yunis Bahri, the Germans broadcast programs that publicized the victories of Axis forces against the Allies as well as speeches by Hitler and Mussolini. Although the British authorities in the Sudan made listening to the German broadcast a punishable offense, people continued to listen to it in coffee shops and public places.[24] As mentioned previously, the Italians failed in their efforts to win Sudanese public support and recruit Sudanese spies.

By and large the Sudanese public remained pro-Allies. Following the Italian occupation of Kassala and their subsequent air raids on Atbara and Omdurman, the Sudanese became convinced that the Italians were determined to occupy their country and turn it into a settler colony to exploit its natural resources. Indeed, the Italian dream about creating an empire stretching from Somalia in the east to Libya in the west and from Eritrea in the north to Kenya in the south was well known. Even before the occupation of Ethiopia, *al-Fajr*, the leading Sudanese journal at the time, published an article entitled "Italian Sudan" in which the author wrote that "all signs show that the Sudan would become an Italian colony." News of Italian atrocities in the Ethiopian invasion intensified Sudanese fears and prompted a strong reaction on both official and unofficial levels. Moreover, Italian designs were considered a major threat to the Sudanese economy. Indeed, the control of the Nile waters and the establishment of plantation agriculture would have been a major threat to the Gezira cotton scheme, the backbone of the Sudanese colonial economy. Sudanese political leaders felt that if they had to choose between the Anglo-Egyptian regime and an Italian settler system, they preferred the former.[25]

As the country was drawn into the war, nationalist leaders and intellectuals felt that they were part of a larger campaign against tyranny and totalitarianism. Local newspapers reported the progress of the military campaigns in Europe and elsewhere. They published articles and commentaries on such topics as Fascism, Nazism, Communism, freedom, democracy, the Muslim response to the war, and so forth. For instance, Shaykh

---

[24] Al-Fatih al-Tahir, *Ana Omdurman: Tarikh al-Musiqa al-Sudaniyya* (Khartoum: Master Inc. 1993).

[25] Hasan Ahmad Ibrahim, *The 1936 Anglo-Egyptian Treaty* (Khartoum: Khartoum University Press, 1976), 53.

Abu Shama 'Abd al-Mahmoud, a prominent religious figure, published an article in one of the local newspapers in which he cited several verses from the Quran, arguing that Islam is against totalitarianism as exemplified by the Fascist and the Nazi regimes and that Muslims should support what he called "democratic" nations.

Arguably one of the most important developments that had a profound impact on Sudanese public opinion was the establishment of Omdurman Radio in April 1941 under the Sudan Broadcasting Service (SBS), whose management team included the director of the intelligence department, his deputy, and three Sudanese officials. From a small room about three by three meters square in Omdurman Post Office, the station began to broadcast news of the war. From the British perspective, broadcasting was a vital tool for countering German and Italian propaganda and rallying the Sudanese public. Program content was carefully controlled, stressing the victories of the Allied forces and the superiority of their airpower.[26] Omdurman radio transmission was strengthened to reach several major cities. At the beginning, there was a limited supply of transistor radios in the country, but they were eventually imported in large quantities. Those who could not afford radios went to coffee shops and public places to hear broadcasts. It was reported that the propaganda campaign of Radio Omdurman so enraged the German radio station that Yunis Bahri declared that "an insect called Radio Omdurman is making noise in the jungles of Africa."[27]

In January 1943, the SBS began to publish *Huna Omdurman*, a monthly (later weekly) magazine, which was closely linked to the radio. In addition to listing broadcast programs, the magazine published a wide range of articles and commentaries on the war as well as social and cultural topics. Realizing the importance of heroic poems and praise songs in Sudanese culture, the British recruited Sudanese singers to perform patriotic songs in support of the Allies. Omdurman broadcasts reached Sudanese soldiers stationed in Eritrea and North Africa. Enthusiastic soldiers pressed their commanders to bring these musicians to the camps. In response, the authorities began to dispatch small groups of singers to the war front: The first group was sent to Tripoli (Libya) and included Muhammad Ahmad Sarour, Ahmad al-Mustafa, and al-Sir Abdalla; and the second group went to Eritrea and included Hasan 'Atiyyah, Ibrahim al-Khasif, and Badr al-Tuhami.

According to Hasan 'Atiyyah, the singers were given military uniforms and were considered army officers without rank. Their uniforms bore SDF insignia so that if they were captured by the enemy, they would be treated as war prisoners. These singers received all the entitlements of officers, including a monthly salary. They traveled in officers' class in train and ship and

---

[26] Fouad Omer, *Mudhakirat Amir al-'Oud* (Omdurman: Abdel Karim Mirghani Center, 2003), 45.

[27] Al-Tahir, *Ana-Omdurman*, 74.

were housed in officers' quarters. 'Attiyyah recalled the great enthusiasm and jubilation they received in the camps in Eritrea. They spent about six weeks performing at various military posts along the war frontier. Performances were held during the day because performing at night with lights would have exposed the military posts to the Italians. In addition to alleviating the anxiety and monotonous life in the camps, the performances boosted the soldiers' morale and confidence. To show their appreciation, the soldiers inundated the singers with gifts and money. The last stop for the group was Keren, a major theater of military operations. 'Attiyyah related that the singers were trapped in the city for several weeks until they were finally taken home.[28]

The war period produced a plethora of patriotic songs praising the Sudanese soldiers. Examples included "*Rijal al-hidoud*" (frontier men) by Hasan 'Atiyyah and "*Al-Mutatwiat*" (volunteers) by Sarour. The most popular war song, which is still revered in the Sudan, was "*Yaju 'Aydein*" ("They Come Home") by Aysha al-Fallatiyya, an iconic figure in the history of Sudanese music. Her family hailed from northern Nigeria. After living in different parts of the Sudan, the family finally settled in Omdurman, where Aysha began to sing at a very young age, accompanying her older sister, Jiddawiyya, a skillful lute player. Although Aysha was preceded by other Sudanese female singers, she attained enormous fame by her distinctive voice and her courage in facing all sorts of social barriers. She became an inspiration and role model for other female singers. The song "*Yaju 'Aydin*" gained such enormous popularity that Aysha was invited to perform for Sudanese soldiers in Eritrea. The song's lyrics included such verses as:

> They come back home
> May God bring them home...
> They come home victorious...
> They come home with the tank and the Maxim [gun]

In addition to praise songs, this period also witnessed a proliferation of what can be described as "humorous" songs, composed mainly by women. For instance, during their air raid on Omdurman, the Italian warplanes missed their targets in Omdurman and instead killed a donkey that belonged to a woman who sold milk. This event gave rise to a song that mocked Italian military capabilities and described Hitler and Mussolini as timid clowns.[29]

The final Allied defeat of the Axis powers sparked a wave of celebrations throughout the Sudan. The SDF victories were glorified and integrated into the nationalist narrative. In the railway town of Atbara, which was a target of an Italian raid and the birthplace of the Sudanese labor movement, the

---

[28] Omer, *Mudhakirat Amir al-'Oud*, 45–46.
[29] Hilal Zahir al-Sadati, *Omdurmaniat: Hikayat 'an Omdurman Zaman wa Qissas Qasira Ukhra* (Khartoum: al-Sharika al-'alamiyya liltiba'a wal Nashr wal Tawzi', 2007), 84.

news of the Japanese capitulation was celebrated by a series of ceremonies and theatrical activities. A play in which Hitler and Mussolini were court-martialed and executed was performed at a social club, followed by poetry readings celebrating the German defeat in North Africa.[30]

The end of the war gave birth to a new discourse among Sudanese nation-alists and intellectuals, who stressed the enormous sacrifices the country had made toward the war effort. A stream of newspaper articles openly debated the Atlantic Charter, demanding that the superpowers recognize the right of colonized nations to liberty and self-determination. On April 21, 1944, Hasib Ali Hasib published an article titled "Signs of Victory" in *al-Sudan al-Jadid* in which he stated that: "Five years have passed during which we endured all forms of hardships, with patience and high spirit and we contributed beyond our capacities so that the nations of the world would achieve this outcome." He urged the British to honor the principles of the Atlantic Charter and to move swiftly toward the realization of self-rule. Shortly afterward, an editorial titled "The War Has Ended: Let's Be Ready, Let the British Remember," in the same newspaper declared:

> Democracy has won and Nazism and Fascism were defeated. We should reflect on this moment and learn lessons from the past. We should remember the pains and the suffering of the past five years. The British should remember the nations that stood by them during those bitter and difficult moments. The British should also remember that the joy they are feeling now is not theirs alone, but is also shared by the nations that supported them.

The author compared the colonized nations to a person who won a marathon and is waiting for his prize, saying that the Sudan is one of those nations. He concluded: "All Sudanese should remember that their reward for this victory should be nothing less than their freedom."

The most vocal nationalist organization that articulated these "rewards" was the GGC. It was mentioned earlier that in 1942 the GGC submitted a petition to the governor-general demanding that the British and the Egyptian governments take the necessary steps to pave the way for Sudan's self-determination after the end of the war. They were swiftly rebuffed and even warned to stop their agitation. As elsewhere in Africa, the hopes of the nationalist movement for self-determination were dashed in the aftermath of the war as the colonial powers continued to cling to power. The sense of betrayal that prevailed among African nationalists and the economic hardships in the postwar era sparked off a wave of protests across the continent and escalated into open confrontation with colonial regimes.

The response to the Allies' victory and the end of the war reveals a great deal about the various ways in which different segments of Sudanese society experienced and perceived the war. The exigencies of the war had a profound

[30] Sikainga, *City of Steel and Fire*, 100.

impact on daily life, particularly in the urban centers. In addition to the atmosphere of fear resulting from Italian raids, severe shortages of consumer goods and austerity measures created major hardships and impacted the daily life of the vast majority of the population. Trenches were dug around public places such as government buildings, schools, and neighborhoods, and people were instructed to rush to these trenches if they heard sirens. Automobiles, bicycles, and motorcycles were painted dark colors and lights were turned off at night.

On May 31, 1945, in the aftermath of the German surrender, *Huna Omdurman* published comments by several individuals from different social backgrounds about their feelings concerning the end of the war. Their responses illustrate how different people viewed the war and their expectations. A working class man responded as follows:

> It is true that the war has ended and the Allies have won. All I hope for now is that this [victory] will mark the beginning of prosperity for all of us. I hope that food and clothes will become available, prices of grain and cloth will be reduced and the Sudanese pound would return to its real value so that we can enjoy life as we did in the past.

Similarly, a university student expressed his delight by this "glorious day in human history." He went on to say that "we have suffered a great deal from this war," which obstructed education as it made it difficult to obtain books and other sources of knowledge. More significant, however, was the response of an educated woman who stressed the contribution of women to the war and the need to recognize their rights. As she put it, "the war has proven the important role that women can play in the life of nations. Women engaged in the field, fought in the frontline, attended the wounded and cheered the fighters." Therefore, she argued, Sudanese women should occupy their proper place in the "marching global caravan."

Although this was just snapshot of Sudanese public opinion, these comments reflect the aspiration of the emerging social forces that would soon confront an unbending colonial regime. As in other African colonies, Sudan became the site of an unprecedented wave of protests in the late 1940s and early 1950s, resulting in the mobilization of four major socioeconomic sectors: workers, peasants, students, and women. Like their counterparts in Mombasa, Lagos, and Dakar, Sudanese railway workers staged a series of strikes over wages and other labor rights. Their confrontations with colonial authorities led to improved working conditions and the legalization of labor unions. Their success opened the door for other workers and civil servants to organize themselves and paved the way for the establishment of one of the largest and most powerful trade union movements in Africa.[31]

---

[31] Tim Niblock, *Class and Power in Sudan: The Dynamics of Sudanese Politics, 1898–1985* (Albany: State University of New York Press, 1987), 123–24.

Another important movement was established by the Sudanese peasants. Using the techniques of industrial workers, the tenants of the Gezira Scheme demanded improvement in their economic conditions and the right to form unions. Suspecting that the scheme management was depriving them of their financial entitlements, the tenants launched a major strike in 1946. After the dispute was settled, the Tenants Representative Body (TRB) was established and played an important role in defending tenant interests. In 1952, it adopted a new constitution and changed its name to the Gezira Tenants' Association (GTA), changing its name again a year later to the Gezira Tenants' Union (GTU). Dominated by leftists associated with the Sudanese Communist Party, it was not surprising that GTU leadership established close alliance with the labor movement.[32]

Equally important was the students' movement, founded by GMC students and then spread to secondary schools. After a great deal of agitation, GMC students established Gordon College Students' Union (GCSU) in 1941. During the height of nationalism the GCSU forged close links with the nationalist movement. Various nationalist organizations, including the Communist Party and the Muslim Brothers, sought to establish a niche in the students' movement. In 1949, a student congress was established as an umbrella organization that included several unions. It was dominated by leftist groups and, in 1954, became the Democratic Front. When GMC became the University of Khartoum in 1956, GCSU changed its name to Khartoum University Students' Union (KUSU) and became one of the most powerful movements in the postindependence period.[33] KUSU played a leading role in the popular uprising that overthrew the military regimes of Ibrahim 'Abboud in 1964 and Ga'far Numeiri in 1985.

Finally, the 1940s also witnessed the birth of the Sudanese women's movement. Despite their small number, educated Sudanese women established a number of organizations, beginning with the Women's League formed in 1947 by the students of Girls' Training College in Omdurman. The following year, a Women Teachers' Association was launched, which became Schoolmistresses Union in 1951. A year later, the Sudanese Women's Union (SWU) was established with the objective to improve the conditions of women through education and cultural activities. The SWU organized literary classes, established schools in various towns to provide adult education, and launched a monthly magazine called *Woman's Voice* in 1955. Like the labor and the tenant movements, SWU aligned itself with the Sudanese left and became increasingly militant in the 1950s and 1960s, participating in several protests organized by labor unions; however, its close alliance with the left and its political activities led some of

---

[32] Ibid., 123–24.
[33] Salah El Din El Zein El Tayeb, *The Students' Movement in the Sudan, 1940–1970* (Khartoum: Khartoum University Press, 1971), 10–12.

its less radical members to split and form rival, but less effective, organizations.[34]

Conclusion: Significance of the Sudan Experience

The response of the Sudanese public to the war illuminates several dimensions of the war experience in Africa. From the preceding narrative it is clear that Italian warfare and occupation in some areas played a pivotal role in shaping Sudanese public opinion. Although the Italian occupation of some Sudanese towns was short-lived, it gave the Sudanese a "taste" of Italian colonialism. It can be argued, therefore, that the Sudanese response was based on real experience, not just a product of British propaganda or an expression of "loyalty." Moreover, the discourse of the Sudanese nationalists during the war reflected a deep understanding of the profound changes taking place across the globe and the emerging trends that were shaping the postwar world. Rather than being a pawn in a European conflict, they considered themselves an integral part of a new world order.

The Sudanese case sheds a significant light on the impact of the war at the grassroots level and on the way noncombatant, ordinary people responded to these events. The story of Kassala during the Italian occupation illustrates the manner in which people used their social capital, kinship ties, religious affiliations, and communal links to cope with and resist the occupation. On another level, ordinary Sudanese used various idioms to express their attitude toward the war. Newspapers, journals, music, poetry, drama, and other artistic expression all played a crucial role. At the same time, the propaganda programs and the development of mass communications gave popular culture a tremendous boost. After the war, *Huna Omdurman* became the main avenue for discussion on music, literature, drama, and the arts. On another level, Radio Omdurman played a pivotal role in the spread of new musical styles that emerged in the 1930s in the urban centers, particularly in Khartoum and Omdurman. *Haqiba* music that featured the tambourine was particularly important, but during and after the war, performers began to rely on instruments such as the mandolin, violin, accordion, trumpet, and piano, which represented a major shift in Sudanese musical styles, pioneered by Ibrahim al-Kashif, Hasan Atiyya, Ahmad al-Mustafa, Hasan Sulayman, and several others. The establishment of the radio station gave this young generation of singers a great opportunity to reach a wide range of audience.

The war had a significant impact on civilian–military relations not only in the Sudan, but also throughout Africa. The combat experience and military victories of the Sudanese soldiers became a source of pride and adulation of the army. As K. D. D. Henderson puts it:

[34] Niblock, *Class and Power in Sudan*, 133–37.

For the Sudanese the war provided a tremendous incentive to national pride. Their troops held off vastly superior forces for six long months and their police kept six hundred miles of frontier more or less intact. They put the Sudan back on the map as a co-belligerent with the rest of the allies and rubbed shoulders with troops from many parts of the world on equal terms and with mutual respect.[35]

The combat experience enhanced the prestige of the army and shaped the self-perception of its members. Soldiers saw themselves as a special group with distinctive traits, such as chivalry, discipline, honesty, and, above all, patriotism. Although the role of African war veterans in the nationalist movement has been the subject of debate, little attention was given to the role of these veterans in the military coups that swept Africa in the postindependence period.[36] General Ibrahim ʿAbound, who staged the first military coup in the Sudan in 1958, was a longtime SDF officer, serving Eritrea and Iraq during the war. Virtually all members of Abboud's junta were World War II veterans.[37] Although the intervention of the military in African politics was a product of complex political, social, and economic factors, this early generation of army officers saw themselves as the harbingers of patriotism and the saviors of their nations, a belief that was undoubtedly born out of their war experience. The war generation in the Sudan still remembers this period as a time of bewilderment, anxiety, and hope. But, as this generation passes, the story of the war may gradually fade from Sudanese public memory. Nonetheless, World War II will remain a pivotal chapter in Sudanese history and a monumental event that transformed and shaped modern Sudan.

[35] K. D. D. Henderson, *Sudan Republic* (New York: Frederick A. Praeger, 1965), 85.

[36] Adrienne M. Israel, "Ex-servicemen at the crossroads: Protest and politics in post war Ghana," *Journal of Modern African Studies*, 3 (1992), 359–68

[37] Elsewhere in Africa, war veterans also led military coups, for example, Jean-Bedel Bokassa of Central African Republic, J. A. Ankrah of Ghana, Idi Amin of Uganda, and Aman Andom of Ethiopia, to name a few.

25

Ugandan Politics and World War II (1939–1949)

Carol Summers

World War II shaped Uganda's postwar politics through local understandings of a global war.[1] Individually and collectively Ugandans saw the war as an opportunity rather than simply a crisis. During the war, they acquired wealth and demonstrated loyalty to a stressed British empire, inverting paternalistic imperial relations and investing loyalty and money in ways they expected would be reciprocated with political and economic rewards. For the 77,000 Ugandan enlisted soldiers and for the civilians who grew coffee and cotton, contributed money and organizational skills, and followed the war news, the war was not a desperate struggle for survival. Ideological aspects of the war, such as Fascism and Nazism, did not produce any widespread revulsion: Even at the height of the war, boys at the country's top school blithely organized a Nazi club.[2] Instead, soldiers, fundraisers, and cotton growers sought *personal* opportunities as they demonstrated their loyalty and competence.

World War II, though, also taught the modern power of *collective* action and the potential exactions and interventions of an ambitious modern state, whether imperial or explicitly Fascist. Impoverished and indebted by the war, Britain was slow to accept Ugandan assessments of themselves as British allies, rather than subordinate clients. As the war ended, therefore, frustrated

---

[1] This paper rests primarily on research about Buganda, the central kingdom of the British protectorate of Uganda. Prior to the 1950s, Baganda regularly conflated Buganda and Uganda. I acknowledge a larger Uganda when referring to Uganda and Ugandans when describing events, ideas, and initiatives extending beyond the kingdom of Buganda. Baganda were prominent in these, but not in exclusive control. I have reserved the labels "Buganda" (the kingdom), "Baganda" (the people), and "Ganda" (the adjective) for things that were connected more specifically to the kingdom.

[2] The drinking and boxing club had officers called "Hitler," "Himmler," and "Goering," CO 536/210/5, 25–26, the National Archives (hereafter TNA), Kew. For discussion, see Carol Summers, "'Subterranean evil' and 'tumultuous riot' in Buganda: Authority and alienation at King's College, Budo, 1942," *Journal of African History*, 47 (2006), 93–113.

Ugandans, individually and collectively, broke with the low-key politics of petition that had characterized earlier years and moved toward a modern mass politics rooted in Ganda culture. This new politics defended Ganda initiative against British planning and demanded generational turnover and structural change from both older Ganda institutions and Uganda's colonial administration.

Background

When World War II broke out in 1939, Uganda was already approaching the end of a colonial era structured around the Uganda Agreement of 1900. The agreement's alliance between a Ganda oligarchy and British official and missionary leaders was losing its ability to define events in the central kingdom of Buganda, much less the protectorate as a whole. World War II and its aftermath – not as a collection of battles, but as a social, economic, and political challenge – brought new actors and aims into the country's politics, and opened political processes while impairing British administrative efforts to adapt.

Ugandans contributed to the imperial war effort by volunteering (or being volunteered by local authorities) for the military, expanding production of cotton and coffee, accepting high taxes and confiscatory pricing controls on cotton and coffee, and raising and "donating" money both as individuals and as groups to help Britain. Ugandans overtly performed wealth, generosity, and loyalty, literally becoming creditors to the British exchequer. In doing so, they upended British ideas of imperial superiority and patronage, creating an imbalance that implicitly called on Britain to reciprocate with its own gifts, loyalty, and opportunities in the war's aftermath.

Unlike Britons, who saw World War II as a desperate struggle for survival against truly dangerous foes, Ugandans drew on older local understandings of war as proving new leaders, pulling new resources into the country, and exposing youth to new ideas and connections capable of remaking politics. Beyond direct military recruitment and propaganda, the fundraising meetings, vernacular newspapers, and popular entertainments that characterized the war years fostered the growth of a modern public sphere. In newspapers, meetings, shops, and buses, Ugandans discussed the war, connected with a broader world, and passed rumors of local scandals and dramas. In this new public sphere, norms, whether of proper colonial civilization and order or of indigenous cultural hierarchy and deference, were threatened from all sides. The war years from 1939 to the end of 1944 brought the final collapse of older elite politics into scandal and ineffectuality as popular activists used the scandal surrounding the pregnancy and marriage of Buganda's moral guardian – the Nnamasole (queen mother) – to discredit older Christian leaders, bringing down a prime minister and affirming the value and power of popular opinion. Thinned and stretched by war, British officials and missionaries increasingly lost control over institutions key to older systems of colonialism, including schools and churches, even as Ugandans demonstrated organizational and leadership skill, political will, and economic resources.

As the war ended, Uganda's 77,000 newly cosmopolitan soldiers began to return home, and a war-impoverished Britain considered how to repay debts to Uganda that included more than a million pounds sterling in direct lending and three million from the Cotton and Coffee Fund, as well as soldiers' wages and more abstract indebtedness. Ugandans joined in an overt, public mass politics that demanded what they believed they were owed. In January 1945, a well-organized general strike forced payment of war bonuses and increased salaries for a range of workers, as well as toppling unpopular local government ministers and chiefs and unsettling imperial complacency. In September 1945, the prime minister of Buganda, Martin Luther Nsibirwa, was assassinated on the steps of Namirembe Cathedral the morning after he had – in opposition to local opinion – forced legislation through Buganda's parliament that provided for government seizure of private land for public purposes, such as the expansion of Makerere University College and the imperial experimental cotton facility. Between 1945 and 1949, cotton growers, motor drivers, and activists of the explicitly political Bataka Union funded and mobilized a pushy and demanding international lobbying effort, mass public meetings in Uganda, and a covert network that embarrassed British officials and culminated in the cotton holdups and mass uprisings of March 1949. Banned, these organizations went underground, but the civil society that fostered them and the mobilizing skills they demonstrated remained in use by activists well into the 1950s as they reshaped Buganda and Uganda in relation to Britain and the world.

War and Opportunity: Ugandan Perspectives

To understand why Ugandans saw the war as an opportunity rather than a danger, it helps to look at how they wrote about it. Robert Kakembo, an elite educated Ugandan veteran from the protectorate's central kingdom of Buganda, produced an English language pamphlet circulated in Uganda to provide officials with some sense of Africans' goals. The pamphlet, "An African Soldier Speaks," described World War II as a time of dramatic opportunity in Uganda. Kakembo described soldiers – often from remote regions – who came into the army ignorant. In his description, though, each returned home as an individual "smartly dressed in His Majesty's uniform and with plenty of money ... he is 100 per cent changed. He is fat and strong, clean and clever, with plenty to talk about and lots of money to spend" Such men, he wrote "proved to Europeans that he [the African soldier] is not inferior." And beyond proving himself to Europeans, a man who "learnt to read and write ... used to reading newspapers, to listening to wireless broadcasts . . . will never submit to the neglect that the uneducated masses, back home in the villages, undergo." Even civilians, Kakembo argues, had been changed as "the war has brought about a great industrial revolution and agricultural improvement. The favourable prices, the assured market . . . all these have brought about a great revolution in the ordinary life of the African, and he is not going back to where he started in 1939."[3]

From this description of war transforming individual African men and European perceptions of their abilities, Kakembo argued for a harnessing of skill, hope, and discontent to produce development and progress. Instead of an administration that muddled by, coordinated by increasingly elderly and out-of-date chiefs, he bluntly asserted that "They must give room to the young generation." Kakembo's politics were not those of simple African-ization, socialism, or modern nationalism as he, like some other returning soldiers, lobbied British patrons to recognize war service as a qualification for chiefships and offices in the protectorate's Native governments. Instead, his vision was one of hard-earned material consumption, and he viewed postwar Ugandans as increasingly educated, sophisticated about consumer goods and commodities markets, thoughtful about the country's future, and aware of gaps in knowledge, but eager and able to learn. "He does not want to accept things blindly, he wants to know why . . . and he wants to give his views. . . . We . . . are very impatient, because we want to grow overnight."[4]

World War II changed Uganda not through violence or collective experi-ences, in Kakembo's analysis, but by remaking individuals and their possi-bilities within a complex local history. Newly tested individuals – whether ex-soldiers or successful cotton farmers – became important as leaders for a new path, but they did so from a thicket of cultural ideals and institu-tions, most notably those of the kingdom of Buganda. British discussions of "demobilization" and hope for a calm return of at least 80 percent of soldiers to rural farms[5] did not describe what Kakembo and others sought as the war ended. Instead, asserting that "The African needs firmness and leadership," Kakembo called for *mobilization* with compulsory education and work that would provide a basis for a new economic, social, and politi-cal order. The ideas of directed development, enforced communal cohesion,

---

[3] Robert Kakembo, *An African Soldier Speaks* (London: Edinburgh House Press, 1946), 9–10, 22, 24. Soldiers eagerly used Army information rooms, learned to read and write, kept in contact with home, and voiced opinions on local political conflicts, according to Army censors in "What the askari thinks," *Fortnightly Review*, copy in CO 536/215/12. CO, TNA, Kew.

[4] Kakembo, *An African Soldier Speaks*, 44.

[5] Officials estimated that only 20% of returning soldiers would find paid employment. "80% will have to return and remain on the land." P. L. O'Brien, "Report on the political situation in Uganda and the events leading up to the Buganda disturbances of January 1945 by G2(I) Northern Area, 13 May 1945," WO 276/504, TNA, Kew.

and the rise of the youth featured in Kalembo's vision of leadership; his program evoked, in some measure, early ideas of Fascist development, rather than the rural romanticism or laissez-faire progressivism of the war's victors. Perhaps alive to such implications, he quoted Winston Churchill's wartime declaration, "Give us the tools and we will finish the job."[6] Development and membership in the new wider world was the job. World War II and Ugandans' experiences as participants in it, he asserted, offered the some of the necessary tools.

Kakembo was far from alone in his sense of himself and other returning soldiers as potential leaders of a new Uganda.[7] In Uganda during the war years not just African activists, but even British officials, most notably two wartime governors, Sir Philip Euen Mitchell and Sir Charles Cecil Farquharson Dundas, were impatient with older doctrines of high colonialism such as indirect rule, and eager to promote the politics of the new educated classes. Mitchell's sponsorship of Makerere College and rejection of any adapted form of education in favor of the broader education of a new African elite was part of his vision that the new Africa required new leadership.[8] His successor, Dundas, had gained prominence in earlier years for fostering of Africanized coffee cooperatives in Tanganyika. In wartime Uganda he struggled energetically for local government reforms that would offer younger, educated activists a public voice at the expense of older kingdom-based institutions.[9] His final gesture before he was replaced by the more conservative Sir John Hathorn Hall was to call for an ambitious program of investment in social welfare and economic development. Dundas dismissed incipient panic over the economic, social, and political effects of returning soldiers on Uganda's stability by asserting the best preparation for demobilization would be to

> improve... conditions of all sorts in the ex-soldiers' [homeland and to] make a land fit for heroes to live in. It will not surprise me if these returning soldiers give some trouble to their own authorities, especially to such as are incompetent and venal. They have lived under the superb leadership of British officers

---

[6] Kakembo, *An African Soldier Speaks*, 46, 47.

[7] Timothy Parsons describes how the Colonial Office originally welcomed Kakembo's pamphlet, but then viewed its political agenda as provocative and banned it. Nevertheless, the East African Command printed and circulated 400 copies as guides to district officers on what to expect from veterans. Parsons, *The African Rank-and-File* (Portsmouth, NH: Heinemann, 1999), 249.

[8] Sir Phillip Mitchell's speech is in the *Proceedings of the Inter-territorial Conference held at Makerere, Uganda, 21–24 May, 1938 on the Establishment of a Higher College* (Entebbe: Government Printer, June 1938).

[9] See Sally Falk Moore, "Encounter and suspicion in Tanzania," in J. Borneman and A. Hammoudi (eds.), *Being There* (Berkeley: University of California Press, 2009), 162; and on Uganda, Sir Norman Whitley, *Report on the Commission of Inquiry into the Disturbances which Occurred in Uganda during 1945* (Entebbe: Government Printer, 1945).

...and have seen inefficiency ruthlessly liquidated. They may not gladly tolerate a regime of muddle...nor defer to incompetent superiors and they may demand to have a voice in the management of affairs. Personally I would consider that a healthy tendency....The influence of thousands of men coming among the people with new ideas and experiences may bring a much needed rousing spirit into native life and body politic.[10]

These critics believed that Uganda, and perhaps especially the protectorate's central kingdom of Buganda, had become stagnant. The late 1940s brought a possibility of dynamic change. Dundas, Kakembo, and others portrayed soldiers and wartime entrepreneurs as energetic potential leaders who could pull Uganda from its backwardness and exhausted crisis to build something new. The generation that had negotiated the Uganda Agreement of 1900 and administered the country under vague British oversight had lost credibility as local observers denounced what they saw as the degeneration of the kingdom.[11] Protectorate and missionary institutions and initiatives, such as those of the kingdom of Buganda, came under increasing overt criticism by activists as both lacked resources and often relied on key personnel who had been young at the beginning of the century when the protectorate was founded and grown old working in Uganda.[12] Britain, stressed by the war, was barely able to staff and administer scant protectorate offices, let alone direct development.[13] The general strike in January 1945, and the assassination of the prime minister later that year, further confirmed observers' sense of the weakness and inadequacy of the older men and longstanding arrangements that had guided Buganda through the early years of colonialism.

In viewing service in a victorious military campaign as a qualification for leadership, Kakembo pointed to soldiers' initiation into the mysteries of new consumer goods, information networks, and technical knowledge. His assertion of victorious warfare as a qualification was not simple militarism. It fit well with older Ugandan ideas of warfare as a profitable activity and way of demonstrating competence and loyalty to the king and those who controlled the kingdom's high offices. Summarizing generations of statecraft within Buganda, a retired official noted that war could be called for when the country was poor and needed more cattle, if an official needed to get rid of a rival or (solving two problems at once) if "the country had lots of young men who might cause trouble, the way to get rid of them was to declare

---

[10] Sir Charles Dundas to Sir A. Dawe, September 7, 1943, CO 536/209/2, TNA, Kew.
[11] See Carol Summers, "Youth, elders, and metaphors of political change in late colonial Buganda," in A. Burton and H. Charton-Bigot (eds.), *Generations Past: Youth in East African History* (Athens: Ohio University Press, 2010), 175–95.
[12] C. E. Stuart, "28 years of happiness in Africa," 5, unpublished memoir, MS 3983, Archives at Lambeth Palace Library, London.
[13] Gardner Thompson argues that during World War II, Britain "all but lost control of" Buganda. See Thompson, *Governing Uganda: British Colonial Rule and its Legacy* (Kampala: Fountain Press, 2003), 222–44.

war; some would be killed and others would return rich in cattle and women which they have plundered from other tribes."[14] In this analysis, war produced prosperity that allowed competent and tested new leaders to emerge, focusing their rapaciousness outside the kingdom, rather than in faction fights within it. War created leaders not directly through some militaristic or heroic model, but practically, as a means of accumulating the resources necessary for prosperous patronage and killing the unqualified. War, progress, and opportunities were closely related concepts for Ugandans.[15]

In 1945, soldiers discussed the appointment of one of their comrades, Mikaeri Kawalya Kaggwa, as Buganda's finance minister and, after Nsibirwa's assassination, prime minister. Kawalya Kaggwa was a returned soldier appointed to restore order to the administration of a kingdom in crisis. Ambitious for their own futures, serving soldiers asserted, "Now the kabaka [king] is fed up with his chiefs and is waiting for the askaris [soldiers] whom he wants to appoint." These soldiers spoke dismissively of aging leaders and arrangements, and saw themselves as solutions to the country's problem: men proven by war, ready to take offices and lead in Buganda's meritocratic system of chiefship or to found building societies, cooperatives, and enterprises to compete with Indian cotton marketing and omnibuses and produce both personal and communal wealth.[16]

This sense of World War II as an opportunity rather than something to fear extended beyond Uganda's soldiers. Far from the war's major combat, Uganda experienced only limited military casualties in its armed forces, felt only minor shortages, and, despite increased taxes and price controls,[17] was prosperous – indeed wealthy – as Britain was bombed, drafted, and rationed. Notable Baganda, including some veterans of World War I, such as Prince Suna, participated in military recruitment drives. Educated, politically connected elites, such as Stanley Kisingiri, coordinated a series of films, concerts, and events designed to simultaneously propagandize

---

[14] Anonymous author, "Leadership study," typescript (1954), Sir Keith Hancock Papers, 29/1/6/4, Institute for Commonwealth Studies, University of London.

[15] Recent histories of precolonial Buganda differ over local meanings regarding the term "war." Richard Reid described precolonial warfare as "fundamental to the process of state-building, to the material basis of state power and to internal cohesion." While acknowledging its inherent violence and disruption, he described war as having "enormous significance as an agency of change and national self-expression"; see *Political Power in Pre-Colonial Buganda* (Oxford: James Currey, 2002) 178–79. Holly Hanson's interpretation is darker, emphasizing war's elevation of successful looters and how they alter the balance of power; see *Landed Obligation: The Practice of Power in Buganda* (Portsmouth, NH: Heinemann, 2003), 59–87, 107–112.

[16] "What the askari thinks," copy in CO 536/215/12. CO, TNA, Kew.

[17] Governor Dundas criticized wartime taxes, citing estimates that "out of an average earning of Shs.110/ derived by a Muganda peasant from his economic cultivation he nets no more than Shs. 27/" after direct and indirect taxation. Sir Charles Dundas, "Memorandum on native taxation," March 19, 1942, CO 536/209/10, TNA, Kew.

Ugandans and elicit voluntary donations. Ugandans from the elite to the ordinary bought tickets and donated money to attend performances that ranged from a display of bicycling tricks to football matches, skits, dance, and singing.[18] With their careful recording and publicizing of organizers and donors, these events allowed Ugandans to display their strength, loyalty, and concern for Uganda's future and their ability to address causes ranging from specific military equipment to impoverished British old people and European refugees. Ugandans expected these displays to lead to postwar acknowledgement and rewards from both local and British elites.

Such displays were not limited to ambitious individuals willing to organize, sing, or donate money. Ugandans mobilized collective organizations for explicit demonstrations of wartime loyalty that reversed paternalistic imperial expectations and called for reciprocity. The Colonial Office was disconcerted, for example, by the decision of Native Government officials in the Eastern province to give Britain thousands of pounds in interest-free loans from their surplus balances, welcoming both the money and the spirit, but nervous about the implications of such a dramatic diversion of local tax money from local concerns to the imperial exchequer.[19] The country's top school, Makerere, established a cadet corps in 1940 that drilled, learned to shoot, and presented itself for inspection by military officials.[20] And the Catholic church, despite or because of the monitoring and intermittent detentions that its Italian clergy were subject to, encouraged its schoolboys to enlist and actively cooperate with propaganda efforts.[21]

Britain lacked the administrative capacity to force Uganda to mobilize for total war.[22] Nonetheless, the country mobilized in its own way, as men "volunteered" for respectable military service while disdaining work in the labor brigades, expanded production of cotton while making concerns about exploitation and Indian control of ginneries clear, and handed over financial surpluses in ways that made indigenous wealth (as opposed to British need) prominent.[23] Despite complaints by some British observers that Ugandans failed to understand the war as desperately serious, anecdotes of their participation in war-related activities show Ugandans connected in personal ways

---

[18] These events were widely covered in the *Uganda Herald*. Beyond fundraisers for general war-fighting, specific events such as a boxing tournament aided thousands of Polish refugees in Uganda.

[19] Sums involved ranged from £15,000 from Teso and £1,250 from Busoga in cotton-growing regions to £1,500 from the marginal Karamojong. Governor of Uganda to colonial secretary, July 20, 1942, CO 536/209/1, TNA, Kew.

[20] File 1, Box 517, MSS. Perham (Papers of Dame Margery Freda Perham), Bodleian Library of Commonwealth and African Studies at Rhodes House (hereafter BLCAS-RH), Oxford.

[21] [Unsigned copy], "Mobile propaganda safari in Uganda," (1943), file 1, Box 530, MSS. Perham, BLCAS-RH, Oxford.

[22] See discussion in Thompson, *Governing Uganda*, 77–79.

[23] Ibid., 96–165.

with what the war meant. Individuals made ostentatiously large donations, such as the £1,200 Christmas donation by the Kabaka in 1942.[24] They also raised money through events. Football matches, boxing tournaments, and bicycle displays allowed both performers and spectators to connect to specific war funds, supporting Greek and Polish refugees in Uganda and a home for the elderly in Bristol, as well as chairs for antiaircraft batteries in Coventry and ultimately specific military supplies, including airplanes and a ship.[25] Along the way, these "loyal" Ugandans emphasized that they were part of a new political class that expected opportunities. Writing from the emerging hub of radical Ugandan politics, Kampala's Katwe neighborhood, A. B. Mukwaya argued:

> A new social class is being born before our very eyes... taking form and shape at a speed that is to some people terrifying. Certainly the war has helped to speed up this growth. This class becomes increasingly self-conscious and excessively vocal every day; and all this to... acquire... a position... in the social and political life of the country.[26]

The exhaustion of the old and the challenges of war offered Ugandans, whether in Buganda or beyond, an opportunity for legitimate authority as individuals and parts of a new Uganda. This authority was accessible in the military, but also beyond it in civic and local government organizations that proclaimed loyalty and abilities, calling, in the historical context of Buganda, for recognition and reciprocity on the part of the British institutions and individuals that received this help. Within Uganda, recruitment campaigns coordinated by Ugandans pulled an estimated 10 percent of men of military age into the armed forces during the war.[27] Ugandans accepted new taxes and unfavorable price regulations, and they donated money for the war effort. Offices, tax abatements, higher cotton and coffee prices for growers, new access to civil service jobs and government preferments dominated by Indians, and higher wages for all – these could provide opportunities for many in the postwar context, and seemed like the least people could expect in return for their generosity and sacrifices.[28]

War as Danger: British Perspectives

During the war, British officials fostered such local understandings of World War II as an opportune moment rather than a crisis or danger. When, in 1940, the war came to East Africa, the governor's press release was curiously blasé, telling Ugandans: do not be afraid. There are Italian forces in Abyssinia but

---

[24] *Uganda Herald*, October 14, 1942.
[25] Private donations and fundraisers were reported in the *Uganda Herald*.
[26] A. B. Mukwaya to editor, *Uganda Herald*, December 28, 1944.
[27] Thompson, *Governing Uganda*, 96.
[28] The concept of reciprocal obligation is a key idea threaded throughout Hanson's *Landed Obligation*.

it is a very long way from you people of Uganda, and there are large armies to prevent them from coming here. It is possible but not likely that you may see an Italian aeroplane or two over some part of Uganda; if you do, do not be frightened. Sit quietly in your banana groves or under any trees until it has gone away. It will do you no harm.[29]

Even as the governor reassured Uganda's people, an imperiled Britain moved away from benign language about imperial partnerships and development for mutual benefit in the context of the war effort, and rather desperately sought to extract as much money and support as possible from Uganda and other parts of the empire not already lost to the Japanese. In the summer of 1940, and even more aggressively in the summer of 1941 and after, Britain demanded money from Uganda, calling for higher taxes and the transfer of revenues to the British exchequer. "Everybody is overtaxed," commented a Colonial Office analyst, "but if the UK taxpayer is to go on accepting heavy sacrifices... it would be only reasonable that the African should accept taxation."[30]

Simultaneously in Uganda, British officials complained that Ugandans were making no real sacrifices for the war and expressed nervousness about the implications of Ugandan war contributions for the country's future politics.[31] Overstretched by the transfer of 20 percent of European administrative personnel to the military, the cancellation of leaves, the addition of new war-related responsibilities such as conscription, disbursement of family allowances and the arrest of deserters, ongoing demands for donations to the war effort, and ordinary wartime shortages of bicycle parts and consumer goods, stressed European officials reacted nervously to African sacrifices, demonstrations of loyalty, or expectations for reciprocity. They held tight to routines and joked with dread about what would happen when "the undisciplined African [came] home from the wars" and made political demands. An observant propaganda officer considered it "unpleasantly sinister" how worried officers "frankly urge us to fire our weapons [in a military exhibition] so that Africans might appreciate the futility of arguing with Bren guns."[32]

As the war began, Uganda's governor dreaded the political and social implications of the country's involvement enough that he had argued for negotiations with Italy to make Africa a demilitarized zone.[33] His successor

---

[29] The message ended "Have no fear, we shall prevail." Governor Philip Mitchell, "Message to the people of Uganda," June 11, 1940, file 2, Box 530, MSS. Perham, BLCAS-RH, Oxford.

[30] Illegible signature, note, October 4, 1943, CO 536/209/15, TNA, Kew.

[31] For example, L. Lawson to Mr. and Mrs. Lawson (Dublin), August 14, 1942, CO 536/209/6; details for the governor's correspondence on contributions can be found in CO 536/209/1, TNA, Kew.

[32] See "Mobile propaganda safari in Uganda," file 1, Box 530, MSS. Perham, BLCAS-RH.

[33] Sir Philip Mitchell to Margery Perham, December 24, 1939, File 3, Box 514, MSS Perham, BLCAS-RH, Oxford.

was more willing to push Uganda for the resources that an embattled empire needed, but remained concerned about putting the empire into Uganda's debt, noting in 1943 that by the end of the war, the empire was likely to owe the protectorate more than a million pounds, not including the full pockets of demobilized soldiers and the unspent savings of Ugandans who had been unable to buy bicycles and other scarce goods during the war owing to restrictions on imports. People, he argued, would be well-off enough to demand more in every area from consumer goods to education, health care, roads, agricultural extension services, and good government.[34]

Far from understanding the war as offering benign opportunities for furthering Britain's partnership with its proven Ugandan allies, wartime British officers grew anxious and suspicious of Ugandan initiative and leadership. Governor Dundas, for example, relied on local elites for both their ability to secure civic peace and their skill in procuring wartime resources, but he neither liked nor respected them. He argued that those in charge of native treasuries had collected taxes, but failed to spend more than half of what they collected, being particularly slow about delivering education and other services. While that meant they had funds to donate to the imperial government, it boded ill for their effectiveness. Local authorities, he asserted, were likely to experience trouble from returning soldiers because many were "incompetent and venal." It would take British authorities, he argued, rather than new powers for African institutions, to serve the masses as opposed to an elite class of chiefs and landowners.

Wartime tensions were particularly acute in the kingdom of Buganda. British leaders might occasionally joke about the war's usefulness in allowing them to banish imperial troublemakers, but the reality was anxiety for the white community as Italians and Germans (including those of Jewish background) were detained, Polish and Greek refugees arrived along with prisoners of war, and a civil labor board drafted local white wives into secretarial and support positions.[35]

The most dramatic breakdown of any hope that service in World War II would lead directly to imperial patronage, though, came in the aftermath of 1945's dramatic events – the January general strike and the September assassination of Buganda's prime minister. Prince Suna, a World War I veteran who had been a prominent military recruiter, died in detention,

[34] Governor Dundas's analysis was as provocative as Kakembo's. See Sir Charles Dundas to Sir A. Dawe, September 7, 1943, CO 536/209/2, TNA, Kew.

[35] See Bishop of Uganda to Max Warren, copy enclosed in Max Warren to Archbishop of Canterbury, January 1,1954, 150: 80–1, Archives at Lambeth Palace Library, London. Dr. Wachsman, a German Jew employed as a school coordinator, was detained as an enemy alien, as were Italian fathers and sisters working in northern Uganda. Polish and Greek refugees were discussed in the *Uganda Herald*. Prisoners of war were deployed within Uganda at tasks that included clearing swampland near Jinja. On white women's war work, see minutes, Civil Defense Board, Mss Afr. S 523, BLCAS-RH, Oxford.

accused of complicity. Stanley Kisingiri, who had led efforts to collect Ugandan donations for the war effort, was deported to the Seychelles. Further, in an articulate collection of petitions, other leading Baganda protested from their detention site at Kitgum that Britain had betrayed them. As a petition from the wives of detainees asserted, "each one of [the detainees] has . . . put in a period of valuable service in the country[;] each one of them set himself out to do his utmost towards the successful prosecution of the war. Each gave freely according to his means."[36] Yet, such prominent and loyal men had been detained without charges or due process. "We should be reluctant to believe that the Uganda Attorney General is naturally a sadist who rejoices in the suffering of people without cause, but it is very curious." The detainees complained that instead of acknowledging loyalty and following "civilized" rules, British officials chose to act like the "Gestapo."[37] As Mrs. Kamulegeya noted, even Axis leaders like Himmler and Goering got trials: her husband, and the other detainees who had helped build British Uganda, did not.[38]

War as Disappointment

As the war ended, individual Africans expected opportunities and rewards for their proven loyalty, while at the same time Britons expressed nervousness about the empire's proven need for Ugandans as allies, not simply subjects. This tension shaped a complicated, experimental popular politics in postwar Uganda, especially Buganda. Britain's wartime allies were not noticeably radical advocates of social change or nationalism. In advocating strong governance and British guidance, they included some of the country's conservatives. The retired Lieutenant Mikaeri Kawalya Kaggwa, who became prime minister, was especially quick to dismiss any popular or youthful pressure for democracy or change, asserting "What Buganda needs is hard work and discipline so that [the people] may be happy with the little things they have." He went on to condemn advocates of rapid change, asking "What have they done . . . Have they improved their country in any way? Have they cultivated and kept good farms? No!!"[39] Even Kakembo's call for "a flying age" was coupled with a call for British guidance, rather than any abrupt autarky. Kakembo and Kawalya Kaggwa,

[36] E. Kamulegeya, A. Wamala, E. Kiingi, and K. Kanyike to A. Creech Jones, July 30, 1946, CO536/211, TNA, Kew.
[37] Detainees at Kitgum prison camp to A. Creech Jones, July 23, 1946, CO 536/211, TNA, Kew.
[38] Kamulegeya, Wamala, Kiingi, and Kanyike to Creech Jones, July 30, 1946, CO536/211, TNA, Kew.
[39] M. E. Kawalya Kagwa to Rev. Canon H. M. Grace, December 5, 1945, Box 281, CBMS A/T. 3/2, Archives and Special Collections, School of Oriental and African Studies Library, University of London, London. Kagwa's title was essentially an honorary rank for Africans in East African military units did not receive commissions.

one hopeful for what he called "the age of speed" and the other rooted in farming, were only two of many intensely political Baganda and Ugandans who sought their own visions of how the country should develop after the war.

> In 1945, the *Uganda Herald* held an essay contest on "The Ideal African Chief for 1945." The top prize went to Seperiya Kisauzi Masembe's carefully balanced essay, which emphasized the ideal chief as an ethical and rational bureaucratic administrator, providing social services and good government, before ending with a brief hint of something more political in vague suggestions that the ideal chief: knows... that he is his people's representative, their mouthpiece. Encourages Societies where his people discuss their affairs and put them before him.... He gives them free speech but he is firm.... He reads books and newspapers, not only of his own country, but of others too.... He willingly changes his opinion if proved to be wrong.... In his private life political controversies have no room.[40]

The reality of a newly complex politics, though, could be seen in the British judge's decision to award prizes as well to at least fourteen other entrants, who ranged from Catholic teaching brothers to detained political activists, at least some of whom rejected the idea that chiefs should work well with British officials or stand as neutral civil servants, instead emphasizing the need for democratically elected chiefs who would educate but also involve people in their country's politics and decisions.[41]

Britain, rationing bread at home and offering development aid slowly and unimpressively, seemed to offer Ugandans little and threatened Ugandan autonomy. The Ugandan "Civil Reabsorption Office" failed to support returning soldiers in their ambitions to form cooperatives and businesses, instead simply reserving entry level positions in the protectorate's police forces, prison service, and post office for "the better type" of returning soldiers and proffering limited technical training that prepared less than 10 percent of returnees in crafts ranging from building to shoemaking.[42] Overall, veterans were so unimpressed by the demobilization process that district archives are full of individual petitions for compassionate leave and early discharge, and district offices found themselves left with last pay packets that

---

[40] "The ideal African chief for 1945," *Uganda Herald*, November 7, 1945.

[41] See coverage in Uganda Herald, 1945. Essays were in English, restricting possible submissions. See also petitions from Fenekansi Musoke, Y. S. Bamutta and I. K. Musazi, 1945, CO 536/211. Without accountability, Musazi noted, "The people pay... leaders, and... get shocking bad value for their money."

[42] Many reserved positions went unfilled – in 1946, the police department reported four applicants for eighty reserved vacancies; for example, see civil reabsorption officer to all district commissioners, September 9, 1945, Box 280; civil reabsorption officer to district commissioners, May 17, 1946, and civil reabsorption officer to district commissioners, May 15, 1947, Box 282, both in Toro District Archive, Mountains of the Moon University, Fort Portal, Uganda.

impatient veterans failed to claim.[43] An embittered detainee, Y. S. Bamutta, delineated a program of economic initiatives that would reward Uganda for its wartime efforts and allow it to develop, but noted that his ideas were blocked:

> Both the Protectorate Government and vested interests have deliberately pursued a policy of criminal negligence in regard to the problem of returning money to the developing economic scheme of the country.... [This is because] the Baganda if developed economically would interfere with the monopolies of cotton, coffee etc from which the Protectorate Government is drawing a huge yearly income.[44]

Thus, the postwar politics of Uganda, most notable in the central kingdom of Buganda, centered on efforts by popular Ganda activists to mobilize for popular control of a changing economic and political world. Instead of loot and offices for returning soldiers and young men, there were new economic initiatives – such as cotton ginneries and bus routes – that Ganda entrepreneurs wanted to seize.[45] Activists organized in the 1940s at least partly simply to demonstrate their administrative capacity and influence.

Cotton growers, whose sterling surpluses and acceptance of submarket prices had contributed to Britain's economic survival during the war, organized during the late 1940s in the African Farmers' Cooperative to advocate "free trade" and market opportunities. They sought to organize their own cooperatives, gin their own cotton, and acquire a greater share of profits from high world prices. Growers were meticulous in their attention to status. They were intensely entrepreneurial and capitalist. But they hosted British socialist politician Fenner Brockway and emphasized in the splendor and organization of their welcome to Brockway that they had the ability and right to administer the country's economy. Overawed by his reception, he wrote that not only had he initially been welcomed by more than 3,000 people who lined his way from the airport, but throughout his visit:

> I have never experienced anything like the succession of meetings to which I was taken.... The arrangements for my tour were perfect... this outlawed Farmers' Union had constructed meeting-places for the occasion in twenty

[43] Compassionate leave was requested on the grounds of houses burning, family members' insanity, unpaid debts, second wives needed, sick parents, etc. Investigation of district officials produced mixed results. Some men whose last pay and gratuities went unclaimed were owed more than 100 shillings. District commissioner Fort Portal to accountant general, May 17, 1947, box 282, Toro District Archive, Mountains of the Moon University, Fort Portal, Uganda.

[44] Y. S. Bamuta to Creech Jones, July 24, 1946, CO 536/211, TNA, Kew. New histories emphasize the austerity that characterized postwar Britain. For example, see David Kynaston, *Austerity Britain: 1945–1951* (London: Bloomsbury Publishing, 2008).

[45] See Parsons, *The African Rank-and-File*. For Kenya, see Hal Brand, "Wartime recruiting practices, martial identity and post World War II demobilization in colonial Kenya," *Journal of African History*, 46 (2005) 103–25. Ugandan patterns were similar.

centres far distant in the country. In two places, where there was no available accommodation, they had actually erected bamboo bungalows, duly fitted with European-style lavatories, for my one-night's stay!

Growers made clear to Brockway that they were men of substance who expected to make their own decisions and earn their own profits, rejecting both the monopoly power of Indian cotton ginners and the administrative fiat of Uganda's administrators. Brockway reported being questioned closely:

> Did governments in England tell farmers what they must grow and how they must grow it? Did the Government fix prices, pool the crops, sell in the world market and keep the profits? My replies shook them. Not all that, I would say, but a good deal of it. They would look at me with astonishment. Why did we put up with it?

Far from petitioning Britain, whether for development assistance, marketing help, or charity, these growers saw themselves as able, organized, and aware, with no need to put up with British interventions. Reading newspapers, holding meetings, and organizing in cooperatives, these growers knew how the protectorate government had accumulated a cotton fund of more than three million pounds. Many mobilized not just economically, but with the political Bataka Union, which asserted that before and during the war, growers had trusted the administration to deal honestly but after the war "they had completely emerged from the 'dark canyon' of ignorance.... This cotton and coffee money was the property of the growers." Frustrated activists complained, however, that "the parties who received money from the cotton and coffee crops" were the protectorate government, the native government, the Europeans, and the growers.[46]

This juxtaposition of entrepreneurialism, organization, and radical rejection of British colonial interventions was not unique to the cotton growers' association. As the war ended in the 1940s, people in Uganda were increasingly political as they read or listened to a variety of local vernacular newspapers and gossip networks, participated in modern organizations ranging from church groups and cooperatives to unions and political associations, and worked to shape both the upcoming generation of Ganda leaders and the future of Uganda's development. Their networks were modern and cosmopolitan in their engagement with a larger world, but very Ganda-centric in their analysis and aims. This local vision of the world rested on several basic understandings. First was the assertion that Buganda was not a British colony, but an ally, tied to Britain for mutual benefit but not subject to Britain or owned as a territory. Second, leading Baganda saw their connections with Britain as significantly helpful to the empire, and expected their

---

[46] Translation of letter from Bataka Union to governor of Uganda, printed in *Gambuze* and reproduced in *Fortnightly Review*, September 9, 1948, CO 537/3601, TNA, Kew.

help in time of Britain's crisis to be reciprocated and indeed pay dividends when the Axis powers had been defeated. Finally, activists, frustrated by Britain's failure to acknowledge and pay its debts and eager to seize new postwar opportunities, regularly compared British recalcitrance to the misgovernance attributed to Nazi Germany. Seperiya Kadumukasa Kaggwa – a former chief, active cotton businessman, and relatively conservative political figure – nevertheless critiqued Britain's response to the 1945 general strike as a move toward a "REIGN OF TERROR as it was in Germany during HITLER'S REGIME."[47] Kadumukasa Kaggwa's activism, like that of many cotton growers and other activists, was almost libertarian in its confident assertion of Ugandans' ability and eagerness to take care of themselves, and rejection of developmentalist or paternalist planning and interventions by British administrators.

Radical Mobilization

The radical politics of the late 1940s in Uganda was an awkward fit with international class-based politics or modernist ideas of state-sponsored development planning. Instead, the 1945 general strike, the cotton activism of the late 1940s, and the Bataka movement leading up to the 1949 insurrection were all movements that crossed classes, from elites to day laborers, and Banyarwanda immigrants. The political language they spoke emphasized betrayed loyalties, poor patronage, and abuses that undermined Ganda ideas of ethical power and governance rooted in reciprocity between generous patrons and hardworking heirs.

Given the meaninglessness of class-based politics among ambitious men seeking social mobility and the alienness of European categories of Fascism and liberal democracy, Ganda political activists worked to develop a Ganda form of political action. One of their most creative initiatives in the late 1940s was the Bataka Union. In the publicity photo in Figure 25.1, it is possible to see a mass meeting that gathered together working men with bicycles to listen and donate funds. Bataka Union meetings could, according to British intelligence estimates, attract thousands of participants who contributed directly by putting money in the baskets circulated in meetings and indirectly by buying the pictures, pamphlets, and badges the movement produced.[48] Its leaders offered Britain advice and called for a postwar future of indigenous modernity. Unlike meetings organized by missionaries, officials, or experts, the agenda was controlled by local activists, not international guides. Platform speakers emphasized Buganda's clans that guarded

---

[47] Emphasis in original, Seperiya R, Kadumukasa Kaggwa to secretary of state for the colonies, October 2, 1945, CO 536/215.9, TNA, Kew.

[48] See reports on these meetings in the fortnightly intelligence reports of 1948 and 1949, CO537/3600, TNA, Kew.

FIGURE 25.1. Publicity photo of Bataka Union mass meeting, enclosed with petitions from the Bataka, [1948], CO 537/3593, TNA, Kew.

the inheritance and security of all Baganda, developing a rhetoric of citizenship not on the basis of individuality, but for people tied together with responsibilities and rights. This rhetoric emphasized the country's senior men as grandfathers who held the past in trust for the grandsons who had a right to their inheritance. Neither Marxist nor nationalist, Bataka activists offered harsh critiques of senior men and of Buganda's Kabaka (king) for collaborating with Britain and eating and enjoying Buganda's resources, rather than acting ethically, guarding the land and preparing the children for the future. Most important, they called for the people to elect their own representatives and officials.

Despite the traditional view of warfare as *resolving* the disorderliness of young men by ensuring that they got either death or opportunities, and the marked willingness of activists to cooperate across expected ideological divides, Uganda's political turmoil increased in the late 1940s. Men who sought offices, unionized for improved conditions and pay, founded cooperatives to market goods or buy and sell cotton, mobilized to challenge inadequacies of mission churches and schools, or even just read and discussed a range of controversial vernacular newspapers, became part of a political scene full of demands and action. Some activists worked with British officials or mission institutions; however, for others, it proved easy to slip

7. 26th APRIL: Section of crowd with banners against
                    tree.

FIGURE 25.2. Police photograph of scene showing part of a massing of thousands of protesters stormed by a police baton charge that left the symbols of social mobility – protesters' bicycles – behind, to be collected by barefoot police in imperial uniforms, dated April 26, 1949, in "Strikes and disturbances in Kampala during April 1949: photographs taken during 1949 riots," CO 537/5864, TNA, Kew.

from petitions to an active citizenship that included lobbying to insurrection. Detained after the 1945 general strike, activists such as Ignatius Musazi, Fenekasi Musoke, Henry Kanyike, Yusuf Bamutta, and others denied any wrongdoing, but many reemerged within the energetic politics of the 1949 uprising, a carefully timed and organized violent conflict that ended with military intervention, thousands of arrests and collective fines for the people of Buganda.

Conclusions

World War II's legacy in Buganda was not simply integration into a broader world and a new worldly class of returned soldiers, but an increasingly widespread – and critical – reevaluation of Buganda's alliance with Britain. While some elites continued to find British allies helpful and productive, more and more Baganda found Britain inadequate. Baganda expressed impatience with Britain as their ally in Uganda's 1945 general strike, in more dramatic mobilizations in an insurrection in 1949, and more loudly during the struggles that shaped the crisis of the 1950s. When they became frustrated with Britain's refusal to listen, they called for acknowledgement of Ganda individual and collective needs, wants, rights, and interests. Buganda's young king, deft in British culture and proud of his honorary commission in Britain's army, complained that Great Britain never told any territory that it was prepared for self-government.[49]

Uganda was not central to World War II. It was well away from all fighting, and avoided mass conscription, but Uganda and its people did more during the war than simply grow cotton for the empire. Ganda officials recruited "volunteer" soldiers. Uganda's donations bought the British air force planes and the navy a ship. Cotton growers loaned Britain millions of pounds from their cotton fund and native government chiefs offered the surplus balances of their treasuries. Everyone suffered a lack of bicycle tires and consumer goods. All this was uncontroversial as what a loyal people did when the king asked and an ally was in danger.

After the war, things changed. In 1946, Kakembo expected a postwar era of leadership and opportunity by young men made modern by their war experiences. His vision highlighted Uganda's tensions, but underestimated the variety of ways those modern men would work with older holders of Ganda values. Far from being a simple place where tradition gave way to modernity through the sponsorship of Britain and its veterans, Uganda, and particularly Buganda, proved spectacularly messy. Traditional values of belonging to land and kin connected with democratic ideals; radical activists learned techniques from Fabian lobbyists, Catholic Action, and the King's African Rifles; and the country's experiment with democratic ideals and rhetoric tumbled into frustration and disarray after an unsuccessful insurrection in 1949.

The legacy of the 1940s proved to be mobilization and mass politics – Kakembo's "impatient" time rather than Kawalya Kaggwa's patronizing call for "hard work" and "little things." The association between returned soldiers and modern nationalism was not simple. But in its challenges and transformation of imperial power and capacity, the spread of new information and worldly ideas, and restructuring of economic relations, production, and commerce, the war remade Ugandans' political worlds. Ugandans found Britain unable or unwilling to reciprocate their loyalty. The new public sphere superseded older relations of loyalty and patronage, leaving contentious Ugandans to fight in new ways, pursuing a sometimes contradictory array of changes.

---

[49] Notes on meeting held November 3, 1953, with the Kabaka, the Omulamuzi, and the governor of Uganda, etc., CO 822/567, TNA, Kew.

SEVEN

CONCLUSION

26

Conclusion

Consequences of the War

Ahmad Alawad Sikainga

The various chapters in this volume have clearly shown Africa's pivotal role in World War II, the profound social, political, and economic changes produced by the war, and the way in which these changes have significantly shaped Africa's post-colonial history. The immediate postwar era in particular witnessed developments that had far-reaching consequences. On the political level, the war weakened the old colonial empires and drastically altered the international balance of power. It also created a new political climate in which the very idea of colonial domination was vigorously questioned, while the concepts of equality and self-determination took the center stage of international politics. Most important, the postwar period opened up new possibilities for colonized people and compelled European imperial powers to reassess their colonial project in Africa and elsewhere. Africans seized this opportunity and used the postwar anticolonial discourse to demand full rights and self-determination.

The political repercussions of the war have been the subject of considerable discussion. However, little attention was given to its myriad economic and social consequences. The imperatives of the war economy led to greater intervention by the colonial state into the lives of ordinary Africans, particularly in the rural areas. This intervention ranged from labor and crop requisition in British and French colonies to elaborate systems of state regulations such as food rationing and price control. Newitt and Clarence-Smith show that even though Spain and Portugal were neutral states during the war, their African colonies still experienced labor and crop requisitions.[1] These policies created severe economic hardships and social dislocation. Schmidt's chapter on Guinea argues that French wartime policies of military recruitment, forced labor, and crop requisitions generated a strong popular reaction and fueled protests that lasted well beyond the end of the war. Impoverished rural farmers resisted labor and crop requisitions and

---

[1] William G. Clarence-Smith, Chapter 9, and Malyn Newitt, Chapter 12, this volume.

embittered forced laborers deserted work, while entire villages fled across colonial borders to avoid military and labor recruitment. These grievances became a catalyst for major changes in the postwar era. They were articulated by the war veterans who returned home with a strong sense of confidence and entitlement and also laid the groundwork for challenging the authority of government appointed chiefs in the postwar period. In the British colony of Nigeria, the colonial state also made relentless efforts to extract and manage resources at a low cost. Judith Byfield's chapter on Abeokuta shows how the efforts of colonial officials to obtain commodities below the cost of production sparked a strong resistance by local producers, particularly women traders who were adversely affected by these policies.[2]

The exigencies of the war and its aftermath prompted colonial powers in Africa to develop new strategies to revamp their regimes and to maximize material benefits. With their battered economies, colonial powers came to rely heavily on their African territories. What is often referred to in the scholarly literature as "the second colonial occupation" meant the exploitation of natural resources with great vigor, the intensification of cash crop production, and the opening of new areas for trade and investment. The new strategies were pursued within the conceptual framework of "development," which was based on the European model of free market, industrialization, and urbanization.

In British West Africa, particularly in the Gold Coast, the government created marketing boards to manage and maximize production and to control prices. Coupled with this was the introduction of capital intensive mechanized schemes. Cash crops generated huge revenues, but the main beneficiaries were the marketing boards, foreign-owned businesses, and a very small percentage of Africans. The overwhelming majority of African producers did not enjoy the postwar boom as a result of the practices of the marketing boards such as price fixing. Although African products commanded high prices in the international market and generated enormous revenue, the surplus was not used to improve the social and economic conditions of rural folks, but was reinvested into new grand schemes. The exploitative policies of the colonial governments triggered several rural protests across the continent. In the Gold Coast, for instance, in 1948 farmers joined other groups such as merchants and war veterans to boycott European- and Syrian-owned businesses.[3] In 1946, the tenants of the Gezira Scheme in the Sudan went on strike after they became convinced that the government was depriving them of their financial rewards. Rural protests erupted in Kenya, Southern Rhodesia, Mozambique, Tanganyika, and South Africa, just to name a few.[4]

---

[2] Judith A. Byfield, Chapter 8, this volume.
[3] D. Austin, *Politics in Ghana, 1946–1960* (London, 1970).
[4] Allen Isaacman, "Peasants and Rural Social Protests in Africa," *African Studies Review*, 33, 2 (1990), 1–120.

The war era witnessed massive growth in urban populations in various parts of Africa. The surge in the transportation of goods, soldiers, military equipment, and supplies led to dramatic expansion of African port cities, military headquarters, and railway centers. A vivid example is Freetown, the capital of the British colony of Sierra Leone, which became one of the most important ports for the Allies during the war, particularly after Great Britain and the United States established a joint staff arrangement for coordinating military operations. Allen Howard's chapter describes how the city became a bustling port that received hundreds of military and cargo ships and tens of thousands of troops. These operations created employment opportunities for thousands of people from Sierra Leone and the neighboring region. According to Howard, the city's population grew steadily from an estimated 10,000 people in the early 1940s to 25,700 and to over 50,000 in November 1942. The chapter illustrates the numerous ways in which the war's demands and opportunities affected Freetown residents and shaped their lives, and how they themselves shaped the city.[5] On another level, urbanization and mobility gave young men and women the opportunity to break away from the gender and age domination that were prevalent in the rural areas. City life allowed these groups to evade the authority and the control of husbands and elders.

One of the most important aspects of the social consequences of the war that has not been explored previously is sexual relations and interracial interaction. Carina Ray's chapter on the sex trade in British West Africa showed how the deployment of a large number of European, American, and local African male soldiers created a huge population of single men and generated a big demand for commercial sex. The "booming" sex trade attracted a large number of African women from the Gold Coast and regional neighbors including Nigeria who engaged in open prostitution in cities such as Accra, Sekondi, and Takoradi. The social and health repercussions of this rampant sex trade, particularly the rise of venereal diseases among both European and African troops, prompted the colonial authority in the Gold Coast to adopt strict antiprostitution laws and to curb the traffic of women and children across colonial boundaries.[6] Ruth Ginio's chapter, on the other hand, focuses on the experience of West African soldiers who fought in France, many of whom developed romantic relationships with French women. The chapter looks at the cases of French women seeking their African lovers who were sent back to West Africa and the response of French authorities to these requests. Ginio argues that the fear of these interracial relationships was one of the many anxieties the French had about the influence of Africa soldiers' experiences during the war on the stability of colonial rule in French West Africa.[7]

---

[5] Allen M. Howard, Chapter 10, this volume.
[6] Carina Ray, Chapter 18, this volume.
[7] Ruth Gino, Chapter 17, this volume.

The postwar period represents a watershed in African labor history. This period saw an unprecedented wave of labor protests that engulfed the entire continent. In addition to the establishment of labor unions and improvement in working conditions, these protests forced colonial powers to rethink their labor policies and to introduce new labor regimes.[8] Although African workers had engaged in various forms of protests since the early days of colonial rule, the postwar uprisings were deeply rooted in the socioeconomic conditions created by the war and reflected much more advanced organizational and mobilization skills and awareness. To meet the growing demand for food and cash crops colonial powers imposed conscripted labor on rural African producers, prompting many to migrate to the cities. Rapid urban growth, shortage of housing, and inflation created serious hardships for city dwellers, particularly wage workers.

The postwar protests were spearheaded by transportation workers, especially dock and railway workers.[9] Railroads and harbors had been the main means for transporting cash crops and other exports. The sheer numbers of railway workers and their strategic position in the colonial economy allowed them to exert considerable influence. Moreover, railway workers were among the most stable, homogenous group of African workers, who embraced the ethos of railway industry and developed a strong sense of community and corporate identity. Strikes occurred in the port city of Mombassa in 1939, 1942, and 1945. Similar protests occurred in Nigeria in 1942, 1945, and 1949; in Sudan in 1947 and 1948; in Dar es Salam in 1947; and in the Gold Coast in 1947 and 1948. In French West Africa, the railway workers of Dakar, the leading port in the region, launched a two-month-long strike in 1947, which shut down the harbor and crippled the transportation system in the whole area.[10]

In addition to workplace grievances, these labor uprisings reflected an acute awareness among African workers about the role of labor in society and workers' struggles worldwide. Carolyn Brown's chapter on the Nigerian coal miners in this volume shows how the political realities of the war in West Africa filtered down into the workplace. With the fall of South Asia in 1942,

[8] Beverly Silver, *Forces of Labor: Workers' Movements and Globalization since 1870* (Cambridge: Cambridge University Press, 2003). Frederick Cooper, *Decolonization and African Society: The Labor Question in French and British Africa* (New York: Cambridge University Press, 1996).

[9] R. D. Grillo, *African Railwaymen: Solidarity and Opposition in an East African Labor Force* (Cambridge: Cambridge University Press, 1973).

[10] Fredrick Cooper, *On the African Waterfront: Urban Disorder and the Transformation of Work in Colonial Mombasa* (New Haven, CT: Yale University Press, 1987); Fredrick Cooper, "Our Strike: Equality, Anti-colonial Politics and the 1947–48 Railway Strike in French West Africa," *Journal of African History*, 37, no. 1 (1996); and Timothy Oberst, "Transport Workers, Strikes, and the 'Imperial Response': Africa and the Post World War II Conjuncture," *African Studies Review*, 31, 1 (1988), 117–34.

Nigeria became an important source of vital minerals such as tin and other tropical products. Realizing their strategic position in the wartime economy, the mine workers in the town of Enugu began to challenge the abuse and the humiliation they were subjected to by British supervisors who practiced what Brown describes as "imperial masculinity." Moreover, the global dimensions of the war encouraged Nigerian workers to see themselves as members of a worldwide group of mine workers, to compare their conditions with those of other workers in Europe, America, and elsewhere, and to demand equal rights.[11]

The postwar strikes resulted in significant improvement in working conditions, including wage increases and the legalization of trade unions. Most important, however, is the fact that these strikes compelled colonial governments to adopt new strategies toward the whole labor question. During the prewar period European colonial powers in Africa were mainly concerned with how many African workers they could obtain and how much labor they could extract from them. African workers were viewed as temporary wage earners who moved back and forth between the city and the countryside. The uprisings of the 1940s awakened colonial officials to the existence of an assertive African working class with ambitions and aspirations. Colonial governments began to reproduce in Africa the legal and administrative institutions used to manage labor problems in Europe, with the hope of creating a more stable, disciplined, and differentiated working class, through the provision of family wages, decent housing, and social services. Instead of relying on the mass of single male migrant workers who oscillated between wage and nonwage employment, the postwar reforms conceived of African workers as individuals with wives and children living in descent houses and imbibed with the work ethics of modern industry.[12]

The postwar labor policies were premised on the European conception of the male worker as head of household and primary breadwinner. Application of these concepts in the African context had serious implications for gender relations and domestic life. In her work on the railway workers in Ibadan in Nigeria, Lisa Lindsay argues that the notion of the male worker as breadwinner conflicted with a Yoruba social structure in which women engaged in various commercial activities and enjoyed a considerable degree of economic independence.[13]

The war period witnessed massive transfer of goods, supplies, and, most importantly, people and ideas. The combat operations and the exigencies of the war entailed the movement of African soldiers from their original

---

[11] Carolyn A. Brown, Chapter 3, this volume.
[12] Frederick Cooper, "From Free Labor to Family Allowances: Labor and African Society in Colonial Discourse," *American Ethnologist*, 16 (November 1989), 745–65.
[13] Lisa A. Lindsay, *Working with Gender: Wage Labor and Social Change in Southwestern Nigeria* (Heinemann: Portsmouth, NH 2003).

homes to various parts of Africa. Moreover, thousands of civilians migrated across colonial borders to escape military conscription or to earn a living. In other words, the war facilitated greater interactions among Africans and provided an opportunity for cross-cultural exchange, connections, networking, and even intermarriage. For instance, the African Line of Communication (AFLOC) brought Congolese and West African soldiers to the Horn of Africa. After the end of the combat operations in northeast Africa, some former soldiers of the Sudan Defence Force established families in Eritrea and settled there permanently. Similarly, the cafés of Cairo became important sites of interaction among African, European, and American servicemen.

One of the most important and yet neglected aspects of the war was the deployment of thousands of African American troops to Africa, which has far-reaching implications. This topic is explored in Hutchinson's chapter. The chapter focuses on the experience of African American soldiers in Africa and the legacy of this experience in the continent of Africa as well as the United States. Hutchinson argues that the war brought African Americans into contact with Africa both physically and symbolically "in ways that had not been experienced since Marcus Garvey's back-to-Africa movement decades earlier."[14] The war experiences of African American soldiers and their presence in Africa and Asia shaped their perspective in a profound way and led them to think about their own struggle for equality in a global context and to develop a sense of solidarity with oppressed people in Africa and worldwide. Many African American war veterans became activists during the civil rights era and employed the tactics and strategies used by the nationalist movements in Africa and Asia during the decolonization era.

One of most significant developments during the war that had a lasting impact on African societies was the introduction of mass media, particularly radio broadcast. As mentioned in Byfield's and Sikainga's chapters, the distribution of radios was a major part of the propaganda campaign of colonial governments to win the support of their subjects. This was the case of Radio Omdurman in the Sudan, which was established in 1941 to counter German and Italian propaganda. On the other side of the continent, in the British colony of Nigeria, a radio station was opened in the town of Abeokuta in June 1943. According to Byfield, the range of the Abeokuta station expanded dramatically during the war years. Like Omdurman, the Abeokuta radio station became an important tool for the dissemination of information about the war and military recruitment. In addition to BBC programs, the station produced local programs and also provided a Yoruba version of the news each day. Radio broadcasts gave Africans an opportunity to become engaged in the war, to share information, and to see themselves as an integral part of the international community.[15]

---

[14] Daniel Hutchinson, Chapter 21, this volume.
[15] Judith A. Byfield, Chapter 8, this volume.

The war opened up new possibilities and ushered in new political imagination. As mentioned earlier, the experience of the war and its aftermath prompted the leading imperial powers – Britain and France – to think about new ways of stabilizing their African colonies. An integral part of the new strategy was to introduce reforms that would facilitate greater African participation and representation. This endeavor was partially derived by the promises that were made during the war. The idea of self-determination and ending colonial rule were considered to be something of the distant future. Both the British and the French saw self-determination as a gradual process that would facilitate the rise of moderate, docile, and educated African leaders who were prepared to compromise and preserve the links between the metropolis and the former colonies.

The French approach was to preserve the unity of the French empire by transferring some responsibilities to educated Africans, a pronouncement that was affirmed by Charles de Gaulle during the Brazzaville Conference in 1944. In French West Africa, a few educated Africans were admitted into the category of "citizens" and a limited number were elected to the French parliament.[16]

The British model, on the other hand, was to integrate Africans into local government and then gradually into some form of self-government within the Commonwealth. Hence, beginning the 1940s, they began to move away from indirect rule, which relied mainly on traditional chiefs, and to give more power to the educated class. The British model colony of the Gold Coast became the testing ground of these policies, which were then applied to other British territories.

While the British and the French were working hard to preserve their empires, African leaders were pursuing diametrically opposite goals. African nationalists, labor movements, peasants, and other social forces saw the postwar climate as an opportunity and used the language of "imperial legitimacy" to demand full rights and self-determination. As Carol Summers argued in her chapter on Uganda, the war was seen by local people as an opportunity rather than a "cataclysmic" struggle. While the British framed the war as a struggle for the triumph of liberalism and democracy over the dark forces of Fascism, Ugandans developed their own understanding of the war and saw it as an opportunity to acquire wealth, to bring new resources into the country, and to expose their youth to new ideas and connections. According to Summers, Ugandans used their money and loyalty to a stressed British empire to gain political and economic rewards. However, after the war, Ugandans became frustrated by British reluctance to see them as equal partners and, hence, moved away from earlier forms of political struggle

---

[16] Frederick Cooper, *Africa since 1940: The Past of the Present* (Cambridge: Cambridge University Press, 2009), 40–41.

such as petition writing and adopted a more assertive and large-scale political mobilization.[17]

By the early 1950s, colonial regimes were facing unprecedented protests that were mounted by broad-based, better-organized, and politically sophisticated movements, and Britain and France finally decided to cede power. With the exception of settler colonies such as Kenya and Algeria, the transition to self-rule was relatively peaceful. Although Portugal and white minority regimes in southern Africa were able to hold on for a few more years, colonial rule began to crumble one decade after the war, a powerful testament to the war's lasting legacy.

[17] Carol Summers, Chapter 25, this volume.

Index